THE
NEW
AMERICAN
NATION
1775–1820

A Twelve-Volume Collection of Articles on the Development of the Early American Republic

Edited by

PETER S. ONUF
UNIVERSITY OF VIRGINIA

A GARLAND SERIES

THE NEW AMERICAN NATION
1775–1820

Volume

9

★

AMERICA AND THE WORLD: Diplomacy, Politics, and War

Edited with an
Introduction by

PETER S. ONUF

GARLAND PUBLISHING, INC.
NEW YORK & LONDON
1991

Library of Congress Cataloging-in-Publication Data

America and the world: diplomacy, politics, and war / edited with an
introduction by Peter S. Onuf.
    p.   cm. — (New American nation, 1776–1815 ; v. 9)
    Includes bibliographical references.
    ISBN 0-8153-0444-7 (alk. paper) : $49.99
    1. United States—Foreign relations—War of 1812. 2. United States—
Politics and government—War of 1812. 3. United States—Foreign relations—1783–1815. I. Onuf, Peter S. II. Series.
    E164.N45   1991 vol. 9   [E358]
    973 s—dc20
    [973.5'2]   91-15487
             CIP

Printed on acid-free, 250-year-life paper.
Manufactured in the United States of America

THE NEW AMERICAN NATION, 1775–1820

EDITOR'S INTRODUCTION

This series includes a representative selection of the most interesting and influential journal articles on revolutionary and early national America. My goal is to introduce readers to the wide range of topics that now engage scholarly attention. The essays in these volumes show that the revolutionary era was an extraordinarily complex "moment" when the broad outlines of national history first emerged. Yet if the "common cause" brought Americans together, it also drove them apart: the Revolution, historians agree, was as much a civil war as a war of national liberation. And, given the distinctive colonial histories of the original members of the American Union, it is not surprising that the war had profoundly different effects in different parts of the country. This series has been designed to reveal the multiplicity of these experiences in a period of radical political and social change.

Most of the essays collected here were first published within the last twenty years. This series therefore does *not* recapitulate the development of the historiography of the Revolution. Many of the questions asked by earlier generations of scholars now seem misconceived and simplistic. Constitutional historians wanted to know if the Patriots had legitimate grounds to revolt: was the Revolution "legal"? Economic historians sought to assess the costs of the navigation system for American farmers and merchants and to identify the interest groups that promoted resistance. Comparative historians wondered how "revolutionary" the Revolution really was. By and large, the best recent work has ignored these classic questions. Contemporary scholarship instead draws its inspiration from other sources, most notable of which is the far-ranging reconception and reconstruction of prerevolutionary America by a brilliant generation of colonial historians.

Bernard Bailyn's *Ideological Origins of the American Revolution* (1967) was a landmark in the new historical writing on colonial politics. As his title suggests, Bailyn was less interested in constitutional and legal arguments as such than in the "ideology" or political language that shaped colonists' perception of and responses to British imperial policy. Bailyn's great contribution was to focus attention on colonial political culture; disciples and critics alike followed his lead as they explored the impact—and limits—of "republicanism" in specific colonial settings. Meanwhile, the social historians who had played a leading role in the transformation of colonial historiography were extending their work into the late colonial period and were increasingly interested in the questions of value, meaning, and behavior that were raised by the new political history. The resulting convergence points to some of the unifying themes in recent work on the revolutionary period presented in this series.

A thorough grounding in the new scholarship on colonial British America is the best introduction to the history and historiography of the Revolution. These volumes therefore can be seen as a complement and extension of Peter Charles Hoffer's eighteen-volume set, *Early American History*, published by Garland in 1987. Hoffer's collection includes numerous important essays essential for understanding developments in independent America. Indeed, only a generation ago—when the Revolution generally was defined in terms of its colonial origins—it would have been hard to justify a separate series on the "new American nation." But exciting recent work—for instance, on wartime mobilization and social change, or on the Americanization of republican ideology during the great era of state making and constitution writing—has opened up new vistas. Historians now generally agree that the revolutionary period saw far-reaching and profound changes, that is, a "great transformation," toward a more recognizably modern America. If the connections between this transformation and the actual unfolding of events often remain elusive, the historiographical quest for the larger meaning of the war and its aftermath has yielded impressive results.

To an important extent, the revitalization of scholarship on revolutionary and early national America is a tribute to the efforts and expertise of scholars working in other professional disciplines. Students of early American literature have made key contributions to the history of rhetoric, ideology, and culture; political scientists and legal scholars have brought new clarity and sophistication to the study of political and constitutional thought and practice in the founding period. Kermit L. Hall's superb Garland series, *United States Constitutional and Legal History* (20 volumes, 1985), is another fine resource for students and scholars interested in the founding. The sampling of recent work in various disciplines offered in these volumes gives a sense of the interpretative possibilities of a crucial period in American history that is now getting the kind of attention it has long deserved.

Peter S. Onuf

INTRODUCTION

The first four decades of the new nation's history were dominated by war, or the threat of war. The struggle for American independence precipitated yet another in a long series of wars between Britain and France, which resumed in 1792 as a British-led coalition of counterrevolutionary powers sought to destroy the new French republic. America's status as a neutral power hung in an evermore precarious balance as the French extended their conquests by land while the British exploited their maritime supremacy. For Jeffersonian oppositionists, the Jay Treaty of 1795 bought relief from British naval depredations at the cost of neutral rights and national independence. But the resolution of the undeclared war with France and a brief interval in the European conflict offered the Jefferson administration an opportunity to chart a new foreign policy.

Despite Federalist fears about his Francophilia, Jefferson was no less committed to American neutrality than his predecessors. He differed, however, in his conviction that the British constituted a greater immediate threat to American rights and interests, and in discounting British claims to be defending the independence of all civilized nations—including the United States—against Napoleon's efforts to establish a despotic "universal monarchy."

Given the subsequent history of Anglo-American friendship, and Europe's more recent experience with designs of world conquest, it is not surprising that most modern commentators endorse the British view of the Napoleonic wars and fault Jefferson for failing to discriminate between the antagonists. Even more damning, from the contemporary "realist" perspective most fully elaborated in Robert Tucker and David Hendrickson's *Empire of Liberty* (1990), the Republicans failed to grasp the international power situation. If, as the dominant naval power, Britain violated America's "neutral rights" more often than France, then it was also true that British power constituted a far greater danger to the new nation's vital interests in the event of war. Finally, the indictment goes, Jefferson and Madison hopelessly exaggerated the efficacy of commercial sanctions as an alternative to war and as a substitute for military preparedness. The ill-fated embargo of 1807–1809, as Burton Spivak shows in *Jefferson's English Crisis* (1979), subverted national unity and depleted the treasury while increasing the likelihood of war.

The historians' negative assessment of Jeffersonian foreign policy stands in striking contrast to the generally adulatory tone of descriptions of his domestic policy. Perhaps this schizophrenic view reflects the special concerns and biases of diplomatic historians who tend to be responsive to the contemporary climate of opinion on foreign policy issues. However this may be, Jefferson's and Madison's efforts to defend American ships and sailors and to vindicate the new nation's honor and independence after the renewal of British depredations in 1805 led to one of the least glorious, and apparently least necessary, wars in American history. Unfavorable assessments of the War of 1812—a war in which Americans found themselves de facto allies of Napoleon in his final struggle for European hegemony—have inevitably colored historical writing on earlier diplomatic failures.

Historiographical debate on the causes and conduct of the war have revolved around conflicting interpretations of American war aims. The essays in this volume discuss an array of motives, from the vindication of neutral rights and American independence to the annexation of British Canada. Roger H. Brown's *The Republic in Peril* (1964) is a plausible account of the interplay of principled commitments and partisan imperatives; interesting recent work by political historians reprinted here illuminates party dynamics during the war years. J. C. A. Stagg's magisterial *Mr. Madison's War* (1983) offers a convincing portrayal of the administration's designs to force a change in British ministerial policy by seizing Canada and so threatening the supply and survival of the British West Indies. Stagg also provides the best treatment of the war's conduct, emphasizing the difficulties of mobilization and policy implementation that effectively subverted Madison's designs. Donald R. Hickey provides an excellent up-to-date narrative of the war's history in his *The War of 1812* (1990).

Despite a few important victories, notably Andrew Jackson's belated triumph at New Orleans (negotiators at Ghent had already concluded a peace agreement), it could hardly be said that the United States "won" the war. As with the original onset of hostilities, British policymakers held the most important cards. Before the war, ministers were persuaded by High Federalist propaganda and their own invincible arrogance that the American union could not survive the outbreak of war and that concessions were therefore unnecessary. By 1815, however, and despite the opportunity now offered by the end of the European war, the British showed little inclination to continue fighting the former colonies. For the vast majority of Americans, this was victory enough. If the American "war machine" barely functioned in the first campaigns, the union held, and independence was secured. Madison's bungling took on a new lustre in hindsight, as Drew McCoy shows in his *The Last of the Fathers* (1989). The Republicans had managed the war effort without the dangerous concentration of power and loss of liberty against which doctrinaire republicans warned.

Peter S. Onuf

ADDITIONAL READING

Roger H. Brown. *The Republic in Peril, 1812*. New York: Columbia University Press, 1964.

Donald R. Hickey. *The War of 1812*. Urbana: University of Illinois Press, 1990.

Lawrence Kaplan. *Jefferson and France: An Essay on Politics and Political Ideas*. New Haven: Yale University Press, 1967.

Drew R. McCoy. *The Last of the Fathers: James Madison and the Republican Legacy*. New York: Cambridge University Press, 1989.

Bradford Perkins. *The First Rapprochement: England and the United States, 1795–1805*. Philadelphia: University of Pennsylvania Press, 1955.

———. *Prologue to War: England and the United States, 1805–1812*. Berkeley: University of California Press, 1961.

Burton Spivak. *Jefferson's English Crisis: Commerce, Embargo, and the Republican Revolution*. Charlottesville: University Press of Virginia, 1979.

J. C. A. Stagg. *Mr. Madison's War: Politics, Diplomacy, and Warfare in the Early American Republic, 1783–1830*. Princeton, NJ: Princeton University Press, 1983.

Robert W. Tucker and David C. Hendrickson. *Empire of Liberty: The Statecraft of Thomas Jefferson*. New York: Oxford University Press, 1990.

Steven Watts. *The Republic Reborn: War and the Making of Liberal America, 1790–1820*. Baltimore: Johns Hopkins University Press, 1987.

CONTENTS

Volume 9—America and the World:
Diplomacy, Politics, and War

Lawrence Delbert Cress, "'Cool and Serious Reflection': Federalist Attitudes Toward War in 1812," *Journal of the Early Republic*, 1987, 7:123–145.

Hickey, Donald R. "American Trade Restrictions during the War of 1812," *Journal of American History*, 1981, 68(3):517–538.

Kagin, Donald H. "Monetary Aspects of the Treasury Notes of the War of 1812," *Journal of Economic History*, 1984, 44(1): 69–88.

J. C. A. Stagg, "Enlisted Men in the United States Army, 1812–1815: A Preliminary Survey," *William and Mary Quarterly*, 1986, 43(4):615–645.

Lee A. Wallace, Jr., "The Petersburg Volunteers, 1812–1813," *Virginia Magazine of History and Biography*, 1974, 82(4): 458–485.

Jeffrey Kimball, "The Fog and Friction of Frontier War: The Role of Logistics in American Offensive Failure During the War of 1812," *Old Northwest*, 1979–80, 5(4):323–343.

John Sugden, "The Southern Indians in the War of 1812: The Closing Phase," *Florida Historical Quarterly*, 1982, 60(3): 273–312.

ACKNOWLEDGMENTS

Volume 9—America and the World: Diplomacy, Politics, and War

Lawrence S. Kaplan, "Jefferson, the Napoleonic Wars, and the Balance of Power," *William and Mary Quarterly*, 1957, 14(2):196–217. Originally appeared in the *William and Mary Quarterly*. Courtesy of Yale University Sterling Memorial Library.

Donald R. Hickey, "The Monroe-Pinkney Treaty of 1806: A Reappraisal," *William and Mary Quarterly*, 1987, 44(1):65–88. Originally appeared in the *William and Mary Quarterly*. Courtesy of Yale University Sterling Memorial Library.

J. C. A. Stagg, "James Madison and the Coercion of Great Britain: Canada, the West Indies, and the War of 1812," *William and Mary Quarterly*, 1981, 38(1):3–34. Originally appeared in the *William and Mary Quarterly*. Courtesy of Yale University Sterling Memorial Library.

Reginald Horsman, "On To Canada: Manifest Destiny and United States Strategy in the War of 1812," *Michigan Historical Review*, 1987, 13(2):1–24. Reprinted with the permission of Indiana University. Courtesy of Yale University Sterling Memorial Library.

George R. Taylor, "Agrarian Discontent in the Mississippi Valley Preceding the War of 1812," *Journal of Political Economy*, 1931, 39:471–505. Reprinted with the permission of the University of Chicago Press. Courtesy of Yale University Sterling Memorial Library.

Stephen M. Millett, "Bellicose Nationalism in Ohio: An Origin of the War of 1812," *Canadian Review of Studies in Nationalism*, 1974, 1(2):221–240. Reprinted with the permission of the *Canadian Review of Studies in Nationalism*. Courtesy of the *Canadian Review of Studies in Nationalism*.

Margaret Kinard Latimer, "South Carolina—A Protagonist of the War of 1812," *American Historical Review*, 1956, 61(4):914–929. Reprinted with the permission of the American Historical Association. Courtesy of Yale University Sterling Memorial Library.

Reginald C. Stuart, "Special Interests and National Authority in Foreign Policy: American-British Provincial Links During the Embargo and the War of 1812," *Diplomatic History*, 1984, 8(4):311–328. Reprinted with the permission of Scholarly Resources, Inc. Courtesy of Yale University Sterling Memorial Library.

J. C. A. Stagg, "James Madison and the 'Malcontents': The Political Origins of the War of 1812," *William and Mary Quarterly*, 1976, 33(4):557–585. Originally appeared in the *William and Mary Quarterly*. Courtesy of Yale University Sterling Memorial Library.

Ronald L. Hatzenbuehler, "Party Unity and the Decision for War in the House of Representatives, 1812," *William and Mary Quarterly*, 1972,

29(3):367–390. Originally appeared in the *William and Mary Quarterly*. Courtesy of Yale University Sterling Memorial Library.

Donald R. Hickey, "Federalist Party Unity and the War of 1812," *Journal of American Studies*, 1978, 12(1):23–39. Reprinted with the permission of the Cambridge University Press. Courtesy of Yale University Sterling Memorial Library.

Lawrence Delbert Cress, "'Cool and Serious Reflection': Federalist Attitudes Toward War in 1812," *Journal of the Early Republic*, 1987, 7:123–145. Reprinted with the permission of Indiana University, Department of History. Courtesy of Yale University Sterling Memorial Library.

Donald R. Hickey, "American Trade Restrictions During the War of 1812," *Journal of American History*, 1981, 68(3):517–538. Reprinted with the permission of the *Journal of American History*. Courtesy of Yale University Sterling Memorial Library.

Donald H. Kagin, "Monetary Aspects of the Treasury Notes of the War of 1812," *Journal of Economic History*, 1984, 44(1):69–88. Reprinted with the permission of Cambridge University Press. Courtesy of Yale University Sterling Memorial Library.

J. C. A. Stagg, "Enlisted Men in the United States Army, 1812–1815: A Preliminary Survey," *William and Mary Quarterly*, 1986, 43(4):615–645. Originally appeared in the *William and Mary Quarterly*. Courtesy of Yale University Sterling Memorial Library.

Lee A. Wallace, Jr., "The Petersburg Volunteers, 1812–1813," *Virginia Magazine of History and Biography*, 1974, 82(4):458–485. Reprinted with the permission of the Virginia Historical Society. Courtesy of Yale University Sterling Memorial Library.

Jeffrey Kimball, "The Fog and Friction of Frontier War: The Role of Logistics in American Offensive Failure During the War of 1812," *Old Northwest*, 1979–80, 5(4):323–343. Reprinted with the permission of Miami University. Courtesy of *Old Northwest*.

John Sugden, "The Southern Indians in the War of 1812: The Closing Phase," *Florida Historical Quarterly*, 1982, 60(3):273–312. Reprinted with the permission of Southern Florida University. Courtesy of Yale University Sterling Memorial Library.

Jefferson, the Napoleonic Wars, and the Balance of Power

Lawrence S. Kaplan*

T HE young American republic of 1800 has been compared by W. Stull Holt to a jackal living off the spoils it steals from more powerful animals diverted by fights among themselves.[1] And like the jackal the United States ran the risk of becoming involved in the struggles of others.

Thomas Jefferson would have appreciated this view of the republic. Indeed, he had used a similar metaphor that placed even greater stress upon the precarious position of the United States in relation to the balance of power in Europe: "Tremendous times in Europe! How mighty this battle of lions and tigers! With what sensations should the common herd of cattle look on it? With no partialities, certainly. If they can so far worry one another as to destroy their power of tyrannizing, the one over the earth, the other the waters, the world may perhaps enjoy peace, till they recruit again."[2] Nevertheless, he expected that the United States would not only survive the strife but would "fatten on the follies of the old [nations]" by winning new territory and new concessions from their wars.[3]

As President of the United States and as unofficial adviser to his successor, James Madison, Jefferson was in a position not only to formulate a concept of the balance of power to be expressed in this kind of metaphor, but also to put into effect, or at least to influence, policy decisions based on his understanding of the balance of power. For him and for many of his colleagues that balance represented the equilibrium achieved by the

---

* Mr. Kaplan is a member of the Department of History at Kent State University. He wishes to thank the American Council of Learned Societies for the opportunity, as an ACLS Fellow in 1950-51, to study the influence of French politics and political ideas on Jefferson's foreign policy.

[1] W. Stull Holt, "Uncle Sam as Deer, Jackal, and Lion; or the United States in Power Politics," *Pacific Spectator*, III (1949), 47-48.

[2] Jefferson to Benjamin Rush, Oct. 4, 1803, *The Writings of Thomas Jefferson*, ed. Andrew A. Lipscomb and Albert E. Bergh (Washington, 1903-04), X, 422.

[3] Jefferson to Edward Rutledge, July 4, 1790, *ibid.*, VIII, 61.

distribution of economic and military strength of the world among the several great powers in such a way that no one of them was strong enough to destroy the others and thereby menace the security of the nonbelligerents. Even if the balance was never exact, the rapacious powers of Europe could check each other sufficiently to assure to smaller nations the maximum degree of peace and stability possible in a world governed by force. A further result of this deadlock was the possibility that a small neutral, such as the United States, might enhance its power and prestige by expanding its territories at the expense of the preoccupied nations of the Old World.

It is important, then, to understand exactly how Jefferson's idea of the national interest can be reconciled with his policy of aiding France by the embargo and by his vigorous espousal of the War of 1812. Did he see a change in the balance of power that favored the lion over the tiger, or did the "common herd" later acquire new strengths or talents that permitted foreign policy to be advanced by other methods? The difference between his often expressed suspicion of Europe and his equally firm support of French war aims has led twentieth-century critics as well as those of his own day to write off his ideas as inconsistent, unrealistic, and Francophile. He recognized the desirability of a deadlock in Europe, and yet, he appeared willing to work toward a French victory at a time when England was fighting a lonely battle to maintain the balance of power on the Continent. He indicated through his embargo program that he understood the risks a small power would run in entangling itself in European wars, and yet he was eager to abandon the path of moderation in 1812. No matter how offensive England's behavior toward the United States, England was fighting a defensive war against an aggressor bent on world conquest: Jefferson never accepted this fact.

The years 1805 to 1815 represent the period in Jefferson's life when his ideas about the balance of power can be fairly treated. Since his attitudes were no longer shaped by the gratitude he once felt for French support in the American Revolution or by sympathy extended to France in her struggle against monarchical invaders, he could look dispassionately at the struggle in Europe and at his country's stake in its outcome. By the time of the Napoleonic Wars, Jefferson realized fully that the United States was facing two powers, both powerful and both hostile to the interests of a small neutral. The course of battle after Britain's naval triumph at Trafalgar and after France's victory at Austerlitz in 1805 turned almost exclusively to economic warfare, which in turn affected the commerce of neutral nations. Britain, deprived of allies on the Continent, and France, lacking sea power, had no other means of coming to grips with each other. In this situation the United States would have been severely tried no matter what the policy of the President had been; but a clear understanding of the relative strength of the two belligerents might have enabled the United States to avoid, or at least to lighten, the burdens it had to suffer during these years.

As each British order in council and Napoleonic decree inflicted increasing damage upon American ships, commerce, and sovereignty, the state of public opinion in the United States made some kind of action necessary. It is clear that the measures Jefferson took deliberately favored France over Britain. From his point of view the contest in Europe was never really one between two titans of equal strength or of equal merit. France, after ceding Louisiana and after losing her fleet, looked less dangerous than Britain, who had the means, through American bases and control of the sea, to insult, plunder, or attack the United States, and who had the motive of revenge to feed her hostility. Jefferson's suspicions of British motives should not be underestimated. The deliberate insolence of her behavior was an important factor in inducing him to choose a weapon that accommodated the war aims of Bonaparte. After the death of Charles Fox, one of America's few friends in the British government, Jefferson's peace moves—the threat of a nonimportation act as well as the blandishment of a special treaty mission—were met with the same contempt by Britain. The crowning insult to American pride was Britain's handling of the impressment issue. One of Monroe's main objectives in seeking a treaty with Britain in 1806 was to end kidnaping of American sailors accused of being British deserters.[4] If Britain had acted with some sense of moderation in this issue, she might have calmed American feeling; Jefferson, even after strong rebuffs, was willing to continue negotiations.[5] Britain, however, abandoned all caution, and the *Chesapeake* incident was the result.

Jefferson was as shaken by this enormity as any of his countrymen.

[4] Monroe and William Pinkney had been dispatched to London in 1806 to make a treaty with Britain upon the expiration of Jay's Treaty of 1794. The result was so unacceptable to Jefferson that he refused to present it to the Senate.

[5] Gallatin to Jefferson, Apr. 13, 1807, Jefferson Papers, CLXVI, Library of Congress. Jefferson to Madison, Apr. 21, 1807, *Writings of Jefferson*, ed. Lipscomb and Bergh, XI, 193.

He immediately summoned his Cabinet to consider measures of retaliation. But angry as the President was, his behavior was not that of a man
carried away by emotional impulse, for an obvious reply to such an insult
was war. Instead, he ordered all armed vessels of Great Britain to depart
from American waters.[6] He talked about war in his correspondence with
du Pont and Lafayette, and even in conversations with the French minister, Turreau.[7] Nevertheless, Jefferson was more interested in "peaceful
means of redressing injustice" than in war, and he eagerly listened to reports that Admiral Berkeley had disavowed the act of the *Leopard* and
that the British in Norfolk had shown only peaceful dispositions toward
the United States.[8] He declared that he wanted to give the offender an
opportunity to make amends for the crime, to grant American merchants
time to bring their ships and property back to American soil in the event
of war, and, finally, to allow the question of war to be determined by the
proper constitutional authority, the Congress.[9]

However, he did not avoid war with Britain at this time because of any
belief that Britain was fighting America's battle against Napoleonic imperialism; in the President's mind, Britain's action in the *Chesapeake*
affair was only an extreme example of the malice she had always borne
the United States. He avoided war because he had a better instrument
with which to strike Britain: an embargo cutting off American commerce
nominally with all of Europe. It was actually directed against the British
Isles, since the British navy had already effectively stifled trade with all

[6] Proclamation of July 2, 1807, in *A Compilation of the Messages and Papers of
the Presidents, 1789-1902*, ed. James D. Richardson (Washington, 1899-1903), I, 423.
   [7] Jefferson to du Pont, July 14, 1807, in *The Correspondence of Jefferson and
du Pont de Nemours*, ed. Gilbert Chinard (Baltimore, 1931), p. 116; Jefferson to
Lafayette, July 14, 1807, *Writings of Jefferson*, ed. Lipscomb and Bergh, XI, 279;
Turreau to Talleyrand, July 18, 1807, Correspondance politique, États-Unis, LX,
166-171, Archives des affaires étrangères, Paris (hereafter cited as Correspondance
politique). When Jefferson failed to take a strong stand with the British, Turreau
bitterly gave up all hope for a people "who have no idea of glory, grandeur, and
justice"; Sept. 4, 1807, *ibid.*, foll. 199-201.
   [8] William Tatham to Jefferson, July 1, 1807; ...... to Jefferson, July 3, 1807,
Jefferson Papers, CLXVII, Lib. Cong. Both presented reasons for moderation, and
Jefferson, in turn, advised Gov. Cabell of Virginia to exercise discretion in applying
the proclamation against British ships in Norfolk. Jefferson to Cabell, July 19 and
24, 1807, *Writings of Jefferson*, ed. Lipscomb and Bergh, XI, 288-290, 294-296.
   [9] Jefferson to George Clinton, July 6, 1807, *ibid.*, p. 258. Henry Adams claimed
that Jefferson would not have delayed calling the Congress into emergency session
if he had really wanted war. Adams, *History of the United States of America* . . .
(New York, 1889-91), IV, 34-35.

countries under Bonaparte's control. This scheme was obviously more than just an answer to the *Chesapeake* affront. Jefferson might have had satisfaction from the British if he had been willing to accept an apology and amends for that crime, but in asking for amends he insisted as well upon the abolition of impressment itself.[10] The incident between the *Leopard* and the *Chesapeake* was merely the occasion that forced him to choose this particular weapon against the enemy, not the reason for his choice.

The embargo came at the time it did because America's position had degenerated so rapidly after the *Chesapeake* affair that an audacious action—war or its equivalent—was imperative. In the period from June to December 1807, when the act went into effect, Jefferson's meek reply to the British atrocity had encouraged the belligerents to continue their attacks on neutral rights. The result was the rejection of American demands for redress, the enforcement of the Berlin Decree, the promise of more rigorous impressment policies, and the order in council of November 11, 1807, forcing American ships into British ports to pay for permission to trade with the Continent.

The embargo was not altogether a new policy for Jefferson. To some degree it was the realization of an old dream that Jefferson shared with other founding fathers: the isolation of the United States from the evils of the Old World. As such, it was a measure that fitted easily into a pattern of behavior which he periodically had advocated for the "common herd" when endangered by the jungle world of international politics. Inasmuch as Britain and France had virtually banned American commerce from the seas, the embargo could be a face-saving means of giving their decrees the force of American law, and thus remove a source of conflict with the belligerents. This conception of the embargo was more in consonance with the ideal role of a small nation than were other considerations that motivated the President and the Secretary of State at this time: namely, the territorial and pecuniary advantages that might be derived from Britain's vulnerability to commercial retaliation.[11] Instead of

[10] *Ibid.*, pp. 39-40.

[11] Jefferson to Hogendorp, Oct. 13, 1785, *Writings of Jefferson*, ed. Lipscomb and Bergh, V, 183. Louis M. Sears seems to have regarded the embargo as a natural outgrowth of Jefferson's philosophy of life and not as a measure of opportunism, as Adams emphasized. Sears, *Jefferson and the Embargo* (Durham, N. C., 1927), pp. 1-2. Sears gives too great a role to Jefferson's pacifism, however, as a cause of the embargo. See also Irving Brant, *James Madison: Secretary of State, 1800-1809* (In-

regarding the embargo as primarily a refuge, Jefferson envisioned it as a panacea which would protect American property, force the belligerents to revoke their decrees, strike a blow for neutral rights, and even help to win the Floridas.

In the embargo message, Jefferson made a point of emphasizing the new construction of the Berlin Decree, as if the embargo were directed against France.[12] This impression was deliberately misleading. Jefferson knew well that its first effect would be to give teeth to the Non-Importation Act against Britain that had gone into effect eight days before the embargo. The President believed that if Britain were deprived not only of her food imports but also of raw materials for her industry, powerful British manufacturers would force the government to yield to American demands.[13] One of Jefferson's aims was to strike a hard blow at Britain without committing his country to war and without bringing upon himself the charge of being a French agent.

It cannot be denied, however, that Jefferson was fully aware that the embargo constituted a service to Napoleon. He more than admitted knowledge that the embargo would not hurt France; he went out of his way to convince Turreau, who had charged him with placing France on the same footing with Britain, that the United States had no intention of treating both countries alike. "The Embargo which appears to hit France and Britain equally," the President told the French minister, "is for a fact more prejudicial to the latter than the other by reason of a greater number of colonies which England possesses and their inferiority in local resources."[14] France, unlike Britain, was reasonably self-sufficient; the supplies she needed from without could be obtained for the most part from her continental tributaries. While the Federalists saw through Jeffer-

---

dianapolis, Ind., 1953), pp. 397-403, and Leonard D. White, *The Jeffersonians; A Study in Administrative History, 1801-1829* (New York, 1951), pp. 423-424.

[12] Three out of the four documents attached to the message dealt with French violations of American neutrality.

[13] In Nov. 1807, Jefferson thought that if no wheat reached England by May, she would be starved into submission. W. E. Dodd, "Napoleon Breaks Thomas Jefferson," *American Mercury,* V (1925), 311; Schuyler D. Hoslett, "Jefferson and England: the Embargo as a Measure of Coercion," *Americana,* XXXIV (1940), 39. Jefferson was gratified in the following spring to learn of complaints in Liverpool about the embargo's effects. Jefferson to Caesar A. Rodney, Apr. 24, 1808, *Writings of Jefferson,* ed. Lipscomb and Bergh, XII, 36.

[14] Turreau to Champagny, June 28, 1808, Correspondance politique, LXI, 166-177. Turreau was reporting this information to Talleyrand's successor as Minister of Foreign Affairs.

7

son's public pose of equal treatment of the belligerents and immediately sought political advantage from his aid to Bonaparte, they were mistaken in looking upon his actions as evidence of a belief that France was more friendly to the United States than was Britain, or that French violations of neutral rights were less hateful.[15]

Jefferson was aware of the deceit and malevolence of Bonaparte. He confessed that it was "mortifying that we should be forced to wish success to Bonaparte, and to look to his victories as our salvation."[16] If Jefferson was willing to accept mortification, it was because the alternative seemed to be British domination and because France was unwittingly serving the cause of neutral rights. "I never expected to be under the necessity of wishing success to Buonaparte. But the English being equally tyrannical at sea as he is on land and that tyranny bearing on us in every point of either honor or interest, I say, 'down with England' and as for what Buonaparte is then to do with us, let us trust to the chapter of accidents. I cannot, with the Anglomen, prefer a certain present evil to a future hypothetical one."[17]

Because he was convinced that France was not an immediate threat to America's security, Jefferson saw the embargo as an offensive as well as a defensive weapon. Remembering Napoleon's pose as a champion of neutral rights, he pretended to offer the embargo as America's blow in behalf of maritime liberty[18] and also as America's equivalent of joining

[15] Adams, *History of the United States,* IV, 232. Pickering was the leading figure in the campaign to prove that Napoleon personally dictated the embargo to Jefferson. See Hervey P. Prentiss, *Timothy Pickering as the Leader of New England Federalism, 1800-1815* (Salem, Mass., 1934).

[16] Jefferson to Col. John Taylor, Aug. 1, 1807, *Writings of Jefferson,* ed. Lipscomb and Bergh, XI, 305.

[17] Jefferson expressed these sentiments in reply to the suggestion that Bonaparte was possibly Providence's instrument for punishing the crimes of kings. Leiper to Jefferson, Aug. 20, 1807, Jefferson Papers, CLXX, Lib. Cong.; Jefferson to Leiper, Aug. 21, 1807, *The Works of Thomas Jefferson,* ed. Paul Leicester Ford (New York, 1904-05), X, 483-484.

[18] Despite the obvious guile, Jefferson was still interested in a maritime pact upholding neutral rights. He corresponded intermittently with Alexander of Russia on the subject and dispatched the Short mission in 1808 in the hope of stimulating Russian interest. He would not have America join such a league, but he thought that it, like the Continental System, served American interests. Jefferson to Paine, Mar. 26, 1806, *Works of Jefferson,* ed. Ford, X, 247; Jefferson to Alexander I, Apr. 19, 1806, *ibid.,* pp. 249-251; Jefferson to William Duane, July 20, 1807, *Writings of Jefferson,* ed. Lipscomb and Bergh, XI, 292; Jefferson to Paine, Oct. 9, 1807, *ibid.,* p. 378.

the Continental System.[19] In return, Jefferson hoped Napoleon would force Spain to cede the Floridas and rectify the western boundary—a hope based on the Emperor's promise to Armstrong, the minister to France, that if the United States made an alliance with France against Britain, Jefferson would be free to intervene in Spanish America.[20] Thus the embargo would teach England that her crimes were costly, and it would inveigle France into working for America's territorial aggrandizement, all without the cost of one American life.[21] If a French victory resulted, the Atlantic Ocean would prevent Bonaparte from attacking the United States, if some other obstacle in the "chapter of accidents" did not stop him first.

Jefferson was outplayed in his dangerous diplomatic game with Bonaparte. The Embargo Act, intended as a fair exchange for the Floridas, in effect made America an ally in the Continental System without securing one square foot of Florida soil in return. Instead, the Emperor's price kept rising: repeal of all restrictions against French commerce, the right to plunder American ships, and ultimate involvement in the war with Britain. In addition, he ordered the Bayonne Decree in April 1808, permitting confiscation of any American ship found in European harbors on the spurious grounds that he was aiding enforcement of the embargo. When Americans complained about the maritime restrictions or about France's procrastination over Florida, they were told that Jefferson himself had stated the embargo was aimed at France, and hence the Emperor's measures represented a natural reprisal. In the same facetious manner French officials refused to listen to American designs on Florida, because Spanish law prevented the king from alienating any of his territory.[22]

Jefferson naturally and openly resented this cavalier treatment. But his retaliation seemed petty and inadequate in view of the provocations. He annoyed Turreau by his talks with British envoys in Washington, by his refusal to capture French deserters in the United States, and by the strict

[19] John Armstrong to Champagny, Feb. 8, 1808, Correspondance politique, LXI, 36-36ᵛᵒ; Turreau to Champagny, June 28, 1808, ibid., foll. 166-177.

[20] Armstrong to Champagny, Feb. 4 and 8, 1808, ibid., foll. 32-33, 36-36ᵛᵒ. Armstrong's hopes for Florida depended upon a promise the French made, before they knew of the embargo, in return for an alliance.

[21] I. J. Cox, "Pan-American Policy of Jefferson and Wilkinson," Mississippi Valley Historical Review, I (1914), 212. Cox claims that Jefferson's desire for Florida influenced his whole relationship with Bonaparte.

[22] Turreau to Champagny, June 28, 1808, Correspondance politique, LXI, 166-177.

accountability to which he held any ship leaving an American port for France on a special mission.[23] Aside from these pinpricks, the President did little to assert America's independence of French foreign policy, certainly nothing to hurt France's war effort. To the very end of his administration he maintained that Britain's sea power made her the greater danger to the United States; the Spanish uprising against French domination in 1808 served only to convince him that France could never carry out a program of overseas aggression.[24] His deep-rooted fear of British power, combined with the temptations offered by co-operation with France, had induced him to throw over his official policy of encouraging a deadlock between the "lions and the tigers" and to risk instead final French victory.

Repeal of the Embargo Act coincided with the expiration of Jefferson's term as President of the United States. Britain, sure that the embargo would damage America more than herself, stubbornly persisted in executing her maritime policies and was rewarded by the opening of Spanish markets in time to offset loss of American trade. France, considering the United States as just another satellite, saw no reason for thanking Jefferson for the Embargo Act. In fact, Napoleon's minister in Washington welcomed the prospect of revocation in the expectation that the next American step would be war with Britain.[25] As for the United States, the embargo did severe damage to agriculture and commerce and brought unpopularity to Jefferson's administration. The loopholes in the act, widespread violations of its provisions, and the threat of secession in New England all contributed to the failure of the program.

Yet Jefferson's despair over the fate of the embargo and of his career was not justified by the facts. During his two terms in office he had assumed responsibility for doubling the territory of the United States and had succeeded in the even more formidable task of keeping his country out of Europe's wars. The embargo itself might have forced concessions from Britain, had it lasted longer.[26] The unhappiness of his last days as

[23] Jefferson to Madison, May 31, 1808, *Writings of Jefferson,* ed. Lipscomb and Bergh, XII, 70; Jefferson to Gallatin, July 4, 1808, *ibid.,* p. 79; Jefferson to Madison, Aug. 12, 1808, *ibid.,* p. 126.

[24] Jefferson to Henry Dearborn, Aug. 12, 1808, *ibid.,* p. 125. Always optimistic in this period, Jefferson wondered if France's difficulties in Spain might make this the proper time to take action against Spanish America.

[25] Turreau to Champagny, July 3, 1809, Correspondance politique, LXI, 238-247[vo].

[26] Sears, *Jefferson and the Embargo,* p. 318.

President was due in part to an overestimation of America's coercive powers and, in larger measure, to circumstances beyond his control. A major difficulty with the embargo was not in its composition or in its general purposes but in the special reasons Jefferson had for adopting it. Designed in part as an instrument to punish Britain, its failure portended a shift to less peaceful means of achieving this objective. In leading directly to the War of 1812, the embargo policy pointed up the flaws in Jefferson's understanding of the balance of power in Europe.

Jefferson's departure from Washington for his home at Monticello brought no change in his views concerning the international scene. As long as Bonaparte remained in power and at war with the British navy, he continued to aver that the "Leviathan of the Sea" was the chief threat to America's security. In the solitude of the Virginia piedmont he dwelt upon his prejudices against Britain and his hopes for a French victory. Instead of acting as a moderating influence upon President Madison, Jefferson helped to stimulate his old friend's wrath against Britain.[27] The weaknesses in Madison's leadership that resulted in a declaration of war received no check from his former chief. In fact, the War of 1812 appeared to Jefferson to be the logical extension of the embargo program, and the results he had expected from the embargo were just those he hoped war would bring in 1812.

Reflecting carefully on the plight of his country, Jefferson weighed the virtues and faults of each belligerent and found the British to be more dangerous than ever before. Aside from the fact that Napoleon, without a navy, could not easily disturb the United States, he noted particularly that the French Empire lacked the stability and permanency of Britain. The Emperor's personality was as distasteful to him as ever, and his regime was admittedly the most violent and most ruthless of Europe. But it was also the most ephemeral. When the dictator died, the flimsy structure he had erected would collapse with him. British power, on the

[27] Federalists and their sympathizers made no secret of their belief that Jefferson controlled Madison's decisions. While Jefferson offered his advice on many issues, there was no conscious effort on his part to dictate policy and no uniform practice of acceptance on Madison's part. See Roy J. Honeywell, "President Jefferson and His Successor," *American Historical Review*, XLVI (Oct. 1940), 64-75. During the War of 1812 Jefferson reduced his correspondence with Madison to avoid charges of meddling. He was human enough, however, to resent the times when he did offer advice and Madison refused it. Jefferson to Monroe, May 30, 1813, *Writings of Jefferson*, ed. Lipscomb and Bergh, XIII, 250-252; Jefferson to Madison, June 18, 1813, *ibid.*, pp. 259-260.

other hand, was all the more intimidating because it could survive the death of its chief of state.[28] The implications of this unpleasant reflection were so inimical to American interests in 1810 and 1811 that Jefferson appeared more disposed to accept a complete French victory over Britain than he had been at the time of the embargo; "a *republican* Emperor" would at least reserve the United States for the last step in his march to world domination.[29] While Jefferson may have felt no more liking for the Emperor as an individual or any more trust in his promises than before, he was not awed by France. Britain, on the other hand, both frightened and angered him.

His disquisitions on the sins of foreign nations, on the mortal sins of Britain in particular, were not made on the sole basis of past experience. He considered them in the light of new actions which the warring powers took against neutral America. Britain once again was the chief offender. The British foreign minister, George Canning, repudiated in 1809 a newly made agreement with the United States whereby each country would repeal punitive laws directed against the other. Canning's recall of Erskine from the post of British minister to the United States was technically justified because Erskine had not followed his instructions, but the tactless way of handling the matter added fuel to the fire of Anglophobia in America. Jefferson was all the more upset by this new evidence of British perfidy, because he had hoped that a real truce with Britain would permit the United States to deal more resolutely with Napoleon.[30]

Seeking revenge for this blow, the United States fell into the next snare of the wily French Emperor by scrapping the nonintercourse system, which had replaced the embargo, in favor of Macon's Bill Number 2 of 1810. Knowing that restoration of American trade with the belligerents would serve the British cause, Napoleon induced Madison to accept a purposely ambiguous announcement of the revocation of the Berlin and Milan Decrees as meeting all the requirements of the Macon Bill.[31] Jeffer-

---

[28] Jefferson to Caesar Rodney, Feb. 10, 1810, *ibid.*, XII, 357-358; Jefferson to Robert Patterson, Sept. 11, 1811, *ibid.*, XIII, 87.

[29] Jefferson to Madison, Apr. 19 and 27, 1809, *ibid.*, XII, 274, 276-277; Jefferson to John Langdon, Mar. 5, 1810, *ibid.*, p. 375. Jefferson's italics.

[30] Jefferson to W. C. Nicholas, May 25, 1809, *Works of Jefferson*, ed. Ford, XI, 107-108; Jefferson to Madison, June 16, 1809, *ibid.*, p. 112.

[31] A. T. Mahan, *Sea Power in its Relations to the War of 1812* (London, 1905), I, 235-241.

son was no less willing to accept these French professions, even if they were not made in good faith.[32]

To trust Napoleon's statements in the face of new hostile actions against American ships and sailors and in the absence of any official document canceling the Berlin and Milan Decrees required the President to shut his eyes to reality. Actually, Madison placed no more faith in Napoleon's pledges than did Jefferson; he frankly expressed his skepticism about France's promises and pondered dolefully over the advisability of declaring war on both countries.[33] He shut his eyes to reality not by trusting the French but by allowing the crimes of the British and the desire for American expansion to push Napoleon's rapacity into the background.[34]

The explosive issues of neutral rights and impressment were not the only ones that brought the United States into war with Britain. America's desire for continental expansion inflamed passions in the West and South, and not the least articulate voice among the expansionists was Jefferson's, urging his countrymen to observe that America had more to gain from a war with Britain than from a war with France. He applauded Madison's decision to send occupation troops into Spanish Florida to protect American interests and advised him to take over East Florida as well as West Florida lest Britain, as Spain's ally, seize it first on the pretext of helping the Spanish against Napoleon.[35]

Florida, however, was small pickings compared with the vast territory to the north which Britain could cede to the United States. Control of Canada would not only give new riches and power to the young republic but also bring security to the pioneers whose lives were constantly being menaced by British-led Indians. "The possession of that country," Jefferson wrote, "secures our women and children forever from the tomahawk and scalping knife, by removing those who excite them."[36] The acquisi-

[32] Jefferson to Mazzei, Dec. 29, 1813, Jefferson Papers, CC, Lib. Cong.

[33] Madison to Jefferson, Mar. 18, 1811, and May 25, 1812, in *The Writings of James Madison*, ed. Gaillard Hunt (New York, 1900-10), VIII, 134-135, 190-191.

[34] C. C. Tansill, "Robert Smith," in *The American Secretaries of State and Their Diplomacy*, ed. S. F. Bemis (New York, 1927-29), III, 177. See also Irving Brant, *James Madison: The President, 1809-1812* (Indianapolis, Ind., 1956), pp. 481-483. Brant places most of the blame, however, on Federalist and British leadership.

[35] Jefferson to John Wayles Eppes, Jan. 5, 1811, *Works of Jefferson*, ed. Ford, XI, 160-161. See Julius W. Pratt, *Expansionists of 1812* (New York, 1925), pp. 69-75.

[36] Jefferson to John Adams, June 11, 1812, *Writings of Jefferson*, ed. Lipscomb and Bergh, XIII, 161.

tion of Canada had long been in his mind, although obscured by other problems that had diverted his energies when he was President. His only objection to Madison's declaration of war was its timing; war should have been declared when the weather first permitted entrance of American troops into Canada.[37]

Jefferson made no move to halt the course of the conflict; rather he anticipated it and welcomed it. He did not prefer war to diplomacy; in his view diplomacy had failed with the downfall of the embargo, and the only method of handling the British thenceforth was war. Having stoically accepted the ultimate necessity of war, he could afford to brush aside the malice and greed of Napoleon as minor problems.[38] Jefferson's pacifism, which had been a dominant factor in his policies as a statesman, had always had a limit. When it was reached, he sought America's advantage from her own war just as in the past he had sought advantage from wars of other powers.

The calmness with which the former President accepted the news of war with Britain was increased by his complacent expectation that American soldiers would have little difficulty in occupying Canada. Britain did not have many men in Canada; she was too absorbed in her European ventures to man her American possessions adequately. "The acquisition of Canada this year, as far as the neighborhood of Quebec, will be a mere matter of marching, and will give us experience for the attack of Halifax the next, and the final expulsion of England from the American continent."[39] To be sure, Jefferson anticipated some hardships, such as the burning of New York and other seaport towns, but he had hopes that incendiaries, recruited from the starving workers of Britain who would be deprived of gainful employment by the lack of markets, would amply compensate for such a catastrophe with retaliatory attacks on London.[40]

[37] Jefferson to Madison, June 29, 1812, *ibid.*, p. 172; Jefferson to Madison, Mar. 26, 1812, Jefferson Papers, CLXLV, Lib. Cong.

[38] The failure of the Erskine Agreement so soon after the failure of the embargo increased his pessimism about future Anglo-American relations. Jefferson to Madison, Aug. 17, 1809, *Writings of Jefferson,* ed. Lipscomb and Bergh, XII, 305-306. Jefferson still thought that the embargo had been the instrument that kept us from "a gripe of the paw" of the Mammoth and "the flounce of the tail" of the Leviathan. But part of the nation rebelled against that program, and "from that moment, I have seen no system which could keep us entirely aloof from these agents of destruction." Jefferson to Walter Jones, Mar. 5, 1810, *ibid.*, pp. 372-373.

[39] Jefferson to Duane, Aug. 4, 1812, *ibid.*, XIII, 180-181.

[40] Jefferson to Gen. Thaddeus Kosciusko, June 28, 1812, *ibid.*, p. 169. Jefferson had long believed that England's industrial system would fall apart once its Ameri-

As for probable British victories on the high seas, American privateers would counterbalance their damage with destruction of Britain's merchant marine. So confident was the squire of Monticello of America's ability to defeat Britain that he was not at all sorry that Congress had learned too late about the revocation of the orders in council which should have removed the immediate cause of hostilities. If the British wanted to have peace now, they should surrender Canada as indemnification for the ships and men seized during the past twenty years and as security against further attacks by them or by their Indian allies.[41] "The British government seem to be doing late, what done earlier might have prevented war; to wit: repealing the orders in Council. But it should take more to make peace than to prevent war. The sword once drawn, full justice must be done."[42]

For the United States to win her objectives—new territory in America, destruction of British commerce, and the humbling of British sea power—complete co-operation with the French Empire should have been the logical result of her entry into the war. The United States and France were fighting a common enemy, and Jefferson counted heavily upon Napoleon's support for success. Only by being assured that British forces would be tied down in Europe could Americans expect free rein in America; only the Continental System could shake the financial structure of Britain. The former President showed his understanding of America's dependence on France by approving Napoleon's invasion of Russia, which coincided with America's initial war moves. "The exclusion of their [British] commerce from the United States, and the closing of the Baltic against it, which the present campaign in Europe will effect, will accomplish the castastrophe already so far advanced on them."[43]

The United States government, nevertheless, maintained the fiction of fighting its own separate war and saw no occasion of making this an excuse to fraternize with the Emperor. Jefferson heartily concurred in this attitude. It was, first of all, good politics to disassociate America's action

can sources of supply were cut off. As late as the summer of 1814 he still had visions of starving workers eager to help America by punishing their ruling classes for the loss of their livelihoods. See Jefferson to Thomas Cooper, Sept. 10, 1814, *ibid.*, XIV, 186.

[41] Jefferson to Thomas Letre, Aug. 8, 1812, *ibid.*, XIII, 185-186.
[42] Jefferson to Robert Wright, Aug. 8, 1812, *ibid.*, p. 184.
[43] Jefferson to William Duane, Aug. 4, 1812, *ibid.*, p. 181.

15

from France's war against Europe. Claims for spoliations and amends for imprisonment of American seamen remained a sore point in Franco-American relations.[44] Any talk of open alliance with the French would have invoked the wrath not only of the Federalists and the Francophobes, but also of those Republicans who detested the Napoleonic dictatorship.[45] Moreover, there was no need for a change of status between the two countries; France, it was felt, would perform the service of tying up the British in Europe no matter what course the United States pursued.

Jefferson's attitude toward the two major adversaries during the War of 1812 was probably more confused than subtle. Clinging to his old theme that Britain was America's principal enemy, he seemed early in the war to look favorably upon a thorough defeat of Britain. The next step was to be war with France if necessary.[46] Singlehandedly, it seemed, the American David could take on the two Goliaths of Europe and defeat them each in turn!

As the war progressed and the invasion of Canada proved more troublesome, Jefferson reflected further upon this scheme and found it wanting. It finally occurred to him that despite all the obstacles Providence might throw in the way of Napoleon's conquest of the United States, a victorious Emperor might easily possess the British fleet and all the resources of the British Empire, combining therewith the power of the Leviathan of the Sea with that of the Mammoth of the Land.[47] "The success of Bonaparte in the battle of Dresden," he observed, "and repair of the checks given by Bernadotte and Blucher, which I have no doubt he will soon effect, added to the loss of Canada, will produce a melancholy meeting between the Executive of England and its parliament. And should it overset the ministry it might give us peace with England, and

[44] Monroe's report to the President, July 12, 1813, in *American State Papers*, ed. Walter Lowrie and others (Washington, 1832-61), *Foreign Relations*, III, 609-612.

[45] The Senate failed by only two votes to include France in its declaration of war against Britain. France, for her part, showed no disposition to treat her republican colleague any more graciously than she had before the United States entered the war.

[46] Jefferson to Robert Wright, Aug. 8, 1812, *Writings of Jefferson*, ed. Lipscomb and Bergh, XIII, 184-185.

[47] Mme. de Staël was the only French liberal to urge Jefferson to take a stand against Napoleon and to warn him against supporting France's war effort. Jefferson's reply was the standard one deploring Napoleon's acts but seeing Britain's as more injurious to the United States. Mme. de Staël to Jefferson, Nov. 10, 1812, in Marie G. Kimball, "Unpublished Correspondence of Mme. de Staël with Thomas Jefferson," *North American Review*, CCVIII (1918), 66-68; Jefferson to Mme. de Staël, May 24, 1813, *Writings of Jefferson*, ed. Lipscomb and Bergh, XIII, 237-245.

consequently war with all those arrayed against her in Europe, which will hardly mend our situation."[48]

Therefore, the United States would do better to let the two powers battle themselves to mutual exhaustion so that neither would have strength left to hurt smaller countries. He decided that it was wise for the United States to send grain to British troops in Spain where they were locked in combat with the French, because the British were fighting America's battles in the Iberian peninsula. Should the British be starved out of Spain, he feared they would be sent to the American theater of operations. On the other hand, the United States should do nothing to interfere with the French campaign in the Baltic, for there France was serving our cause by shutting off Britain's manufactures from that sea and hence from the Continent, thereby "assisting us in her reduction to extremity."[49] So difficult was the choice that "we know not what to fear, and, only standing to our helm, must abide, with folded arms, the issue of the storm."[50]

While the devious course of Jefferson's opinions on foreign policy pointed toward a stalemate in Europe as the desirable result for America, the logic of his country's position in Europe's war indicated service to French interests. Understandably, his followers were never so mystified about his views as they were at this time. If a French conquest of Europe was inimical to the United States, why make common cause in war? How was he to explain a policy that advocated a French victory, but not too much of a victory? And Jefferson was forced to make explanations, for even in retirement he was considered the fountainhead of all wisdom in the Republican party and as such was expected to exert considerable influence upon the Madison administration.[51] The issue of friendship with

[48] Jefferson to T. M. Randolph, Nov. 14, 1813, Jefferson Papers, CC, Lib. Cong.
[49] Jefferson to James Ronaldson, Jan. 12, 1813, *Writings of Jefferson,* ed. Lipscomb and Bergh, XIII, 205-206. A year later Jefferson changed his mind about a French invasion of Russia when he realized that a Napoleonic victory would "lay at his feet the whole continent of Europe." Jefferson to Thomas Leiper, Jan. 1, 1814, *ibid.,* XIV, 43-44.
[50] Jefferson to Mrs. Trist, June 10, 1814, Jefferson Papers, Massachusetts Historical Society.
[51] The Republican journalist, William Duane, had even assumed that the old master would replace James Monroe as Secretary of State after the fiasco in Canada. Jefferson was gratified by this show of loyalty and deemed it honorable "for the general of yesterday to act as a corporal today, if his service can be useful to his country." But he claimed that he was too old to be of service. William Duane to Jefferson, Sept. 20, 1812, Jefferson Papers, CXCVI, Lib. Cong.; Jefferson to Duane, Oct. 1, 1812, *Writings of Jefferson,* ed. Lipscomb and Bergh, XIII, 186-187.

France divided Republicans into two groups: those whose contempt for Bonaparte as a destroyer of liberty made them as anxious for his defeat as for Britain's, and those whose hatred for Britain transformed Bonaparte into an agent of republicanism. Since Jefferson's ideas on America's re-lations with France were susceptible to both interpretations, it was not surprising that both groups claimed him for their patron.

The consequence of a misunderstanding arising from the intraparty confusion of war aims could have been political embarrassment to the country's war effort as well as personal grief for Jefferson. For the most part he was successful in reconciling the two factions without bringing the issues into the public eye, but in one instance he was forced to admit to hostility toward both major belligerents so openly that he feared the French minister would lodge a protest claiming his statements were lend-ing comfort to the enemy.[52] The cause of this storm was the controversial figure, George Logan, an ardent supporter of the French Revolution until the rise of Bonaparte. He was the idealistic and perhaps naïve Pennsyl-vania Quaker who had made a visit to Europe in the summer of 1798 to find out for himself whether the French government intended to make war upon the United States. Although the Federalists had reprimanded him by passage of the Logan Act penalizing private citizens undertaking such missions to foreign governments, Logan's report of the friendliness of the Directory influenced many Americans, including Thomas Jefferson. Fifteen years later, Logan's missionary zeal was no less strong, except that his love for France had been converted into hatred for the dictator. Mak-ing another trip to Europe, this time to England, he found, in 1810, con-firmation for his prejudices, just as he had in 1798. England was free and powerful and much less under the control of the sordid commercial class than most Americans imagined.[53] Hence, when the Anglo-American war broke out, Logan considered it his duty to inform Jefferson that an honor-able treaty could be made with the British if the former President as-serted his influence on Madison.[54]

Jefferson had standard answers for Republican critics who opposed America's fighting alongside France. He would usually marshal his old arguments admitting the villainies of Napoleon and France's animosity toward the United States, while at the same time claiming that British

[52] Jefferson to Thomas Leiper, Jan. 4, 1814, Jefferson Papers, CC, Lib. Cong.
[53] Logan to Jefferson, Sept. 18 and Dec. 9, 1813, *ibid.*
[54] Logan to Jefferson, Sept. 18, 1813, *ibid.*

enmity was more immediate and more threatening to national security. Possibly in deference to Logan's emotional state, his reply in this instance emphasized more forcefully than was customary his own horror of the imperial regime: "No man on earth has stronger detestation than myself of the unprincipled tyrant who is deluging the continent of Europe with blood." The letter also contained the usual qualifying remarks about his hope of "seeing England forced to just terms of peace with us," a hope that could be realized only through the agency of Napoleon.[55] Whether Logan misunderstood the qualification or purposely misconstrued the letter is not clear. What is clear was his release to the press of an excerpt that presented the former President as an enemy of France and an apparent opponent of the war.[56]

Publication of Jefferson's condemnation of Napoleon immediately antagonized Republicans, like Thomas Leiper of Philadelphia, who considered the French to be performing a noble service, if unwittingly, in fighting Britain and forces of monarchical reaction. Leiper wrote Jefferson a letter of rebuke, lecturing him on the consequences of a British victory. The triumphant British, he foresaw, "would not suffer a Cockboat of any other nation to swim the Ocean." The only consolation he could find in the old statesman's apparent Anglophilism was the possibility that the letter was a forgery.[57] Jefferson did not fail him. Shocked "by the infidelity of one with whom I was formerly intimate, but who has abandoned the American principles out of which that intimacy grew, and become the bigoted partisan of England," he explained the details of Logan's "infidelity" to Leiper.[58] Despite the unpleasantness that this contretemps caused him,[59] the incident made it perfectly clear that when he was forced to choose between Britain and France, his choice fell to the latter.

[55] Jefferson to Logan, Oct. 3, 1813, *Writings of Jefferson,* ed. Lipscomb and Bergh, XIII, 384-387.
[56] It appeared in *Poulson's American Advertiser,* Philadelphia, Dec. 6, 1813.
[57] Leiper to Jefferson, Dec. 9, 1813, Jefferson Papers, CC, Lib. Cong.
[58] Jefferson to Leiper, Jan. 1, 1814, *Writings of Jefferson,* ed. Lipscomb and Bergh, XIV, 41-45. Jefferson did not give his opinions specifically on America's ties with France in the Logan letter, as he had in less publicized ones. In the Leiper letter he actually enlarged on the evils of Bonapartism. He hoped for a stalemate but implied that British defeat would be his second choice.
[59] It is worth noting that Jefferson's cry of betrayal did not signify the severance of his relations with Logan. Jefferson never wanted to lose a friend; he went out of his way to renew ties with Logan as he had done with others—Paine, Monroe, William Short—who had abused his friendship on various occasions. It is possible that Logan had not realized what he had done. He actually wrote Jefferson, thanking

The fact that the Treaty of Ghent in December 1814 ended the War of 1812 without entailing the loss of any American territory testified to the essential truth of one of Jefferson's favorite theses: Europe's troubles were America's opportunity. With Napoleon brought to heel and banished to the island of Elba, Britain was master of Europe as well as of the high seas and hence was in a position to impose her will upon the hapless United States whose campaigns against British America had failed even while the French Emperor was still ruler of the Continent. If Britain did not complete her reconquest of America, a prominent deterrent was the difficulties facing her in the redivision of Europe. Worn out by long years of warfare, Britain envisaged sufficient obstacles at the Vienna peace tables —potential squabbles among the victorious allies and the possible return of Napoleon—to dampen her ardor for revenge upon the Americans.

The retired statesman of Monticello saw none of this at first. When the Emperor departed for Elba in the spring of 1814, Jefferson expected that his country would be exposed to the unchecked wrath of the British, to their lust for reconquest.[60] Contemplation of this frightening prospect, in which the burning of Washington seemed to have been only a prelude, made him regard Bonaparte in an almost favorable light. He remembered that "he gave employment to much of the force of the nation who was our common enemy" and that "diabolical as they paint that enemy, he burnt neither public edifices nor private dwellings. It was reserved for England to show that Bonaparte, in atrocity, was an infant to their ministers and their generals."[61]

But while Jefferson mourned the loss of French power and expressed his fear of the anger of Britain, he observed Britain's disposition to talk peace and urged Americans to meet her efforts at least halfway. The invasion of Canada having ended in ignominious failure, Jefferson made little mention of territorial ambitions as being obstacles in the way of American reconciliation with Britain. As for the issues of neutral rights

---

him for what he obviously considered to be support of his views. Logan to Jefferson, Dec. 9, 1813, Jefferson Papers, CC, Lib. Cong. Not until after the war did Jefferson express to Logan his resentment over the incident, and then he couched it in gentle terms. Jefferson to Logan, May 19, 1816, *Works of Jefferson*, ed. Ford, XI, 525-526.

[60] Jefferson to John Melish, Dec. 10, 1814, *Writings of Jefferson*, ed. Lipscomb and Bergh, XIV, 219.

[61] Jefferson to Thomas Cooper, Sept. 10, 1814, *ibid.*, p. 186; Jefferson to William Crawford, Feb. 11, 1815, *ibid.*, p. 240; Jefferson to Monroe, Jan. 1, 1815, *ibid.*, pp. 226-227.

and impressment, he hoped that the conclusion of the European war would make them academic. He personally was happy to do his part in calming British passions by letting it be known that he had never really been hostile to the British people; he merely disliked some of the principles, such as their interpretation of neutral rights, and even those principles would be acceptable if the United States might thereby escape from the war.[62] He approved of the work of the peace negotiators, although the posthumous victory of American arms at New Orleans gave him back some of his old boldness: "I presume that, having spared to the pride of England her formal acknowledgment of the atrocity of impressment in an article of the treaty, she will concur in a convention for relinquishing it."[63] The last was only face-saving bluster.

As soon as the United States was released from war with Britain, Jefferson's attitude toward France gradually became more hostile. Not that he admitted his mistake in having supported the imperial regime in the past. On the contrary, his disgust for the stupidity of the restored Bourbons made him welcome for a moment the return of Napoleon from Elba as a defender of "the cause of his nation, and that of all mankind, the rights of every people to independence and self-government."[64] But with the British threat removed, these thoughts were no more than an expression of anger at the greed of the Coalition and its Bourbon puppet; he knew that France could never enjoy lasting peace under a Bonaparte. No matter how democratic his guise, the result would be military despotism for France and renewal of conflict for the world. Jefferson did not regret Waterloo for long.[65]

It is obvious that Jefferson understood the importance to American security of an equilibrium in Europe. As he had asserted many times, the objective of the United States in any European struggle should be ultimate stalemate, leaving the belligerents too weak to affect to any important degree the sovereignty of small neutrals. Nevertheless, his con-

---

[62] Jefferson to Short, Nov. 28, 1814, *ibid.*, pp. 212-213; Jefferson to John Adams, July 5, 1814, *ibid.*, pp. 146-147; Jefferson to Caesar Rodney, Mar. 16, 1815, *ibid.*, pp. 285-286.

[63] Jefferson to Madison, Mar. 23, 1815, *ibid.*, pp. 291-292.

[64] Jefferson to Correa de Serra, June 28, 1815, *ibid.*, p. 330; Jefferson to Adams, Aug. 10, 1815, *ibid.*, p. 345; Jefferson to Mazzei, Aug. 9, 1815, *Works of Jefferson*, ed. Ford, XI, 483.

[65] Jefferson to du Pont, May 15, 1815, *Writings of Jefferson*, ed. Lipscomb and Bergh, XIV, 297-298; Jefferson to Adams, June 10 and Aug. 11, 1815, *ibid.*, pp. 299-300, 346.

fidence in America's powers of coercion and his preoccupation with the British menace led him to adopt a foreign policy that misread the scales of power. The freedom of action which he enjoyed in dealing with embattled Europe stemmed from an assumption that the balance was fundamentally in favor of the British. Thus he could risk supporting France's ambitions, secure in the knowledge that the services he was rendering Napoleon would not affect the desired stalemate. While he recognized the evils of the dictator's regime, he saw an imbalance in the comparative postions of France and Britain which allowed diplomatic maneuvers that would not have been ventured had he been dealing with two countries equally dangerous to the United States.

He was not without his doubts about his balance-of-power policy. Periodically, he expressed fear concerning the consequences of a victory for either belligerent, but even in his darkest moods he would still take his chances with a victorious France, if such a choice had to be made. Those rare occasions when he spoke out in favor of an alliance with Britain or on the benignity of British sea power were prior to the intensification of the European wars and reflected either a devious gambit designed to extract concessions from the French or an errant faith in the friendliness of the short-lived Fox ministry.[66]

Jefferson's activities on behalf of Napoleon are difficult to explain on the basis of national interest. Granting the material and psychological damage done by British maritime practices and granting also the threat to American's sovereignty inherent in their actions, one may still claim that Britain's war was essentially a defense against the continuous pressure of Napoleonic imperialism, and the policies which disturbed or injured Americans were essentially by-products of Britain's response to that pressure. To illustrate the difference between the two nations, one need only speculate as to what Jefferson's foreign policy might have been if France and not Britain had been a neighbor in Canada during this ten-year period. His behavior in the Louisiana crisis suggests that he would have been far more disturbed over potential French aggression than he actually had been over a British attack in 1812. Britain's war with the United States was fought reluctantly—despite the malevolence of Canning—and her war aims were limited. As to Napoleon's plans in event of victory, Jefferson had no illusions, whatever he might have felt about the Emperor's ability to carry them out.

[66] Jefferson to Madison, Aug. 27, 1805, *ibid.*, XI, 87; Jefferson to Monroe, May 4, 1806, *ibid.*, p. 111.

Even if the United States had been buttressing the weaker power, the idea of competing so vigorously in the international arena was exceedingly dangerous when all adversaries were so much more powerful than herself. But Jefferson's policies, centering as they did on retaliation against Britain and on using France to win new Louisianas, pushed the country inexorably into the European maelstrom. Only by keeping out of Europe's wars could the plan of playing one country against the other be executed with any real success; by engaging in the war as a cobelligerent if not as an open ally, the country deprived itself of the advantages Jefferson had anticipated. Once involved, the danger of being either overwhelmed by the superior force of the enemy or treated as a satellite by the powerful ally was far greater than the opportunity for making gains at the expense of Europe.

Ironically, the isolationism for which he has been criticized—specifically, abstention from European quarrels—best suited the national interest at this time. Isolationism was not necessarily opposed to realism in foreign policy and, in Jefferson's case, was not in practice equated with ideological rigidity. His greatest successes as a statesman were characterized by an appreciation for the importance of the European balance of power to America's fortunes, the need for freedom from foreign entanglements, and the value of a cautious diplomacy in advancing westward expansion. His rationalizations for the embargo and for American participation in the Napoleonic Wars represent a departure from this policy.

The Monroe-Pinkney Treaty of 1806:
A Reappraisal

Donald R. Hickey

ON March 3, 1807, David M. Erskine, the British minister in Washington, received from London the draft of an Anglo-American treaty. The American envoys who had negotiated it—James Monroe and William Pinkney—had urged dispatch so that the agreement might reach the United States before Congress adjourned.[1] The treaty arrived just in the nick of time.

Erskine hastened to James Madison's office to show the document to the secretary of state. According to Erskine, when Madison learned that the treaty did not provide for an end to impressment, he "expressed the greatest astonishment and Disappointment." Moreover, when the secretary read a note appended to the treaty reserving to Great Britain the right to retaliate against France for the recently issued Berlin Decree, he insisted that this note alone "would have prevented . . . the ratification of the Treaty even if all the Articles of it had been satisfactory."[2]

That night a joint committee of Congress waited on President Thomas Jefferson to find out whether he had any further business for Congress to transact. Jefferson was in unusually bad humor. Not only was he vexed by the terms of the treaty, but he was suffering from one of his recurring migraine headaches. When a member of the committee asked if the treaty would be submitted to the Senate, the president angrily replied, "Certain-

Mr. Hickey is a member of the Department of History at Wayne State College in Nebraska. This article is an offshoot of a study of the War of 1812 that will be published by the University of Illinois Press. Acknowledgments: I would like to thank all who commented on a version of this article at meetings of the Mid-America American Studies Association in Urbana, Ill., in April 1985, and the Society for Historians of the Early American Republic at Gunston Hall, Va., in July 1985. I owe a special debt to Morton Borden, Lawrence S. Kaplan, Robert McColley, Bradford Perkins, and William Stinchcombe for helpful criticisms of drafts, and to Clifford Egan for bringing valuable source materials to my attention.

[1] Monroe and Pinkney to Lords Holland and Auckland, Nov. 20, 1806, and Monroe to Auckland, Dec. 17, 1806, Monroe Papers, New York Public Library, New York, N.Y.

[2] Erskine to Lord Howick, Mar. 6, 1807, Foreign Office Papers, 5/52, Public Record Office.

ly not." Instead, the draft was returned to England for renegotiation that, in the event, proved utterly futile.[3]

The Monroe-Pinkney Treaty dealt with a host of issues that had long troubled Anglo-American relations. Ever since the outbreak of the Wars of the French Revolution in the early 1790s, Great Britain and the United States had repeatedly clashed over neutral rights on the high seas. As one of the leading belligerents, Britain favored a narrow definition of neutral rights, while the United States, the leading neutral, favored a much broader one. The two nations had resolved some of their differences in the Jay Treaty of 1794, but most of the articles in that treaty had expired in 1803, and a number of new issues had surfaced.[4] The Monroe-Pinkney Treaty was designed to resolve these issues. It was a maritime agreement that defined neutral and belligerent rights in time of war and established the terms of trade between the United States and the British Empire.

The treaty put America's reexport trade with the West Indies on a secure footing and recognized an extension of America's territorial waters. It also established a narrow definition of contraband, assured proper notice of blockades, and reduced duties paid by American ships in British ports. In addition, it provided for compensating American merchants who suffered from British violations of the treaty. In exchange for these concessions, the United States promised to employ no commercial sanctions against Great Britain, to give up the doctrine of free ships–free goods, to accept greater restrictions on American trade with the British East Indies, and in general to treat the British in a friendly manner. In effect, the United States secured a broader definition of neutral rights in exchange for a promise of benevolent neutrality.

Nonetheless, to Republican leaders the treaty seemed one-sided. You may depend on it, Jefferson wrote Monroe, "that it will be considered as a hard treaty when it is known. The British commis[sione]rs appear to have screwed every article as far as it would bear, to have taken everything, & yielded nothing."[5] Jefferson's advisors concurred. A month before the

---

[3] Samuel Smith to Wilson Cary Nicholas, Mar. 4, 1807, in Henry Adams, *History of the United States of America*, 9 vols. (New York, 1889-1891), III, 431-432; *Federal Gazette* (Baltimore), reprinted in *Aurora* (Philadelphia), Mar. 10, 1807; *Commercial Advertiser* (New York), reprinted in *Enquirer* (Richmond), Mar. 20, 1807; Merrill D. Peterson, *Thomas Jefferson and the New Nation: A Biography* (New York, 1970), 861.

[4] The Jay Treaty was scheduled to expire either two years after the preliminaries of peace were signed in Europe or twelve years after the exchange of ratifications. Some historians have accepted the latter date (1807), but both the United States and Britain agreed (the latter reluctantly) that the treaty actually expired Oct. 1, 1803—two years after the preliminaries of peace were signed between England and France. See Madison to Monroe, Mar. 5, 1804, in Diplomatic Instructions (M-77), reel 1, State Department Records, Record Group 59, National Archives, and Monroe to Madison, Aug. 7, Sept. 8, 1804, in Dispatches from United States Ministers to Great Britain, 1791-1906 (M-30), reel 9, *ibid.*

[5] Jefferson to Monroe, Mar. 21, 1807, in Paul Leicester Ford, ed., *The Writings of Thomas Jefferson*, 10 vols. (New York, 1892-1899), IX, 36. See also Jefferson's

treaty arrived, members of the cabinet had unanimously agreed that the United States should reject any treaty that gave up the right of commercial retaliation without providing for an end to impressment.[6] Republican experts who later studied the treaty were uniformly critical of its commercial provisions. All agreed that the new restrictions on trade to the British East Indies would work a particular hardship on American merchants.[7]

Federalists took a different view. The Boston *Centinel* considered it *"extraordinary"* that the president should reject the work of envoys whom he himself had appointed and even *"more extraordinary"* that he should fail to submit the treaty to the Senate.[8] Federalist criticism increased after the treaty was published in early 1808, and rose to a torrent during the War of 1812. In early 1812 the *Alexandria Gazette* declared that "the rejection of that treaty, the responsibility of which act Mr. Jefferson has boldly taken to himself, has been the fruitful source of all the evils, which we have suffered from embargoes and non-importation acts, and may soon suffer from war."[9] Federalists often compared the Monroe-Pinkney Treaty to the Jay Treaty and reminded Americans how much the nation had prospered under the latter. Indeed, they came to see the rejection of the 1806 treaty as a great turning point in Jeffersonian diplomacy, for it killed any chance of Anglo-American rapprochement and opened the way to a contest of economic sanctions ending in war.[10]

---

memorandum on the treaty [Mar. 1807], Jefferson Papers microfilm, reel 38, Library of Congress.

[6] Cabinet notes, Feb. 3, 1807 (filed under Mar. 5, 1806), Jefferson Papers microfilm, reel 35.

[7] Madison to ———, Mar. 27, 1807, and Tench Coxe to Madison, Apr. 1, 2, and [?], 1807, Madison Papers microfilm, reel 9, Lib. Cong.; statement of William Jones [Apr. 1807] (filed under Dec. 31, 1806), Monroe Papers; Samuel Smith to Madison, Mar. 14, Apr. 3, 18, 1807, Samuel Smith Family Papers microfilm, reel 1, Lib. Cong. See also Madison to Jefferson, Apr. 13, 1807, and Albert Gallatin to Jefferson, Apr. 13, 1807, Jefferson Papers microfilm, reel 38.

[8] *Columbian Centinel* (Boston), Mar. 21, 1807.

[9] *Alexandria Daily Gazette, Commercial and Political*, Jan. 31, 1812.

[10] Speech of James A. Bayard, Feb. 14, 1809, in *[Annals of Congress], Debates and Proceedings in the Congress of the United States, 1789-1824,* 42 vols. (Washington, D.C., 1834-1856), 10th Cong., 2d sess., 391-399, hereafter cited as *Annals of Congress;* speech of Nicholas Van Dyke, Feb. 1, 1809, *ibid.,* 1296-1298; speeches of Abijah Bigelow, Feb. 9, 1814, Joseph Pearson, Feb. 16, 1814, and Zebulon Shipherd, Feb. 18, 1814, *ibid.,* 13th Cong., 2d sess., 1275-1283, 1461, 1522-1523; *Minerva* (Raleigh), Nov. 1, 1811; *Supporter* (Chillicothe, Ohio), Nov. 16, 1811; *New-England Palladium* (Boston), Oct. 4, 1811; *Columbian Centinel* (Boston), Oct. 26, 1811; *Boston Gazette,* Apr. 6, 1812, Nov. 7, 1814; *Federal Republican* (Baltimore), Oct. 27, 1814; *Alexandria Gaz.,* Oct. 3, 1811, Jan. 9, 1812; *Connecticut Mirror* (Hartford), Jan. 20, 1812; *Boston Daily Advertiser,* reprinted in *United States' Gazette* (Philadelphia), Nov. 25, 1814; *Virginia Patriot* (Richmond), reprinted in *Providence Gazette,* Sept. 10, 1814; *American Republic* (Frankfort, Ky.), reprinted in *Pittsburgh Gazette,* Jan. 31, 1812; *Connecticut Herald* (New Haven),

Republicans were not immune to the sting of criticism. The envoys had agreed not to publish the treaty until ratifications had been exchanged, but Jefferson seemed reluctant to publicize its terms at all.[11] Not until March 1808, after American newspapers had picked up the gist of the agreement from English sources, did he send the treaty and supporting documents to Congress for its information.[12] Even then, Republican congressmen tried to manipulate public opinion by limiting the number of copies printed and by insisting that a paper outlining the administration's view of the treaty be read in the House before either the treaty itself or an explanatory note penned by Monroe and Pinkney.[13] Nevertheless, it proved impossible to bury the treaty. In 1812, rumors were spread by a Republican newspaper in Baltimore that the British were planning to resurrect the agreement with certain changes favorable to the United States.[14] Even after war was declared, Republican editor Hezekiah Niles felt obliged to publish the treaty in his widely read magazine. The treaty, Niles said, was "frequently referred to;—and its insertion in the *Register* has been earnestly solicited."[15] Indeed, it was not until after the Peace of Ghent closed this era of troubled diplomacy that the Monroe-Pinkney Treaty was finally forgotten. When historians began to study the treaty, the debate was renewed.

---

reprinted in *Providence Gaz.*, Oct. 22, 1814; *Delaware Gazette* (Wilmington), reprinted in *Pittsburgh Gaz.*, Sept. 14, 1814; *Balance* (Albany), reprinted in *Alexandria Gaz.*, Nov. 6, 1812; Resolutions of Loudon Co., Va., Aug. 21, 1812, in *Federal Republican*, Sept. 9, 1812; Address of Staunton, Va., Sept. 21, 1812, *ibid.*, Oct. 5, 1812; George Cabot to Timothy Pickering, Apr. 14, 1807, in Henry Cabot Lodge, *Life and Letters of George Cabot* (Boston, 1877), 373; John Quincy Adams, "To the Citizens of the United States," in Henry Adams, ed., *Documents Relating to New-England Federalism, 1800-1815* (Boston, 1877), 177.

[11] *Enquirer*, Mar. 3, 1807.

[12] Jefferson to Monroe, Mar. 10, 1808, in Ford, ed., *Writings of Jefferson*, IX, 180n; Jefferson to Congress, Mar. 22, 1808, in *American State Papers: Documents, Legislative and Executive, of the Congress of the United States*, 38 vols. (Washington, D.C., 1832-1861), *Class I: Foreign Relations*, III, 80. The terms of the treaty were first aired in a pamphlet entitled *The British Treaty*, dedicated to members of Congress and published anonymously without indication of date or place of publication. Internal evidence suggests that it was written by a northern Federalist in late 1807. According to British consul Phineas Bond, Rufus King may have acquired a copy of the treaty from English friends and passed it on to the author of the pamphlet—probably Gouverneur Morris. This pamphlet is the only Federalist attack on the treaty I have come across. It can be found in F.O. 97/7. See also Phineas Bond to George Canning, Oct. 5, 1807, F.O. 5/53.

[13] John Randolph to Joseph Bryan, Mar. 29, 1808, John Randolph Papers, William R. Perkins Library, Duke University, Durham, N.C.; *Annals of Congress*, 10th Cong., 1st sess., Mar. 22-29, 1808, 1870-1874. The administration's view of the treaty is in Madison to Monroe and Pinkney, May 20, 1807, Diplomatic Instructions (M-77), reel 1.

[14] *American* (Baltimore), reprinted in *Boston Gaz.*, Feb. 17, 1812; *Minerva*, Feb. 21, 1812.

[15] *Niles's Weekly Register*, III (Nov. 28, 1812), 196-201.

One group, including Richard Hildreth and a number of modern diplomatic historians, has taken a favorable view of the treaty. Although Hildreth was thoroughly pro-Federalist, he could muster the sort of ri;hteous indignation at the practice of impressment that was more typical of Republicans. It was an "outrage," he said, "too flagrant to be palliated." Nevertheless, he regarded the treaty as "very favorable" to the United States and the decision to reject it as "precipitate" and "disastrous." The arguments for ratification, he insisted, "were even stronger than in the case of Jay's Treaty."[16] A. L. Burt agreed. He praised Monroe and Pinkney for displaying "unusually sound judgment" and criticized the administration for its "well-meaning yet narrow-minded repudiation of the wise decision made in London." Taken together with a stillborn supplementary convention negotiated the following year, Burt said, the Monroe-Pinkney Treaty would have "provided a settlement for almost all the outstanding issues between the United States and the British Empire." Bradford Perkins's position is more equivocal, but he too sided with the envoys. While conceding that the price exacted by the British "seemed exorbitant" and that the treaty "implied American inferiority," he nonetheless concluded that the American envoys "spoke the traditional accents of American realism" and "opened the door to peace and uneasy friendship," even though "at the cost of important moral considerations."[17]

Other historians, including Henry Adams and most Republican biographers, have taken a more hostile view. According to Adams, the treaty contained "offensive" stipulations that "no self-respecting government could admit." The English Whigs, he concluded, intended to impose "on the United States terms which would have been hard as the result of war." Dumas Malone, Jefferson's most eminent biographer, expressed a more restrained opinion. "Viewed in retrospect from the American angle," he wrote, "the treaty does appear to have been a hard one." Jefferson's rejection of the agreement was "wholly understandable" for "there were entirely too many things wrong with it." Similarly, Marshall Smelser claimed that the treaty "bound Britain in no realistic way and was clearly inferior to the Jay Treaty. At best it would have established a nervous peace by reducing the country to a British satellite." More recently,

[16] Hildreth, *The History of the United States of America*, 6 vols., rev. ed. (New York, 1854-1855), V, 535, 658-662.

[17] Burt, *The United States, Great Britain, and British North America: From the Revolution to the Establishment of Peace after the War of 1812* (New Haven, Conn., 1940), 236; Perkins, *Prologue to War: England and the United States, 1805-1812* (Berkeley, Calif., 1961), 135-139. For similar sentiments see Anthony Steel, "Impressment in the Monroe-Pinkney Negotiation, 1806-1807," *American Historical Review*, LVII (1952), 364-366, 368-369, and Patrick C. T. White, *A Nation on Trial: America and the War of 1812* (New York, 1965), 32-33. For a copy of the supplementary convention mentioned by Burt see Observations on the Proposed Treaty of Boundaries, and Intercourse, between His Majesty's Territories in North America and Those of the United States, F.O. 95/515.

Burton Spivak has characterized "the concrete gains" of the treaty as "scant" and Monroe's defense of the agreement as "excuses and apologies."[18]

Why have scholarly assessments varied so much? One reason is that because the treaty was never implemented there is no way of knowing what it would have meant to either side in practice. Moreover, scholars have allowed their view of the treaty to be colored by their biases. Historians sympathetic to Jefferson and Madison have generally assumed that the Republican leaders were right to reject the agreement, while those sympathetic to the British have taken the opposite view. As a result, the actual terms of the treaty have been largely neglected. The only extended treatments we have are those presented by Perkins in *Prologue to War* and Spivak in *Jefferson's English Crisis*, and these studies focus only on the main points.[19]

What is the best way to evaluate the treaty? First, one can seek to understand the conditions under which it originated. Next, one can examine its terms with an eye to determining as far as possible what they actually meant. Finally, one can compare it to the Jay Treaty, the only other Anglo-American agreement dealing with commerce and neutral rights in that era. Since the Monroe-Pinkney Treaty was designed to replace the Jay Treaty, the earlier agreement provides a suitable standard against which the later one can be measured.[20]

Like the Jay Treaty, the Monroe-Pinkney Treaty grew out of a crisis in Anglo-American affairs precipitated by British seizure of large numbers of American ships, primarily in the Caribbean Sea, for violating the Rule of 1756, a British maritime doctrine that prohibited neutrals from carrying

[18] Adams, *History of the United States*, III, 409-410, 415; Malone, *Jefferson and His Time*, 6 vols. (Boston, 1948-1981), V, 411; Smelser, *The Democratic Republic, 1801-1815* (New York, 1968), 156; Spivak, *Jefferson's English Crisis: Commerce, Embargo, and the Republican Revolution* (Charlottesville, Va., 1979), 60. For similar sentiments see Peterson, *Jefferson*, 865, and Irving Brant, *James Madison*, 6 vols. (Indianapolis, Ind., 1948-1961), IV, 374-379.

[19] Perkins, *Prologue to War*, 114-139; Spivak, *Jefferson's English Crisis*, 53-67. Perkins used sources on both sides of the Atlantic, while Spivak relied solely on American sources.

[20] Since the Monroe-Pinkney Treaty dealt exclusively with trade and neutral rights, the two treaties can be compared only on these issues. It should not be forgotten, however, that the Jay Treaty offered the United States other significant benefits. It bound the British to evacuate their forts in the Northwest, and it established commissions to determine indemnifications for pre-Revolutionary War debts and spoliations on the high seas. British merchants subsequently received $2,807,000 in compensation from the United States, while American merchants were awarded $10,345,000 from Great Britain. The latter was the largest award ever made by one country to another up to that time. See Samuel Flagg Bemis, *Jay's Treaty: A Study in Commerce and Diplomacy*, 2d ed. (New Haven, Conn., 1962), 441.

on trade in time of war that was closed to them in time of peace. This rule was intended to exclude Americans from France's colonial commerce, but American ships sailing between France and the West Indies circumvented it by making a stopover in the United States. At first tacitly, and then officially in the *Polly* decision (1800), the British held that such broken voyages did not violate the rule. Hence the United States captured much of the trade between Europe and the Caribbean, and its reexport trade rose from $500,000 in 1790 to $53,000,000 in 1805.[21] Such was Britain's restraint in the face of this mushrooming trade that by 1804 Monroe, the American minister in London, could report: "The truth is that our commerce never enjoyed in any war, as much freedom, and indeed favor from this govt. as it now does."[22]

Little more than a year after Monroe delivered this judgment, he accused the British of adopting a plan "to subject our commerce at present and hereafter to every restraint in their power."[23] What had happened in the interval? British officials, jealous of American commercial success and suspicious of frauds in the reexport trade, had grown much less indulgent of neutral commerce.[24] In keeping with the government's restrictive policy, the High Court of Admiralty ruled in the *Essex* decision (1805) that landing goods and paying duties in the United States was no longer proof of bona fide importation. Thenceforth, American merchants would have to provide additional though unspecified proof that ships stopping over in the United States actually broke their voyages.[25]

Given the *Essex* decision, the Royal Navy began seizing American ships engaged in the reexport trade, with paralyzing effect. Insurance rates quadrupled and American merchants faced staggering losses. Merchants in Philadelphia alone reported over a hundred captures, valued at $500,000, in the second half of 1805.[26] The total number of vessels seized in 1805-

[21] Madison to Monroe, Apr. 12, 1805, Diplomatic Instructions (M-77), reel 1; Bradford Perkins, *The First Rapprochement: England and the United States, 1795-1805*, 2d ed. (Berkeley, Calif., 1967), 87-89; Curtis P. Nettels, *The Emergence of a National Economy, 1775-1815* (New York, 1962), 396.

[22] Monroe to Madison, July 1, 1804, in Stanislaus Murray Hamilton, ed., *The Writings of James Monroe . . .*, 7 vols. (New York, 1898-1903), IV, 218. See also Monroe to Madison, Aug. 7, 1804, *ibid.*, 235.

[23] Monroe to Madison, Oct. 18, 1805, in *Am. State Papers: For. Relations*, III, 107.

[24] On the question of fraudulent practices see [James Stephen], *War in Disguise; or, The Frauds of the Neutral Flags*, 2d ed. (London, 1805); *Aurora*, Feb. 19, 1807; and W. Alison Phillips and Arthur H. Reede, *Neutrality: Its History, Economics and Law* (New York, 1935-1936), II, 118.

[25] Perkins, *Prologue to War*, 80-81. Perkins puts the date of the *Essex* decision at May 22; the correct date is May 23. See George Joy to Monroe, Dec. 31, 1805, Monroe Papers microfilm, reel 10, Lib. Cong.

[26] "Exhibit of Captures by the Belligerent Powers of Property Insured . . . in Philadelphia" [Dec. 1805], in *Am. State Papers: For. Relations*, II, 742-745; Joseph Dorr to Monroe, Oct. [?], 1806, Monroe Papers microfilm, reel 3; Anthony Merry to Lord Mulgrave, Sept. 30, Nov. 3, 1805, F.O. 5/45.

1806 was probably three or four hundred, roughly the same number taken by the British in 1793-1794 before the Jay negotiations. But in the case of the *Essex* seizures, the number of actual condemnations was small, probably no more than 10 or 20 percent. Admiralty courts in England, hearing original cases or cases on appeal from the West Indies, released most of the vessels. Great Britain, Monroe wrote home, "seeks to tranquillize us by dismissing our vessels in every case that she possibly can."[27] The Whig ministry that assumed office in 1806 under Lord Grenville and Charles James Fox found the *Essex* decision an embarrassment and quickly moved to set it aside. By an order in council issued in May 1806 proclaiming a blockade of northern Europe (the "Fox Blockade"), the reexport trade was implicitly restored to its old status.[28] The trade subsequently rose to new heights—$60,000,000 in 1806 and just slightly less in 1807. Thereafter it fell off sharply, not because of British harassment but because of American economic sanctions and the War of 1812.[29]

In 1805, American merchants could not have known that the British lion's growl would be worse than its bite. They only knew that they faced heavy losses if their ships were condemned. Accordingly, in every major seaport they banded together to petition the federal government for relief.[30] Congress responded with a partial nonimportation act aimed at Great Britain, but this law was suspended to permit negotiations first.[31] The Senate called on the president "to enter into such arrangements with the British Government, on this and all other differences subsisting between the two nations, and particularly respecting the impressment of American seamen, as may be consistent with the honor and interests of the United States."[32]

Up to this point, the chain of events was remarkably similar to what had

[27] Monroe to Madison, Sept. 25, 1805, in *Am. State Papers: For. Relations*, III, 106. See also Monroe to [Madison], Aug. 20, Sept. 2, 1805, Dispatches from U.S. Ministers (M-30), reel 9. American vessels were restored whenever their owners could show that the cargoes in question were put up for sale in the United States. See *Cobbett's Political Register* (London), reprinted in *Enquirer*, Feb. 8, 1806.

[28] Monroe to Madison, Apr. 18, 20, May 20, June 9, 1806, Dispatches from U.S. Ministers (M-30), reel 9; Fox to Monroe, May 16, 1806, and Monroe to Madison, May 17, 1806, in *Am. State Papers: For. Relations*, III, 124-125.

[29] Nettels, *National Economy*, 396; Anna Cornelia Clauder, *American Commerce as Affected by the Wars of the French Revolution and Napoleon, 1793-1812* (Philadelphia, 1932), 90-91.

[30] See petitions in *Am. State Papers: For. Relations*, II, 737-773. See also *Annals of Congress*, 9th Cong., 1st sess., Feb. 17, 20, 1806, 113, 483; *Memorial of the Inhabitants of the Town of Salem* ... (Washington, D.C., 1806); *Memorial of the Merchants of the Town of Boston* ... (Washington, D.C., 1806); and Merry to Mulgrave, Feb. 2, 1806, F.O. 5/58.

[31] *Annals of Congress*, 9th Cong., 1st sess., Apr. 18, 1806, 1259-1262.

[32] *Ibid.*, Feb. 12, 14, 1806, 90-91, 109, 112, quotation on p. 91. See also Merry to Mulgrave, Feb. 24, 1806, F.O. 5/48.

occurred before the Jay negotiations, as the president was no doubt painfully aware.[33] By this time Jefferson had soured on all commercial agreements, having concluded that mutual interest was the only reliable guarantee for trade. The day was not distant, he said in 1801, when the United States could dictate international law on the high seas. "In the meantime, we wish to let every treaty we have drop off without renewal."[34] Jefferson had little love for the Jay Treaty—"a millstone round our necks," he once called it—and his administration refused British overtures to renew its commercial clauses when they expired.[35] He was willing to sanction a limited treaty with England covering neutral rights—impressment, blockades, contraband, the reexport trade, and the right of search—but he wanted to leave the negotiations to Monroe and to exclude Anglo-American commercial issues altogether.[36] However, such was the pressure from Congress that he felt obliged to appoint a special mission to work out the whole range of differences between the two nations. "I found it necessary," he later said, "to yield my own opinion to the general sense of the national council."[37]

To join Monroe in the negotiations, Jefferson selected William Pinkney, a Baltimore Federalist who had penned a vigorous memorial against the Rule of 1756 after the *Essex* seizures.[38] Pinkney arrived in London on June 19, 1806.[39] The talks with the British envoys, Lord Holland (Fox's

[33] An *Enquirer* article noted "a strong resemblance between these relations as they were in the year '94 and as they are at present" ("Relations to Great-Britain," reprinted in *National Intelligencer, and Washington Advertiser,* Feb. 28, 1806). The parallel was heightened by the fact that the British ministry in 1806 was headed by Grenville, the man who had negotiated the Jay Treaty twelve years earlier. See Malone, *Jefferson,* V, 397.

[34] Jefferson to William Short, Oct. 3, 1801, in Ford, ed., *Writings of Jefferson,* VIII, 98. See also Jefferson to Madison, Sept. 12, 1801, *ibid.,* 93, and Henry S. Randall, *The Life of Thomas Jefferson,* 3 vols. (New York, 1858), III, 112.

[35] Randall, *Jefferson,* III, 315; Lord Harrowby to Anthony Merry, Aug. 4, 1804, in Bernard Mayo, ed., *Instructions to the British Ministers to the United States, 1791-1812* (Washington, D.C., 1941), 207.

[36] See Madison to Monroe, Jan. 5, 1804, Diplomatic Instructions (M-77), reel 1.

[37] Jefferson to Monroe, Mar. 10, 1808, in Ford, ed., *Writings of Jefferson,* IX, 179n. See also Joseph H. Nicholson to Monroe, May 5, 1806, Monroe Papers microfilm, reel 3; Anthony Merry to Lord Mulgrave, Feb. 2, 1806, and Samuel Smith to Wilson Cary Nicholas, Apr. 1, 1806, in Adams, *History of the United States,* III, 150, 169.

[38] Jefferson to the Senate, Apr. 19, 1806, Jefferson Papers microfilm, reel 35; [William Pinkney], "Memorial of the Merchants . . . of Baltimore . . . ," Jan. 21, 1806, in *Am. State Papers: For. Relations,* II, 750-756; William Pinkney, *The Life of William Pinkney . . .* (New York, 1853), 158. Pinkney also had served from 1796 to 1804 on one of the Jay Treaty commissions. See Mayo, ed., *Instructions to British Ministers,* 224n. Pinkney's appointment was a surprise to some Republicans, but Madison gave assurances that he was "an excellent Republican." See Samuel Smith to [?], Apr. 29, 1806, Smith Family Papers microfilm, reel 1.

[39] Pinkney to Monroe, June 19, 1806, Monroe Papers microfilm, reel 3.

nephew) and Lord Auckland, began on August 27 and lasted until December 31.[40] The American commissioners worked very well together. "In the management of the business," Monroe later said, "we acted with the greatest harmony."[41]

The instructions that Madison drew up to guide the envoys called for a host of concessions from the British and were largely an exercise in wishful thinking. But the administration considered only two items essential to a settlement: an end to impressment and the restoration of the reexport trade.[42] The British had recently conceded a broad range of neutral rights to Russia, Denmark, and Sweden, and the United States hoped for the same consideration.[43] Britain, however, proved unwilling to grant these terms to such a formidable commercial rival. It acted as though Jay's clauses were still in effect, and its envoys expressed the hope "that in the form & wording of the Commercial Regulations, the Treaty of 1794 should be followed as closely as circumstances would allow." The Americans demurred. Monroe said "that neither He nor his Colleague, had personally any objection—But that several of the Stipulations of the Treaty of 1794 were so offensive to the People of the United States that a Treaty nearly similar to that, not only in substance but in form, could not be favorably received on the other side of the Atlantic."[44] Thus the agreement that emerged from the negotiations followed the general outlines of the Jay Treaty but contained a number of changes, almost all of which favored the United States.

The first two and a half months were devoted primarily to the impressment issue.[45] The Americans insisted that the British give up the

[40] Am. State Papers: For. Relations, III, 133n.

[41] Monroe to Madison, Feb. 28, 1808, ibid., 173. For similar sentiments see Monroe to John H. Purviance [Jan. 1807], Purviance-Courtenay Papers, Perkins Lib.

[42] Madison to Monroe and Pinkney, May 17, 1806, Diplomatic Instructions (M-77), reel 1. See also Madison to Monroe, Jan. 5, 1804, ibid.

[43] James Madison, "An Examination of the British Doctrine, Which Subjects to Capture a Neutral Trade, Not Open in Time of Peace" (1806), in Gaillard Hunt, ed., The Writings of James Madison . . . , 9 vols. (New York, 1900-1910), VII, 257-261; Phillips and Reede, Neutrality, II, 108-109; Monroe to Fox, Feb. 25, 1806, in Am. State Papers: For. Relations, III, 113-114.

[44] Journal of Holland and Auckland, Aug. 24, 1806, Admiralty Papers, 80/117, P.R.O.; Harrowby to Merry, Aug. 4, 1804, in Mayo, ed., Instructions to British Ministers, 206-207.

[45] Steel presents a good discussion of the impressment negotiations in "Impressment," AHR, LVII (1952), 352-369, but he overrates the problem of binationalism. Very few British seamen actually became naturalized Americans. From 1796 to 1807, only 1,139 foreign seamen became American citizens. Estimates of the size of the American merchant marine in 1805-1807 (which were peak years) range from 45,000 to 110,000. See "Naturalized Seamen Registered," Jan. 6, 1813, in American State Papers: Class IV: Commerce and Navigation, I, 955; speech of Langdon Cheves, Jan. 17, 1812, in Annals of Congress, 12th Cong., 1st sess., 818; Gallatin to Madison, Apr. 13, 1807, Madison Papers microfilm, reel 25; and Adams, History of the United States, VI, 455.

practice and in exchange offered to return all British deserters in American jurisdiction. The British envoys showed an interest in this proposal but backed away when resistance in the cabinet stiffened.[46] Grenville, for one, opposed the quid pro quo "from my strong sense of the impossibility of obtaining anything like a fair execution of the American part of this stipulation."[47] The most the British would offer publicly was a solemn pledge to exercise "the greatest caution" when impressing British subjects from American ships and to afford "immediate and prompt redress" to any American mistakenly forced into service.[48] The American negotiators claimed that privately the British went much farther, even promising that if deserters were returned, the practice of their government would be "strictly conformable" to the spirit of the American proposal, and that impressment would be resorted to only "in cases of an extraordinary nature."[49] When later quizzed by their government, Holland and Auckland denied making any such promise. The written declaration, they said, contained "a full and authentic statement of what was settled between us and the American Commissioners, with respect to the impressment of British Seamen from on board American ships."[50]

Whatever verbal assurances they may have received, Monroe and Pinkney felt they had come close to meeting the spirit of their instructions.[51] Indeed, the administration in Washington later indicated that an informal arrangement on impressment was perfectly satisfactory as long as the United States was not bound by treaty to surrender the right of commercial retaliation.[52] The American envoys, however, decided to sign a treaty that gave up this very right because the British showed such a

[46] Journal of Holland and Auckland, Aug. 24, Nov. 5, 1806, Adm. 80/117; Holland and Auckland to Howick, Oct. 27, 1806, *ibid.*

[47] Grenville to Holland, Oct. 30, 1806, in Walter Fitzpatrick, ed., *Report of the Manuscripts of J. B. Fortescue, Esq., Preserved at Dropmore*, 10 vols. (Historical Manuscripts Commission, *Fifteenth Report* [London, 1892-1927]), VIII, 410, hereafter cited as *Fortescue MSS.* See also Henry Richard Lord Holland, *Memoirs of the Whig Party during My Time*, ed. Henry Edward Lord Holland, 2 vols. (London, 1852-1854), II, 102.

[48] Holland and Auckland to Monroe and Pinkney, Nov. 8, 1806, Dispatches from U.S. Ministers (M-30), reel 10.

[49] Monroe and Pinkney to Madison, Jan. 3, Apr. 22, 1807, and Monroe to Madison, Feb. 28, 1808, in *Am. State Papers: For. Relations*, III, 146, 160-161, 174, quotations on pp. 160, 174.

[50] See George Canning to Holland and Auckland, July 25, Aug. 6, 1807, and Holland and Auckland to Canning, July 28, Aug. 10, 1807, F.O. 5/54, quotation from Aug. 10 letter. See also Steel, "Impressment," *AHR*, LVII (1952), 365-366.

[51] Monroe and Pinkney to Madison, Nov. 11, 1806, Dispatches from U.S. Ministers (M-30), reel 10; Monroe and Pinkney to Madison, Apr. 22, 1807, and Monroe to Madison, Feb. 28, 1808, in *Am. State Papers: For. Relations*, III, 160, 176.

[52] Madison to Monroe and Pinkney, Feb. 3, 1807, Diplomatic Instructions (M-77), reel 1.

conciliatory spirit on the other issues. Knowing that the Americans had settled for less than their instructions called for on impressment, the British evidently sought to make the treaty as palatable as possible in other respects.[53] The result was an agreement that, for the United States at least, was a decided improvement over the Jay Treaty.[54]

The most important point gained by the United States was protection for the reexport trade. Although Britain sometimes invoked the Rule of 1756 to injure its enemies, in this case its sole aim was to share in the profits. According to the British negotiators, "the point at issue with the United States on this subject, is not a question of great importance, but a mere consideration of how the profit taken from the Enemy is to be divided." If Americans were allowed to trade freely with the French and Spanish West Indian colonies, the advantages of neutrality would enable them to dominate the trade. Hence Great Britain's aim was to clog the trade "with further impediments, which will in some degree counterbalance the advantages accruing to the Americans from their Neutrality."[55]

The problem the British faced was to obstruct the trade without destroying it. In the *Polly* decision the High Court of Admiralty had ruled that landing goods in the United States and paying duties there was sufficient to break the continuity of such voyages, but that the *intention* of the shipper was critical.[56] American merchants preferred hard and fast rules, but they often skirted such rules when they could. The issue was further clouded by an act of Congress in 1805 changing the transit duty. Before that year, the reexport trade was subject to a 3.5 percent transit duty, which meant that the United States retained 3.5 percent of the duties paid on imported goods that were subsequently shipped out of the country. In 1805 Congress eliminated all duties on goods clearly intended for reexport.[57] This convinced some British observers that American merchants paid no duties at all on their reexports, but as Samuel Smith, a Baltimore merchant and Republican senator, pointed out, few merchants actually took advantage of this law for fear of driving their insurance rates

[53] See Holland and Auckland to Howick, Nov. 8, 1806, Adm. 80/117.

[54] The Monroe-Pinkney Treaty is printed in *Am. State Papers: For. Relations*, III, 147-151. For an explanatory note see Monroe and Pinkney to Madison, Jan. 3, 1807, *ibid.*, 142-147. The Jay Treaty can be found *ibid.*, I, 520-525.

[55] Holland and Auckland to Howick, Oct. 20, 1806, F.O. 5/51. For an identical statement see Holland and Auckland to Howick, Oct. 27, 1806, Adm. 80/117. Americans recognized the commercial motivation behind the Rule of 1756. See [Pinkney], "Memorial of the Merchants of Baltimore," in *Am. State Papers: For. Relations*, II, 753, and [Gouverneur Morris?], *The British Treaty* (n.p., n.d.), 62-65.

[56] Holland and Auckland to Howick, Oct. 20, 1806, F.O. 5/51. See also Thomas P. Courtenay, *Additional Observations on the American Treaty, with Some Remarks on Mr. Baring's Pamphlet* (London, 1808), 8-18; [William Loughton Smith], *The Numbers of Phocion . . .* (Charleston, S.C. [1806]), 53-61.

[57] *Annals of Congress*, 8th Cong., 2d sess., Feb. 22, 1805, 1667; speech of David R. Williams, Mar. 8, 1806, *ibid.*, 9th Cong., 1st sess., 650.

to ruinous heights. "The merchant understands his interest too well," he said, "to commit such an act of folly."[58]

In the negotiations with Monroe and Pinkney, the British initially insisted that they could formally sanction the trade only if cargoes were landed in the United States, stored for a month, subjected to a 4 percent transit duty, and shipped out of the country in a different vessel. The Americans countered by proposing that the cargoes be landed and the ship changed.[59] A compromise was reached that provided for landing the goods and subjecting them to a 2 percent transit duty en route to Europe and a 1 percent duty en route to the West Indies.[60] Since this tax was less than the old duty, American merchants were unlikely to find it burdensome. Moreover, since British courts occasionally applied the Rule of 1756 to French or Spanish colonies elsewhere in the world (particularly in the Orient), the British agreed that this provision could be used to protect trade with those colonies as well.[61]

In another clause, the British recognized an extension of American territorial waters to five miles in favor of American vessels and the unarmed vessels of other powers acknowledging this limit.[62] In their headier moments, Republican leaders in Washington talked of gaining the Gulf Stream but were willing to accept anything more than the customary three-mile limit.[63] Because searches and seizures conducted close to the American coast were so galling, Monroe and Pinkney represented this issue as being extremely important to the United States, and the British conceded the new limit to show their "conciliatory disposition."[64] It is true that other belligerents were unlikely to recognize the new limit, and that

[58] Courtenay, *Additional Observations*, 44n; speech of Samuel Smith, Mar. 10, 1806, in *Annals of Congress*, 9th Cong., 1st sess., 173-174.

[59] Journal of Holland and Auckland, Sept. 17, 22, 1806, Adm. 80/117; Holland and Auckland to Howick, Oct. 27, 1806, *ibid.*; Madison to Monroe and Pinkney, May 17, 1806, in Diplomatic Instructions (M-77), reel 1; Monroe and Pinkney to Madison, Nov. 11, 1806, Dispatches from U.S. Ministers (M-30), reel 10; Monroe and Pinkney to Madison, Jan. 3, 1807, in *Am. State Papers: For. Relations*, III, 145.

[60] Monroe-Pinkney Treaty, Art. 11; Journal of Holland and Auckland, Dec. 1, 6, 1806, Adm. 80/117.

[61] Monroe and Pinkney to Madison, Jan. 3, 1807, in *Am. State Papers: For. Relations*, III, 145; Monroe and Pinkney to Holland and Auckland, Dec. 31, 1806 (unsent), and to John Armstrong, Jan. 16, 1807, Monroe Papers microfilm, reel 3.

[62] Monroe-Pinkney Treaty, Art. 12.

[63] Madison to Monroe and Pinkney, May 17, 1806, Diplomatic Instructions (M-77), reel 1.

[64] Holland and Auckland to Howick, Nov. 14, 1806, F.O. 5/51. See also Monroe and Pinkney to Madison, Jan. 3, 1807, in *Am. State Papers: For. Relations*, III, 145; Sir John Nicholl to Howick, Nov. 17, 1806, Adm. 80/117. Auckland said that this concession was "not unreasonable, in consideration of the peculiar shelvings of the North American shores"—that is, the shallow waters that forced coasting vessels to sail beyond the three-mile limit. Auckland to Grenville, Nov. 28, 1806, in *Fortescue MSS*, VIII, 445.

Britain would therefore retain the right to stop and search ships between the three- and five-mile limits in order to establish their nationality. But this did not mean that Britain could seize or impress from American vessels within this zone.[65] Madison later said that British naval officials stopping American ships in the zone would find it difficult to resist the temptation to seize cargo that, by their lights, was subject to confiscation.[66] This may be true. But then the injured merchant would be entitled to compensation under another clause in the treaty, which is discussed below.

The contraband article also favored the United States. To enhance its commercial opportunities, the United States preferred to abolish contraband altogether or, at least, to secure a narrow definition limited to war matériel and expressly excluding all non-enumerated goods. The British had conceded such a narrow, exclusive definition to Russia in a treaty of 1781.[67] In the Jay Treaty the contraband list was non-exclusive, which meant that the British could seize items that were not on the list. Indeed, a proviso was included that authorized the seizure of unlisted items that were not generally considered contraband (such as food), provided the owner received compensation.[68] In the Monroe-Pinkney Treaty, the list was slightly narrower: tar and pitch were excluded as long as they were not headed for a port equipped to repair warships. More important, the clause authorizing the seizure of unlisted articles was dropped, and another was substituted that prohibited the detention of any vessel for carrying contraband unless some of the listed items were found on board. This came very close to transforming the list into an exclusive one. Moreover, in another concession the British renounced the practice, recently adopted, of seizing vessels *after* they had deposited contraband at an enemy port.[69]

The United States also won concessions in the articles governing Anglo-American trade.[70] Like the Jay Treaty, the Monroe-Pinkney Treaty accorded most-favored-nation status to the ships of each nation in the ports of the other. However, the provision governing the structure of duties was changed. In 1794, American duties on foreign ships—50¢ a ton—were considerably higher than duties paid by foreign ships in British

[65] Monroe and Pinkney to Madison, Jan. 3, 1807, in *Am. State Papers: For. Relations,* III, 145.

[66] Madison to Monroe and Pinkney, May 20, 1807, Diplomatic Instructions (M-77), reel 1.

[67] Madison to Monroe, Jan. 5, 1804, and to Monroe and Pinkney, May 17, 1806, *ibid.*

[68] Jay Treaty, Art. 18.

[69] Monroe-Pinkney Treaty, Art. 9. See also Madison, "Examination of the British Doctrine," in Hunt, ed., *Madison Writings,* VII, 300-310; Madison to Monroe and Pinkney, May 17, 1806, and May 20, 1807, Diplomatic Instructions (M-77), reel 1; and Monroe to Madison, Feb. 28, 1808, in *Am. State Papers: For. Relations,* III, 176-177.

[70] See Jay Treaty, Arts. 11, 14, 15, and Monroe-Pinkney Treaty, Arts. 4, 5, 23.

ports. To equalize this burden, the Jay Treaty authorized the British to raise their duties on American ships while it froze American duties on British ships. To gain a competitive edge over American carriers as well as to raise revenue, the British had used this provision as a pretext for raising duties on American ships to 6s. 5d. or about $1.42 per ton. This was 30 percent more than the ships of Great Britain or other nations paid in British ports. The United States had regained the right to retaliate when Jay's commercial clauses expired, and this right was retained in the Monroe-Pinkney Treaty. However, to forestall a drastic increase in the duties paid by British ships in American ports, the British were expected to lower the duties paid by American ships in their ports to the same level as those paid by all other nations.[71] The United States also gained from a provision that equalized all duties, bounties, and drawbacks on goods, whether carried in English or American ships. Hitherto, the British imposed considerably higher duties on goods imported in American ships than the 10 percent surcharge imposed by the United States on goods imported in British ships.[72]

Another article dealt with American commercial privileges in the British East Indies. Of the many terms carried over in modified form from the Jay Treaty, this was the only one that offered the United States less rather than more. American merchants trading with India had to ship bullion since this was the principal import of the Indies. Under the Jay Treaty, Americans could sail to India indirectly, stopping in Europe en route to fill out their cargoes. The return trip, however, had to be direct to some port in the Western Hemisphere.[73]

Monroe and Pinkney were instructed to secure most-favored-nation status in this trade in order to enable American merchants to sail indirectly (and thus trade along the way) on both legs of the trip.[74] The East India Company, however, raised an alarm, claiming that Americans took such liberties with the trade (often with the cooperation of British merchants and the connivance of British officials) that company ships could not

[71] Monroe and Pinkney to Madison, Jan. 3, 1807, and Monroe to Madison, Feb. 28, 1808, in *Am. State Papers: For. Relations*, III, 143, 181; "Mem° of British Tonnage Duties," n.d., Dispatches from U.S. Ministers (M-30), reel 10.

[72] Monroe and Pinkney to Madison, Jan. 3, 1807, in *Am. State Papers: For. Relations*, III, 143. Samuel Smith criticized the treaty for not ending the additional tax that Britain imposed on exports headed for the Western Hemisphere rather than Europe. "To remedy this grievance," he claimed, "was considered by the Senate as one of the great objects of the extraordinary mission." But since the surcharge was only 2.5%, it is hard to believe that this issue was so critical. See statement of Samuel Smith [Apr. 1807] (filed under Dec. 31, 1806), Monroe Papers.

[73] Jay Treaty, Art. 13; John H. Reinoehl, ed., "Some Remarks on the American Trade: Jacob Crowninshield to James Madison, 1806," *William and Mary Quarterly*, 3d Ser., XVI (1959), 102, 113.

[74] Madison to Monroe, Mar. 5, 1804, and to Monroe and Pinkney, May 17, 1806, Diplomatic Instructions (M-77), reel 1.

effectively compete.[75] Indeed, such were the advantages of neutrality and such was the availability of American ships that even company agents sometimes used them.[76] Hence instead of broadening American privileges in this trade, the British insisted on a clause in the treaty that required both legs to be direct.[77]

This article elicited more criticism than any other from Republican commercial experts who studied the treaty. They pointed out how important it was for American merchants to pick up specie in Europe and to trade with other ports beyond the Cape of Good Hope en route to India. On the other hand, at least one of the experts—Tench Coxe—concluded that in time of war Americans could still make a profit under the new stipulation.[78] Monroe and Pinkney believed that the trade was better off if subject to treaty regulation, especially since the treaty guaranteed that American ships would be admitted to India on favorable terms, paying British instead of alien duties. "We acceded to that agreement," Monroe later said, "from a conviction that it secured us better terms than we should be likely to enjoy if left to depend on the pleasure of the British Government."[79]

The United States secured favorable modifications in several other articles borrowed from the Jay Treaty. The British agreed, as they had in 1794, to give proper notice of blockades, but this time they explicitly recognized that American merchants were entitled to special consideration because of the distance of the United States from the theater of war in Europe.[80] In addition, the article governing search and seizure on the high seas was modified to enjoin the commanders of British warships and privateers to conduct themselves "as favorably [toward American merchants] as the course of the war . . . may possibly permit" and to observe the rules and principles of international law. The security bonds required

[75] Statement of East India Company, Oct. 27, 1806, Adm. 80/117. See also Holden Furber, "The Beginnings of American Trade with India, 1784-1812," *New England Quarterly*, XI (1938), 251-256. One British observer claimed that Americans "now supply almost the whole world, except Great Britain and Ireland, with East India manufactures." See Observations on the American Treaty [summer 1807], F.O. 95/515.

[76] Joseph Dorr to Monroe, Oct. [?], 1806, Monroe Papers microfilm, reel 3.

[77] Monroe-Pinkney Treaty, Art. 3.

[78] Tench Coxe to Madison, Apr. 2, 1807, Madison Papers microfilm, reel 9; statements of William Jones [Apr. 1807] and Samuel Smith [Apr. 1807] (filed under Dec. 31, 1806), Monroe Papers.

[79] Monroe to Madison, Feb. 28, 1808, in *Am. State Papers: For. Relations*, III, 179. In this case Monroe may have been wrong. Although the East India Company issued an order restricting American merchants to direct voyages in 1808, the order was not implemented until 1811. By then, however, America's trade with India had been crippled by the Embargo and the Nonintercourse Act. See Furber, "American Trade with India," *NEQ*, XI (1938), 257, 263-264.

[80] Jay Treaty, Art. 18; Monroe-Pinkney Treaty, Art. 10; Monroe and Pinkney to Madison, Jan. 3, 1807, in *Am. State Papers: For. Relations*, III, 144.

of commanders of privateers were also increased.[81] Finally, in a clause that was entirely new, the British agreed not to seize enemy subjects from American ships unless they were enrolled in the military or naval forces of the enemy. This conceded a point long claimed by the United States—that enemy civilians on neutral vessels were immune to capture.[82]

Another clause in the Monroe-Pinkney Treaty was in some ways the most important because it gave teeth to all the rest. This provision, which was inserted at the insistence of the American envoys, stipulated that the owner of any vessel detained in violation of the treaty was to be fully indemnified for damages suffered, including the costs of legal proceedings.[83] Although recognizing the propriety of such compensation in theory, the British courts often ignored the theory in their decisions. As Monroe and Pinkney put it, "There is, perhaps, no principle in the maritime pretensions of this country which has been more abused in practice than that which this provision is intended to remedy."[84] In Halifax and the West Indies especially, the vice-admiralty courts were notorious for compelling shipowners to bear their own costs and their captors' as well, even when the vessels in question were acquitted.[85] Since trial costs typically ran from $2,000 to $5,000, the British concession was an important one.[86] It ensured that shipowners would be reimbursed not only for their losses but for their legal expenses as well.

These, then, were the benefits the Monroe-Pinkney Treaty offered to the United States. What did they add up to? To American merchants seeking to make a profit in a war-torn world, the treaty offered considerable security: security against interference with the East or West Indian trade, against hazy definitions of contraband or unannounced blockades, and against impressment or seizure within five miles of the American coast. The treaty also offered a favorable revision of duties paid by American merchants trading in British ports. Above all, it provided

[81] Jay Treaty, Art. 19; Monroe-Pinkney Treaty, Art. 13. The British assured the American envoys that Parliament would regulate the subject of visitation and search in a manner satisfactory to the United States. See Monroe and Pinkney to Madison, Jan. 3, 1807, in *Am. State Papers: For. Relations*, III, 145.

[82] Monroe-Pinkney Treaty, Art. 10; Madison to Monroe, Jan. 5, 1804, Apr. 12, 1805, Diplomatic Instructions (M-77), reel 1.

[83] Monroe-Pinkney Treaty, Art. 8; Notes on Art. 11 (filed under Dec. 31, 1806), Monroe Papers.

[84] Monroe and Pinkney to Madison, Jan. 3, 1807, in *Am. State Papers: For. Relations*, III, 144.

[85] The normal British practice was to award costs to the captors whenever they had good cause for bringing a ship in for adjudication. See [Smith], *Numbers of Phocion*, 59; *Enquirer*, Oct. 1, 1805; and *Natl. Intelligencer*, Sept. 30, 1805, Jan. 6, 1806.

[86] Monroe and Pinkney to Madison, Jan. 3, 1807, in *Am. State Papers: For. Relations*, III, 144; Jonathan M. Taylor to Monroe, Aug. 2, 1806, Monroe Papers microfilm, reel 3; Reinoehl, ed., "Remarks on the American Trade," *WMQ*, 3d Ser., XVI (1959), 114.

insurance by guaranteeing that the British would indemnify merchants who suffered from a violation.

What did the United States have to give up to gain these advantages? When the concessions are tallied, they add up to little more than a promise of benevolent neutrality. As far as Republican leaders were concerned, the most important concession was a commitment (carried over from the Jay Treaty) to employ against Great Britain no commercial sanctions—such as nonimportation, nonexportation, or nonintercourse—that did not apply to all other nations as well.[87] This stipulation, which did not preclude an embargo, was designed to prevent the United States from resorting to the sort of commercial warfare presaged by the partial nonimportation act of 1806. Republicans always considered the nation's economic leverage its greatest weapon, and they were unwilling to yield this weapon in any treaty that did not go far toward meeting their foreign policy goals. Yet given the futility of the commercial restrictions later employed against Britain and the enormous harm they did to the American economy, one might well argue that the treaty's prohibition of sanctions was as beneficial to the United States as to England.

By virtue of another article lifted from the Jay Treaty, the United States surrendered the principle of free ships–free goods, thus recognizing Britain's right to take enemy property from American vessels.[88] Although historians have long considered this to be one of the pivotal diplomatic issues of the period, the principle was of little practical importance and was seen by the United States as simply a bargaining counter to secure concessions in other areas, particularly the reexport trade.[89] Although Americans had freighted property for the European belligerents in the 1790s, by 1800 they had sufficient capital to purchase any goods they transported. This americanized the property and thus protected it from seizure even under the British interpretation of international law. "We are no longer mere freighters for foreigners," said a Republican congressman in 1806, "but have become the carriers of foreign as well as native produce, on our own capital, and for our own account."[90] Federalists even argued that the United States benefited from the British doctrine that

---

[87] Jay Treaty, Art. 15; Monroe-Pinkney Treaty, Art. 5.

[88] Jay Treaty, Art. 17; Monroe-Pinkney Treaty, Art. 8.

[89] Madison to Monroe and Pinkney, May 17, 1806, Diplomatic Instructions (M-77), reel 1. See also Madison to George Joy, Jan. 17, 1810, in Hunt, ed., *Madison Writings*, VIII, 88-89, The doctrine of free ships–free goods loomed large in Samuel Flagg Bemis's works on the 18th century. Other scholars have carried this theme into the 19th century. See Bemis, *The Diplomacy of the American Revolution*, 2d ed. (Bloomington, Ind., 1957), 46, 61, 132-134, 154, 169-170, 250; *Pinckney's Treaty: America's Advantage from Europe's Distress, 1783-1800*, rev. ed. (New Haven, Conn., 1960), 299; and *Jay's Treaty*, 207-208, 293, 328, 335-336, 358. See also Burt, *United States and Great Britain*, 216-217; White, *Nation on Trial*, 7; and Spivak, *Jefferson's English Crisis*, 15.

[90] Speech of Barnabas Bidwell, Mar. 8, 1806, in *Annals of Congress*, 9th Cong., 1st sess., 653. See also speech of Jacob Crowninshield, Mar. 12, 1806, *ibid.*, 754;

enemy goods on neutral ships were subject to seizure. "The boasted principle of free ships, free goods," said Fisher Ames in 1802, "would deprive the United States of a great part of the fair profits of their neutrality. Belligerent nations could in that case transact their own affairs, and neutrals would have no gains but freight."[91] Even Republicans accepted the British doctrine. "If any of our ships are found carrying the property of the enemies of Great Britain," said Samuel Smith, "let them be punished, we mean not to defend them."[92] The administration did not object to the seizure of such property, and Madison later conceded that, in spite of the virtues of free ships—free goods, "it seems to have been generally understood, that the British doctrine was practically admitted."[93]

At the insistence of the British, a number of other clauses were carried over from the Jay Treaty without change. One bound the United States to seek satisfaction through diplomatic channels before initiating reprisals for alleged wrongs. Another pledged the United States to bar its citizens from committing hostile acts against Britain on behalf of a foreign power. Others guaranteed British warships and privateers a hospitable reception in American ports, denied the use of American ports to privateers belonging to Britain's enemies, and prohibited the seizure of British ships by enemy warships or privateers in American waters.[94] Most of what the United States promised in these clauses was already embodied in American law or was accepted practice under international law.[95] In other words,

---

Fisher Ames, "War in Disguise," in W. B. Allen, ed., *Works of Fisher Ames*, 2 vols. (Indianapolis, Ind., 1984), I, 387; and Madison to Edward Everett, Feb. 18, 1823, in Hunt, ed., *Madison Writings*, IX, 122.

[91] Ames, "Political Review III," reprinted from *N.-E. Palladium*, in Allen, ed., *Works of Ames*, I, 472-473. See also *Repertory* (Boston), cited in *Enquirer*, Oct. 11, 1805.

[92] Speech of Samuel Smith, Mar. 10, 1806, in *Annals of Congress*, 9th Cong., 1st sess., 168.

[93] Madison to Monroe, Jan. 5, 1804, and to Monroe and Pinkney, May 20, 1807, Diplomatic Instructions (M-77), reel 1; Madison to Charles J. Ingersoll, July 28, 1814, in Hunt, ed., *Madison Writings*, VIII, 283, quotation from letter to Ingersoll. For similar sentiments see Albert Gallatin, "Notes on Mr Dallas's opinions," in Gallatin Papers microfilm, reel 25, New York University, New York, N.Y. In the *Nereide* case, adjudicated in 1815, the United States Supreme Court held that enemy property on a neutral ship was subject to seizure. This doctrine, said the Court, is "believed to be a part of the original law of nations" and "has been fully and unequivocally recognized by the United States." See Carlton Savage, *Policy of the United States toward Maritime Commerce in War*, 2 vols. (Washington, D.C., 1934-1936), I, 289.

[94] Jay Treaty, Arts. 21-25; Monroe-Pinkney Treaty, Arts. 15-19.

[95] The Neutrality Acts of 1794 and 1797 (which were not repealed until 1818) barred American citizens from enlisting in foreign service and prohibited foreign privateers from fitting out in American ports. See *Annals of Congress*, 3d Cong., 1st sess., June 5, 1794, 1461-1464, and 5th Cong., 1st sess., June 14, 1797, 3685.

the United States conceded very little here that constituted a new obligation.

Other clauses dealt with routine matters and represented no great gain or loss to either side. Some were taken without change from the Jay Treaty. These authorized appointment of consuls, provided for treatment of pirates and extradition of certain classes of felons, protected merchants in the event of a diplomatic rupture, and provided against contradictions with previous treaties.[96] Other articles, new in this treaty, dealt with the salvage of wrecked ships, exchange of information on the slave trade, and confirmation of the permanent clauses in the Jay Treaty.[97] The last clause in the Monroe-Pinkney Treaty set a ten-year limitation on the agreement from the date that ratifications were exchanged.[98]

All in all, the terms of the Monroe-Pinkney Treaty were quite favorable to the United States, especially compared to those of the Jay Treaty. The United States gave up the right of commercial retaliation and the doctrine of free ships—free goods. It accepted greater restrictions on its trade with India and agreed to treat Great Britain in a friendly and favorable manner. In exchange, the United States received almost all the privileges and guarantees of the Jay Treaty and many more. The reexport trade was guaranteed, the nation's territorial waters were extended, a narrow definition of contraband was established, a more favorable structure of commercial duties was secured, and a number of smaller points were gained as well. Best of all, the treaty contained an insurance clause that guaranteed indemnification in the event of violations.

The envoys from the two nations signed the treaty on December 31, 1806. Several weeks earlier, however, British officials had learned of Napoleon's Berlin Decree, which proclaimed a paper blockade of the British Isles, excluded from French-occupied harbors all neutral vessels that had touched at a British port, and declared all British-made products lawful prize even when owned by neutrals. This undermined Britain's willingness to suspend the Rule of 1756, and its envoys insisted on appending a note to the treaty reserving Britain's right to retaliate against France if the United States acquiesced in the decree.[99] The British hoped this reservation would not vitiate the treaty and even solicited suggestions from the American envoys to make their note "as conciliatory in form as . . . it is in substance."[100] The note was extraordinary and put a cloud over

[96] Jay Treaty, Arts. 16, 20, 25-27; Monroe-Pinkney Treaty, Arts. 7, 14, 20, 21, 25.

[97] Monroe-Pinkney Treaty, Arts. 2, 6, 22, 24. The British were especially interested in abolishing the slave trade. Parliament had expressly urged the crown to seek the cooperation of other powers. See Journal of Holland and Auckland, Oct. 15, 1806, Adm. 80/117, and Monroe and Pinkney to Madison, Jan. 3, 1807, in *Am. State Papers: For. Relations*, III, 147.

[98] Monroe-Pinkney Treaty, Art. 26.

[99] Journal of Holland and Auckland, Dec. 9, 1806, Adm. 80/117; note of Holland and Auckland, Dec. 31, 1806, Dispatches from U.S. Ministers (M-30), reel 10.

[100] Holland to Monroe, Dec. 29, 1806, Monroe Papers.

the whole treaty. Nevertheless, it was not without redeeming features. As Monroe and Pinkney pointed out, although the British were unwilling to give a definition of blockade in the treaty proper, they supplied one in the note that was "tolerably correct."[101] When officials in Washington first read the reservation, they were outraged. Later, however, Republican leaders indicated a willingness to accept some such stipulation if it were made reciprocal and put in a more palatable form.[102] Thus the British reservation need not have killed the treaty even though Madison initially thought it would do so.

What effect the British reservation would have had is difficult to say. Great Britain certainly lost no time in retaliating against France. On January 7, 1807, barely a week after signing the Monroe-Pinkney Treaty, the government issued an order in council prohibiting the coasting trade between enemy ports on the Continent.[103] Although this did not violate any provision in the treaty, it ran counter to an implicit pledge to await America's response before acting against France. But even with this hasty British action, the United States was in a strong position diplomatically. By ratifying the treaty and making a gesture against the Berlin Decree, it could still demand that the entire agreement be implemented.

Jefferson, however, chose not to submit the treaty to the Senate. His decision was based in part on mistrust of that body. The year before, just as he was buckling to pressure to appoint a special mission, he indicated his reluctance to submit a British treaty to the Senate. Such was the influence of Federalists Uriah Tracy and James Bayard among their fellow senators, he confided to a friend, that "very much do I dread the submitting to them at the next session any treaty which can be made with either England or Spain."[104] Given the political culture in which Jefferson had been reared, any commercial agreement with Britain was likely to seem unpalatable. The Revolution had generated a powerful current of anglophobia in the United States. Many Republicans, Jefferson included, regarded British society as corrupt and decadent and saw the Jay Treaty as an insidious agreement that bound the United States to Great Britain, undermined the republican spirit, and contributed to the anglicizing of

---

[101] Monroe and Pinkney to Madison, Jan. 3, 1807, in *Am. State Papers: For. Relations*, III, 147.

[102] Madison to Monroe and Pinkney, May 20, 1807, Diplomatic Instructions (M-77), reel 1.

[103] Adams, *History of the United States*, III, 416. The British later said that this measure was not intended to prevent neutrals from trading from port to port on the continent in their own goods. See Howick to J. Rist (Danish chargé d'affaires in London), Mar. 17, 1807, in Courtenay, *Additional Observations*, lxvi-lxvii.

[104] Jefferson to Wilson Cary Nicholas, Apr. 13, 1806, Jefferson Papers microfilm, reel 35. Both Madison and Samuel Smith favored consulting the Senate on the treaty, though Madison pointed out the futility of doing so if the president was determined to reject the agreement. See Smith to Nicholas, Mar. 4, 1807, in Adams, *History of the United States*, III, 432, and Smith to Madison, Mar. 14, 1807, Madison Papers microfilm, reel 25.

American society.[105] Given this view, perhaps the Monroe-Pinkney Treaty was doomed from the beginning.

After studying the treaty, Jefferson told Madison he was "more & more convinced that our best course is to let the negociation take a friendly nap."[106] Instead, the administration returned the treaty to England for revision. The president called for a series of changes, six of which were deemed "essential." These dealt with impressment, the reexport trade, trade with India, indemnification for the *Essex* spoliations, treatment of the belligerents, and the Berlin Decree.[107] But to secure these changes, the president was willing to offer few concessions. Earlier the administration had hoped to secure an end to impressment by promising to return all British deserters. Now it considered barring all British seamen from American service. But Gallatin's research showed that British subjects constituted 9,000 of the 24,000 able-bodied seamen in the merchant marine. This figure, Gallatin said, was "larger than we had estimated," and the exclusion of so many men "would materially injure our navigation."[108] Jefferson was inclined to drop all propositions respecting the employment of British seamen, but in the end the administration decided to offer to bar those British subjects who had not been in continuous service on American ships for two years or more.[109]

The president set his diplomatic goals high because, even if the British refused to cooperate, he expected American views on neutral rights to prevail. "With respect to the rights of neutrality," he wrote in 1806, "we have certainly a great interest in their settlement[,] but this depends exclusively on the will of two characters, Buonaparte & [Czar] Alexander."[110] Republican leaders even feared that a British treaty might tie the United States to a more narrow definition of neutral rights than Britain conceded to her enemies in Europe. According to notes taken at a cabinet meeting held in early 1807, Jefferson's advisors agreed that the points sought by the United States were all matters of right. "They are points

[105] For the evolution of Republican political culture see Drew R. McCoy, *The Elusive Republic: Political Economy in Jeffersonian America* (Chapel Hill, N.C., 1980), esp. 164, 185-186.

[106] Jefferson to Madison, Apr. 21, 1807, Madison Papers microfilm, reel 25.

[107] Copy of treaty marked "Alterations proposed by The President of the United States," F.O. 5/51; Madison to Monroe and Pinkney, May 20, 1807, Diplomatic Instructions (M-77), reel 1.

[108] Gallatin to Jefferson, Apr. 13, 1807, Gallatin Papers microfilm, reel 14; Gallatin to Madison, Apr. 13, 1807, Madison Papers microfilm, reel 25, quotations from letter to Jefferson.

[109] Jefferson to Madison, Apr. 21, 1807, Madison Papers microfilm, reel 25; Jefferson to Gallatin, Apr. 21, 1807, Gallatin Papers microfilm, reel 14; Madison to Monroe and Pinkney, May 20, 1807, Diplomatic Instructions (M-77), reel 1.

[110] Jefferson to Thomas Paine, Mar. 25, 1806, in Jefferson Papers microfilm, reel 35. See also Jefferson to Czar Alexander, Apr. 19, 1806, *ibid.*; Jefferson to Gallatin, Apr. 21, 1807, Gallatin Papers microfilm, reel 14; Madison to John Armstrong, Mar. 14, 1806, Diplomatic Instructions (M-77), reel 1; Merry to Mulgrave, Mar. 2, 1806, F.O. 5/48; Erskine to Howick, June 3, 1807, F.O. 5/52.

which Bonaparte & Alexander will concur in settling at the Treaty of peace, & probably in more latitude than Gr. Br. would now yield them to us, & our treaty w^d place [us] on worse ground as to them than will be settled for Europe."[111]

Even if Britain's enemies failed to force it to agree to a broad definition of neutral rights, Republicans could always resort to commercial restrictions. Although implementation of the partial nonimportation act of 1806 was repeatedly postponed, the law was held over the British as a threat during the Monroe-Pinkney negotiations. It is probably no coincidence that documents from the 1790s calling for commercial discrimination against England were reprinted in 1806.[112] Moreover, when the United States pressed for revision of the Monroe-Pinkney Treaty, Madison freely brandished the economic sword. The British, he said, "must know that, apart from the obstacles which may be opposed here to the use of British manufactures, the United States, by a mere reciprocation of the British navigation and Colonial laws, may give a very serious blow to a favorite system"—namely, Britain's colonial empire. Moreover, if the British retaliated with war, they would suffer even more. "[I]t is enough to observe," Madison continued, "that a war with the United States involves a complete loss of the principal remaining market for her manufactures, and of the principal, perhaps the sole, remaining source of supplies, without which all her faculties must wither."[113] The Republicans, of course, would later have ample opportunity to test their theories of economic coercion and war, although the results would be quite different from what they expected.

As it happened, the British were unmoved by the threat of economic warfare in 1807 and showed no interest in revising the terms of the Monroe-Pinkney Treaty. The treaty had come under heavy attack, and the Tory ministry that assumed office in 1807 was happy to let it go.[114] In a letter dated October 22, 1807, the new foreign minister, George Canning, told the American envoys that the president's proposal to revise the treaty was "wholly inadmissible." Characteristically, he chided the United States

[111] Cabinet notes, Feb. 3, 1807 (filed under Mar. 5, 1806), Jefferson Papers microfilm, reel 35. See also Jefferson to James Bowdoin, Apr. 2, 1807, in Andrew A. Lipscomb and Albert Ellery Bergh, eds., *The Writings of Thomas Jefferson*, 20 vols. (Washington, D.C., 1903-1905), XI, 184-185.

[112] See Thomas Jefferson, *Report of the Secretary of State, on the Privileges and Restrictions on the Commerce of the United States in Foreign Countries* [Dec. 16, 1793] (Washington, D.C., 1806), and Madison's congressional resolutions, Jan. 3, 1794, reprinted in *Natl. Intelligencer*, Feb. 17, 1806.

[113] Madison to Monroe and Pinkney, May 20, 1807, Diplomatic Instructions (M-77), reel 1.

[114] See Observations on the American Treaty [summer 1807], and [George Rose], Notes respecting the American Treaty, July 20, 1807, both in F.O. 95/515; Lord Aberdeen to A. J. Foster, Jan. 13, 1807, in Vere Foster, ed., *The Two Duchesses . . .* (London, 1898), 306; [Thomas P. Courtenay], *Observations on the American Treaty* (London, 1808), 72, and *passim; Enquirer*, Mar. 3, 1807; *Columbian Centinel* (Boston), May 18, 1807; and Perkins, *Prologue to War*, 133-134, 188.

for assuming "to itself the privilege of revising and altering agreements concluded and signed on its behalf by its agents duly authorized for that purpose; of retaining so much of those agreements as may be favorable to its own views, and of rejecting such stipulations, or such parts of stipulations, as are conceived to be not sufficiently beneficial to America."[115]

Many years after the War of 1812, Richard Hildreth pointed out that while the Jay Treaty "secured to the country thirteen years of peace and of unexampled commercial prosperity," the rejection of the Monroe-Pinkney Treaty was followed by "four years of vexatious and ruinous commercial restrictions, to which succeeded two years and a half of most disastrous and aimless war."[116] It was not that the Jay Treaty resolved all Anglo-American differences, but rather that it created a climate of understanding that allowed American commerce, and hence the American economy, to boom.[117] Monroe hoped that his treaty would lead to the same kind of accord. "We flatter ourselves," he wrote in early 1807, "that the treaty will meet the approbation of our gov' & country. It was the best that under existing circumstances it was possible to obtain. By it some points of real utility will be arranged, and it may be considered as paving the way to a perfect good understanding in future between the two countries."[118]

Just how close the treaty would have drawn the two nations is impossible to say. When the Tories assumed power in 1807, the British posture stiffened. Even so, it is undeniable that, in the realm of commerce and neutral rights, the Monroe-Pinkney Treaty was far superior to the Jay Treaty and in all likelihood would have benefited the United States. Scholars often echo the Republican claim that the only options for the United States in this era were submission, commercial sanctions, or war. But the Monroe-Pinkney Treaty offered another alternative, that of accommodation. The rejection of this treaty was an important turning point in the Age of Jefferson, for with this decision the United States missed an opportunity to reforge the Anglo-American accord that had served the nation so well in the previous decade, and to substitute peace and prosperity for commercial sanctions and war.

[115] Canning to Monroe and Pinkney, Oct. 22, 1807, in *Am. State Papers: For. Relations*, III, 199. Twice before, the United States had modified Anglo-American agreements before ratifying them: the Jay Treaty in 1795 and a boundary convention in 1803. The British accepted the changes in the Jay Treaty but not in the boundary agreement. For British assessments of the proposed changes to the 1806 treaty, see Alterations proposed in the depending Treaty by the Government of America [summer 1807], [George Rose], Observations on the Alterations made by the American Government to the Treaty ... [Aug. 1807], and notes by *C* (probably Canning), *B* (probably Earl Bathurst), and what looks like *MP*, all in F.O. 95/515. All of these assessments were critical of the American changes. It is "hopeless," concluded the author of Alterations, to expect "any fair and reasonable Arrangement with America."

[116] Hildreth, *History of the United States*, V, 665.

[117] American exports rose from $33,000,000 in 1794 to more than $108,000,000 in 1807. See Nettels, *National Economy*, 396.

[118] Monroe to [Fulwar Skipwith], Jan. 20, 1807, Monroe Papers.

James Madison and the Coercion of Great Britain: Canada, the West Indies, and the War of 1812

J.C.A. Stagg

D URING the War of 1812 the United States invaded Canada to obtain redress for injuries suffered on the high seas from the Royal Navy's enforcement of British maritime policies. Some fifty years ago, Julius W. Pratt attempted to account for this strategy by arguing that the American concern with Canada in 1812 originated in a complex combination of resentment by frontier congressmen at British links with the northwestern Indians, an incipient sense of "Manifest Destiny," and a tacit sectional bargain that traded off the promise of northern expansion into Canada against the prospect of southern expansion into Spanish East Florida.[1] Many of the elements in Pratt's explanation have now been discarded as unconvincing or have not been given the same emphasis that Pratt gave to them, but in rejecting the "expansionist" thesis historians have lost sight of the larger problem that it addressed: the nature of the American interest in Canada in 1812 and its relationship to the maritime grievances that the second war with Great Britain was intended to settle.[2] Most historians now seem satisfied with the explanation of American policy offered by Secretary of State James Monroe in a letter of June 1812

Mr. Stagg is a member of the Department of History at the University of Auckland. Earlier versions of this article were presented at the Library of Congress on Apr. 4, 1979, and at the University of Maryland, College Park, on May 2, 1979. The author would like to thank all present on those occasions for their comments and assistance, particularly James M. Banner, Jr., and Alison Gilbert Olson, and to acknowledge as well a debt of gratitude to Ronald L. Hatzenbuehler for reading an early draft. He would also like to thank the American Historical Association and the Library of Congress for their administration of the J. Franklin Jameson Fellowship, under the auspices of which this article was researched and written. The article represents part of a larger study of politics, diplomacy, and warfare in the early republic with special reference to the War of 1812.

[1] *Expansionists of 1812* (New York, 1925).

[2] Reginald Horsman, *The Causes of the War of 1812* (Philadelphia, 1962), 158-177; Paul A. Varg, *Foreign Policies of the Founding Fathers* (East Lansing, Mich., 1963), 267-270; Roger H. Brown, *The Republic in Peril: 1812* (New York, 1964), 120-130.

that "it might be necessary to invade Canada, not as an object of the war but as a means to bring it to a satisfactory conclusion."[3]

Monroe's statement, however, explains very little about Canada's role in the War of 1812. Possibly, the secretary of state meant to suggest that the United States, lacking the naval power to challenge its enemy on the seas, had to take advantage of Canada's proximity and vulnerability, and seize the region in order to use it as a bargaining point in negotiations that might secure British respect for American maritime rights. If so, the logic of the argument seems plausible, but it did not satisfy John Taylor of Caroline, the recipient of Monroe's letter. Taylor had written to Monroe in May 1812 to state his reasons for opposing the impending war, among them his conviction that Great Britain would never sacrifice its maritime policies to save Canada from an American invasion. He argued that as Britain had been unwilling to renounce any of its maritime and imperial pretensions during the Revolutionary War in order to preserve its American colonies, it was unlikely now to surrender its methods of commercial and naval warfare in a much more desperate struggle with Napoleonic France simply to retain Canada, a collection of colonies that were of far less value to the empire than the lost thirteen had been.[4] Taylor's argument thus exposed some very large assumptions in the American strategy of invading Canada as a means of coercing Great Britain. When Monroe's response ignored the objection, Taylor repeated in a second letter that the war "may gain Canada and nothing beneficial."[5]

Taylor's views were echoed by most opponents of the War of 1812, and his doubts were shared even by some advocates of the conflict.[6] Senator Jesse Franklin of North Carolina, for example, supported both the preparations for war and its declaration, yet he privately confessed in February 1812 that he could not see how the seizure of Canada would "settle the dispute about which we are now like to get to war, that is our *Commercial Rights*." As for territory, he added, "God knows we [have] enough already."[7] Americans who questioned the wisdom of administration policies

[3] James Monroe to John Taylor, June 13, 1812, James Monroe Papers, Lib. Cong.

[4] Taylor to Monroe, May 10, 1812, *ibid.*

[5] Taylor to Monroe, June 18, 1812, *ibid.*

[6] See, for example, the following statements by opponents of the war: for the "Old Republicans," John Randolph to Richard K. Randolph, Feb. 7, 1812, John Randolph Papers, Lib. Cong.; for the Clintonian view, *Albany Register* (N.Y.), Oct. 25, 1811; for the Federalist view, the protest of the Massachusetts legislature against the war, June 5, 1812, in Walter Lowrie and Walter S. Franklin, eds., *American State Papers: Documents, Legislative and Executive ... Miscellaneous*, II (Washington, D.C., 1834), 186-187, and James H. Broussard, *The Southern Federalists, 1800-1816* (Baton Rouge, La., 1978), 158-161.

[7] Jesse Franklin to William Lenoir, Feb. 15, 1812, Lenoir Family Papers, University of North Carolina, Chapel Hill. See also Burwell Bassett to Josiah Bartlett, Jan. 13, 1813, Josiah Bartlett Papers, Lib. Cong.

would, no doubt, have been even more concerned had they been aware of Monroe's instructions to the American chargé d'affaires in London, Jonathan Russell, shortly after the war began. The secretary of state told Russell to warn the British government that a successful American war against Canada would "present very serious obstacles on the part of the United States to an accommodation which do not now exist," and he predicted that it might be "difficult to relinquish territory which had been conquered."[8] The Madison administration thus seems to have presumed that the occupation of Canada in 1812 would be sufficient to bring Great Britain to terms. The question is why, especially when so many Americans were not convinced that it would do so but believed that the possession of Canada would scarcely repay the cost of acquiring it.

The purpose of this essay is to suggest an answer to that question. It will proceed on the assumption that the motive for the War of 1812 was not so much to enlarge the boundaries of the United States as to deprive Great Britain of Canada in the expectation that this action would affect Britain's capacity to exercise its commercial and naval powers against Americans in harmful ways that they could not otherwise control. The essay will try to demonstrate that assumption by reconstructing, as far as possible, President James Madison's understanding of the potential impact of the loss of Canada on the British empire. The focus on Madison is justified on the ground that he was, after all, the commander-in-chief and the official most responsible for conceiving a war strategy. Moreover, he has enjoyed a deserved reputation as a systematic thinker who was ever conscious of the relationship between the ends and means of politics; accordingly, it is difficult to imagine that he gave no thought at all to how a Canadian war might relieve the United States from the effects of British maritime policies, especially when he had spent much of his public career studying those policies as they had operated against the interests of his country.[9] The task of reconstructing Madison's thinking, though, is by no means easy, principally because the president seldom made comments in his correspondence during the war years that directly addressed the issue in point.

Among the reasons why Madison's surviving correspondence is silent here is the fact that the war failed to produce the military victories necessary for Madison to engage in successful diplomatic bargaining with Great Britain over the problems of maritime rights; as a consequence, the president's wartime statements invariably centered on problems of a different

---

[8] Monroe to Jonathan Russell, June 26, 1812, Diplomatic Instructions: All Countries (M-77), Reel 2, Records of the Department of State (RG 59), National Archives.

[9] See Madison's remark of 1790 that the injuries the United States received from Great Britain formed "a copious subject" that always led him to "serious and important considerations" (Joseph Gales, comp., [Annals of Congress] Debates and Proceedings in the Congress of the United States [Washington, D.C., 1834-1856], 1st Cong., 1st sess., 213, hereafter cited as Annals of Congress).

order. Furthermore, whenever he sought to explain his conduct during the war he was usually more preoccupied with demonstrating to Americans the malignant nature and consequences of the British policies he wished them to resist than he was with revealing his strategic view of the effect of a Canadian war.[10] Nonetheless, Madison's papers contain a number of statements on Canada, and these are most suggestive about his understanding of the role that Canada played in Anglo-American relations. Indeed, the context in which these statements occur makes it evident that Madison, as a close observer of British affairs, was well aware of Canada's significance in the minds of the most determined defenders in Great Britain of the anti-American aspects of that nation's maritime policies. It was against these men that Madison's Canadian war was really waged, and he had good reason to believe that, had the war been successful, the British government would have been compelled to pay greater respect to American maritime rights.

The argument of this essay accordingly depends less on anything that Madison wrote or said during the War of 1812—as distinct from what he tried to do—than on the thesis that the American attempt to conquer Canada was both a logical sequel to Madison's entire mode of thinking about the relationship between the United States and the British empire after 1783, and a natural reaction to the problems he encountered in trying to translate that thinking into effective policy. Once the problem of Canada has been placed in a longer-term perspective, it becomes apparent that there was considerable continuity in the assumptions underlying all the policies that Madison attempted to pursue toward Great Britain throughout his long public life between 1779 and 1817. And, paradoxical though it may seem, Madison's decision to make war on Canada was not basically inconsistent—as historians have so often supposed—with the reasons for the belief he held before 1812 that the diplomacy of commercial restriction would enable the United States to avoid hostilities with Britain. In fact, given the circumstances Madison had to confront by 1812, the policy of a Canadian war followed logically from his previous diplomatic strategies that assumed that efforts to restrict British access to vital American resources would be instrumental in compelling Britain to moderate its anti-American policies. For by 1812, Canada had become an integral part of the larger question of British access to American resources, and Madison could therefore believe that to strip Britain of its North American possessions was a reasonable response to the maritime disputes that had long disturbed Anglo-American relations.

Underlying most of the disputes that led to the war was the problem of how far British merchants and shippers should enjoy access to American

---

[10] For the way in which Madison and other Republicans justified American resistance to Britain see Robert L. Ivie, "The Republican Dramatization of War in 1812," paper delivered at the Western Speech Communication Association Convention, 1976, at San Francisco.

markets, natural resources, and agricultural produce. The dimensions of this problem were clearly defined in 1783 by the British decisions—embodied particularly in the Order in Council of July 2 of that year—to deny the United States any of their former commercial privileges in the trade of the empire, especially the West Indian trade, as well as by the polemical arguments put forward in defense of those decisions by John Baker Holroyd, first earl of Sheffield, in his pamphlet *Observations on the Commerce of the American States*.[11] The outline of most of Lord Sheffield's ideas is well known, particularly his assertion that the United States were by definition not a nation and his peculiar notion that America had no future, while its independence was for Great Britain a blessing in disguise. Less appreciated has been the distinctive impact on an entire generation of Englishmen, Canadians, Americans, and West Indians of Sheffield's defense of the navigation system after 1783 and his vision of how to reconstruct the economy of the empire.[12] This impact was central to Madison's understanding of the problems of Anglo-American relations, and his policy of commercial restriction was conceived very much in response to it.

In the *Observations* Sheffield developed a number of justifications for attempting to keep the United States commercially subordinate. These he put forward in an analysis of commerce under two main headings: British exports to America and American exports to Britain. Many of the goods, Sheffield believed, that Britain had traditionally sent to the United States, notably manufactures, would continue to be bought by Americans because they had no alternative supply and could not manufacture them locally. Even where Americans could establish manufactures, Sheffield dismissed them as expensive shoddy, incapable of competing with British products in cost and quality. American exports to Britain, largely bulky raw materials, posed more difficulty, but Sheffield claimed that tobacco alone had appreciable value, and then only as an item in Britain's entrepôt trade. Other important raw materials, such as timber, naval stores, pipe staves, and even wheat, Sheffield believed would soon be in short supply in the United States, and for this reason he argued that it would be better for Britain to obtain them from alternative sources, either from other parts of the empire or from the Baltic region.[13]

This line of argument led to a discussion of American trade with the British West Indies, designed by Sheffield to support the claim that after 1783 the empire could be reconstituted as a self-sufficient economic unit. Crucial to this claim was Sheffield's belief that Canada could be developed to fill the role previously played by the revolted colonies. Nowhere was

[11] 2d ed. (London, 1784). For the background see Vincent T. Harlow, *The Founding of the Second British Empire, 1763-1793*, I (London, 1952), 146-311, 448-492.
[12] See, for example, the decision to exclude from publication all documents on the West Indies, in William R. Manning, ed., *Diplomatic Correspondence of the United States: Canadian Relations, 1784-1860*, I (Washington, D.C., 1940), viii.
[13] Sheffield, *Observations*, 9-105.

the need for a substitute for the American contribution to empire greater than in the matter of West Indian supply, and Sheffield attempted to demonstrate in detail that Canada could produce the timber, livestock, fish, and other provisions that the islands needed in order to furnish the mother country with the greatly valued staples of sugar and coffee. Indeed, so optimistic was his vision of Canada's future that he even predicted substantial northward emigration from the United States. Many of his writings on British maritime rights through to 1809 continued to assert Canada's economic potential in the most fulsome tones. The means for developing Canada were basically simple; Sheffield believed that the enforcement of the navigation laws against the United States, together with some bounties on Canadian exports, would be sufficient.[14]

Yet, as Sheffield made abundantly clear, more than rivalry for trade and development was at stake. His primary goal in advocating the application of the navigation laws against the United States was to preserve the effectiveness of those laws as the basis of Great Britain's naval power. Few Englishmen seriously questioned that the navigation laws, by augmenting British shipping and the nation's pool of trained seamen, did serve this function, though some—of whom the earl of Shelburne was the most prominent—were prepared by 1783 to consider loosening parts of the system in order to guarantee American supplies to the West Indies and to inaugurate a new era of Anglo-American harmony and cooperation.[15] Sheffield, however, believed that relaxation of the laws would permit ruinous competition for trade that would ultimately destroy Great Britain as a naval power. This fear drove him to argue that the empire could— indeed, must—function as a coherent economic unit despite the loss of the American colonies. His claims were made all the more attractive to his countrymen by his prediction that Britain could continue to dominate the American market by carrying its trade there.

Nor did Sheffield expect that the United States were capable of demonstrating any of his views to be ill founded, mainly because their government under the Articles of Confederation was no more effective than the Diet of Germany. He dismissed as ridiculous the idea that they might close their markets or withhold their produce in protest. Even if such attempts were made, he saw Britain's possession of Canada as the means to undermine them. Many of the northern parts of the United States had little option but to trade with Canada through the St. Lawrence River as a means of reaching the outside world, while control of that waterway would also enable Britain to transport its exports into the American interior.[16]

[14] *Ibid.*, 107-217.

[15] Even Adam Smith defended the navigation laws for their provision for the national defense (*An Inquiry into the Nature and Causes of the Wealth of Nations*, ed. Edwin Cannan [New York, 1937], 429-431). For Shelburne's views see Harlow, *Founding of the Second British Empire*, I, 228-232, 308-311.

[16] Sheffield, *Observations*, 145, 185, 188-191, 198. The belief that Canada was valuable as a channel for British manufactures into America was widely held by English officials. Harlow, *Founding of the Second British Empire*, I, 440, 483.

The restrictive policies of Great Britain after 1783, as well as the arguments of Lord Sheffield, provoked strong reactions on both sides of the Atlantic, resulting in a sizeable polemical literature not unlike that produced by the controversy over annexing Canada or Guadaloupe after 1760.[17] Among the best-known pamphlets published in Britain were those by Edward Long and Bryan Edwards, both writing as spokesmen for the West India planters. The most comprehensive assault on Sheffield's doctrines was written by Richard Champion, a Bristol china manufacturer of liberal opinions who had been deputy paymaster of the forces in the early 1780s until he resigned his office in disgust at the Treaty of Paris and moved, in 1784, to South Carolina.[18] In the United States, Tench Coxe's seven essays, assembled as *A Brief Inquiry into the Observations of Lord Sheffield*, were the most extended American response.[19] Madison, too, had been in the forefront of protests against the British decision to subject the American states to the navigation laws, both with his sponsorship of the Virginia Port Bill of 1784 and with his support of attempts to strengthen

[17] Cf. William L. Grant, "Canada Versus Guadeloupe, an Episode of the Seven Years' War," *American Historical Review*, XVII (1912), 735-743.

[18] [Edward Long], *A Free and Candid Review of a Tract, Entitled "Observations on the Commerce of the 'American States' "; Shewing the Pernicious Consequences, both to Great Britain, and to the British Sugar Islands, of the Systems Recommended in That Tract* (London, 1784); Bryan Edwards, *Thoughts on the Late Proceedings of Government, Respecting the Trade of the West India Islands with the United States of North America* (London, 1784); Richard Champion, *Considerations on the Present State of Great Britain and the United States of America with a View to Their Future Commercial Connections, Containing Remarks upon the Pamphlet Published by Lord Sheffield . . . and Also on the Act of Navigation as It Relates to Those States. Interspersed with Some Observations upon the State of Canada, Nova Scotia, and the Fisheries; and upon the Connexions of the West Indies with America* (London, 1784). Other pamphlets attacking Sheffield's views were James Allen, *Considerations on the Present State of the Intercourse between His Majesty's Sugar Colonies and the Dominions of the United States of America* (London, 1784); [William Bingham], *A Letter from an American Now Resident in London to a Member of Parliament on the Subject of the Restraining Proclamation and Containing Strictures on Lord Sheffield's Pamphlet on the Commerce of the American States* (London, 1784); and [anonymous, but attributed to Mr. Ruston], *Remarks on Lord Sheffield's Observations on the Commerce of the American States; by an American* (London, 1784). Sheffield repeated his views in *Observations on the Manufactures, Trade and Present State of Ireland* (London, 1785), 88-91, and received support from George Chalmers, *Opinions on Interesting Questions of Public Law and Commercial Policy Arising from American Independence* (London, 1784); John Stevenson, *An Address to Brian Edwards, Esq., Containing Remarks on His Pamphlet. . . . Also Observations on Some Parts of a Pamphlet, Lately Published by the West India Planters Entitled "Considerations on the Present State of Intercourse etc. etc."* (London, 1784); and Arthur Young, comp., "Considerations of the Connection between the Agriculture of England and the Commercial Policy of Her Sugar Islands, Particularly Respecting a Free Trade with North America," *Annals of Agriculture*, I (1784), 437ff.

[19] (Philadelphia, 1791).

the powers of the Continental Congress to regulate foreign trade.[20] The failure of Congress or the states to achieve significant commercial reform after 1783 led Madison to support the more sweeping changes put forward in the Constitutional Convention of 1787. One of the first duties of the new government, he declared to George Washington in 1788, would be to pass a retaliatory navigation act, and he introduced in Congress between 1790 and 1794—as an accompaniment to Thomas Jefferson's reports on the state of American fisheries and commerce—a series of discriminatory duties against nations, principally Great Britain, that refused to trade with the United States on reciprocal terms.[21]

Madison's arguments in his public defense of this course were shaped to a considerable degree by his reactions to Sheffield's views. Alarmed by the appearance of the *Observations* so soon after the establishment of American independence, Madison noted that the pamphlet's prescriptions, put into effect, would preclude Anglo-American commercial harmony.[22] His alarm was tempered, however, by his awareness that many of Sheffield's more extreme claims were not very plausible: to the extent that they were erroneous he concluded that British commercial policies were based on false premises. In reaching this position, Madison was clearly influenced by the polemical writings that the *Observations* had provoked—especially those by Champion, Coxe, and Edwards—from which he frequently lifted statistical information and key ideas, integrating these with opinions derived from his wider reading and experiences in public affairs.[23] In particular, he was greatly offended, as were all American nationalists in the

[20] On the Virginia Port Bill see Robert Bittner, "Economic Independence and the Virginia Port Bill of 1784," in Richard A. Rutyna and Peter C. Stewart, eds., *Virginia in the American Revolution: A Collection of Essays* (Norfolk, Va., 1977), 73-92.

[21] Madison to Washington, Aug. 24, 1788, in William T. Hutchinson, William M. E. Rachal, and Robert A. Rutland *et al.*, eds., *The Papers of James Madison* (Chicago and Charlottesville, Va., 1962-   ), XI, 241; hereafter cited as *Papers of Madison*.

[22] Madison to Edmund Randolph, Aug. 30, 1783, *ibid.*, VII, 295-296.

[23] Thomas Jefferson obtained a copy of Bryan Edwards's pamphlet in 1784 and appears to have been influenced by it in drawing up some notes on Sheffield's views. Jefferson then sent Edwards's pamphlet to Madison (Jefferson to Madison, July 1, 1784, in Julian P. Boyd *et al.*, eds., *The Papers of Thomas Jefferson* [Princeton, N.J., 1950-   ], VII, 356-357; hereafter cited as *Papers of Jefferson*. Jefferson also lent Madison his notes on Sheffield in 1790-1791, and a copy of them may be found in "Notes on Exports and Navigations," James Madison Papers, microfilm, Reel 28, Lib. Cong. Jefferson, Madison, and Coxe obviously reread much of this polemical literature between 1790 and 1794, drawing on it in preparing their speeches and reports for Congress. See *Papers of Jefferson*, XIX, 121-139. At this time Madison also read Champion's pamphlet and reread the one by Edwards. He relied on them both extensively in compiling data on British imports, insurance rates in war time, and the costs of supplying the West Indies.

1780s, by Sheffield's belief that the United States was a weak nation condemned by diminishing economic resources to a bleak future, including the loss of both trade and population to Canada. It was for this reason, no doubt, that Madison heartily approved of Coxe's detailed refutation of Sheffield's arguments on this score and made a considerable effort to send a copy of Coxe's pamphlet to England, possibly in the hope that Sheffield would see it.[24]

Of greatest importance in shaping Madison's diplomacy was his response to Sheffield's argument that Canada could replace the United States in the West Indian trades. This point attracted the most attention in the polemical controversies after 1783, and the majority of pamphleteers took very strong issue with Sheffield. In fact, the notion that Canada could ever be as valuable as America had already been rejected, even before American independence, by many British political economists who had stressed the vital economic contribution of the American colonies to British commercial and naval power.[25] From this viewpoint, it seemed illogical for Sheffield to suggest that Britain had less need of American trade after independence than before, and no one was quicker to develop this objection than the West Indian planters. Those planters found no substance in the claim that Canada could provide them with timber and provisions, and even Sheffield himself could publish trade figures for only one year—1774—that demonstrated Canada's ability to produce a surplus of wheat for export.[26] Equally vulnerable was Sheffield's tacit admission that exploitation of Canada's resources of timber would require more capital, people, and shipping than the region possessed. For these reasons, West Indians, especially after the hardships they had suffered from starvation,

---

[24] Madison to Jefferson, July 24, 31, 1791, Madison Papers, Reel 4. For a discussion of Coxe's *Brief Examination* and evidence of its coming into Sheffield's hands see Jacob E. Cooke, *Tench Coxe and the Early Republic* (Chapel Hill, N.C., 1978), 202-208.

[25] The importance of the American colonies to Britain was stressed by a number of writers including Adam Anderson, Benjamin Franklin, Joshua Gee, and Josiah Tucker. See Anderson, *An Historical and Chronological Deduction of the Origin of Commerce, from the Earliest Accounts . . . Containing an History of the . . . Commercial Interests of the British Empire*, 2 vols. (London, 1764); Gee, *The Trade and Navigation of Great Britain Considered*, 5th ed. (London, 1750 [orig. publ. 1729]); and Tucker, *A Brief Essay on the Advantages and Disadvantages which Respectively Attend France and Great Britain, with Regard to Trade*, 2d ed. (London, 1750). Madison was familiar with all these works, having recommended them for purchase by the Continental Congress in 1783. For a discussion of Franklin's thought here see Gerald Stourzh, *Benajamin Franklin and American Foreign Policy* (Chicago, 1954), 66-104.

[26] See Allen, *Considerations on the Present State*, 26-39; Edwards, *Thoughts on the Late Proceedings*, 15-21, 34; and Long, *A Free and Candid Review*, 10-89. In the appendices to his *Observations* Sheffield provided trade figures to support his claims.

hurricanes, and trade disruption during the Revolution, were most reluctant to risk relying on Canada for supply, and their demands that the United States be exempted from the navigation laws for that purpose were accordingly presented as a sustained assault on Lord Sheffield's political economy and vision of Canada.[27]

The planters' polemic depicted Canada as an ice-bound, snow-covered, windy, foggy desert where crops froze in the ground and agricultural surpluses could not be produced. As Bryan Edwards bluntly declared, "Canada is shut up six months of the year and the other six months is devoted to everlasting sterility."[28] So outraged were the planters at being asked, as they believed, to risk starvation and ruin for the Canadian fantasies of a man who understood nothing of their situation that, led by Edwards, they continued their attacks on Sheffield and the navigation laws well into the early nineteenth century. In successive editions of his voluminous history of the West Indies, Edwards offered the dead bodies of thousands of slaves as evidence for the folly of Sheffield's attempts to promote Canada, while he produced trade figures for the years after 1783 to prove that Canada was unable to provide the surplus wheat that Sheffield had predicted.[29]

[27] See the works cited in n. 26 and also [Bingham], *Letter from an American*, 7, 17; Champion, *Considerations*, 23, 107-122, 259; and Coxe, *A Brief Examination*, 21-23. On the problems of the planters in the West Indies see Lowell Joseph Ragatz, *The Fall of the Planter Class in the British Caribbean, 1763-1833: A Study in Social and Economic History* (New York, 1928), 142-173, and Richard B. Sheridan, "The Crisis of Slave Subsistence in the British West Indies during and after the American Revolution," *William and Mary Quarterly*, 3d Ser., XXXIII (1976), 615-641.

[28] Edwards, *Thoughts on the Late Proceedings*, 21.

[29] Bryan Edwards, *The History Civil and Commercial of the British Colonies in the West Indies*, II (London, 1794), 393-500. The *History*, which was reissued in 1798, 1801, 1806, 1810, and 1818, was a major contribution to a large body of literature on the West Indies that appeared in this period, much of which also attacked the views of Lord Sheffield. See, for example, Simon Cock, *An Answer to Lord Sheffield's Pamphlet on the Subject of the Navigation System Proving That the Acts Deviating Therefrom which His Lordship Censures Were Beneficial to Our Trade and Navy in the Last War and Ought to be Renewed in the Present* (London, 1804); Gibbes W. Jordan, *The Claims of the British West India Colonists to the Right of Obtaining Necessary Supplies from America and Employing the Necessary Means of Effectually Obtaining These Supplies Under a Limited and Duly Regulated Intercourse, Stated and Vindicated in Answer to Lord Sheffield's Strictures* (London, 1804); Joseph Lowe, *An Inquiry into the State of the British West Indies*, 4th ed. (London, 1808); Macall Medford, *Oil without Vinegar and Dignity without Pride: Or, British, American, and West-India Interests Considered*, 2d ed. (London, 1807); and William Spence, *The Radical Cause of the Present Distresses of the West-India Planters Pointed Out; and the Inefficiency of the Measures which Have Been . . . Proposed for Relieving Them Demonstrated* (London, 1808). Madison was familiar with many of the works, having requested the American minister in London to forward copies for deposit in the State Department library. See Madison to William Pinkney, Mar. 21, Apr. 4,

Even Richard Champion, who did not have the same personal stake in the issue as the West Indians, agreed that Sheffield's views were both "extravagant" and "mischievous." "Till we can force Nature to make," he added, "a free and open navigation and to soften the climate, we will not derive any advantage from Canada or Nova Scotia in any degree equal to the hopes that are held out to us."[30]

Madison was thoroughly familiar with this criticism of Sheffield, and many of his notes as well as his speeches in Congress indicate that he assimilated it into the arguments he put forward in favor of commercial discrimination from 1790 to 1794. He revealed his doubts about the ability of Canada to replace the United States in the West Indian trade by including in his preparation for a major speech in 1790 a rhetorical question aimed at the defenders of Sheffield's system: how had the West Indies fared for supply during the Revolution? The answer, as Madison pointed out on several occasions, was "very badly indeed," and he noted also that the planters had to divert labor "to less profitable cultivation to avoid starving."[31] Madison also knew from Coxe's pamphlet that trade between Canada and the West Indies did not increase significantly in the years immediately after 1783, and that to cope with this situation the British government, especially during wartime, had to exempt the islands from the navigation laws in order to allow them to receive supplies in American bottoms.[32] Indeed, at times the situation in the Canadian provinces themselves seemed so unpromising, even in the Newfoundland fishery, that Canadians had to import food from the United States.[33] It is hardly surprising therefore that Madison observed, in 1790, that should Britain ever be forced to attempt to supply the islands during wartime without American aid, "she could not afford to keep them."[34]

1808, and Apr. 21, 1809, William Pinkney Papers, Princeton University Library, Princeton, N.J. Madison's personal copy of Medford's pamphlet is in the collection of Madison pamphlets in the Alderman Library, University of Virginia, Charlottesville. Even when it is not possible to prove with certainty that Madison owned copies of particular works, he would have been familiar with their contents from his regular reading of the *Edinburgh Review*, which devoted much space to the problems of neutral rights and the West Indies.

[30] Champion, *Considerations*, 123.

[31] See Madison's "Notes on Trade and Shipping for a Speech in Congress," May 14, 1790, Madison Papers, Reel 4. Here Madison again took notes from the writings of Sheffield and Champion, and he may even have taken his rhetorical question about the West Indies from Champion's *Considerations*, 160-161.

[32] Coxe, *A Brief Examination*, 21-22. See also Alice B. Keith, "Relaxations in the British Restrictions on the American Trade with the British West Indies, 1783-1802," *Journal of Modern History*, XX (1948), 1-19.

[33] Gerald S. Graham, *British Policy and Canada, 1774-1791: A Study in 18th-Century Trade Policy* (London, 1930), 72-76.

[34] "Notes on Trade and Shipping," May 14, 1790, Madison Papers, Reel 4.

Such knowledge gave Madison much of his confidence in retaliatory commercial discrimination, and he singled out for attack in a speech in January 1794 both Sheffield and William Knox, a Georgia loyalist who had been responsible for incorporating Sheffield's views into British policy in the Order in Council of July 2, 1783, charging them with egregious error in their arguments about the self-sufficiency of the empire.[35] Madison assumed that experience would demonstrate that the theory of the navigation system did not fit the economic realities of the North Atlantic and Caribbean regions. This prospect, in turn, encouraged his desire to resort to commercial discrimination. He declared, for example, that a formal demand that American produce be taken to the West Indies only in American bottoms would soon lead to "very different language" from the British government about the terms of American trade.[36] Madison believed such a course would not expose the United States to risk of war. Great Britain's policies since 1783, he pointed out, had been designed to exploit American commerce, whereas "war would turn the arrangement ag[ains]t her by breaking up the trade with her."[37] And because Britain's policies seemed based on calculating just how much the United States would bear, Madison repeatedly argued between 1790 and 1794 that above all else the Republic should demonstrate that it had both the ability and the disposition to retaliate against the navigation laws.[38]

To accomplish this goal, Madison argued that commercial restrictions could operate on the imperial economy in a number of ways. His study of the situation led him to conclude that Britain was by no means as independent of the need for American raw materials and markets as Sheffield's *Observations* had supposed.[39] By restricting its imports, therefore, the United States could strike directly at Britain's prosperity, and Madison spent some energy on calculating how many people across the Atlantic would be "driven to poverty and despair" by such action.[40] But he admitted that Britain was not totally dependent on America for either raw mate-

[35] *Annals of Congress*, 3d Cong., 1st sess., 223. For Knox's contributions to Sheffield's cause see Leland J. Bellot, *William Knox: The Life and Thought of an Eighteenth-Century Imperialist* (Austin, Tex., 1977), 192-195.

[36] *Annals of Congress*, 1st Cong., 1st sess., 248.

[37] Madison to Horatio Gates, Mar. 24, 1794, in Gaillard Hunt, ed., *The Writings of James Madison . . .* , VI (New York, 1906), 208-209; quotation on p. 209.

[38] *Annals of Congress*, 1st Cong., 1st sess., 107, 190, 197, 209, 213, 247; *ibid.*, 2d sess., 1631; *ibid.*, 3d Cong., 1st sess., 155, 157, 211.

[39] For a more detailed discussion of this point see Drew R. McCoy, "Republicanism and American Foreign Policy: James Madison and the Political Economy of Commercial Discrimination, 1789 to 1794," *WMQ*, 3d Ser., XXXI (1974), 633-646.

[40] *Annals of Congress*, 3d Cong., 1st sess., 215. On the basis of material taken from Anderson's *History of Commerce*, Madison calculated that nonimportation could put as many as 300,000 people out of work in Great Britain.

rials or markets.[41] The real weakness in the imperial economy was the supply of the West Indies, and because Madison could see no source alternative to the United States, he began after 1794 to consider further ways of turning this situation to advantage. Initially, the pressure of circumstances as much as abstract considerations of political economy drove him along this path; in particular, he faced the problem of relating his theories of commercial discrimination to the preservation of American neutrality after the outbreak of war between Great Britain and France in 1793. As the neutrality crisis worsened in 1794, Madison felt some doubts about the ability of commercial restrictions to deal with the realities of war, but he was at the same time deeply upset that Britain was able to continue drawing supplies for its Caribbean colonies from the United States while under the "rule of '56" it simultaneously denied American merchants the right of a neutral trade with the colonies of France.[42] Eventually, he reached a tentative solution by suggesting that "perhaps the last step would be to declare that so long as Great Britain will not allow France to be supplied by us, we will not allow our supplies to go to her."[43]

Because of the protests that merchants, farmers, and shipowners would raise in response to this last suggestion, Madison hesitated to advocate it as public policy, though Congress did adopt in March 1794 an embargo on American shipping in order to preserve it from further British seizures. After a period of two months, however, a majority of legislators, including Madison, decided to abandon the measure, partly because it discriminated against France as well as Britain (though Madison noted at the time that the resumption of American trade would "save the W. Indies from famine without affording any sensible aid to France").[44] Yet as he reflected on the subject, Madison came to regret the repeal of the 1794 embargo, for he concluded that the measure, although short-lived, had been instrumental in effecting some moderation in British seizures of American shipping because of its "known effect in the West Indies."[45] These thoughts reinforced his opposition to the Federalist policies of increasing military and naval preparedness and sending John Jay to London to negotiate trade problems. He felt that this tactic would not work for it amounted, as he wrote in 1795, to saying no more to Great Britain than "do us justice or we will seize on Canada, though the loss will be trifling to you, while the

[41] *Annals of Congress*, 3d Cong., 1st sess., 216.
[42] For background see Samuel Flagg Bemis, *Jay's Treaty: A Study in Commerce and Diplomacy*, rev. ed. (New Haven, Conn., 1962), 253-278. See also Madison to Jefferson, Mar. 12, 14, 1794, Madison Papers, Reel 5.
[43] Madison to Jefferson, Mar. 2, 1794, Madison Papers, Reel 5.
[44] *Annals of Congress*, 3d Cong., 1st sess., 529, 597, 682-683; Madison to Jefferson, May 25, 1794, Madison Papers, Reel 5.
[45] See Madison's "Political Observations," Apr. 20, 1795, in *Letters and Other Writings of James Madison*, IV (Philadelphia, 1865), 500.

cost will be immense to us."[46] This remark expressed the essence of Madison's developing thought about the problems of Anglo-American relations and revealed the extent to which he had incorporated into his conception of the political economy of republicanism his earlier view that Lord Sheffield had been incorrect in believing that Canada could be employed to preserve the British navigation system from the pressures of American competition. In this form, Madison's thinking would have vital importance in the shaping of American diplomacy in the years of Republican ascendancy after 1800.

The belief that Canada was of little economic value to the British empire can be detected behind many of the diplomatic policies Madison advocated as secretary of state from 1801 to 1809. After the resumption of Anglo-French war in 1803, Madison, along with many other Americans, became greatly alarmed at the rising incidence of British impressment of American seamen and the seizure of American merchantmen in the West Indies under the "rule of '56." In Madison's opinion, this growing severity of British policy toward neutrals that culminated in the Orders in Council of November 1807 had very little to do with making war on France but was designed instead to serve the purposes of the West India interest in Great Britain. This loose alliance of bankers, merchants, and factors—widely regarded as one of the most formidable pressure groups in British politics—became greatly agitated over the rapid growth of American shipping in the colonial trades, which was not only depriving British shipping of cargoes but harming the West Indies by enabling Americans to dump sugar and coffee on European markets.[47] Many of the notoriously anti-American pamphlets that appeared in Britain after 1805—such as James Stephen's *War in Disguise* and Joseph Maryatt's *Concessions to America the Bane of Britain*—originated with this interest group, often with the blessing of the ministry.[48] These writings catalogued the economic ills of the British West Indies, occasionally suggested remedies such as cutbacks in production or alternative uses for sugar and molasses, but more commonly advocated that American shipping be driven out of all the colonial trades. Needing to encourage the growth of shipping to meet the demands of war, the British government gradually adopted these suggestions, first by rigorous enforcement of the "rule of '56" to control vessels in the colonial trades, and, ultimately, by the Orders in Council of November 1807,

[46] Madison to Jefferson, May 25, 1794, Madison Papers, Reel 5. "Political Observations," *Letters and Other Writings of Madison*, IV, 498.
[47] On the organization of the West India interest see Lillian M. Penson, "The London West India Interest in the Eighteenth Century," *English Historical Review*, XXXVI (1921), 373-392, and B. W. Higman, "The West Indian 'Interest' in Parliament, 1807-1833," *Historical Studies*, XIII (1967), 1-19.
[48] Horsman, *Causes of the War of 1812*, 33-43, 112-117, 119, 129.

which were designed to regulate the disposal of cargoes of colonial produce carried by American vessels.[49]

This perception of the motives behind British policy became firmly fixed in Madison's mind during the summer of 1805 as he began research into the origins of the "rule of '56," which, even as he started work, he denounced for threatening "more loss and vexation to neutrals than all the other belligerent claims put together."[50] His conclusions that the rule had no standing in international law and that the British violated it at their own convenience he expressed in a lengthy pamphlet, released late in 1805, and also in conversations with the British minister in Washington, Anthony Merry.[51] Madison told Merry that the "rule of '56" could not be defended as legitimate warfare against France for it was in reality a fraudulent legalism devised to justify "a pure and manifest commercial monopoly" for British shippers. In time, the secretary of state worked up a considerable animosity against the West India interest that finally found release in his outburst that West India merchants had less morality than African slave traders.[52] He had, though, no difficulty in prescribing the remedy, which was to strike at the heart of the problem in the British West Indies themselves.

Pursuing the conclusions he had reached in the 1790s, Madison suggested in March 1805 that the United States demand reciprocity with Great Britain in its West Indian trade, and stated his belief that Britain could not resist the demand because its Canadian colonies seemed no more prosperous than they had been a decade earlier and could not therefore be an alternative source of supply.[53] He then extended the logic of

[49] These motives for British policy were openly avowed in Parliament. See particularly the remarks by Earl Bathurst on Mar. 22, 1808, in *Cobbett's Parliamentary Debates* ... (London, 1806-1820), X, 1239-1240. They were also discussed in detail by Alexander Baring, *An Inquiry into the Causes and Consequences of the Orders in Council; and an Examination of the Conduct of Great Britain towards the Neutral Commerce of America* (London, 1808). Madison found this to be an "able and comprehensive pamphlet" (Madison to Pinkney, May 1, 1808, Pinkney Papers) largely because it confirmed a viewpoint that he himself had reached before 1808.

[50] Madison to Jefferson, Sept. 14, 1805, Thomas Jefferson Papers, microfilm, Reel 34, Lib. Cong.

[51] The pamphlet was *An Examination of the British Doctrine which Subjects to Capture a Neutral Trade Not Open in Time of Peace* (Philadelphia, 1805).

[52] Anthony Merry to Lord Mulgrave, Dec. 2, 1805, F.O. 5/45, Public Record Office (photostats in Lib. Cong.). Madison to Monroe and Pinkney, May 20, 1807, Dipl. Instructions, Reel 1; Madison to Albert Gallatin, July 28, 1809, in Carl Prince and Helen Fineman, eds., *The Papers of Albert Gallatin*, microfilm, Reel 19, Lib. Cong.; Madison to Jefferson, Aug. 16, 1809, Madison Papers, Reel 11; Madison to Pinkney, Oct. 23, 1809, Pinkney Papers.

[53] Madison to Monroe, Mar. 6, 1805, to John Armstrong, June 6, 1805, Dipl. Instructions, Reel 1. Madison to Jefferson, Aug. 20, 1805, Jefferson Papers, Reel 34. See also Merry to Mulgrave, June 2, 1805, F.O. 5/45.

this thinking to advocate by September 1805 an embargo on American trade to the Caribbean islands. "If indeed a commercial weapon can be shaped for the executive hand," he argued to Jefferson, "it is more and more apparent to me that it can force all nations having colonies in this quarter of the globe to respect our rights."[54] That Britain might react by "forcing the growth of the Continental provinces of Nova Scotia etc" and thus risking the sources of "wealth and power" that the West Indies contributed to the "revenue, commerce, and navigation of the parent state," Madison had already dismissed as simply "preposterous."[55]

Jefferson's response to this suggestion—reflected in the nonimportation law of April 1806 and in the decision to continue negotiations with Great Britain even after his rejection of the Monroe-Pinkney treaty—was less forceful than Madison would have liked, but he remained constant in his view that the problems of the West Indies should be exploited as the key British weakness.[56] Issuing instructions in May 1807 for the American ministers in London, James Monroe and William Pinkney, Madison observed that it was within the power of the United States to destroy the value of the West Indies to the British empire since it could no longer be unknown, even "to the most sanguine partisan of the colonial monopoly that the necessaries of life and cultivation can be furnished to those Islands from no other source than the United States, [and] that immediate ruin would ensue if this source were shut."[57] The course of events after the *Chesapeake* incident of June 1807, culminating in the adoption of the embargo in December, then created a situation where Madison's views were to receive a fair trial. As early as October 1807 the administration had learned—from the receipt of parliamentary reports on the West India trade—that Britain was contemplating new and drastic measures against neutral commerce, and when the Orders in Council of November 1807 went into effect, along with the Berlin and Milan decrees of France, Madison was successful in his advocacy of an embargo as the American response.[58]

[54] Madison to Jefferson, Sept. 14, 1805, Jefferson Papers, Reel 34. See also *National Intelligencer and Washington Advertiser* (Washington, D.C.), Nov. 18, Dec. 11, 1805.

[55] Madison to Monroe, Mar. 6, 1805, Dipl. Instructions, Reel 1.

[56] For Madison's doubts about the 1806 nonimportation law see his letter to Richard Cutts, July 11, 1806, Cutts Collection of the Papers of James and Dolley Madison, University of Chicago (microfilm in Lib. Cong.). Madison's opinions about Canada and the West Indies at this time were confirmed by Jacob Crowninshield in a report that stated that "the British provinces in America can by no means in their present state furnish important supplies to the British West Indies" (John H. Reinoehl, "Some Remarks on the American Trade: Jacob Crowninshield to James Madison, 1806," *WMQ,* 3d Ser., XVI [1959], 83-118; quotation on p. 83).

[57] Madison to Monroe and Pinkney, May 20, 1807, Dipl. Instructions, Reel 1.

[58] Pinkney to Madison, Aug. 13, 1807, Madison Papers, Reel 25. Madison to Pinkney, Oct. 2, 1807, Pinkney Papers. For Madison's role in the imposition of the

Madison's colleagues, particularly Jefferson, appear to have accepted the embargo, at least initially, for its value in preserving American commerce from the danger of seizures by the European belligerents, but the secretary of state's emphasis was rather different.[59] Believing that Britain's policies posed a more serious threat to American neutral rights than did those of France, Madison hoped, if the editorials in the *National Intelligencer* are to be believed, that the embargo would "coerce the settlement of long-standing and complicated accounts." The administration journal predicted that Great Britain would feel the effects of the loss of American trade "in her manufactures, in the loss of naval stores, and above all in the supplies essential to her colonies."[60] On the basis of Madison's previous arguments, the embargo would achieve these effects provided that Britain lacked alternative sources for the supplies it needed. So far as Madison could see, Canada, all Lord Sheffield's hopes notwithstanding, had failed to develop sufficiently, while by the end of 1807 the Baltic region—the only other source from which Britain might draw grain, timber, and naval stores—had been closed to British trade by the decision of Alexander I to join Napoleon's Continental System.[61]

In these circumstances, Madison's confidence in the coercive efforts of an embargo seemed reasonably well founded, and throughout 1808 he calmly waited for the measure to accomplish its purpose. Indeed, he could scarcely believe that Britain would adhere to the Orders in Council so far as to jeopardize the foundations of the West Indian commercial system; as early as May 1808, and again in July, he predicted the repeal of the Orders because of "distress" in the West Indies.[62] By August, however, the embargo was in serious difficulty, mainly because Madison and his colleagues had miscalculated both its popularity in the northern states and the prob-

embargo see Dumas Malone, *Jefferson the President: Second Term, 1805-1809* (Boston, 1974), 475-489.

[59] For a discussion of differences within the administration over the purposes of the embargo see Burton Spivak, *Jefferson's English Crisis: Commerce, Embargo, and the Republican Revolution* (Charlottesville, Va., 1979), x, xi, 102-111.

[60] *Natl. Intelligencer,* Dec. 21, 25, 28, 1805. For the claim that Madison wrote these editorials see Irving Brant, *James Madison: Secretary of State, 1800-1809* (Indianapolis, 1953), 402.

[61] The *Natl. Intelligencer,* Aug. 7, 19, Sept. 9, 11, 16, Dec. 7, 1807, noted that Britain could draw on neither Canada nor the Baltic for supplies, while Gallatin gave Jefferson figures on "how little Canada affords of what in British official returns appears as being the exports of that colony" (Gallatin to Jefferson, Feb. 13, 1808, Jefferson Papers, Reel 40).

[62] Madison to Pinkney, May 1, July 21, 1808, Pinkney Papers. The same point was made by *The Monitor* (Washington, D.C.), May 31, 1808, a paper edited in Madison's interest by John B. Colvin. See Brant, *Madison: Secretary of State,* 461. Macall Medford also argued that to bring Great Britain to terms, America "has nothing to do *but not to let a barrel of provisions go out of her ports for eighteen months,* and the West India islands will declare themselves independent" (*Oil without Vinegar,* 2d ed., 66).

lems of enforcement there. Beginning in March with the Treasury Department's attempts to cut off all exports by land, there developed down the St. Lawrence and Richelieu rivers a massive clandestine trade, principally in timber, provisions, and potash, much of which ultimately found its way through Canada to Great Britain and the West Indies.[63] To stop this traffic, Treasury Secretary Albert Gallatin first demanded a "little army on the lakes," but by August he had come to believe that the embargo had failed in this region and should therefore be abandoned.[64]

The evasions of the law alarmed Madison, and he fully grasped their implications. But for "lawlessness" on the part of the smugglers, he complained to Jefferson, there would have been "an uproar in the West Indies far more operative [on the British government] than the disturbance among the weavers."[65] The embargo, "if persisted in," he declared, "must soon reach [Britain's] vital interests"; even very late in his life he still held that view.[66] He was therefore reluctant to accept Gallatin's view that enforcement problems required repeal, and in the period immediately before his inauguration as president in March 1809 he hoped that the Republican majority in Congress would rally behind such anti-British policies as "an invigoration of the embargo, a prohibition of imports, *permanent* duties for encouraging manufactures, and a *permanent* navigation act."[67] Unfortunately for Madison, however, political support for the embargo in Congress collapsed; its members, between March 1809 and March 1811, were only prepared to endorse successively weaker measures of commercial restriction, principally the Non-Intercourse law of March 1809 and the so-called Macon's Bill #2 of April 1810.[68]

These developments distressed Madison, who found himself in the unenviable position of having to respond to British maritime policies with commercial and diplomatic weapons that he regarded as inadequate. A return to his favored policy of the embargo was, he reluctantly admitted, out of the question since popular prejudice and enforcement problems

[63] Louis Martin Sears, *Jefferson and the Embargo* (Durham, N.C., 1927), 90, 93, 95, 201. H. N. Mueller, "Smuggling into Canada: How the Champlain Valley Defied Jefferson's Embargo," *Vermont History*, N.S., XXXVIII (1970), 5-21. Israel Ira Rubin, "New York State and the Long Embargo" (Ph.D. diss., New York University, 1961), 107-140.

[64] Gallatin to Jefferson, July 29, Aug. 6, 1808, Jefferson Papers, Reel 41.

[65] Madison to Pinkney, July 3, 21, 1808, Pinkney Papers; Madison to Jefferson, Aug. 7, 14, 1808, Jefferson Papers, Reels 41, 42.

[66] Madison to Pinkney, Jan. 3, 1809, Pinkney Papers; Madison to Henry Wheaton, July 11, 1824, Madison Papers, Reel 20. See also *Monitor*, Sept. 12, 1808, and Spivak, *Jefferson's English Crisis*, 189.

[67] Madison to Pinkney, Nov. 10, 1808, Pinkney Papers.

[68] For a study of congressional voting behavior between 1809 and 1811 see Ronald L. Hatzenbuehler, "Foreign Policy Voting in the United States Congress, 1808-1812" (Ph.D. diss., Kent State University, 1972), 41-387.

had "incapacitated [it] for future use."[69] The Non-Intercourse law was increasingly evaded by Great Britain through an entrepôt trade opened to Americans in Amelia Island off the coast of Georgia, in Halifax in Nova Scotia, and even in Montreal in Lower Canada itself.[70] Nor did the practical consequences of the nonimportation clauses of Macon's Bill #2—which Madison invoked in November 1810 in response to Napoleon's offer of the Cadore letter and which Congress enacted into law on March 2, 1811—at first seem any better. The United States was now attempting to alter British maritime policies largely by coercing that nation's manufacturing interests, and Madison, although quite willing to try this tactic, was somewhat doubtful about its prospects, probably because it would take time for the manufacturers to organize an effective campaign against the better-represented shipping and West Indian interests that supported the Orders in Council.[71] Aided by a severe depression in Great Britain, nonimportation, ironically, did finally bring down the Orders in Council in June 1812, but long before that date Madison, for a variety of reasons, had concluded that the policy was ineffective and had shifted, after July 1811, toward preparations for war.[72] As with the embargo, the roots of the apparent failure of nonimportation could be traced back to Canada.

The difficulties of enforcing nonimportation throughout 1811 were felt in two areas: the first was in the trade from Passamaquoddy through Eastport and from there to other major American ports; the second, in the region between lakes Ontario and Champlain. A growing number of American merchants sailed to Eastport to import British merchandise under fraudulent bills of lading for local plaster of paris, while British West Indian rum was extensively smuggled into the United States as Spanish produce, especially in New England where there was a sudden absence of experts to testify in the courts as to its true British origins.[73] Equally serious was the smuggling of British manufactures from Montreal through the

[69] Madison to Pinkney, Feb. 11, Apr. 17, 1809, and Jan. 20, 1810, Pinkney Papers; Madison to Jefferson, Apr. 23, 1810, and to Pinkney, May 23, 1810, Madison Papers, Reels 12, 26. See also *Natl. Intelligencer*, May 23, June 1, 4, Aug. 24, 1810.

[70] Henry Dearborn to Gallatin, July 28, 1809, *Gallatin Papers*, Reel 19; Madison to Pinkney, Oct. 30, 1810, Madison Papers, Reel 26. See also Eli F. Heckscher, *The Continental System: An Economic Interpretation*, ed. Harald Westergaard (Oxford, 1922), 137-138.

[71] This point was made by Baring in *Inquiry into the Causes and Consequences of the Orders in Council*, 7.

[72] J. C. A. Stagg, "James Madison and the 'Malcontents': The Political Origins of the War of 1812," *WMQ*, 3d Ser., XXXIII (1976), 557-585.

[73] Dearborn to Gallatin, Aug. 31, 1811; Gallatin to James McCulloch and Larkin Smith, Sept. 6, 1811, all in *Gallatin Papers*, Reel 23. See also Gerald S. Graham, "The Gypsum Trade of the Maritime Provinces: Its Relation to American Diplomacy and Agriculture in the Early Nineteenth Century," *Agricultural History*, XII

lakes region, a business which the Treasury reported gave all the indications of having a determined and large-scale organization behind it. Only one officer of the Treasury Department—Peter Sailly at Champlain—showed any zeal in enforcing the law; the others lacked either the will or the means to stop the smuggling.[74] By October 1811, Gallatin felt compelled to report to Madison, as he had done to Jefferson three years earlier, that nonimportation could not be enforced without considerable expansion of the numbers of customs officers and of their powers, including the right to search private houses. The administration's attorney general, Caesar A. Rodney of Delaware, also urged this course.[75]

Madison did not oppose these suggestions, though he may have doubted their effectiveness. He was well aware of the difficulties of implementing nonimportation and had regretted as early as May 1811 that Congress had not banned American exports to Nova Scotia to lessen the inducements for British merchants to come there with imports.[76] By the end of the year, too, he knew that Britain had decided to assist further the smugglers of both British manufactures and West Indian produce by throwing open some free ports in Canada to American shipping.[77] Moreover, these problems would worsen over the winter of 1811-1812 as the freezing of roads and rivers multiplied the opportunities for smugglers to evade customs officers, and it promised to be a nice question how those officers were going to do their duty without running the risk of being shot as highwaymen by Americans who were obviously determined to trade

---

(1938), 212-218, and Herbert Heaton, "Non-Importation, 1806-1812," *Journal of Economic History*, I (1941), 193-198.

[74] Nathan Sage to Gabriel Duvall, Aug. 10, 1811; Peter Sailly to Gallatin, Aug. 24, Sept. 10, Oct. 8, 15, 1811; Samuel Buell to Gallatin, Sept. 13, 1811, all in *Gallatin Papers*, Reel 23. In documents he sent to Congress, Gallatin included a report "from an intelligent agent sent to Montreal" that contained descriptions of disguised American merchants purchasing British goods and arranging for their movement to the United States. See Legislative Records of the United States Senate, Sen. 12 A-D 1'(RG 46), Natl. Archs.

[75] Gallatin sent Madison an annotated copy of a Treasury circular dated Oct. 7, 1811, describing and warning about the infractions of the law. See Madison Papers, Reel 13. See also Gallatin to Thomas Newton and Samuel Smith, Nov. 26, 1811, *Gallatin Papers*, Reel 23, and Caesar A. Rodney to Gallatin, Oct. 20, 1811, *ibid.*

[76] Madison to Cutts, May 23, 1811, Cutts Coll., Papers of James and Dolley Madison. The *Natl. Intelligencer*, on the same day, declared that the U.S. could no longer tolerate the smuggling organized by the "colonial operations from Canada and Nova Scotia."

[77] George Joy to Madison, Oct. 18, 1811, Madison Papers, Reel 26. Here Joy informed Madison of the successful applications by British merchants to the Board of Trade to open the ports of St. Andrews and St. John in New Brunswick and Halifax in Nova Scotia to American merchants in order to allow them to receive British manufactures and West India produce in exchange for American supplies.

with Canada.[78] There was, moreover, the undesirability of tolerating a situation where Britain could encourage American citizens to flout American laws to the detriment of republican virtue. Madison also believed that widespread smuggling encouraged Britain to resist America's demands for redress of its maritime grievances. As he told the Twelfth Congress when it met to consider war in November 1811, "the practice of smuggling . . . is odious," especially "when it blends with a pursuit of ignominious gain a treacherous subserviency in the transgressors, to a foreign policy adverse to that of their own country," and he called on Congress to pass whatever measures were necessary to suppress all forms of illicit trade.[79]

Following this injunction, Gallatin requested from Congress at the end of November 1811 several laws to tighten nonimportation, including authorization of customs collectors to search private houses and the creation of an additional district court on the New York frontier.[80] But by now the administration was committed to preparing for war, and it could have hardly escaped Madison's notice that belligerency, too, was another way of dealing with the difficulties of enforcing restraints on trade. Indeed, the president may have concluded that the occupation of Canada was the only way to seal off the North American continent from British trade, though he did not publicly justify the War of 1812 on this ground. To have done so, given the disfavor into which commercial restrictions had fallen by late 1811, would have been politically unwise and would have weakened his case for war against Britain.[81] Shortly after the war ended, however, Madison pointed out to Monroe that "interested individuals," presumably in Britain, had "dwelt much on [Canada's] importance to G. Britain as a channel for evading and crippling our commercial laws"; as such, he continued, Canada "must ever be a source of collision between the two nations." To remove these and other causes of friction, he stressed, was "in truth the only reason we can have to desire Canada."[82] The fact, however, that Madison was willing to call for war after the summer of 1811 strongly suggests that he had reached the conclusion that Canada was of considerable value to Great Britain as a vent for trade long before he made this written admission to Monroe. If so, a war in Canada had become necessary in order to reinforce restrictive policies by which Madison had originally intended to avoid resorting to such a drastic remedy for the nation's grievances.

[78] See Sailly to Gallatin, Nov. 12, 1811, and Hart Massey to Gallatin, Nov. 8, 12, 1811, *Gallatin Papers*, Reel 23.

[79] James D. Richardson, *A Compilation of the Messages and Papers of the Presidents, 1789-1896*, I (New York, 1897), 480.

[80] Gallatin to Newton and Smith, Nov. 26, 1811, *Gallatin Papers*, Reel 23. The bill giving effect to this request was rejected by the Senate on Jan. 23, 1812. See *Annals of Congress*, 12th Cong., 1st sess., 105.

[81] See Stagg, "Madison and the 'Malcontents,'" *WMQ*, 3d Ser., XXXIII (1976), 583-584.

[82] Madison to Monroe, Nov. 28, 1818, Madison Papers, Reel 19.

Madison's belief that the United States should seize Canada in 1812 emerged from concerns that were broader than the practical problems of enforcing commercial restrictions. These concerns, which centered on Canada's position in the British empire, reflected the fact that after 1808 Madison could no longer be confident that Sheffield's predictions about the Canadian contribution to the empire were as erroneous as he had initially supposed. Sheffield had continued to assert his claims for Canada, and after the resumption of the Anglo-French war in 1803 he was again one of the earliest pamphleteers to warn of the dangers in making concessions to Americans in the West Indian trades.[83] At this time, though, he came to appreciate that the West India interest—toward which his earlier feelings had been somewhat ambivalent—could provide some important allies in his campaign to uphold the navigation acts. He therefore endorsed warmly in 1806 James Stephen's pamphlet *War in Disguise*, while many of the pamphleteers for the West India interest, particularly the merchants, in return adopted Sheffield's enthusiasm for Canada to assist their argument for driving neutral commerce out of the colonial trades.[84]

One result of this alliance was the parliamentary investigation into the condition of the West Indies in 1807, during which an assortment of West Indian merchants and Canadian traders, as well as the British governor of New Brunswick, all produced testimony both on the increasing involvement of Americans in carrying colonial produce to Europe and on Canada's "inexhaustible" ability to supply the British islands with food and timber. This testimony led to a report that summarized and reaffirmed the message of *War in Disguise* while adding to it the conclusion that the United States should no longer be regarded as "essential" to the supply of

[83] John Baker Holroyd, earl of Sheffield, *Strictures on the Necessity of Inviolably Maintaining the Navigation and Colonial System of Great Britain* (London, 1804). Other contributions to this debate in support of Sheffield's position included Jerome Alley, *A Vindication of the Principles and Statements Advanced in the Strictures of the Right Hon. Lord Sheffield on the Necessity of Inviolably Maintaining the Navigation and Colonial System of Great Britain* (London, 1806); N[athaniel] Atcheson, ed., *Collection of Interesting and Important Reports and Papers on the Navigation and Trade of Great Britain, Ireland, and the British Colonies in the West Indies and America* (London, 1807); and Atcheson, *American Encroachments on British Rights; Or Observations on the Importance of the British North American Colonies* (London, 1808). Atcheson was a Canadian merchant who was later appointed by the merchants of Montreal and Quebec to lobby in London against British concessions to the U.S. Many of his pamphlets were dedicated to Lord Sheffield.

[84] See Sheffield, *Strictures*, 2d ed. (London, 1806), 105. See also [Joseph Marryat], *Concessions to America the Bane of Britain, or the Cause of the Present Distressed Situation of the British Colonial and Shipping Interests Explained and the Proper Remedy Suggested* (London, 1807), and *Hints to Both Parties: Or Observations on the Proceedings in Parliament upon the Petitions against the Orders of Council* (London, 1808).

the West Indies.[85] This report reached Madison in October 1807 and drew from him his sharpest statement ever about the "infatuating prejudices" that led Great Britain to overvalue Canada. "Nothing is known with more certainty here," he reminded Minister Pinkney in London, "than the impossibility of drawing supplies for the West Indies from the British colonies in our neighbourhood." Only the United States, he repeated, could provide the raw materials and food the empire needed so badly.[86] But toward the end of 1808, as he confronted the failure of the embargo, Madison began to sense that this "infatuating prejudice" about Canada was more dangerous to the United States than he had realized, and he never again made any remarks suggesting that he still felt Canada was of little or no value to the British empire.

Sheffield, in this continuing advocacy of Canada, had challenged, indeed almost begged, the United States to adopt an embargo because it would stimulate the growth of Canadian shipping.[87] This point was taken up by the influential West India merchant, Joseph Marryat, in his pamphlet *Hints to Both Parties* that spoke of the need to raise "our much neglected provinces in North America to that prosperity and importance of which they are capable of attaining" in order to render the West Indies "independent of the caprice of any foreign power." Marryat took the argument one stage farther by suggesting that the development of Canada would enable Great Britain to enforce its maritime rights so stringently that it could totally subordinate all neutral commerce to its wartime needs. For this purpose he advocated adherence to the Orders in Council for the duration of the war with France, regardless of whether France repealed its decrees against neutral commerce and despite the fact that until then the Orders had been publicly justified as no more than fair retaliation against the French decrees.[88] In London, Pinkney seized on Marryat's pamphlet and sent Madison a copy in September 1808, pointing out that its author had been instrumental in shaping Britain's anti-neutral policies. Madison abstracted Marryat's arguments in the *National Intelligencer*—with special reference to the sections on Canada, the West Indies, and the Orders in Council. The administration newspaper concluded its summary with the observation that if a perpetual enforcement of the Orders in Council and the development of Canada should prove to be "the real object of the British ministry it is important that the American people should know it as in that case very different measures might be required than those called

---

[85] British Parliamentary Papers, *Report from the Committee on the Commercial State of the West India Colonies* (n.p., 1807), report on pp. 3-7; testimony is on pp. 9-85.

[86] Madison to Pinkney, Oct. 2, 1807, Pinkney Papers. Madison received two copies of this report, one from Pinkney and one from Joy, who also enclosed notes from Marryat's *Concessions to America*. See Joy to Madison, Aug. 25, 1807, Madison Papers, Reel 9.

[87] Sheffield, *Strictures*, 2d ed., 155, 191, 197, 200.

[88] [Marryat], *Hints to Both Parties*, 37-38.

for by a *temporary* restriction or suspension of neutral trade."[89] The implication, though unspoken, seemed clear: the United States might under
such circumstances have to consider depriving Great Britain of its Canadian possessions.

In the fullness of time, a British minister, Augustus J. Foster, did declare to Madison in July 1811 that his government would refuse to repeal
the Orders in Council almost regardless of the status of Napoleon's decrees, but long before that occurred Great Britain had taken the decision
to force the economic growth of Canada. This was not done in accordance
with dictates of the West India merchants or because of Lord Sheffield's
enthusiasm for Canada, but rose instead from a desperate need to obtain
timber and naval stores for the Royal Navy after Napoleon had induced
Russia to close the Baltic to British trade.[90] Nor was this new British
interest in Canada merely a temporary one since British timber companies
demanded a long-term commitment in return for their willingness to invest in a difficult enterprise. The government gave this commitment in
1809 and 1810 by doubling the duties on timber imports from the Baltic
into Great Britain and by increasing them again in 1811 and 1812.[91] Under this stimulus the Canadian economy, and the timber trade in particular, began to expand very rapidly. The increase in production and export
of timber between 1808 and 1812 was enormous and sustained the Royal
Navy for the duration of the war with France.[92] This development shifted

[89] Pinkney to Madison, Sept. 7, 1808, Dispatches from United States Ministers
to Great Britain (M-30), Reel 12, Recs. of the Dept. of State (RG 59), Natl. Archs.
Natl. Intelligencer, Nov. 23, 25, 1808. Madison would have recognized Marryat for
his important testimony in the 1807 West India Committee report on the volume
of colonial sugar and coffee being carried to Europe by American merchants. It was
the British desire to stop this trade that led to the Orders in Council of Nov. 1807
and Apr. 1809; hence Madison's outraged remarks on the "London smugglers of
sugar and coffee." See Madison to Gallatin, July 28, 1809, Gallatin Papers, Reel
19.
[90] Gerald S. Graham, "Napoleon's Baltic Blockade and the Birth of the Canadian Timber Trade," *Baltic and Scandinavian Countries*, V (1939), 28-30. See also
John Quincy Adams to Robert Smith, May 19, 26, 1811, pointing out that with the
closure of the Baltic, Canada became Great Britain's only source of timber. Worthington Chauncey Ford, ed., *The Writings of John Quincy Adams*, IV (New York,
1914), 83, 87.
[91] Robert G. Albion, *Forests and Sea Power: The Timber Problem of the Royal Navy*,
1652-1862 (Cambridge, Mass., 1926), 353-355, and Arthur R. M. Lower, *Great
Britain's Woodyard: British America and the Timber Trade, 1763-1867* (Montreal,
1973), 52-56.
[92] Albion, *Forests and Sea Power*, 346, 356. Figures on the timber trade can be
seen in British Parliamentary Papers, *An Account of the Quantity of Timber Imported
into Great Britain from British North America in Each Year from 1800 to 1819* (n.p.,
1819). Between 1807 and 1811, the volume of Canadian exports of oak and plank
timber rose by 549%, of great and middling masts by 519%, and of fir and pine
timber by 556%. In each case, the volume of timber taken from Canada by 1811
exceeded British timber imports from the Baltic for any year before 1807.

much of Britain's commercial interest in Canada away from the fisheries and fur trade toward Quebec, Montreal, and the hitherto undeveloped region of Upper Canada, which became the center for the supply of great and middling masts for the navy. But even in the maritime provinces, the demands of the new trade also encouraged the production of food surpluses for export.[93] It was, in short, a classic case of a discriminatory system multiplying the benefits of colonies to the mother country, and the point could hardly have been lost on Madison.

Even worse, from the American point of view, was the fact that the growth of Canada was also stimulated by, and in turn contributed to, the growth of the United States itself. The volume of oak cut in Vermont after 1808 for shipment down the Richelieu and St. Lawrence rivers actually increased as Anglo-American tensions rose, and Americans who had neither the means nor the wish to obtain land from the landlords of upstate New York moved into the southwest corner of Lower Canada and into Upper Canada in steadily increasing numbers.[94] Land was far cheaper and easier to obtain in many parts of Canada than in the United States, and by 1812 around the northern shore of Lake Ontario there existed an unbroken chain of settlements where there had been almost none in 1800. These settlements quickly began to produce surpluses of timber, staves, flour, wheat, meat, and potash, all of which could contribute significantly to the economies of both Great Britain and the West Indies.[95] Furthermore, the trade in the products in both Canada and the Unites States was conducted across the Great Lakes and down the St. Lawrence to Montreal and Quebec, where it was ultimately Canada rather than the United States that derived the benefit from it. The British diplomat Francis James Jackson, whom Madison had dismissed from Washington in November 1809 for his overbearing conduct, visited Canada in 1810 and reported to the British Foreign Office that the number of vessels clearing from Quebec had increased fivefold between 1805 and 1810 and yet could still not cope with the volume of timber and agricultural produce that was coming down

[93] W. T. Easterbrook and Hugh G. J. Aitken, *Canadian Economic History* (Toronto, 1956), chaps. 7, 9. See also John Bartlet Brebner, *North Atlantic Triangle: The Interplay of Canada, the United States and Great Britain* (New Haven, Conn., 1945), 81; Gerald S. Graham, *Sea Power and British North America, 1783-1820: A Study in British Colonial Policy* (Cambridge, Mass., 1941), 143, 189; and W. S. MacNutt, *The Atlantic Provinces: The Emergence of Colonial Society, 1712-1857* (Toronto, 1965), 129-144.

[94] H. N. Mueller III, "A 'Traiterous and Diabolic Traffic': The Commerce of the Champlain-Richelieu Corridor during the War of 1812," *Vt. Hist.*, N.S., XLIV (1976), 78-96. See also John Lambert, *Travels Through Lower Canada and the United States of North America, in the Years 1806, 1807, and 1808*, 2d ed., I (London, 1813 [orig. publ. 1810]), 244-255.

[95] Marcus Lee Hansen, *The Mingling of the Canadian and American Peoples*, comp. John Bartlet Brebner (New Haven, Conn., 1940), 70, 73, 81, 86, and Gerald M. Craig, *Upper Canada: The Formative Years, 1784-1841* (Toronto, 1963), 43-54. See also the works cited in n. 93 above.

the St. Lawrence. Nor did it escape Jackson's attention that the growth of Upper Canada was a significant step toward freeing the empire from the pressure of American economic restrictions. "Without going into detail," he wrote to Foreign Secretary Lord Wellesley, "Great Britain and her colonies are already in a great degree, and shortly will be still more so, independent of the produce of the United States."[96]

As Madison himself recalled some years later, there had swiftly developed after 1807 "in the portion of the United States connected with the [St. Lawrence] and the inland seas a world of itself" where patterns of trade and personal allegiances cut across political boundaries.[97] And it was in this "world" that the policies of embargo and nonimportation were failing. If anything, American restrictive policies, with the enormous boost they gave to smuggling, stimulated rather than retarded the Canadian economy. Canadian officials and merchants boasted to British companies that it would be business as usual during the nonimportation period, while the withdrawal of American vessels from the sea during the embargo gave Canadian shippers a strong incentive to develop a trade with the West Indies. And despite the heavy demands made on Canadian shipping to carry timber to Great Britain, Canadian navigation to the West Indies did increase significantly, albeit with some fluctuations, after 1807, so that the British North American provinces began to supply the islands to a greater degree than they had done before.[98] The president of the Board of Trade,

[96] Francis James Jackson to Earl Bathurst, Jan. 23, 1810, and to Lord Wellesley, Sept. 15, 1810, F.O. 5/69.
[97] Madison to Richard Rush, Nov. 13, 1823, Madison Papers, Reel 20. As the *Annual Register* for 1810 observed: "Canada has . . . risen to a degree of importance and prosperity altogether unexampled. In 1810, upward of 600 sail of ships arrived at Quebec for timber; and sawmills every where sprung up, worked by steam engines. Our navy is supplied with her timber; our West-India islands with her lumber; large and every year increasing quantities of corn, the growth both of the Upper Province, and of the States bordering upon the Lakes, and the river St. Lawrence, supply the deficiency of what had before been obtained from New York, Philadelphia, and the towns situated within the Virginian Cape" (LII, 260-261). See also W. A. Mackintosh, "Canada and Vermont: A Study in Historical Geography," *Canadian Historical Review*, N.S., VIII (1927), 9-30.
[98] The figures for Canadian trade in the early 19th century are not wholly reliable, but all the available estimates reflect sizeable increases for the years after 1807. The most comprehensive estimates of the trade of Quebec up to 1810 have been made by Gilles Paquet and Jean-Pierre Wallot, "International Circumstances of Lower Canada, 1786-1810: Prolegomenon," *Can. Hist. Rev.*, LIII (1972), 371-401, esp. 383, and their "Aperçu sur le commerce international et les prix domestiques dans le Bas-Canada (1793-1812)," *Revue d'Histoire de l'Amérique Française*, XII (1967), 447-473. For the trade of Halifax see David Sutherland, "Halifax Merchants and the Pursuit of Development, 1783-1850," *Can. Hist. Rev.*, LIX (1978), 1-17, esp. 4. Figures for the trade of all the Canadian colonies in this period are provided in the appendices of Graham's *Sea Power and British North*

Earl Bathurst, produced figures in Parliament in February 1809 demon-strating that the commerce between British North America and the West Indies "was in a rapid state of increase," and both Lord Sheffield and Wil-liam Knox at last had the satisfaction of seeing their predictions begin to come true.[99] As Knox wrote in 1808: "I applaud Jefferson very much, as an Englishman and especially as a New Brunswick Agent and Planter, for the measure of the embargo, as it . . . raises our continental colonies at the expense of the American States. I hope it will continue during the war with France."[100] Sheffield, it hardly need be pointed out, was equally de-lighted.[101]

The beginning of Canada's transition from a "few acres of snow" to a collection of "respectable" colonies was a development of considerable significance for Anglo-American relations, and Madison, in the years after 1815, explicitly stated his belief that this growth encouraged Britain to resist claims for more liberal definitions of American maritime rights.[102] From the outset, moreover, he was aware of the changing nature of Cana-da's contribution to the empire, having been warned by Pinkney in June 1808 that one way Britain intended to evade the effects of American com-mercial restrictions was "to look to the carriage from New Brunswick etc to the British Islands of commodities previously smuggled, in violation of our embargo, from the United States."[103] Very probably, Madison at first

---

America. These indicate that the number of ships entering British North America from the West Indies rose by 126% between 1806 and 1811, while the number clearing for the West Indies increased by 109%. See also J. Holland Rose, "British West India Commerce as a Factor in the Napoleonic War," *Cambridge Historical Journal,* III (1929), 42-43. The exact amount of wheat and flour exported from Canada to the West Indies is difficult to ascertain. The figures in Graham, *Sea Power and British North America,* show that the volume of wheat exported from Quebec rose by 171% between 1806 and 1812, and the volume of flour by 74%. Fernand Ouellet, who has minimized the agricultural potential of Lower Canada in the early 19th century, believes that while Quebec exported relatively little of its surplus wheat to the West Indies, it was, after 1808, sending 60% of its surplus flour to the islands (*Histoire économique et sociale du Québec, 1760-1850: Structure et conjuncture* [Montreal, 1966], 181).

[99] *Cobbett's Parliamentary Debates,* XI, 786.

[100] William Knox to Edward Winslow, May 4, 1808, in W. O. Raymond, ed., *Winslow Papers, A.D. 1776-1826* (St. John, New Brunswick, 1901), 622.

[101] John Baker Holroyd, earl of Sheffield, *The Orders in Council and the American Embargo Beneficial to the Political and Commercial Interests of Great Britain* (London, 1809). As Sheffield pointed out, "These are opinions I offered to the attention of the public twenty five years ago, and everything that has happened since proves that they were well founded" (p. 45).

[102] H. A. Innes and A.R.M. Lower, eds., *Select Documents in Canadian Economic History, 1783-1885* (Toronto, 1933), 3-4. Madison to Tench Coxe, Mar. 20, 1820, Madison Papers, Reel 19.

[103] Pinkney to Madison, June 22, 1808, Dispatches from U.S. Ministers to Great Brit. (M-30), Reel 12.

dismissed this possibility as he had done on a number of occasions in the past, but the dispatches to the State Department from American consuls throughout the Caribbean during the embargo period left little doubt that Canadian-West Indian trade had grown very rapidly and that the impact on the islands of the withdrawal of American shipping was not as severe as Madison had predicted.[104] The consul in Kingston, Jamaica, for example, reported at the beginning of 1809 that while the embargo had caused the planters some hardship, "the Canadas [had] furnished through the navy of Quebec flour to a greater magnitude than anticipated as also the article of lumber which comprises the implement of conveyance of the produce of the colonies to the mother country."[105]

Admittedly, many of these new Canadian exports, especially in 1808, were American rather than Canadian in origin, but Madison could have derived little comfort from that fact. He had long been aware that even if Canada itself seemed to lack potential for development, the waterway of the Great Lakes and the St. Lawrence had the capacity to command much of the trade of the American interior, and, as early as 1780, he had predicted that should the commerce of the American hinterland ever be channeled down the St. Lawrence the commercial benefit to Great Britain would be enormous. "So fair a prospect," he then wrote, "could not escape the commercial sagacity of that nation [and] she would embrace it with avidity [and] cherish it with the most studious care." If Britain did succeed in fixing America's inland commerce in the St. Lawrence "channel," Madison added, "the loss of her exclusive possession of the trade of the United States might prove a less decisive blow to her maritime pre-eminence and tyranny than has been calculated."[106] The failure of the embargo and the consequences of that failure turned this prediction into a growing reality. After 1808 Gallatin began to collect statistics on the trade of Quebec, and these confirmed other reports of rising exports in lumber and provisions as well as a steady growth in Canadian tonnage and seamen. In fact, the figures on Canadian trade compiled by John Jacob Astor for the Treasury

[104] See Spivak, *Jefferson's English Crisis*, 168-169.

[105] William Savage to Madison, Jan. 20, 1809, Dispatches from United States Consuls in Kingston, Jamaica (T-31), Reel 1, Recs. of the Dept. of State (RG 59), Natl. Archs. Savage also mentioned that the planters were trying to develop their own sources of supply, and added that "many properties now supply themselves with staves."

[106] Madison to [John Jay], Oct. 17, 1780, in *Papers of Madison*, II, 134. Madison drafted this letter while serving as chairman of the committee of the Continental Congress entrusted with issuing instructions to Jay and Benjamin Franklin on negotiations with Spain over the navigation of the Mississippi. He was comparing and contrasting the merits of the Mississippi and St. Lawrence river systems, noting that the former was "manifestly the most natural and by far the most advantageous." The latter, though, he wrote, "will be found far from . . . impracticable." More than 40 years later, Madison made the same point again in his letter to Richard Rush on Nov. 13, 1823 (see n. 97 above).

Department in 1810 were higher than those reported to the British Foreign Office by Francis James Jackson.[107]

Additional news about the rising prosperity of Canada, moreover, was readily available in the United States, and it is inconceivable that Madison was not familiar with this information. Many Republican congressmen after 1809, as well as several American newspapers such as the *National Intelligencer,* made references to the growth of Canada, speculated on its importance to Great Britain, and hinted that the United States should lose no time in depriving that nation of such a vital resource.[108] The editor of the Philadelphia *Aurora General Advertiser,* William Duane, after denouncing Britain's encouragement of smuggling from Canada, predicted in October 1811 that the British government would never renounce its anti-American policies voluntarily and suggested that his readers consult the pamphlets of Sheffield and Stephen for the reason.[109] At the same time, the Richmond *Virginia Argus* claimed that "many of the effects of a successful naval warfare would result to us from the conquest of the British provinces adjacent to us," though the editor hastened to add that this did not mean that the United States would have any territorial ambitions in a war with Britain.[110] In Washington, the administration journal reported that some of the assemblies of the West Indian islands—which had usually been as skeptical as Madison about the claims made for Canada's economic potential—were now considering resolutions that they should rely in future on Canadian rather than American timber.[111] Furthermore, it was apparent that after 1807 the British government was far less disposed to grant West Indian governors the powers to exempt American shipping from the navigation laws. Among the indications of this hardening attitude were the decisions in 1809 to authorize all West Indian assemblies to adopt discriminatory duties against American produce and to institute an enlarged convoy system to protect Canadian-West Indian trade from French privateers.[112] Finally, in an Order in Council dated September 6,

---

[107] John Jacob Astor to Gallatin, Jan. 14, 1811, *Gallatin Papers,* Reel 22.

[108] See, for example, the remarks of Ezekiel Bacon of Massachusetts in Feb. 1809 on the extent to which Canada, by supplying the West Indies, enabled Great Britain to escape the effects of the embargo. "Now," Bacon declared, "if by getting possession of Canada you could in that way affect the other possessions and interests of Great Britain, it is important to have possession of it" (*Annals of Congress,* 10th Cong., 2d sess., 1283).

[109] *Aurora General Advertiser* (Philadelphia), Oct. 26, 1811. See also *ibid.,* Sept. 25, Oct. 21, Nov. 4, 1811, and July 8, 1812.

[110] *Virginia Argus* (Richmond), Nov. 11, 1811.

[111] *Natl. Intelligencer,* Sept. 14, Oct. 22, Nov. 12, 1811, and Feb. 22, 1812. For similar statements in other newspapers see *Democratic Press* (Philadelphia), May 27, July 6, Nov. 18, 1812; *Baltimore Whig,* Dec. 14, 1811; *Weekly Register* (Baltimore), May 30, 1812; *Albany Republican* (N.Y.), May 27, 1812; and *Ontario Repository* (Canandaigua, N.Y.), Jan. 15, 1811, and Jan. 21, 1812.

[112] For a copy of the Order in Council of Aug. 16, 1809, authorizing West Indian assemblies to impose discriminatory duties see Francis James Jackson Pa-

1811, Britain excluded American salt fish from the West Indies and imposed heavy duties on all other articles imported into the islands from the United States. As the *National Intelligencer* observed, this measure could only have been designed to promote Canadian-West Indian trade at the expense of the United States.[113]

Discussing the Order in Council of September 6, the administration newspaper, on November 2, 1811, argued that the West Indies could only be supplied from the United States, but the significance of the growth of Canada after 1808 was not to be mistaken, and the *National Intelligencer* admitted as much very shortly afterwards. In a series of articles in late November and early December 1811, the *Intelligencer* commented at length on the problem of Canada. To remove any impression among the members of the Twelfth Congress—who were on the point of considering a report from the House Foreign Relations Committee on preparations for war—that the comments were merely occasional pieces, the editor stated that they came from a "valuable correspondent whose sources of information are unquestioningly correct and whose statements may therefore be relied on." More significantly, that correspondent, after providing detailed discussions of the economy, soils, waterways, and population of Canada, noted that his information about the Canadians was "the more necessary as it is intimately connected with their reduction and affiliation with the United States." Admitting that former ideas about Canada as a "sterile" region, useful only in so far as it produced furs, had been proved "erroneous" by Canada's rise to "wealth and importance," the author declared that "in the present state of the world" Canada was "of more vital importance to Great Britain than one half her West India colonies." This rapid rise in Canada's value he attributed to recent changes "effected by settlements, by commerce, and by war," particularly the growing needs of Britain's West India colonies, the exclusion of that nation's trade from the "north of Europe" by France and Russia, the operation of "our embargo and other restrictive laws," and, above all, the expansion of American settlements, especially in New York, "to those places which naturally communicate with Canada." This last cause, he feared, "will continue to increase the trade down the St. Lawrence till it will be equalled only by that of the Mississippi," and he added the warning that should the growth of Canada go unchecked and "should Great Britain be allowed to retain possession of [it] she may laugh at any attempts to distress her West Indies or exclude her from the Baltic, for she will have more than a Baltic of her own."[114]

---

pers, F.O. 353/59, P.R.O. (microfilm in Lib. Cong.). See Gerald S. Graham, *Empire of the North Atlantic: The Maritime Struggle for North America* (Toronto, 1950), 234-235.

[113] *Natl. Intelligencer*, Nov. 2, 1811.

[114] *Ibid.*, Nov. 23, 28, Dec. 3, 1811.

These editorials were the closest that Madison's administration ever came to admitting openly by word, as distinct from deed, that the growth of Canada had the potential to destroy the very basis of Madison's diplomacy of commercial restriction—the assumption that Britain and its empire were dependent on the United States for "necessaries." Without such dependence between the two nations, the United States, as Madison understood its position, would have few means of bringing effective pressure on Britain other than by trying to build up its own naval and military forces to match those of the enemy. This would not have been an attractive proposition for Madison, and, given the considerations that he knew had justified British policies toward the United States since 1783, it was entirely logical for him to conclude by 1812 that the time had come to deprive Britain of Canada. As he recalled on more than one occasion after the War of 1812, a developing Canada presented "serious difficulties . . . in self-denying contests with Great Britain for commercial objects."[115] To Tench Coxe, who, like Madison, had dismissed Sheffield's claims for Canada in the 1780s and 1790s, he observed in 1820 that "the supplies attainable *from* Canada and from the contiguous parts of the United States, now become so productive *through* Canada, may render the contest [between Great Britain and the United States] more obstinate than might have happened at periods when the dependence of the Islands on our exports was more acutely felt."[116] With this remark, and others like it, Madison tacitly conceded that events in Canada had undermined the diplomacy of commercial restriction and, as he pointed out to Churchill C. Cambreleng in 1827, that "future contests" between the two nations would have to take "a different character."[117]

The British government, as it took steps to foster the growth of Canada after 1808, also counted on being able to draw increasing amounts of grain, timber, and naval stores from the Baltic region as the nations there struggled to break away from Napoleon's Continental System, but it was the belief of many Americans, including Madison and his minister to Russia, John Quincy Adams, that Napoleon would probably succeed in 1812 in excluding British commerce from the north of Europe.[118] This develop-

[115] Madison to Churchill C. Cambreleng, Mar. 8, 1827, Madison Papers, Reel 21.

[116] Madison to Coxe, Mar. 20, 1820, *ibid.*, Reel 19.

[117] Madison to Cambreleng, Mar. 8, 1827, *ibid.*, Reel 21.

[118] John Quincy Adams to Monroe, June 22, Aug. 16, 1811, and May 9, 1812, in Ford, ed., *Writings of John Quincy Adams*, IV, 115, 117, 179, 325. Madison to Henry Wheaton, Feb. 26, 1827, Madison Papers, Reel 21. Monroe even told the British minister, Augustus Foster, that France, as a sine qua non for a peace with Russia in 1812, would place a garrison in every port town to enforce the Continental System (entry of May 24, 1812, Augustus Foster Journal, Augustus Foster Papers, Lib. Cong.). For a more general discussion see Lawrence S. Kaplan, "France and Madison's Decision for War, 1812," *Mississippi Valley Historical Review*, L (1964), 652-671.

ment promised to leave Britain almost wholly dependent on Canada for resources that were essential for maintaining its navigation system, and it was for this reason that Madison could believe that a Canadian war would be an effective solution to the problem of compelling British respect for American maritime rights. American victory in Canada would leave little alternative but to accept American terms for trade if Britain wished to preserve the remnants of its empire and its naval power from further damage. The defenders of the navigation system, such as Lord Sheffield, could have presented critics of that system, both in America and in Britain, with no answer to the argument that the empire, without Canada, would be unquestioningly dependent on the resources of the United States. It was therefore by no means unreasonable for James Monroe to explain American policy to John Taylor of Caroline and Jonathan Russell as he did in June 1812. To the former he could state in good faith that the republic was not going to war for the sake of territorial expansion, while to the latter he could give authority to warn the British government that if it did not speedily make a settlement with the United States, American forces would have to occupy Canadian soil and then refuse to relinquish it.

On To Canada: Manifest Destiny and United States Strategy in the War of 1812

by
Reginald Horsman

WAR ᎾᏁ GREAT LAKES
Canada and the United States
in the War of 1812

When, in July 1812, General William Hull crossed the Detroit River and invaded Canada, he issued a grandiloquent proclamation in which he told the Canadians that he was offering them "the invaluable blessings of Civil, Political, & Religious Liberty." After promising them protection in their *"persons, property, and rights,"* he went on to tell them that they were to be "emancipated from Tyranny and oppression and restored to the dignified station of freemen." To Hull the choice was clear. "The United States offer you *Peace, Liberty,* and *Security,"* he proclaimed, "your choice lies between these, & *War, Slavery,* and *destruction."*[1] In the next month Hull had to eat his words as he surrendered his northwestern army, but he had set the tone for the American invasion. When in November of the same year General Alexander Smyth prepared to invade Canada on the Niagara front, he was also ready with bombastic proclamations, culminating in the exhortation: "Be strong! Be brave! And let the ruffian power of the British King cease on this continent."[2]

Reginald Horsman is Distinguished Professor of History at the University of Wisconsin - Milwaukee. This essay was presented originally at the symposium, *War on the Great Lakes: Canada and the United States in the War of 1812* at Monroe County Community College, January 1987.

[1] William Hull proclamation, 13 July 1812, *Michigan Pioneer and Historical Collections,* 40 vols. (Lansing: 1877-1929), 15: 106-107. There was no "Canada" in 1812. There were four separate British colonies on the mainland: Upper Canada, Lower Canada, New Brunswick, and Nova Scotia. When the Americans wrote and talked of Canada, their immediate objectives were Upper and Lower Canada, but they also wrote and talked of eliminating British power on the North American continent.

[2] Alexander Smyth proclamation, 27 November 1812, *American State Papers, Military Affairs* (Washington: 1832), 1:501. See also Henry Adams, *History of the United States during the Administrations of Jefferson and Madison,* 9 vols. (New York: Charles Scribner, 1889-1891), 6: 354-56.

Michigan Historical Review 13 (Fall 1987)
Copyright © Central Michigan University 1987

In September 1814, far away in Ghent, the British peace commissioners cited proclamations by Hull and Smyth as evidence that the Americans, in spite of their assertion that they were fighting a defensive war to protect their neutral rights, had in reality intended to conquer and annex Canada. This was denied by the American peace commissioners who stated that the statements by Hull and Smyth were neither authorized nor approved by the American government.[3]

That there should be some confusion regarding the intentions of the American government in the War of 1812 is not surprising. These intentions were argued about at the time— both before and during the War of 1812—and they have been argued about since. Among American historians the intentions of the American government along the Canadian border have usually been considered in the context of the causes of the War of 1812, rather than in the context of long-term American interests in the British North American Provinces and general American ambitions on the North American continent. During the past century American historians have delighted in arguing about the causes of the War of 1812, and the role of Canada in the coming of the war has been particularly controversial. I intend to argue that the form this argument about the causes of the war has taken has brought confusion to the subject of American intentions in regard to Canada. To understand the causes of the War of 1812 it is necessary to focus in detail on the events from 1803 to 1812; but, to understand American attitudes toward Canada in that war it is necessary to understand American fears about the British in Canada that had existed since the Revolution, American dreams of a continent free of British influence and dominated by the United States, and the course of American arguments regarding Canada during the War of 1812.

The historiographical argument about the causes of the War of 1812 is a familiar one. In the nineteenth century it was generally assumed that the United States declared war on England to defend American neutral rights and the national honor. Canada was simply the arena in which the war was

---

[3] The British to the American Commissioners, 19 September 1814; the American to the British Commissioners, 13 October 1814; James F. Hopkins and Mary W. M. Hargreaves, eds., *The Papers of Henry Clay* (Lexington: University of Kentucky Press, 1959-), 1: 978, 983.

fought.[4] For the past sixty years that simplicity has disappeared. In 1925 Julius Pratt argued in his book *The Expansionists of 1812* that a decisive factor in the declaration of war was the western demand that the British should be expelled from Canada to prevent their instigating Indian hostilities on the American frontier. He also maintained that southern support for the war came from a belief that the acquisition of Canada to the North was to be balanced by the acquisition of the Floridas to the South.[5]

Although Pratt's arguments were challenged in the fifteen years after his book was published, it was not until the 1960s that maritime problems and national honor again became dominant in the discussions of the coming of the war. Both Bradford Perkins in his *Prologue to War* and myself in *The Causes of the War of 1812* argued that the causes of the war were to be found on the sea not on the land, and I argued that the invasion of Canada was a method of waging the war not a reason for starting it. The arguments have continued since that time, but discussions of Canada have continued to revolve around the question of how Canada fitted into the specific question of the causes of the war. In one of the latest books on the subject, J.C.A. Stagg argues that President James Madison pressed for war and the invasion of Canada because the growing importance of exports from Canada to Great Britain combined with Republican disunity threatened American policies of commercial restriction. By conquering Canada the United States would better be able to force Great Britain to acknowledge American neutral rights.[6]

---

[4] For early writing on the causes of the war, see Warren H. Goodman, "The Origins of the War of 1812: A Survey of Changing Interpretations," *Mississippi Valley Historical Review* 28 (September 1941-42): 171-86.

[5] See Julius W. Pratt, *Expansionists of 1812* (New York: The Macmillan Company, 1925), 12-13.

[6] Bradford Perkins, *Prologue to War: England and the United States, 1805-1812* (Berkeley: University of California Press, 1961); Reginald Horsman, *The Causes of the War of 1812* (Philadelphia: University of Pennsylvania Press, 1962); J.C.A. Stagg, *Mr. Madison's War: Politics, Diplomacy, and Warfare in the Early American Republic, 1783-1830* (Princeton: Princeton University Press, 1983). For a discussion of other historians and the causes of the war, see Reginald Horsman, "Western War Aims, 1811-1812," *Indiana Magazine of History* 53 (March 1957): 1-18, and Clifford L. Egan, "The Origins of the War of 1812: Three Decades of Historical Writing," *Military Affairs* 38 (April 1974): 72-75.

When discussing American intentions in regard to Canada, rather than simply the causes of the War of 1812, a problem with all these arguments, including mine, is that later historians have too often allowed Julius Pratt to set the framework of the discussion. Since the publication of Pratt's work in 1925, historians discussing the causes of the war have been anxious to point out that the war was caused by a whole series of maritime acts that were bitterly resented by nationalistic Americans, not by a western desire to conquer Canada to prevent British support for the Indians. But, while it is correct to argue that the United States did not cynically declare war in 1812 to invade and conquer Canada, this does not mean that there was not a strong desire to annex Canada in the United States. Many hoped that a war declared largely for other reasons was likely to have the major collateral benefit of ending the British occupation of Canada.[7]

In disagreeing with those interpretations that have simply stressed expansionism and minimized maritime causation, historians have ignored deep-seated American fears for national security, dreams of a continent completely controlled by the republican United States, and the evidence that many Americans believed that the War of 1812 would be the occasion for the United States to achieve the long-desired annexation of Canada. The United States would not have declared war in 1812 without the British maritime aggressions of almost twenty years, but many believed that a possible benefit of the war would be the annexation of all or substantial parts of the British North American colonies.

From the very beginning of the revolutionary era, the Americans had an acute sense of the importance of Canada for their future security. Nearly a century of conflict with the French and their Indian allies had demonstrated the vulnerability of the American colonies to attack from Canada, and there was also a developing realization of the importance of the St. Lawrence and the Great Lakes system to the trade of northern New England and the whole region south of the Great Lakes.

---

[7] Writing primarily from the perspective of Canada and the military operations along the United States-Canadian frontier, George F. G. Stanley argues that "the incorporation of Canada into the American union was among the aims of the men who dominated Congress in 1812," *The War of 1812: Land Operations* (Ottawa: Macmillian of Canada, 1983), 29.

In October 1774, even before the outbreak of hostilities in the American colonies, Congress had invited the Canadians to join the Americans in resisting British abuses. "Your province," it told them, "is the only link wanting to compleat the bright and strong chain of union."[8] Further efforts to enlist Canadian support having failed, the Americans in 1775, before declaring their independence from Great Britain, launched an attack on Canada. Montreal was taken, and the invasion only failed before the walls of Quebec.[9] No better indication could have been given of the dangers the revolutionaries perceived from Canada remaining in the hands of the British.

With independence declared, there was no doubt in the minds of American leaders of the necessity of expelling the British from Canada. As early as September 1776, when Benjamin Franklin drafted a set of possible peace terms, he included a provision for the British cession of the Canadian provinces, East and West Florida, Bermuda, and the Bahamas. "It is absolutely necessary for us to have them," he wrote, "for our own security."[10] In this same summer of 1776 the Continental Congress was engaged in discussing a model treaty to provide guidelines for shaping a hoped-for French alliance. One of its provisions was that, in return for American trade, the French should agree to American claims to all the British possessions on the North American continent and nearby British islands. When the French alliance was signed in February 1778, article 5 stated that should the United States see fit to attack the British mainland colonies or the Bermudas "those countries or islands, in case of success, shall be confederated with, or dependent upon, the said United States."[11]

There were high hopes in America in 1778 that the French alliance would enable the United States to conquer Canada. In

---

[8] "A Letter to the Inhabitants of the Province of Quebec," 26 October 1774, in James H. Hutson, ed., *A Decent Respect to the Opinions of Mankind: Congressional State Papers, 1774-1776* (Washington: U.S. Government Printing Office, 1975), 67.

[9] Ibid., 84-87; also Richard Van Alstyne, *The Rising American Empire* (1960; reprint Chicago: Quadrangle Books, 1965), 37-38.

[10] Quoted in Gerald Stourzh, *Benjamin Franklin and American Foreign Policy*, 2d ed. (Chicago: University of Chicago Press, 1969), 200.

[11] Worthington C. Ford, et al., eds., *Journals of the Continental Congress*, 34 vols. (Washington: U.S. Government Printing Office, 1904-1937), 5:770; 11:450.

May 1778 George Washington corrected a rumor that Canada
had joined the union, but added: "It is a measure much to be
wished, and I believe would not be displeasing to the body of
that people." He went on to say that he believed Canada was
of major importance to the American Union: "If that country
is not with us, it will, from its proximity to the eastern States,
its intercourse and connexion with the numerous tribes of
western Indians, its communion with them by water and other
local advantages, be at least a troublesome if not a dangerous
neighbor to us; and ought, at all events, to be in the same
interests and politics, of the other States."[12]

Independence without Canada was perceived as creating a
major security problem for the United States. In July 1778
George Mason of Virginia argued that though it was natural
to wish for peace, war was in the present interest of the United
States. It was necessary because the union was "yet incomplete,
& will be so, until the inhabitants of all the territory from Cape
Breton to the Mississippi are included in it." Canada and
Florida were essential, he argued, to stop the British inciting
the Indians, and St. Augustine and Halifax were essential for
the safety of America's coasts and American trade.[13] John
Adams agreed with Mason. At this time in his career Adams
was so convinced of the danger presented by British possessions
in North America that he was advocating a permanent alliance
with France. The basic problem, he believed was contiguity, for
"neighboring nations are never friends in reality." Only France
could provide the necessary counterweight to the British, for
"as long as Great Britain shall have Canada, Nova Scotia, and
the Floridas, or any of them, so long will Great Britain be the
enemy of the United States, let her disguise it as much as she
will."[14] When in October 1778 Congress appointed Franklin
minister to France, they provided him with fresh instructions.
Congress wanted France to cooperate in a plan for the capture

---

[12] Washington to Landon Carter, 30 May 1778, *The Writings of George
Washington*, 37 vols. (Washington, D.C.: U.S. Government Printing Office,
1931-1940), 11:492-93.

[13] George Mason to Richard Henry Lee, 21 July 1788, quoted in Van
Alstyne, *Rising American Empire*, 54-55.

[14] John Adams to Samuel Adams, 28 July 1778, Francis Wharton, ed., *The
Revolutionary Diplomatic Correspondence of the United States*, 6 vols.
(Washington: U.S. Government Printing Office, 1889), 2:667-68.

of Halifax and Quebec. This, it was argued, would give the United States two new states — Quebec and Nova Scotia.[15]

American hopes of annexing Canada during the revolution were dashed. France supported the United States for her own purposes, and had no desire to enhance the power of the new republic. The French never supplied the assistance necessary for the United States to be able to take Canada. Congress realized that in the immediate future it was more important to obtain the eastern half of the Mississippi Valley than Canada; and, when possible peace terms were drawn up in 1779, it was argued that a boundary on the Mississippi was essential. Although Canada was desirable, and of great importance, peace would not depend on its cession.[16] In the preliminary peace talks in April 1782, Franklin suggested that the British should cede Canada, but in the eventual peace treaty the American commissioners had to accept the reality that the United States did not yet have the power to force the British out of Canada.[17]

Canada, however, remained of vital importance in American thinking. When the Articles of Confederation went into effect in March 1781 they contained a provision that Canada could enter the union whenever it wanted to, but that other new states would require the agreement of nine of the thirteen states.[18] The desire to remove the British presence to the north remained strong in the years after 1783, but before 1789 American weakness meant that the British in Canada were a much bigger threat to the United States than the Americans were to Canada. In the 1780s and early 1790s, the British in Canada retained the Northwest posts, controlled navigation on the lakes, and encouraged the Indians within American territory to resist the frontier advance. The Americans also suspected them of attempting to split the republic by plotting in Vermont and Kentucky.[19]

---

[15] *Journals of the Continental Congress,* 12:1046.

[16] Ibid., 14: 959-60, 14 August 1779.

[17] Richard B. Morris, *The Peacemakers: The Great Powers and American Independence* (New York: Harper & Row, 1965), 262-63 and passim.

[18] *Journals of the Continental Congress,* 19:221.

[19] See John Jay to Thomas Jefferson, 14 December 1786, William R. Manning, ed., *Diplomatic Correspondence of the United States: Canadian Relations, 1784-1860,* 4 vols. (Washington, D.C.: Carnegie Endowment for International Peace, 1940-45), 1:32. See also J. Leitch Wright, Jr., *Britain and*

In the years after 1789, as the American government grew in strength, it again became possible to envisage the expulsion of the British from North America. In the eyes of the leaders of the United States it was not simply a matter of the British in Canada harassing American frontiers by backing the Indians, it was a belief that the British were pursuing a specific course of blocking America's ultimate triumph and destiny on the North American continent. Washington wrote in 1792 that he did not believe the Indians would ever be in "a quiescent state so long as they may be under an influence which is hostile to the rising greatness of these States."[20]

A remarkable feature of the young United States was the degree to which there was confidence in the future continental destiny of the American people. Since the mid-eighteenth century it had been common for both European and American observers to forecast the future greatness of the American states and the transference of power from the old to the new world. Even in the weak, disunited years of the 1780s these hopes of future destiny had persisted. Thomas Jefferson had written in 1786 that "Our confederacy must be viewed as the nest from which all America, North and South is to be peopled," and in the same year a minor government official in what was to be the state of Tennessee asked: "Is not the continent of America one day to become one consolidated government of United States?"[21] In 1789, as the new American constitution went into effect, geographer Jedediah Morse wrote that "we cannot but anticipate the period, as not far distant, when the AMERICAN EMPIRE will comprehend millions of souls, west of the Mississippi. Judging upon probable grounds, the Mississippi was never designed as the western boundary of the American empire. The God of nature never intended that

---

the American Frontier, 1783-1815 (Athens, Ga.: University of Georgia Press, 1975).

[20] Washington to Gouverneur Morris, 20 October 1792, Manning, ed., *Diplomatic Correspondence: Canadian Relations*, 1:53-54.

[21] Jefferson to Archibald Stuart, 25 January 1786, Julian P. Boyd, ed., *The Papers of Thomas Jefferson* (Princeton: University of Princeton Press, 1950-), 9:218; Judge David Campbell to Governor Richard Caswell, 30 November 1786, in James G. M. Ramsey, *The Annals of Tennessee to the End of the Eighteenth Century* (1853; reprint Knoxville: Steam Power Press of Walker and James, 1926), 350.

some of the best part of his earth should be inhabited by the subjects of a monarch, 4000 miles from them."[22]

The outbreak of war between England and France in 1793 led to twenty years of crisis in the Atlantic, and it also renewed the American fears of the British that had made the Americans so determined to conquer Canada during the American Revolution. In the 1790s the Federalists made every effort to avoid war with England, but after 1803, as the crisis at sea intensified, the Democratic-Republicans began to consider the possibility of reacting with force to British policies.

In 1807 the *Chesapeake* affair brought demands for war within the United States, and Canadian fears of American invasion. These fears were real, for had war been declared in 1807 the United States intended to attack Canada. The primary reason for this was, of course, that Canada was the only accessible British possession, and British sea power combined with Democratic-Republican reluctance to enhance the power of the navy, appeared to preclude an effective maritime response. Yet, the general strategy of an attack on Canada was also supported because it promised the possibility of ending a British threat to American security that had been feared since 1774, and because it would help to further the aim of a continental republic.

In July 1807 President Thomas Jefferson told a visitor that "if the English do not give us the satisfaction we demand, we will take Canada, which wants to enter the Union." A Tennessee politician wrote to Jefferson in the fall supporting an attack on British possessions, and stating that "it will be a sublime spectacle to spread liberty and civilization in that vast country, Canada." When in 1808 John Howe was sent by the Governor in Chief of Canada to report on the situation in the United States, he reported back from Washington that no man in either party seemed to think that there would be any difficulty in taking Canada, Nova Scotia, and New Brunswick.[23] Many in the United States were willing to take advantage of what they considered a just war to end the threat

---

[22] Jedediah Morse, *The American Geography; or, A View of the Present Situation of the United States of America* (1789; reprint New York: Arno, 1970), 469.

[23] Jefferson's comment to Turreau is quoted in Henry Adams, *History of the United States,* 4:36. For the Tennessee quote, see Arthur Campbell to Jefferson,

from the north and to further the aim of a continent freed from European control and dedicated to republicanism.

Jefferson and the Democratic-Republicans, fully aware of the military weakness of the United States, chose economic coercion rather than war in 1807, but the crisis continued. Great Britain would not change her maritime policies to accommodate the desires of the neutral United States, and by her intransigence increased the Democratic-Republican feeling that Great Britain was an inveterate enemy of the United States. Moreover, in the aftermath of the *Chesapeake* affair the British in Canada responded to the maritime crisis, as they had in 1793-1794, by trying to make sure that the Indians on the frontiers of the American Old Northwest would fight for the British should the Americans invade.[24] This, in turn, intensified the American feeling that the British in Canada were a constant threat to American security and bad neighbors. The United States would no more have risked a war with Great Britain simply to end British support for the Indians than they would have declared war simply to annex Canada, but, given the impasse regarding British maritime policies, the possibility of an invasion of Canada that would respond to British maritime aggressions since 1793 while offering the possibility of achieving other long-desired American goals became increasingly attractive.

William A. Burwell of Virginia stated the position very well in Congress early in 1809 when complaining of the renewed British activity among the Indians. He said that he "would not risk the peace of the country to free us from evils of that kind, yet if we were forced into war, by more irresistible causes, I should certainly consider this collateral advantage gained by it important." He went on to say that the "expulsion of the British from Canada has always been deemed an object of the first importance to the peace of the United States, and their security against the inroads of an enemy."[25]

---

10 October 1807, Thomas Jefferson Papers, Library of Congress. Also, John Howe to Sir George Prevost, 27 November 1808, in "Secret Reports of John Howe, 1808," *American Historical Review* 17 (January 1912): 342-343.

[24] See Reginald Horsman, "British Indian Policy in the Northwest, 1807-1812," *Mississippi Valley Historical Review* 45 (1958-59): 51-66.

[25] *Annals of Congress*, 10th Cong., 2d sess., 1 February 1809, p. 1283.

From 1810 the American Congress and President James Madison gradually and painfully reached the conclusion that war was the only solution to the difficulties with Great Britain. It was painful and difficult because it was known that American military forces were weak, that a war would ruin American trade, and because the opposition Federalist party bitterly opposed the conflict. An important factor in convincing a majority that a war with Great Britain was even possible was the argument of the War Hawks that England was vulnerable in Canada. Oddly, although the desire for Canada did not cause the War of 1812, it is difficult to imagine the United States declaring war if Great Britain had not possessed that region. There would have been nowhere to attack. The only other possibility was to fight the type of naval war that had been fought by the Federalists against France in the late 1790s, and that was out of the question given the attitude of the Democratic-Republican majority toward the use of naval power. As it was, Canada could be attacked, and a successful attack opened up the possibility of permanent possession and the ending of a long-perceived British threat to American security.

When in February 1810 the young Henry Clay first made a fiery speech in favor of war, he said that the United States had just causes for war against both England and France, but that the injuries from England had been greater. There was a solution, said Clay: "The conquest of Canada is in your power." Clay said "conquest" not "invasion," and pointed out that such a conquest would eliminate British support for the Indians and give the United States control of the entire fur trade.[26] In the 11th Congress Clay's appeal fell on deaf ears, but when the 12th Congress met in November 1811 Clay and his War Hawk friends, with the cooperation of President James Madison, were able slowly to move the nation toward war. There was never any doubt that the Democratic-Republicans intended to fight this war by invading Canada. They even voted down a proposal to increase the strength of the tiny American navy.[27]

In the debates of the 12th Congress from November 1811 to June 1812, those who advocated war justified it on the grounds of a long history of British maritime aggressions, which had

---

[26] Ibid., 11th Cong., 1st sess., 22 February 1810, pp. 579-80.
[27] See Horsman, *Causes of the War of 1812*, 241.

hindered American trade, harmed American seamen, and besmirched American national honor. They also made it quite clear that they believed Great Britain could only be injured by the invasion of Canada. It was stressed that such an invasion was a retaliation against British policies, but throughout the debates there is ambiguity about whether the War Hawks and their allies are discussing invasion or conquest. Often it is simply argued that Britain will be forced to change her maritime policies because of American success in Canada, but at other times it seems conquest not simply invasion is envisioned. Echoing the speech that Burwell of Virginia had made in 1809, advocates of war often appeared to feel that the conquest and retention of Canada was a "collateral advantage" to be gained from being forced into just war.

Several of the War Hawks were quite overt in their intention to conquer and retain Canada, both as retaliation for the long history of British maritime aggression and to fulfill long-expressed American desires. Felix Grundy of Tennessee said that he was "willing to receive the Canadians as adopted brethren; it will have beneficial political effects." It would preserve the equilibrium of the government by balancing off the peopling of Louisiana. He said that he was "anxious not only to add the Floridas to the South, but the Canadas to the North of this empire."[28] This particularly infuriated maverick Virginian John Randolph who said he could see the American capitol on the move. It would alight at Darien, "which, when the gentleman's dreams are realized, will be a most eligible seat of Government for the new Republic (or Empire) of the two Americas!"[29]

Richard M. Johnson of Kentucky was not affected by Randolph's sarcasm. On the following day he said he wished to force Great Britain to cease to violate America's neutral rights and treat her Americans as an independent people, but he went on to say "I shall never die contented until I see her expulsion from North America, and her territories incorporated with the United States." He accepted fully the idea of a divine plan for the United States on the North American continent. "The waters of the St. Lawrence and the Mississippi interlock in a

---

[28] *Annals of Cong.*, 12th Cong., 1st sess., 9 December 1811, pp. 426-27.
[29] Ibid., 10 December 1811, p. 446.

number of places, and the great Disposer of Human Events intended those two rivers should belong to the same people."[30] Randolph lashed back, arguing that the War Hawks were driven by "agrarian cupidity." He was wrong. In wanting to invade Canada the War Hawks were driven not by a desire for land, but by a desire to retaliate against British maritime policies and by a desire for security and for a continent controlled by a republican United States.[31]

War Hawk John A. Harper of New Hampshire was particularly keen that if war was to come with England then this war should end the British possession of Canada. Like Richard Johnson, Harper was able to see a divine plan in the future of the United States on the American continent: "The northern provinces of Britain are to us great and valuable objects. Once secured to this Republic, and the St. Lawrence and the Lakes become the Baltic, and more than the Baltic to America; north of them a population of four millions may easily be supported; and this great outlet of the northern world, should be at our command, for our convenience and future security. To me, sir, it appears that the Author of Nature has marked our limits in the south, by the Gulf of Mexico; and on the north, by the regions of eternal frost."[32] As a representative from New Hampshire, Harper was more aware than the southerners of the importance of the lakes and the St. Lawrence to the trade of the northern states.

Shortly before the war began, Harper revealed the extent to which he was committed not simply to the invasion of Canada but also to its conquest and retention. He told the governor of his state that he had worked hard and used all his influence to have the idea accepted that Canada should be incorporated into the Union. "I have no idea of having a war for several years to conquer the British Provinces," he wrote "and then surrender them by negociation and unless we can have a pledge that once conquered, they shall be retained, I will never give my vote to send an army there."[33] Harper was more overt than most War Hawks in the extent to which he was willing to press

---

[30] Ibid., 11 December 1811, pp. 457-58.

[31] Ibid., 16 December 1811, p. 533.

[32] Ibid., 4 January 1812, p. 657.

[33] Harper to William Plumer, 13 May 1812, quoted in Pratt, *Expansionists of 1812*, 148-49.

for a commitment that if Canada was conquered it should be kept. Federalist Senator James A. Bayard reported that westerners and southerners were disturbed by this insistence that Canada, when conquered, should be divided into states and incorporated into the union.[34]

Most who pressed for or supported war simply took the line of argument that the only way to fight a war that had been caused by a long history of British aggressions and insults against the United States was by invading Canada, and then in their speeches talked of the advantages that would be gained by conquering Canada even independent of the causes of the war. When in March 1812 Andrew Jackson issued division orders, he summarized why the United States was going to fight. He said it was to reestablish the national character, to protect American seamen from impressment, to defend the American right to a free trade, and open a market for American agricultural products, "in fine, to seek some indemnity for past injuries, some security against future aggressions, by the conquest of all the British dominions upon the continent of north america."[35] It is hard to believe that Jackson was contemplating handing these dominions back to the British.

In June 1812, as the United States went to war, American Secretary of States James Monroe well-expressed the ambiguity of the American position in two of his statements. Less than a week before the war began he told Virginian John Taylor that Canada was to be invaded "not as an object of the war but as a means to bring it to a satisfactory conclusion." Two weeks later in writing to Jonathan Russell, the United States chargé d'affaires in London, he told him to point out to the British the danger for them of allowing the war to persist for any length of time. If American troops entered Canada, this might mean commitments to the Canadian inhabitants, and in the United States the effect of success on the public mind would make it "difficult to relinquish Territory which had been conquered."[36]

---

[34] See the discussion in ibid., 147-48.

[35] Andrew Jackson, Division Order, 12 March 1812, in John Spencer Bassett, ed., *The Correspondence of Andrew Jackson,* 6 vols. (Washington: Carnegie Institute of Washington, 1926-33), 1:221-22.

[36] Monroe to John Taylor, 13 June 1812, Monroe to Jonathan Russell, 26 June 1812, Stanislaus M. Hamilton, ed., *The Writings of James Monroe,* 7 vols. (New York: G.P. Putnam's Sons, 1898-1903), 5:207, 212-13.

In retirement at Monticello, Thomas Jefferson, as often before, well-summarized majority American opinion. Writing to Thaddeus Kosciusko about the war which had just begun, he commented that Great Britain would control the sea but "we shall be equally predominant at land, and shall strip her of all her possessions on this continent." He went on to say that British intrigues to destroy the American government, and among the Indians, "prove that the cession of Canada, their fulcrum for these Machiavelian levers, must be a sine qua non at a treaty of peace." In August Jefferson told another of his correspondents that "the acquisition of Canada, this year, as far as the neighborhood of Quebec, will be a mere matter of marching, and will give us experience for the attack of Halifax the next, and the final expulsion of England from the American continent."[37]

The conquest of Canada was not a question of marching. Canadian inhabitants did not welcome the Americans as liberators, and in 1812 the invasion of Canada was an abysmal failure. For nearly forty years Americans had talked and written of the desirability of the acquisition of Canada, and there had never been the slightest question that the invasion of Canada would be the main way of fighting the War of 1812, yet the preparations for such an invasion had been grossly inadequate. Many Democratic-Republicans wanted the expansion of the republic, and the expulsion of European powers from North America, but they did not want either to pay for or to risk having a military establishment. They wanted to be welcomed as republican liberators bringing liberty from European tyranny.

The failures of the 1812 campaigns did not end American dreams of conquering and retaining Canada. Indeed, one result of the disasters was to make American politicians shun ambiguity and point out that if the nation could unite itself and successfully invade Canada, it might well be able to retain it. James Monroe's reaction to General William Hull's surrender of Detroit was to state that this "most disgraceful event" might have good results. "It will rouse the nation," he wrote. "We

---

[37] Jefferson to Kosciusko, 28 June 1812, Jefferson to Col. Duane, 4 August 1812, Andrew A. Lipscomb and Albert E. Bergh, eds., *The Writings of Thomas Jefferson*, 20 vols. (Washington: Thomas Jefferson Memorial Association, 1905), 13:168-72, 180-82.

must efface the stain before we make peace, and that may give us Canada." In writing to Henry Clay about the same event, he was even clearer in his conclusions. The American people, he argued falsely, had been drawn together by military defeats and naval victories. If Great Britain did not offer peace with honor, he was convinced that the war would become a national one, and would "terminate in the explusion of her force and power from the continent."[38]

Later in the year, in drafting a plan for the military requirements of the United States, Monroe reached the conclusion that "if a strong army is led to the field early in the Spring the British power on this Continent must sink before it, and when once broken down it will never rise again. The reconquest of Canada will become, in the opinion of all enlightened men, and of the whole British nation, a chimerical attempt. It will therefore be abandoned." When Albert Gallatin was sent as a peace commissioner to Europe in May 1813, Monroe asserted that if his mission failed, and Great Britain prolonged the war, it would simply lead to greater American efforts and "the complete expulsion of the British from the Continent."[39]

In Congress too the failures of 1812 brought the desire for Canada far more into the open. In the winter of 1812-13 Congress debated the necessity of increased military forces. The most important bill for the invasion of Canada—a bill to raise an additional 20,000 troops for one year—was discussed and passed in January 1813 after lengthy debate. What is striking about the debate, compared to those before the war began, is that now there was much less ambiguity about the purposes of the invasion of Canada. Both Democratic-Republicans and their Federalist opponents now seemed to assume that if Canada was conquered it was unlikely to be given up.

Surprisingly, Henry Clay was somewhat more cautious than some of his expansionist suppporters. His argument in supporting the increased military force was that he wished to "negotiate the terms of a peace at Quebec or Halifax."[40] This

---

[38] Monroe to Jefferson, 31 August 1812, and Monroe to Henry Clay 17 September 1812, Hamilton, ed., *Writings of Monroe,* 5:220-23.

[39] "Explanatory Observations," enclosed in Monroe to George W. Campbell, 23 December 1812, and Monroe to Gallatin, 6 May 1813, ibid., 5:235, 258.

[40] *Annals of Congress,* 12th Cong., 2d sess., 8 January 1813, p. 676.

was more along the lines of pre-war arguments that the invasion of Canada would force the British to make concessions regarding neutral rights at sea, but other Democratic-Republicans were now ready to throw caution to the winds in regard to the advantages to be gained from an annexation of Canada. Thomas Robertson of Louisiana dismissed any doubts his southern constituents might have about an extension of northern power in an impassioned speech in favor of the bill. He said that the British possessions in America invited a conquest:

> The power of Britian must be extinguished in America. She must no longer be permitted to corrupt the principles and disturb the peace and tranquillity of our citizens. Our frontier inhabitants must not be kept in dread and danger from her Indian allies. And never shall we be secure among ourselves, and exempt from the mischievous intrigues of Europeans, until European power is expelled across the Atlantic.

He argued that no citizen would have consented to an unprovoked attack on Canada just to get possession of it, but that now the United States had the opportunity to drive Great Britain from the continent she should take advantage of the situation. Robertson also used the common argument that contiguity bred trouble, and that when Great Britain was no longer a neighbor a great number of difficulties would be removed.[41]

Although the gaining of security by the expulsion of Great Britain from the continent continued to be the most important argument for the retention of Canada, there was again some discussion of the importance of the whole St. Lawrence-Great Lakes system to American trade. Silas Stow of New York pointed out that the St. Lawrence was the outlet for many United States exports, and that these could be taxed. He also expressed a fear that Canada could draw off United States settlers. Willis Alston of North Carolina also pointed out the benefits of enhancing internal American trade by uniting eastern and western waters.[42] All of this discussion clearly had

---

[41] Ibid., 11 January 1813, p. 709.
[42] Ibid., 14 January 1813, (Stow), p. 809; 14 January 1813, (Alston), p. 822.

little to do with invasion as a means of coercing Great Britain but much to do with the desirability of conquering and annexing Canada.

One of the best summaries of the expansionist view in this debate was that given by experienced politician Nathaniel Macon of North Carolina. He differed with those who said that the United States was incapable of conquering Canada, and insisted that not only could it be conquered but that it was "worth conquering, if it was only to get clear of a meddling and bad neighbor, who is always willing to make a strife in our family." The St. Lawrence was needed by the United States, he argued, and whether it was obtained in the present war or not, it would be obtained on some future occasion. "It is absolutely necessary, in my opinion," he said, "to the peace and happiness of the nation, as much so as the mouth of the Mississippi was. These two great rivers seem to have been intended by Providence for an inland navigation from North to South." Not only Canada but also Florida were needed, and their occupation would rid the United States of bad neighbors. Both would be obtained, he said, before many years were up.[43]

The Federalists, who were already completely disgusted at a war which they had opposed, which was ruining American trade, and which had proved ineffective on the Canadian frontier, were now additionally shocked at the overtness with which the Democratic-Republican majority talked of the annexation of Canada. The Federalists spoke at length in opposition to the invasion of Canada and were bitterly opposed to its annexation. In discussing the invasion itself the Federalists drew a distinction between Great Britain and the Canadians themselves, arguing that it was wrong to attack unoffending Canadians to retaliate against British offenses at sea. Josiah Quincy of Massachusetts said: "I consider the invasion of Canada as a means of carrying on this war, as cruel, wanton, senseless, and wicked." Laban Wheaton of Massachusetts objected to the killing of "the harmless Canadians."[44]

The Federalists also delighted in pointing out that the Canadians had not welcomed the American troops as liberators.

---

[43] Ibid., 12 January 1813, pp. 758, 768.

[44] Ibid., 5 January 1813, (Quincy) p. 545; 8 January 1813, (Wheaton), p. 656.

Elijah Brigham of Massachusetts asked why the United States was bothering the Canadians, who were obviously not panting for American liberties as had vainly been argued at the last session of Congress. Lyman Law of Connecticut said the pretence had been that the United States would not conquer Canada; it would merely be taken from welcoming inhabitants, and then exchanged for maritime rights. This, he said, had been proved false.[45]

The main objection of the Federalists, however, was to the effect the annexation of Canada would have on the United States, for the Federalists now strongly expressed fears for the republic and American liberty. Much of the theoretical writing on republics in the eighteenth century had been concerned with the problem of whether republics had to be small to survive. Montesquieu had argued that a republic that did not have a small territory could not long exist. All authorities agreed that republics were fragile, liable to be destroyed by internal dissent or by external enemies. This problem had much concerned the Revolutionary generation, particularly in the dangerous decade of the 1780s, and the historical difficulties experienced by republics formed a large part of the discussions surrounding the Constitutional Convention in 1787 and the debates on the ratification of the new document. James Madison had maintained that the United States had solved the problem of size by adopting representative rather than direct democracy, but the fear remained. From the time of the Louisiana Purchase a group within the Federalist party launched a bitter attack on the idea of an ever-expanding republic. To the traditional fears of size necessitating a more despotic government, was added a specific Federalist fear that every new state enhanced the power of the Democratic-Republican party.[46]

In the military debates of early 1813 the Federalists strongly took up the cry that the annexation of Canada would bring a major threat to American constitutional government. Josiah Quincy argued that such an annexation would have a dire effect on American liberties and the Constitution. It would

---

[45] Ibid., 4 January 1813, (Brigham), pp. 513-14; 5 January 1813, (Law) pp. 537-38.

[46] See Gordon S. Wood, *The Creation of the American Republic, 1776-1787* (Chapel Hill: University of North Carolina Press, 1969), 499-505.

create a veteran army and a military leader to subvert American liberties. Elijah Brigham of Massachusetts used a similar argument, maintaining that the conquest of Canada would be "fatal to the civil liberties of the country, and change the character of our Government." Henry Ridgeley of Delaware said that the strength of the United States was already too much scattered, and would be weakened still further by a greater expansion of territory and population. Hermanus Bleecker of New York argued that Canada should not be accepted even if Great Britain would willingly give it to the United States, for the United States was already too extensive.[47]

Some of the Federalists were shocked at the shift from public statements arguing that Canada was merely to be a hostage for British good behavior to public assertions of the desirability or the necessity of annexing Canada. Daniel Sheffey, one of the few remaining southern Federalists, was puzzled to hear of conquests in the North and South as essential to American "security and happiness," and he questioned the real objects of this bill to increase the military forces. Congress, he said, had sometimes been told that Canada was merely to be conquered to be exchanged for American maritime rights, at others that it was to be retained to prevent future collisions and Indian attacks. Sheffey said he had come to the conclusion from the conduct of American military commanders that this was "a war for the conquest of Canada."[48]

In responding to the Federalists, the Democratic-Republicans took issue with the distinction that the opposition was drawing between the government of Great Britain and the inhabitants of Canada. Joseph Desha of Kentucky wanted to know why there was all this sympathy for "the poor Canadians." The sympathy should be saved for the victims of the Indians. Nathaniel Macon was also puzzled at hearing of the "unoffending Canadians."[49] In general, the Democratic-Republicans talked of Canada as simply part of the power of Great Britain while the opposition Federalists drew a

---

[47] *Annals of Congress,* 12th Cong., 2d sess., 5 January 1813, (Quincy), pp. 546-49; 4 January 1813, (Brigham), p. 513; 4 January 1813, (Ridgely) p. 518; 7 January 1813, (Bleeker), p. 628.

[48] Ibid., 11 January 1813, pp. 689-90.

[49] Ibid., 14 January 1813, (Desha), p. 826; 12 January 1813, (Macon), p. 768.

distinction between the British government and the Canadian inhabitants.

For the most part, however, the Democratic-Republicans let the Federalists talk, and spent little time answering their specific arguments. They were no longer concerned with drawing careful distinctions between the invasion of Canada as a means of changing British maritime policies and the invasion of Canada as the way to conquest and the removal of a permanent British threat. They simply merged the objectives. Matthew Clay of Virginia, an old Jefferson supporter, expressed this plainly when he discussed Great Britain early in January 1813.

> We have the Canadas as much under our command as she has the ocean; and the way to conquer her on the ocean is to drive her from the land. I am not for stopping at Quebec or anywhere else; but I would take the whole continent from them, and ask them no favors. Her fleets cannot then rendezvous at Halifax as now . . . . It is as easy to conquer them on the land, as their whole Navy could conquer ours on the ocean . . . . We must take the continent from them. I wish never to see a peace till we do. God has given us the power and the means; we are to blame if we do not use them. If we get the continent, she must allow us the freedom of the sea.[50]

Matthew Clay's speech was a triumph of rhetoric over reason. It melded earlier Democratic-Republican arguments that Canada was to be a pawn to be exchanged for maritime rights with later arguments that Canada was to be conquered and kept. It never addressed the question of how the conquest of Canada would force the British to allow the Americans freedom of the seas, and it never addressed the question of how if Canada were kept it could be used in an exchange of such doubtful results. But Clay's statement well-revealed the ambiguities with which the Democratic-Republicans began the war. They were fighting because of British infringements of American maritime rights, but they were hoping to use the war to solve the lingering problem of the British possession of Canada.

---

[50] Ibid., 2 January 1813, p. 498.

The additional troops voted for in January 1813 solved nothing. Although the United States gained some consolation for earlier defeats by victories on Lake Erie and at the battle of the Thames, the conquest of Canada came no nearer. When James Monroe gave instructions to peace commissioners in June 1813 he had to assume that Great Britain would insist on the restoration of Canada at the end of the war. He did, however, state that the peace commissioners should suggest to the British commissioners the advantages of avoiding future controversies by ceding the upper parts of Canada or even the whole of Canada to the United States.[51]

Moreover, the victory of the Thames restored in the West the hope that perhaps Canada or at least western Canada could be kept. This feeling was so strong that Henry Clay found it necessary to deny "a very unpopular opinion" that had been attributed to him that the conquered region should be given up as a price of peace. Clay's explanation was that in the summer of 1813, when the United States had none of Canada, and the British had Michigan Territory, he had stated that he would be willing for the present to forego the conquest of Canada if the United States could make a peace securing the points in controversy. Clay pointed out that when the war began "Canada was not the end but the means." But he also stated that "it has ever been my opinion that if Canada is conquered it ought never to be surrendered if it possibly can be retained."[52]

With the impending collapse of Napoleon in the winter of 1813-1814, it was becoming obvious that any opportunity of conquering Canada was fast disappearing, but even at this juncture the advantages and disadvantages of such an acquisition were again debated in the American Congress. The Federalist opposition once more launched a major attack on the idea that additional troops were to be used for the invasion and conquest of Canada; this "crusade against Canada" as Morris Miller of New York called it. Miller attacked the proclamations issued by Generals Hull and Smyth in 1812, saying that Hull's proclamation "avows principles and intentions which might

---

[51] Monroe to the United States Commissioners, 23 June 1813, Manning, ed., *Diplomatic Correspondence: Canadian Relations,* 1:214-15.

[52] Clay to Thomas Bodley, 18 December 1813, Hopkins and Hargreaves, eds., *Papers of Clay,* 1:841-42.

well become a robber and a bandit." Daniel Webster said that the United States had failed in dividing the people of the Canadian provinces from their government; they were still hostile to the American cause.[53]

The Federalists again made it clear that they did not want either a larger federal republic or military control of a conquered territory, and in this way foreshadowed arguments to be used by the New England Whigs in the period of the Mexican War. William Gaston of North Carolina asked what the South would think of half a dozen new northern states made out of Canada, and incorporating people who did not want to enter the Union. Artemus Ward of Massachusetts said that if the Canadians were to be admitted to all the privileges of freemen "we shall then have a motley mixture of citizens, ignorant of their rights and of their duties, added to a population already too heterogenous." But if Canada was kept as a conquered province, then the United States would have to maintain an armed force there, led by a Caesar or Bonaparte who could overturn the American government.[54]

Even in this bleak period of the war some of the Democratic-Republicans still talked as though the conquest of Canada was within the power of the United States. John C. Calhoun, in a rather ineffective speech, stressed the peace and security that could be secured by the acquisition of Canada. Nathaniel Macon pointed out that the United States had wanted Canada in the Revolution, that George Washington had wanted Canada, that it was envisioned admitting it to the American Union, and that even now the acquisition of Canada and Florida "would add much to the probability of a peace being lasting."[55]

The clearest statement of how Canada had figured both in the coming of the war and in its prosecution was by Charles Ingersoll of Pennsylvania, who argued that his constitutents were certainly interested in the acquisition of Canada. "As a separate cause of war, independent of all others, I will not undertake to say what the popular sentiment may be with

---

[53] *Annals of Congress,* 13th Cong., 2d̄ sess., 14 January 1814, (Miller), pp. 975-76; 14 January 1814, (Webster) p. 947.

[54] Ibid., 18 February 1814, (Gaston), p. 1569; 5 March 1814 (Ward), p. 1819.

[55] Ibid., 15 January 1814, (Calhoun) p. 996; 3 March 1814, (Macon), pp. 1778-80.

regard to the invasion and conquest of Canada; but, as an instrument for waging it effectually, and as a desirable acquisition in the course of its prosecution, most certainly we do look upon those British provinces in our neighborhood as all-important in the account." The United States should persist in its attempts to take Canada, said Ingersoll, "otherwise we may postpone the conquest to the next generation." He also, in answer to those Federalists who claimed that in their areas the invasion of Canada was unpopular, gave his estimate of general public opinion on this question. "With a large majority of the country, the conquest, I am confident, is not unpopular, but looked upon as even a strong independent inducement to the war." A fellow representative from Pennsylvania, Thomas Wilson, agreed with him, saying that Canada had never been a motive to commence the war or a primary objective, but that it was "an incidental but indispensable object."[56]

This debate in early 1814 was even more futile than that of the previous year, for the main problem of the United States in 1814 was not the conquest of Canada but how to prevent being dismembered by a British invasion. Yet, these debates of the war period were revealing of the motivations of the Democratic-Republican party in voting for war. The Democratic-Republicans had reached the decision to support war against England because of a long history of British interference with American trade and American seamen, an interference which infuriated these young republicans who viewed Great Britain as hostile to the rising greatness of their nation. They intended to invade Canada to retaliate against Great Britain and to hurt Great Britain, but they were happy to invade Canada because it had long been perceived as a threat to American security and hated as a surviving example of British power on a continent now dedicated to a new republicanism. The United States did not declare war because it wanted to obtain Canada, but the acquisition of Canada was viewed as a major collateral benefit of the conflict.

---

[56] Ibid., 14 January 1814, (Ingersoll), pp. 952, 954; 17 January 1814, (Wilson), p. 1040.

AGRARIAN DISCONTENT IN THE MISSISSIPPI
VALLEY PRECEDING THE WAR OF 1812

GRARIAN discontent has so often played an important part in our history that it is surprising that its importance in the Mississippi Valley preceding the War of 1812 has not been recognized. Western agriculture suffered, as this paper will show, a severe economic depression in the years just before the war, and this depression was an important factor in determining the support which the frontier gave first to the Embargo and Non-intercourse acts and finally to war. To understand western discontent, something of the situation in earlier years must be known. The examination of western economic conditions may well begin, therefore, with the period of prosperity which preceded the hard times of 1808–12.

In the first decade of the nineteenth century, the hunting and trapping frontier receded to the west and north, and, over wide areas, the valleys of the Ohio and lower Mississippi became definitely a farming country. For several years following the Louisiana Purchase this new agricultural West experienced a pronounced boom. The usual optimism and exaggerated anticipations of wealth which we have since learned to expect in such periods were abundantly present. The depression which accompanied the Peace of Amiens had been largely attributed by western farmers to Spanish interference with the Mississippi trade at New Orleans. When, therefore, news reached the West that the United States had purchased Louisiana, the frontiersmen believed that serious obstacles to western prosperity were a thing of the past.

Everywhere on the frontier people now believed that they saw the dawn of a new and prosperous day. A Kentucky editor declared that the undisturbed right to navigate the Mississippi insured in itself ". . . . a perpetual union of the states, and lasting prosperity to the Western country."[1] And a contributor to the *Scioto Gazette* wrote: ". . . . No ruinous fluctuations in com-

[1] *Guardian of Freedom* (Frankfort, Kentucky), July 20, 1803.

471

merce need now be apprehended. Agriculture may depend upon those steady markets which trade shall open to industry."[2]

With this spirit abroad it is not surprising that settlers came crowding to the frontier in unprecedented numbers. Soon after the transfer of Louisiana to the United States, a great influx of pioneer farmers and adventurers began into the area bounded by New Orleans on the south and the frontier settlements in central Ohio on the north, and reached its crest in the boom years of 1805 and 1806.

One of the first parts of the West to feel the effect of this movement was New Orleans. Governor Claiborne reported, "Every boat from the western country and every vessel from the Atlantic States bring hither adventurers."[3] Tennessee was receiving more immigrants than ever before in her history, the influx being described by Governor Sevier as exceeding "anything of the kind that has heretofore taken place."[4]

But settlers migrated in greatest numbers in the years before the embargo to the region north of the Ohio River. They came not only from the Atlantic states but even from Kentucky and Tennessee. Opposition to slavery or inability to own slaves brought many from the upland regions of the South Atlantic states.[5] An Ohio editor reported in 1805 that the number of immigrants exceeded "all reasonable bounds of calculation,"[6] Fig-

[2] Chillicothe, Ohio, October 1, 1803. See also the *Farmers Register* (Greensburg, Pennsylvania), July 16, 1803.

[3] Claiborne to Madison, New Orleans, February 13, 1804, in J. A. Robertson, *Louisiana under the Rule of Spain, France, and the United States, 1785–1807*, II, 251. Claiborne's letters show that many French fugitives from Santo Domingo sought asylum in New Orleans at this time.

[4] *Senate Journal*, Tennessee, 7 Ass., 1 Sess., p. 13.

[5] Josiah Espy, *Memorandums of a Tour in Ohio and Kentucky in 1805*, "Ohio Valley Historical Series," No. 7 (Cincinnati, 1871), pp. 22–23. A record which was kept at Kennedy's ferry opposite Cincinnati in Kentucky showed the following migration into Ohio from April 1 to December 31, 1805: South Carolina, 669; Kentucky, 568; Virginia, 465; North Carolina, 463; Georgia, 264; Tennessee, 200; Illinois, 10; total, 2,639. On the basis of these figures it was estimated that 30,000 people entered the state in 1805 in addition to those who came down the Ohio River. The *Commonwealth* (Pittsburgh, Pennsylvania), March 12, 1806.

[6] *Scioto Gazette* (Chillicothe, Ohio), November 7, 1805. See also the same paper for April 22, 1805; Rufus Putnam to John May, Marietta, January 17, 1806, *The*

ures given by Cist show that the population of Cincinnati increased 28 per cent from 1800 to 1805 and 142 per cent from 1805 to 1810. As there was but little movement in 1808 and 1809, this Ohio town apparently more than doubled its population in the three years—1805, 1806, and 1807.[7]

Not only was the westward migration in the period between the Purchase and the embargo greater than ever before; but settlers, and speculators as well, gave earnest of their faith in the new country by purchasing, chiefly on credit, large tracts of western land. In the decade before the war, the amount of public land sold in the territory north of the Ohio River reached its highest point in 1805, when 619,000 acres were purchased. In 1806 sales continued high (473,000 acres), but in no other year for the period did they reach the 400,000 mark.[8] State lands also in Kentucky and Tennessee were bought on time, and debtors were to lament in the lean years to come of obligations entered into at this boom period "when commerce was flattering hope."[9]

A wave of optimism once started by a propitious event—in this case the removal of Spanish control over Mississippi River trade—may, as subsequent crazes and booms have shown, go far on its own momentum. Moreover, the ambitious hopes of the frontier farmers had some solid basis. Good land was cheap; and, the land once cleared, crops flourished and harvests were abundant. What could be more encouraging to the farmers who had just left exhausted soils on the eastern coast or the infertile lands of the Appalachian Plateau?

And, for a time at least, the problem of marketing did not seem over-serious. As long as immigration continued at full tide, those producers living along the line of travel found a ready market by

John May Papers, Western Reserve Historical Society Tract No. 97, p. 191; *Stewart's Kentucky Herald* (Paris, Kentucky), December 16, 1805, Governor Tiffin to Ohio state legislature; and Daniel Drake, *Natural and Statistical View or a Picture of Cincinnati and the Miami Country, Etc.* (Cincinnati, 1815), p. 131.

[7] Charles Cist, *Cincinnati in 1841: Its Early Annals and Future Prospects* (Cincinnati, 1841), p. 38.

[8] *American State Papers, Finance*, Vol. II, *passim*.

[9] *Carthage Gazette* (Carthage, Tennessee), December 15, 1809.

supplying the needs of the migrants. And farmers already established in the areas to which the new settlers came found the newcomers good customers for that season at least until their lands were cleared and their first crops harvested. Few, if any, worried about this metamorphosis, and everywhere new settlers were welcomed not only because they purchased the surplus produce but also because they brought money into the country.[10]

But especially stimulating to the high hopes of 1805 was the behavior of prices for western staples. The whole price situation has been dealt with in detail elsewhere.[11] Here it will suffice to point out that the extremely low prices of 1802 and 1803 had improved in 1804 and had reached in 1805 the highest level to be attained before the war. The year following saw slightly lower levels; and in 1807 the downward trend was clearly evident, though not to be compared with the precipitous decline of the embargo year which succeeded it.

From the vantage point of over one hundred years after the event, the fact is clear enough that the western agriculturist of 1805 was, despite elimination of Spanish interference on the Mississippi, abundant harvests, increased immigration, and high prices for western products, much more sanguine in his expectations of prosperity than fundamental conditions justified. Even without the embargo and non-intercourse of 1808 and 1809, it cannot be doubted that the bubble of 1805 would soon have burst. Time, it is true, was to iron out many of the obstacles to western prosperity; in the long run the West was in truth a land of promise. But underlying weaknesses existed in the immediate situation; and the most important of these must now be considered, although extended comment is not possible within the limits of this article.

Most serious was the problem of transportation. The physical obstacles to getting western products to market in the days before the steamboat and the railroad were even greater than is gen-

[10] See, for example: *Scioto Gazette* (Chillicothe, Ohio), October 1, 1803; *Guardian of Freedom* (Frankfort, Kentucky), June 9, 1804; and *Clarion* (Nashville, Tennessee), February 16, 1808.

[11] See the author's "Wholesale Prices in the Mississippi Valley Preceding the War of 1812," *Journal of Economic and Business History*, III, 148–63.

erally realized.[12] Some furs and peltries were being sent up the Ohio and over the mountains as late as 1811; but as the hunting and trapping areas moved westward, most of these products were exported by way of either the Mississippi or the St. Lawrence route.[13] When flax and hemp were bringing extremely high prices in 1809 and 1810, considerable quantities of rope, yarn, cordage, country linen, and twine were carried overland.[14] Cattle, horses, and even swine were sometimes driven literally hundreds of miles from Ohio, Kentucky, and Tennessee to Atlantic markets.[15] But the difficulties which attended this transmontane exportation are so patent that the small overland trade which did take place is chiefly a testimony to the obstacles by the Mississippi route. So great were the drawbacks to land transportation from western Pennsylvania, to say nothing of the vast region farther west, that the wagons which brought the needed imports from Philadelphia to Pittsburgh customarily returned empty.[16] Such frontier staples as hemp, flour, bacon, and even whiskey simply could not stand the cost of carriage over the mountain roads.

In consequence, Ohio Valley produce had to be sent a thousand miles or more down the Ohio-Mississippi river system to Natchez or New Orleans. This trip usually took about a month, and was beset with perils and hardships from beginning to end. To begin

[12] Not until after the War of 1812 did the steamboat become a real factor in Mississippi River commerce.

[13] See, for example, *Louisiana Gazette* (New Orleans), April 16, 1810, and Letter Book of Joseph Hertzog, Joseph Hertzog to Christian Wilt, Philadelphia, Pennsylvania, May 2, 1811, in the Hertzog Collins Collection, Missouri Historical Society Library, St. Louis, Missouri.

[14] Zadok Cramer, *Cramer's Pittsburgh Magazine Almanack for 1809*, p. 29; *Star* (Raleigh, North Carolina), September 27, 1810; *Supporter* (Chillicothe, Ohio), February 2, 1811, from the *Commonwealth* of Pittsburgh. See also correspondence of James Wier, especially during 1808 and 1809, Letter Book of James Wier in the Draper Collection of the Wisconsin Historical Society.

[15] There are many contemporary references to this trade. For interesting statements regarding it see *Carthage Gazette* (Carthage, Tennessee), March 22, 1811; *Palladium* (Frankfort, Kentucky), January 28, 1808; *Kentucky Gazette* (Lexington, Kentucky), December 8, 1807; and *Ohio Centinel* (Dayton, Ohio), December 13, 1810.

[16] *Kentucky Gazette* (Lexington, Kentucky), January 9, 1800, and F. A. Michaux, *Travels to the Westward of the Allegany Mountains, Etc.* (London, 1805), p. 73.

with, flatboats must be built at no little trouble or bought by the farmer who typically lived not far from some small tributary of the Ohio River.[17] Then the flats must be ready and loaded to take advantage of the first high water. This part of the journey, often several hundred miles down small tributaries to the Ohio, was full of hazards. If the waters were at flood, the boats often became unmanageable, and there was loss of boat and cargo. If the season was unusually dry, the flat might never even get started for market. If the rains were of too short duration or the trip delayed a few days too long, the river might go down before the Ohio was reached and flatboats be caught high and dry on sandbars, there to remain for months while their cargoes spoiled and their owners returned to their farms to raise more produce which must again run similar risks.

The perils of the trip down the Ohio and Mississippi can be hardly more than suggested. No river improvements had yet been made. Snags and bars were a constant menace. Travel at night, especially over the most dangerous sections, was extremely perilous; yet the river was liable to such sudden changes in the height of its water that tying up to the bank for the night might mean, at best, delay, at worst, loss of the entire cargo.

As the end of the journey approached, new dangers arose. The wideness of the river, combined with the frequency of storms accompanied by strong winds, was often fatal to the low-sided, wallowing flats. Every storm took its toll of these clumsy craft. If it was accompanied by rain, the cargo of flour or cotton, tobacco or cordage, might be ruined by water. If other hazards were avoided, the warm and humid climate of the south might cause the flour or pork to spoil before the market was reached.

But physical hazards were not all. From Cairo to Natchez the trip was made through a wild, unsettled region. Indians, and

[17] If the flatboat was bought, it cost from fifty dollars to more than twice that figure. It was an operating expense, for at New Orleans flats were abandoned or broken up and sold for lumber. *Palladium* (Frankfort, Kentucky), July 15, 1802; J. S. Bassett (ed.), *Correspondence of Andrew Jackson*, I, 94; Christian Schultz, *Travels on an Inland Voyage* (New York, 1810), I, 132 and 138; John Melish, *Travels in the United States of America, in the years 1806 and 1807, and 1809, 1810, and 1811, Etc.* (Philadelphia, 1812), II, 85, and F. A. Michaux, *op. cit.*, p. 224.

more especially renegade whites, preyed on the river trade. River pirates throve, and their exploits have become legendary.

The crew of each flat numbered from three to five men. They must be paid for their services and supplied with food on the journey. If the farmer accompanied his own shipment, as was often the case, he must be absent for months from his farm. If he left home in December or January (most started even later), he was fortunate if he got to market, disposed of his cargo, and returned safely by land over the robber-infested Natchez trace in time to plant his crops for the next season. Many, indeed, never returned, for the Ohio Valley farmers were especially susceptible to the fevers common in the lower Mississippi. Each year as spring advanced into summer Natchez and New Orleans were full of flatboat men too sick to attempt the journey home and for whom no hospital facilities were available.[18]

The same difficulties of transportation which hindered western producers from getting their surplus to market made the bringing in of their imports very costly. Though self-sufficing to a considerable extent, the frontier was dependent upon the eastern states and foreign countries for a great variety of products, including most manufactured goods. For example, the letter books of James Wier, a leading merchant of Lexington, Kentucky, show that he imported coffee, tea, sugar, chocolate, prunes, spices, wines, needles, velvet ribbons, muslins and other kinds of cloth, men's slippers, crockery, lead, brimstone, glue, and a host of other commodities which even the unpretentious people of the frontier regarded as necessary to their happiness.

Except to ports on the lower Mississippi, such as Natchez and

[18] A wealth of contemporary material exists on the conditions of the early river trade. Many interesting descriptions are to be found not only in the correspondence of James Wier and Andrew Jackson referred to above but also in the writings of early western travelers such as John Bradbury, Fortescue Cuming, H. B. Fearon, Timothy Flint, Henry Ker, John Melish, and Christian Schultz. Illuminating side lights on the river trade are to be found in the following: *Palladium* (Frankfort, Kentucky), April 8 and 22, 1802, and March 17, 1808; *Ohio Centinel* (Dayton, Ohio), August 9, 1810, and May 15, 1811; *Scioto Gazette* (Chillicothe, Ohio), August 12, 1805; and the *Mississippi Herald and Natchez Gazette* (Natchez, Mississippi Territory), September 23, 1806. Most valuable of all perhaps are the New Orleans customs records in the Library of Congress.

New Orleans, importations up-river remained relatively small until the advent of the steamboat. Forcing a barge up the Mississippi was a peculiarly difficult task. Not only was the current strong and treacherous, but the river bottom was often too soft for poling and the banks unsuited for towing. Every device then known for forcing a craft through water was attempted. Oars, sails, setting poles, treadmills operated by horses, "bush-whacking," and the cordelle, all were tried, and still the journey remained so slow, arduous, and uncertain that the passage from New Orleans to Louisville took three months and freight charges were from three to five times as high as down-river rates.[19]

Little wonder, then, that despite the inherent difficulties of land transportation most western imports were hauled three hundred miles by Conestoga wagon to Pittsburgh or Wheeling and then floated on the rivers often several hundred miles farther to local distributing centers. But the burden upon the frontier was great which ever route was used. The cost of carriage over the mountains is illustrated in the dealings of the Lexington merchant mentioned above. In 1808 he appears to have paid a little over two hundred dollars to have two wagon loads of goods brought from Philadelphia to Pittsburgh.[20]

The fact emerges from a survey of the physical conditions of the overland and river trade that the frontier suffered a severe handicap by reason of transportation difficulties. It has been insufficiently appreciated that, in point either of time or cost of carriage, Philadelphia was in the first decade of the nineteenth century nearer to Liverpool, Lisbon, or Havana than it was to Chillicothe, Lexington, or Nashville.[21]

[19] One of the best descriptions of the difficulties of this up-river trade is to be found in Timothy Flint, *Recollections of the Last Ten Years*, pp. 91–92. Down-river rates were usually given as a cent or a little more a pound. See *Tennessee Gazette* (Nashville, Tennessee), February 18, 1801; Wier, *op. cit.*, James Wier to Thomas Fitzpatrick, Lexington, Kentucky, February 23, 1805; Christian Schultz, *op. cit.*, II, 186–87. Up-river rates from New Orleans to both Tennessee and Kentucky as quoted in the *Louisiana Gazette* of New Orleans were ordinarily five cents a pound.

[20] Wier, *op. cit.*, James Wier to Abner Barker, Lexington, Kentucky, September 10, 1805.

[21] Freight rates from Philadelphia and Baltimore to Pittsburgh were usually given as $5.00 per hundred or even higher. Shipments to Lexington cost $7.00 or

Slow and unreliable communication of market information also added to frontier difficulties. This was due in part to the obstacles to travel emphasized above and in part also to the undeveloped trade organization of the frontier community. For news of market conditions the western merchant or farmer depended upon prices current either printed in the newspapers or communicated privately by letter. By 1810 the good-weather time for post riders from Philadelphia to Lexington was still at least two weeks. From New Orleans letters could, under favorable conditions, be delivered in Kentucky in twenty-five days.[22] Obviously the slow movement and frequent delays of the mails were of great disadvantage to those who shipped goods down the Ohio, for, as a result, they had to select their cargoes in the light of market information already nearly a month old, in addition to shipping goods which would, in all probability, be at least four or five weeks in getting to market.

This handicap was made all the more serious by the presence of eastern speculators. The editor of the *Kentucky Gazette* complained that because of the slowness of the mail:

A speculator . . . . can hasten [from Philadelphia or New Orleans] . . . . purchase our production on his own terms, and lay the whole western country under contribution . . . . before we can have any information as to the change in price of produce in the markets of those places . . . . fortunes have often been made in this way . . . . when the loss of a battle, the death of a Bonaparte, or the fall of a minister of state, may change the course of business, and improve or depress markets.[23]

The undeveloped financial organization of the West can hardly be more than mentioned here as still another of those factors which contributed to the fundamental economic difficulties of the frontiersman. A scarcity of money often existed for the payment of taxes or to meet the ordinary needs of trade. Barter, everywhere common for small payments, was almost the only mode of

---

$8.00 and to Cumberland $9.00 or $10.00 per hundred pounds. See for example, *American State Papers*, Miscellaneous II, 117; John Melish, *op. cit.*, II, 52; *Farmers Register* (Greensburg, Pennsylvania), September 1, 1804; and Letter Book of Joseph Hertzog, Joseph Hertzog to Christian Wilt, Philadelphia, March 20, 1811.

[22] *Kentucky Gazette* (Lexington, Kentucky), October 9, 1810.   [23] *Ibid.*

exchange in the more remote settlements.[24] Public officers' receipts and land warrants were commonly issued by the frontier states; and, although helping somewhat to make up for the scarcity of other media, they were often unsatisfactory because subject to depreciation.[25]

Banking facilities developed beginning with the establishment of the Kentucky Insurance Company in 1802.[26] But, for most of the West, banks were just getting well started by 1812. Despite help from merchants who dealt in exchange and branches of the First Bank of the United States which were set up at Pittsburgh and New Orleans, payments at a distance were often costly and difficult to make.[27]

↝ Probably more serious than the imperfect financial machinery

[24] See, for example, *Scioto Gazette* (Chillicothe, Ohio), October 1, 1803; *Dayton Repertory* (Dayton, Ohio), December 14, 1809; *Natchez Gazette* (Natchez), October 17, 1811; and Marshall to Bosseron, Vincennes, June 7, 1800. Lasselle Collection, Indiana State Library. For an example of the almost complete absence of money in the more isolated regions, see Jonathan S. Findlay to James Findlay, Natchez, November 24, 1805, "Selections from the Torrence Papers," *Quarterly Publications of the Historical and Philosophical Society of Ohio*, IV, 108–9. Major William Stanley, when he was about to start on a trip down the Ohio River, made this matter of fact notation in his diary: "sell my horse for 650 lbs. Bacon" ("The Diary of Major William Stanley, 1790–1810," *Quarterly Publications of the Historical and Philosophical Society of Ohio*, XIV, 29).

[25] *Stewart's Kentucky Herald* (Paris, Kentucky), December 16, 1805; *Independent Gazetteer* (Lexington, Kentucky), June 14, 1805; *Western Herald* (Steubenville, Ohio), December 27, 1806; and *Western American* (Bardstown, Kentucky), April 5, 1805. See also C. C. Huntington, "A History of Banking and Currency in Ohio before the Civil War," *Ohio Archaeological and Historical Society Quarterly*, XXIV, 262; and R. T. Durrett, "Early Banking in Kentucky," *Proceedings of the Kentucky Bankers' Association, 1892*, p. 37.

[26] The original act chartering the Kentucky Insurance Company may be found in the *Kentucky Gazette* (Lexington, Kentucky), January 18, 1803, and in *Acts of Kentucky*, 11 Ass., 1 Sess., pp. 149–59. Although, as the name implies, this company wrote marine insurance, it does not appear that most western farmers insured their river shipments. See *Palladium* (Frankfort, Kentucky), April 10, 1806, and *Louisiana Gazette* (St. Louis, Missouri), August 16, 1810.

[27] Notes on eastern banks often brought a premium on the frontier because of their superiority to specie in making distant payments. Western merchants found it necessary at times to assume the risk and expense of transporting the heavy silver specie over the mountains. *Palladium* (Frankfort, Kentucky), January 12, 1805, and March 6, 1806; F. A. Michaux, *op. cit.*, pp. 157 ff.; Charles Cist, *The Cincinnati Miscellany*, I, 6; Fortescue Cuming, "Sketches of a Tour to the Western Country, Etc., 1807-1809" in Thwaites' *Early Western Travels*, IV, 183–84.

was the scarcity of capital. The settlers did not bring much capital with them, nor had the country been settled long enough to develop its own surplus. As yet little eastern capital flowed westward except as Atlantic merchants gave long credits to their frontier customers. The complaint of scarcity of money so frequently found in western newspapers no doubt often arose in reality from a scarcity of capital. Even in western Pennsylvania, one of the earliest settled portions of the West, the farmers did not, according to a newspaper account, have capital to invest even in such needed improvements as turnpikes.[28]

Finally, as a new, extensive, and sparsely settled region, the frontier suffered, as we should expect, from an imperfectly developed business and marketing organization. Importing was largely in the hands of small firms, usually partnerships, which were dependent upon Philadelphia or Baltimore merchants for long-term credits. As time went on, the function of receiving and forwarding goods was placed more and more in the hands of commission houses at such centers as Pittsburgh and Cincinnati. But for many years these small-scale western merchants commonly carried out the whole process, purchasing in Philadelphia, superintending transportation to the frontier, storing, retailing, and carrying back to the Atlantic Coast money, bills of exchange, or, more rarely, west-country produce.[29]

But especially in the disposal of his exportable surplus did the frontier argiculturist suffer from lack of adequate marketing machinery. In order to get his produce to market, the farmer had often to assume the risk of carrying his own produce to New Orleans and there disposing of it as best he could. In the words of a contributor to the Frankfort *Palladium* the producer became "a navigator, and a trader."[30]

[28] *Commonwealth* (Pittsburgh, Pennsylvania), May 28, 1806, and *Western Spy* (Cincinnati, Ohio), November 10, 1802. A Kentuckian stated in 1805 that private lenders received from 10 to 50 per cent on loans. *Independent Gazetteer* (Lexington, Kentucky), June 14, 1805.

[29] See the correspondence of James Wier and Andrew Jackson referred to above, also Christian Schultz, *op. cit.*, II, 22; Morris Birkbeck, *Notes on America* (2d ed., London, 1818), pp. 89-90, and Henry B. Fearon, *Sketches of America, Etc.* (2d ed., London, 1818), p. 231.

[30] April 10, 1806. See also *Western American* (Bardstown, Kentucky), March 29, 1805.

Had this farmer-trader found a well-organized market at Natchez or New Orleans, he might not have fared so badly when he arrived at the lower river port. But one who had probably engaged in this trade himself wrote:

He there meets with strangers—his time is precious—new expences ensue —the climate is unfriendly both to his own health, and the preservation of his cargo. The market may be dull—he cannot wait—he sells of necessity at what he can get, and he returns home after a long and fatiguing journey, with but little money, and less health. . . . .

. . . . when the whole profit and loss is summed up, there are few I believe who do not find it a bad business. What is here said of the adventuring farmer, may be applied to all exporters on a small capital.[31]

Especially disadvantageous must have been what the writer quoted above described as "the want of some established mode of doing business between the citizens and traders." Is it surprising that the farmer-adventurer often made hurried and bad bargains at New Orleans? In a market glutted with produce, he was a stranger, often unused to the forms of trade and ignorant as to the state of the market. Fearful of the oncoming "sickly season" or even of "the danger of robbery and assassination," he sold quickly for whatever he could get and returned to Kentucky to tell of the "unprincipled speculators" and "rapacious agents" at New Orleans or to attribute the low prices to combination among the purchasers.[32]

Complaint that west-country merchants did not help the farmers to market their produce was repeatedly voiced in western newspapers; and when a merchant did engage in exporting farm produce down the rivers, he was hailed in the press as a public benefactor.[33] Numerous attempts were made to establish some agency which would be primarily concerned in marketing the farmers' surplus produce. In Ohio a number of attempts were

[31] *Palladium* (Frankfort, Kentucky), April 10, 1806.

[32] *Kentucky Gazette* (Lexington, Kentucky), October 18, 1803, Aristides; and *Palladium* (Frankfort, Kentucky), April 15, 1802.

[33] See for example the *Reporter* (Lexington, Kentucky), December 5, 1809; *Scioto Gazette* (Chillicothe, Ohio), October 1, 1803; *Clarion* (Nashville, Tennessee), February 16, 1808; and *Democratic Clarion and Tennessee Gazette* (Nashville, Tennessee), August 10, 1810.

made to set up stock companies for this purpose.[34] And at Nashville (1810) a newspaper published a long series of articles urging that the state take over the marketing function which, according to the writer, the farmer could not and the merchant would not assume.[35]

As a result, in part at least, of the absence of old, established firms and accepted ways of doing business, western products were usually poor in quality and bore a bad reputation.[36] Ohio River Valley flour usually sold at New Orleans for several dollars less than the Atlantic product. A New Orleans merchant declared, "There is . . . . a manifest repugnance shewn by the merchants, to ship it to foreign markets, where the quality is always found inferior to that of the Atlantic States, and almost invariably proves rotten at the end of two or three months."[37] Nor were other products much better. Kentucky producers were accused of putting up "everything that ever looked like tobacco."[38] Despite many attempts at state regulation, complaints were frequent of western corn and hemp and the "extreme bad quality" of Ohio

[34] *Western Spy and Hamilton Gazette* (Cincinnati, Ohio), August 17, 1803; *Liberty Hall* (Cincinnati, Ohio), August 29, September 26, October 3, 10, and 17, 1810.

[35] *Democratic Clarion and Tennessee Gazette* (Nashville, Tennessee), May 4–Oct. 26, 1810, series signed "A Farmer." Of course, some down-river exportation was done by the west-country merchants, and even Philadelphia houses occasionally engaged in it. In so far, however, as the merchants did enter this trade, they confined their operations largely to cotton, tobacco, hemp products, and, in western Pennsylvania, to flour. Practically all exporting from New Orleans was done by local merchants and agents or factors for mercantile houses in Atlantic Coast cities or Great Britain. *Mississippi Herald and Natchez Gazette* (Natchez, Mississippi Territory), July 26, 1805; *Palladium* (Frankfort, Kentucky), February 10, 1803; *Candid Review* (Bairdstown, Kentucky), December 9, 1807; and New Orleans customs records, Library of Congress.

[36] Other factors, such as the crudeness of western flour mills and cotton gins, were of course important. Emphasis on quantity rather than fine quality is perhaps typical of frontier regions.

[37] *Louisiana Gazette* (New Orleans), August 8, 1806. It was reported from New Orleans that "the reputation of Kentucky flour, formerly bad enough, is this year ten times worse than ever, so much Weavel eaten flour; and even *old flour with boles filled with fresh flour*, has been sold here . . . ." (*Kentucky Gazette* [Lexington, Kentucky], June 21, 1803; italics in the original text). For other references to the inferior grade of this frontier product see for example, *Palladium* (Frankfort, Kentucky), July 15, 1802, and February 4 and March 17, 1808.

[38] *American State Papers*, Miscellaneous, I, 709.

Valley pork.[39] Baltimore merchants threatened to boycott Louisiana sugar producers unless their product was shipped in proper
casks; and at Liverpool cotton importers deplored the presence
of leaves, dirt, and considerable quantities of seed in bales of
western cotton.[40]

No one of the drawbacks described above nor all of them together were necessarily fatal to western hopes, for, though difficulties are great and costs high, if prices are still higher, prosperity
may yet be obtained. Still these difficulties surely tended to make
the West of this period a sort of marginal area in relation to
world-markets. When world-prices ruled high, Monongahela and
Kentucky flour could be disposed of in competition with that
from Virginia and Maryland. Likewise, when cotton and tobacco
brought good prices, the Kentucky and Tennessee product could
be sold along with that of the Atlantic states and still yield a
profit to distant western farmers. But when markets were dull
and prices falling, western producers not only saw the fading of
their roseate hopes but often enough found themselves in desperate straits to secure necessary imported commodities or to
meet obligations for land bought on credit when hopes ran high
with prices.

Free navigation of the Mississippi, unprecedented immigration, and unusually high prices had brought a great wave of
optimism to the West following 1803, despite the underlying
difficulties just considered. The peak year proved to be 1805,
but times were relatively good in 1806 and 1807 except for those
parts of the West which were adversely affected by glutted markets and lower prices for west-country provisions. Acute depression did not come until 1808.[41] The price situation of that year
speaks for itself. Since 1805 the index of wholesale prices of

[39] See the *Orleans Gazette* (New Orleans), April 20, 1805; the *Louisiana Gazette*
(New Orleans), August 8, 1806; *Liberty Hall* (Cincinnati, Ohio), April 9, 1808; and
the *Kentucky Gazette* (Lexington, Kentucky), February 28, 1804.

[40] See the following New Orleans newspapers: *Orleans Gazette*, August 3 and
September 18, 1805; *Union*, January 23, 1804; *Louisiana Gazette*, September 23,
1804.

[41] The building of seagoing ships at Ohio Valley river ports, which had generated
tremendous enthusiasm earlier in the decade, had been proved an impractical venture several years before the embargo. This ship-building boom is one of the few
local matters upon which the student may find very full comment in the western

western products at New Orleans had fallen over 20 per cent. Except for hemp growers in Kentucky and infant manufacturing interests at Pittsburgh and Lexington, practically the whole West was prostrated.[42]

Immigration into Ohio seems virtually to have ceased, and land sales north of the Ohio River were greatly reduced.[43] Those who had previously purchased lands now found it impossible to meet their obligations. In a petition to Congress the legislature of Ohio stated:

> . . . . the unprovoked aggressions of both England and France, which could neither be foreseen or evaded, has so materially affected the whole commerce of the United States, that it has almost put a stop to our circulat-ing medium, and rendered the payment of the installments of the purchase money for the . . . . lands almost impracticable; forfeitures of interest for two, three and four years, are daily accruing.[44]

Stay-laws and relief for debtors were the rule in Kentucky, Tennessee, and Mississippi Territory,[45] and depressed conditions were reported at New Orleans as early as April, 1807.[46]

---

press. The authoritative study of this episode in Ohio Valley history is Archer B. Hulbert's "Western Ship-Building," *American Historical Review*, XXI, 720–33. Hulbert's suggestion that the failure of the experiment was due to the embargo is not acceptable. The insuring of the right of deposit at New Orleans by the Louisiana Purchase, combined with the repeated disasters experienced in getting seagoing ships down western rivers, had brought about a decline certainly before the embargo and probably as early as 1805.

[42] Probably Kentucky suffered less from the embargo than other parts of the frontier. See Samuel G. Adams to Harry Innes (?), Richmond, July 15, 1809, *Harry Innes Papers*, Vol. XXI, Library of Congress, and the author's *Prices in the Mississippi Valley* referred to above.

[43] Jarvase Cutler, *A Topographical Description of the State of Ohio, Indiana Territory, and Louisiana, Etc.* (Boston, 1812), p. 11; *Liberty Hall* (Cincinnati, Ohio), July 11, 1810; Daniel Drake, *loc. cit.*; and *American State Papers, Finance*, Vol. II, *passim*. On May 7, 1808, a resident of Marietta, Ohio, wrote that no land could be sold at that place "on account of the scarcity of money & the stoppage of business." Rufus Putnam to John May, Marietta, John May Papers, Western Reserve Historical Society Tract No. 97, p. 202.

[44] *Acts of Ohio*, 7 Ass., 1 Sess., pp. 222–23.

[45] *Palladium* (Frankfort, Kentucky), February 16, 1809; *Senate Journal*, Tennessee, 7 Ass., 2 Sess., pp. 6–8; *Annals of Congress*, 10 Cong., 2 Sess., 1246; and *Weekly Chronicle* (Natchez, Mississippi Territory), October 12 and December 14, 1808.

[46] *Palladium* (Frankfort, Kentucky), June 11, 1807, see a copy of a letter from Sanderson and White. New Orleans Commission merchants dated April 6 1807

Two main remedies for the situation received increasingly enthusiastic support from the frontiersmen in the period of falling prices and hard times, which began for parts of the West as early as 1806, became general by 1808, and continued down to the War of 1812 with but partial and temporary relief in 1809–10. One was the development of manufactures; the other was forcing the European powers to repeal their restrictions on our foreign commerce. Of course, still other remedies were advocated from time to time. Occasionally, some one saw clearly enough that fundamental difficulties of marketing, of transportation, and of business and financial organization must be overcome.[47] Some violent partisans believed all would be well if only the Federalists might be returned to power and the national government thereby saved "from the incapacity . . . . of our own rulers, and the want of that pure patriotism" which distinguished the time of Washington.[48] Even the moralists were present to attribute economic ills to the laxity of the laws and the absence of a feeling of moral responsibility on the part of the people.[49] These, and other solutions were suggested, but the two most popular measures of relief were those intended to stimulate manufactures and those designed to force Great Britain to modify her commercial system.

The enthusiasm for manufacturing cannot be dwelt on here. The following statement from the *Western Spy and Miami Gazette* may be regarded as typical of this western attitude:

Raise articles of produce, which can be manufactured, rather than such as require a foreign market; Rye to distill; Barley to brew; Flax and Wool to spin, rather than Wheat to ship.

Above all *observe* the household manufactures of your neighbors. *Observe* the accounts of them in the newspapers. Immitate what you see manufactured. . . . . Shew our foreign spoliators we can live in comfort without their finery.[50]

[47] See for example, *Democratic Clarion and Tennessee Gazette* (Nashville, Tennessee), August 10, 1810, contribution signed "A Farmer"; and *Palladium* (Frankfort, Kentucky), April 10, 1806.

[48] *Natchez Gazette* (Natchez), October 17, 1811.

[49] *Louisiana Gazette* (New Orleans), March 7, 1811.

[50] August 13, 1808; italics in the original text. See also for similar statements: *Reporter* (Lexington, Kentucky), September 8, 1810, and February 23, 1811, and *Carthage Gazette* (Carthage, Tennessee), April 25, 1811.

Our attention in this paper is centered primarily upon western attempts to mend their failing fortunes through supporting commercial coercion and war. An understanding of the course of frontier opinion in respect to these measures involves, first, a realization of the degree of support which the West gave to the Embargo Act of December, 1807, and, second, an appreciation of the importance of economic motives in prompting the West to support a measure accompanied, as this one was, by widespread depression. An examination of the situation reveals that in his policy of commercial coercion President Jefferson received no more faithful support than that which came from western congressmen. Almost to a man, they voted for the original act of December, 1807, which placed a general embargo on foreign trade; and they supported him loyally in the numerous measures which followed to make its operation effective. When, in November, 1808, the House of Representatives by the very close count of fifty-six to fifty-eight voted to continue the measure in effect, the western members were solidly with the majority.[51] And the next spring, when others weakened, western congressmen stood out for the continuance of the embargo, or, failing that, for the adoption of a non-intercourse act. A westerner, George W. Campbell, of Tennessee, was one of the Senate leaders who held out most firmly against any loosening of commercial restrictions.[52]

On the whole, the citizens of the western states were just as enthusiastic for commercial restrictions as their representatives in Congress. Yet some frontier opposition did appear. At Pittsburgh and Presque Isle (Erie) in Pennsylvania, and in parts of Ohio where some Federalism still survived (e.g., Dayton and Chillicothe), newspaper writers vigorously attacked the measure.[53]

[51] *Annals of Congress*, 10 Cong., 2 Sess., p. 500.

[52] See for example, *ibid.*, pp. 1475–87, 1499, and 1541. Matthew Lyon, of Kentucky, was the only western representative in Congress who opposed the embargo and deprecated talk of war with England. *Annals of Congress*, 10 Cong., 1 Sess., p. 1222, and 2 Sess., pp. 1504–5. In spite of his early services to his party, his constituents were unwilling to have such a representative, and August 18, 1810, the Lexington *Reporter* announced that "the apostate Lyon" had failed of re-election. See also the *Reporter* (Lexington, Kentucky) for July 1, 1809.

[53] On Federalism in Ohio before the War of 1812, see Homer C. Hockett, *Western Influences on Political Parties to 1825*, pp. 54–62.

In Kentucky, the *Western World* of Frankfort, a paper with an extremely small following, was the only one in the state antagonistic to the embargo.[54] As might be expected from the presence of commercial and shipping interests, some active disapproval appeared at New Orleans, where at least two of the newspapers attacked the measure.[55] Even here probably the group opposed to the embargo formed but a small minority. Its size, however, may have been minimized by the intensely partisan Governor Claiborne, who wrote to Madison: "Two or three British Factors, and some violent Federalists censure the Embargo, but the better informed, and worthy part of Society, appears highly to approve the measure."[56]

Despite the opposition noted above, the frontier was, as a whole, no less favorable to the embargo than its representatives in Congress. The commercial boycott had been successfully used against England in our earlier struggles, and it now seemd to westerners a natural and powerful weapon.[57] State legislatures, local political leaders, and public meetings expressed their enthusiastic approval.[58] Most western newspapers printed articles which ardent-

[54] The attack on the embargo which one finds most often in these opposition papers is to the effect that the Democrats are ruining the country in an attempt to help the French.

[55] *La lanterne magique* and the *Louisiana Gazette.*

[56] Claiborne to Madison, New Orleans, June 8, 1808, D. Rowland, ed., *Official Letter Books of W. C. C. Claiborne*, IV, 176. The suggestion in a New Orleans paper that the people of Orleans Territory were opposed to the restrictions on trade brought a vigorous denial in the *Courrier de la Louisiane* for June 3, 1808.

[57] In what was perhaps the first book of a political character printed in the Trans-Appalachian region, Allan B. Magruder advocated the so-called "Chinese policy" and expressed the belief that foreign nations could best be coerced by depriving them of the benefits of commerce with us. *Political, Commercial and Moral Reflections on the Late Cession of Louisiana to the United States* (Lexington, 1803), pp. 56–65. The importance which the frontiersmen attached to our foreign relations may be illustrated by the assertion of a Kentucky farmer that ". . . . if our relations with foreign countries go on well, we are likely to have good markets at home, especially during the continuance of a European War." *American Republic* (Frankfort, Kentucky), June 21, 1811.

[58] See, for example, Mann Butler, *A History of the Commonwealth of Kentucky* (Louisville, 1834), p. 330; *Acts of Ohio*, 7 Ass., 1 Sess., pp. 223–24; *Scioto Gazette* (Chillicothe, Ohio), February 13, 1809; *Acts of Kentucky*, 17 Ass., 1 Sess., p. 129; *Reporter* (Washington, Pennsylvania), December 19, 1808; and the *Carthage Gazette* (Carthage, Tennessee), February 6, 1809.

ly championed the embargo.[59] Opinion was so united in its favor
in Tennessee as to call forth the following statement: "We never
witnessed a greater unanimity to prevail in any considerable district of country, and relative to any important question, than now
prevails throughout the state of Tennessee respecting the measures of the General Government. The voice of approbation is universal."[60] Two months after the measure had been superseded by
the Non-Intercourse Act, they were still drinking toasts to it in
Vincennes.[61] Perhaps at that distant frontier outpost they had
not yet learned of its repeal.

Two American students, Professor L. M. Sears and Professor
W. W. Jennings, have given special attention to the embargo of
1808. Both emphasize the traditional hatred for England, and
the former specifically denies the significance of economic factors.
Approval of the embargo, he tells us, was the result of the "simple
trust" in Jefferson which filled the hearts of southern Democrats.
As for the approval which was given the embargo in Mississippi
Territory, Sears regards it as the pure flower of disinterested
logic.[62]

It cannot be denied that traditional attitudes and party loyalty
played some part in determining western support for the embargo.
To some extent the westerner was playing the rôle of a good Democrat and supporting his president. In part he was acting as a
good patriot and a high-spirited frontiersman who resented insults to the national honor either by France or England. The
traditional friendship of Democrats for France doubtless made
the westerner quick to resent untoward acts by Britain and slow
to see evil in the French aggressions. But these explanations are,
at most, not the whole story, for an examination of western opinion clearly indicates that the support which was given the em-

[59] *Western Sun* (Vincennes), August 13, 1808; *Mississippi Messenger* (Natchez),
February 4 and March 24, 1808; *Political Theatre* (Lancaster, Kentucky), December
10, 1808; *Wilson's Knoxville Gazette* (Knoxville, Tennessee), May 13, 1808; and
Commonwealth (Pittsburgh, Pennsylvania) March 16, 1808.

[60] *Carthage Gazette* (Carthage, Tennessee), February 6, 1809.

[61] *Western Sun* (Vincennes), July 8, 1809.

[62] Louis Martin Sears, *Jefferson and the Embargo*, pp. 100 and 126; and W. W.
Jennings, *The American Embargo, 1807–1809*, pp. 201–2.

bargo on the frontier had in it a considerable element of economic self-interest.

The western farmer was quite willing to admit his lack of interest in the carrying trade. Even impressment of seamen, though to be deplored, did not seem to him very important.[63] But he did want adequate markets and good prices for his produce, and these he believed impossible so long as Great Britain restricted the West Indian market, forbade direct trade with the Continent, and placed exceedingly burdensome duties upon American imports into Great Britain. In the eyes of the western farmer, the depression of 1808 was primaily the result of the belligerents' decrees and orders in council, not of the embargo which he regarded as a highly desirable act, designed as a measure of retaliation to force the abandonment by foreign nations of their destructive interference with the marketing of our surplus products. "Who now blames the embargo?" demanded a Cincinnati editor. "Who considers it a matter of French interest or procurement? Who does not allow it to be a *saving measure?* . . . . The embargo was produced by the foreign belligerent powers. They made it wise, just and necessary. They made its continuance necessary."[64]

In Congress western representatives made no effort to conceal their economic interest in the embargo. Said Senator Pope of Kentucky, in stating the very core of the argument in defense of this measure:

What, Mr. President, is our situation? . . . . The dispute between us and the belligerents is not about the carrying trade, but whether we shall be permitted to carry our surplus produce to foreign markets? The privilege of carrying our cotton to market, is one in which, not only the growers themselves are interested, but one which concerns every part of the nation.

He then went on to show that if the embargo were taken off while the orders in council remained in force, cotton would be confined alone to the British market and the price would fall to a ruinously

[63] *Annals of Congress*, 10 Cong., 2 Sess., pp. 204–6; *Reporter* (Lexington, Kentucky), October 3, 1808, and *Kentucky Gazette* (Lexington, Kentucky), August 30, 1808.

[64] *The Western Spy and Miami Gazette* (Cincinnati, Ohio), August 13, 1808. Italics in original text.

low level. "The necessity," he continued, ". . . . of resisting the British orders and forcing our way to those markets where there is a demand for the article, must be evident to every one who will consider the subject." In conclusion he added that if England did not change her course war might be necessary.[65]

When the question of continuing the embargo was again debated in the spring of 1809, much was said of markets and prices by those favoring a continuance of restrictive measures. In arguing in the House of Representatives against the proposed repeal of the Embargo Act, George W. Campbell, of Tennessee, declared:

. . . . though you relieve your enemy, you do not furnish any substantial relief to your own people. No, sir, I am convinced that, in less than three months from this day, should this measure succeed, produce will sink below the price which it now bears, or has borne for the last year. There are but few places to which you can go, and those will naturally become glutted for want of competition; and, in a short time, the prices will not pay the original cost. It will, therefore, afford no substantial relief. The relief, too, which it may afford will be partial, confined to certain portions of the Union, and not equally beneficial to the whole. Tobacco will find no market; cotton a temporary market only—for, although Great Britain will receive it, yet, as we have more on hand than she will immediately want, or can make use of, and as we cannot go to France, and our trade to the Continent will undoubtedly be interrupted by Great Britain, she has nothing to do but wait a few days, weeks, or months, and buy it at her own price.[66]

If the inhabitants of Mississippi Territory gave, as has been held, a completely disinterested support to the embargo, one must conclude that their delegate in Congress failed somehow to understand the position of his constituents. George Poindexter, the delegate in Congress from Mississippi Territory, wrote the editor of the *Natchez Chronicle* that nothing could be gained by remov-

[65] *Annals of Congress*, 10 Cong., 2 Sess., pp. 1592–93. The West was outraged not only that English restrictions should keep our goods from Continental markets but also that heavy duties should be levied on the most important of our goods marketed in her ports. A contributor to a Kentucky newspaper declared: " . . . . the *tax* in '74 was imposed on the article of *tea* alone, & whilst we were colonies of that country—in 1808, it is imposed on *every article of our commerce*, and that too while we occupy the ground of an *independent nation*." *Palladium* (Frankfort, Kentucky), November 3, 1808, from the *Western World;* italics in the original text.

[66] *Annals of Congress*, 10 Cong., 2 Sess., pp. 1481–82. See also *The Mississippian* (Natchez, Mississippi Territory), February 2, 1809.

ing the embargo, for British taxes and trade restrictions would so limit the market for cotton as greatly to depress the price.[67]

By the Non-Intercourse Act, which superseded the Embargo Act in the spring of 1809, direct trade with England and France and their colonies was prohibited. Although there was nothing now to stop an indirect trade with England, the British orders in council still kept American produce from reaching the Continent. On the whole the West did not like the change, and their representatives were right in predicting that such partial opening of trade would glut markets with our products and bring prices still lower. Poindexter denounced England's attempt to monopolize world-trade and "tax the product of our farms when exported to foreign markets." He even advocated war against her if necessary, and did not hesitate to recommend to his constituents that cotton be shipped immediately to England via a neutral port so as to get a fair price before markets were glutted.[68]

The course of events during the summer of 1809 was well calculated still further to inflame western hatred for Great Britain and convince the frontier farmers that their surplus could never be exported at a profit until England was somehow forced to permit free trade upon the seas. Prices, although somewhat improved, continued low as compared with pre-embargo years. The Spanish West Indies were now open to American trade; but as early as June 5, 1809, Havana, the most important Spanish port, was reported surfeited with exportations from New Orleans.[69] Erskine's treaty (April 19, 1809) by which direct trade was to be reopened with England was, at least in some quarters, regarded with suspicion. If it should not result in opening trade with the Continent, it was held that there would be loss for us and gain for England. The editor of the *Lexington Reporter* wrote:

What will be the price of our produce confined and concentrated totally in British warehouses?

Where will be our carrying trade? Why, British merchants and British

[67] *Weekly Chronicle* (Natchez, Mississippi Territory), December 14, 1808, letter dated Washington, November 12, 1808.

[68] *The Mississippian* (Natchez), May 1, 1809, Poindexter to his constituents, Washington, D.C., March 5, 1809.

[69] *Louisiana Gazette* (New Orleans), June 27, 1809.

manufacturers will purchase our productions for the mere expense of shipping and the duties and commissions to London and Liverpool merchants! *Our manufactures will be annihilated.* Britain will have gained a most glorious victory. . . . .

What is become of the 100,000 hogsheads of Tobacco exported from the United States?

Will Britain consume and manufacture all our cotton?

No, not one tenth of our Tobacco—not one half of our Cotton; and our flour, our grain, our ashes, our staves, and every other property must center there, and be held as a *pledge for our allegiance.*[70]

In July news reached the West of the extension of the British continental blockade and of the new duties to be levied upon cotton. The *Reporter*, while bitterly attacking England, held that her insults were the results of our weak policy. "Submission only encourages oppression," wrote the editor, "and Britain will follow up her blow, 'till our chains are fully rivetted."[71] Probably this writer's attitude was extreme. Some westerners were inclined to look with considerable hope upon the Erskine arrangements.[72] But when, in the late summer of 1809, word was carried over the Appalachians that England had repudiated the acts of her minister, the frontier was thoroughly aroused. Public gatherings were called for the denunciation of British perfidy. Editors joined in the clamor, and state legislatures sent communications to the president denouncing England and declaring their willingness to resort to arms.[73]

The editor of the Lexington *Reporter* was not slow to drive home the moral. In a long analysis of the situation he said in part:

The *Farmer* who is complaining of the low price of Cotton, of Tobacco, of any other produce cannot now be deceived of the real cause, he will not

[70] May 13, 1809; italics in the original text.

[71] Lexington, Kentucky, July 1, 1809.

[72] Johnson of Kentucky, for example, was one of the chief supporters of the administration in its negotiations with Erskine. *Annals of Congress*, 11 Cong., 1 Sess., pp. 156–61. But most western representatives were not very enthusiastic. See *ibid.*, pp. 187 ff.

[73] *Carthage Gazette* (Carthage, Tennessee), August 17, September 1, and November 17, 1809; *Independent Republican* (Chillicothe, Ohio), September 8, 1809; *Reporter* (Lexington, Kentucky), September 9 and November 11, 1809; *House Journal*, Tennessee, 8 Ass., 1 Sess., pp. 147–49; *Acts of Ohio*, 8 Ass., 1 Sess., p. 347.

attribute it to embargo systems, or to French decrees, for French decrees were in full force when we so anxiously made the experiment of *confining* our trade to Britain, the farmers will see clearly that the orders in council prohibiting and interrupting all commerce to the continent is the only cause for his embarrassments.

. . . . The farmer who wishes a market for his produce, must therefore charge his representative in Congress to cast off all temporising. . . . .[74]

The winter of 1809–10 found hard times on frontier farms and western sentiment more bitter than ever against the British as the chief cause of the farmers' troubles.[75] The attempt at commercial coercion had failed, but Congress was not yet ready to declare war. Beginning May 1, 1810, commerce was freed from the restrictive measures of our own government. On the whole, conditions seemed on the mend in the following summer, and western farmers were busy harvesting crops which they hoped might be floated down the river to good markets in 1811. Some thought they perceived a promise of better times, while others saw no assurance of prosperity until foreign restrictions should be withdrawn.[76]

But, instead of improving, conditions actually grew seriously worse during the next two years. Wholesale prices of western products were below even those of 1808 in the year before the war. In this new period of general depression on the frontier, the northern part of the Ohio River Valley appears to have suffered less than other parts of the West. Frequent newspaper notices of the building of flour mills in Ohio and increased advertising by

[74] October 24, 1809; italics in the original text. See also *Carthage Gazette* (Carthage, Tennessee), December 15, 1809.

[75] *Carthage Gazette* (Carthage, Tennessee), December 15, 1809; *Reporter* (Lexington, Kentucky), November 11 and December 30, 1809, and February 24, 1810; *Independent Republican* (Chillicothe, Ohio), February 8 and March 8, 1810; *Liberty Hall* (Cincinnati, Ohio), February 7, 1810. The plight of the settlers living west of the Great Miami River in Ohio may be regarded as typical. They could not, so they reported to Congress, make payments on lands which they had bought because (1) specie could not be commanded, (2) laws for the relief of debtors made it impossible for them to collect payments which were due, (3) immigrants were no longer coming into the country and bringing money with them, and (4) there were no markets for their produce. *Dayton Repertory* (Dayton, Ohio), December 14, 1809.

[76] *Ohio Centinel* (Dayton, Ohio), May 31, 1810; *Kentucky Gazette* (Lexington, Kentucky), July 31, 1810; *Reporter* (Lexington, Kentucky), June 15 and 30 and July 14 and 21, 1810.

those wishing to buy wheat and flour indicates at least some optimistic sentiment. Also, advantage must have resulted from a considerable increase which now took place in the number of cattle and hogs driven eastward over the mountains.[77] Although some settlers still came via Kentucky or by the river route, the fact which now called forth newspaper comment was the large number of wagons bringing immigrants to Ohio which were to be met on the Pennsylvania turnpikes and on the Zanesville Road in Ohio.[78] Along with this new wave of immigration, land sales rose, though not to their pre-embargo peak. So, at least a temporary market must have been afforded for considerable quantities of country produce.[79]

In so far as contemporary appraisals of the economic situation in this northern area are available, they show little or no reflection of the favorable factors just noted. Dulness of business, scarcity of money, "poverty, disappointment, embarrassment," "the present disastrous state of our affairs"—these are typical of contemporary statements. Taken along with what we know of the price situation, the disorganization of the Mississippi commerce in the winter of 1811–12, and the fact that settlers on public lands were still petitioning for relief, the indications are that, although there was some promise of better times, the region north of the Ohio River was certainly not enjoying general prosperity in the year or two immediately preceding the war.[80]

Judging from the extremely low prices brought by tobacco, hemp, and cotton, one might suppose that the frontier south of

[77] *Muskingum Messenger* (Zanesville, Ohio), November 24, 1810; *Ohio Centinel* (Dayton, Ohio), December 13, 1810; *Supporter* (Chillicothe, Ohio), March 30, 1811.

[78] *Ohio Centinel* (Dayton, Ohio), December 13, 1810; *Supporter* (Chillicothe, Ohio), March 30, 1811; and the *Muskingum Messenger* (Zanesville, Ohio), November 13 and December 18, 1811.

[79] *American State Papers, Finance*, Vol. II, *passim*.

[80] See: William Rufus Putnam to John May, Marietta, Ohio, March 15, 1810, *The John May Papers*, Western Reserve Historical Society Tract No. 97, p. 211; *Commentator* (Marietta, Ohio), April 3, 1810; *Advertiser* (Cincinnati, Ohio), June 27, 1810; *Ohio Centinel* (Dayton, Ohio), March 7 and May 15, 1811; *Western Telegraphe* (Washington, Pennsylvania), July 18, 1811; James McBride to Mary McRoberts, "Mississippi River, April 1, 1812," *Quarterly Publication of the Historical and Philosophical Society of Ohio*, V, 27–28; and *Acts of Ohio*, 9 Ass., 1 Sess., pp. 90–91, and 10 Ass., 1 Sess., pp. 190–91.

the Ohio River suffered from a more serious depression than that to the north. The records clearly show this to have been the case. The Kentucky farmers, who had turned so enthusiastically to hemp culture in 1809 and 1810 that hemp had become the most important staple of the state, now complained even more loudly than those who produced wheat, cotton, or tobacco. There is hardly an issue of the Frankfort and Lexington papers which does not give voice to the despair and resentment of these unfortunate frontiersmen. In spite of public resolutions and even co-operative action to keep up the price by refusing to sell (probably one of the first efforts of this kind among American farmers), ruin was not averted and prices continued their disastrous decline.[81]

In western Tennessee and Mississippi Territory where cotton was almost the only sale crop, the plight of the frontier farmers was most desperate of all. Tennessee cotton planters were reported in the fall of 1810 as so discouraged that to a considerable extent they had ceased the cultivation of their staple.[82] An able contributor to Nashville papers wrote:

Ask a Tennessee planter why he does not raise some kind of crop besides corn! His answer is—if he were to do it he could get nothing for it—that he could not sell it for money, unless he carried it to Natchez or Orleans—and that was out of his power—therefore he was content to make just what would do him, (as the saying is.) Hence it is undeniable that the want of encouragement forms the principal cause of the indolence of our inhabitants.[83]

This was written in 1810. In the next year conditions were, if changed at all, worse; and "hardness of times and scarcity of money" continued to be the farmer's story.[84]

As for Mississippi Territory, conditions there were also "very dull."[85] Planters were heavily in debt for slaves as well as for

[81] See files of the Lexington *Reporter* and the Frankfort *Palladium* especially for January and February of 1811.

[82] *Western Chronicle* (Columbia, Tennessee), November 17, 1810.

[83] *Democratic Clarion and Tennessee Gazette* (Nashville, Tennessee), September 21, 1810.

[84] *Carthage Gazette* (Carthage, Tennessee), August 21, 1811.

[85] *Palladium* (Frankfort, Kentucky), November 8, 1811, from the *Baltimore Whig*.

land, and in the autumn of 1811 they petitioned Congress to permit them to defer payments due on public lands because of "the severe pressure of the times" and the "reduced price of cotton."[86]

In Orleans Territory the picture was much the same except that cattle raisers in the central and western part of the territory and sugar planters along the river received fair prices for their produce. But cotton growers were as hard pressed as elsewhere. And business at New Orleans experienced a severe crisis in 1811. The editor of the *Louisiana Gazette* declared:

> The numerous failures lately in this city, has not alone been distressing to the adventurous merchant, but it has in a great measure paralized commerce, by destroying that confidence which is the grand key stone that keeps the commercial world together. This city is young in business, we have but few capitalists in trade amongst us, and a shock of adversity is severely felt.[87]

Increased bitterness toward Great Britain and a renewed determination to force her to repeal her commercial restrictions accompanied the depression of 1811–12. But frontiersmen showed no desire to repeat the attempt at commercial coercion; past failures had shaken their faith in pacific measures. The new attitude is epitomized in the following toast offered at a Fourth of July celebration held at Frankfort in 1811: "Embargoes, nonintercourse, and negotiations, are but illy calculated to secure our rights. . . . . Let us now try old Roman policy, and maintain them with the sword."[88]

Although it cannot be questioned that this toast expressed the predominant feeling of the West, the existence of an opposition must not be overlooked. Two western senators, one from Ohio and the other from Kentucky, cast ballots against the declaration of war.[89] Letters to newspapers and editorial comments opposing a definite break with England are not uncommon in the Ohio and western Pennsylvania press. In Allegheny County, which includ-

---

[86] *Ibid.*, and *Natchez Gazette* (Natchez), October 17, 1811.

[87] March 7, 1811.

[88] *American Republic* (Frankfort, Kentucky), July 5, 1811.

[89] The junior senator from Ohio was not present. His attitude toward the war is not known. See *Muskingum Messenger* (Zanesville, Ohio), July 1, 1812.

ed Pittsburgh, the peace party was actually in the majority.[90] Elsewhere in the Mississippi Valley, with the possible exception of New Orleans, where, as during the embargo, the *Louisiana Gazette* was outspoken in its attack on all administration policies, the opposition was of very little consequence.[91]

Taking the frontier as a whole, the predominance of the war spirit cannot be doubted. All of the congressmen from western states voted for war, and the delegate to Congress from Mississippi Territory repeatedly showed himself an enthusiastic advocate of hostile measures toward Great Britain. Both the governor and the state legislature of Ohio took occasion publicly to approve the aggressive stand taken by the Twelfth Congress.[92] In a vote regarded as a test of the peace sentiment the rural elements in Pennsylvania showed themselves strongly for war.[93]

In no part of the Union was the demand for war more clamorous or determined than in Kentucky.[94] The *Reporter*, which had long called for war, now demanded it more insistently than ever, and the other papers of the state followed its lead.[95] Before Congress met in the autumn of 1811 the Georgetown *Telegraph* declared: "We have now but one course to pursue—a resort to arms. This is the only way to bring a tyranical people to a sense of justice."[96] And the next spring the editor of the *Kentucky Ga-*

[90] *Pittsburgh, Gazette* (Pittsburgh, Pennsylvania), October 23, 1812. See also *ibid.*, May 15 and 27 and September 18, 1812.

[91] The *Natchez Gazette* of Natchez, Mississippi Territory, and the *American Republic* of Frankfort, Kentucky, were opposed to war, at least in the manner proposed by the party in power.

[92] *Belmont Repository* (St. Clairsville, Ohio), December 21, 1811; and *Muskingum Messenger* (Zanesville, Ohio), July 1, 1812.

[93] *Pittsburgh Gazette* (Pittsburgh, Pennsylvania), October 23, 1812.

[94] John Pope, of Kentucky, who voted against war with England paid the penalty for acting contrary to the clearly expressed wishes of his constituents. He was defeated by an overwhelming majority when he came up for re-election in 1813. John Bowman to Stephen F. Austin, August 5, 1813, *Annual Report* of the American History Association, 1919, II, 227–28.

[95] See especially, *Reporter* (Lexington, Kentucky), November 2, 1811, and January 11 and April 14, 1812.

[96] *Telegraph* (Georgetown, Kentucky), September 25, 1811.

zette expressed the impatience of the frontier when he wrote: ". . . . we trust no further delay will now take place, in making vigorous preparations for War. Indeed those who believed Congress in earnest, expected a declaration of war long ago. . . . ."[97] The Kentucky state legislature, which had declared itself ready for war at least as early as December, 1808, now insisted upon a break with England and condemned further "temporising."[98]

To one familiar with the situation on the frontier in 1808–10 it can hardly come as a surprise that, in the same breath in which the farmers deplored their ruined agriculture, they urged war against England. Both on the frontier and in the halls of Congress westerners now demanded war as a necessary measure for economic relief.

When word of President Madison's warlike message to the Twelfth Congress reached western Pennsylvania, the editor of the Pittsburgh *Mercury* declared himself attached to peace but if necessary ready to fight for commerce.[99] And at the other end of the frontier, Governor W. C. C. Claiborne, in his inaugural address before the Louisiana state legislature, declared: "The wrongs of England have been long and seriously felt; they are visible in the decline of our sea towns, in the ruin of our commerce and the languor of agriculture."[100] Perhaps the statements of the somewhat bombastic governor must not be taken too seriously. But the following by a Louisiana cotton planter seems to come directly, if not from the heart, at least from the pocketbook:

Upon the subject of cotton we are not such fools, but we know that there is not competition in the European market for that article, and that the British are giving us what they please for it—and, if we are compelled to give it away, it matters not to us, who receives it. But we happen to know that we should get a much greater price for it, for we have some idea of the

[97] March 3, 1812.

[98] *Acts of Kentucky*, 17 Ass., 1 Sess., p. 129, and 20 Ass., 1 Sess., pp. 252–54. For other expressions of frontier demand for war see for example: *Mercury* (Pittsburgh, Pennsylvania), September 26, 1811; *Commonwealth* (Pittsburgh, Pennsylvania), April 14, 1812; *Muskingum Messenger* (Zanesville, Ohio), July 1, 1812.

[99] November 12, 1811.

[100] Charles Gayarré, *History of Louisiana, The American Domination* (New York, 1866), p. 283.

extent of the Continent, and the demand there for it; and we also know that the British navy is not so terrible as you would make us believe; and, therefore, upon the score of lucre, as well as national honor, we are ready.[101]

In Kentucky even the editor of the lone Federalist paper the *American Republic* denounced foreign restrictions as the cause for the depressed prices for western produce. He differed from the Democrats only in that he blamed not England but France, and also, of course, the Democratic administration for the hard times.[102] But this editor had almost no popular following. His paper, which went out of existence in the spring of 1812, represented little more than his own personal opinions.[103]

When aggressive action toward England seemed imminent late in 1811, the *Reporter*, which had advocated war to secure markets as early as 1809, printed an editorial saying: "It appears likely that our government will at last make war, to produce a market for our Tobacco, Flour and Cotton."[104] And as Congress hesitated over the fatal step, the *Reporter* continued to clamor for war. In April a communication printed in that paper violently attacked England as the source of western difficulties and declared that western hemp raisers would be completely ruined by English measures.[105] And the editor himself wrote in similar vein:

We are . . . . aware that many circumstances combined to reduce the price of produce. The *British Orders in Council*, which still prevent the exportation of cotton, tobacco, &c. to the continent of Europe, *are the chief*—(at the same time confining every thing to their own glutted market) whilst those continue, the carrying trade will be very limited, and bear down considerably the consumption and price of hemp, yarns, &c.[106]

[101] *Time Piece* (St. Francisville, West Florida [Louisiana]), July 25, 1811.

[102] *American Republic* (Frankfort, Kentucky), October 4, 1811. Also *ibid.*, July 19, 1811.

[103] It is interesting to note that the frontier opposition to the war in western Pennsylvania and Louisiana emanated not from the farmers but apparently from the commercial interests in Pittsburgh and New Orleans, and that in Ohio it came from a part of the West in which economic conditions were least depressed and in which a similar Federalist opposition to the embargo has been noted.

[104] *Reporter* (Lexington, Kentucky), December 10, 1811.

[105] *Ibid.*, April 25, 1812.

[106] April 13, 1811; italics in the original text. Also *ibid.*, February 23, 1811.

In what was perhaps the most curious and at the same time most revealing article to appear in the West, this same editor wrote:

Should those *quid* representatives and *quid* members of the administration support war measures after Britain has forced us into war, they support it only for *popularity*, and fear of *public* opinion. Not that their hearts are with their country—But with the British agents and U. States aristocracy. —But the scalping knife and tomahawk of *British savages, is now, again devastating our frontiers.*

Hemp at three dollars.

Cotton at twelve dollars.

Tobacco at nine shillings.

Thus will our farmers, and wives and children, continue to be *ruined* and *murdered*, whilst those half-way, *quid*, execrable measures and delays preponderate.

Either *federal* or democratical energy would preserve all.[107]

When it is remembered that the streets of Lexington were safely distant from the nearest conceivable point of Indian depredation, the editor's reference to economic ruin and the depressed price of commodities appears somehow more sincere than his dramatic reference to danger of tomahawk and scalping knife.

Nor did the economic aspect of the situation fail to find emphasis in the debates at Washington. In the discussions there on declaring war, western congressmen repeatedly emphasized the economic argument. Said Felix Grundy, of Tennessee, a leader of the western War Hawks second only to Henry Clay: ". . . . inquire of the Western people why their crops are not equal to what they were in former years, they will answer that industry has no stimulus left, since their surplus products have no markets."[108] And Samuel McKee, of Kentucky, expressed frontier exasperation with those who counseled delay, in the following words:

How long shall we live at this poor dying rate, before this non-importation law will effect the repeal of the Orders in Council? Will it be two years or twenty years? The answer is in the bosom of futurity. But, in the meantime, our prosperity is gone; our resources are wasting; and the present state of things is sapping the foundations of our political institutions by the demoralization of the people.[109]

[107] *Reporter* (Lexington, Kentucky), March 14, 1812 (italics in the original text).
[108] *Annals of Congress*, 12 Cong., 1 Sess., p. 426.   [109] *Ibid.*, p. 508.

So much has been made of the youthful enthusiasm of the War Hawks, of their national feeling and keen resentment of foreign insults, that it may possibly appear to some that these western leaders were great hypocrites who talked of national honor but acted secretly from economic motives. By way of extenuation it may be suggested that national honor and national interest seldom fail to coincide. Furthermore, the western leaders made no secret of their "interests" even though they did have much to say of "honor." Clay demanded vigorous measures against England, declaring that through failure to fight we lost both commerce and character. "If pecuniary considerations alone are to govern," he said, "there is sufficient motive for the war."[110] Three months later, when writing to the editor of the *Kentucky Gazette* assuring him that war would yet be declared, Clay did not hesitate to state in a letter which was probably intended for publication: "In the event of war, I am inclined to think that article [hemp] will command a better price than it now does."[111]

Confusion has sometimes arisen from the failure to realize that commercial privileges were as essential to those who produced goods for foreign exportation as for the merchants who gained by performing the middleman service. John Randolph did accuse the Democratic majority in Congress of being the dupes of eastern merchants. But one has only to read the words of the southern and western advocates of war to find that their position was clear and straightforward enough. Said Felix Grundy:

It is not the carrying trade, properly so called, about which this nation and Great Britain are at present contending. Were this the only question now under consideration, I should feel great unwillingness. . . . . to involve the nation in war, for the assertion of a right, in the enjoyment of which the community at large are not more deeply concerned. The true question in controversy, is of a very different character; it involves the interest of the whole nation. It is the right of exporting the productions of our own soil and industry to foreign markets.[112]

[110] *Ibid.*, pp. 599–600.

[111] Clay to the editor of the *Kentucky Gazette*, March 14, 1812, printed in the *Kentucky Gazette* (Lexington, Kentucky), March 24, 1812.

[112] *Annals of Congress*, 12 Cong., 1 Sess., p. 424. For the position of John Rhea, another Tennessee congressman, see *ibid.*, p. 637.

Repeatedly this matter came up, and as often western representatives clearly stated their position. Henry Clay left the speaker's chair to explain:

> We were but yesterday contending for the indirect trade—the right to export to Europe the coffee and sugar of the West Indies. Today we are asserting our claim to the direct trade—the right to export our cotton, tobacco, and other domestic produce to market.[113]

Too much has been made of Randolph's charge against the War Hawks that they sought the conquest of Canada, and not enough of his declarations that western representatives were much influenced by consideration of their own advantage.[114] It is true that pro-war Democrats of the coast states hurried to deny that their western colleagues were actuated by "selfish motives."[115] But Calhoun's reply to Randolph is worth quoting, for, although apparently intended as a denial, it is actually an admission of the charge. He is reported as saying:

> . . . . the gentleman from Virginia attributes preparation for war to everything but its true cause. He endeavored to find it in the probable rise of the price of hemp. He represents the people of the Western States as willing to plunge our country into war for such base and precarious motives. I will not reason on this point. I see the cause of their ardor, not in such base motives, but in their known patriotism and disinterestedness. No less mercenary is the reason which he attributes to the Southern States. He says, that the non-importation act has reduced cotton to nothing, which has produced feverish impatience. Sir, I acknowledge the cotton of our farms is worth but little; but not for the cause assigned by the gentleman from Virginia. The people of that section do not reason as he does; they do not attribute it to the efforts of their Government to maintain peace and independence of their country; they see in the low price of the produce, the hand of foreign injustice; they know well, without the market to the Continent, the deep and steady current of supply will glut that of Great Britain; they are not prepared for the colonial state to which again that Power is endeavoring to reduce us.[116]

Not only were westerners accused of seeking war for their own economic advantage, but many held they were mistaken in believing that war with England would bring them the results they

[113] *Ibid.*, p. 601.

[114] *Ibid.*, pp. 450 and 533.

[115] *Ibid.*, pp. 467–75.

[116] *Ibid.*, p. 482.

sought. Federalists and anti-war Democrats repeatedly declared in Congress that war would not open markets or restore the price of hemp, tobacco, or cotton.[117] These speeches, cogent as they often were, failed in their purpose of dissuading the frontiersmen from demanding war, but they are convincing evidence to us that the anti-war minority, no less than the majority which favored the conflict, recognized clearly enough the important relation of economic motives to the war spirit.

As noted at the outset, factors other than those emphasized in this study undoubtedly played a part in bringing on the war. The expansionist sentiment, which Professor Julius W. Pratt has emphasized, was surely present.[118] English incitement to Indian depredations and Spanish interference with American trade through Florida should be noted, as should also the fact that the frontiersmen sought every possible pretext to seize the coveted Indian lands. Restrictions on the carrying trade, even impressment of seamen, may have had some effect in influencing western opinion. No doubt the traditional hostility of the Republican party toward England played a part. Many veterans of the Revolutionary War had settled upon western lands, and time had not failed to magnify the glory of their achievements or to add to the aggressive ardor of their patriotism.

But important as these factors may have been, the attitude of the western settler can hardly be evaluated without an understanding of his economic position. He was, after all, typically an ambitious farmer who moved to the Mississippi Valley in order to make a better living. In the boom times following the Louisiana Purchase he had regarded the western frontier as a veritable promised land. Moreover, the fertile river valleys rewarded his toil with luxuriant harvests. But somehow prosperity eluded him. When, in spite of tremendous difficulties, he brought his produce to market, prices were often so low as to make his venture a failure.

[117] See, for example, *Annals of Congress*, 12 Cong., 1 Sess., pp. 626, 674, 676, and 710.

[118] *Expansionists of 1812* (New York, 1925); and "Western Aims in the War of 1812," *Mississippi Valley Historical Review*, XII, 36–50.

We know now that the farmers' troubles were, in no small degree, fundamentally matters of transportation, of communication, and of imperfect marketing and financial organization. But is it unexpected that in their disappointment (and not unlike their descendants of today who still are inclined to magnify political factors) they put the blame for their economic ills upon foreign restriction of their markets and supported the Embargo and Non-Intercourse acts as weapons to coerce the European belligerents to give them what they regarded as their rights? And when peaceful methods failed and prices fell to even lower levels, is it surprising that the hopeful settlers of earlier years became the War Hawks of 1812?

GEORGE ROGERS TAYLOR

AMHERST COLLEGE

Stephen M. Millett

BELLICOSE NATIONALISM IN OHIO:
AN ORIGIN OF THE WAR OF 1812

Perhaps no other aspect of early American diplomatic historiography has been argued as much as the causes of the War of 1812. The argument has raged largely among professors who have tried over the years to explain the war in terms contemporary to their own biases. Patriotic historians have seen the war in terms of altruistic national honour; Western historians have viewed it from the frontier perspective; economic determinists have interpreted it according to economic dialectics. Historians have argued much, but agreed seldom. No single interpretation has satisfied the entire community of diplomatic historians.

A major methodological problem in dealing with the causes of the War of 1812 is that scholars have too often researched the national sources rather than examine the evidence of the seventeen states of the Union. Even regional studies have been often too general to adequately explain the war fever of 1812 at the individual state or local level. This paper will review the principal theories of the causes of the War of 1812 and demonstrate why they fail to apply to the Western state of Ohio. It presents an alternative interpretation which stresses the psychological aspects of American frontier nationalism in the early nineteenth century.

I

There are two general schools of War of 1812 historiography. The first emphasizes the maritime controversy with Great Britain and American national honour. This school is further divided between the early group of writers (1815-1911) and the neo-maritime group (1940-1970). The second school stresses the Western origins of the war. It is divided into three groups accord-

ing to different perspectives: land hunger (1855, 1911, 1924);
the Indian menace (1911, 1920, 1925); and economic depression
(1930, 1931, 1956).

For the war's early chroniclers there was no question that the
conflict had been caused by British encroachments on American
sovereignty on the high seas. Robert B. McAfee, a captain of Kentucky militia under General William Henry Harrison, asserted that
Americans had fought against British ambitions to reconquer the
United States. While he took into account the Indian problem on
the frontier, he stated that "the evils we experienced on the ocean
were now infinitely more intolerable than those of the interior."[1]
The idea of British designs to regain her former colonial possessions ·
south of the Great Lakes appeared repeatedly in the patriotic
ante-bellum histories. [2] Besides British challenges to American
sovereignty on the high seas, tangential ideological reasons pitted
the republican United States against the encroachments of British
monarchism. [3]

The most sophisticated group of the early maritime school were
the historians who placed the Anglo-American commercial conflict
in the perspective of the Napoleonic Wars in Europe. Theodore
Lyman, writing the first comprehensive American diplomatic
history in 1826, pictured the self-conscious American republic
caught between the harsh maritime policies of London and Paris.
He asserted that neutrality was the Jefferson administration's key
policy to keep the United States out of the maelstrom of European
politics; yet its stance directly clashed with British naval warfare
against France. [4] His thesis was elaborated in Henry Adams'
famous multi-volume history of the Jefferson and Madison administrations. Although critical of Madison, Adams concluded that
war with England was the only honourable alternative in 1812
after numerous British violations of the President's commercial
policy. He conceded that the Indian threat to the frontier was a
consideration, but only as a possible complication in Anglo-
American diplomatic relations. [5] The prominent naval historian
Alfred Thayer Mahan offered much detail to support the thesis
that the War of 1812 was but an episode in the history of English
naval domination of the Atlantic. In Mahan's eyes, impressment
and the blockade were the sole reasons for the second war with
England.[6] In 1906 Professor Kendric Charles Babcock restated
Adams and Mahan in what was widely accepted then as the authoritative explanation of the causes of the 1812 War. [7]

In the early decade of this century, some historians began to
challenge the maritime thesis. Following the pioneering scholarship
of frontier historian Frederick Jackson Turner, professors became

more aware of Western influences on national policy. They began to pay more attention to the Indian question and American territorial ambitions which Babcock had dismissed as "mere perplexities." During the 1920s and 1930s, the theses of Western war origins eclipsed the maritime thesis to the point where some historians believed that the West and South had dragged the nation into a war for its own peculiar interests.

Meanwhile Professor A. L. Burt, an expert on American-Canadian relations, revived the maritime thesis in 1940. The War of 1812, he argued, had to be seen as a peripheral action of the Napoleonic Wars. Britain could not allow free American trade with France, and therefore harassed American merchant ships and seamen. Impressment, Burt continued, became the principal conflict between the United States and Great Britain because it raised the fundamental question of American sovereignty and national identity; London viewed Washington's policy as benefiting France and Washington viewed London's policy as an attack on the independence it had won in 1783. Burt concluded that Canada was the object of American invasion as the only strategic way to strike at England, rather than a goal in itself. [8]

The neo-maritime group has concentrated on how the maritime issue directly affected different aspects of national life. Reginald Horsman has argued that the commercial problems on the seacoast caused by the British navy had a depressing effect on the nation's infant economy.[9] Norman K. Risjord and Roger H. Brown have interpreted the maritime issue in relation to Republican Party politics and doctrine and the effect it had on the national ideology.[10] Harry L. Coles, in his 1965 military history of the war, reviewed the various theses for the war causes and concluded that the maritime school had the strongest argument.[11] In 1968 Anglo-American diplomatic expert Bradford Perkins, sounding very much like Lyman, Adams, and Mahan, concluded after extensive research in English archives that the maritime issue was indeed so important to both sides that it was the primary *casus belli* in 1812.[12]

In 1911 two different theses about Western war origins inaugurated the second historiographical school. As early as 1855 a Canadian had argued that the 1812 war had been one of American aggression against Canada to seize more land.[13] Frederick Jackson Turner, who delivered his famous frontier thesis in 1893, gave a new stimulus to historians to examine Western influences on national affairs. In 1901, the Wisconsin professor referred to Western land cupidity and the Indian tensions of 1811-1812 on the Wabash River as a cause for the War of 1812.[14] Howard T. Lewis in 1911 asked a penetrating question that perplexed historians: if the war was for neutral maritime rights, why did the shipping interests oppose it and the distant interior support it? Lewis restated the whole war question in terms of regional interests rather than abstract national pride. His answer was that the West wanted to conquer Canada and the South desired to annex Florida, and they used the maritime issue as a pretext to force war on the old North. [15]   D. R. Anderson, writing the same year as Lewis, approached the problem from the same viewpoint, but concluded that the West wanted war primarily to eliminate the Indian threat to its security. [16]

Lewis' thesis was rediscovered after the First World War by economic determinist Louis M. Hacker, who raised the same "disturbing and unconvincing situation" as to sectional alignment as had Lewis. Hacker flatly rejected the national honour thesis, and he portrayed the war as resulting solely from the desire of Westerners for annexation of Canadian agricultural land. [17]

Four years before Hacker's article, however, Christopher B. Coleman had argued that Westerners had wanted to conquer Canada, not for land, but to eliminate British influence over the Indian tribes of the Great Lakes. [18]   In 1925 Julius Pratt, elaborating on the works of Anderson and Coleman, presented a thesis that dominated historical thinking for twenty years. In direct response to Hacker, Pratt rejected Western hunger for Canadian land as the principal cause of war. He defined the West not merely as the Ohio Valley but as the entire frontier crescent from Maine through western New York to Illinois and south through Mississippi to Florida. To the Westerners, the primary concern was Indians, and the conquest of Canada was a means to that end. Pratt argued that while there was no real reason for alarm, Westerners feared possible Indian attacks after the Battle of Tippecanoe in November 1811. To the Southerners, the Indian menace was of great concern along with the desire to annex Spanish Florida. As a result of a political understanding, the young Republican expansionists of the West and South voted for war in June 1812 over the opposition of the Northeast. [19]

Hacker had argued that the West had had no economic interest in the maritime issue, therefore it went to war for its own peculiar interest in land. Pratt had stressed politics and fear of Indians, more or less avoiding the economic situation. Economist George Rogers Taylor argued in 1930 and 1931 that the West was critically affected economically by the Anglo-American commercial war. In examining retail price indices from 1804 to 1812 at New Orleans, the principal port of Western produce export, Taylor discovered that a depressed condition in the West ensued after the Embargo Act of 1808. Economic recovery was only slight and irregular during the next four years, slumping again in 1812. Economic depression thus created rising discontent among Westerners, who sought recovery by war with England. [20]

Taylor's thesis replaced Pratt's in popularity until the neo-maritime studies of the 1960s. Margaret Latimer applied the Taylor thesis to South Carolina and presented impressive arguments for the war's commercial origins in the cotton-exporting South. [21] Taylor also had great influence on Horsman's studies of the Ohio Valley and the 1812 War. [22] Taylor's work remains today substantially unrevised.

II

As the first state created out of the Northwest Territory and the third most populated one west of the Alleghenies, Ohio figured prominently in the origins of the War of 1812. One way to test the validity of the four basic theses about Western war aims (land hunger, Indians, depression, and national honour) is to apply them to the Ohio case.

The Hacker thesis has been challenged so often that it seems needless to refute it once more. There is no evidence of any land hunger in Ohio or popular desire to conquer Canada prior to June 1812. On the contrary, newspaper advertisements for land give the impression that much rich land was still available. An editorial from a Marietta paper in August 1811 mentioned specifically the "fertility and cheapness of our lands" and the vast tracts not yet cultivated. [23] The editor of the Franklinton *Freeman's Chronicle* in his inaugural editorial in June 1812 also referred to Ohio's "immense quantities of fertile land."[24] Two English travellers who toured the state before the war marvelled at the quantity of fertile land still available to immigrants. [25]

There is evidence, however, that some Ohioans wanted to conquer Canada as a means to strike at the British. This strategic approach to Canada as a means to wage war against England has been mentioned by several historians. [26] Ohio newspapers frequently referred to conquering Canada as a means of revenge for British wrongs against the United States on the high seas. After the declaration of war the Cincinnati *Western Spy* published a speech which urged the conquest of British North America: "If then the Canadas be so valuable as a place of traffic in the hands of another government, why not at this time take them to ourselves, and add them to the union?"[27]

There is substantial but conflicting evidence to show that Ohioans were deeply concerned about the Indian menace, particularly after the Battle of Tippecanoe. [28] Behind the hostile tribes, Ohioans thought they detected the conspiratorial intrigues of omnipresent British agents. Was the Indian threat real or imaginary? Hacker did not take it seriously because there were only three thousand Indians spread over six million acres in contrast to some 230,000 whites. [29] Pratt argued that while there was no reasonable Indian menace to white settlements, it was a psychological fear that motivated Westerners to combat it, real or not. [30] On the other hand, Burt, having examined material in the Canadian archives, found no evidence that British authorities were encouraging the tribes to attack the Americans before June 1812. On the contrary, British agents were restraining the chiefs hostile to the Americans from initiating a frontier war. [31]

Except for the eastern and northern periphery of the state, where farms were scattered and isolated, there was no Indian threat to Ohio. Ohio historians for fifty years have stated that Ohioans in 1812 did not go to war *because* of the Indian problem. [32] Ohioans saw the Indian threat in relation to their deep-seated animosities toward England; they viewed the Indian scare within the perspective of fifty years of Anglophobia. Captain McAfee, writing in 1816 about the British intrigues with the chiefs, recorded that "although this interference with the Indians was not an obvious and ostensible cause of the war, yet it may fairly be considered as a very efficient cause . . .", although he considered the neutral rights issue as more important. [33]

Interestingly enough, there was a definite relationship between partisan politics and the Indian scare in the newspapers and private correspondence of the period. This may have indicated that the Indian issue was part of a larger question. Pro-administration Republicans viewed the Indian trouble after 1811 with great alarm; conservatives, Anglophiles, and Federalists did not.

The center of the political controversy was William Henry Harrison, governor of the Indiana Territory. Harrison was a major Republican figure north of the Ohio River and anything he did drew the fire of Federalists. Son of a Virginian signatory of the Declaration of Independence, and son-in-law of Judge John Cleves Symmes, land speculator of the Miami Valley, he had played a prominent role before 1800 in the political contest between the obstructionist Federalist Governor of the Northwest Territory and the Republican settlers in Ohio who wanted statehood. Harrison had been the Territorial Delegate to Congress, where he had successfully lobbied for the Land Act of 1800. That same year, he became the first territorial governor of Indiana. His clash with Tecumseh and the Shawnees eleven years later was largely over land surveying and selling, in which Harrison had a personal interest. The Governor's pre-emptive campaign against the Prophet's Village on the Wabash River resulted in the bloody battle of Tippecanoe on November 7, 1811.[34]

Harrison was bitterly criticized for precipitating an Indian war by those who were also critical of President Madison's policies. He also drew the fire of some Republicans. The death on the Wabash of James H. Davies, an important Kentucky Republican politician and militia leader, produced a sharp reaction against Harrison in parts of Kentucky.[35] In Dayton, Ohio, the anti-Madison *Ohio Centinel* unfavourably contrasted Harrison's blunders with General "Mad" Anthony Wayne's victory at Fallen Timbers in 1794.[36] Harrison was initially so discouraged by outspoken criticism that he considered resigning his command.[37]

Republican partisans, on the other hand, portrayed the Prophet's attack on Harrison at Tippecanoe as the introduction of a major crisis. The Cincinnati *Western Spy* ran an extra announcing "War! War! War! The Blow Is Struck."[38] In the eyes of Anglophobe Republicans, the British were fully responsible for the battle. "We are then persuaded that the Indian war will be found to be really *British*. The Savages [are] only the allies of GREATER *Savages*," declared the Lexington *Reporter*.[39] The uproar created in Ohio by Tippecanoe prompted Ohio Senator Thomas Worthington to write to his state's governor, Return Jonathan Meigs, Jr., "The late unfortunate occurrence on the Wabash I fear will be the means of exciting the greatest alarm on the frontiers of Ohio and if it ends in alarms only I shall be thankful."[40]

Throughout the first half of 1812 the same Ohio newspapers that protested against British insults to American rights on the seas raised the spectre of a British-inspired Indian war. The Steubenville *Western Herald*, a zealous pro-Madison paper, reported in November 1811 that British agents had approached the Chickasaws for an anti-American alliance.[41] The Circleville *Fredonian*, a Republican journal circulated throughout the state, claimed that the Wabash tribes were threatening a frontier war.[42] This paper considered such a threat more of an outrage than a menace. It demanded the removal of "those treacherous and perfidious savages" from Ohio's border and revenge for Indian atrocities.[43] In April 1812 the *Fredonian* called for another General Wayne to deal with the Indians and another George Washington to drive the English out of Canada.[44]

Yet as war came closer, newspapers on the periphery, where communities were exposed to Indian attack, were wary of war scares. When the *Western Spy* published a letter from the Governor of the Illinois Territory predicting an Indian war,[45] the Dayton *Ohio Centinel* dismissed it as "alarmist."[46] The Worthington *Western Intelligencer* took a dim view of a rumour of an Indian attack that had created panic in the town.[47] The papers also printed information to relieve the tension. The *Ohio Centinel* reprinted a letter from Indian agent John Johnson to the Cincinnati *Liberty Hall* in January 1812 reporting that the tribes were unfavourable to the Prophet's attack on Harrison and that "there is not any danger to be apprehended at present on any part of our frontiers."[48] It also published Johnson's letter to Governor Meigs that there were only 2,000 red men, women, and children inside Ohio.[49] The newspapers gave full details of the Massasinwee Indian Council of May 15 and the Urbana Council with Meigs on June 6, when the chiefs of twelve tribes pledged neutrality in case of an Anglo-American war.[50]

The real significance of the Indian scare in Ohio was that it frightened defenseless farmers from their land and stunted settlement of the frontier areas. As one paper put it, this was not in the "interests" of Ohioans.[51] The whole town of Sandusky was threatened with extinction as people moved away.[52] Governor Meigs received several petitions from remote settlements that warned of de-population and abandoned crops if they did not receive militia protection. The petition from Danbury in Huron County is particularly revealing. Within the last year, it reported, a hundred settlers had emigrated to the town from the Eastern states, and they were the ones most anxious about the Indian scare. Danbury's distress stemmed from the lack of defense in the case of a national war rather than fear of an immediate Indian attack.[53] During the spring of 1812, Meigs deployed rangers along the western frontier and mustered 5,000 militia — more than enough to handle the Indians.[54] But when the militia left camp in Dayton on June 1, it did not march west to the Indiana Territory, but north toward Detroit and Canada.[55]

To most Ohioans, the Indian threat, whether they took it seriously or not, was only another source of irritation caused by the British. It was not by itself a major cause of war, but only a part of a much larger nationalistic mood. The Indian menace was added to British impressment of sailors and the blockade in the list of English wrongs against the United States.[56] In December 1811 the state General Assembly stated that "when we reflect on recent occurrences on the Wabash new sources of grief and sympathy are open" in a resolution supporting Madison in a firm stand against London. [57] In an April 1812 address to the militia, Colonel James Denny referred to the Indian problem as "additional proof of their [British] determined hostility towards this country . . . of their hatred to the free institutions which form the basis of our happy constitution."[58] Ohioans did not view the Eastern maritime grievance as an excuse to wage war against the tribes. They saw the Indian question as another British threat to American security and sovereignty.

All factors considered, Ohioans on the whole favoured war in 1812 principally because of maritime issues. Hacker and Pratt could not accept this fact as they found no concrete Ohioan interest in the commercial problems of the East. Taylor and Horsman tried to show that the West was economically hurt by the commercial depression in the East as a result of Republican policy and the British blockade. Roger H. Brown suggested that since the West was predominantly Republican, it had a political stake in the success of Madison's foreign policy. These theories apply to Ohio no better than those of Hacker and Pratt.

There was no depression in 1812 that would have motivated Ohioans for a war, a fact which Taylor recognized. In his 1931 article, Taylor specifically excluded Ohio from his generalizations about Western economic difficulties. [59] That depression did occur in several parts of the country and that some blamed their economic plight on the British appears to be true. Taylor's argument, however, was based primarily on Kentucky and Tennessee, states which had a much greater interest in exporting produce than Ohio. Bernard Mayo's examination of Kentucky newspapers gave much support to Taylor's analysis of that state [60] and Latimer has successfully applied Taylor's thesis to South Carolina. [61] Ohio, however, was not exporting produce before 1812 in any significant amount and it was certainly not dependent on export trade for its prosperity.

Taylor made several other observations about the West as a whole which were not true of Ohio. [62] Prosperity was not gauged by money received for selling agricultural produce at New Orleans prices. Sending produce down the Ohio and Mississippi Rivers was dangerous and infrequent before the introduction of steamships. Cincinnati, not New Orleans, was the market for Ohio goods. Taylor erred when he implied that Ohio farmers paid all land purchase obligations and debts in hard money. The economy before 1815 was still so underdeveloped that many transactions were done by barter. Cincinnati merchants frequently received produce in return for finished goods. They in turn exported produce for money, but this does not support Taylor's generalizations about money-poor agrarian Ohioans. [63]

Horsman, who borrowed heavily from Taylor's works, asserted that while trade was small it was vital as it represented the difference between subsistence and prosperity. [64] This was not true in Ohio. Ohio farmers were not dependent on export prices as they sold their surpluses internally to the wave of immigrants who came to Ohio during this period. In 1800 there had been only 45,365 people in the Ohio region; by 1810 the state's population had grown five fold. [65] The peculiar aspect of Ohio's economy was that imported finished goods, as well as settlers, came over the mountains from the East while Ohioan flour was shipped down the Mississippi. There was virtually no upstream trade. Ohio was more closely linked economically with Baltimore and Philadelphia than with New Orleans. Moreover, the Embargo and Non-Importation laws gave the Ohio economy an enormous lift by stimulating domestic manufacturing, especially in Cincinnati. The internal market was further enriched by farmers exchanging produce for goods made in the local towns. [66]

There is no evidence of any depression in the Ohio newspapers of the time. On the contrary, they were highly optimistic about the future. The Cincinnati *Western Spy* was filled with advertisements of new shops and factories. In January 1812 a brewery opened in Cincinnati and advertised to buy grain. [67] By the end of the war, breweries were consuming over 40,000 bushels of local barley. [68] The Dayton *Ohio Centinel*, in May 1811, bemoaned the fact that international relations had dampened the *prospect* of a rich market at New Orleans, but in August it stated that while there was no regular export market, flour could always be sold locally. [69] In Meigs' address to the legislature in December 1811, he referred to Ohio's "copious abundance" and he observed that the state was "as prosperous as the unexampled disorder of the political world will permit." [70] Ohioans may have felt that all the riches for which they had staked their lives in the wilderness were yet unfulfilled because of foreign policy difficulties, but they did not want war in 1812 principally for commercial reasons.

Nor did Ohio support the war out of any political consensus or uncritical loyalty to Madison. Ohio was overwhelmingly Republican, but the state party had two factions, one of which contained former Federalists hostile to the administration. The New Englanders who settled in Marietta, the Western Reserve, and Cincinnati were torn between their previous political loyalties to the party of Hamilton and Adams and their new Western interests championed by the party of Jefferson. Ohio Federalists who became conservative Republicans had an important influence on elections. Chillicothe, in the heart of the Virginia Military District, was the center of southern, pro-administration Republicans. By 1812 the Ohio party was split between a liberal faction labeled "Tammany," and a coalition of conservatives, called "Quids." Senator Thomas Worthington, a native of Virginia, belonged to the former; Governor Meigs, a Connecticut Yankee, to the latter. [71]

Neither faction benefitted from the war to the exclusion of the other. The liberal faction was confident that a war declaration would be so well received in Ohio that it would unite the party behind it for the 1812 elections. [72] Worthington had lost the gubernatorial election of 1810 to Meigs, and he hoped to run again in 1812. If he had been motivated by personal political considerations, he would have voted for the war resolution. Because of the lack of preparation for war in Ohio and its defenselessness against an Anglo-Indian invasion, Worthington refused to vote for total war. He voted for a maritime war with England, and France, but against the motion that the Senate finally passed. Ohio's other Senator, Alexander Campbell, did not vote at all because he was home with a sick child. Jeremiah Morrow, Ohio's only Representative, probably voted for war more out of loyalty to the administration than conviction. In the 1812 election, four months later, Meigs (whom the Jeffersonians wanted to defeat) won re-election easily. Worthington had lost so much popularity by his negative vote that he did not even run for Governor. All six new Congressmen were Republicans, but only one came from the Tammany faction. President Madison also carried all of Ohio's electors. While the party as a whole benefitted from the war declaration, the pro-Madison faction within Ohio did not. [73]

The maritime issue in its own right held the continued interest of the public. All the major Ohio newspapers carried front page news from Washington on the negotiations with London. They gave much more space to national events than to regional or even local news. While opinion was divided on war itself, it was unified in its indignation toward British insults to national honour. In September 1811 (two months before Tippecanoe) the editor of the *Western Intelligencer* wrote in reference to the maritime conflict:

> Does England suppose that we are too cowardly, or too impotent to defend ourselves; too stupid, too passive to assert our rights; too submissive and humble to resent such unparalleled wrongs? Or does she consider us so far beneath her imperial dignity that she may, with impunity continue her injurious conduct? If these are her calculations, will not the zeal of our forefathers, that spirit of '76, arouse us to reassert our country's rights? [74]

The editor of the *Ohio Centinel*, who was no war hawk, urged the frontiersmen to "stand firm on your own soil, the only land of liberty on the map of the civilized world."[75]   In December 1811 the Republican *Fredonian* requested Congress to take a firm stand against London and regain America's national character and dignity in the eyes of other nations. [76]

In the state capital, Zanesville, the out-going Governor Samuel Huntington addressed the legislature in January 1811 on the national crisis with England. He did not mention either Indians or the economy. Huntington (and later his successor, Meigs) urged the state assembly to continue their patient support of President Madison's "impartial and pacific conduct of our government."[77] Huntington and Meigs, so it seems, were cautioning bellicose Ohioans not to press for a war that they were not prepared to fight. The General Assembly, however, passed a resolution enumerating grievances against England, of which neutral rights violations were primary: "We will suffer every hardship — submit to every privation in support of our country's rights and honor."[78]

As Anglo-American diplomatic tension grew worse, Ohio editors became more bellicose in tone. The *Fredonian* editor praised Congress for increasing the size of the army and declared: "Having, from a love of peace, and an indisposition to engage in European warfare, been for five years past reluctantly content with measures of commercial restriction; and now, perceiving that forebearance and remonstrance have failed to procure a respect of our rights; the people, their spirit aroused by the indignities they have witnessed, loudly call for measures of a strong character."[79]   The *Western Intelligencer* asked: "Is there an American who can behold with indifference, much less approves the frequent captures and condemnation of our ships? Every breast that possesses the least spark of humanity or patriotism must glow with indignation at the savage barbary [sic] with which thousands of the American people are detained on board British men of war . . ."[80]

The editor of the *Fredonian* highly praised the Twelfth Congress "who have so generously determined to repel the unjust and unparalleled depredations of Great Britain on the high seas, and her infamous violations of the most sacred of our national rights..."[81] As early as March 1812, he called on Ohioans to support Congress in a war with England as a "redress from all our grievances" and "to secure to our beloved country the full enjoyment of all her rights."[82]

Not all editors wanted war, but never did they favour the continuation of unsatisfactory relations with London. When war was declared in June, no important editor in Ohio opposed it. "Let us convince Great Britain that, though we were divided on the propriety of the measure, when once adopted it shall be seconded by the united energies of the nation," wrote the editor of the *Ohio Centinel.* [83] The Chillicothe *Supporter*, after commenting on the enthusiastic popular reaction to the war announcement, concluded that "It appears that Congress have, at last, taken a firm and decided stand — they have *declared war*, and however we may differ in political sentiments it now becomes the duty of every citizen to cling to his country and rise or fall with it." [84] An editorial from the Cincinnati *Freeman's Journal* was widely republished and seems to reflect a consensus: "Since war is declared, duty will impel every citizen, with no distinction of party, to obey; and honor, and patriotism, and love of country (for we know no country on earth but America) will now steel every honest heart and nerve every arm, to support our country through her present difficulties." [85]

This paper has attempted to show that many Ohioans favoured war with England before June 1812. Ohioans did not want war because of land hunger, or to end the Indian tension, or to relieve a non-existing depression, or for partisan political reasons. Ohio went to war primarily because of national honour. [86] But what stake *did* Ohioans have in that issue?

The psychology of bellicose nationalism was probably the fundamental reason why Ohioans went to war in 1812. To the first generation frontiersmen, patriotism was no mere abstract concept to cover other, selfish interests. Nationalism was their sense of identity in the wilderness, of belonging to something solid and respectful. Ohioans were no longer New Englanders, Pennsylvanians, Virginians, or Europeans. Yet they were not exactly "Ohioans" in that they belonged to an established state with a fully developed character, like Virginians or New Yorkers. Nationalism meant that they belonged to the United States of America, no matter where they were or who they were, and enjoyed all the rights and immunities of American citizenship.

Nationalism, in part, is a psychological product of social mobility. [87] In the American frontier experience, this was predominantly horizontal mobility from one well-established locale to an underdeveloped region. In 1775 there had been less than 30,000 people in the Pittsburgh-Upper Ohio Valley area. Fifteen years later there were only two settlements in Ohio, Marietta and Cincinnati. The census of 1800, the first to record an Ohio population, listed 45,365 people in seven counties along the north bank of the Ohio River. A tremendous migration hit Ohio after it became a state in 1803. By 1810 the state's population was 227,843 with 52% of it

in the interior counties.[88]   These were first-generation Ohioans
eager to make new livings in the frontier, but also anxious of their
new social status and identity.

The people of Ohio were of mixed origins and predominantly
young in age. New Englanders settled in Marietta, the Connecticut
Western Reserve, and the Miami Valley. Virginians settled in the
Scioto Valley. Cincinnati was a blend of immigrants from New
England and the Middle States, principally New Jersey. Manchester
on the Ohio was founded by Kentuckians. Germans and Scots-
Irish from Pennsylvania came to Youngstown and the Mahoning
Valley. A colony of French founded Gallopolis. All of these people
did not lose their native identities immediately. In the search for a
common social identity, they were Americans before they became
Ohioans. [89]

One-third of all Ohioans in 1810 were between the ages of sixteen and forty-four. A full 18% of the state's population were free
white males of that age group. Less than 10% of Ohioans were over
forty-four years old (20,443 as compared with 89,707 under the
age of ten!) [90]   For these young people from various backgrounds,
nationalism was no doubt a very comforting emotion. It gave them
not only identity but also a feeling of security. Having lost the
security of the community from which they left, they often felt
alone when they moved to an area populated by strangers. The
bond between scattered frontiersmen was their common national
identity. [91]

In Europe, nationalism was based on common descent, religion,
language, or history.[92]   In the United States, nationalism arose
from the common experience, and that was the struggle for the
present and a better future. A general faith in their republican
ideals and democratic institutions was a common trait among
frontiersmen, the ones who carried American values to the
interior. [93]

British attacks on American sovereignty on the high seas raised
serious anxieties to Ohio's first generation citizens. Impressment
of sailors humiliated patriots who wanted to establish a firm basis
in international law for American national identity. When sailors
were denied their rights of American citizenship, their plight was
shared by Ohioans. [94]   Perhaps they feared that a national government that abandoned the rights of seamen would also forsake the
rights of pioneers. Congressman John McLean of Lebanon summarized well the empathy of Ohioans for impressed sailors in
January 1814: ". . . Suppose the Orders in Council are repealed,
does that act heal the bleeding wounds of our country? Are the
thousands of American seamen held in British servitude — taken by

force — and compelled to fight the battles of our enemy, are these to be neglected and forgotten? ... The strong arm of the community must be raised in behalf of one of its members; a Government that refuses this is unworthy of confidence, the sooner it is dissolved the better."[95]

The British infringements of American citizens at sea by forceful impressment and their insults to American sovereignty deeply wounded national pride in the hinterland. The security of a common identity in a highly mobile society afforded in nationalism would mean nothing if American sovereignty meant nothing in international law. Some of the expected benefits of nationalism were internal law and order and security from outside threats.[96] This was precisely what was at stake in the Anglo-American crisis of 1812. Anglophobia also provided a common enemy for Americans which linked frontiersmen with each other and with their eastern countrymen. To Ohioans, the strength and dignity of the United States reflected on their own psychological and physical security.[97]

Perhaps the greatest fallacy of Hacker and Pratt (and Taylor to a lesser degree) was in viewing the West as one region with common interests. A region is not unified unless there is constant communication and trade within it.[98] As it has already been seen, Ohio was more closely connected in terms of population flow, finished goods, and news with Washington and Philadelphia than with Lexington and New Orleans. The common bond between Ohioans and Kentuckians was simply their mutual connection with the Eastern seaboard and their common loyalty to the government in Washington.

Besides the covert psychology of nationalism, Ohioans had an overt interest in national affairs in Washington. Ohio, unlike the original states, was national real estate whose statehood was created by the general government. National finances determined land prices in Ohio; national military strength determined the security of the borders (it had been General Wayne and a national army that had defeated the Ohio tribes at Fallen Timbers in 1794); national politics and administrative policies determined the social and economic progress of the state. Ohioans were very much concerned with how well Madison handled national problems, particularly how effectively he conducted foreign affairs.[99]

By 1812 many Ohioans wanted Congress to take a firmer stand against British violations of American sovereignty. They generally applauded the election of Henry Clay as Speaker of the House in 1811, which guaranteed all Westerners a loud voice in the conduct of national affairs. "It is worthy of remark," wrote an Ohio politician to Senator Worthington, "that the Western country will now command respect abroad, both for its talents and its numbers . . . and the supposed 'wilds of America' will no longer be looked upon with indifference." [100] Two others advised Worthington that only a hard-line policy (as personified by Clay), even war, was the only way to avenge British insults to national honour. [101]

In 1811 Governor Meigs expressed well Western nationalism in his inaugural address: ". . . Our strength is our union; to cultivate sentiments of union is then a duty, worthy of being cherished with a holy zeal, commensurate to the importance of national independence," and "A fervent attachment to our country and its free institutions, is a principle of predominant obligation. — Foreign influence is the harbinger of destruction to states which are free." [102] A year later, the *Fredonian* called on Congress to show the frontier as much consideration as it did for other sections, and frontiersmen to show their mettle in times of national crisis.[103] In April 1812 the *Supporter* reprinted "What Is Patriotism?" from the *Boston Centinel*. The article pointed out that patriotism in America replaced the role of subjects' loyalty in England as a social cement, and the time to prove one's patriotism was in war.[104] After the declaration of war, the *Western Intelligencer* observed that the war would contribute much to the promotion of patriotism throughout the country. [105]

In order to understand the causes of the War of 1812, historians must look at the state level first before drawing conclusions about regional or national war origins. The United States in 1812 was not a tightly unified nation. Indeed, the war itself was conducted as a series of regional actions with little national coordination. Likewise, historians sometimes must apply psychological models to understand human behaviour in an historical context. In this one case, the psychology of nationalism explains better than any other theory why Ohioans wanted war in 1812.

U. S. Air Force Institute of Technology,
Wright-Patterson A.F.B., Ohio

1. Robert B. McAfee, *History of the Late War in the Western Country* (n.p., 1816 [Reprinted, Bowling Green, Ohio, 1919]), pp. 9-16.

2. H. M. Brackenridge, *History of the Late War Between the United States and Great Britain* (Philadelphia, 1839), pp. 13-15; John Armstrong, *Notices of the War of 1812*, 2 vols. (New York, 1840), I, pp. 9-13; J. T. Headley, *The Second War with England*, 2 vols. (New York, 1853), I, pp. 15-16.

3. Brackenridge, *ibid.*, pp. 15-17 and 27-28; Samuel Perkins, *A History of the Political and Military Events of the Late War Between the United States and Great Britain* (New Haven, Conn., 1825), pp. 16-17.

4. Theodore Lyman, Jr., *The Diplomacy of the United States*, 2 vols. (Boston, 1828), II, pp. 2, 8 and 49-50.

5. Henry Adams, *History of the United States of America During the First Administration of James Madison*, 2 vols. (New York, 1891), II, pp. 109-112, 114-115, 225-226 and *passim*.

6. A. T. Mahan, *Sea Power in its Relations to the War of 1812*, 2 vols. (London, 1905), I, pp. vii and 2.

7. Kendric Charles Babcock, *The Rise of American Nationality, 1811-1819. The American Nation: A History*, 26 vols. (New York, 1906), XIII, pp. xv, 37 and 55.

8. A. L. Burt, *The United States, Great Britain, and British North America from the Revolution to the Establishment of Peace after the War of 1812* (New Haven, 1940), pp. 207-208, 211-212 and 223-224.

9. Reginald Horsman, "Western War Aims, 1811-1812," *Indiana Magazine of History*, 53, No. 1 (March 1957), 1-18; *The Causes of the War of 1812* (New York, 1962); *The War of 1812* (New York, 1969); and *The Frontier in the Formative Years, 1783-1815* (New York, 1970), pp. 166-188. Horsman has written more on the 1812 War than any other current historian. In each work he has become more emphatic in his assertion that the maritime issue, for different reasons, was the primary cause of war.

10. Norman K. Risjord, "1812: Conservatives, War Hawks, and the Nation's Honor," *William and Mary Quarterly*, 18, No. 2 (April 1961), 196-210; Roger H. Brown, *The Republic in Peril: 1812* (New York, 1964).

11. Harry L. Coles, *The War of 1812* (Chicago, 1965), p. 33.

12. Bradford Perkins, *Prologue to War. England and the United States, 1805-1812* (Berkeley and Los Angeles, 1968), pp. 2-3, 5, 67-69, 284-285 and 437.

13. G. Auchinleck, *A History of the War Between Great Britain and the United States of America During the Years 1812, 1813, and 1814* (Toronto, 1855), pp. 38-39.

14. Frederick Jackson Turner, "The Middle West," (1901) in Turner, *The Frontier in American History*. With Foreword by Ray Allen Billington (New York, 1962), p. 134; also see Turner, "The Ohio Valley in American History," (1909) *ibid.*, p. 168.

15. Howard T. Lewis, "A Re-analysis of the Causes of the War of 1812," *Americana*, 6 (1911), 507, 511-514, 577-579 and 584.

16. Warren H. Goodman, "The Origins of the War of 1812: A Survey of Changing Interpretations," *Mississippi Valley Historical Review*, 28, No. 2 (September 1941), 174.

17. Louis Morton Hacker, "Western Land Hunger and the War of 1812: A Conjecture," *ibid.*, 10, No. 4 (March 1924), 365-395.

18. Christopher B. Coleman, "The Ohio Valley in the Preliminaries of the War of 1812," *ibid.*, 7, No. 1 (June 1920), 39-50.

19. Julius W. Pratt, "Western Aims in the War of 1812," *ibid.*, 12, No. 1 (June 1925), 36-50; Pratt, *Expansionists of 1812* (Gloucester, Mass., 1957 [1925]), pp. 9, 11-14, 54, 58 and 135-152.

20. George Rogers Taylor, "Prices in the Mississippi Valley Preceding the War of 1812," *Journal of Economic and Business History*, 3 (1930), 148-163; Taylor, "Agrarian Discontent in the Mississippi Valley Preceding the War of 1812," *Journal of Political Economy*, 39, No. 4 (August, 1931), 471-505. Statistical evidence for Taylor's thesis is in Arthur Harrison Cole, *Wholesale Commodity Prices in the United States, 1700-1861* (Cambridge, Mass., 1838), pp. 155, 158, 161-162. A similar article showing the economic effects of American trade policy is Herbert Heaton, "Non-Importation, 1806-1812," *Journal of Economic History*, 1, No. 2 (November 1941), 178-198.

21. Margaret Kincaid Latimer, "South Carolina - A Protagonist of the War of 1812," *American Historical Review*, 61, No. 4 (July 1956), 914-929.

22. See note 9.

23. *Ohio Centinel*, 22 August 1811. Editorials and stories of one paper were frequently reprinted by other papers, thus giving them state-wide circulation.

24. J. B. Gardiner, *Freeman's Chronicle*, 24 June 1812. Franklinton, on the west bank of the Scioto River opposite the site of Ohio's future capital, later became part of the city of Columbus.

25. Fortescue Cuming, *Sketches of a Tour to the Western Country* (Pittsburg, 1810) in Reuben Gold Thwaites, ed., *Early Western Travels, 1748-1846*, 32 vols. (Cleveland, 1904), IV, pp. 201 and *passim;* John Bradbury, *Travels in the Interior of America in the Years 1809, 1810, and 1811* (London, 1819), *ibid.*, V, pp. 285-286.

26. Pratt, *Expansionists of 1812, ibid.*, p. 188; Burt, *ibid.*, p. 207; Risjord, *ibid.*, 202; Horsman, *Causes of the War of 1812, ibid.*, pp. 169-170, 183 and 267; Perkins, *ibid.*, pp. 284-285.

27. William Hendricks at Hamilton County Courthouse, 4 July 1812; quoted in *Western Spy*, Cincinnati, 18 July 1812.

28. John F. Cady, "Western Opinion and the War of 1812," *Ohio Archaeological and Historical Publications*, 33 (1924), 427-474; W. M. Heflinger, "The War of 1812 in Northwest Ohio. Background and Causes," *Northwest Ohio Quarterly*, 22, No. 1 (Winter 1949-1950), 8-24; Donald Walter Curl, "Ohio Opinion During the War of 1812 Until the Victory of the River Thames," unpublished M.A. thesis,(Ohio State University, 1958), pp. 39-52.

29. Hacker, *ibid.*, 373.

30. Pratt, "Western Aims in the War of 1812," *ibid.*, 38-39.

31. Burt, *ibid.*, pp. 302-305 and 309.

32. Emilius O. Randall and Daniel J. Ryan, *History of Ohio. The Rise and Progress of an American State*, 5 vols. (New York, 1912), III, pp. 257-258; William T. Utter, *The Frontier State: 1803-1825. A History of the State of Ohio*, 6 vols. (Columbus, 1942, 1968), II, pp. 78-87; Eugene H. Rosebloom and Francis P. Weisenburger, *A History of Ohio* (Columbus, 1964), pp. 78-80.

33. McAfee, *ibid.*, pp. 10 and 16.

34. For biographies of Harrison, see Freeman Cleaves, *Old Tippecanoe. William Henry Harrison and His Times* (New York, 1939); and James A. Green, *William Henry Harrison. His Life and Times* (Richmond, 1941). In reference to Harrison's land speculation, see Cleaves, *ibid.*, pp. 69-84.

35. Adams, *ibid.*, II, pp. 106-107.

36. *Ohio Centinel*, 28 November 1811.

37. Harrison to Secretary of War William Eustis, 7 January 1812, in Richard C. Knopf, Jr., transcriber, *William Henry Harrison and the War of 1812. Document Transcriptions of the War of 1812 in the Northwest* (Columbus, 1957), I, p. 1.

38. *Western Spy*, 21 November 1811.

39. Articles from Lexington, Kentucky, *Reporter*, carried in *Ohio Centinel*, 28 November 1811.

40. Senator Thomas Worthington to Governor Return Jonathan Meigs, Jr., 30 November 1811, in Richard C. Knopf, Jr., transcriber, *Return Jonathan Meigs, Jr., and the War of 1812, Document Transcriptions of the War of 1812 in the Northwest* (Columbus, 1957), II, p. 92.

41. *Western Herald*, 6 November 1811.

42. *Fredonian*, 15 January 1812.

43. *Ibid.*, 26 February and 18 March 1812.

44. *Ibid.*, 8 April 1812.

45. *Western Spy*, 7 March 1812.

46. *Ohio Centinel*, 19 March 1812.

47. *Western Intelligencer*, 29 May 1812.

48. *Ohio Centinel*, 2 January 1812.

49. *Ibid.*, 5 March 1812.

50. *Western Intelligencer*, 26 June 1812; *Freeman's Chronicle*, 24 June 1812; *Ohio Centinel*, 4 June and 18 June 1812; *Trump of Fame*, 22 July 1812, reprinted in the *Ohio Archaeological and Historical Publications*, 28 (1919), 299-304 and 354-355.

51. *Western Intelligencer*, 20 November 1811.

52. *Ibid.*, 22 May 1812.

53. Petition to Meigs from Danbury (Huron County), 3 June 1812, in Knopf, *ibid.*, II, p. 8.

54. Isaac Van Horn to Meigs, 9 May 1812, *ibid.*, p. 135.

55. McAfee, *ibid.*, pp. 64-72.

56. *Western Intelligencer*, 11 September 1811.

57. Quoted by *Fredonian*, 25 December 1811.

58. *Ibid.*, 25 April 1812.

59. Taylor, *ibid.*, 494-495.

60. Bernard Mayo, *Henry Clay. Spokesman of the New West* (Boston, 1966 [1937]), pp. 382-383.

61. Latimer, *ibid.*, 924-929.

62. Taylor, *ibid.*, 148, 156, 162 and 163.

63. Randolph C. Downes, "Trade in Frontier Ohio," *Mississippi Valley Historical Review*, 16, No. 4 (March 1930), 467-494; Richard T. Farrell, "Cincinnati, 1800-1830: Economic Development-through Trade and Industry," *Ohio History*, 77, No. 4 (Autumn 1968), 111-129; Richard C. Wade, *The Urban Frontier. Pioneer Life in Early Pissburgh, Cincinnati, Lexington, Louisville, and St. Louis* (Chicago, 1959); Horsman, *The Frontier in the Formative Years, ibid.*, pp. 149-163. Unfortunately, there are no price indices for Cincinnati before 1815.

64. Horsman, "Western War Aims," *ibid.*, 5, 6, 9 and 18; *Causes of the War of 1812, ibid.*, pp. 175-176.

65. Beverley W. Bond, Jr., *The Foundations of Ohio. History of the State of Ohio*, 6 vols. (Columbus, 1941), I, pp. 394-395.

66. Wade, *ibid.*, pp. 26, 39, 41-42, 53, 54 and 55; Horsman, *Frontier in the Formative Years, ibid.*, pp. 154-155, 157 and 160-163; Farrell, *ibid.*, 111-114.

67. *Western Spy*, 25 January 1812.

68. Wade, *ibid.*, p. 58.

69. *Ohio Centinel*, 9 May and 22 August 1811.

70. *Ibid.*, 19 December 1811.

71. Homar C. Hockett, "Western Influences on Political Parties to 1825," *The Ohio State University Bulletin*, 22, No. 3 (August 1917), 51-62; Alfred Byron Sears, *Thomas Worthington. Father of Ohio Statehood* (Columbus, 1958), pp. 94, 98, 111, 137-138, 147 and 150-154; Utter, *ibid.*, pp. 32-62.

72. James Caldwell to Worthington, 14 December 1811; Lewis Cass to Worthington, 13 April 1812; John Hamm to Worthington, 18 June 1812, in Richard C. Knopf, Jr., transcriber, *Thomas Worthington and the War of 1812. Document Transcriptions of the War of 1812 in the Northwest* (Columbus, 1957), III, pp. 18, 79 and 98, respectively.

73. Sears, *Worthington, ibid.*, pp. 156-157 and 167-170; William R. Barlow, "Ohio's Congressmen and the War of 1812," *Ohio History*, 72, No. 3 (July 1963), 175-194; Leland R. Johnson, "The Suspense Was Hell: The Senate Vote for War in 1812," *Indiana Magazine of History*, 65, No. 4 (December 1969), 247-267.

74. *Western Intelligencer*, 11 September 1811. What aroused the editor's wrath was news of the presence of British agents among the Indians. This, together with the maritime crisis, was too much for him to endure.

75. *Ohio Centinel*, 10 October 1811.

76. *Fredonian*, 25 December 1811.

77. *Ohio Centinel*, 3 January 1811.

78. Quoted by *Western Intelligencer*, 8 January 1812.

79. *Fredonian*, 29 January 1812.

80. *Western Intelligencer*, 10 April 1812.

81. *Fredonian*, 18 March 1812.

82. *Ibid.*, 25 March 1812.

83. *Ohio Centinel*, 15 July 1812.

84. *Supporter*, 4 July 1812.

85. *Ibid.; Ohio Centinel*, 15 July 1812.

86. A study about Pennsylvania has come to the same conclusions as this paper has for Ohio. See Victor A. Sapio, *Pennsylvania and the War of 1812* (Lexington, Ky., 1970). After concluding that that state had gone to war for national honour, the author neglected to explain why.

87. Karl W. Deutsch, *Nationalism and Its Alternatives* (New York, 1969), pp. 21-25.

88. Bond, *ibid.*, pp. 181-182 and 395.

89. *Ibid.*, pp. 280-309, 321 and 351-371.

90. *Third Census, 1810* (Washington, 1811 [1919]), Book I, p. 70.

91. See Deutsch, *ibid.*, pp. 23-27; Hans Kohn, *The Idea of Nationalism. A Study in Its Origins and Background* (New York, 1944), pp. 10-14; Hans Kohn, *Nationalism: Its Meaning and History* (Princeton, 1965), pp. 9, 19-20 and 30; Kenneth E. Appel, "Nationalism and Sovereignty: A Psychiatric View," *Journal of Abnormal and Social. Psychology,* 40, No. 4 (October 1945), 355-367; Floyd H. Allport, "The Psychology of Nationalism. The Nationalistic Fallacy as a Cause of War," *Harpers Magazine,* 155 (August 1927), 291-301.

92. Kohn, *Nationalism, ibid.*, pp. 19-20. Also see Boyd C. Shafer, *Nationalism. Myth and Reality* (New York, 1955), pp. 7-8 and 56.

93. Frederick Jackson Turner, "The Significance of the Frontier in American History," (1893) in Turner, *ibid.*, p. 29; Merle Curti, *Roots of American Loyalty* (New York, 1967), pp. 42-45, 50 and 60-61.

94. S. Perkins, *ibid.*, pp. 16-17; Burt, *ibid.*, pp. 211-212; B. Perkins, *ibid.*, pp. vii-viii, 2-3 and 67-68.

95. McLean quoted by Francis P. Weisenburger, *The Life of John McLean* (Columbus, 1937), p. 13.

96. Boyd C. Shafer, *Faces of Nationalism. New Realities and Old Myths* (New York, 1972), p. 344. Also see p. 130.

97. See David M. Potter, "The Historian's Use of Nationalism and Vice Versa," *American Historical Review,* 67, No. 4 (July 1962), 925-926 and 936-937; and Leonard W. Doob, *Patriotism and Nationalism: Their Psychological Foundations* (New Haven, 1965), pp. 6 and 253-260.

98. Deutsch, *ibid.*, pp. 6-8, 14, 96 and 102. Also see Karl W. Deutsch, *Nationalism and Social Communication* (New York, 1953).

99. Curti, *ibid.*, pp. 118-119 and 148-150; B. Perkins, *ibid.*, pp. 172 and 437; Utter, *ibid.*, pp. 63-87.

100. Jessup N. Couch to Worthington, 16 November 1811, in Knopf, *ibid.*, III, p. 8.

101. Benjamin Hough to Worthington, 21 December 1811, and W. C. Nicholas to Worthington, 10 February 1812, *ibid.*, pp. 23, 24 and 56, respectively.

102. Meigs quoted by *Ohio Centinel,* 3 January 1811.

103. *Fredonian,* 18 March 1811.

104. *Supporter,* 25 April 1812.

105. *Western Intelligencer,* 3 July 1812.

South Carolina—A Protagonist of the War of 1812

Margaret Kinard Latimer

YOUNG Mr. Calhoun entered Congress prepared for a showdown. It was June 3, 1812, and the ambitious congressman from South Carolina would recommend war against England. The Foreign Relations Committee, of which he was chairman, had deliberated only two days on President Madison's message, but, after a forceful report in favor of war, John C. Calhoun presented a bill of declaration. A majority of the House followed his lead and on June 4 passed the act, the Senate concurring with some reluctance on June 18. Madison's signature, also of June 18, marked the official beginning of war.

The grievances against European powers for interfering with American ships and sailors on the high seas had gathered momentum in a continuous stream of events for more than a decade. The Jeffersonian policy of conciliation, restrictive measures, minimum armaments, and "peace at any price" had generally insured against violent ruptures.

Until the Twelfth Congress, legislation aimed at France or England had in reality been a jockeying of party strength in Congress. Although party voting was far from regular, the major portion of the Republicans and the Federalists debated hotly on the embargo and the succeeding restrictive measures. The erratic stands of the Quids accentuated the hodgepodge nature of congressional opinion as did certain courses taken by the New Englanders. Believing that the Republicans would never be forced into a war, Josiah Quincy of Massachusetts and many of his fellow New England Federalists voted steadily for armament and naval increases in order to antagonize the administration. Quincy wrote to Harrison Gray Otis on November 26, 1811, even suggesting that New England stand for war.[1] However, when it became evident that the young Republicans in the Twelfth Congress had plunged their peace-loving party into just that war, the Federalists pitched their tents in the opposite camp.

Henry Adams estimated that only a third of Congress was in favor of war early in 1812, yet on June 4 the bill in the House was carried 79-49.[2] The crystallization of sentiment had been the work of an enthusiastic group

---

[1] Samuel E. Morison, *Letters of Harrison Gray Otis* (Boston, 1913), II, 33-34.
[2] Henry Adams, *History of the United States of America* (New York, 1889–91), VI, 170.

914

of leaders in the Twelfth Congress who were responsible for a notable change in congressional foreign policy within the span of a few months. The story of the "War Hawks" is familiar, but still eminently impressive. It is important enough to warrant amplification and correction.

Of the five or six major "War Hawks" prominent in most accounts of the war, three were young South Carolina Republicans in Congress for the first time. John C. Calhoun, William Lowndes, and Langdon Cheves arrived in Washington with a motive in mind; they came if not pledged, at least committed, to oppose the prevailing Republican foreign policy. These three leaders in the war group frequently initiated actions so far from the old Jeffersonian line that even their fellow War Hawks sounded some misgivings.

Calhoun made his real debut in the Twelfth Congress on December 12, 1811, when he spoke in opposition to the mercurial John Randolph. The subject before the House was the recommendation for armament made by the Foreign Relations Committee, which in the opinion of Mr. Randolph and many others had veered well off the Jeffersonian course. In an effective rebuttal, Calhoun presented ideas still further from the original tenets of the Republican party, which he nominally represented. "I know of but one principle to make a nation great," reasoned the South Carolinian, ". . . and that is to protect every citizen in the lawful pursuit of his business. . . . Protection and patriotism are reciprocal."[3] These sentences seemed almost to echo a phase of Hamiltonianism.

The second South Carolinian, Langdon Cheves, as chairman of the Naval Committee spoke at length in January maintaining the power of the President to use voluntary militia forces in time of war. Such nationalization, obviously anathema to old-line Jeffersonians, also appeared unduly risky to some of Cheves's belligerent cohorts. Later that month when Cheves requested an appropriation for twelve seventy-fours and twenty frigates at the cost of seven and a half million dollars, he was supported by a large number of the war group as well as the Federalists, but the bill failed by a close vote of 62-59. Clearly prompting Cheves's individual efforts were the underlying objectives of the South Carolinians—an effective navy and its complement, free-flowing international trade. William Lowndes of South Carolina, speaking on behalf of the frigates, well illustrated their policy:

The Constitution was not formed for the exclusive protection of commerce, but for the defense of all the interests of the United States. . . . But is it in this nation, and at this time that the profits of commerce are confined to the merchant? Your trade was, a few years ago unrestrained and flourishing—did it not enrich the

[3] *Annals of Congress*, 12 Cong., 1 sess., p. 479. All subsequent references to *Annals* except where specified denote the Twelfth Congress, First Session.

most distant parts of your country? It has since been plundered and confined. Does the industry of the country languish? Is not the income of every man impaired?[4]

The concern of South Carolina with commerce became increasingly obvious. When the Committee on Foreign Relations in March, 1812, planned a ninety-day emergency embargo—information about which was supposedly to be withheld from public notice until passage—Calhoun opportunely informed Josiah Quincy, leader of the New England commercial interests. Eastern longshoremen were consequently set at work to load as many ships as possible and clear them from the ports, and undoubtedly the southern waterfronts were in the midst of similar activity.[5]

The joint efforts of Lowndes, Cheves, and Calhoun were directed in April toward a measure to authorize the importation of goods from Great Britain which had been contracted for before February, 1811. Having no success with this, on June 19 Cheves introduced a bill for the suspension of non-importation, and Calhoun hastened to its support: "The restrictive system, as a mode of resistance . . . has never been a favorite one with me. . . . I object to the restrictive system."[6] In essence, Calhoun was rejecting on the floor of Congress the major basis of the Jeffersonian foreign policy.

When Calhoun led his fellow congressmen in requesting a declaration of war, he was displaying not only the views of the three most aggressive South Carolina representatives but a real solidarity in the constituents whom he represented. True, not all eight South Carolinians in the House voted as a bloc on every measure. David R. Williams, chairman of Military Affairs, had been in Congress during most of the Jeffersonian decade and accepted in general such established party measures as restriction, yet he had always acted independently and as early as the Tenth Congress had looked favorably toward war. He spoke forcefully for the cause of armaments and resistance to Great Britain: "It has been said our Constitution is not calculated to sustain a war. It surely is not calculated for submission."[7] The other representatives, Moore, Earle, Butler, and Winn, had also been in earlier Jeffersonian Congresses, the latter two prominent Revolutionary soldiers. They belonged to a different generation from the young Calhoun, Cheves, and Lowndes, and their approaches to problems were similarly varied, but they shared fundamental principles based on the desires of their constituents at home. A majority of South Carolina representatives did support Cheves's bill for

[4] *Ibid.*, p. 886.
[5] For Quincy's report of the incident, see *Niles' Weekly Register*, II, 110.
[6] *Annals*, pp. 1281–1312, 1511, 1539.
[7] *Ibid.*, p. 682. Williams was a Charleston planter. See James H. Wolfe, *Jeffersonian Democracy in South Carolina* (Chapel Hill, 1940), p. 218; *Dictionary of American Biography*, XX.

frigates, and all voted for the added military forces. When the crucial vote was taken, South Carolina cast a solid eight for war. The two senators, Gaillard and Taylor, likewise voted in its favor. Kentucky, Tennessee, and Georgia, casting in the House five, three, and three votes respectively, were the only other states which were unanimously in favor of war with England.[8]

The "War Hawks"—primarily from the four above-mentioned states—were given special emphasis by Julius W. Pratt in his *Expansionists of 1812,* which set forward in 1925 what has become one of the most popular and widespread theories regarding the War of 1812. Basically, Pratt asserts that the Southwest and its war-minded leaders gave a major impetus to the war. Singling out the war group in Congress is highly significant in tracing the origins of the war sentiment, but the further direction taken by the Pratt school is more open to question: the "Southwest," including South Carolina as well as the inland states, is depicted as desirous of war largely because of an urge for frontier expansion and a concern with the Indian question. These basic ideas repeatedly occur in historical literature, most recently in a 1954 popularized account of the war, even though varying shades of doubt have from time to time been cast on the Pratt thesis. Not well enough known perhaps is the work of George Rogers Taylor in 1930 describing the dire economic conditions in the Mississippi Valley preceding the war and the resulting attitude of the western farmer toward international affairs.[9]

In A. L. Burt's study, *The United States, Great Britain and British North America* (1940), it is maintained that the War of 1812 was fought primarily for maritime rights; Burt discusses with thoroughness the diplomatic wrangles with Britain and France from the turn of the century onward, as an offshoot suggesting pertinent objections to Pratt. A historiographical article of 1941 by Warren H. Goodman gives a good progressive account of theories regarding the causes of the war, although it was unhappily prepared before the publication of Burt's work. Goodman does, however, make several elucidating observations about the Pratt thesis and takes successful issue with various of its aspects. Pointing to the need for much further investigation, Goodman concludes that the causes of the War of 1812 are still "singularly uncertain."[10]

[8] *Annals,* pp. 287, 1637. There were no negative votes from these states. Senator Pope of Kentucky, however, did not favor war and refrained from voting on the issue. He did not thereby represent the feelings of his constituents, because his action resulted in disgrace at home and defeat in the next election. See John Bowman to Stephen F. Austin, Aug. 5, 1813, *Austin Papers,* ed. E. C. Barker, American Historical Association, *Annual Report, 1919,* II, 227–28.

[9] See currently, Glenn Tucker, *Poltroons and Patriots* (Indianapolis, 1954). The Taylor work appeared in two articles: "Agrarian Discontent in the Mississippi Valley Preceding the War of 1812," *Journal of Political Economy,* XXXIX (1931), 471–505; and "Prices in the Mississippi Valley Preceding the War of 1812," *Journal of Economic and Business History,* III (1930), 148–63.

[10] Warren H. Goodman, "The Origins of the War of 1812," *Mississippi Valley Historical*

Although South Carolina is included as an integral segment of the "South" and "Southwest" in the Burt and Pratt theses respectively, little has been said specifically about South Carolina's part in the drive for war. Nor in the many studies of John C. Calhoun has more than scant attention been given to his basic stands in the Twelfth Congress. During this era, South Carolina has been simply catalogued with the Jeffersonian states because of its nominal support of the Republican party in national elections from 1796 onward, and Calhoun and his fellow South Carolina "War Hawks" are neatly fitted into the same package. Many of the ambiguities associated with "Jeffersonian democracy" are regularly applied to South Carolina, which did of course share in the countrywide liberalizing trends. Sufficient attention has been given to the formal rise of the Republican party to control within the state;[11] yet too often overlooked in this period of history have been the other factors which explain South Carolina's important relation to the war and which at the same time elucidate the state-centered aims of the "young nationalist" Calhoun.

A unity had developed in the life of South Carolina which helped it achieve a share in the leadership of the nation at this critical period and which was to give impetus to its sectional prominence down to the Civil War. At the core of this unity was a fundamental political oneness which persisted despite the interplay of the two political parties. The spread of the electorate as settlement moved into the upcountry after 1800 indicated a liberalizing trend in South Carolina as did the election of an increasing number of young men to state offices; but the coming of age of the younger generation, who called themselves Republicans, had no effect on the ever-lingering conservatism in South Carolina which is normally associated with the Federalists. The upcountry farmer either young or old was severe and puritanical; he was also ambitious to gain the position in which he saw the planter slightly more prosperous than he. The planter as well as the farmer felt at all times that it was the purpose of government to maintain the orderly social and economic system, to protect the status quo. The representatives of the newer political alignment, led by the inherently conservative Charles Pinckney,

---

Review, XXVIII (1941), 171–86. Goodman's conclusion is based on the fact that nineteenth-century authors dealt primarily with military events and the twentieth century has netted only monographs on restricted phases of the question. No writer has attempted to "correlate and synthesize the various sets of causes," weighing the relative importance of the factors. Goodman makes an able suggestion of some eleven fields for investigation.

[11] J. H. Wolfe in his *Jeffersonian Democracy in South Carolina* gives a thorough factual discussion of this movement. Although the term "Jeffersonian democracy" has come into popular use, I question its preciseness of meaning for any area and especially with regard to South Carolina. Wolfe, however, is making in his title a correct distinction between the liberalism of this era and that of Jackson's, which South Carolina never accepted. See Wolfe, p. 286.

were never enthusiastically "Republican" as a party group; they were indeed a distinct political faction increasingly dominant in South Carolina, but they upheld an all-pervading South Carolina political philosophy in much the same measure as their forerunners, the Federalists.[12]

Even though there were overwhelming numbers of Republicans in the state after 1800, many prominent conservatives of the purely Federalist variety were not without significant influence. The original solons of South Carolina politics had operated under the Federalist banner, and the presence of a Republican majority did not mean that the respect offered the older men came to an end. Thomas and Charles Cotesworth Pinckney, of course, were venerated elders. Abraham Blanding, William Crafts, William Drayton, Stephen Elliott, Daniel E. Huger, Keating Simons, and Henry W. DeSaussure, all notable Federalists, continued to wield a considerable power in state politics well after 1800.[13]

Of the thirty-four men recorded in the *Dictionary of American Biography* as outstanding in South Carolina political life from 1800 to 1812, one finds, surprisingly enough, that fifteen professed themselves Federalists. Contemporary accounts also indicate the political activity of these men: documents from Josiah Quincy were circulated by William Crafts among many "friends who still dare to call themselves Federalists, of whom there yet are many," and Henry W. DeSaussure wrote to Quincy that "many wise and good men view the course pursued by the Administration as you do. . . . They take a moderate share in the affairs of our own state, and are respected and permitted to have some share in the management."[14] DeSaussure, incidentally, had just been appointed to the Equity Bench by the Republican legislature. National crises during this period called forth widespread town meetings in which citizens joined together to pass resolutions. Participating on the local committees were as many nominal Federalists as Republicans—Keating Simons, William L. Smith, and Thomas Pinckney in company with Langdon Cheves, William Lowndes, and Peter Freneau.[15]

Major issues in state politics brought to the fore a rather uncanny agree-

[12] Certain items in early South Carolina politics are interesting in this respect, in particular South Carolina's relation to the Virginia-Kentucky Resolutions, the vote on the Jefferson-Burr tie of 1800 in the Federal House of Representatives, and the nature of the Republican leader Charles Pinckney. On the latter, see Irving Brant, *James Madison, Father of the Constitution* (Indianapolis, 1950), pp. 79, 132.

[13] There is a discussion of the South Carolina Federalists from the Revolution to 1800 in Ulrich B. Phillips, "The South Carolina Federalists," *American Historical Review*, XLV (1909), 742.

[14] Edmund Quincy, *Life of Josiah Quincy of Massachusetts* (Boston, 1867), pp. 191, 192.

[15] Charleston *Courier*, Aug. 30, 1809, May 21, 1912, etc. In Georgia, similar public meetings also included representative Federalists. See John E. Talmadge, "Georgia's Federalist Press and the War of 1812," *Journal of Southern History*, XIX (November, 1953), 496–97.

ment between the Federalist and the Republican members of the legislature. In fact, the part played by Federalist legislators in passing measures which are considered liberal and "Jeffersonian" is little short of amazing. The founding of South Carolina College in 1801 was a very special monument not only to the progress but to the unity of the state; it was located in Columbia, clearly a part of the upcountry, yet the impulse for the college was a patrician one solidly supported in the lowcountry Federalist circles.[16] The bill calling for a change in proportionment of representation was passed in 1807 with only two votes against it in each house. Some of the major pressure in its behalf had been exerted by Federalists, Robert Goodloe Harper having been especially active in this realm during the 1790's. The legislative act itself was introduced in 1807 by Abraham Blanding, a Federalist legislator from Kershaw, and had probably been prepared by Judge Daniel E. Huger, Federalist of Charleston.[17] Another notable gesture by a Federalist was the bill for free schools introduced into the legislature in 1811 by the botanist Stephen Elliott.[18] There seemed to be no particular clash of interests on basic issues between the majority Republican party and the minority Federalist party within the state. Their respective philosophies merged in concerted activities which were subsequently issued under the name of Republicanism.

The preponderance of Republicans in South Carolina politics within the state obviously was not the result of a distinct break with the older South Carolina Federalist school, nor did the South Carolina Republicans in national circles represent a close tie to national Republican policies. Actually the Republican party was so diverse that its national objectives defied accurate definition. Few would claim that Jefferson himself was consistent in political philosophy and actions. As an administrator, he initiated a duality which underlay the whole Republican era. His first inaugural spoke for restraint in government; the second showed the Jefferson who would negotiate the Louisiana Purchase and plan numbers of prospective states across the Mississippi, the Jefferson who found in the Constitution powers during the embargo which rivaled the hated Alien and Sedition Acts. The Jeffersonian

[16] J. L. Petigru in later years claimed that the college was a work of the Federalists. Whether or not this was strictly true, Hollis describes it as an undertaking of lowcountry aristocrats. See Daniel W. Hollis, *South Carolina College* (Columbia, 1951), pp. 5–6. The patrician influence in the South Carolina legislature is interesting as contrasted with the rampant Republican Assembly of 1800 in North Carolina; the University of North Carolina was deprived of a portion of its income for fear the institution was drifting toward aristocracy. Delbert H. Gilpatrick, *Jeffersonian Democracy in North Carolina, 1789–1816* (New York, 1931), p. 142.

[17] William A. Schaper, "Sectionalism and Representation in South Carolina," A.H.A. *Annual Report*, 1900, I, 408, 428. This bill became a Constitutional amendment in 1808. See David D. Wallace, *History of South Carolina* (New York, 1934), II, 373, for information on Huger's preparation. Harriet Ravenel, *Life and Times of William Lowndes* (Boston, 1901), pp. 70–71, less convincingly ascribes the authorship to Lowndes.

[18] Wolfe, *Jeffersonian Democracy*, p. 175.

tradition to which his followers have pointed sets up a noble set of social values, the secret of which is an appeal to America's better self, to her idealism and simplicity. However, Jefferson made no headlong attack upon established institutions to make his principles work; Leonard White points out that "the Jeffersonian era in the field of administration was in many respects a projection of Federalist ideas and practice. . . . The ambivalence reflects the duality of the Republican party and of Jefferson himself."[19] The Jeffersonian party drew to it a tremendous variety of interests, and South Carolina had become a part of this group.

South Carolina's agrarian economy was one of the major factors which drew her originally into the Republican fold. But it was the growing preoccupation of South Carolina with the international commerce necessary to make agriculture profitable that took her somewhat off the path envisaged by Jefferson. Attacking the traditional Jeffersonian international policy, the Republican William Lowndes said to Congress, "The interests of agriculture and commerce are inseparable. What is commerce but the exchange of the surplus produce of . . . one nation for those of another? . . . it is this commerce which makes agriculture valuable."[20] Such a positive stand was not unusual, for South Carolina never demonstrated a very close adherence to the national party. The local Republican group so well represented the interests of the planting-business community of the state as a whole that its standard-bearers received almost no opposition from the Federalists in elections for national representatives, and the delegates in turn exercised a notable independence and lack of partisanship in Congress. Edward Hooker's description of Wade Hampton, one of the prosperous upcountry Republicans, was almost generally applicable to South Carolinians: "In his politics he is, I hardly know what. He is called a republican; yet he certainly has many notions and sentiments which are more characteristic of federalism. And he does not hesitate to condemn openly, and unequivocally some measures of the republican party."[21]

[19] Leonard D. White, *The Jeffersonians: A Study in Administrative History, 1801–1829* (New York, 1951), p. vii.

[20] *Annals*, pp. 805–806.

[21] J. Franklin Jameson, ed., "Diary of Edward Hooker, 1805–1808," A.H.A. *Annual Report, 1896*, I, 847. Among other South Carolinians in Congress who acted independently was Senator John Gaillard, who broke from his party in voting against the Chase impeachment. Thomas Sumter consistently voted against nonintercourse and the embargo; he and D. R. Williams have been singled out as particularly nonpartisan spirits among the Republicans. Senator John Taylor, concerned by the depressing effects of the embargo, worked for less extreme measures; he was the real author of Macon's Bill No. 2, which did grant some relief. See Albert J. Beveridge, *The Life of John Marshall* (Boston, 1919), III, 218; Anne King Gregorie, *Thomas Sumter* (Columbia, S. C., 1931), p. 260; Wolfe, *Jeffersonian Democracy*, pp. 203–206; letter to Joseph H. Nicholson from Nathaniel Macon, Apr. 10, 1810, in William E. Dodd, *Nathaniel Macon* (Raleigh, N. C., 1903), p. 259.

Calhoun, Cheves, and Lowndes had come to prominence in this era of independent Republicanism and conservative political unanimity. Calhoun was from Scotch-Irish upcountry stock, although the holdings of his father put him easily in the category of "planter."[22] After early training at the academy of Moses Waddell in Georgia, Calhoun went to Yale, where his seriousness and sternness must have made him well fitted for Timothy Dwight's domain. This Federalist president had a prevading influence over the students at Yale College, and it seems unlikely that Calhoun was untouched by his ideas. Experience in the Charleston law office of Henry W. DeSaussure and formal study at Litchfield Law School in Connecticut under Federalists James Gould and Tapping Reeve contributed further to Calhoun's background of conservatism. In 1811, his marriage to Floride Calhoun, a cousin who belonged to wealthy Charlestonian society, gave the Republican uplander a direct tie to the older, more staid South Carolina lowcountry.

Calhoun was a lawyer in the Piedmont region at the time that the Chesapeake-Leopard affair provoked indignant public meetings in many localities. His first chance at public oratory came when he was requested by the Abbeville committee to write and present its resolutions denouncing the incident; shortly thereafter he was elected to the state legislature, and in 1810 he became a representative to the United States Congress.

Langdon Cheves, also newly elected to Congress in 1810, had both upcountry and lowcountry connections as did Calhoun. He was born in Abbeville, a Piedmont district, and later became a lawyer in Charleston. The third new congressman, William Lowndes, was of lowcountry planting origin, and his attractive and intelligent wife was a confirmed Federalist, the daughter of Thomas Pinckney.[23]

Calhoun, Cheves, and Lowndes, Republicans with backgrounds strongly marked by conservative influences, expressed in the Twelfth Congress the conservatism which had become characteristic of South Carolina's "Federal"-Republicanism. All three were men of outstanding leadership abilities; and, when they made demands in the interest of their state, they also revealed a strong bent toward nationalization. Though nationalism can be the manifestation of both liberal and conservative movements, in 1811 nationalizing measures were definitely the latter. The conservatives during the Constitution-making era were the nationalists, and the South Carolinians were of this

---

[22] Patrick Calhoun is credited with over 1000 acres of land and 31 slaves in 1790. Charles M. Wiltse, *John C. Calhoun*, II (Indianapolis, 1944), 17–23. See also Wallace, *History of South Carolina*, II, 386.

[23] See *DAB*, IV, XI, for biographies of Cheves and Lowndes; also Ravenel, *Life and Times of William Lowndes*.

breed—conservatives in their desire to preserve the prevailing socio-economic system of their state. They sought federal power to protect this way of life.[24] Their nationalism was thus, in a sense, a sectionalism in disguise.

Calhoun, Cheves, and Lowndes were elected to Congress in 1810 with "reference to the critical condition of the country."[25] They were all in a belligerent mood, and they had spoken vigorously in pre-election campaigns. A clear statement of Calhoun's views on international affairs had been set forward as early as the Republican caucus in 1808: reviewing the struggle between the United States and European powers, he labeled the resort to the restrictive system an inefficient means of preserving American rights and pointed out that war with England was unavoidable. He later saw "in the low price of the produce, the hand of foreign injustice."[26] British minister Augustus J. Foster, who met the representatives in Washington, noted that the South Carolina members of Congress were "resolute," "particularly the younger Deputies . . . who seemed to have great influence and were very cool and decided on the propriety of going to war in order to protect the Commerce of the Country."[27] The South Carolina congressmen had a vital interest in the "Commerce of the Country," because on it depended the future of the prosperous economic developments which had taken place in South Carolina during the first decade of the nineteenth century.

By 1811 the entire state was in the middle of a tremendous cotton boom. The value and practicability of upland-grown short-staple cotton had become immediately apparent upon invention of the cotton gin and were demonstrated after the introduction of the gin into South Carolina in 1801; at the same time the demand for cotton went up as machine methods of manufacture became standard in England. When the slave trade was reopened in 1803, cotton production proceeded at full speed. South Carolina doubled its cotton output in the ten years following 1801, producing forty million pounds in 1811; the state had begun to export approximately forty per cent of the total cotton exports of the United States.[28] As David Ramsay wrote in 1808, cotton "has trebled the price of land suitable to its growth, and when the crop

---

[24] Whether nationalization was a rightist or leftist move perhaps became questionable during the Jacksonian period. If one assumes Calhoun always to have been a conservative, his inconsistencies which appeared during the Jackson era have some basis for explanation.

[25] [John C. Calhoun], *Life of John C. Calhoun* (New York, 1843), p. 8.

[26] *Annals*, p. 482. For Calhoun's own description of the 1808 caucus at which he opposed the nomination of George Clinton for Vice President, see *Life of John C. Calhoun*, p. 7.

[27] MS Notes, Augustus J. Foster Papers, Library of Congress; see also MS Diary, Apr. 15, 1812, L.C.

[28] The amount of cotton produced in South Carolina is an approximation made by Frederick J. Turner, *Rise of the New West* (New York, 1906), p. 47, based on a group of figures. See Matthew B. Hammond, *The Cotton Industry* (New York, 1897), Appendix I, p. 358, for total yearly cotton production and exports of the United States in 1811. See *Niles' Weekly Register*, I, 399, for exports of each state in 1811.

succeeds and the market is favorable, the annual income of those who plant it is double to what it was before the introduction of cotton."[29]

The increased use of the Negro slave was of course necessary for the phenomenal expansion of upland cotton, and during these years a constantly growing number of farmers and planters acquired property in slaves. It is important to note, however, that in twenty-three out of twenty-eight districts in 1810 whites still outnumbered blacks, the popular image depicting masses of Negroes working on all the farm lands being far from correct.[30] True, in coast districts such as Charleston and Colleton the black population was actually much greater than the white, but here cotton and rice production had probably been expanded to the limit before 1800 since the percentage of slave population even decreased slightly in the period 1800–1810. It was the upcountry legislators who insisted on the reopening of the slave trade in 1803, for it was their region in which cotton and slavery were spreading. A look at the United States Census figures for 1790, 1800, and 1810 shows as expected a steady increase in slaves for upcountry districts, the largest proportional gain coming after 1800. The following are sample Piedmont districts:[31]

	York		Greenville		Edgefield	
	Slaves	Whites	Slaves	Whites	Slaves	Whites
1790	923	5,652	606	5,888	3,619	9,805
1800	1,804	8,417	1,439	10,029	5,006	13,063
1810	3,164	7,828	2,391	10,739	8,576	14,433

When the upland area like the coast became a significant producer of cotton, South Carolina could boast an amazing unity of economic interest. Corollary to this economic development was of course the spread of political power into the upcountry and the resulting era in which political and cultural oneness increased steadily. This unanimity of interest, political and economic, exhibited itself under the name of Republicanism.

The enactment of the embargo by the federal government in 1808 exactly coincided with the full realizations of South Carolinians that the primary economic interests of the state were much the same from coast to hill country, that a continuance of the cotton-planting system was essential to all areas. The discomforts brought on by the embargo gave the state an even greater unity as both sections were prey to the economic forces which made prices go

[29] David Ramsay, *History of South Carolina* (Newberry, S. C., 1858), II, 121.
[30] Schaper, *Sectionalism and Representation*, p. 392, gives a map of the enlarging "Black belt" which shows a much greater preponderance of Negroes in South Carolina at this date. However, he lists no source. Census of 1810 bears out the above statement. See *Niles' Weekly Register*, I, 309.
[31] *Ibid.*, I, 309. See also Wiltse, *Calhoun*, II, 146.

up at the same time that profits decreased. The southern agriculturalists incurred constant expenses whether or not their products sold, but the traditional planting system had to be kept. Manufacturing had no chance to develop because after 1803 the capital of the South had gone into buying slaves; the area was already in debt to New England.[32]

The Charleston *Courier* reported on January 20, 1808, that cotton was down to twenty-five cents per pound, and on February 10, 1810, that it had fallen to fourteen cents. A contemporary observer reported that in order to make ends meet, the South Carolinians had to get at least twenty cents for their cotton.[33] One should note that the critical drop in price came between 1808 and 1810; this difference may partially account for South Carolina's growing concern with the world situation during that period, for attitudes which varied from passive endurance to active belligerence. The South Carolina legislature in June, 1808, had expressed its willingness to enforce the embargo, but in reporting the resolutions to Jefferson, Speaker Joseph Alston did tell the President that they represented a wholehearted patriotism, not necessarily a "perfect unanimity of political opinion."[34] As economic conditions became tighter, there was growing resistance to the embargo and to its successor, nonintercourse.

Calhoun's public speech against the embargo in 1808 has already been cited. Governor Charles Pinckney in December, 1807, blamed disputes with Great Britain for "an almost total stagnation of commerce and stoppage of the sale of produce"; this caused "the great inconvenience of merchants and planters."[35] Fear that the international situation would bring the loss of markets gave impetus to such news stories as that which noted the phenomenal growth of South American cotton sales in Liverpool. By June, 1812, there were reports that cotton planters had been forced to turn to corn, that some upcountry men were turning to wheat.[36] The situation in Charleston is well mirrored in the letters of Margaret Izard Manigault to her mother: cotton prices of 1811 were down to eight cents; money in town was almost nonexistent; and worst of all, since early 1809 there had scarcely been a party.[37]

South Carolina depended on unrestricted trade—on "commerce" as British minister Foster called it—because this was a region where people cultivated

[32] *Ibid.*, II, 45.
[33] MS Notes, Foster Papers.
[34] Note Wade Hampton's letter of April, 1808, and other comments in Wolfe, *Jeffersonian Democracy*, pp. 222–25.
[35] Charleston *Courier*, Dec. 2, 1807.
[36] *Ibid.*, Sept. 26, 1809; June 2, July 3, 1812.
[37] Margaret I. Manigault to Alice Izard, February, 1809, Dec. 1, 1811, Ralph Izard Papers, II, III, Library of Congress.

the soil, sold most of what they produced, and purchased most of what they consumed.' Although the nonimportation law which succeeded the embargo in 1809 was often unenforced, general economic conditions kept on the down-grade as long as there was a controversy with England, the chief purchaser and provider in the South.[38] By the time of the Twelfth Congress, the tone of the South Carolina legislature had changed notably from that of 1808. This group sent resolutions to President Madison demanding that definite action be taken to protect commerce and the honor of the nation. A firm stand from the beginning, it was explained, might have prevented much loss to agriculture. 'D. R. Williams vigorously expressed the sentiments of his state before Congress:

> But what is the condition of the commerce with Great Britain. . . . Truly miserable. . . . How is tobacco affected? . . . Inquire into the state of the cotton market; where is the crop of 1810? A curse to him who meddled with it. Where is that of 1811? Rotting at home in the hands of the grower, waiting the repeal of the Orders in Council.[39]

, South Carolina had developed a decided urge for war. Excited by considerations of her primary livelihood, the export trade in cotton, South Carolina became one of the main protagonists of the conflict. This was not the largest or wealthiest state in the union, but it had one special qualification for national leadership in 1812—the most at stake in the domestic export trade; •South Carolina had more exports per individual white person than any other state in the union. With only 3.6 per cent of the total white population of the United States, South Carolina exported 10.3 per cent of the domestic goods.[40] Whether or not fighting a war with England was the logical step to take as a remedy to the commercial and thus agricultural distress is not the question—the South Carolinians of 1812 were convinced that a war would help. .

To assess the total internal and external forces which produced the War of 1812 will call for the investigation of a multitude of factors not yet understood. The effort in this paper has been primarily to set forth the position of

---

[38] Wolfe, *Jeffersonian Democracy*, p. 236; *Niles' Weekly Register*, I, 133. Incidentally, Great Britain received 60 per cent of the American cotton exports in 1811. Hammond, *Cotton Industry*, p. 358.

[39] Speech of Jan. 6, 1812, *Annals*, p. 686. See also speech of Governor Henry Middleton giving a justification for war. *Niles' Weekly Register*, III, 275–76.

[40] *Ibid.*, I, 237, for figures from the Census of 1810; I, 399, for exports, domestic and foreign, for each state in 1811. South Carolina had 214,196 white population of the total 5,905,782 whites in the United States. (Counting the slave population full value, South Carolina had 5.8 per cent of the total.) South Carolina's domestic exports were valued at $4,650,934, while the total was $45,294,043. Maryland came close to South Carolina in trade per individual; with 3.9 per cent of the white population, her domestic trade was 10 per cent. However, she also had over 14 per cent of the total shipping trade, a factor which would greatly complicate her attitude toward war.

South Carolina with regard to the war, thereby pointing out in particular the significant part played by the direct trade of the United States, by foreign markets for staple products, in determining the course of events.

In the realm of international diplomacy, A. L. Burt's study goes farther than any other in explaining how the United States, entangled with both Great Britain and France, finally chose war with Britain. Burt's suggestions regarding the attitudes of the various sections of the United States toward going to war are also well directed. Making note of the fact that the South was sorely pinched for markets (and South Carolina indeed received considerable support in her war effort from Georgia, Virginia, and North Carolina), Burt further points out that the Northeast was "betraying national honor . . . for selfish profit." All sources indicate in fact that New England experienced a great shipping and commercial boom because of continuing European hostilities; the United States government went to war to "champion maritime interests . . . in spite of their opposition."[41] Burt's observations, apparently sound, are directly supported by the conclusion of this paper that South Carolina, which played a significant role in the congressional campaign for war, had as its primary concern an alleviation of commercial distress.

The thesis of Julius W. Pratt, on the other hand, seems considerably weakened by the findings here reported. The coupling together of the South and Southwest in interpreting the war sentiment is certainly justifiable, but this alliance was not altogether natural, and in many respects the relationships that have been singled out are not the significant ones. Indian troubles may have had some bearing on western sentiment, but these did not pose a serious problem in the South at this date; expansion into Florida was likewise an unimportant urge.[42] The developing political philosophy of Kentucky

[41] A. L. Burt, *The United States, Great Britain, and British North America* (New Haven, 1940), p. 306. Burt explains that Great Britain, in command of the sea, pressed harder on American neutrality than France, which had no foothold on the American continent and therefore was less vulnerable.

[42] Warren H. Goodman, taking issue with Pratt's thesis, grants that Pratt had sufficient evidence to justify listing the Indians as a definite problem, but not as an "overmastering" concern. In line with Goodman's statement on the Indian question, if sample data from middle Tennessee in this writer's files are of value, there seems to have been no particular concern with Indians or any other British-inspired difficulties in the Williamson County frontier settlement in the years before 1812; see Williamson County MS Records, 1800–1812, Court House, Franklin, Tennessee. It is also interesting to note from a slightly different angle that Ohio, which was closer to the British-Indian sphere of influence than Kentucky and Tennessee, cast one vote for war in the House yet one against war in the Senate, the negative vote being given by Senator Thomas Worthington, a future governor of the state. See *DAB*, XX. Pratt's contention that the southern desire for war was a part of its acquisitive impulse toward Florida is weak. No evidence can be found in congressional debates that Florida was a motive for war. Actually, part of Florida was taken without a thought of conflict with Britain, and in June, 1812, a move by the House of Representatives to permit the occupation of East and West Florida was blocked by the Senate (*Annals*, pp. 1684–92). The Florida thesis can certainly not be applied in any sizable measure to South Carolina; Thomas Sumter had opposed even the purchase of Florida in 1806 because too large a portion of seacoast would be left undefended. (Everett S.

and Tennessee could rarely be equated with that of conservative cotton-producing South Carolina, nor was the latter by 1812 in a position to share the frontier sentiments of the West. Indeed, the support of these states for similar measures in Congress lasted only a few years.

' The significant basis of alliance between the South and the Southwest in 1812 was their common cry against foreign depredations on American shipping: As well-explained by G. R. Taylor, when depression replaced the early western prosperity of 1808 and 1809, discontent was rampant and settlers looked madly about them for the causes of their troubles: Economic analysts believe today that these were primarily difficulties within the frontier area itself—matters of transportation, communication, imperfect marketing, and insufficient financial organization.' However, the westerners of 1808–1812 grasped for a time at the first likely cause; they began to be painfully aware of foreign restrictions on American commerce, and to these they directed more and more blame for their economic ills. Although western markets were actually far less directly connected to European trade than those of South Carolina, increased demands for western hemp, tobacco, cotton, and flour were hopefully anticipated as results of a war with Great Britain. In 1812, "the right of exporting the productions of our own soil and industry to foreign markets" seemed as real to the hemp and tobacco growers of Kentucky as to the large-scale cotton producers of South Carolina.[43]

The internal scene in South Carolina was ripe for a burst of political activity on behalf of commerce. Contrary to the impression left by authors who have elected to discuss in isolation the rise of the Republican majority in South Carolina, the state's over-all outlook was largely a conservative one based on an established political and economic philosophy. The South Carolina Republican party itself could only in a superficial sense be described as Jeffersonian; more specifically it was a state-centered group which kept well in line with the prevailing statewide views, these marked by ambition for

---

Brown, ed., *William Plumer's Memorandum of Proceedings in the United States Senate, 1803–1807* [New York, 1923], p. 421.) In November, 1812, William Lowndes expressed the opinion that no law would be recommended for the occupation of Florida because Spain was likely to cede it anyway. (Lowndes to [Thomas Pinckney], Nov. 27, 1812, William Lowndes Papers, Library of Congress.) There was certain agitation in Georgia over the question of Florida because of the common boundary, but it seems unwise to visualize the entire South as an expansive-minded area. The contention that a sectional bargain was made between North and South regarding the acquisition of Canada and Florida has been left completely without basis by W. H. Goodman, who has pointed out that the conquest of Canada was openly advocated in the South as early as 1807, no particular opposition to this move being voiced thereafter. Canada was often regarded in many parts of the country as possible remuneration for British damages to American commerce. See Goodman, "Origins of the War of 1812," pp. 177–82.

[43] The quotation is from a speech by Felix Grundy of Tennessee in which he singled out this right as the "true question in controversy." *Annals*, p. 424.

gain yet an innate distrust of substantial change. Such conservatism, prompted by the immediate need to preserve the prosperous economic system of the state, was expressed by South Carolina in a nationalistic impulse for war.

In a sense the war marked the end of one era of Jeffersonianism and the beginning of a change in the nature of the Republican party. South Carolina, one of the foremost war-minded leaders, was a state whose Republicanism had never been more than an independent, local movement. The new generation in the Republican party, with an aim to protect and promote the direct commerce of the country that seemed more Federalist than Jeffersonian, was strongly spearheaded by men from the South and the Southwest who worked together successfully in a congressional drive for war. The effective leadership of Henry Clay in the Speaker's chair supplemented by other representatives of the frontier regions must never be minimized, but that provides matter for another paper. Working with Clay, the new delegation from South Carolina was the most aggressive force in Congress.

Paradoxical as it may seem, the desire of South Carolina to preserve and extend the status quo produced a determination not to be undone by the caprices of warring European powers. Going to Congress with the conviction that the older Republican measures would not solve the problems of 1812, South Carolina's young Congressmen Calhoun, Cheves, and Lowndes spoke for the protection of America's foreign commerce and not at all incidentally for the well-being of South Carolina's trade in cotton.

Stanford, California

Special Interests and National Authority in Foreign Policy: American-British Provincial Links During the Embargo and the War of 1812

REGINALD C. STUART*

Students of American foreign policy in the early national period tend to focus on the national government and political parties to explain the internal dynamics of their subject and its successes and failures. Local studies generally have reinforced this historiographical tendency and further illuminated the political center of foreign policymaking and execution. We also have a rich literature on the international context of early American foreign policy, its ideological backdrop, the interplay of personalities, and the views of particular Founding Fathers. What we lack is much understanding of how the outlook in the territorial peripheries related to the course and conduct of external relations in the early United States.

In *New England and Foreign Relations 1789–1850*, Paul Varg states that "historians of American foreign relations concentrate their attention on decision making in the nation's capital and give only slight attention to the role of regions in asserting their foreign policy interests."[1] Seeking to redress this imbalance, Varg traces in detail New England's changing character and its perspective on foreign policy down to 1850. By then, he argues, New England's outlook had lost its distinctiveness. This article presents another region of the United States—the American borderland along the northern frontier—for similar, albeit briefer consideration. In particular, it surveys the reaction of the more thickly settled and economically developed sectors of this American-provincial borderland to two policies of the Jeffersonian era, the embargo and the War of 1812. The evidence suggests that historians

*The author is grateful for the generous support of the Social Sciences and Humanities Research Council of Canada and the Senate Research Committee of the University of Prince Edward Island in the research and presentation of this paper. Valuable criticism came from Thomas Spira and Ron Hatzenbuehler. A version of this paper was read at the Organization of American Historians meeting in Los Angeles, April 1984.
[1]Paul A. Varg, *New England and Foreign Relations 1789–1850* (Hanover, 1983), p. vi.

311

would do well to develop the subject of local-central relations further to deepen their appreciation of how foreign policy operates in a democratic federal structure.

First, it is necessary to establish the accuracy of Varg's claims for this period. Historians have long recognized the importance of sectionalism in American history, but recently they have questioned how swiftly or deeply nationalism sank into the roots of American society following the Revolution.[2] Separatist schemes floated in the West and Vermont in the early national period, and in New England during the War of 1812. Julius Pratt's *Expansionists of 1812* and Arthur P. Whitaker's studies of early western interests are classics. Pratt's thesis about an intersectional alliance for expansionism has been much mauled by revisionism, but this process has not invalidated his argument about regional outlooks. Isaac Cox focused on the West Florida controversy down to 1815, and James W. Hammack, Jr., has recently published a study of Kentucky in the War of 1812. There are many articles on the relations of states and regions to the coming of the war, and to the embargo, but most of them discuss national politics and policies as much as local perspectives.[3] In sum, the list seems brief, and Varg's observation must command attention.

No scholar has studied the northern borderland as a comprehensive geographic-political-economic unit. Despite the existence of a (subsequently revised) line after 1783, the society and economy along the border developed as a blend of British-American and American characteristics and interests. Remote from the national center of power in the United States until the construction of the Erie Canal and its tributary system after 1815, this northern American borderland from Vermont west viewed the St. Lawrence River as its natural outlet and the provinces as natural markets. To the east, northern New Englanders saw the British Maritime Provinces as extensions of their own landed and maritime enterprises. A full consideration of this borderland is beyond the scope of this paper, but it is necessary to establish a context within which to see its relationship to the issue of national authority in foreign policy.

The British provinces were scattered and feeble in 1783, except for the French settlements along the St. Lawrence, but by 1800, the borderland

---

[2]Paul C. Nagel, "Historiography and American Nationalism: Some Difficulties," *Canadian Review of Studies in Nationalism* 2 (Spring 1975): 225–40; Kenneth M. Stampp, "The Concept of Perpetual Union," *Journal of American History* 65 (June 1978): 5–33.

[3]Julius Pratt, *Expansionists of 1812* (1925; reprint ed., New York, 1957); Arthur P. Whitaker, *The Spanish-American Frontier 1783–1795: The Westward Movement and the Spanish Retreat in the Mississippi Valley* (1927; reprint ed., Lincoln, 1969); Isaac Cox, *West Florida Controversy 1789–1813: A Study in American Diplomacy* (Baltimore, 1918). For examples relating to the War of 1812 see Stephen Millett, "Bellicose Nationalism in Ohio: An Origin of the War of 1812," *Canadian Review of Studies in Nationalism* 1 (Fall 1974): 221–40; Robert Hayne, "The Southwest and the War of 1812," *Louisiana History* 5 (1964): 41–51; Sarah Lemmon, *Frustrated Patriots: North Carolina and the War of 1812* (Chapel Hill, 1973); and James W. Hammack, Jr., *Kentucky and the Second American Revolution: The War of 1812* (Lexington, 1976).

comprised two distinct and well-established regions, and a third section that was less well defined because it was on the fringes of settlement both in the United States and Upper Canada. First, there were the New England-Maritimes links. Second, there were the connections running up the Champlain Valley, including the Vermont and New York lake shores, to Lower Canada. Third, there were the land necks and river crossings joining British and American territory along the Great Lakes waterways, principally on the St. Lawrence, Niagara, and Detroit rivers.

The New England-Maritimes link originated with northward colonial expansion before 1775. The imperial schism of 1776 brought regular interchange to a halt and Nova Scotia largely sat out the American War for Independence. But in 1783 Sir Guy Carleton's fleets arrived in Halifax from New York bearing a sad cargo of refugees. These loyalist exiles immediately proved too much for local agricultural production or British stores. In 1783 and 1784 the British therefore turned to the United States for supplies to avoid mass tragedy. New Englanders sold foodstuffs and lumber under special licenses. The emergency quickened what would have evolved naturally—the resumption of New England-Maritimes trade.

No general regulations covered this exchange, despite American efforts to reach a broad agreement on trade with Britain and her dominions. But the needs continued, and so did the traffic. In addition, woodsmen pushed north through Maine's forests to find employment in the St. John River Valley. As lumbering developed in this region, both logs and timber moved back and forth across the line, finding markets as conditions warranted. The British consumed American wood products in local construction for the navy and for export to the British West Indies. In 1790, over one million board feet of lumber went from New England mills to Nova Scotia. At the same time, New England fishermen worked Maritimes waters and conducted trade over the sides of their vessels both for supplies and as a subsidiary source of profit. Finally, Nova Scotia and New Brunswick grindstones and gypsum found markets in the United States as far away as southern plantations.[4]

The extensive waterways of the Bay of Fundy provided ample opportunity for the "schooner trade" of fishermen and more concerted smuggling. Halifax became an entrepôt for Yankees denied access to the British West Indies. Massachusetts politicians, disgruntled over their merchants' exclusion

---

[4]W. S. MacNutt, *The Atlantic Provinces: The Emergence of Colonial Society* (Toronto, 1957), pp. 107–8, 114, 132–34, 150–53; Gerald S. Graham, "The Gypsum Trade of the Maritime Provinces: Its Relation to American Diplomacy and Agriculture in the Early Nineteenth Century," *Agricultural History* 12 (July 1938): 209–23; Harold Davis, *An International Community on the St. Croix (1604–1930)* (Orono, 1950), pp. 62–64, 103–12, develops the borderland idea for a restricted area over a long time span. See also Arthur J. Mekeel, "The Quaker-Loyalist Migration to New Brunswick and Nova Scotia in 1783," Friends Historical Association, *Bulletin* 32 (1943): 65–76; George Butler, "Commercial Relations of Nova Scotia with the United States 1783–1830" (M.A. thesis, Dalhousie University, 1934), p. 83; and Timothy Pickering to Thomas Pinckney, 5 March 1796, William R. Manning, ed., *The Diplomatic Correspondence of the United States: Canadian Relations 1783–1860*, 4 vols. (Washington, DC, 1940–45), 1:96.

from this coveted market, interdicted exchange with the Maritimes as retaliation. But smuggling enlarged as an easy alternative. Federal authorities tried to curtail the illegal trade, but lacked the men and vessels for effective patrols. The federal government eventually authorized, built, and manned Fort Sullivan at Eastport, Maine, on Moose Island in Passamaquoddy Bay to control this smuggling, but to no avail.[5] The locals easily evaded both state and federal authorities. Frustrated, Massachusetts legislators withdrew their ordinances and left policing the smugglers to the largely helpless federal officers.

Farther west a similar pattern developed as settlement crept north along both shores of Lake Champlain. In addition, from 1796 to 1810, some 15,000 New Englanders migrated to the eastern townships of Lower Canada to farm, start businesses, or join relatives, and they maintained old links, as well as established new personal and commercial ties, with the United States. The valley settlers early developed a northern orientation. British merchants and officials in Montreal provided profitable markets, and the St. Lawrence River was a natural outlet for Americans separated from the centers of their country by a vast wilderness. Political factionalism in Vermont reinforced this northern gaze when the federal government failed initially to accept Vermont's claims to statehood. Some frustrated radical Vermonters even spoke of rejoining the British empire.[6]

The Allen family in particular was linked with the hints of repatriation and dabbled actively in cross-border schemes on several levels. One of the Allens had been a loyalist during the Revolution. As early as 1786 Ira Allen negotiated with British officials in Montreal to conduct business, implying that he might be able to persuade Vermont to return to the fold. Lord Dorchester, the governor, listened, although he did not take Allen's allusions about political fusion seriously. He did open the border and created a free-trade zone that trafficked in grains, foodstuffs, pot and pearl ashes, timber, and iron ore in exchange for British manufactured goods and specie. Lake Champlain was a natural highway, and timber rafts negotiated the Richelieu River to the St. Lawrence Valley and Montreal. Their cargoes were consumed locally and exported to the Maritimes and other British destinations. By 1806 this trade seemed sufficient to some to warrant speculation in a Montreal-Boston turnpike. Horatio Gates, son of a Vermont trader who went to Montreal as an agent for his father, helped to found the Bank of Montreal with his profits. Occasionally British finance capital moved south to invest in small industrial enterprises, such as sawmills. Vermont became a state in 1791 and

[5]Davis, *International Community*, pp. 70–73, 91–94; Tristam Dalton to John Adams, 11 April 1785, in Julian P. Boyd, ed., *The Papers of Thomas Jefferson*, 21 vols. (Princeton, 1950–), 7:468–69; Lorenzo Sabine, "Moose Island," in William Kirby, comp., *Eastport and Passamaquoddy: A Collection of Historical and Biographical Sketches* (Eastport, 1888), pp. 142–74.

[6]Peter Onuf, "State Making in the Revolutionary Crisis: Independent Vermont as a Case Study," *Journal of American History* 67 (March 1981): 797–815; W. A. Mackintosh, "Canada and Vermont: A Study in Historical Geography," *Canadian Historical Review* 8 (March 1927): 9–30.

acquired a customs collector, but this official was unable to control the contraband trade in tea, furs, specie, tobacco, and rum that had developed parallel to the open commerce.[7]

This American-provincial link extended to New York City, despite the difficulties of travel between Lake Champlain and Albany, as the head of navigation on the Hudson River. Montreal businessmen traded on the New York money markets and Americans, such as John Jacob Astor, joined with provincials to exploit the northwestern fur trade. Astor looked north to speculate in Canadian township grants in 1796, but soon moved into furs. By 1808 he had trusted Montreal partners. Provincials even outnumbered Americans in his ill-fated venture to the mouth of the Columbia River in Oregon in 1811. Astor made annual trips north himself and became so knowledgeable about provincial affairs that Secretary of the Treasury Albert Gallatin had him compile statistics on the British North American economy for government use; Gallatin even had Astor spy on British garrisons in 1812 while the businessman negotiated with British officials to supply their troops. He was a prominent example of American businessmen who saw opportunity in the provinces and disregarded the American-British political frontier. Another example lay in promoters of the Erie Canal who, even before 1812, dreamed of Canada as part of the hinterland that would transform New York into America's queen city of commerce.[8]

The third American-provincial borderland sector was not well developed, even by 1812. It extended from the New York side of the St. Lawrence frontier west. Once it reached Lake Ontario, however, a large body of water separated the American and provincial sides until one reached the Niagara region. This area was only recently settled by the time of the embargo, and even by the War of 1812, it did not have much commerce. At the farthest western point, along the Detroit River, there were only small garrisons and a few hundred settlers in Detroit.

The eastern part of Upper Canada had many American immigrants by 1800, on the other hand. Attracted by British offers of free land, Americans migrated in the 1790s and freely swore oaths of loyalty to the crown, which most of them probably did not take seriously. In Canadian history, these

---

[7] Aleine Austin, *Matthew Lyon: "New Man" of the Democratic Revolution 1749–1822* (Philadelphia, 1981), pp. 59–62, 76, 83–87; H. N. Muller, III, "The Commercial History of the Lake Champlain-Richelieu River Route 1760–1815" (Ph.D. diss., University of Rochester, 1969); "The Act of Incorporation and the Bye Laws of the Boston and Montreal Turnpike Company" (Peacham, 1806); Adam Shortt, "Founders of Canadian Banking," *The Canadian Banker* 30 (October 1922): 34–37.

[8] K. W. Porter, *John Jacob Astor: Businessman,* 2 vols. (Cambridge, MA, 1931), 1:249–71, 279–83; Ronald Shaw, *Erie Water West: A History of the Erie Canal 1792–1854* (Lexington, 1966), pp. 72, 80, 101–2, 402–4; Chilton Williamson, "New York's Impact on the Canadian Economy Prior to the Completion of the Erie Canal," *New York State History* 24 (January 1943): 24–38, and Williamson, "New York's Struggle for Champlain Valley Trade 1760–1825," *New York State History* 20 (October 1941): 426–36; William Campbell, *The Life and Writings of DeWitt Clinton* (New York, 1849), pp. 72–82; *Report of the Commissioners to Explore the Route of an Inland Navigation* (New York, 1811), pp. 7–9.

people appear under the title of "late loyalists," of suspect motives in British notations of the time and under a cloud as far as ultrapatriotic Canadians were concerned. This is not entirely fair. Most settlers were migratory frontiersmen whose sense of nationalism was not strong and who simply responded to what seemed to be an opportunity. The late loyalists were not advance agents of an American empire seeking to subvert British rule, although subsequent events made such a construction of their motives reasonable from a British or Canadian perspective. The migrants went to join friends and relatives and speculate in land. Some even went to seek political asylum. Among the last were ex-Whiskey rebels who had a religious parallel in Quakers, Dunkards, and Mennonites from New York and Pennsylvania.[9] As the borderland became settled, however spottily, several towns along the American side of the frontier had provincial opposite numbers—Ogdensburg/Prescott, Sackett's Harbor/ Kingston, Lewiston/Queenston, and Detroit/Malden are four examples. It was between such centers that trade developed along the inland borderland, using the natural highways of lakes and rivers.

The influx of American settlers worried many British officials and implied that future possession of the Canadian provinces might go either way. Early travelers through the Canadas, betraying an optimism about new settlements common on the nineteenth-century frontier, believed that the region would flourish. These travelers also found a variety of loyalties, and often read into locals' remarks perspectives that suited their own prejudices. Some noted an anti-Americanism among the provincials; others noted an anti-monarchism; still others noted an eagerness to join the United States.[10] When the War of 1812 broke out, Americans in the Canadas faced an uncomfortable choice of loyalties. Some drifted back to the United States, but many remained.

National foreign policymakers knew relatively little about this border-land and its interests and seemed not to appreciate that local loyalties and inclinations might take precedence over national or political sympathies. The American government had official relations with the British in Canada, such as the postal agreement the Continental Congress passed in July 1785. The Congress also noted British efforts to lure American settlers north.[11] In the 1790s, George Washington's administration resented British activity with the

---

[9]Marcus L. Hansen and John B. Brebner, *The Mingling of the Canadian and American Peoples* (New Haven, 1940), p. 92; Gerald M. Craig, *Upper Canada: The Formative Years 1784–1841* (Toronto, 1963), chaps. 3 and 4; E. A. Cruikshank, "Immigration from the United States to Upper Canada 1784–1812—Its Character and Results," *Proceedings of the Thirty Ninth Annual Convention of the Ontario Educational Association* (1900), pp. 263–83.

[10]J. C. Ogden, *A Tour Through Upper and Lower Canada* (Litchfield, 1799), pp. 36–37, 52, 84–85, 88, 102; Timothy Bigelow, *Journal of a Tour to Niagara Falls in the Year 1805* (Boston, 1876), pp. 66, 69, 71; Christian Schultz, *Travels on an Inland Voyage 1807 and 1808* (New York, 1968), pp. 50, 55, 95–97; Michael Smith, *Geographical View of the Province of Upper Canada* (New York, 1813).

[11]Worthington C. Ford, ed., *Journals of the Continental Congress*, 34 vols. (Washington, DC, 1934–37), 29:86–87; postal agreement, 12 July 1785, ibid., 32:79–80. Virginia delegates to Edmund Randolph, 19 March 1787, William T. Hutchinson and William M. E. Rachal, eds., *The Papers of James Madison*, 13 vols. (Chicago, 1962–), 9:325.

Indians in the Old Northwest, knew of the value of the fur trade, wanted to expel the British garrisons from the Northwest posts (until the Jay Treaty settled this issue), and generally believed that the British were using Canada as a base to contain American expansion. Local jurisdictional disputes could threaten international peace. In 1794, for example, when Anglo-American tensions ran high over seizures of vessels and impressment in the West Indies because of the wars of the French Revolution, Lord Dorchester feared that clashes between provincial woodcutters and American settlers near the line might precipitate a war.[12]

The possibility of northern American separatism appeared in different guises. When Edmond Genêt, the flamboyant and impetuous Girondist representative from France, arrived in America, he tried to enlist volunteers for expeditions against British and Spanish territories to the north and south as part of his country's war effort. Ethan, Levi, and Ira Allen, along with other Vermonters, responded eagerly. Matthew Lyon, a rising Jeffersonian Republican, was among them. American anger over British maritime seizures and fear of frontier war inspired by British agents generated some sympathy among local democratic societies for ending British rule in Canada. But the Washington administration adopted a policy of neutrality that local adventurism was too weak, or ill-inclined, to challenge.[13]

In 1797, another separatist plot involving Vermonters, the French, and Canada came to light. The Directory, the successor to the Girondists, wanted to use Americans with Montreal business contacts as the germ of a movement to oust the British. Ira Allen again conspired with French officials and arranged a shipment of arms for use in the campaign. One of the merchants, William Barnard of Deerfield, Massachusetts, warned the American government, and independently, British officials caught wind of the plot and seized Allen's weapons en route. John Adams's administration was alarmed because Franco-American relations were descending into the Quasi-War. Nevertheless, Secretary of State Timothy Pickering accepted Vermont Governor Martin Chittenden's explanation that Allen was only speculating to appease his creditors. Allen had debts, but he was also in a political speculation to create a new republic comprising Canada and Vermont.[14] The peculiar ambitions of the

---

[12]Gouverneur Morris to George Washington, 29 May 1790, Manning, *Diplomatic Correspondence*, 1:376–7; Washington to John Jay, Randolph to Jay, 30 August, 6 May, 30 July, 30 August 1794, ibid., 1:64–65, 77, 79–80; instructions to Jay, Henry P. Johnston, ed., *The Correspondence and Public Papers of John Jay*, 3 vols. (New York, 1890–93), 4:15–17; Randolph to George Hammond, 20 May, 2 June 1794, Walter Lowrie and Matthew St. Clair Clarke, eds., *American State Papers: Foreign Affairs*, 5 vols. (Washington, DC, 1832), 1:461, 465–66; Samuel Flagg Bemis, *Jay's Treaty: A Study in Commerce and Diplomacy* (New Haven, 1923), chap. 8, and pp. 456–58.

[13]Useful background is in S. F. Bemis, "Relations between Vermont Separatists and Great Britain 1789–91," *American Historical Review* 21 (October 1916): 547–60.

[14]Jeanne Ojala, "Ira Allen and the French Directory 1796: Plans for the Creation of the Republic of United Columbia," *William and Mary Quarterly* 36 (July 1979): 436–48; Austin, *Lyon*, pp. 83–87; Rufus King to Pickering, 15 December 1796, same to same, 6 April, 16 and 20 June 1797, Manning, *Diplomatic Correspondence*, 1:103, 109–11, 111–12, 478.

Allens notwithstanding, a local group felt sufficiently confident to challenge national authority in foreign policy on this occasion, aligning itself with a country that had become a national enemy. To be sure, this was a controversial point in American politics, since the Jeffersonian Republicans believed that Adams's French policy imperiled the country's future.

Some early foreign policymakers did develop views on the provinces that went beyond the image of a northern British base. Young James Monroe, Thomas Jefferson's protégé, traveled to the Great Lakes and Montreal in 1784. He argued to Jefferson that Americans should make Canada as expensive a possession as possible for the British, even to the point of refusing to trade with the provincials. He did not advocate forcible expansion north, but did suggest that Britain's hold on her American provinces might weaken and that eventually a provincial-American merger might ensue.[15] He held a similar view as the War of 1812 got under way, although as one disastrous campaign followed another, he lost his interest in acquiring Canada.

James Madison, Jefferson's political partner, was early concerned over the potential value of the provinces in Britain's American empire. Madison disagreed with John Baker Holroyd, first Earl of Sheffield, that the provinces would be able, by careful nurturing, to supply the West Indies. To the contrary, these colonies seemed to Madison so dependent upon the United States that economic sanctions would force Britain to acquiesce in American interests. Madison did realize that the St. Lawrence River would be a valuable outlet for the northwest, although he did not seem much aware of the growth of the provincial-American commerce. J. C. A. Stagg argues that Madison had reversed his estimation of provincial development by 1811 and 1812. He planned an invasion of Canada to cut off supplies to the West Indies and curtail the American smuggling that was undermining his policies of economic coercion against the British. Some years after the war, Madison would acknowledge that the borderland had become a "world of itself" that had doomed the embargo, but there is no evidence that he realized this in 1807 when the issue of an embargo arose.[16]

Jefferson said little about Canada and less about the borderland until the embargo. In the 1790s he was primarily concerned about asserting American control over the Indians in the northwest. Once British influence had been removed from American soil, he believed that western dissidents would no longer find British patrons and that local militia would provide any necessary defense. Beyond that, he too thought of subtly eroding provincial loyalties to Britain, referred idly to the population of Tories to the north, and

---

[15] James Monroe to Thomas Jefferson, 1 November 1784 and 12 April 1785, Boyd, *Papers of Jefferson*, 7:459–62, 8:78.

[16] James Madison to King, 8 June, 20 July 1802, Manning, *Diplomatic Correspondence*, 1:157–60; J. C. A. Stagg, "James Madison and the Coercion of Great Britain: Canada, the West Indies and the War of 1812," *William and Mary Quarterly* 38 (January 1981): 12–16, 20–21. See also Stagg, *Mr. Madison's War: Politics, Diplomacy, and Warfare in the Early American Republic 1783–1830* (Princeton, 1983), chap. 1, passim.

thought that over time Canadians would cease to compete with Americans and perhaps even join the United States.[17]

Jefferson's great rival, Alexander Hamilton, learned much more about the borderland economy because of his New York origins and because as secretary of the treasury he had direct reports from his northern officers and agents. He had no part in Jeffersonian foreign policy, but he argued that reciprocal trade with the provinces would develop as a matter of course and benefit both New York in particular and the United States in general. He also realized that the border could never be effectively closed to honest trade, to smugglers, or to potential separatists, such as those in Vermont.[18]

Gallatin, Jefferson's secretary of the treasury, also had the reports of border agents on northern trade and additional information, such as that prepared for him by Astor, but he failed to appreciate how this commercial link would translate into reactions toward national authority in foreign policy. In recommendations for military preparations following the *Chesapeake-Leopard* Affair of 1807, for example, he assumed that the northern states would cheerfully provide volunteers for expeditions to conquer the provinces. Indeed, any strategy of military assault on Canada or the Maritimes had to be based upon the anticipated cooperation of American settlers along the border or it would not work without enormous effort, as the War of 1812 was to show. Gallatin assumed, in other words, strong local support for whatever foreign policy the national government followed.[19] The northern reaction to the embargo therefore came as a shock to both Gallatin and Jefferson, although Gallatin knew a great deal about the smuggling that existed by that time between Americans and their provincial neighbors.

The embargo remains a controversial subject in the historiography of the early national period. How much it benefited or damaged the American economy and ideology remain unclear. Nor is it certain that, as Jefferson believed, stricter enforcement would have forced the British to yield on American demands over freedom of the seas and impressment. What does seem clear is that local resistance to, and defiance of, national authority frustrated

---

[17]Jefferson to Adams, 19 November 1785, Boyd, *Papers of Jefferson,* 9:44; "Reply to representations of Affairs in America by British Newspapers," before 20 November 1784, ibid., 7:542; Dumas Malone, *The Sage of Monticello* (Boston, 1981), pp. 22, 109, 339; Jerald Combs, *The Jay Treaty: Political Battleground of the Founding Fathers* (Berkeley, 1970), pp. 73–74, 90–91.

[18]Hamilton to David Sewall, 13 November 1790, Harold C. Syrett, ed., *The Papers of Alexander Hamilton,* 27 vols. (New York, 1960–82), 8:150–53; "Broadside to Citizens of New York," 22 April 1796, ibid., 20:133–34; "Remarks on the Jay Treaty for Washington," 9–11 July 1795, ibid., 18:404–11, 453. In his "Defence" series on the Jay Treaty, Hamilton revealed considerable knowledge of American-provincial trade. For information from correspondents see Medad Mitchell to Hamilton, 27 August 1793, ibid., 16:296; Benjamin Lincoln to Hamilton, 9 and 17 July 1790, ibid., 6:489, 499–500; and Gilbert Lycan, *Alexander Hamilton and American Foreign Policy: A Design for Greatness* (Norman, 1970), pp. 176–77, 200–202, 260.

[19]Albert Gallatin to Jefferson, 25 July 1807, Henry Adams, ed., *The Writings of Albert Gallatin,* 3 vols. (New York, 1960), 1:345–51; Gallatin to Jefferson, 1806, on intended negotiation with Great Britain, ibid., 1:286–87; Madison to Pinkney and Monroe, 17 May 1806, Manning, *Diplomatic Correspondence,* 1:172–73.

and undermined Jefferson's foreign policy. Madison seriously underestimated how unpopular the measure would be in the northern states. As he and Jefferson conceived the embargo, it was simultaneously protective, coercive, a step on the road to stronger retaliation against Great Britain if it failed, and an example of how republicans should conduct foreign affairs. Jefferson and Madison believed that the British West Indies depended heavily on American supplies and that denying this trade would induce the British to stop seizing American ships and impressing American sailors.[20]

Initially, the embargo seemed to go well. Congress put the previously suspended Non-Importation Act of 1806 into effect in December 1807. Jefferson's cabinet then expanded the concept and Republican majorities passed a total embargo on ocean trade 21 December 1807.[21] Through 1808, these same majorities obediently passed supplementary acts to close loopholes or provide for enforcement. Evasion made police work increasingly cumbersome and morally questionable. But defiance approached insurrection along the provincial frontiers, and coastal smuggling to the north and south through such smugglers' entrepôts as Eastport and Amelia Island replaced much of New England's interdicted high seas trade. Into the fall of 1808, the Republican party lost support on local and national levels, especially in the north, and the partisan furor ripped into the session of 1808 to 1809, producing the cloud under which Jefferson departed the presidency in March.[22] The story of the embargo's failure is complex, but the borderland interests contributed significantly to the collapse of national policy. Opposition fueled partisanship, defiance forced Jefferson's administration to apply severe enforcement procedures; these in turn evoked greater defiance, and the local popular fury translated into a political liability that cost the Republicans ground in New England and the north generally. All the while, Americans who had become dependent on exporting to the provinces continued to move their goods.

The original Embargo Act referred to ocean trade. Shipmasters, however, simply sailed where they wished once they had cleared port. At first, coastal trade continued, but Congress closed this in an effort to stop evasion, granting state governors the power to issue special licenses so that outlying coastal hamlets could receive supplies. Massachusetts's Governor James Sullivan wrote licenses out wholesale, thus nullifying the edict. Coastal trade

---

[20]Louis M. Sears, *Jefferson and the Embargo* (Durham, 1927); Bradford Perkins, *Prologue to War: England and the United States 1805–1812* (Berkeley, 1961), chap. 5; Walter Johnston, Jr., *Jefferson and the Presidency: Leadership in the Young Republic* (Ithaca, 1978), chap. 8; Dumas Malone, *Jefferson the President: Second Term 1805–1809* (Boston, 1974), pp. 472–89, 565–607; Burton Spivak, *Jefferson's English Crisis: Commerce, Embargo and the Republican Revolution* (Charlottesville, 1979); Jeffrey A. Frankel, "The 1807–1809 Embargo against Great Britain," *Journal of Economic History* 42 (June 1982): 291–308.

[21]Jefferson to Congress, 18 December 1807, James D. Richardson, comp., *A Compilation of the Messages and Papers of the Presidents 1789–1902*, 12 vols. (Washington, DC, 1903), 1:433.

[22]Richard Mannix, "Gallatin, Jefferson, and the Embargo of 1808," *Diplomatic History* 3 (Spring 1979): 151–72; Reginald C. Stuart, "James Madison and the Militants: Republican Disunity and Replacing the Embargo," *Diplomatic History* 6 (Spring 1982): 145–68.

from Boston in 1808 was more than double that of 1807, and overall movements of vessels in the port rose by just over 14 percent. Many of those
vessels shipped goods to the provincial maritime ports. Wilson Cary Nicholas,
a Virginia congressman and Jefferson's intimate, eventually voted to rescind
the embargo. He noted to his constituents as a rationale its evident futility.
"Many vessels escaped from New England. Immense quantities of American
produce, not only of the neighboring states, but also of the cotton and tobacco
of the south, were collected in Canada, ready to be shipped to G. Britain, as
soon as the St. Lawrence should be free from ice." Throughout 1808, reports
flowed into Jefferson's office from political friends along the border and into
the Treasury Department from Gallatin's collectors and informants about
scandalous violations of the embargo. The act of 12 March 1808 that closed
exchange with Canada, except in furs, made scant difference.[23]

The Champlain Valley was a hive of activity during 1808. Valley people
trading north ignored the embargo at first, assuming that it referred only to
ocean traffic. British agent John Henry, on his way through Swanton, Vermont, as part of his intelligence gathering travels in New England prior to
the War of 1812, noted in February 1808 that "the roads are covered with
sleighs and the whole country seems employed in conveying their produce
beyond the line of separation." New York pot and pearl ash producers and
Vermont lumbermen and farmers continued to export to Montreal. The 12
March act that ostensibly closed the border was ignored. Jefferson requested
New York Governor Daniel Tompkins to use the militia as a border police,
but Tompkins was fearful of the political consequences of attempting to
enforce a locally unpopular federal law. On 16 April, Burlington, Vermont,
residents met to repudiate the "land embargo" while the press denounced
federal policy.[24] Valley residents with Canadian trade connections effectively
nullified a national foreign policy and created federal-state tensions at the
same time, no less than South Carolinians would do in 1832 over the tariff.

Jefferson was caught in the grip of his own ideology and its assumptions
about the law-abiding character of good republicans. He therefore attributed

[23]Butler, "Commercial Relations," pp. 17–19; Nicholas to constituents, March 1809,
Noble E. Cunningham, Jr., *Circular Letters of Congressmen to their Constituents 1789–1829*,
3 vols. (Chapel Hill, 1978), 2:670. Pinkney to Madison, 22 June 1808, cited in Stagg, "Madison
and Canada," warned that the British were counting on smuggling to maintain their West Indies
plantations. Robin Higham, "The Port of Boston and the Embargo of 1807–1809," *American
Neptune* 16 (July 1956): 191–92, 196–98, 200; John D. Forbes, "Boston Smuggling, 1807–
1815," *American Neptune* 1 (April 1950): 145–49; *New England Palladium*, 18 March, 1 July,
26 August 1808, and 6 January 1809.

[24]John Henry to Herman Ryland, 13 February 1808, E. A. Cruikshank, *The Political
Adventures of John Henry: The Record of an International Embroglio* (Toronto, 1936), cited on
p.18; Gallatin to Jefferson, 30 March, 1 April, 16, 23, and 28 May 1808, Adams, *Writings of
Gallatin*, 1:390–93; Tompkins, general orders, 19 August 1808, H. H. Hastings, ed., *Public
Papers of D. D. Tompkins* (Albany, 1898–1902), 1:194–97; Sears, *Jefferson and Embargo*,
pp. 92–95; Richard Casey, "North Country Nemesis: The Potash Rebellion and the Embargo of
1807–1809," *The New York Historical Society Quarterly* 64 (January 1980): 31–49; H. N. Muller,
"Smuggling into Canada: How the Champlain Valley Defied Jefferson's Embargo," *Vermont
History* 38 (Winter 1970): 5–21; "Ethan Allen," *Vermont Sentinel*, 15 April 1808.

this defiance to "unprincipled agents," lax customs officers, defective legislation, avaricious individuals, and conspiring Federalist politicians, who combined were subverting a virtuous citizenry. Gallatin referred to the "criminal party-rage of the Federalists and Tories," although he appreciated the pull of profits for the locals more than the president. At the same time, Gallatin could see that American supplies were still reaching the West Indies by smuggling, and this undercut the cornerstone of Madison's belief that it was there, rather than in Britain herself, that Americans could create hardship. In the Champlain Valley, party labels were applied to supporters and violators of the embargo, but Jefferson and Gallatin got things reversed. Defiance contributed more to party divisions, than partisanship to defiance. The local economic orientation of the American borderland people and the established maritime interests of New Englanders, rather than partisanship on its own, shaped views on national policy. Jefferson's administration knew what was happening, but did not understand fully why.[25]

Enforcement measures failed. Jefferson proclaimed on 19 April 1808 that

> Sundry persons are combined or combining and confederating together on Lake Champlain and the country thereto adjacent for the purposes of forming insurrections against the authority of the laws of the United States . . . . and that such combinations are too powerful to be suppressed by the ordinary course of judicial proceedings. . . .[26]

Jefferson commanded "such insurgents and ordered all concerned in such combination" to disperse and all officers in the vicinity to "quell and subdue such insurrections" and arrest any who refused to obey the law. A public meeting at St. Albans, Vermont, rejected this proclamation openly. Customs officers increasingly looked the other way as their neighbors smuggled. Local judges and juries displayed great reluctance to convict arrested smugglers and often goods seized in evidence vanished from storerooms. A few collectors hired thugs as enforcers, but these men usually went into the smuggling business on the side. If the militia did act as police, violence, bitterness, and desertions followed, but no consistent enforcement of the law was possible. Some local judges even smuggled themselves. Eventually, the Jefferson administration used regulars along the border, but they were too few to be effective, and they found smugglers willing to shoot it out rather than submit. In January 1809 Jefferson presented Congress with stringent enforcement

---

[25]Ez Hill to William Duane, 29 July 1808, from Buffalo Creek, New York, cited in Frankel, "1807–1809 Embargo"; Gallatin to Jefferson, 29 July 1808, Adams, *Writings of Gallatin*, 1:397–99, and same to same, 17 August 1808, ibid., 1:406; Gallatin to William B. Giles, 24 November 1808, ibid., 1:428–35; Spivak, *Jefferson's English Crisis*, pp. 163, 223–24; Malone, *Jefferson 1805–1809*, pp. 603–4; Stagg, *Mr. Madison's War*, pp. 22–26.

[26]Jefferson, "Proclamation," 19 April 1808, Richardson, *Messages and Papers*, 1:450–51.

measures. The regulations passed, but valley residents met to condemn the administration.[27]

National support for the embargo wilted through the fall of 1808. The administration had assumed a national consensus, not counting partisan opponents. It failed to appreciate that a national policy requires a consensus of interests in a democratic-federal system. The American border people wanted business as usual, although local Federalists were more eager to evade the embargo than local Republicans. Regardless of federal law, however, valley trade north persisted in its accustomed channels.[28] The similar absence of a national consensus in foreign policy from March 1809 to June 1812 was clear to members of Congress and the Madison administration. So was the British encouragement of smuggling and the ability of the provinces to supply the West Indies, partly with their own produce, and partly with illegal goods from the United States.

Stagg argues that this realization led Madison to adopt a strategy of Canadian conquest in his efforts to defend national interests against British pressure. The argument is intriguing, but Stagg's evidence unfortunately seems circumstantial at crucial moments. Nevertheless, in June 1812 Madison appealed to American nationalism for a policy of force that all could see would be directed toward the provinces, but Americans did not respond as he hoped. The congressional session of 1811 and 1812 produced a majority of Republicans behind a policy of war, but that partisan support did not translate into a national consensus, especially at the local level along the border. Federalist partisanship or ideological disagreements sparked opposition to the war in New England and in pockets of the South and West. Along the northern border, opposition grew from a combination of partisanship, self-interest, local contacts, and fear of cross-border attacks. In Congress, the opposition decried a war of conquest contrary to national interests. Whatever Madison's dreams about the future of North America, the provinces seem primarily to have been hostages, targets for retaliation.[29]

---

[27]Ibid.; Muller, "Champlain Route," pp. 210–39, 242–45.

[28]"Evasions of the Non-Importation Act," 28 November 1811, *American State Papers: Commerce and Navigation*, 5 vols. (Washington, DC, 1832), 1:873–74.

[29]Monroe to John Taylor, 13 June 1812, S. M. Hamilton, ed., *The Writings of James Monroe*, 7 vols. (New York, 1901), 5:207; Monroe to Jacob Brown, 10 February 1815, C. P. Stacey, ed., "An American Plan for a Canadian Campaign," *American Historical Review* 46 (March 1941): 348–58; Madison to William Dearborn, 7 October 1812, Gaillard Hunt, ed., *The Writings of James Madison*, 10 vols. (New York, 1906), 8:218; Reginald C. Stuart, "Canada in the American Mind: The Era of the War of 1812," unpublished paper presented at the Canadian Historical Association, Vancouver, British Columbia, 6 June 1983. The opposition to the war is covered in Samuel Eliot Morison, "Dissent in the War of 1812," in Morison, et al., *Dissent in Three American Wars* (Cambridge, MA, 1970), pp. 1–31; Myron Wehtje, "Opposition in Virginia to the War of 1812," *Virginia Magazine of History and Biography* 78 (January 1970): 65–86; Sarah E. Lemmon, "Dissent in North Carolina during the War of 1812," *North Carolina Historical Review* 49 (April 1972): 103–18; Edward Brynn, "Patterns of Dissent: Vermont's Opposition to the War of 1812," *Vermont History* 40 (Winter 1972): 10–27; and Harvey Strum, "New York Federalists and Opposition to the War of 1812," *World Affairs* 142 (Winter 1980): 169–87. See also Stagg, *Mr. Madison's War*, pp. 31, 45–47.

Economic interdiction was part of Madison's policy of force, and the administration directed this to trade in general, as well as exchange with the enemy. Congress passed a protective embargo immediately prior to declaring war, and a bill of 6 July 1812 prohibited exports to the provinces and maritime exchange with any part of the British Empire. At the same time, Gallatin recognized the need to guard or rescue American property in the provinces against possible confiscation.[30] Members of Congress knew that commerce would continue with the British, edicts and the war notwithstanding. Treasury collectors would continue to be helpless. As during the embargo, locals conspired with federal agents and British officials alike to maintain trade, and Congress could do little save pass additional legislation. In partial capitulation to this reality and because the downfall of Napoleon in 1814 freed Europe to trade and brought pressure from merchants who wanted to be unleashed before they would subscribe to the administration's call for loans, Madison requested Congress on 31 March 1814 to repeal the general prohibition of trade. Exchange with the enemy was still banned.[31]

The Champlain Valley was once again the scene of flagrant violations of national law. Some thirty-five of the American merchants in Montreal at the outbreak of the war took an oath of allegiance to the crown so that they could remain in Lower Canada and carry on business. They also continued to trade on the New York money markets. On the Vermont frontier, locals declared a neutrality among themselves and in 1813 Federalists took control of Vermont's legislature and worked to maintain commercial links with the British despite the campaigns being waged along the border. Before those campaigns got started, federal contractors roamed the border region trying to purchase supplies for the future armies, but they found that most of the local production flowed north for sale to the British. Smugglers clashed with Treasury agents, who once again reported a stream of violations of federal laws passed to support national foreign policy. Frequently, the militia, who were supposed to act as border police, were conspirators in the smuggling operations. When General George Izard moved with regulars into the Champlain Valley in 1814, he expressed his own outrage over this traffic:

> From the St. Lawrence to the ocean an open disregard prevails for the laws prohibiting intercourse with the enemy. The road to St. Regis is covered with droves of cattle, and the river with rafts destined for the

---

[30]Gallatin to Langdon Cheves, 23 June 1812, Adams, *Writings of Gallatin,* 1:521–22; U.S., Congress, *The Debates and Proceedings in the Congress of the United States,* 42 vols. (Washington, DC, 1834), 12th Cong., 1st sess., pp. 2354–56; Donald R. Hickey, "American Trade Restrictions During the War of 1812," *Journal of American History* 68 (December 1981): 517–38; Stagg, "Madison and Canada,' pp. 32–34.

[31]John C. Calhoun, "Speech," 24 June 1812, Robert L. Meriwether and W. Edwin Hemphill, eds., *The Papers of John C. Calhoun,* 15 vols. (Columbia, 1962–), 1:132; *Debates and Proceedings,* 13th Cong., 2nd sess., p. 2002; Treasury Department, "Circular to Collectors," October 1812, *Military Monitor and American Register,* 9 November 1812, p. 97; Hickey, "Trade Restrictions," pp. 527–30, 533; Madison to Congress, 31 March 1814, Richardson, *Messages and Papers,* 1:542–43, and "Proclamation," 29 June 1814, ibid., 1:543–44.

enemy. The revenue officers see these things but acknowledge their inability to put a stop to such outrageous procedures. On the eastern side of Lake Champlain, the high roads are found insufficient for the supplies of cattle which are pouring into Canada. . . . Nothing but a cordon of troops from the French Mills to Lake Memphremagog could effectively check the evil.[32]

The Lake Champlain smuggling network during the War of 1812 reached far into the United States. One chain linked Moses and Guy Catlin, Burlington merchants, with Lynde Catlin and Astor in New York City, and C. P. Van Ness, the Vermont collector of customs. Other merchants hired the services of Ramon Manzuco, who ran a ship across the line on the lakes under the neutral Spanish flag to protect contraband. Bogus "privateers" on the lake "captured" cargoes for shipment south. Astor maintained his fur trade, albeit at a reduced level, throughout the war. In July 1812 he removed his furs personally and in 1813 sent up an agent who collected nearly 50,000 more pelts for export. Even as federal troops gathered around Plattsburg in 1814 for what became one of the final campaigns of the war along the northern frontier, the traffic continued. One detail of regulars arrested some smugglers, but civilian authorities released the accused and jailed the officer in charge of the arresting detail for exceeding his authority.[33]

The New York border along the St. Lawrence River contributed other examples of locals defying federal policy. Local reaction to the advent of war was mixed, but subdued. The frontier economy depended upon access to Montreal, and upstate New Yorkers displayed no enthusiasm for invading their provincial neighbors. British garrisons lay just across the river and the 40,000 scattered western New York settlers feared Indian attacks. Buffalo and other settlements on the lakes foresaw bombardment from British ships. In late February 1812, the British captured Ogdensburg and Canadians crossed on the ice to plunder the town. Subsequently, Ogdensburgers resisted having American troops stationed among them for fear of being a target again. David Parish, a prominent local businessman and banker, openly opposed war. At the same time, he conducted a brisk trade through a string of agents on both sides of the border. One of these, John Ross, wrote to Parish in July 1813, "it is incredible what quantities of cattle & sheep are driven into Canada. We can hardly get any for love or money; the day before yesterday upwards of 100 oxen went through Prescott, yesterday about 200." British officers visited Ogdensburg, not to fight, but to shop and dine, and visitors went back and

---

[32]Izard to John Armstrong, 31 July 1814, cited in Allan Everest, *The War of 1812 in the Champlain Valley* (Syracuse, 1981), p. 151. See also ibid., pp. 41–42, 57, 139; and H. M. Muller, "A 'Traitorous and Diabolical Traffic': The Commerce of the Champlain-Richelieu Corridor During the War of 1812," *Vermont History* 44 (Spring 1976): 78–96.

[33]Muller, "Champlain Route," pp. 313–17; Porter, *Astor*, 1:250–83; Strum, "New York Federalists," pp. 177–78; Craig, *Upper Canada*, pp. 70–75.

forth across the river. Canadians even came down to pick up tea and other supplies unobtainable in the provinces because of wartime shortages.[34]

The New England-Maritimes sector had greater flexibility for maintaining peacetime traffic during the War of 1812. New England was virtually neutral, where it was not downright hostile, to Madison's war. No campaigns occurred on land east of the Champlain Valley, although many New Englanders enlisted in federal regiments and fought on the northern frontier farther west. Some of those who enlisted spent part of the war on the Maine-New Brunswick border attempting to stop their fellow New Englanders from running supplies to the British. At the beginning of the war local pressure in Eastport, Maine, forced the removal of an army officer who had pursued the Passamaquoddy Bay smugglers too zealously. Yankees supplied British military contractors in Halifax and New England fishermen found licenses freely available from Nova Scotia and New Brunswick authorities. American-Nova Scotian trade rose after hostilities officially began, and plaster of paris, a bulky cargo, continued to flow through Boston to American markets. The British navy protected smugglers who eluded Boston's federal agents, and when Britain tightened the blockade in 1814, its forces occupied eastern Maine and established a customs post at Castine, where they found locals freely willing to take oaths of loyalty to King George III and stay in business.

Coastal smuggling perforce declined, but some traffic continued overland through British-occupied territory. New England merchants frequently followed "captured" cargoes to Halifax where they secured prompt redress for their "losses." As secretary of state, Monroe reflected the Madison administration's unwillingness to antagonize merchants any more than necessary and issued special passes to those who petitioned for travel to the Maritimes to recover such property. New Englanders also frequently paid for illegal British goods in cash, and Christopher Gore noted to Rufus King in 1814 that between the provinces and "the Eastern States, especially this, there is an uninterrupted trade in Bills of the British gov't—from two banks in Boston there have departed 1,800,000 Dollars since the first of June."[35]

The War of 1812 almost collapsed of its own weight. A reluctant belligerent, the Madison administration was a willing, albeit cautious suitor at the peace table. This, and the larger context within which the war had emerged, produced unusual results for all parties. The Canadians won because in the west, at least, they had repelled a republican invader and saved their

[34]Harry Landon, *Bugles on the Border: The Story of the War of 1812 in Northern New York* (Watertown, 1954), pp. 7, 12, 32–36; Beverly W. Bond, *The Civilization of the Old Northwest: A Study of Political, Social, and Economic Development* (New York, 1934).

[35]Gore to King, 28 July 1814, Charles R. King, ed., *The Life and Correspondence of Rufus King*, 7 vols. (New York, 1898), 5:403; "War of 1812 Papers," Department of State, National Archives, Washington, DC, RG 59, M 588, Reel 5, frames 50, 52, 55; Jacob Varnum presenting petition of Boston merchants, 18 December 1815, *Debates and Proceedings*, 14th Cong., 1st sess., pp. 23–24; Forbes, "Boston Smuggling," pp. 152–54; MacNutt, *Atlantic Provinces*, pp. 135–53; Walter R. Copp, "Nova Scotian Trade During the War of 1812," *Canadian Historical Review* 18 (June 1937): 141–55; Butler, "Commercial Relations," p. 22, n. 64, p. 24.

homeland. The British won because they lost nothing. The Americans won because they stood up to the British and vindicated their national honor. The professed causes, the grievances against British maritime policies before 1812, were remarkably absent in the peace document, although the trade issue continued to dog Anglo-American diplomats and merchants for years. If the results of the conflict seem largely psychological, that is fitting, because Republican psychology had much to do with the coming of the war in the first place. As a venture in national policy for the Madison government, war had proven to be an equivocal instrument.

Along the northern border of New England and New York, the defiance of federal law was one of the factors contributing to the ambivalent outcome of the struggle. True, armies marched, fought, bivouacked, countermarched, and departed from the Champlain Valley west. The campaigns proved enormously difficult and embarrassed the Madison administration because of military ineptitude, political jealousies, administrative inadequacies, combined with the lack of necessary local bases, supplies, and volunteers. In the far west, once westerners had recovered from the disaster of General William Hull's surrender, the war was more successful. This did not apply to the Maine-New Brunswick border, however, where no campaigns occurred except against New England smugglers. In the St. Croix Valley, where a strong borderland spirit had developed by 1812, the locals observed a neutrality. New England fishermen and traders still viewed the provincial Maritimes as part of their economic hinterland and operated despite the war, heartily assisted by New England's neutrality and obliging British officials. Supplies that should have gone to American armies in a national war effort went instead to the British. Federalists would not even cooperate to recover regional territory occupied by the British in 1814. The smuggling continued from Eastport under the British gaze until they withdrew in 1818 after an arbitration established by the Treaty of Ghent awarded Moose Island to the United States.

The Champlain Valley residents found attempted neutrality impossible because of the early presence of troops mustering for assaults on Canada. Valley people nevertheless continued their trade with the provinces in defiance of federal policy and power. The end of the war removed the obstacle of federal troops as border police, but it did not alter the character of local interests as much as did the opening of the Erie Canal in 1825. That waterway, not federal authority or agents, redirected the economic life of the entire northern tier of American states and competed as a commercial conduit in the provinces with the St. Lawrence River.

Some bitterness toward the provinces existed farther west, where most of the fighting had occurred, but in general, Americans in the borderland were relieved when the war ended and swiftly returned to business with the provincials. After all, the aggressive westerners had achieved their primary goal of breaking Indian power in the northwest and discrediting the British with the tribes. American diplomats at Ghent had confirmed this triumph by refusing to consider the British efforts to revive the old idea of an Indian buffer state between British settlements in Canada and the United States.

Taken together, the war and the embargo demonstrated that a sector of the American periphery could circumvent, defy, and frustrate federal authority in the conduct of foreign policy, the Constitution notwithstanding, if locals decided that national policy contradicted their interests. Aggressive policies could not be prosecuted against a neighboring region unless the Americans along the border were behind them. National authority was one thing; local interests another. The success of a given policy rested on their harmonious interaction. Trade with the enemy was not treason to the borderlanders, just good business, even though their defiance helped to riddle the embargo and undermined the war effort after 1812. Without American supplies from the Champlain Valley, for example, the British would not have been able to feed their people farther west and hence defend Canada against American assaults across the Detroit and Niagara rivers, not to mention along the St. Lawrence frontier. New England's neutrality rendered a vast stretch of border secure for the British, and provincial militia from New Brunswick and Nova Scotia could be shipped west for duty where American armies threatened in Upper and Lower Canada.

Finally, the idea of an Anglo-American borderland between the provinces and the northern states requires careful and consistent investigation. Even this brief synthesis suggests how Americans reflected their emerging agrarian-mercantile national culture as they pushed past their borders, not simply through the agents of war and diplomacy, but with their settlers and businessmen. This in turn suggests an important perspective on the American-Canadian sharing of North America beyond the familiar triangular diplomatic surveys.

James Madison and the "Malcontents": The Political Origins of the War of 1812

J. C. A. Stagg

F OR the past eighty years the question of the causes of the War of 1812 has been a subject of controversy in the historiography of the early American Republic. Historians have usually approached the subject by trying to isolate the causes of the war from a broad complex of problems that complicated Anglo-American relations in the early nineteenth century. The number of possible causes has now become large indeed; they include violation of American maritime rights, impressment of American seamen, British incitement of hostile Indians, American designs on Canada and Florida, the depressing effects of British policy on American farm prices, American concern for both the dignity and the future of the Republic, and the desire of the dominant Republican party to maintain its control of the federal government.[1]

Yet when all the possible grievances and motives have been discussed, there remains the feeling that a truly satisfactory explanation for the outbreak of the war has eluded its students. This is because all of the explanations proposed to date have dealt with these grievances and motives in a way that has presented them only as *necessary* antecedents for war. With the possible exception of the continual violation of American maritime rights resulting from the British Orders in Council of 1807 and 1809, it has seemed doubtful whether these problems, either singly or in combination, were *sufficient* causes for war. And although the Orders in Council must be given priority in any explanation of the coming of the war, there has been the nagging question of why the United States delayed so long before insisting on their repeal at all costs. In fact, all of the disputes over maritime rights, although providing legitimate enough reasons for war, were old grievances in 1812, and

Mr. Stagg is a lecturer in history at the University of Auckland, New Zealand. He would like to acknowledge the assistance of James M. Banner, Jr., and the Research Grant Committee of Auckland University in the preparation of this article.
[1] See the summaries by Warren H. Goodman, "The Origins of the War of 1812: A Survey of Changing Interpretations," *Mississippi Valley Historical Review*, XXVIII (1941), 171-186, and Clifford L. Egan, "The Origins of the War of 1812: Three Decades of Historical Writing," *Military Affairs*, XXXVIII (1974), 72-75.

none of these grievances were as burdensome in that year as they had been earlier.[2]

Historians have not yet seriously concerned themselves with the problem of why the "necessary antecedents" for war did not produce the final event until 1812. Usually they have argued that the movement toward war came in 1811 and 1812 because the earlier policies of commercial restriction had by then clearly failed to obtain redress of American grievances.[3] This answer is not so much wrong as circular; it begs the question about the timing of the war while also failing to make clear who concluded that the earlier policies were inadequate and for what reason. No doubt the rejection of Thomas Jefferson's foreign policies was a gradual process as Americans came to see the need for change at different times from 1808 to 1812, but the decisive shift in policy from economic coercion to war might nevertheless be described more exactly than it has been. Indeed, the major problem in explaining the coming of the war is not to single out its possible causes but to make intelligible the dynamics behind the movement to war. This approach requires a political analysis in which the main American decisions leading to war can be located and explained as precisely as the surviving evidence will permit.

A political analysis can also deal with another critical problem in the historiography of the subject—the relative responsibility of President James Madison and the "War Hawk" Congress for precipitating the final crisis. Here most historians have placed the responsibility with Congress rather than the president. The old notion that a reluctant Madison was coerced into war by Congress dies hard. While this version of events in its cruder forms has long been regarded as misleading, there is still considerable uncertainty about the role of the president.[4] The belief that Madison failed to exercise presidential leadership during his first term has invariably led historians to locate in Congress the impetus toward war. However, the crucial assumptions in the case for Congress as the prime agent can be shown to have been already undermined or to be simply erroneous.

First, the research of Roger H. Brown and Ronald L. Hatzenbuehler has failed to identify in the first session of the twelfth Congress—the session that voted for war—a distinct faction of "War Hawks" pursuing belligerent policies which were believed to be at variance with the wishes of Madison.[5]

[2] Bradford Perkins, *Prologue to War: England and the United States, 1805-1812* (Berkeley and Los Angeles, 1961), 3, 432.

[3] See, for example, Reginald Horsman, *The Causes of the War of 1812* (Philadelphia, 1962), 265-266.

[4] For a discussion of this point see Egan, "Origins of the War," *Military Affairs*, XXXVIII (1974), 73-74.

[5] Roger H. Brown, *The Republic in Peril: 1812* (New York, 1964), 44-46; Ronald L. Hatzenbuehler, "Party Unity and the Decision for War in the House of Representatives, 1812," *William and Mary Quarterly*, 3d Ser., XXIX (1972), 375-378, 383.

Yet the existence of the "War Hawks" is essential to most explanations of the coming of the war. Even Bradford Perkins, the first scholar to doubt whether the congressional elections of 1810 and 1811 hatched a nest of "War Hawks," continues to use the term, largely because of the difficulty of discarding the image of a fumbling and indecisive Madison.[6] Undeniably, Madison was cautious, but this should not be overemphasized. Throughout his career he combined a consistently analytical and rational approach to the problems of government with a deeply ingrained stubbornness that could lead him to take a position and adhere to it at almost any cost. As Albert Gallatin remarked on the eve of the president's taking office, "Mr Madison is slow in taking his ground, but firm when the storm arises."[7]

Secondly, the belief that congressional actions played a vital part in pushing the administration to war rests on a misconception about the relations between executive and legislature in the early Republic. Congress at that time was a loosely organized body, seldom capable of initiating or adopting major policy decisions independently of the executive. Congressional proceedings, moreover, were strongly influenced by the wishes of the administration which were usually communicated to select and standing committees by members of the executive departments. The Republican presidents and their cabinets were, within the conventions of their time and with the limited means at their disposal, political managers, informally but actively engaged in influencing the legislative process.[8]

The so-called "War Hawks" of the twelfth Congress, who can best be identified not as a faction but as a loose group of the most prominent members of the committees of the House of Representatives, played only an intermediary role.[9] They received in committee policy recommendations

[6] Perkins, *Prologue to War*, 262-267, 378-381, 425.

[7] Albert Gallatin to Joseph H. Nicholson, Dec. 29, 1808, in Henry Adams, ed., *The Writings of Albert Gallatin*, I (Philadelphia, 1879), 449.

[8] Joseph Cooper, "Jeffersonian Attitudes Toward Executive Leadership and Committee Development in the House of Representatives, 1789-1829," *Western Political Quarterly*, XVIII (1965), 45-63. Cooper's analysis seems preferable to that of James Sterling Young, *The Washington Community, 1800-1828* (New York, 1966), esp. 202-210. By emphasizing how the committee system in Congress ultimately became a barrier to executive influence, Young overlooks evidence that suggests that the committee system, at least in its early stages, was an instrument of executive policy.

[9] For evidence of regular contact between the administration and House committee members see "Minutes of the Committee on Foreign Relations," Feb. 6, 11, Mar. 9, 24, 1812, Peter B. Porter Papers, Buffalo and Erie County Historical Society, Buffalo, New York. See also William Eustis to David R. Williams, Nov. 30, 1811, and Jan. 9, 1812, and Eustis to Langdon Cheves, Dec. 3, 5, 10, 1811, Reports to Congress from the Secretary of War, 1803-1870 (M-220), Roll 2, Records of the Office of the Secretary of War (RG 107), National Archives. Attempts to identify the "War Hawks" using legislative roll-call analysis have not proved to be wholly satisfactory, but all of the "War Hawks" can be located on the various committees of

from the administration, then reported them as bills to the floor of the House. As committee members had done in previous congresses, they frequently took the lead in the ensuing debates to make a case for the policies which the executive wished to have adopted. The program of military preparations and the bellicose oratory of these Republican party House leaders after November 1811 in reality reflected not simply their own wishes but, more significantly, those of President Madison.

The role of Congress in the coming of the War of 1812 was thus far less decisive than most historians have believed, while the role of the president was far more important. Madison, in his joint capacities as president and as leader of the Republican party, must be the focus of any study of the coming of the war. Like his predecessors in office, Madison was unable to conduct foreign policy independently of any consideration of its impact on American domestic politics. Indeed, the nature of the first American party system, originating as it did in the interaction of events within and beyond the United States, imposed this situation on his administration.[10] Madison's actions throughout his first term are therefore best described in the context of reaction and response to the many diplomatic and political pressures which were brought to bear on him. In this sense, the coming of the War of 1812 can be understood not merely as the termination of a long crisis in Anglo-American relations but also as the outcome of the politics of the first American party system.

Politics during Madison's first administration were shaped by two overriding considerations: the need for a new foreign policy to replace Jefferson's discredited embargo, and the fact that Madison had not been the unanimous choice of the Republican party in 1808. Both problems caused considerable dissension within the party, and the election of 1808 defined a relationship between diplomatic and political issues that thereafter dominated Madison's presidency. The general outline of events during Madison's first two years in office is well enough known to require only summary restatement, but it is important to stress that the continuing interplay between foreign policy and domestic politics determined Madison's handling of the dispute over maritime rights with Great Britain. Ultimately, the exigencies of domestic politics were to provide a sufficient cause for the president's decision to prepare for war.

---

the House. See Ronald L. Hatzenbuehler, "The War Hawks and the Question of Congressional Leadership in 1812," *Pacific Historical Review*, XLV (1976), 1-22. I am grateful to Professor Hatzenbuehler for allowing me to read this article in manuscript.

[10] See Joseph Charles, *The Origins of the American Party System: Three Essays* (Williamsburg, Va., 1961), 91-140.

Those Republicans who refused to accept Madison as Jefferson's successor, notably the supporters of Vice President George Clinton of New York and of James Monroe of Virginia, also rejected the foreign policies of the Jefferson administration, in which Madison had been secretary of state. The Clintonians attacked the embargo as a "southern" measure intended to harm the other sections of the nation. They thus integrated foreign policy issues into their main campaign argument that another Virginian should not be allowed to succeed to the presidency. Clinton appears to have believed that he could win the election by welding an alliance of his supporters in the middle states with the Federalists and Monroe's supporters in Virginia, thereby recreating the "germ of the true Republican party" as an alternative to the existing one.[11] The candidacy of Monroe was more personal and more localized, but the main issue was similar: he was seeking vindication against Jefferson and Madison for their rejection of the treaty which he and William Pinkney had negotiated with Britain in 1806.[12]

Madison's candidacy survived these challenges, but his presidency nearly foundered on the problems they had raised. The Clintonians remained constant in their hostility to the president, their estrangement again entailing a repudiation of his foreign policy. In the columns of the *Albany Register* George Clinton's son-in-law, Edmond Genet, assumed a belligerent position, persistently attacking the administration for not making naval and military preparations to defend American rights.[13] Madison, however, not only failed to reconcile the Clintonians but during 1809 and 1810 also lost the support of other important Republican politicians such as William Duane of Pennsylvania, Robert and Samuel Smith of Maryland, and Wilson Cary Nicholas and William Branch Giles of Virginia. The efforts of all these Republican state party leaders had been essential to Madison's election in 1808, and their subsequent defection was a serious matter, reflecting considerable dissatisfaction with the president's conduct of foreign affairs, the composition of his administration, and, in some cases, the distribution of power within the Republican party itself.

In Maryland and Pennsylvania Madison's troubles arose from his attempt to appoint Jefferson's Treasury secretary, Albert Gallatin of Pennsylvania, as his secretary of state. This move alienated Duane and the Smith brothers; all three disliked Gallatin, and his promotion not only threatened

---

[11] Josiah Masters to Edmond Genet, Mar. 29, 1808, Edmond Genet Papers microfilm, Roll 9, Library of Congress.

[12] Harry Ammon, "James Monroe and the Election of 1808 in Virginia," *WMQ*, 3d Ser., XX (1963), 33-56.

[13] E. Wilder Spaulding, *His Excellency George Clinton: Critic of the Constitution* (New York, 1938), 177-178; Harry Ammon, *The Genet Mission* (New York, 1973), 177-178.

their ambitions but seemed to ignore the services they had rendered Madison in staving off the Clintonian challenge.[14] Although Robert Smith and not Gallatin finally gained the appointment, the affair left a legacy of bitterness and sparked a premature struggle for the succession in the Republican party. Gallatin and the few Republicans who were sympathetic to him suspected that the Smith brothers were out to destroy the administration, partly out of pique and partly as a prelude to an attempt by Robert Smith to claim the presidency for himself in 1812.[15]

To ward off this perceived threat, Gallatin, who reluctantly remained at the Treasury, waged unrelenting war on the Smith brothers. He accused the Baltimore firm of Smith and Buchanan of mishandling government funds, tried to prevent Samuel Smith's re-election to the Senate, and rejected the Smiths' beliefs that the nation should strengthen its defenses and vindicate its neutral rights more forcefully. Occasionally he even snubbed them socially, while the cabinet wives, in the confined atmosphere of Washington society, indulged in unpleasant, petty recriminations. After one rebuff from Gallatin, Robert Smith swore that had it not been necessary to preserve appearances, he would have "shot him the next morning."[16]

The administration's failure either to continue the embargo or to prepare for war further alienated William Duane and his Clintonian ally, Senator Michael Leib of Pennsylvania. By the middle of 1810 their longstanding dislike of Gallatin had hardened into implacable hatred. After learning of the Treasury secretary's unofficial role in negotiations with Britain throughout 1809, Duane became convinced that Gallatin had misled Madison into adopting a foreign policy of "base submission" in order to replenish the Treasury from the flow of customs receipts. Thereafter he called for both the dismissal of Gallatin and the adoption of a policy of armed neutrality and retaliation against Britain.[17] Admittedly, Duane was frequently carried away by the excesses of his own rhetoric, but his intense Anglophobia was probably shared by most Republican leaders in Pennsylvania. He was, moreover, a

[14] Frank A. Cassell, *Merchant Congressman in the Young Republic: Samuel Smith of Maryland, 1752-1839* (Madison, Wis., 1971), 144-147; Sanford W. Higginbotham, *The Keystone in the Democratic Arch: Pennsylvania Politics, 1800-1816* (Harrisburg, 1952), 156-161.

[15] Gallatin to Thomas Jefferson, Nov. 8, 1809, in Adams, ed., *Writings of Gallatin*, I, 465; Nathaniel Macon to Thomas Worthington, Apr. 9, 1810, Miscellaneous MSS, Alderman Library, University of Virginia, Charlottesville.

[16] Cassell, *Merchant Congressman*, 147-153; [Joseph Gales], "Recollections of the Civil History of the War of 1812 by a Contemporary," *Daily National Intelligencer* (Washington, D.C.), Sept. 12, 1857.

[17] William Duane to Madison, Dec. 1, 8, 1809, and to Jefferson, July 16, 1810, in Worthington C. Ford, ed., "Letters of William Duane," Massachusetts Historical Society, *Proceedings*, XX (1906-1907), 325-328, 331, 338-339, hereafter cited as Ford, ed., "Letters of Duane."

brilliantly effective publicist; his newspaper, the *Aurora General Advertiser*, was, as a rival editor conceded, "the oldest and most influential Republican newspaper in Pennsylvania [which] probably had as much, or more, influence with that party in the Union than any other paper."[18]

In Virginia, Madison lost the support of the two Republican leaders, Wilson Cary Nicholas and William Branch Giles, who had outmaneuvered Monroe and his "Old Republican" followers in 1808. While Monroe never altered his conviction that Madison's attitude toward Britain was fundamentally wrong and more likely to bring war than peace, Nicholas and Giles came to condemn the president for not making a more aggressive defense of America's neutral rights.[19] Nicholas withdrew from politics in disgust, while Giles, who had also been offended by the attempt to promote Gallatin, joined forces occasionally in the Senate with Samuel Smith and a handful of "factious" Republicans to oppose administration-sponsored foreign measures as too weak.[20] Smith and Giles feared that Britain and France would reduce the United States to a "makeweight," and, like the Clintonians, they believed that the navy should be increased.[21] This course of action, however, was unlikely to win the president's approval as long as Gallatin remained in the cabinet and kept the federal budget in balance by cutting down expenditures.

Toward this growing disunity in the party and rising criticism of his policies Madison was outwardly forbearing. He had always felt that "schisms" would occur in the party as the Republicans "lost the cement given to their union by the rivalship of the Federal party." He even regarded such "breaches" as permissible, provided that the Republic was confronted with no serious threats to its barely consolidated stability. Should "new dangers" ever arise from abroad, Madison believed that the Republican party would

---

[18] Higginbotham, *Keystone in the Democratic Arch*, 243-246; Martin Kaufman, "War Sentiment in Western Pennsylvania: 1812," *Pennsylvania History*, XXXI (1964), 436-448; John Binns, *Recollections of the Life of John Binns* (Philadelphia, 1854), 191.

[19] Wilson Cary Nicholas to Jefferson, Dec. 22, 1809, Smith-Carter Papers, Alderman Lib., Univ. of Va.; Dice Robins Anderson, *William Branch Giles: A Study in the Politics of Virginia and the Nation, 1790 to 1830* (Menasha, Wis., 1914), 146-170.

[20] Ronald L. Hatzenbuehler, "Foreign Policy Voting in the United States Congress, 1808-1812" (Ph.D. diss., Kent State University, 1972), 313, 317, 346, 354, 373-387. This loose group of Republicans in the 11th Congress, generally referred to as the "invisibles" or the "malcontents," included, in addition to Samuel Smith and Giles, Senators John Smith and Obadiah German of New York, Elisha Matthewson of Rhode Island, Nicholas Gilman of New Hampshire, and Michael Leib of Pennsylvania.

[21] Samuel Smith to Wilson Cary Nicholas, Jan. 13, 1810, Randolph Family Papers, Alderman Lib., Univ. of Va.; Hatzenbuehler, "Foreign Policy Voting," 155.

close ranks to carry the nation through the crisis.[22] But reality did not conform to these expectations. After 1809 Republican unity vanished with the rising tensions between the administration and the party's factional and regional components. In the process, foreign policy issues came to bear the burden of many of the differences among quarrelling Republicans, a development that made it unlikely that the many disputes within the party could be resolved independently of each other.

The difficulty was not that the president lacked a coherent analysis of foreign policy problems, but that he was unable to find a stable Republican majority either in Congress or in the cabinet to support any consistent policy. Shortly before he became president, Madison had concluded that, failing a negotiated settlement of American grievances, the broad alternatives before him were either war with Britain or submission to its Orders in Council. Since he was not prepared to accept submission or its consequences, Madison recognized that war was an imminent possibility. In fact, he believed that both Congress and the merchant community would welcome war after a brief experience of British restrictions. The British market would soon become glutted with American products, forcing merchants to seek European markets and thus run the risk of seizure by the Royal Navy. "It cannot be doubted," the president wrote early in 1809, "[that] if the orders be enforced, war is inevitable."[23]

Unfortunately, the effects on American trade of the policies that replaced the embargo, embodied in the Non-Intercourse Act of 1809 and Macon's Bill No. 2 of 1810, did not produce the strong reaction against Britain for which Madison had hoped. The American desire for trade, even on British terms, was so great that the volume of commerce—though not the prices of American staples—actually increased.[24] France and its satellites retaliated, not against Britain but against the United States, thus failing, as Madison bitterly complained, to put their mutual enemy in the wrong.[25] Under the decrees of Milan and Rambouillet during the five years before 1812, French officials and privateers seized more American vessels than did the Royal Navy.[26] This intolerable impasse placed Madison in a very dangerous position. By the middle of 1810 his diplomacy had clearly become ineffective; his principal advisor, Gallatin, was isolated within the party and brought no significant support to the administration; and, worst of all, the coalition of

[22] Madison to James Monroe, May 17, 1806, July 6, 1807, James Madison Papers, Lib. Cong.

[23] Madison to William Pinkney, Feb 11, 1809, ibid.

[24] George R. Taylor, "Prices in the Mississippi Valley Preceding the War of 1812," Journal of Economic and Business History, III (1930), 148-163.

[25] Madison to Jefferson, Apr. 23, May 7, 1810, Madison Papers, Lib. Cong.

[26] For the figures see Brown, Republic in Peril, 18.

state Republican interests that had elected him to the presidency had completely gone to pieces.

The Republican party, its ranks swollen by continual success at the polls, had become increasingly unable to serve the interests of all its constituents or even to reflect adequately in its own structures their relative degrees of political strength. The rapidly rising population of the middle states, especially New York, gave Republicans from that region ever greater voting strength in Congress and in the electoral college, but it did not give them equivalent influence on the formation of national policy.[27] Effective political power, as reflected in the distribution of federal patronage and the committee structure of Congress, was largely held by Republicans from south of the Potomac.[28] Republicans whose views and interests went unheeded complained of neglect. As one prominent Madisonian in Pennsylvania pointed out to Gallatin, it was difficult in such circumstances "to maintain the Republican cause or vindicate the administration from reproach."[29]

Consequently, many prominent Republican politicians, especially in the middle states, came to resent the domination of Virginia in national politics. They felt dissatisfied both with Madison and with a party system that could not generate fresh alternatives to the policies of "free trade" advocated by the Federalists or to the commercial restrictions practiced by the administration. They therefore ceased to support consistently the old Jeffersonian coalition that had cast the Federalists from power in 1800. Yet the disposition of these Republican leaders was often critical in determining the political complexion of their own regions, and their support for the administration was vital in

[27] Between 1790 and 1810, the population of the Middle Atlantic states of New York, New Jersey, and Pennsylvania rose by 110%, while that of the New England and South Atlantic regions increased by only 46% and 44% respectively. The number of presidential electors from the Middle Atlantic states rose by 4% between 1796 and 1812, while that from the New England and South Atlantic states fell by 6% and 1.5% respectively. Figures calculated from U.S. Bureau of the Census, *Historical Statistics of the United States: Colonial Times to 1957* (Washington, D.C., 1960), Ser. A, 123-180.

[28] The Middle Atlantic states were poorly represented in Madison's cabinet and underrepresented in the congressional power structure. With 31% of the membership of the House, middle state representatives held during Madison's administrations only 24% of the committee assignments and 19% of the chairmanships. Southern congressmen, however, received 38% of the committee assignments and 56% of the chairmanships on the basis of the House membership. See Harry W. Fritz, "The Collapse of Party: President, Congress, and the Decline of Party Action, 1807-1817" (Ph.D. diss., Washington University, 1971), 243-247.

[29] Alexander James Dallas to Albert Gallatin, July 24, 1811, Albert Gallatin Papers, New-York Historical Society, New York City. For a discussion of congressional factionalism that highlights the importance of the role of middle state representatives in maintaining Republican unity see Hatzenbuehler, "Foreign Policy Voting," 74, 85, 109, 114, 182, 197, 230, 254-283.

maintaining a national party structure. The impact of their disaffection was therefore serious; it hampered American diplomacy, threatened the future of the Republican party, and thus undermined the political stability of the nation in a period of crisis. In a long letter to Henry Dearborn of Massachusetts in July 1810, Duane diagnosed the nation's problems and prescribed their remedy. Unless the president acted to resolve the disputes over men and measures in his administration, the editor predicted that "everything must go to disorder . . . the Republican party must go to destruction . . . [and] Mr Madison will be thrown out at the next election."[30]

In August 1810 Napoleon made a move that seemed to give Madison the chance both to reactivate his foreign policy and to restore his standing in the Republican party. In the Cadore letter the emperor offered to repeal his edicts against neutral shipping on condition that by November 1810 either Great Britain would withdraw the Orders in Council or the United States would make its rights respected by that nation. Although the wording of this letter did not exactly meet Madison's terms for a settlement of Franco-American differences, the president nonetheless chose to accept it as evidence of an actual change in French policy. Hoping that France would not give him any reason to insist on further clarification of these matters, Madison reimposed non-intercourse against Britain in November 1810.[31]

Madison's reasons for taking this gamble are difficult to ascertain, but it seems probable that he believed that Britain could be induced to match the French concession by revoking the Orders in Council. The president did not expect Britain to give up completely its efforts to control the flow of trade to Europe, but he anticipated that the policy would be continued by the means of a series of more limited blockades. Such a development would have amounted to a· considerable diplomatic triumph for the United States; it would have spared American shipping from the worst of the seizures by the belligerents while leaving Madison free to contend with Britain over the legality of specific blockades, a far more manageable subject than the Orders in Council. Indeed, Madison hoped that it would be possible for Britain to conduct its policies so as to "irritate France against our non-resistance without irritating this country to the resisting point."[32] On the home front the announcement of the French concession promised to have a favorable

[30] Duane to Henry Dearborn, July 3, 1810, Miscellaneous MSS, Lib. Cong. For similar observations see Nicholas to Giles, Dec. 10, 1810, Edgehill-Randolph Papers, Alderman Lib., Univ. of Va.; Macon to Nicholson, Feb. 9, 1811, and John Randolph to Nicholson, Feb. 14, 1811, Joseph H. Nicholson Papers, Lib. Cong.

[31] Perkins, *Prologue to War*, 245-250.

[32] Madison to John Armstrong, Oct. 29, 1810, and Madison to Jefferson, Oct. 19, 1810, Madison Papers, Lib. Cong.

effect on the congressional elections to be held in eight states later in the year.[33]

Madison's gamble failed. The Cadore letter was a fraud. Not only did Napoleon not release previously seized American vessels but his officials continued their old policies, citing "municipal regulations" as justification. The miscalculation seriously weakened Madison's case against Britain and greatly intensified the factionalism within the Republican party, finally leading to the political crisis which both Duane and Gallatin had been dreading so long. This political crisis, as Joseph Gales of the *National Intelligencer* later recalled, was "an important link in the chain of circumstances which led to the declaration of war with Great Britain."[34] The secretary of state, Robert Smith, although no Anglophile, opposed Madison's decision. He did not believe that the Cadore letter furnished a firm basis for a major change in American foreign policy.

Smith favored taking no action until further news was received from France on the status of American shipping there. In the meantime he intended to prod the new French minister in Washington, Louis Sérurier, into admitting that there had been no change in French policy at all. Madison, according to Gales, appeared "to be afraid to *think* that France would not fulfill her engagement," and he tried to prevent Smith from going ahead with his plan.[35] The secretary, however, was not to be deterred and even conveyed his opinions to the British *chargé d'affaires*, John Philip Morier. Smith told Morier that Congress, realizing that Madison had erred, would shortly do away with "the whole of their restrictive commercial systems."[36]

At the same time the American minister to France, John Armstrong of New York, who believed that his own brand of diplomacy had been responsible for the offer of the Cadore letter, resigned and returned to the United States. He had been away from home for a long period, and his diplomatic career had not been entirely successful. French officials resented Armstrong's "morose, captious, and petulant moods" expressed in the "peevish notes" he penned on the seizure of American vessels, while Armstrong, in constant contact with Napoleon's duplicity, had difficulty in restraining his

---

[33] [Gales], "Recollections," for Sept. 27, 1810, *Daily Nat'l. Intelligencer*, July 30, 1857.
[34] *Ibid.*
[35] *Ibid.*, for Jan. 30, 1811, Aug. 8, 1857.
[36] John Philip Morier to Lord Wellesley, Dec. 28, 1810, and Feb. 4, 1811, F.O. 5/70, 5/74, Public Record Office (photostats in Lib. Cong.). Louis Sérurier to duc de Cadore, Feb. 7, 1811, Archives des Affaires Étrangères, Correspondence Politique, États Unis, LXV (photostats in Lib. Cong.).

own bellicose instincts.[37] Privately Armstrong was disgusted with Madison's policies, fearing that they would reduce the Republic to a "proverb of weakness and irresolution." There were advantages, he told Samuel Smith, in going to war with France, and on occasion he had even exceeded his instructions by suggesting that war would result if France did not redress American grievances.[38] Living in constant worry that the administration would disgrace both him and itself by revealing his position to be one of "mere gasconade," Armstrong may have used the extraction of a concession from Napoleon, albeit an ambiguous one, as the occasion for withdrawing from a potentially embarrassing situation.

Madison and Gallatin were undoubtedly aware of Armstrong's views on foreign policy, but, surprised by his sudden return, they suspected ulterior motives in his resignation. Gallatin believed that the minister was "returning on the invitation of a party, probably the Vice President," to assist in organizing dissident middle state Republicans against Madison in the 1812 election. Madison's supporters had reluctantly accepted Clinton as vice president in 1808 in the belief that he would be too old to oppose Madison again in 1812, yet, as Gallatin remarked, Clinton "seemed to increase in ambition the older he grew."[39] There were also rumors that Armstrong, especially if he took up residence not in New York but in Pennsylvania, might be seeking the vice presidency himself. His reception in the middle states on his return from France did nothing to remove this impression. He was honored with public dinners in all the major cities, and, according to William Lee, there was much talk of him "for Governor of Pennsylvania, Secretary of State, and even for President."[40]

It is almost certain that Armstrong was approached by some "malcontent" Republicans, probably the Clintonians, but he appears to have expressed no immediate interest in the election of 1812.[41] He was probably not much disposed to be schismatic, believing as firmly as Madison that anything that disrupted the Republican party was "not merely unwise, but . . . absolutely and morally wrong." He did not settle in Pennsylvania but retired to his wife's estates in New York, content simply to observe the

[37] John Quincy Adams to Robert Smith, Apr. 13, 1811, in Worthington Chauncey Ford, ed., *The Writings of John Quincy Adams*, IV (New York, 1914), 51-53.

[38] Armstrong to Samuel Smith, Sept. 1809, and Jan. 17, 1810, Ferdinand Dreer Autograph Collection, Historical Society of Pennsylvania, Philadelphia.

[39] [Gales], "Recollections," for Nov. 13, 1810, *Daily Nat'l. Intelligencer*, July 30, 1857.

[40] William Lee to Susan Lee, Dec., 12, 18H, in Mary Lee Mann, ed., *A Yankee Jeffersonian: Selections from the Diary and Letters of William Lee of Massachusetts* . . . (Cambridge, Mass., 1958), 134; Morier to Wellesley, Nov. 21, 1810, F.O. 5/70.

[41] John Smith to [Nicholas], Mar. 3, 1811, Randolph Family Papers, Alderman Lib., Univ. of Va.

growing diplomatic and political problems of the administration. War, he was convinced, was the best remedy for the nation's ills, though he felt that the "spirit" to attempt it was lacking in the administration. "We are," he lamented, "a nation of quakers, without either their morals or their motives."[42]

By early 1811, however, Madison and Gallatin concluded that Armstrong would help organize and possibly even head an anti-Madison ticket in 1812.[43] While this belief credited the "malcontent" Republicans with far more unity of purpose than they actually possessed, the potential for such a development undeniably existed. Armstrong, because of his role in the half-hearted mutiny of the Continental army in 1783, was notorious both as an intriguer and as a polemicist of considerable ability. Added to these talents were his connections by friendship and marriage with some of the leading Republican families of New York—the Clintons, the Livingstons, the Lewises, and the Spencers. George Clinton bitterly resented his lack of influence in the administration and, according to Sen. John Smith of New York, still felt as "competent and ambitious" as ever to end the domination of Virginia in national politics.[44] To realize this goal Clinton would not lack potential allies in the Republican party. Duane, as he moved into open revolt against the administration, was inclining more and more to support the Clintonian faction of the party. Even Robert Smith, in an incautious conversation with the French minister, stated that Clinton would make a far better president than Madison.[45]

The badly strained relations between Madison and the Smith brothers now reached the breaking-point. Robert justified his preference for Clinton as president on the ground that the New Yorker would not have lacked the nerve to go to war with Britain, while Samuel angrily denounced Madison

[42] Armstrong to Ambrose Spencer, June 8, 1807, Misc. MSS, N.-Y. Hist. Soc.; Armstrong to Spencer, Feb. 15, 1811, William Astor Chanler Collection of John Armstrong Photostats, *ibid.*

[43] Duane to Jefferson, Jan. 25, 1811, in Ford, ed., "Letters of Duane," 344. Here Duane narrated that George W. Erving had warned him that Jefferson's "nearest friends" in Washington, that is, Madison and Gallatin, were "persuaded that [he] had entered into some arrangements with General Armstrong to promote him to the Presidency." Duane denied this, though he did admit that rumors of schemes to "blow up" the administration were not without foundation. See also Irving Brant, *James Madison: The President, 1809-1812* (Indianapolis, 1956), 273-277.

[44] John Smith to [Nicholas], Mar. 3, 1811, Randolph Family Papers, Alderman Lib., Univ. of Va.; George Clinton to Genet, Mar. 3, 1811, Genet Papers microfilm, Roll 9, Lib. Cong.

[45] *Aurora General Advertiser* (Philadelphia), Mar. 1, 5, 16, 29, 1811; Sérurier to Cadore, Mar. 5, 1811, Arch. des Affaires Étrangères, Corresp. Politique, États Unis, LXV.

for failing to nominate him to replace Armstrong in France.[46] Moreover, their capacity to indulge in anti-administration intrigue almost equalled that of the Clintonians. The Smith and Nicholas families were united by three marriages, and their friends and relations were politically influential in New York, Maryland, and Virginia. Jefferson, although in retirement at Monticello, quickly sensed the drift of events: he feared that Madison's Republican opponents would coalesce and oppose the administration by advocating policies of military preparedness and war. So alarmed was the former president by the possibility that the Republican party would "break into squads, every one pursuing the path he thinks most direct," that he wrote to Duane imploring him not to quarrel with the administration on either "men or measures." The nation would require, Jefferson argued, "the union of all its friends to resist its enemies within and without. If we schismatize . . . , if we do not act in phalanx, I will not say our *party*, the term is false and degrading, but our *nation* will be undone. For the republicans are the *nation*."[47]

The suspicions of the administration about Armstrong and the other "malcontents" soon became Washington gossip, spreading among Republicans generally. So too did the news that Robert Smith and Madison had disagreed over how to respond to the Cadore letter, with Gales noting at the time that Smith did "not seem sorry that such a *report* had got abroad."[48] And it was in this political climate, poisoned by fear and suspicion, that Gallatin finally came to believe that his enemies were uniting to force him out of the cabinet. In February 1811 the Senate rejected the bill to recharter the Bank of the United States. The vice president and the Republican senators from New York, New Jersey, Pennsylvania, Maryland, and Virginia all voted against recharter and the known wishes of the secretary of the Treasury. Gallatin, who had frequently contemplated withdrawing from the cabinet, could stand no more. He sent the president a letter of resignation,

[46] Brant, *Madison: The President,* 279, 310.

[47] Jefferson to Duane, Mar. 28 and Apr. 30, 1811, Thomas Jefferson Papers, Lib. Cong. The network of alliances among the Randolph, Jefferson, Nicholas, Smith, Clinton, Livingston, Lewis, and Armstrong families provided the Republican party with much informal and organized support. Jefferson immediately realized that the quarrel between Madison and the Smiths was fraught with immense personal and political consequences, and it is hardly surprising that he begged to be considered neutral by all concerned. See Jefferson to Robert Smith, Apr. 30, 1811, Robert and Samuel Smith Papers, Maryland Historical Society, Baltimore.

[48] [Gales], "Recollections," for Feb. 18, 1811, *Daily Nat'l. Intelligencer,* Aug. 8, 1857. See also William Burwell to Nicholas, Feb. 14, 1811, Wilson Cary Nicholas Papers, Lib. Cong.; Charles Cutts to William Plumer, Feb. 25, 1811, William Plumer Papers, *ibid.*; Dearborn to Jefferson, Apr. 14, 1811, Jefferson Papers, *ibid.*; Morier to Wellesley, Feb. 22, 1811, F.O. 5/74.

complaining of the growing strength of "personal factions" within the party, and waited for the reaction.[49]

The ultimatum implied in the resignation was reinforced by a group of Republican senators, probably led by William H. Crawford of Georgia, who called on the president early in March 1811 to urge him to do something to unify the party. Madison, though well aware of the threats to his administration, had so far avoided action in the hope that his Republican opponents would be unable to agree among themselves. But his hand was forced. Should Gallatin insist on the acceptance of his resignation, the president would be left almost entirely dependent on the Smith brothers and their connections for advice and political support. Since Madison had never been enthusiastic about having Robert Smith in the cabinet, he quickly made a crucial decision. He resolved to offer James Monroe, now governor of Virginia, the position of secretary of state.[50]

This decision promised to solve some of Madison's problems, although only at the expense of aggravating others. There was no point in dismissing Smith if Madison intended to pursue the same foreign policies which Smith and many other Republicans disliked. In this respect the invitation to Monroe seemed to indicate that the president would make a new attempt to settle with Britain. Indeed, it became widely believed that this would be Madison's future policy.[51] Monroe's appointment might also help in restoring the support of the "Old Republicans" of Virginia to the administration, but there Monroe's usefulness would probably end. It was the schisms in the middle states that posed the most serious threat to the party, and in this context Monroe, as a Virginian, was a distinct liability. In fact, the news that Monroe might succeed Smith jolted Armstrong out of his retirement, drawing him back into involvement in politics.

The cabinet change annoyed Armstrong. Not only did he question Monroe's talents as a diplomat, but he feared that Monroe would now be placed in a favorable position to seek the presidency after Madison. This would do more, he complained to Justice Ambrose Spencer of New York, to

[49] Brant, *Madison: The President*, 265-270. Gallatin probably talked with Madison after writing his resignation. Joseph H. Nicholson urged Gallatin to do so and to point out that the opponents of the Treasury were also opponents of the president himself. The "cabal," Nicholson added, was "just beginning their attack more openly on Mr Madison by holding up Clinton." Nicholson to Gallatin, Mar. 6, 1811, Gallatin Papers, N.-Y. Hist. Soc.

[50] Brant, *Madison: The President*, 277-278, 282-283.

[51] Littleton Tazewell to Monroe, Mar. 24, 1811, James Monroe Papers, Lib. Cong.; Philip Norbonne Nicholas to Samuel Smith, Apr. 3, 1811, Samuel Smith Papers, *ibid.*; John Randolph to James Mercer Garnett, Mar. 25, 1811, Randolph-Garnett Letterbook, *ibid.*; Henry St. George Tucker to Garnett, James Mercer Garnett Papers, Duke University Library, Durham, N.C.; *The Enquirer* (Richmond, Va.), May 10, 1811.

disrupt the Republican party and the Union than "anything that has yet occurred." The strength of the Union, Armstrong felt, was no more than that of a mere "bundle of twigs," and he predicted that if Monroe should attempt to succeed Madison, the ascendancy of the Republican party "must and will go. Neither western, middle, nor northern states," in his opinion, would "consent to take a third President in succession from Virginia." Armstrong hoped that Monroe and his Virginian supporters "would steer us clear of this rock" by turning down Madison's offer.[52]

For his part Monroe had no desire to refuse the offer, but he was keenly aware of the problem of credibility which his appointment would raise. As a public figure with a reputation as a critic of administration policy, he was somewhat surprised by Madison's move, realizing also that the "near connections" of Robert Smith would "naturally feel some sensibility and would be apt to indulge some portion of resentment." Indeed, he feared that acceptance under such circumstances could lead to a crisis that would threaten "the overthrow of the whole Republican party."[53] Accordingly, Monroe sought assurances from Madison about the role he would play in making foreign policy, wishing to know to what extent that policy had been fixed by actions already taken. Believing privately that the Cadore letter was a fraud, Monroe clearly stated to the president that he favored a settlement with Britain "even on moderate terms rather than hazard war or any other alternative." He also requested a written answer which he could lay before the Virginia Council of State to justify his resignation from the governor's office.[54] In other words, Monroe was tentatively asking whether the president was prepared to concede that the acceptance of the Cadore letter might have been a mistake.

Madison declined to be drawn out on these questions. He already had enough trouble without adding to it by admitting that Napoleon might have deceived him. At the time, though, the president did think that the recent assumption by the Prince of Wales of the powers of the Regency could lead "to a material change" in Britain's policy toward the United States. He even hoped for a repeal of the Orders in Council as well as for a settlement of the dispute on blockades, but he concealed this optimism in a vague reply to Monroe that merely expressed his desire for an honorable arrangement with the British government. Monroe's previous differences with the Jefferson administration, Madison added, would not be an obstacle to this goal.[55] This

[52] Armstrong to Spencer, Mar. 19, 1811, Chanler Coll., N.-Y. Hist. Soc.

[53] Monroe to Charles Everett, Apr. 23, 1811, *Tyler's Quarterly Historical and Genealogical Magazine*, IV (1922), 101; Monroe to Richard Brent, Mar. 18, 1811, Gallatin Papers, N.-Y. Hist. Soc.

[54] Monroe to Madison, Mar. 23, 1811, Madison Papers, Lib. Cong.

[55] Madison to Jefferson, Mar. 18, 1811, to Monroe, Mar. 26, 31, 1811, *ibid*. For the Regency in Great Britain see J. Steven Watson, *The Reign of George III, 1760-*

reply in no way committed the president to accept Monroe's views on foreign policy, since the issues he wished to settle were not identical to those which Monroe claimed to have successfully negotiated with Britain in 1806. Nevertheless, Monroe accepted the State Department post on this basis, believing that a successful venture in Anglo-American diplomacy would help reunite the Republican party. His willingness to join the cabinet thus freed Madison to dismiss Smith.

In two final meetings with the secretary of state at the end of March 1811, Madison reviewed their differences, especially those concerning the wisdom of the "restrictive system." Madison severely reproved Smith for consenting to decisions taken in the cabinet and then organizing opposition to them "out of doors." Evidence of these activities, he added, had been brought to his attention "from so many sources and with so many corroborations that it was impossible to shut [his] mind against them." To smooth Smith's departure and to avoid offending his many friends and relatives, Madison offered him the position of minister to Russia. Smith at first agreed to consider the offer but then refused it, imprudently admitting that he had done so on the advice of "his friends in Baltimore, Pennsylvania and New York." The *Aurora*, in the interval, had declared that Smith "owed it to his friends" not to accept the Russian mission and warned Madison to abandon Gallatin or risk being abandoned by the voters in 1812. At the end of the second interview Smith broke off relations with Madison, remarking as he did so that his dismissal would seriously injure the "Republican cause." Smith also told the president that "he should be supported by a body of friends and that he knew he could stand on good ground in justifying himself to his country."[56]

Madison could only have interpreted this last statement by Smith as a barely concealed threat to disrupt the party by carrying their foreign policy differences to the public. Shortly afterwards Jefferson warned the president against the "secret workings of an *insatiable* family" and their allies who would "sound the tocsin against the *antient* dominion" in the elections of 1812.[57] The warning was hardly necessary, for evidence of intrigue against the administration was apparent everywhere by April 1811. Duane attributed Smith's dismissal to the machinations of Gallatin, then spread false rumors that Madison would get rid of his navy and war secretaries in order to divide

1815 (Oxford, 1960), 489-491. Madison had always believed that changes in British maritime policies were dependent on fundamental changes in the nature of the British government itself. He had hopes that the Prince of Wales would introduce reforms, but from the Tory prime minister, Spencer Perceval, he feared that the United States could expect nothing but "quackeries and corruptions." Madison to Jefferson, Nov. 6, 1809, Madison Papers, Lib. Cong.

[56] "Memorandum as to R. Smith," Apr. 1811, Madison Papers, Lib. Cong.; *Aurora*, Mar. 25, 1811.

[57] Jefferson to Madison, Apr. 7, 24, 1811, Madison Papers, Lib. Cong.

his New York opponents by offering the War Department to Armstrong. Armstrong's brother-in-law, Morgan Lewis of New York, informed the president, however, that his former minister to France had been in contact with the Smith brothers and was now working with the vice president's nephew, DeWitt Clinton, on electoral strategy for 1812. Armstrong and the Clintonians were in fact brought together by Ambrose Spencer in Albany in April 1811 to discuss ways in which the "weight" of New York might "be felt in the national scale."[58]

These discussions in Albany, centering in the scheme that Armstrong should move to Pennsylvania to stand as vice president on a Clintonian ticket, were inconclusive. Although Spencer argued that Armstrong's "personal interests" and those of the Clintonians were "not in opposition," Armstrong seems to have preferred to watch developments from New York without committing himself too openly. Madison, however, was aware of the meetings and, already deeply upset by Robert Smith's conduct, expected both Armstrong and the Smiths to declare "open warfare" on the administration any day. He made ready for battle by gathering all the information he could about his adversaries, including the preparation of a memorandum on Robert Smith with a view to releasing it to the public. The president also suspected that Armstrong might have had some influence on Smith's refusal to accept the Russian mission.[59]

These developments in New York had their counterparts in Philadelphia and Baltimore. The *Aurora* offered an "authorized" version of the dismissal of Smith which Madison believed had been provided by none other than the former secretary himself. Duane denied this charge but, by doing so, only further exasperated Madison, who concluded that the editor showed a regrettable "want of candor" in his politics. Gallatin then received a warning that the "Philadelphia Junto" of Duane and Leib was planning to deprive Madison of Pennsylvania's electoral votes in 1812 by exploiting the bad relations that had always existed between the administration and the supporters of Gov. Simon Snyder over the long-standing Olmstead affair.[60] Madison

---

[58] *Aurora*, Apr. 4, 1811; John Smith to Gallatin, Apr. 15, 1811, Gallatin Papers, N.-Y. Hist. Soc.; Morgan Lewis to Madison, Apr. 8, 1811, Madison Papers, Lib. Cong.; Armstrong to Spencer [Mar. 1811?], and Spencer to Armstrong, Mar. 20, 1811, Chanler Coll., N.-Y. Hist. Soc.; Sérurier to duc de Bassano, Apr. 26, 1811, Arch. Affaires Étrangères, Corresp. Politique, États Unis, LXV.

[59] Spencer to Armstrong, Mar. 20, 1811, Chanler Coll., N.-Y. Hist. Soc.; Madison to Jefferson, Apr. 11, 19, 1811, Madison Papers, Lib. Cong.; [Gales], "Recollections," *Daily Nat'l. Intelligencer*, Aug. 8, 1857.

[60] *Aurora*, Apr. 5, 1811; Madison to Jefferson, May 3, 1811, Madison Papers, Lib. Cong.; John Binns to Gallatin, Apr. 27, 1811, Gallatin Papers, N.-Y. Hist. Soc. The Olmstead affair involved a dispute between federal and state courts in Pennsylvania over claims to a prize captured in 1778. For the details and how they contributed to dislike of the Madison administration and disunity in the Pennsylvania Republican party see Higginbotham, *Keystone in the Democratic Arch*, 182-204.

undertook to forestall this possibility by promoting the "pro-Smith" comptroller of the Treasury, Gabriel Duval of Maryland, to the Supreme Court and replacing him with a "Snyderite," Richard Rush of Pennsylvania. Gallatin acted to prevent Leib from securing control of important patronage positions in Philadelphia.[61]

These moves, amounting to the formation of an alliance between the administration and the majority Republican faction in Pennsylvania, brought Madison some badly needed political support. Yet changing the personnel of the cabinet and paying greater attention to the political uses of federal patronage within the states would not necessarily stem the rising tide of criticism of Madison's foreign policy. The administration's troubles with the "malcontents" had always involved disputes over both men and measures. As John Wayles Eppes had observed to Jefferson at the time of Smith's dismissal, "only a change in our foreign relations would enable Mr Madison to ride triumphant, put down his opponents in Congress, and silence the growlings of those who ought to possess his entire confidence."[62]

Duane, for example, was still calling for stronger measures against Britain, convinced that the appointment of Monroe signified that the administration would continue the policy of attempting to negotiate agreements peacefully. The *Baltimore Whig*, a paper controlled by the Smith brothers, indirectly took up the same theme with a series of criticisms of Monroe's abortive treaty of 1806 with Britain, arguing that it was more shameful than the Jay Treaty of 1795. The *Baltimore Whig* also began to adopt the anti-Gallatin rhetoric of the *Aurora*, claiming that Gallatin and Madison had made a "corrupt" bargain with Monroe to "sustain themselves in that power which their tergiversation ought to have forfeited." Both papers then published laudatory editorials about the Clinton family and deplored the administration's hostility to all such "true Republicans."[63]

As the "malcontents" warmed to the business of accusing Madison of being soft on Britain, the president received the news that the American minister in London, William Pinkney of Maryland, was returning home because he had failed to win any concessions on neutral rights.[64] The coincidence of these external and internal developments forced Madison to begin a reconsideration of the effectiveness of the policies of economic coercion. The president now needed alternative policies, not only to be able to deal with a new British minister, Augustus Foster, who was already on his

[61] J. H. Powell, *Richard Rush: Republican Diplomat* (Philadelphia, 1942), 13-16.

[62] Eppes to Jefferson, Mar. 20, 1811, Edgehill-Randolph Papers, Alderman Lib., Univ. of Va.

[63] *Aurora*, Mar. 29, Apr. 13, 30, 1811; *Baltimore Whig*, Mar. 22, 23, Apr. 3, 1811.

[64] This was announced in a postscript to the *Nat'l. Intelligencer*, Apr. 9, 1811.

way to the United States, but also to relieve his administration from the pressure of mounting public criticism. On April 13, 1811, a day on which the *Aurora* predicted that Madison would succumb to British "duplicity" and "insults" instead of firmly upholding American maritime rights, the president invited the editor of the *National Intelligencer* to a private dinner for a lengthy discussion of foreign policy problems. Three days later Gales presented a summary of the president's thoughts in the editorial columns of the administration newspaper. Their tone suggested that Madison had abandoned his earlier hopes for a settlement with Britain and considerably hardened his attitude toward that nation's continuing infringement of neutral rights.[65]

The editorial accused the British government of bad faith in its negotiations with Pinkney and stated that the forthcoming talks with Foster would fail for the same reason. Madison's purpose, according to Gales, was "to prepare the public mind" for that failure. The president then went on to define his conditions for an agreement with Britain, making them as favorable to the United States as possible. As "preliminary points for adjustment," wrote Gales, Britain would have to accept American demands that it abandon the Orders in Council, alter its system of blockades so far as it affected the maritime rights of the United States, and end the practice of impressment, the last item being one which Madison had recently implied to Monroe would not necessarily be a bar to a settlement. Now, however, the president was suggesting that Britain and the United States could never agree on any of these matters, to say nothing of any "minor points of difference." The editorial therefore concluded with the warning that measures far stronger than economic coercion might be required from the twelfth Congress after the failure of Foster's mission.[66]

This editorial of April 16 was, as Gales recalled, "the first indication from any source approaching to official authority of a disposition to resort to any more effective measures than Embargoes and non-importation acts." Its contents, however, greatly upset Monroe, although he never knew that Gales had only been summarizing the president's views; ironically, he suspected that the editorial had been written by Robert Smith's department clerk as a way of embarrassing the administration's quest for a negotiated settlement.[67] The new secretary of state had commenced his duties in April 1811 under the impression that he had a free hand to make a settlement with Britain. Late in April he accepted in principle a plan outlined by his son-in-law, George Hay,

[65] [Gales], "Recollections," for Apr. 16, 1811, *Daily Nat'l. Intelligencer* Aug. 8, 1857; see also Madison to Jefferson, Apr. 19, 1811, Madison Papers, Lib. Cong.
[66] *Nat'l. Intelligencer,* Apr. 16, 1811.
[67] [Gales], "Recollections," for Apr. 16, 1811, *Daily Nat'l. Intelligencer,* Aug. 8, 1857.

which was based on the assumption that the Republican party schisms in the middle states could be ended only by some decisive stroke of foreign policy. That stroke, Hay argued, should be a settlement with Britain in the summer of 1811, even if that meant risking war with France.[68]

Monroe first attempted to bring the supporters of his 1808 presidential candidacy to unite with the administration by claiming that he could moderate Madison's attitudes toward Britain. A settlement, Monroe argued, would unify the party and help keep "a certain Yorker [Armstrong] from the Presidency," a prospect which James Mercer Garnett reported was gravely troubling the secretary. The other "Old Republicans," however, were not convinced. They could see little evidence that Madison favored their Anglo-philic way of thinking. John Randolph simply dismissed all talk of a peaceful settlement with the remark that either Monroe was trying to dupe his friends or that Madison was duping his new secretary of state.[69]

The rough treatment Monroe accorded the French minister between April and July 1811 over the repeal of Napoleon's decrees further strength-ened the impression that he was contemplating a breach with France.[70] The president, meanwhile, was steadily moving in the opposite direction. Madi-son had not yet completely abandoned his faith in the "restrictive system," but in May 1811 he admitted to his kinsman, Richard Cutts, that it had been "extremely difficult to keep the public mind awake" to the distinctions which he had drawn between the major effects of the British Orders in Council on American trade and the lesser inconveniences arising from French "munici-pal irregularities." This amounted to a further acknowledgment on the part of the president that the application of non-intercourse against Britain on the basis of the Cadore letter had caused severe problems which, he wrote, could be "turned against the government of the United States."[71]

In the meantime, Madison's Republican opponents kept up their criti-cism of his foreign policy. Duane, who had continued to editorialize on the dismissal of Smith, finally reduced the episode to one issue, while raising the tone of outrage in his columns to new heights. Smith was removed, he cried, for his opposition to the *"feeble, faithless, dishonest, degrading* and *tempo-rizing* system pursued since the repeal of the Embargo." The president, Duane warned, should no longer postpone the inevitable and necessary decision to go to war with Britain. If he continued to temporize, the editor

[68] George Hay to Monroe, Apr. 22, 1811, Monroe Papers, Lib. Cong.; Hay to Monroe, Jan. 23, 1812, James Monroe Papers, New York Public Library, New York City.

[69] Randolph to Garnett, Mar. 25, Apr. 11, May 27, 1811, and Garnett to Randolph, Apr. 15, 30, May 21, 1811, Randolph-Garnett Letterbook, Lib. Cong.

[70] Sérurier to Bassano, June 30, 1811, Arch. Affaires Étrangères, Corresp. Politi-que, États Unis, LXV.

[71] Madison to Richard Cutts, May 23, 1811, Cutts Coll., Lib. Cong.

foresaw political disaster for both the administration and the nation.[72] Madison also learned from his private secretary, Edward Coles, that the "little clan" of the Smiths, believing that they could "make and unmake any administration," intended to "spur on their relations and friends to attack the President and Colonel Monroe."[73] Thus did the increasing pressures of domestic politics threaten to limit the diplomatic choices open to the president, a fact which he himself fully recognized. By June 1811, on the eve of Foster's arrival, Madison knew that he had to insist that Britain settle the grievances of the United States. If this did not happen, there would be, he predicted, "new shapes" in American foreign policy, including the possibility of an "open rupture" with Britain.[74]

The climax to the diplomatic and political events which had been set in motion by Madison's acceptance of the Cadore letter and his dismissal of Robert Smith came in July 1811. In the first week of that month the new British minister arrived in Washington for fresh negotiations, while Smith, in his pamphlet, *Address to the People of the United States*, openly attacked the administration. Republicans throughout the nation were horrified by the evidence which Smith provided of the disunity that had prevailed in the cabinet. Madison, however, could hardly have been taken by surprise. For some months he had been expecting Smith to protest his dismissal; and the publication of the *Address* was probably timed to coincide with Foster's arrival and the Independence Day celebrations. At the same time, there was renewed speculation that Armstrong would also publish a book exposing the errors of Madison's diplomacy as a prelude to seeking the presidency in 1812. Monroe, after reading Smith's *Address*, remarked that "Armstrong will probably follow him and the sooner the better."[75]

The *Address* reargued the differences between Smith and Madison with many embellishments to make the circumstances seem more favorable to the former. The pamphlet included arguments which, while not wholly consistent, were intended to convey the impression that Madison was averse to preparing the nation for war, that Smith had always supported such a policy, and that Madison had been wrong both in his belief that the French edicts had been repealed and in his subsequent policy toward Britain.[76] Coming as it did on the eve of further talks with Britain, the publication of the *Address* was as serious as Smith's earlier sabotage of Madison's diplomacy. Madison

---

[72] *Aurora*, May 2, 3, 11, 1811.

[73] Edward Coles to Dolley Madison, June 10, 1811, James Madison Papers, N.Y. Pub. Lib.

[74] Madison to Jefferson, June 7, 1811, Madison Papers, Lib. Cong.

[75] Monroe to Hay, July 3, 1811, Monroe Papers, N.Y. Pub. Lib.; Samuel Smith to John Spear Smith, June 13, 18, 1811, Samuel Smith Papers, Lib. Cong.; *Nat'l. Intelligencer*, July 25, 1811.

[76] The *Address* appeared in the *Nat'l. Intelligencer*, July 2, 1811.

described it as a "wicked act which could not be allowed to escape with impunity."[77] Equally serious was the political threat contained in the *Address*. Although the former secretary of state had publicly denied that he was engaged in organizing opposition to Madison's re-election, he concluded his observations with the suggestion that the continued ascendancy of the Republican party required a president of stronger views than Madison to maintain American neutral rights. Privately Smith confessed that his object was indeed Madison's overthrow and vowed that he would accomplish it.[78]

The *Address* was immediately attacked by Joel Barlow, friend of the president and minister-designate to France, who asserted that Smith *was* organizing an opposition party to work himself "at the next Presidential election . . . into a higher station than he did at the last." The reason why Smith refused the mission to Russia, Barlow claimed, was that he could not put "the machinery of opposition into motion from the bottom of the Gulph of Finland as he thought he could do from Baltimore."[79] If Smith's charges won widespread acceptance, however, the administration would be in trouble. Duane applauded the *Address*, while Giles circulated it in Virginia, informing his "most confidential friends that republicanism was not safe in [Madison's] hands." Both the *Aurora* and the *Baltimore Whig* followed the *Address* with accusations that Monroe was engaged in making a humiliating arrangement with Britain and was submitting to insults from Foster in the process.[80] The editor of the *Baltimore Whig*, Baptist Irvine, wrote privately to a State Department clerk, expressing his hope that Madison would not come to an agreement with Britain. Surely, Irvine thought, the president "has too many warnings before him to allow him to swerve from the right track. Should he deviate, however, it is not in the power . . . of *coalitions* between *Virginia* and *Massachusetts* or of *bargains* in *Pennsylvania* to re-elect him."[81]

The Independence Day celebrations provided the Republican "malcontents" with an opportunity to publicize their views. On July 4, Samuel Smith's Baltimore militia company not only pointedly omitted to toast the president's health but drank toasts with cheers to Robert Smith, Armstrong, George and DeWitt Clinton, and the *Aurora*. A few days later the *Baltimore Whig* bluntly stated that Madison was not entitled to re-election because of his "pusillanimous" conduct of the nation's foreign affairs. In Rhinebeck, New York, Independence Day was celebrated with Armstrong and Chancellor Robert Livingston as the guests of honor at a public dinner. The toast list,

[77] Madison to Jefferson, July 8, 1811, Madison Papers, Lib. Cong.
[78] Robert Smith to Samuel Smith, Mar. 26, 1811, Samuel Smith Papers, *ibid.*
[79] *Daily Nat'l. Intelligencer*, July 4, 6, 9, 11, 1811.
[80] *Aurora*, July 3, 8, 1811; Giles to Robert Smith, July 5, 1811, Dreer Coll., Hist. Soc. Pa.; *Baltimore Whig*, July 6, 10, 13, 19, 31, 1811.
[81] This letter, dated July 17, 1811, was written to John B. Colvin, an appointee of Robert Smith. It appeared in the *Nat'l. Intelligencer*, Aug. 8, 1811.

which was almost identical to that of the Baltimore militia, included some volunteered remarks about "unfettered commerce" and a vigorous defense of American rights. An embarrassed Swedish consul at the dinner proposed a toast to the president, only to find that the name of Madison drew no cheers from the guests. Morgan Lewis then informed the president that Armstrong was now "in the field" for 1812.[82]

Given these developments in domestic politics in July 1811, it would have been extremely difficult for the administration to make any agreement with Britain short of that power's total capitulation to American demands. Barlow, as he penned his replies to Robert Smith, complained that the conduct of the former secretary of state had crippled the negotiations at the outset, while Monroe fretted over how to respond to the distorted accounts of his actions that were appearing in the *Aurora* and the *Baltimore Whig*.[83] The administration felt that it could not even risk sending a new minister to London for fear that any nominee would be rejected by the anti-Madison Republicans in the Senate.[84] When Madison formally received Foster on July 6, he had already learned that the British minister was empowered only to settle the four-year-old *Chesapeake* affair and to state that agreement on the legality of specific British blockades might be possible after the removal of the blanket blockades imposed by the Orders in Council. On this last question, however, Foster made no concessions. Pointing to the continuing seizure of American vessels by France after the supposed repeal of her restrictive decrees, he declared that Madison's imposition of non-intercourse against Britain was unjustified. He further announced that his government would be convinced of the fact of French repeal and remove the Orders in Council only when American merchants could carry British goods as neutral property into European ports and when France had restored neutral commerce to the condition in which it stood prior to the operation of the Berlin and Milan decrees.[85]

As Madison had predicted in April, Britain had failed to meet American demands. The responsibility for the next move now lay with the president. He summoned the cabinet to a meeting on July 9, 1811, undoubtedly for the

[82] *Baltimore Whig*, July 6, 12, 18, 1811; Morgan Lewis to Madison, July 15, 1811, Madison Papers, Lib. Cong. On Aug. 13, 1811, the *Nat'l. Intelligencer* called on Armstrong to deny the charge that he had allied himself with the Smith brothers.

[83] James Woodress, *A Yankee's Odyssey: The Life of Joel Barlow* (Philadelphia, 1958), 280-281; Monroe to Madison, Aug. 11, 1811, Madison Papers, Lib. Cong.

[84] Foster to Wellesley, July 18, Aug. 5, 1811, F.O. 5/76. In his final conversations with Robert Smith in Mar. 1811, Madison had implied that the United States would continue to maintain a minister in London. After Pinkney returned home in June, however, he was not replaced. See "Memorandum as to R. Smith," Apr. 1811, Madison Papers, Lib. Cong.

[85] Perkins, *Prologue to War*, 276-282.

purpose of discussing the response to be made to Foster.[86] Shortly afterwards, on the basis of conversations with members of the cabinet, Foster reported that the secretaries of state, war, and the Treasury were opposed to taking any step that might worsen relations with Britain, while Madison had not immediately committed himself to any decision. The minister also noted that Madison was showing considerable "asperity in his remarks" on British policy, although he failed to attach any significance to the president's obviously angry mood.[87] As the talks between Foster and Monroe continued fruitlessly throughout July, Madison made the decision, probably by the third week of the month, to call the twelfth Congress into early session on November 4, 1811, one month before the constitutionally appointed time.[88] A proclamation was issued to this effect on July 24, after which the president left for vacation in Virginia.

The motives behind this decision were complex, and Madison's action was not governed solely by the unsatisfactory state of Anglo-American relations. In fact, Foster's diplomacy had been easily and quickly rejected by the administration. To the demand that American merchants ship British goods as neutral property into Europe, Madison and Monroe replied that Britain could not rightly compel Americans to carry British cargoes or make the United States government responsible for ensuring that French officials accept them. They dismissed as "preposterous" the British declaration that France should restore neutral commerce to the state in which it stood prior to the operation of the French decrees as a condition for the repeal of the Orders in Council. Foster's attempt to counter Madison's enforcement of non-intercourse against Britain by stressing French violations of American rights was thus brushed aside in a series of strongly worded notes on the extravagance and injustice of British maritime pretensions.[89]

Foster had supported his position with a vague threat of retaliation against American commerce if the United States did not provide proof acceptable to the British government of the repeal of the Berlin and Milan decrees.[90] This development, though more serious, did not greatly worry Madison. Foster delivered the threat in as "mild" a tone as possible and with "great regret"; he found that Madison and Monroe ignored it altogether. Madison, with one eye on British diplomatic difficulties in Europe, observed that the situation there did "not favor temerity" on the part of the British government.[91] Yet even if Madison had felt that Britain would not violate

[86] Madison to Gallatin, July 9, 1811, Gallatin Papers, N.-Y. Hist. Soc.
[87] Foster to Wellesley, July 12, 1811, F.O. 5/76.
[88] Madison to Dearborn, [July 1811], Charles Roberts Autograph Collection, Haverford College Library, Pa.
[89] Monroe to Foster, July 23, 26, Oct. 1, 29, 1811, F.O. 5/76, 5/77.
[90] Foster to Monroe, July 14, 1811, ibid., 5/76.
[91] Foster to Wellesley, Aug. 5, 1811, ibid.; Madison to Eustis, Sept. 8, 1811, Daniel Parker Papers, Hist. Soc. Pa. Since Madison was closely watching devel-

American neutral rights to any greater degree than it had done in the past, he could not have ignored Foster's diplomacy and continued the established Republican policies of peaceable coercion. Mounting political pressures had compelled the president after April 1811 to begin considering new ways to obtain concessions from Britain, and it was the potential impact of Foster's conduct on the domestic political scene that led him to the decision to call Congress into early session.

Madison was infuriated with Foster, not simply because the British government had refused to settle American grievances, but also because he suspected that the minister was trying to exploit political divisions in the United States, especially those within the Republican party. Madison's stand against the Orders in Council was based on the belief that the French edicts against neutral shipping had been repealed, but Foster, like Robert Smith, was questioning his word on this point. As the minister admitted, his notes to Monroe were designed to throw onto the United States the burden of proof that "even any part of the decrees had ceased to operate."[92] Madison, in order to have responded positively to Foster's demands, would have been required either to acknowledge that Napoleon's decrees were still in force or to have begun challenging the legality of the French "municipal regulations." In both cases the president would also have been admitting the charges in Smith's *Address* that he had been tricked by Napoleon and that his attempts to use the Cadore letter to persuade Britain to make concessions were futile and mistaken.

Madison was only too well aware of his predicament and was not prepared to become the instrument of his own humiliation. Foster, he complained, seemed "more disposed to play the diplomatist than the conciliatory negotiator. His letter, though not very skilfully made up, is evidently calculated for the public here, as well as for his own g[overnmen]t." "In this view," the president warned Monroe, "his evasion and sophistical efforts may deserve attention."[93] Given Madison's troubles with the "malcontent"

---

opments in Europe, it is more than likely that he detected changes in the balance of power there that promised to assist his efforts to change British maritime policy. The steady drift of France and Russia toward war throughout 1811 created a situation that caused Britain many internal and external difficulties while allowing American diplomacy more scope for success than at any time since the imposition of the embargo. The fact that the two major efforts of the United States to solve the problems of neutral rights—the embargo and the War of 1812—coincided with Napoleon's two attempts to include Russia within his Continental System has not yet received sufficient attention from diplomatic historians. See J. C. A. Stagg, "The Revolt Against Virginia: Republican Politics and the Commencement of the War of 1812" (Ph.D. diss., Princeton University, 1973), 83-96.

[92] Foster to Wellesley, July 18, 1811, F.O. 5/76.

[93] Madison to Monroe, [Aug.] 2, 1811, Monroe Papers, Lib. Cong. The letter is misdated July. See also Madison to Monroe, Aug. 11, 1811, *ibid.*, in which the

Republicans, he was in no position to release to Congress and the newspapers the correspondence between Foster and Monroe—including the British view that the president was the dupe of France—and leave his foreign policy unchanged. Such conduct would only have given substance to the charges of the *Aurora* and the *Baltimore Whig* that Madison was weak enough to submit to anything, including deceit from France and insults from Britain at the same time. Even if the president had desired to retract his measures against Britain, he would still have had to request Congress to repeal the non-intercourse law which it had passed against Britain in March 1811. This step, too, would have played directly into the hands of his bellicose enemies in the Republican party.

Diplomatically and politically, therefore, Madison was in an intolerable position in the summer of 1811. He had, furthermore, every reason to believe that both Foster and the "malcontents" would continue their attacks on his foreign policy.[94] Foster fully appreciated the president's dilemma and attempted to turn it to Britain's advantage. Precisely because Madison did not stand on "high ground" in the Republican party, Foster believed that he could ultimately force the president to make some concessions for the sake of peace.[95] For Madison, though, there seemed to remain only one course of action that would be both honorable and effective. He could regain the initiative at home and abroad by moving toward the positions advocated for so long by his Republican opponents. If he did not do so, there was the possibility that they would coalesce into a formidable anti-administration party, make the issues of war and preparedness wholly their own, and turn them against him in the months to come.

The early calling of Congress was Madison's first step in breaking out of the political and diplomatic deadlock of 1811. The action amounted to no less than a decision to prepare the United States for war with Britain. The political situation was such that Madison could hardly have planned to arouse public expectation by calling an early session of a new Congress only to announce the failure of yet another series of negotiations and then to recommend another embargo or a stricter enforcement of non-intercourse as the American response. Had he done so, the "malcontents," as Monroe later pointed out, would have treated "with vast asperity and contempt such an inefficient expedient" and would have probably been able to defeat it.[96]

president pointed out that any public comments by the administration on Foster's mission had to be judged by "considerations both foreign and domestic."

[94] See Madison to Cutts, Aug. 24, 1811, Cutts Coll., *ibid.*, "The hostile effusions from Baltimore," Madison wrote, "having a source not to be mistaken . . . will be renewed in every shape that deadly hatred can prompt."

[95] Foster to Wellesley, Aug. 5, 1811, F.O. 5/76.

[96] Monroe to John Taylor, June 13, 1812, Monroe Papers, Lib. Cong. Monroe described these "habitual" Republican opponents of the administration as "more

Instead, the nation's honor, the president's political salvation, and the unity of the Republican party required that American policy now be directed toward war.

When the twelfth Congress assembled in November 1811, the president and his cabinet greeted them with a call to arms and a specific list of military preparations. To be sure, the president never appeared to close the door on negotiations that might have preserved peace, but he had already decided that peace could continue only on his terms, and he thought it unlikely that Britain would meet them.[97] This fundamental shift in policy helped curb much of the dissidence within the Republican party. Between November 1811 and June 1812 the Republicans in the House were goaded by the "War Hawk" committee leaders into translating the wishes of the executive into legislation, while the "malcontents" in the Senate tried to obstruct the drift to war by quarrelling over the details of military policy. Madison, however, was not to be dissuaded from his course, and his stubborn persistence, if not the adroitness of his tactics, eventually compelled a majority of congressional Republicans to agree with him. By the end of the session a sufficiently large Republican majority had emerged in both houses to renominate Madison in May and to declare war against Britain in June.[98]

While the United States moved toward war, the "malcontent" Republicans found themselves caught in an embarrassing quandary. After November 1811, Madison's actions, in effect, presented them with the choice of rejecting the aggressive measures they had long called for or of supporting a president whom they despised.[99] In these altered circumstances Armstrong and Duane proved to be the most adaptable. In 1812 first Armstrong, then Duane broke with the Clintonians and announced their support both for the war with Britain and for Madison as the Republican candidate for president. Their flexibility was duly rewarded when Madison reluctantly took Armstrong into his cabinet as secretary of war in January 1813 and allowed him not only

violent" than the Federalists. Samuel Smith also realized that the events of July 1811 were crucial for the administration. If Madison could not quickly negotiate the disputes with Britain and France, Smith wrote, "he must take some new course hostile to his natural temper to reinstate himself in public opinion." Smith to John Spear Smith, July 11, 1811, Smith Papers, *ibid.*

[97] Madison to John Quincy Adams, Nov. 15, 1811, Madison Papers, *ibid.* The British government, Madison wrote, "shews a predetermination to make her Orders in Council co-durable with the war." For additional evidence on this point, though of a much later date, see Edward Coles to William Cabell Rives, Jan. 21, 1856, "Letters of Edward Coles: Third Installment," *WMQ*, 2d Ser., VII (1927), 162-164.

[98] For an account of the first session of the 12th Congress that emphasizes the effect of political maneuvering in delaying the declaration of war until June 1812 see Stagg, "The Revolt Against Virginia," 45-82. Throughout the session, support among congressional Republicans for military preparations and war was somewhat stronger than was support for the president's renomination.

[99] Monroe to Taylor, June 13, 1812, Monroe Papers, Lib. Cong.

to guide the war effort but to elevate Duane and his political allies in Pennsylvania to important positions in the federal government.[100]

The Clintonians and the Smith brothers were less able to suppress either their ambitions or their dislike of the president. For the first half of 1812 they could not decide whether to attack Madison personally or to oppose the movement to war—a dilemma which was clearly reflected in the divided votes on the war by the anti-Madison Republicans in the Senate.[101] After June 1812, however, they found it impossible to challenge either Madison or his war from within the party. Consequently, they were forced not only into opposing the war but also into making an awkward and unrewarding alliance with the Federalists. As his Republican opponents thus divided and found themselves deprived of any politically effective combination of issues, Madison emerged triumphant at the head of a refashioned majority Republican coalition united in support of the war.[102]

In this manner the coming of the War of 1812 restored a degree of order and stability to the highly factionalized politics of Madison's administration. Yet the degree of unity within the Republican party, reflecting as it did the minimal degree of integration within the nation itself, was always precarious. The declaration of war, while affirming the unity of the party on some issues, only served to expose fresh, and perhaps more serious, divisions on other matters. Many Republicans feared—and events were shortly to bear them out—that neither the party nor the American people were sufficiently united to carry the nation through the ordeal of combat. Moreover, the decision to go to war with Britain did not include any agreement among the nation's leaders on how the war was to be fought. It is hardly surprising, therefore, that the conduct of the War of 1812 was characterized by confusion and uncertainty as the administration grappled with the problems of defining war policies and of arousing sufficient support for their implementation. But that is a separate and very different story.

[100] Armstrong to Duane, Aug. 20, 1812, "Selections from the Duane Papers," *Historical Magazine*, 2d Ser., IV (1868), 60-61; Higginbotham, *Keystone in the Democratic Arch*, 267-268.

[101] The dilemma was made all the more acute by the fact that the "malcontents" held the balance of power between the Federalists and the supporters of the administration. Among the most prominent "malcontent" Republicans in the Senate, Giles, Leib, John Smith, and Samuel Smith finally voted for war, while German, Gilman, and Lambert (of New Jersey) voted against it. When the final vote was taken, John Randolph reported that "Leib and [Samuel] Smith exhibited the strongest symptom of perturbation." To Edward Cunningham, June 24, 1812, John Randolph Papers, Lib. Cong.

[102] In July 1811 Samuel Smith complained that the president was "engaged in putting down a family who put him where he now is." In Oct. 1812 he conceded that Madison had won his struggle with the Smith family. Smith to John Spear Smith, July 1811, Smith Papers, Lib. Cong., and Smith to Leib, Oct. 14, 1812, Misc. MSS, *ibid.*

Party Unity and the Decision for War in the House of Representatives, 1812

Ronald L. Hatzenbuehler*

A REVIEW of recent scholarship relating to origins of the War of 1812 reveals a growing interest in an examination of partisan politics in the Twelfth Congress in explaining the final votes for war. In the mid-1950s the work of two scholars, John S. Pancake and Margaret K. Latimer, inaugurated the move away from standard interpretations for war compiled by Warren H. Goodman.[1] Pancake's research centered around a group of Republicans who followed the leadership of Gen. Samuel Smith of Baltimore, Senator from Maryland, and frequently opposed the policies of the Madison administration. In Pancake's view, these "Invisibles" combined forces with the War Hawks in 1811 and pushed President Madison to take strong measures against Great Britain—even as far as war.[2]

Margaret Latimer also focused on a "bloc" in Congress during Madison's first administration. She assessed the influence of three young congressmen from South Carolina—John C. Calhoun, William Lowndes, and Langdon Cheves—who were elected to the House "with reference to the critical condition of the country." Because of the unusual cohesion of opinion within South Carolina, these young congressmen came to Washington committed to the promotion of a vigorous foreign policy. By working with the Speaker of the House, Henry Clay, the new delegation from South Carolina became the most aggressive

* Mr. Hatzenbuehler is a graduate student at Kent State University. He is especially indebted to Robert P. Swierenga for his encouragement and critical readings of the draft. Joel H. Silbey of Cornell University and John T. Hubbell and Lawrence S. Kaplan of Kent State University provided valuable editorial assistance. Eileen Rickard of the Computer Center at Kent State kindly formulated the programs used in calculating the Q statistic and agreement scores for the cluster-bloc analysis.

[1] Warren H. Goodman, "The Origins of the War of 1812: A Survey of Changing Interpretations," *Mississippi Valley Historical Review*, XXVIII (1941-1942), 171-186.

[2] John S. Pancake, " 'The Invisibles': A Chapter in the Opposition to President Madison," *Journal of Southern History*, XXI (1955), 17-37.

force in Congress and was primarily responsible for plunging their "peace loving party" into war.[3]

Both authors emphasized that influential members of the Republican party produced the movement toward war. Norman K. Risjord was one of the first historians to suggest another explanation for Republican party voting. Attacking Latimer's South Carolina position, Risjord argued that the election of Calhoun, Lowndes, and Cheves represented an addition not of numbers but of talent to the House of Representatives. More significant to Risjord was the gradual shift of older Republican members of Congress away from Jeffersonian peaceful coercion to a vigorous defense of American neutral rights. The only unifying factor in all parts of the country to explain this conversion and the eventual decision for war, said Risjord, was "the realization that something had to be done to vindicate the national honor." The majority of the Republicans who voted for war were men who had been in Congress for many years, and the younger War Hawks were primarily catalysts rather than determinants of the war.[4] Bradford Perkins's detailed account of Anglo-American relations from 1805 to 1812 stressed that the majority of the Republicans moved toward war slowly and with deep misgivings about the prudence of their course. He presented the War Hawks as an ineffective, though persistent, force in breaking the deadlock in Congress between Federalist opposition to restrictions against Great Britain and Republican continuation of peaceful coercion.[5]

Perhaps the most significant study of activity in the Twelfth Congress has been that of Roger H. Brown. Brown took the final votes for war recorded in the House and Senate and showed that "with some exceptions the congressional split followed party lines."[6] Moving beyond

[3] Margaret Kinard Latimer, "South Carolina—A Protagonist of the War of 1812," *American Historical Review*, LXI (1955-1956), 914-929.

[4] Norman K. Risjord, "1812: Conservatives, War Hawks, and the Nation's Honor," *William and Mary Quarterly*, 3d Ser., XVIII (1961), 196-210; Risjord, *The Old Republicans: Southern Conservatism in the Age of Jefferson* (New York, 1965), 122-126.

[5] Bradford Perkins, *Prologue to War: England and the United States, 1805-1812* (Berkeley and Los Angeles, 1961), 373-377.

[6] Roger H. Brown, *The Republic in Peril: 1812* (New York, 1964), 45. His count revealed that only Republicans voted for war (98) and that all the Federalists (40) voted against it. He used the list in *Niles' Weekly Register*, Nov. 30, 1811, to determine party affiliation. My calculations are somewhat different, based on the criterion detailed in note 11, and tend to be more conservative than those obtained by following Brown's method.

nationalistic explanations of congressional action, Brown stressed Republican party unity as the primary motivation in the decision for war. To Republicans, the situation in 1812 was the end result of a defense of republicanism born in 1800. Submission to the British Orders in Council would threaten their party's control of the presidency and could even destroy republican government in the nation.[7] Jefferson and Madison, according to Brown, had committed their party repeatedly to a program that would permit no foreign government to regulate American commerce, which is precisely what the Orders sought to do. When peaceful policies of diplomacy and commercial restrictions no longer offered any hope of redress, Republicans in Congress viewed war as the only policy which would save their imperiled nation.[8]

Although studies of congressional voting in this period have been too individualistic to constitute a new school in the historiography of the war's causes, one may isolate three explanations for legislative behavior: (1) Pancake and Latimer contended that blocs of common interest, both sectional and personal, determined legislative voting; (2) Risjord and Perkins indicated that attitudes, primarily on the issue of national honor, motivated the majority of the Republicans to vote for war; (3) Brown emphasized the role of political parties in the war declaration. The validity of each of these evaluations is confirmed in the congressional debates. To date, however, no historian has expanded his investigation of the traditional sources of political rhetoric, newspapers, and manuscripts to include a systematic analysis of the voting behavior of the lawmakers in 1812. A rigorous study of the roll call votes in Congress relating to foreign affairs can help to break the deadlock in conflicting interpretations and assess the relative strengths of geographical blocs, factional groupings, and party cohesion in influencing political activity in the Twelfth Congress.[9]

[7] Brown, *Republic in Peril*, 73.

[8] *Ibid.*, 39-48. Reginald Horsman has argued that the wars of Europe caused the War of 1812. Had there been no war between France and England, there would have been no Orders, no impressment, and hence no war. *The Causes of the War of 1812* (Philadelphia, 1962), 14-23, 265-267.

[9] Although most of the roll-call analyses of the U. S. Congress have dealt with recent times, several historians have demonstrated the utility of such studies for Congresses prior to and during the Civil War. See Thomas B. Alexander, *Sectional Stress and Party Strength: A Study of Roll-Call Voting Patterns in the United States House of Representatives, 1836-1860* (Nashville, 1967); Joel H. Silbey, *The Shrine of Party: Congressional Voting Behavior, 1841-1852* (Pittsburgh, 1967); and

Social scientists have developed several statistical methods of investigating sectional, factional, or partisan motivations for voting. An index of cohesion measures the strength of party unity.[10] After dividing the members of a legislative body into self-conscious political groupings (Republicans and Federalists in the Twelfth Congress), one calculates the difference in percentages between the members of a party who voted yea and those who voted nay.[11] In order to evaluate the relative strengths of the parties on particular roll calls, an index of fifty (a 75-25 percent split) may be operationally used as a basis of comparison.

In a cluster-bloc analysis, the researcher counts how many times each pair of legislators voted together on related roll calls and then fits the pair-wise agreement scores into a matrix to form groups of like-minded legislators (Figures 3 and 4 in Appendix).[12] A series of identical votes to individual roll calls indicates that similar considerations prompted the legislators to vote alike. Cross-party voting and sectional groupings are uncovered in this manner.

Scaling, developed by Louis Guttman in the 1940s to analyze opinion surveys in social psychology, is applied to political studies to evaluate quantitatively a legislator's position toward a particular issue.[13] Using

---

Allan G. Bogue, "Bloc and Party in the United States Senate: 1861-1863," *Civil War History*, XIII (1967), 221-241.

[10] Developed by Stuart A. Rice, *Quantitative Methods in Politics* (New York, 1928), 208-209. For applications, see Jerome M. Clubb and Howard W. Allen, "Party Loyalty in the Progressive Years: The Senate, 1909-1915," *Journal of Politics*, XXIX (1967), 567-584.

[11] The criterion for determining party identification was the party label that the individual used in his campaign for Congress as recorded in the *Biographical Directory of the American Congress, 1774-1961* (Washington, D. C., 1961), supplemented by the *Dictionary of American Biography*. Nine legislators were not identified in these sources. Because of general voting behavior, I assigned 8 (David Bard, Josiah Bartlett, Jr., Howell Cobb, Isaiah L. Green, George C. Maxwell, Thomas Moore, William Piper, and George Smith) to the Republican party, and Edwin Gray to the Federalist party. See Table II for party affiliations.

[12] See David B. Truman, *The Congressional Party, A Case Study* (New York, 1959), 46. The 63 roll calls were the same as those to which the Q statistic was applied.

[13] George M. Belknap, "A Method for Analyzing Legislative Behavior," *Midwest Journal of Political Science*, II (1958), 377-402. See also Bogue, "Bloc and Party," *Civil War Hist.*, XIII (1967), 224; and Silbey, *Shrine of Party*, 14-15. Not every roll call should be included in the scale. Only those which dichotomize the members into two groups, pro and con, plus those whose voting pattern cannot be better explained by other reasons, namely unanimity or sharp partisanship, can be used. Unanimity was operationally defined as 90% of those voting either favoring or oppos-

roll calls relating to a certain topic, scaling ranks legislators according to their positions toward the issue in question and allows the researcher to divide them into groups which range, in this case, from aggressive to moderate to non-aggressive categories. In addition to the issue orientation of scaling, the scales can play a double role due to the variety of information which they contain when party affiliation and geographical representation of the legislators are also considered (Tables I and II).

Scaling is a more versatile tool than either a cohesion index or cluster-bloc analysis because attitudinal rankings can also be grouped in terms of partisan or sectional considerations. By using all three techniques, however, each of which considers the roll-call data differently, historians have arrived at a fuller picture of legislative behavior.

The present study utilizes an index of cohesion, scaling, and cluster-bloc analysis to study roll calls related to foreign policy in the House of Representatives during the first session of the Twelfth Congress, from November 4, 1811, to June 18, 1812, the date of the final votes on the bill declaring war. This presentation involves a wider range of roll-call behavior within a larger universe than has previously been attempted, but the special tactical problems arising from such a decision do not outweigh the potential benefits. For the purpose of a more nearly complete roll-call analysis, the House provides greater possibilities than the Senate for three reasons: (1) the larger number of roll calls dealing specifically with foreign affairs which the House recorded during the first session; (2) the larger sectional groupings; and (3) the larger number of Federalists potentially in opposition to the Republican majority.[14]

Of the 166 roll calls in the House during this timespan, 113 non-

---

ing the subject of the roll call, and partisanship was based on a 90% agreement in both parties (cohesion indexes above 80) or a cohesion index of one party above 95 on a particular vote. In addition, roll calls were excluded if less than 80% of the legislators voted so as not to inflate spuriously the reproducibility of the scale, and finally according to their level of association measured by the Q statistic. Of the 63 roll calls for which Q values were calculated, 26 (Table I) were mutually scalar at the .8 level. See Lee F. Anderson et al., Legislative Roll-Call Analysis (Evanston, Ill., 1966), 89-106; Charles D. Farris, "A Method of Determining Ideological Groupings in the Congress," Jour. Pol., XX (1958), 308-338; and Duncan MacRae, Jr., "A Method for Identifying Issues and Factions from Legislative Votes," American Political Science Review, LIX (1965), 909-926.

[14] For the most recent study of the Senate in the first session, see Leland R. Johnson, "The Suspense Was Hell: The Senate Vote for War in 1812," Indiana Magazine of History, LXV (1969), 247-267.

unanimous votes were generally related to foreign affairs, with Federalists and Republicans in opposition to one another on 98 of the votes (87 percent). From a graph of the two parties' indexes of cohesion over time (Figures 1 and 2 in Appendix), one sees this divergence of party policies even more clearly. In particular, two trends are obvious. First, both parties were able to maintain a relatively high degree of unity throughout the session. Republicans fell below an index of fifty (a 75-25 percent split) forty-two times from November through June 18. The Federalists fell below it only twenty times. Secondly, a point arose in the session when the cohesion of both parties increased sharply. In *Prologue to War*, Bradford Perkins argued that the nadir in the movement for war came in March and was not closely related to any one issue.[15] The cohesion indexes indicate, however, that the crisis occurred earlier—the Republican jump corresponding with the second reading of a bill to borrow $11 million on February 24, and the Federalist tightening with the first war tax resolution on February 27. From February 24 through the final war votes, Republicans fell below the fifty mark only fifteen times (20 percent of the votes as compared to 68 percent prior to this point). Once again, the Federalists attained a higher degree of party unity as they fell below the mark only three times after February 27, a miniscule 4 percent.[16]

The loan and the war taxes were direct responses by the Republican majority in the House to President James Madison's State of the Union Message presented to Congress on November 5, 1811.[17] In his message, the President asked the lawmakers to "feel the duty of putting the United States into an armor and an attitude demanded by the crisis, and corresponding with the national spirit and expectations." Specifically, he recommended that the military establishment be strengthened and that new sources of revenue be tapped to provide for military preparedness.[18] After nearly a four-month delay, on February 26 the Ways and Means

[15] Perkins, *Prologue to War*, 373-376.
[16] [Annals of Congress.] *Debates and Proceedings in the Congress of the United States, 1789-1824* (Washington, D. C., 1853), 12th Cong., 1st sess., 1086-1087, 1108.
[17] *Ibid.*, 11-15, 331.
[18] *Ibid.*, 13-15. One week later, the House resolved itself into a Committee of the Whole on the State of the Union to consider the president's message, and John Smilie (R., Pa.) submitted six resolutions. Two of his motions related explicitly to preparations for war: that a select committee be appointed to study foreign relations and that the Committee of Ways and Means be charged with implementing the financial section of the president's message. *Ibid.*, 334-335.

Committee finally presented fourteen resolutions for raising taxes to support a war with a European nation.[19]

The financing of the war marked an especially significant stage for the Federalists in cementing their party unity. As a whole, the Federalist congressmen generally took no part in the debates of the first session, believing that the Republicans used Federalist opposition only to consolidate their own party's position. As one Federalist explained, "The cry of British party, and British influence has been managed with great adroitness and success. This [silence] has stript them of this weapon, and now they have not to plead . . . Federal opposition as an apology for the continuance of the restrictive system."[20]

Some Federalists, however, led by Josiah Quincy of Massachusetts, supported the Republicans in the early part of the session. In two letters to Massachusetts Federalist Harrison Gray Otis, Quincy revealed his motives for such a drastic change in policy on the part of the pro-British Federalists. Shortly after the opening of the session, Quincy declared to Otis that "the fault of the conduct of the federalists has been the zeal with which they have advocated every point between this country and Great Britain, in favour of the latter." He felt that Federalists could destroy the administration by pressing for war with Great Britain, and he informed Otis that he was "very far from being alone in these sentiments."[21] A fortnight later, he reiterated his stance: "Let them [Federalists] set themselves about convincing the people of our section of the country that the present situation of the commercial part of the country *is worse than any war, even a British,* and that if [the] administration mean to force us to take the one, or the other, that although they cannot justify the principle of such war, yet that in its political effects, foreign war in any supposable calamity is preferable to the evils we now feel and may fairly anticipate."[22]

Even Quincy, however, abandoned his plan when the taxes became

---

[19] *Ibid.,* 1106-1107.

[20] Samuel Taggart to John Taylor, Dec. 14, 1811, "Letters of Samuel Taggart: Representative in Congress, 1803-1814," American Antiquarian Society, *Proceedings,* N.S., XXXIII (1924), 369-370.

[21] Josiah Quincy to Harrison Gray Otis, Nov. 8, 1811. Quoted in David Hackett Fischer, *The Revolution of American Conservatism: The Federalist Party in the Era of Jeffersonian Democracy* (New York, 1965), 174.

[22] Quincy to Otis, Nov. 26, 1811, in Samuel Eliot Morison, *The Life and Letters of Harrison Gray Otis, Federalist, 1765-1848,* II (Boston, 1913), 34.

the issue of debate. As Abijah Bigelow of Massachusetts explained to his wife, Federalists would know that the Republicans were truly determined upon war only when they voted the taxes necessary for its prosecution: "The great difficulty is raising taxes. They dare not do it. They are too cunning to risk their popularity by a land tax, loans, etc.,

TABLE I

SAMPLE OF FOREIGN POLICY ROLL CALLS

Q = .8 OR HIGHER

Scale Number	Volume and Page (Annals)	Date	Subject	Positive Response	Cohesion Index Rep. Fed.		Number of Ties
1	1/545-6	Dec. 16	Raise additional troops for a period of three years.	Y	91	3	6
	1/800-1	Jan. 17	Raising a volunteer corps--final vote.	Y	88	20	
2	1/716-7	Jan. 9	Postpone consideration on bill to raise additional troops as amended by the Senate.	N	87	44	3
	1/1092	Feb. 25	Borrow $11 million--final reading.	Y	91	43	
3	1/617	Jan. 2	Raise additional troops--second reading.	Y	76	45	0
	1/691	Jan. 6	Raise additional troops--final reading.	Y	75	44	
4	2/1636-7	June 4	Motion to adjourn.	N	74	82	0
	2/1635-6	June 4	Postpone decision on bill to declare war until June 5.	N	67	89	
	2/1635	June 4	Postpone decision on bill to declare war until the first Monday in October.	N	73	82	
5	1/340	Nov. 12	Motion to send Madison's State of the Union Message to a special committee on the state of the union.	N	91	76	6
	1/341	Nov. 12	Motion to read the documents connected with Madison's State of the Union Message.	N	77	61	
6	2/1632	June 3	Defeat bill declaring war.	N	68	82	1
	2/1634-5	June 4	Second reading of bill to declare war.	Y	69	82	
7	2/1681-2	June 18	Postpone declaration of war to the first Monday in October.	N	69	84	2
	2/1682	June 18	Postpone declaration of war to the first Monday in July.	N	65	84	

when they raise the taxes necessary to carry on a war I shall think them in earnest, not before."[23]

Another way to test the strength of party unity than a cohesion index is to compare party loyalty with other explanations for a legislator's vote, such as attitudinal or sectional reasons. In a scale reflecting a representative's position toward roll calls related to foreign policy (Tables I and II), the diversity one might expect within rankings from zero to fourteen does not occur. The construction of the scale purposely em-

8	2/1637	June 4	Final vote for war.	Y	63	83	
9	1/1108	Feb. 27	War Taxes, Resolution 1. Add to duties on imports.	Y	79	82	5
	2/1470-8	May 29	Resolution: Inexpedient to resort to war against Great Britain at this time.	N	75	86	
10	2/1630-1	June 3	Vote to remove secrecy on the bill declaring war.	N	68	88	0
	2/1631-2	June 3	Open the doors of the House to discussion of the bill declaring war.	N	72	89	
11	1/1111-2	Feb. 27	War Taxes, Resolution 3. Add to tax rate on foreign ships per ton.	Y	81	73	7
	1/1148	Mar. 4	War Taxes, Resolution 6. Tax on licenses to retailers of wines, etc.	Y	65	81	
12	1/793-4	Jan. 15	Amendment on bill to raise a volunteer corps.	N	76	84	
13	1/1111	Feb. 27	War Taxes, Resolution 2. Retain 25 per cent of the drawbacks on exports.	Y	73	89	12
	1/1150-1	Mar. 4	War Taxes, Resolution 9. Duties on carriages for transport of persons.	Y	78	89	
14	1/1161	Mar. 6	Resolution to cut funds from maritime defenses.	Y	57	89	

Note: In forming a scale, roll calls of similar subject matter and voting patterns can often be combined to form "contrived items," thereby minimizing the number of absences of legislators in the scale. Items 12 and 14 could not be combined with roll calls of similar content or voting pattern without an excessive number of tied votes occurring (13 dichotomous responses represent about a 10% error). The final vote for war (item 8) stands alone because of its special content. For a discussion of "contrived items," see Anderson *et al., Roll-Call Analysis,* 107.

[23] Abijah Bigelow to Hannah Bigelow, Jan. 1, 1812, "Letters of Abijah Bigelow, Member of Congress, to His Wife, 1810-1815," Am. Antiquarian Soc., *Procs.,* N.S., XL (1931), 323.

TABLE II

SCALE OF FOREIGN POLICY ROLL CALLS

FIRST SESSION, TWELFTH CONGRESS: HOUSE OF REPRESENTATIVES

Representative	Party-State	Scale Type	1	2	3	4	5	6	7	8	9	10	11	12	13	14
Alston	R-NC	14	+	+	+	+	+	+	+	+	+	+	+	+	+	+
Bard	R-Pa	14	+	+	+	+	+	+	+	+	+	+	+	+	+	+
Bibb	R-Ga	14	+	+	+	+	+	+	+	+	+	+	+	+	+	+
Brown	R-Pa	14	+	+	+	+	+	+	+	+	+	+	+	+	+	+
Burwell	R-Va	14	+	+	+	+	+	+	+	+	+	+	+	+	+	+
Butler	R-SC	14	+	+	+	+	+	+	+	+	+	+	+	+	+	+
Calhoun	R-SC	14	+	+	+	+	+	+	+	+	+	+	+	+	+	+
Crawford	R-Pa	14	+	+	+	+	+	+	+	+	+	+	+	+	+	+
Davis	R-Pa	14	+	+	+	+	+	+	+	+	+	+	+	+	+	+
Desha	R-Ky	14	+	+	+	+	+	+	+	+	+	+	+	+	+	+
Earle	R-SC	14	+	+	+	+	+	+	+	+	+	+	+	+	+	+
Hall, O.	R-NH	14	+	+	+	+	+	+	+	+	+	+	+	+	+	+
Harper	R-NH	14	+	+	+	+	+	+	+	+	+	+	+	+	+	+
Kent	F-Md	14	+	+	+	+	+	+	+	+	+	+	+	+	+	+
Lacock	R-Pa	14	+	+	+	+	+	+	+	+	+	+	+	+	+	+
Lyle	R-Pa	14	+	+	+	+	+	+	+	+	+	+	+	+	+	+
Moore	R-SC	14	+	+	+	+	+	+	+	+	+	+	+	+	+	+
McCoy	R-Va	14	+	+	+	+	+	+	+	+	+	+	+	+	+	+
Morrow	R-Oh	14	+	+	+	+	+	+	+	+	+	+	+	+	+	+
Rhea	R-Te	14	+	+	+	+	+	+	+	+	+	+	+	+	+	+
Roane	R-Va	14	+	+	+	+	+	+	+	+	+	+	+	+	+	+
Sage	R-NY	14	+	+	+	+	+	+	+	+	+	+	+	+	+	+
Seaver	R-Ma	14	+	+	+	+	+	+	+	+	+	+	+	+	+	+
Smith, G.	R-Pa	14	+	+	+	+	+	+	+	+	+	+	+	+	+	+
Troup	R-Ga	14	+	+	+	+	+	+	+	+	+	+	+	+	+	+
Findley	R-Pa	14	+	+	+	+	+	+	+	+	+	+	+	+	+	+
Cheves	R-SC	14	+	+	+	+	+	+	+	+	+	+	+	+	+	0
Johnson	R-Ky	14	+	+	+	+	+	+	+	+	+	+	+	+	+	0
Lowndes	R-SC	14	+	+	+	+	+	+	+	+	+	+	+	+	+	0
New	R-Ky	14	+	+	+	+	+	+	+	+	+	+	+	+	+	0
Ormsby	R-Ky	14	+	+	+	+	+	+	+	+	+	+	+	+	+	0
Piper	R-Pa	14	+	+	+	+	+	+	+	+	+	+	+	+	+	0
Cochran	R-NC	14	+	+	+	0	+	+	+	+	+	+	+	+	+	+
Taliaferro	R-Va	14	+	+	+	0	+	+	+	+	+	+	+	+	+	+
Whitehill	R-Pa	14	+	+	0	+	+	+	+	+	+	+	+	0	+	+
Winn	R-SC	14	+	+	0	+	+	+	+	+	+	+	+	0	+	+
Goodwyn	R-Va	14	+	+	0	+	+	+	+	+	+	+	+	0	+	+
Ringgold	R-Md	14	+	+	+	+	0	+	+	+	+	+	+	0	+	0
Dawson	R-Va	14	+	+	+	+	0	+	+	+	+	+	+	0	+	+
Clopton	R-Va	14	+	+	+	+	0	+	+	+	+	0	+	0	0	0
Franklin	R-NC	14	+	+	+	0	+	0	+	0	+	0	+	+	+	+
Clay, M.	R-Va	14	+	+	+	0	+	0	0	0	+	0	+	+	+	+

phasizes the extreme positions (zero and fourteen), and yet one finds 46.5 percent of the total number of scaled legislators (58 of 125) in these most extreme categories (Table II).

When one adds to these two groups of legislators others whose scale positions may be viewed as similarly extreme, the division between aggressives and non-aggressives becomes even more striking, and the moderate position virtually disappears (Table III).[24]

[24] A division of scale types into three simple categories—aggressive, moderate,

Representative	Party-State	Scale Type	1	2	3	4	5	6	7	8	9	10	11	12	13	14
Hall, B.	R-Ga	13	x	+	+	+	+	+	+	+	+	+	+	+	+	+
Pond	R-NY	13	+	+	+	+	+	+	+	+	+	+	x	+	+	+
Smith, J.	R-Va	13	+	+	+	+	+	+	x	+	+	+	+	+	+	+
Dinsmoor	R-NH	13	+	+	+	+	+	+	+	+	+	+	+	+	x	+
Morgan	F-NJ	13	+	+	+	+	+	+	+	+	+	+	+	+	x	+
McKim	R-Md	13	+	+	+	+	+	+	+	+	+	+	+	+	x	+
Seybert	R-Pa	13	x	+	+	+	+	+	+	+	+	+	+	+	+	o
Anderson	R-Pa	13	+	+	+	+	+	+	+	+	+	+	+	+	x	o
Strong	R-Vt	13	+	+	+	+	+	+	+	+	+	+	+	o	x	+
Lefever	R-Pa	13	+	+	+	+	+	+	+	+	+	+	x	+	x	+
Pleasants	R-Va	13	o	+	o	+	x	+	+	+	+	+	+	o	+	+
Blackledge	R-NC	13	+	+	+	+	+	+	+	+	+	+	+	+	+	-
Condict	R-NJ	13	+	+	+	+	+	+	+	+	+	+	+	+	+	-
Green	R-Ma	13	+	+	+	+	+	+	+	+	+	+	+	+	+	-
Little	R-Md	13	+	+	+	+	+	+	+	+	+	+	+	+	+	-
Newton	R-Va	13	+	+	+	+	+	+	+	+	+	+	+	+	+	-
Roberts	R-Pa	13	+	+	+	+	+	+	+	+	+	+	+	+	+	-
Sevier	R-Te	13	+	+	+	+	+	+	+	+	+	+	+	+	+	-
Hyneman	R-Pa	13	+	+	+	+	+	+	+	+	+	+	-	+	+	+
Grundy	R-Te	13	+	+	+	+	+	+	+	+	+	+	-	+	+	+
McKee	R-Ky	13	+	+	+	+	+	+	+	+	+	+	+	+	+	+
Pickens	R-NC	13	+	+	+	+	+	+	+	+	+	+	+	+	+	+
Gholson	R-Va	13	+	+	+	+	o	+	+	+	+	+	+	+	+	+
Shaw	R-Vt	13	+	+	+	+	+	+	+	+	+	+	o	+	-	+
Porter	R-NY	13	+	+	+	o	+	o	o	o	+	o	+	-	+	+
Wright	R-Md	13	+	+	+	+	+	+	+	+	+	x	+	+	+	+
Bacon	R-Ma	13	x	+	+	o	+	o	o	o	+	o	+	-	+	+
Smilie	R-Pa	13	+	+	-	+	+	o	+	+	+	o	+	+	+	+
Turner	R-Ma	12	+	+	+	+	+	+	+	+	x	+	+	+	x	-
Widgery	R-Ma	12	+	+	+	+	+	+	+	x	+	-	o	+	+	x	+
Archer	R-Md	12	+	+	+	+	+	+	+	+	-	+	+	+	+	-
Bassett	R-Va	12	+	+	+	+	+	+	+	+	-	+	+	+	+	-
Hawes	R-Va	12	+	+	+	+	+	+	+	+	+	-	+	+	+	-
Williams	R-SC	12	+	+	+	+	+	+	+	+	-	-	o	+	o	o
Metcalf	R-NY	12	+	+	+	+	+	-	+	-	+	+	x	+	+	+
Richardson	F-Ma	12	o	+	o	+	o	+	+	+	-	+	o	x	-
Fisk	R-Vt	11	x	+	+	+	+	+	+	+	x	+	x	+	-	-
Nelson	R-Va	11	+	+	+	+	x	+	+	+	x	+	+	+	-	-
Macon	R-NC	11	+	x	-	+	x	+	+	+	x	-	+	+	+	+
King	R-NC	11	+	+	+	+	-	+	+	+	+	+	-	+	-
Sammons	R-NY	10	+	+	+	-	+	+	o	-	+	+	-	+	-
Mitchill	R-NY	9	+	+	+	+	+	x	-	-	+	+	-	-	o
Van Courtlandt	R-NY	6	+	+	+	+	+	-	-	-	o	-	-	+	-	o
Sullivan	F-NH	4	+	+	+	-	-	-	-	-	-	-	+	o	o	o
Tracy	R-NY	4	+	+	+	-	+	-	-	-	-	-	+	o	x	-
Stow	F-NY	4	+	+	-	-	+	o	-	-	-	o	x	-	-	-
Rodman	R-Pa	4	+	-	-	-	o	-	-	-	x	-	x	+	x	+

and non-aggressive—reflects the polarity of the data without undue constriction of the moderate position. A grouping of the types 14 to 11 as aggressives, 10 to 4 as moderates, and 3 to 0 as non-aggressives represents approximately a 25% division of the total scale types in the extreme categories and approximately 50% in the moderate range. Scaling tends to push individuals to the extreme positions, especially when a "minimum error score" is used. (For an example of this type of scor-

Representative	Party–State	Scale. Type	1	2	3	4	5	6	7	8	9	10	11	12	13	14
Reed	F-Ma	3	+	+	+	-	-	-	-	-	-	-	-	-	-	-
Emott	F-NY	3	+	+	+	-	-	-	-	-	-	-	-	0	-	-
Gold	F-NY	3	+	+	+	-	-	-	-	-	0	-	-	-	-	-
Quincy	F-Ma	3	+	+	+	-	-	-	-	-	-	-	-	0	-	0
Bleecker	F-NY	3	+	+	+	-	0	-	-	-	-	-	-	0	-	-
Milnor	F-Pa	3	+	x	+	-	-	-	-	-	-	-	-	0	-	-
McBryde	R-NC	2	+	-	-	-	0	-	-	-	-	-	-	-	+	- 0
Baker	F-Va	1	+	-	-	-	-	-	-	-	-	-	-	+	-	-
Wilson	F-Va	1	+	-	-	-	-	-	-	-	-	-	-	+	-	-
Breckinridge	F-Va	1	+	-	-	-	-	-	-	-	-	-	-	-	-	-
Ridgely	F-De	1	+	-	0	-	-	-	-	-	-	-	-	-	-	-
Goldsborough	F-Md	1	+	-	0	-	0	-	-	-	-	-	-	0	-	-
Key	F-Md	1	+	-	-	-	-	-	-	-	-	-	-	-	-	0
Randolph	R-Va	1	-	-	-	-	-	-	-	-	-	-	-	+	-	0
Chittenden	F-Vt	1	-	-	-	-	x	-	-	-	-	-	-	-	-	-
Ely	F-Ma	1	-	-	-	-	x	-	-	-	-	-	-	-	-	-
Taggart	F-Ma	1	-	-	-	-	x	-	-	-	-	-	-	-	-	-
Fitch	F-NY	1	x	-	-	-	-	-	-	-	-	-	-	-	-	-
Potter	F-RI	1	-	x	-	-	0	-	-	0	-	-	0	-	0	-
Stanford	R-NC	1	x	-	-	-	-	-	-	-	-	-	-	-	x	-
Jackson	F-RI	0	-	-	-	-	-	-	-	-	-	-	-	-	-	-
Law	F-Ct	0	-	-	-	-	-	-	-	-	-	-	-	-	-	-
Lewis	F-Va	0	-	-	-	-	-	-	-	-	-	-	-	-	-	-
Moseley	F-Ct	0	-	-	-	-	-	-	-	-	-	-	-	-	-	-
Sturges	F-Ct	0	-	-	-	-	-	-	-	-	-	-	-	-	-	-
Wheaton	F-Ma	0	-	-	-	-	-	-	-	-	-	-	-	-	-	-
White	R-Ma	0	-	-	-	-	-	-	-	-	-	-	-	-	-	-
Brigham	F-Ma	0	-	-	-	-	-	-	-	-	-	-	-	0	-	-
Champion	F-Ct	0	-	-	-	-	-	-	-	-	-	-	-	0	-	-
Davenport	F-Ct	0	-	-	-	-	-	-	-	-	-	-	-	0	-	-
Pearson	F-NC	0	-	-	-	-	-	-	-	-	-	-	-	-	-	0
Stuart	F-Md	0	0	-	-	-	-	-	-	-	-	-	-	-	-	-
Tallmadge	F-Ct	0	-	-	-	-	-	-	-	-	-	-	-	0	-	-
Pitkin	F-Ct	0	-	-	-	-	-	-	-	-	-	-	-	0	-	-
Bigelow	F-Ma	0	-	-	-	0	-	0	-	0	-	0	-	-	-	-
Sheffey	F-Va	0	-	-	-	0	-	0	-	0	-	0	-	-	-	-

Total Positive Responses =
Total Respondents = 125

96 92 87 80 77 77 77 77 77 74 74 73 70 56

Notes: + = positive response; — = negative response; ✕ = tied response. Two tied responses per individual raise or lower the scale type one rank. Tied responses were treated as error responses when computing the coefficient of reproducibility (CR = .94). Adam Boyd, Jacob Hufty, George C. Maxwell, and Thomas Newbold (all Republicans from New Jersey) were eliminated because their responses would not scale; other missing legislators did not respond to two-thirds of the scale items.

In our own day, issues of foreign policy often evoke a comparable polarization of attitudes. Are there other explanations for this extreme divergency? A breakdown of the legislators into sectional groupings

ing, see Bogue, "Bloc and Party," *Civil War Hist.*, XIII [1967], 230.) Therefore, in calculating an individual's scale type, I used a simple score based on the number of positive responses recorded.

TABLE III

FOREIGN POLICY ISSUE, ATTITUDE FREQUENCY
TWELFTH CONGRESS, FIRST SESSION: HOUSE OF REPRESENTATIVES

	Scale Type	Number	Percentage
Aggressive	(14-11)	82	65.6
Moderate	(10- 4)	7	5.6
Non-aggressive	(3- 0)	36	28.8
	totals	125	100.0

(Table IV) revealed that the South and West section was most favorable to war and the Northeast was least favorable. The Middle States were the most diverse with five of the six moderates in the scale belonging to this section:

A division of the legislators by party as well as section, however, proved to be more informative than the attitudinal or sectional groupings alone (Table V). Two patterns are evident from such a presentation. First, Republicans and Federalists opposed one another diametrically in every section. This opposition appears to have been especially intense in the South and West and Northeast as both factions attained approximately 90 percent cohesion. More diversity was evident in the Middle States, but the party division was virtually the same as in the other two

TABLE IV

FOREIGN POLICY ISSUE, SECTIONAL DIVISION
TWELFTH CONGRESS, FIRST SESSION: HOUSE OF REPRESENTATIVES

Scale Type		South and West No. Per Cent		Middle No. Per Cent		Northeast No. Per Cent	
Aggressive	(14-11)	42	82.4	28	65.1	12	38.7
Moderate	(10- 4)	---	----	6	14.0	1	3.2
Non-aggressive	(3- 0)	9	17.6	9	20.9	18	58.1
	totals	51	100.0	43	100.0	31	100.0

South and West	Virginia, North Carolina, South Carolina, Georgia, Tennessee, Kentucky, and Ohio.
Middle	Pennsylvania, Maryland, New York, New Jersey, and Delaware.
Northeast	Massachusetts, New Hampshire, Vermont, Connecticut, and Rhode Island.

TABLE V

FOREIGN POLICY ISSUE DIVIDED BY SECTION AND PARTY

TWELFTH CONGRESS, FIRST SESSION: HOUSE OF REPRESENTATIVES

Scale Type		Republicans No. Per Cent		Federalists No. Per Cent	
South and West					
Aggressive	(14-11)	42	93.3	--	----
Moderate	(10- 4)	--	----	--	----
Non-aggressive	(3- 0)	3	6.7	6	100.0
totals		45	100.0	6	100.0
Middle					
Aggressive	(14-11)	26	83.9	2	16.7
Moderate	(10- 4)	5	16.1	1	8.3
Non-aggressive	(3- 0)	--	----	9	75.0
totals		31	100.0	12	100.0
Northeast					
Aggressive	(14-11)	11	91.7	1	5.3
Moderate	(10- 4)	--	----	1	5.3
Non-aggressive	(3- 0)	1	8.3	17	89.4
totals		12	100.0	19	100.0

sections. Secondly, the polarization of attitudes evidenced in Table III may be best explained in terms of these partisan divisions. In other words, the attitudinal diversity is of less importance than the two parties' differing views on the conduct of foreign policy.

It could be argued that party would naturally appear from this scale as more revealing of voting patterns than either issue or section because the roll calls which the Q statistic selected for inclusion in the scale were those with high cohesion scores (Table I). Thus, a new scale composed of roll calls with lower cohesion scores tested the validity of the original scale. A frequency distribution by issue revealed 56.2 percent aggressives, 19.0 percent moderates, and 24.8 percent non-aggressives—a gain in the moderate position. A division by party and section revealed a tendency for Federalists in the Middle States and Republicans in the Northeast to be influenced more by sectional considerations than in the first scale (Table VI), but party still appeared to explain more of the voting than either section or issue:[25]

[25] I selected another group of roll calls from the initial group of 113 non-unanimous roll calls by eliminating those with either party possessing an index of 80 or

240

TABLE VI

Scale Type		Republicans No. Per Cent		Federalists No. Per Cent	
South and West					
Aggressive	(6-5)	32	74.4	—	—
Moderate	(4-2)	7	16.3	—	—
Non-aggressive	(1-0)	4	9.3	6	100.0
totals		43	100.0	6	100.0
Middle					
Aggressive	(6-5)	23	69.7	4	40.0
Moderate	(4-2)	9	27.3	3	30.0
Non-aggressive	(1-0)	1	3.0	3	30.0
totals		33	100.0	10	100.0
Northeast					
Aggressive	(6-5)	7	58.3	2	11.8
Moderate	(4-2)	4	33.3	—	—
Non-aggressive	(1-0)	1	8.3	15	88.2
totals		12	99.9	17	100.0

A cluster-bloc analysis of the sectional groupings also emphasized a partisan voting pattern rather than factional or geographical ones, especially in the South and West and Northeast where Republicans and Federalists were most heavily concentrated (Figures 3 and 4 in Appendix). In each matrix a near perfect division existed between the two parties. At the 80 percent cohesion level, the diverse Republican blocs are intriguing but at lower levels collapse due to the absence of moderate scale types and the lack of cross-party voting. For example, at the 70 percent cohesion level, the left corner of Figure 3 becomes one bloc. Extensive manuscript research would be necessary before much significance could be assigned to the specific differences between the Republican groups in each section.

One additional observation from the results of the cluster-bloc analy-

---

above (90-10% split). Only 30 of the 113 roll calls remained. Once again I chose a Q score of .8 as the minimum level of association and found 6 roll calls mutually scalar at this level. The fact that in both cases the Q statistic selected roll calls in which party explained the association more than issue or section is quite significant. This second scale is available from the author on request.

sis relates to James Sterling Young's scrutiny of the Washington society of this period. Young discovered that "boarding house fraternities" which developed among the legislators were often more influential in determining political attitudes than partisan or sectional ties. For example, during the Twelfth Congress Abijah Bigelow roomed in Washington with Elijah Brigham and dined with Brigham and William Ely from Massachusetts, Epaphroditus Champion, Jonathan O. Moseley, Lewis B. Sturges, and Lyman Law from Connecticut, Martin Chittenden from Vermont, and Asa Fitch from New York. Figure 4 in the Appendix shows the high voting cohesion of this group (minus Fitch) and would seem to support Young's perceptive insights.[26] The fact that they were all Federalists, however, would also indicate that by the Twelfth Congress party ties had become more important than Young would admit.

There are three questions not central to this presentation which are worthy of extended investigation. The scale itself contains at least two definable "sub-issues" relating to Madison's State of the Union Address, additional military personnel and loans and taxes for war. An intensive examination of each of these issues which are connected with but inferior to the main problem of an overall view of foreign policy in the Twelfth Congress would provide additional information on the positions of individual congressmen as well as the interaction of the political parties on specific instances of conflict. Secondly, the political diversity of the Middle States both along attitudinal and party lines is most intriguing. In particular, preliminary research would indicate that the Republicans in the Middle States were extremely sensitive to the issue of the war taxes and other legislation which might hamper their advantageous position as a "breadbasket" for the participants in the Napoleonic Wars. Federalist newspapers in the Northeast blasted what they viewed as clear evidence of political expediency and favoritism in the application of Republican foreign policy. One Boston newspaper even suggested that President Madison's dependence on the support of the Middle States (and particularly Pennsylvania) in his reelection bid in 1812 was the reason for their preferential treatment.[27] Thirdly, concerning the War

[26] James Sterling Young, *The Washington Community, 1800-1828* (New York, 1966), Chap. 7. Young does not include in his study roll calls from 1809 to 1815. A. Bigelow to H. Bigelow, Nov. 4, 1811, "Letters of Abijah Bigelow," Am. Antiquarian Soc., *Procs.*, N.S., XL (1931), 317.

[27] Thomas Jefferson wrote to Madison on one occasion on the importance of keeping markets open for American farmers: "Our farmers are cheerful in the ex-

Hawk controversy, one may easily distinguish from the voting scales a group of representatives who may be classified as "hawks" as well as a group of "doves."[28] And yet, these same divisions may best be labeled Republicans and Federalists as only one Federalist was included in the forty-two legislators in the most aggressive scale type of fourteen, and only one Republican was in the most non-aggressive scale type of zero (Table II).[29] Republican voting became especially cohesive after the war taxes were introduced, but the voting scales indicate that a warlike attitude was present from the beginning of the session. An analysis of the Eleventh Congress and previous Congresses would be necessary to help resolve the larger question of when this party transformation occurred.

In summary, the three statistical techniques—index of cohesion, cluster-bloc analysis, and scaling—although they organized the data differently, each presented overwhelming evidence to support the conclusion that Republican party unity was the determining factor in the decision of the House of Representatives to declare war on Great Britain in June of 1812. This study, therefore, supports Roger H. Brown's contentions, based on the final war vote, that a division of legislators by party explains the voting pattern better than one by geographical blocs or attitudinal considerations. From an analysis of the foreign policy related roll calls over the entire session, however, it is

---

pectation of a good price for wheat in Autumn. Their pulse will be regulated by this, and not by the successes or disasters of the war. To keep open sufficient markets is the very first object towards maintaining the popularity of the war." Jefferson to Madison, Aug. 5, 1812, in Andrew A. Libscomb and Albert E. Bergh, eds., *The Writings of Thomas Jefferson*, XIII (Washington, D. C., 1907), 132; *New England Palladium*, Aug. 28, 1812. See also Irving Brant, *James Madison: Commander in Chief, 1812-1836* (Indianapolis, 1961), 104.

[28] The *Ind. Mag. of Hist.* devoted its June 1964 issue (Vol. LX) to the question of the War Hawks in the Twelfth Congress. The participants, Reginald Horsman, Roger H. Brown, Alexander DeConde, and Norman K. Risjord, observed that those legislators who should be termed hawks will long be the subject of debate because of the complex of factions and personalities composing the Republican party. For a recent study emphasizing the role of the War Hawks in the decision for war, see Harry W. Fritz, "The Collapse of Party: President, Congress, and the Decline of Party Action, 1807-1817" (Ph.D. diss., Washington University, 1971).

[29] Joseph Kent, the Federalist exception, is classified as a Republican by Roger Brown, *Republic in Peril*, 45; and Norman Risjord, "1812," *WMQ*, 3d Ser., XVIII (1961), 197. Leonard White, the Republican in the non-aggressive group, was actively involved in Federalist party activities in Massachusetts. Daniel A. White Collection, Essex Institute, Salem, Mass.

apparent that Brown understated his evidence in support of his major thesis of Republican concerns over their imperiled nation.

The importance of the search for party solidarity should not be lightly regarded. Although an aggressive attitude existed from the beginning of the session, there were numerous opportunities in the Twelfth Congress for divisive opinions on such topics as the timing of the declaration, the mobilization of a standing army before the outbreak of the war, and the means of financing the war effort to wreck the movement toward war. Felix Grundy of Tennessee spoke to his Republican colleagues on December 9, 1811, on the need for developing and adhering to a consensus:

My business at present is to address a particular portion of the members of this House—I mean, sir, the Republican members—and although what I am about to say might be deemed impolitic on ordinary subjects of legislation, yet, at this time and on this occasion, it would be criminal to conceal a single thought which might influence their determination. We should now, Mr. Speaker, forget little party animosities, we should mingle minds freely, and, as far as we are able, commune with the understandings of each other; and, the decision once made, let us become one people, and present an undivided front to the enemies of our country. Republicans should never forget that some years ago a set of men of different politics held the reins of this Government, and drove the car of State. . . . By a national sentence, the men then in power were taken down from their high places, and Republican men were put in their seats. If your minds are resolved on war, you are consistent, you are right, you are still Republicans; but if you are not resolved, pause and reflect, for should this resolution pass, and you then become faint-hearted, remember that you have abandoned your old principles, and trod in the paths of your predecessors.[30]

Late in the session, however, consensus ceased to attract a least one candid Republican congressman. Thomas Sammons of New York, a supporter of the additional troop levies and most of the war tax legislation (Table II), opposed the timing of the war declaration as potentially disastrous to the nation. Stressing the unprepared state of the country to conduct an offensive war, he attacked the majority of the Republican

[30] Grundy's speech came in response to John Randolph's objection to raising a standing army in peacetime because of accusations during John Adams's administration of Federalist intentions to use troops to curb internal dissent. Grundy argued that the army could be raised only for war purposes, if the Republicans were to be consistent in their thinking. *Annals of Congress*, 12th Cong., 1st sess., 423-424.

legislators as determined "to go to war at all events or under any circumstances whatever." Sammons, a staunch Republican who endorsed the war's legitimacy if not its timing, bitterly lamented the partisanship which he felt had contaminated the war issue: "The prejudices and self will of parties and party men to support principles and measures right or wrong if it is brought forward by their political friends has appeared to me for some time verry dangerous, in perticular when it concerns our for[e]ign relations, including Mr. Adams administration to the present. [T]he federalists and republicans have each in turn supported and opposed the same acts and measures with but few exceptions—no reformation appears to take place every one is just all parties are right at Least in their own opinion."[31]

In a similar vein, one of the older Federalists in the House, Daniel Sheffey of Virginia, viewed circumstances leading to the declaration of war in 1812 as being the same type of situation that the nation faced in 1798. He depicted both occasions in terms of the deleterious impact of partisan politics on foreign policy decision making: "It is but about fourteen years ago, when the very men who now brand every person with the name of tory and British partisan, merely because they think the war impolitic—themselves opposed a war contemplated by their government, and partially entered into against France. . . . We had abundant cause for war—the only difference then and at present, is, that the war then was waged against *France,* now it is waged against *England.* Then Federalists were the war spirits, now republicans (so called) have stept into their principles. With the people, these *distinctions* can make no difference; the effect on them will be the same, whatever nation may be the enemy."[32]

When historians debate the conflicting reasons for the declaration of war in the House of Representatives in 1812, they generally minimize

[31] Thomas Sammons to James Lansing, May 9, 1812, Thomas Sammons Letters, The Old Fort, Fort Johnson, N. Y. Writing to New York Governor Daniel B. Tompkins the same day as the war was formally declared, he said: "I voted against the declaration believing the United States were not prepared to prosecute the war Immediately which in my opinion the safety and good of our country required." Sammons to Tompkins, June 18, 1812, Daniel B. Tompkins Collection, Box 3, Package 3, New York State Library, Albany, N. Y.

[32] Daniel Sheffey, *The Honorable D. Sheffey (Member of Congress from Virginia) to His Constituents* (Washington, D. C., 1813), 15. This circular was evidently printed at several places. The one to which I refer was printed in Lexington, Ky., at the press of Thomas T. Skillman.

the importance of the legislators' partisan motivations. However, a congressman who broke party ties was an exceptional case, and both parties exhibited remarkably strong wills to survive as organizations when confronted with potentially disruptive pressures within or outside their ranks. The victorious Republican faction molded a consensus at the beginning of the session which favored a declaration of war and either adjusted or abandoned positions which threatened to destroy the cohesion necessary to realize its goal. By June the war issue had become so thoroughly entangled with partisan political strategies that the decision for war must be viewed in terms of Republican party unity.

Figure 1

Republican Party Index of Cohesion Values for Non-unanimous Foreign Policy Roll Calls
Twelfth Congress, First Session: House of Representatives

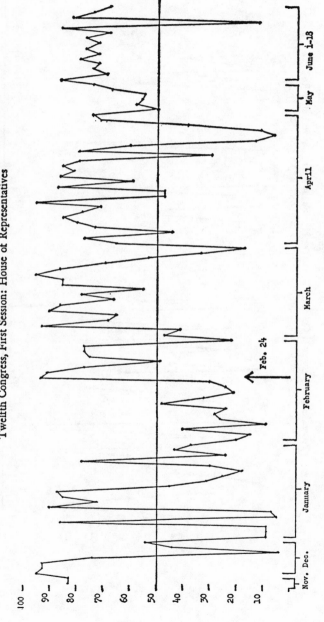

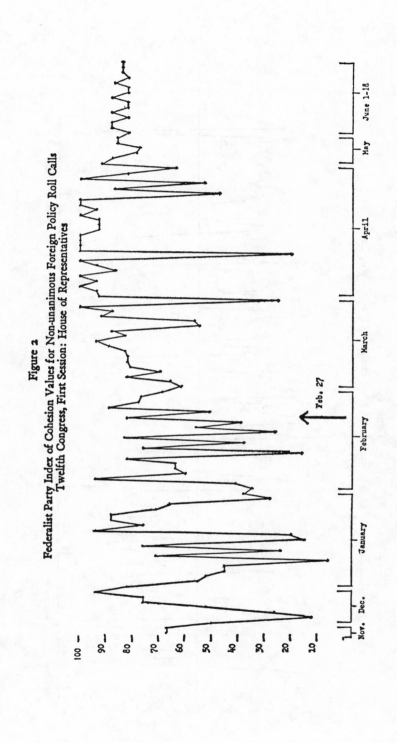

Figure 2

Federalist Party Index of Cohesion Values for Non-unanimous Foreign Policy Roll Calls
Twelfth Congress, First Session: House of Representatives

Figure 3
South and West Section
Pair-wise Voting Scores on Sixty-three Foreign Policy Roll Calls
Twelfth Congress, First Session: House of Representatives[a]

	Alston, R-NC	Bassett, R-Va	Lowndes, R-SC	Troup, R-Ga	Cheves, R-SC	Calhoun, R-SC	Roane, R-Va	Bibb, R-Ga	Ormsby, R-Ky	Grundy, R-Te	Desha, R-Ky	New, R-Ky	Morrow, R-Oh	Johnson, R-Ky	Butler, R-SC	Hall, R-Ga	Pickens, R-NC	King, R-NC	Gholson, R-Va	McCoy, R-Va	McKee, R-Ky	Moore, R-SC	Franklin, R-NC	Earle, R-SC	Dawson, R-Va	Newton, R-Va	Cochran, R-NC	Sevier, R-Te	Rhea, R-Te	Winn, R-SC	Hawes, R-Va	Blackledge, R-NC	Burwell, R-Va	Smith, R, Va	Clay, R-Va
Alston, R-NC		51		53	50	52	55																	52								51			
Bassett, R-Va	51		57		52	52	53																			50									
Lowndes, R-SC		57		53	56	54	51																				52	51	50						
Troup, R-Ga	53		53		52	52	52		54	54			52														52	51	50						
Cheves, R-SC	50	52	56	52		53	50	51	50							50																			
Calhoun, R-SC	52	52	54	52	53		52	51	50	51					50	50						52											51		
Roane, R-Va	55	53	51	52	50	52		54	55	56	56	53	53		52	54	53	51	53	50		50													
Bibb, R-Ga						51	51		54		53	55	52	54	54		53	50		54	50	52													
Ormsby, R-Ky						50	50	55		54		54	52	53	53	53		52		51								51	50						
Grundy, R-Te						54		51			56	53	54		51	52	52	50	51	51															
Desha, R-Ky				54				66	55	52		51	54	52	53	53	53	54	50	50	51	50	50												
New, R-Ky								53	52	53	52		54		51	55	52	50	51		50														
Morrow, R-Oh						50		53	54	53	50	52		51	51	50		51				53		52		50									
Johnson, R-Ky								54	53	54	52	55	51		54									51											
Butler, R-SC			52					52		51	53	52	50	51				50	51											50					
Hall, R-Ga								54	53	52		53	50				50	50																	
Pickens, R-NC					50	53	50				54	51	51		50			53	53		51			50											
King, R-NC					50	50	51		51		50						50	53													53				
Gholson, R-Va							53						50				50	53															53		
McCoy, R-Va							50						51	50			51																		
McKee, R-Ky								54					50		53																				
Moore, R-SC								50							51												50								
Franklin, R-NC				50		50	52																												
Earle, R-SC	52			52											52										50	51									
Dawson, R-Va			51	52									51											50		50			50						
Newton, R-Va	50	50																						51	50										
Cochran, R-NC							50							50						50															50
Sevier, R-Te				51																							52								
Rhea, R-Te				50																							52								
Winn, R-SC																							50												
Hawes, R-Va							53																												
Blackledge, R-NC	51																																		
Burwell, R-Va																50																			
Smith, R, Va				51																															
Clay, R-Va																						50													

[a] 80% agreement matrix

Figure 3
Continuation of Original Matrix

	McBryde, R-NC	Pearson, F-NC	Randolph, R-Va	Lewis, F-Va	Wilson, F-Va	Breckinridge, F-Va	Baker, F-Va	Stanford, R-NC	Gray, F-Va	Sheffey, F-Va
McBryde, R-NC		50								
Pearson, F-NC	50			50	50					
Randolph, R-Va				55	53		50			
Lewis, F-Va			55		53	51	52			
Wilson, F-Va	50	57	52			54	55			
Breckinridge, F-Va			51	54			60			
Baker, F-Va	50		52	55	60					
Stanford, R-NC				50						
Gray, F-Va										50
Sheffey, F-Va									50	

Figure 3.1
Two Additional Blocs
Hidden in the Original Matrix

	Troup, R-Ga	Earle, R-SC	Dawson, R-Va	Newton, R-Va	Grundy, R-Te	Sevier, R-Te	Rhea, R-Te
Troup, R-Ga		52	51	50			
Earle, R-SC	52		50	51			
Dawson, R-Va	51	50		50			
Newton, R-Va	50	51	50				
Grundy, R-Te						51	50
Sevier, R-Te					51		52
Rhea, R-Te					50	52	

Figure 4
Northeast Section
Pair-wise Voting Scores on Sixty-three Foreign Policy Roll Calls
Twelfth Congress, First Session: House of Representatives[a]

	Fisk, R-Vt	Shaw, R-Vt	Dinsmoor, R-NH	Green, R-Ma	Hall, R-NH	Seaver, R-Ma	Strong, R-Vt	Harper, R-NH	Turner, R-Ma	Quincy, F-Ma	Reed, F-Ma	White, R-Ma	Brigham, F-Ma	Moseley, F-Ct	Sturges, F-Ct	Bigelow, F-Ma	Champion, F-Ct	Chittenden, F-Vt	Davenport, F-Ct	Ely, F-Ma	Jackson, F-RI	Law, F-Ct	Pitkin, F-Ct	Potter, F-RI	Taggart, F-Ma	Wheaton, F-Ma	Tallmadge, F-Ct
Fisk, R-Vt		52	51																								
Shaw, R-Vt	52		52																								
Dinsmoor, R-NH	51	52		52			52																				
Green, R-Ma			52		55	50	51																				
Hall, R-NH				55		54	50																				
Seaver, R-Ma				50	54		55																				
Strong, R-Vt				50		55																					
Harper, R-NH		52																									
Turner, R-Ma			51																								
Quincy, F-Ma											59																
Reed, F-Ma										59		50	51	51	51												
White, R-Ma											50		60	62	62	53	57	58	60	60	60	60	58	55	59	60	55
Brigham, F-Ma											51	60		61	61	54	58	57	61	59	59	59	59	58	58	59	56
Moseley, F-Ct											51	62	61		63	54	58	59	61	61	61	61	59	56	60	61	54
Sturges, F-Ct											51	62	61	63		54	58	59	61	61	61	61	59	56	60	61	54
Bigelow, F-Ma												53	54	54	54		51	50	52	52	52	52	50	51	51		54
Champion, F-Ct												57	58	58	58	51		56	60	56	60	58	56	53	55	58	53
Chittenden, F-Vt												58	57	59	59	50	56		57	61	57	57	59	56	60	59	54
Davenport, F-Ct												60	61	61	61	52	60	57		59	61	61	59	56	58	59	54
Ely, F-Ma												60	59	61	61	52	56	61	59		59	59	61	58	62	59	52
Jackson, F-RI												60	59	61	61	52	60	57	61	59		61	57	54	58	59	54
Law, F-Ct												60	59	61	61	52	58	57	61	59	61		58	54	58	59	54
Pitkin, F-Ct												58	59	59	59	50	56	59	59	61	57	57		58	60	57	52
Potter, F-RI												55	58	56	56	51	53	56	56	58	54	54	58		57	56	51
Taggart, F-Ma												59	58	60	60	51	60	58	62	58	58	60	57			58	53
Wheaton, F-Ma												60	59	61	61	54	58	59	59	59	59	59	57	56	58		54
Tallmadge, F-Ct												55	56	54	54	53	54	54	52	54	52	54	52	51	53	54	

[a] 80% agreement matrix

Amer. Stud. **12**, 1, 23–39 *Printed in Great Britain*

Federalist Party Unity and the War of 1812

DONALD R. HICKEY

There is no comprehensive study of Federalist opposition to the War of 1812. The fragmentary studies that exist suggest a party divided between New England extremists on the one hand and moderates in the Middle and Southern States on the other. In this interpretative framework, Federalists to the south and west are invariably portrayed as " good " Federalists, that is, as patriots who consciously and decisively rejected New England's leadership in order to support the war or at least maintain a discreet neutrality.[1] A closer examination of the subject, however, sug-

Donald R. Hickey is a member of the History Department at Texas Tech. University, Lubbock, Texas. A version of this paper was read at the Annual Convention of the Organization of American Historians in Atlanta, Georgia, April 1977. For helpful criticism of earlier drafts. the author is indebted to Robert McColley of the University of Illinois, Morton Borden of the University of California at Santa Barbara, Jerry Martin of the University of Colorado, and Vance Burke of Chicago.

[1] The older studies focus on New England's opposition, giving the impression that Federalists elsewhere supported the war. See Henry Adams, *History of the United States during the Administrations of Jefferson and Madison,* 9 vols. (New York: Charles Scribner's Sons, 1889–91), **6**, 399–403, **8**, 1–23, 287–310; John Bach McMaster, *A History of the People of the United States,* 8 vols. (New York: D. Appleton, 1883–1913), **3**, 543–53, **4**, 210–52; James Schouler, *History of the United States under the Constitution,* 7 vols., rev. ed. (New York: Dodd-Mead, 1894–1913), **2**, 395–96, 461–76; Edward Channing, *A History of the United States,* 6 vols. (New York: Macmillan, 1905–25), **4**, 543–63; Samuel Eliot Morison, *The Life and Letters of Harrison Gray Otis, Federalist, 1765–1848,* 2 vols. (Boston and New York: Houghton Mifflin, 1913), **2**, 53.

More recent studies show a greater awareness of Federalist opposition in the Middle and Southern States, but still tend to discount this opposition or to emphasize its tame and patriotic cast. See Albert J. Beveridge, *The Life of John Marshall,* 4 vols. (Boson and New York: Houghton Mifflin, 1916–19), **4**, 30–31; Dixon Ryan Fox, *The Decline of Aristocracy in the Politics of New York* (New York: Columbia Univ. Press, 1919), pp. 176–77; Sanford W. Higginbotham, *The Keystone in the Democratic Arch: Pennsylvania Politics, 1800–1816* (Harrisburg: Pennsylvania Historical and Museum Commission, 1952), p. 279; Norman K. Risjord, " The Virginia Federalists," *Journal of Southern History,* 33 (1967), 510–11; Marvin R. Zahniser, *Charles Cotesworth Pinckney, Founding Father* (Chapel Hill: Univ. of North Carolina Press, 1967), p. 260; John A. Munroe, *Federalist Delaware, 1775–1815* (New Brunswick: Rutgers Univ. Press, 1954), p. 259, and *Louis McLane: Federalist and Jacksonian* (New Brunswick: Rutgers Univ. Press, 1973), p. 52; Thomas P. Abernethy,

gests that this view is largely false. New England did indeed oppose the war, but instead of abandoning her, Federalists elsewhere followed her lead. Far from degenerating into sectional factions, the Federalist party presented a united front. The result was the most vigorous and sustained party opposition to a war the United States has ever experienced.

I

The declaration of war against England in June of 1812 jolted most Federalists. Convinced that Republicans would never take the step, they were unprepared for the news. It struck them, as Samuel Goodrich remembered, "like a thunderbolt." [2] The initial shock caused considerable confusion, especially among Federalists in the Middle and Southern States. Everywhere Republicans were claiming that with war declared all opposition must cease. Many Federalists were inclined to accept this dictum, especially since they had taken a similar position during the French War of 1798. In New York City and Albany, they talked of pursuing a policy of benevolent neutrality, of not obstructing war measures. [3] Elsewhere in the Middle and South Atlantic States they gave more positive pledges of support. Most agreed with Georgia Federalist Felix H. Gilbert that even though the declaration of war was an "astounding act of Madness," everyone ought to "rally round the Standard" and contribute to the nation's success. [4] As the Charleston *Courier* put it, offensive war was ill-advised, but since the die was cast, it was the duty of everyone "to join the standard of our Country, to rally around the Rulers of the Nation, and

The South in the New Nation, 1789–1819 ([Baton Rouge] : Louisiana State Univ. Press, 1961), pp. 406–11; L. Marx Renzulli Jr., *Maryland: The Federalist Years* (Rutherford : Fairleigh Dickinson Univ. Press, 1972), pp. 269–71, 295–96; Marshall Smelser, *The Democratic Republic, 1801–1815* (New York : Harper and Row, 1968), pp. 287–97.

  For exceptions to this pattern, see S. E. Morison, *Harrison Gray Otis, 1765–1848: The Urbane Federalist* (Boston : Houghton Mifflin, 1969), pp. 325–26; Sarah M. Lemmon, *Frustrated Patriots: North Carolina and the War of 1812* (Chapel Hill : Univ. of North Carolina Press, 1973), pp. 162–86.

[2] Samuel G. Goodrich, *Recollections of a Lifetime*, 2 vols. (New York and Auburn : Miller, Orton and Mulligan, 1856), I, 439. See also Richard Sedgwick to Henry D. Sedgwick, 20 June 1812, in H. D. Sedgwick Papers, Massachusetts Historical Society, Boston, Mass.; Henry Lee to Patrick T. Jackson, 30 Jan. 1813, in Kenneth W. Porter, ed., *The Jacksons and the Lees: Two Generations of Massachusetts Merchants, 1765–1844*, 2 vols. (Cambridge : Harvard Univ. Press, 1937), 2, 1076.

[3] Theodore Sedgwick Jr. to Henry D. Sedgwick, 30 June 1812, in H. D. Sedgwick Papers, Massachusetts Historical Society, Boston, Mass.

[4] Felix H. Gilbert to Sarah Hillhouse, 20 June 1812, in Alexander-Hillhouse Papers, Southern Historical Collection, University of North Carolina Library, Chapel Hill, N.C.

to use every means which we possess to aid in bringing [the war] to a speedy and honorable conclusion." [5]

Federalists in New England, however, took a different view. They could not brook supporting the administration or remaining neutral, believing that the best way to bring the war to a speedy end was to oppose it. They were willing to defend their homes against invasion, and to support the navy and other forms of maritime defense. But in all other respects they were determined to oppose the war. Hence from the beginning, they wrote, spoke, and preached against it, discouraged efforts to raise men or money, and in general threw the weight of their authority on the side of peace. [6]

Resolved to make their own opposition felt, New England Federalists were disturbed by the posture of their friends to the south and west. The doctrine of non-opposition was considered "heresy" in New England, Harrison Gray Otis of Massachusetts reminded a friend in South Carolina. The declaration of war was like any other law: "It must be obey[e]d but its mischief may be and ought to be freely discuss[e]d and all due means taken to procure its repeal." [7] The strictures of Otis, re-enforced by the words and deeds of other New Englanders, did much to encourage Federalist opposition elsewhere. The decision of the New England governors to withhold their militia from national service reportedly "enlivened the drooping spirits of the federalists in New York," and probably had the same effect in other states as well. [8] The Baltimore riots also had an impact.

5 Charleston *Courier*, 25 June 1812. For similar sentiments, see oration of William Winder, 4 July 1812, in Wilmington *American Watchman*, 15 July 1812; B. D. Rounsaville to Citizens of Rowan County (N.C.), 1 July 1812, in Raleigh, *Minerva*, 10 July 1812; Resolutions of Fayetteville (N.C.) Town Meeting, 27 June 1812, in Charleston *Courier*, 10 July 1812; Address of Isaac Auld, cited in Charleston *Courier*, 21 July 1812; Baltimore *Federal Gazette*, reprinted in Chillicothe *Supporter*, 11 July 1812; Philadelphia *Freeman's Journal*, reprinted in Wilmington *American Watchman*, 1 July 1812; Philadelphia *United States Gazette*, 23-29 June 1812.

6 See William Gribbin, *The Churches Militant: The War of 1812 and American Religion* (New Haven: Yale Univ. Press, 1973), pp. 24-34; Address of Mass. House, 25 June 1812, in *Boston Gazette*, 29 June 1812; Resolutions of Boston Town Meeting, 15 July 1812, in Boston *New-England Palladium*, 17 July 1812; Address of Middlesex County (Mass.) Convention, 10 Aug. 1812, in Providence *Gazette*, 22 Aug. 1812; Boston *Columbian Centinel*, 11 July 1812; Boston *New-England Palladium*, 9-26 June 1812; Hartford *Connecticut Courant*, 7 July 1812; Hartford *Connecticut Mirror*, 17 Aug. 1812; Petition of Bridgeport (Conn.), 28 Jan. 1814, in Thompson R. Harlow, *et al.*, eds., *John Cotton Smith Papers*, 7 vols. (Hartford: Connecticut Historical Society, 1948-67), 2, 168-69.

7 Otis to John Rutledge Jr., 31 July 1812, in Rutledge Papers, Southern Historical Collection, University of North Carolina Library, Chapel Hill, N.C.

8 Theodore Sedgwick Sr. to Henry D. Sedgwick, 9 July 1812, in H. D. Sedgwick Papers, Massachusetts Historical Society, Boston, Mass. See also Philadelphia *United States*

The destruction of the office of the Baltimore *Federal Republican*, and the bloody assault on those who sought to defend it, shocked and frightened Federalists everywhere. Was this, they wondered, the beginning of a reign of terror? Was the war being fought for freedom of the seas, as Republicans claimed, or was the real object an end to freedom of the press? [9]

As the summer of 1812 wore on, Federalists in the Middle and Southern States grew steadily more disillusioned with the conflict, and ever more responsive to New England's chord. Some Federalists in these areas publicly avowed a change of heart without disguising the source of their inspiration. The Charleston *Courier*, for example, which in June had pleaded with everyone to support the war, in early August noted the growing ascendancy of the peace party and called on all Americans to work for its success. Five days later the paper praised as " excellent " a piece it reprinted from the Windsor (Vermont) *Washingtonian* advising Federalists of their right to oppose the war as long as they obeyed the laws and the Constitution.[10] Other Federalists to the south and west made no such public declaration. They simply stopped talking about supporting the war, and no longer hesitated to attack the administration and its policies, or to work for a change of leaders. In short, they remained Federalists and, once they understood New England's position and appreciated the logic behind it, they toed the party line.

II

In Congress, most Federalists had enlisted under the New England banner even before war was declared, and they showed no sign of wavering after the decision was made.[11] The party voted unanimously against the declaration of war and most of the war legislation taken up during the remain-

---

Gazette, 29 June 1812; Resolutions of Md. House, 24 Dec. 1812, in *Niles' Register*, 2 Jan. 1813, p. 273. For an analysis of the militia problem, see D. R. Hickey, " New England's Defense Problem and the Genesis of the Hartford Convention," *New England Quarterly*, 50 (1977), 587–604.

[9] See D. R. Hickey, " The Darker Side of Democracy: The Baltimore Riots of 1812," *Maryland Historian*, 7 (Fall, 1976), 1–19.

[10] Charleston *Courier*, 5 and 10 Aug. 1812.

[11] For identification of the Federalists in the war Congresses, see D. R. Hickey, " The Federalists and the War of 1812," Ph.D. dissertation (University of Illinois, 1972), Appendix A. In the Twelfth Congress (1811–1813), there were 36 Federalists in the House (19 from New England, 6 from the Middle States, and 11 from the South), and 6 in the Senate (4 from New England and 2 from the South). In the Thirteenth Congress (1813–1815), there were 64–68 Federalists in the House (30–31 from New England, 20–23 from the Middle States, and 14 from the South), and 8–10 in the Senate (4–6 from New England, 1 from the Middle States, and 3 from the South). The number of Federalists fluctuated in the Thirteenth Congress because of resignations and contested elections.

der of the session. In the three sessions that followed, from late 1812 to early 1814, Federalists continued to vote as a bloc on all war measures. In each area of legislation, the party's cohesion was consistently high (see table on p. 28). Their position was not simply one of mindless opposition, however, for while Federalists opposed all military measures (affecting the army, volunteers, or militia), and all financial and trade limitation proposals, they supported maritime defense.

They opposed all military measures, mainly because the troops were being raised for service in Canada. Josiah Quincy called the invasion of Canada " cruel, wanton, senseless, and wicked," and most other Federalists agreed.[12] The Canadians had done no injury to the United States, and Federalists believed they deserved none in return. " Canada has issued no Orders in Council which obstruct our commerce to any part of the world," said Samuel Taggart of Massachusetts. " She has not impressed our seamen, taken our ships, confiscated our property, nor in any other respect treated us ill. All the crime alleged against Canada or the Canadians, is that, without any act of their own, they are connected with, and under the protection of a nation which has injured us on the ocean." [13]

Federalists considered the invasion not only unjust but also unwise. As the Maryland House of Delegates put it, the conquest of Canada would be " worse than a doubtful boon." [14] Federalists were convinced that Great Britain would never surrender her maritime rights to regain the province, and that annexation was fraught with danger. Drawing on the arguments of Montesquieu, they claimed the addition of such a vast expanse of territory would render the United States too large, and thereby threaten the American form of government, American civil liberties, and the Union itself. Incorporating Canada into the Union, said John Lowell Jr. of Massachusetts, would " enfeeble " the United States by increasing " the jarring materials " that composed the country and were " already too discordant for our peace or safety." [15]

Federalist agreement on military measures, as the table indicates, was

[12] Speech of Josiah Quincy, in *Annals of Congress*, 12 Cong., 2 Sess., p. 545.

[13] Speech of Samuel Taggart, in *Annals of Congress*, 12 Cong., 1 Sess., p. 1640. For similar sentiments, see speeches, ibid., 12 Cong., 2 Sess., pp. 512–14 (Elijah Brigham); 13 Cong., 2 Sess., p. 1818 (Artemas Ward). Also Gribbin, *Churches Militant*, p. 28.

[14] Memorial of Md. House, [Jan. 1814], in *Annals of Congress*, 13 Cong., 2 Sess., p. 1207.

[15] A New-England Farmer [John Lowell Jr.], *Mr. Madison's War* (Boston: Russell and Cutler, 1812), p. 41. See also Memorial of Mass. House, [Spring 1812], in *Niles' Register*, 20 June 1812, p. 259; speeches in *Annals of Congress*, 12 Cong., 2 Sess., pp. 512–14 (Elijah Brigham), 516–18 (Henry M. Ridgely), 537–38 (Lyman Law), 646 (Benjamin Tallmadge), 653–56 (Laban Wheaton), 692–93 (Daniel Sheffey); 13 Cong., 2 Sess., pp. 1286–87 (Timothy Pitkin), 1453–54 (Joseph Pearson), 1516–19 (Z. R. Shipherd), 1569–70 (William Gaston).

FEDERALIST COHESION LEVELS ON WAR MEASURES IN CONGRESS
1 JUNE 1812–13 FEB. 1815

Congress & Session	Type of Legislation	House		Senate	
		No. of Roll Call Votes Taken	Cohesion Index * %	No. of Roll Call Votes Taken	Cohesion Index * %
12C 1S	Declaration of War	15	99.2	18	100.0
(1 June 1812–	Military Measures **	8	100.0	5	78.9
6 July 1812)	Privateering	—	—	1	100.0
	Trade Restrictions	11	90.8	1	100.0
	Loans & Treas. Notes	4	100.0	2	100.0
	Tax Proposals	5	94.8	5	93.1
	Totals	43	96.5	32	96.5
12C 2S	Military Measures **	12	94.2	21	85.6
(2 Nov. 1812–	Naval Measures	8	90.6	5	100.0
3 Mar. 1813)	Privateering	3	97.6	1	100.0
	Trade Restrictions	23	98.2	1	100.0
	Loans & Treas. Notes	8	99.2	9	93.3
	Tax Proposals	4	83.2	—	—
	Totals	58	95.6	37	89.7
13C 1S	Privateering	3	99.2	5	100.0
(24 May 1813–	Trade Restrictions	7	98.8	10	96.3
2 Aug. 1813)	Tax Proposals	36	93.3	25	85.1
	Totals	46	94.3	40	89.7
13C 2S	Military Measures **	11	97.8	16	82.8
(6 Dec. 1813–	Naval Measures	3	90.3	2	84.6
18 Apr. 1814)	Privateering	1	97.9	1	100.0
	Trade Restrictions	36	97.4	27	95.5
	Loans & Treas. Notes	5	95.0	2	90.0
	Tax Proposals	2	81.8	—	—
	National Bank	1	70.9	—	—
	Totals	59	95.9	48	91.0
13C 3S	Military Measures **	24	98.4	13	95.3
(19 Sept. 1814–	Naval Measures	—	—	3	100.0
13 Feb. 1815)	Trade Restrictions	6	99.6	8	100.0
	Loans & Treas. Notes	3	90.6	1	88.9
	Tax Proposals	34	84.1	21	87.3
	National Bank	32	95.7	24	97.7
	Totals	99	92.7	70	94.6
All Sessions	Declaration of War	15	99.2	18	100.0
	Military Measures **	55	97.7	55	87.2
	Naval Measures	11	90.5	10	96.0
	Privateering	7	98.4	8	100.0
	Trade Restrictions	83	97.3	47	96.6
	Loans & Treas. Notes	20	96.2	14	93.1
	Tax Proposals	81	88.8	51	86.6
	National Bank	33	94.9	24	97.7
	Totals	305	94.4	227	92.5

256

fairly high. In the first four sessions of the war, their cohesion on this legislation ranged between 94.2 and 100 per cent in the House, and 78.9 and 85.6 per cent in the Senate. The range was lower in the Senate because Federalists there sometimes differed over amendments or issues only marginally related to the war. On proposals to raise troops, however, there was little disagreement in either house.

Just as they opposed Republican measures to raise troops, so too did Federalists resist efforts to raise money, whether by imposing taxes, or by authorizing loans or the issue of treasury notes. They objected to such legislation because it was designed to support the Canadian venture and for other reasons as well. At the beginning of the war, Republicans had doubled the tariff and tonnage duties but had postponed a plan for internal taxes. Federalists argued that the complete program was necessary to maintain public credit, and to force the backcountry (which consumed few imported goods) to pay its share of taxes. Any new taxes, however, were likely to be unpopular, and Federalists had no intention of supporting them. For the sake of consistency and political expediency, they voted against all taxation just as they opposed other measures designed to further the war in Canada.[16]

As the table shows, Federalist agreement on financial measures in the first four war sessions was generally high. On loan and treasury note proposals, their cohesion was always over 95 per cent in the House and over 90 per cent in the Senate. On tax measures, the range was somewhat lower: between 81.8 and 94.8 per cent in the House, and 85.1 and 93.1 per cent in the Senate. But the disagreement here was over amendments and tactics, and not over the tax bills proper. When these bills were put to a final vote, Federalist opposition in both houses was close to 100 per cent.

Federalist opposition extended not only to men and money bills but to commercial restrictions as well. American economic sanctions of one sort

---

16 See speeches in *Annals of Congress*, 12 Cong., 1 Sess., pp. 1517–18 (Abijah Bigelow), 1522–24 (Harmanus Bleecker), 1526–27 (Elijah Brigham); 12 Cong., 2 Sess., pp. 873–78 (Bigelow), 895–902 (Thomas R. Gold), 902–07 (Timothy Pitkin); 13 Cong., 1 Sess., pp. 381 (Z. R. Shipherd), 405–09 (Brigham), 458–62 (A. C. Hanson); 13 Cong., 2 Sess., pp. 1274 (Bigelow), 1290–98 (Pitkin), 1298–1311 (Daniel Sheffey), 1371–79 (Hanson), 1447–53 (Joseph Pearson), 1504–07 (Shipherd), 1732–33 (Timothy Pickering).

* This figure shows the unity of the party. It is arrived at by dividing the party majority on roll call votes by the party's total vote, and then converting the result to a percentage. If, for example, on three roll call votes, Federalists voted 44–6, 45–5, and 46–4, then the cohesion index would be 135/150 or 90%.

** That is, legislation affecting the army, volunteers, or militia.

Source: *Annals of Congress*, 12 Cong., 1 Sess., through 13 Cong., 3 Sess. (Vols 23–28). Figures under each class of legislation are based on *all* recorded votes, *i.e.* those on amendments and procedures as well as on bills and resolutions.

or another had been on the statute books since 1806, and Federalists had hoped that the system would be scrapped with the declaration of war. But Republicans had refused to repeal the non-importation law, the latest of the restrictive measures; and over the next two years Congress took up a host of other proposals for embargoing trade, limiting exports or imports, and preventing intercourse with the enemy. Federalists opposed limitations on trade, as they always had, because they thought these measures injured America more than England, worked a hardship on merchants and farmers alike, destroyed government revenue and encouraged smuggling, and gave public officials excessive powers to probe into private life.[17] As the table shows, Federalist agreement on trade restrictions was consistently high throughout the first two years of the war. Their cohesion was usually over 95 per cent in both houses of Congress, and often it was closer to 100 per cent.

Although Federalists opposed the war party's troop, tax, and trade program, they took a more co-operative position on maritime defense. They opposed privateering, believing that in an unjust war it was little better than piracy, and against this species of warfare their level of agreement was invariably over 97 per cent. The navy and coastal fortifications, on the other hand, had their full support. Federalists never wavered in their support of maritime defense, in peace or in war. Always the maritime party, they had tried in early 1812 to limit the war to a defensive maritime contest in the tradition of 1798.[18] Although disappointed in this hope, they continued to support maritime defense in the interest of protecting commerce and their constituents on the seaboard.[19] There were no roll call votes on coastal fortifications during the war. These bills simply went through uncontested with full Federalist support. On naval measures, however, there were numerous votes. In this area of legislation, Federalist cohesion was usually over 90 per cent, and on the question of fleet expansion (which separated the staunch navalists from the timid), it was actually close to 100 per cent.

Federalists, in sum, voted *en bloc* on all war measures during the first two years of the war, opposing military, financial, and trade limitation

---

[17] See speeches in *Annals of Congress*, 12 Cong., 2 Sess., pp. 381–93 (Josiah Quincy), 1134–42, 1157–63 (T. P. Grosvenor); 13 Cong., 2 Sess., pp. 554–61 (Jeremiah Mason), 602–11 (Christopher Gore), 937–38, 2020 (Cyrus King), 1135–37 (William Gaston), 1137–39 (Grosvenor), 1965–73 (Daniel Webster), 2034–42 (Richard Stockton), 2042–46 (Timothy Pitkin).

[18] See D. R. Hickey, "The Federalists and the Coming of the War, 1811–1812," *Indiana Magazine of History*, forthcoming.

[19] See speeches in *Annals of Congress*, 12 Cong., 1 Sess., pp. 131–47 (James Lloyd), 895–99 (Lyman Law), 933–38 (Thomas R. Gold), 949–68 (Josiah Quincy); 12 Cong., 2 Sess., pp. 170 (Quincy), 414–17 (Gold), 866–69 (James Milnor).

proposals while supporting maritime defense. In each session, the cohesion they achieved on war legislation was high. The average over all four sessions was 95·6 per cent in the House, and 91·7 per cent in the Senate. Such disagreements as occurred were usually over minor issues: votes on amendments or tactical procedures, or on issues not directly related to the war. On the main issues, Federalists from the Middle and Southern States almost always voted with New England.

III

Such accord was possible as long as the nature of the war remained clear. Although unwilling to support an " offensive " war against Canada, all Federalists agreed on the propriety of supporting defensive measures. " Let it not be said," Morris Miller of New York told the Republicans in Congress, " that we refuse you the means of defence. For that we always have been – we still are – ready to open the treasure of the nation. We will give you millions for defence; but not a cent for the conquest of Canada – not the ninety-ninth part of a cent for the extermination of its inhabitants." [20]

Just how fine the line between offensive and defensive warfare could be, Federalists discovered in the latter half of 1814. With the arrival of news in June that Napoleon had been driven from Europe, the United States found itself alone in the field against England. While Britain was bringing her military and naval might to bear – dispatching thousands of Peninsular veterans and scores of ships-of-the-line to the New World – America's own war-making capacity appeared to be declining. The failure of the administration's loan in the late summer, coupled with the suspension of specie payments among banks in the Middle and Southern states, threw the nation's finances into chaos. Unable to transfer funds across country or to meet its growing bills, the administration had no choice but to rely on treasury notes that declined rapidly in value.

The nation's deteriorating military situation forced Federalists to ask themselves whether the war had changed in character and thus merited their support. When in September 1814, Congress convened for its fifth and last session during the war, a cleavage was evident in Federalist ranks. At a caucus of House and Senate Federalists held on 8 October, suggestions that the party support men and money bills won the endorsement of Federalists from the Middle and Southern states but not of New Eng-

---

[20] Speech of Morris Miller, in *Annals of Congress*, 13 Cong., 2 Sess., p. 958. See also speeches and proposals for defensive warfare, ibid., 12 Cong., 2 Sess., pp. 170, 560 (Josiah Quincy); 13 Cong., 2 Sess., pp. 939 (Daniel Sheffey), 941, 951 (Daniel Webster), 1054-56, 1545 (William Gaston), 1364 (John Culpepper).

landers. In the hope of working out a common policy, the caucus appointed a committee of seven, instructing it to study the matter and issue a report. On the panel were four Federalists from the middle and southern states — Rufus King and Thomas J. Oakley of New York, Richard Stockton of New Jersey, and Joseph Pearson of North Carolina — and three from New England — Timothy Pickering and Christopher Gore of Massachusetts, and David Daggett of Connecticut. The committee met and, over the objections of the New England members, recommended cautious support for the war.[21]

Just as the committee was drawing up its report, news of diplomatic developments in Europe threatened to drive a wedge still further into Federalist ranks. In a deft move to bolster support for the war, President James Madison in mid-October submitted documents to Congress showing the state of the peace negotiations at Ghent. These revealed that while America had dropped her own demands, Great Britain would not restore peace without certain concessions. Confident of victory, England demanded the establishment of a permanent Indian reservation in the Northwest Territory, cessions of land in northern Maine and Minnesota, American demilitarization of the lakes, and the surrender of fishing privileges in British North American waters.[22]

These terms need not have surprised anyone, since they had been anticipated by articles in the American press picked up from English and Canadian sources.[23] But as Madison had anticipated, the disclosure had an explosive effect. Alexander Contee Hanson, the fiery Maryland editor who had been beaten and tortured by a pro-war mob in 1812, rose in Congress to condemn the terms, pledging his support for " the most vigorous system of honorable war, with the hope of bringing the enemy to a sense of justice." [24] Other Federalists from outside New England joined in the cry, calling the terms " arrogant," " inadmissible," " humiliating," and " disgraceful." Most agreed with the Alexandria *Gazette* that whatever the

---

[21] A. C. Hanson to Robert Goodloe Harper, 29 Sept. and 9 Oct. 1814, in Harper-Pennington Papers, Maryland Historical Society, Baltimore, Md.; Memorandum of Rufus King [Oct. 1814], in Charles R. King, *The Life and Correspondence of Rufus King*, 6 vols. (New York: G. P. Putnam's Sons, 1894–1900), 5, 422–24; Timothy Pickering to Gouverneur Morris, 21 Oct. 1814, in Pickering Papers (microfilm), Massachusetts Historical Society, Boston, Mass., reel 15. The Pickering letter can also be found in Henry Cabot Lodge, *Life and Letters of George Cabot*, 2nd ed. (Boston: Little, Brown, 1878), p. 536, although the date is erroneously given as 29 Oct.

[22] See *American State Papers: Foreign Relations*, 3, 695–710.

[23] See New London *Connecticut Gazette*, 17 Aug. and 7 Sept. 1814; Portland *Eastern Argus*, 18 Aug. 1814; Boston *Gazette*, 1 Sept. 1814; New York *Evening Post*, 23 Sept. 1814.

[24] Speech of A. C. Hanson, in *Annals of Congress*, 13 Cong., 3 Sess., pp. 381–82.

war's origins, it had "from the arrogance of the enemy, become a war of necessity." [25]

New England Federalists, by contrast, responded to the terms with much greater equanimity. Astonished more by the reaction of their friends to the south and west than by the terms themselves, most New Englanders believed the proposals offered a reasonable basis for negotiation. [26] The Boston *Gazette* said that, having declared war and failed, the nation must now pay the price. [27] This was a common view in New England. Harrison Gray Otis claimed that 90 per cent of the people in Massachusetts preferred "*treating* on the proposed basis *at least*, to the continuance of the war one day." Although his estimate ignored the state's Republican population, it was a good indication of Federalist thinking. [28]

New Englanders had little trouble accepting the proposal for an Indian barrier, not only because of their traditional anti-western and anti-expansionist bias, but also because of their sympathy for the native and his plight. Historians have paid little attention to Federalist views on the Indian and thus have failed to appreciate how significantly they differed from those held by Republicans. Most Republicans attributed the nation's recurring border wars to British intrigue or Indian savagery. New England Federalists, on the other hand, put the blame on the white man for coveting the Indian's land. [29] "The spirit of cupidity," said the Massa-

[25] Alexandria *Gazette*, 15 Oct. 1814. See also speech of Thomas J. Oakley, in *Annals of Congress*, 13 Cong., 3 Sess., pp. 382–83; Charles Cotesworth Pinckney to F. D. Petit de Villers, 31 Oct. 1814, in Pinckney Papers, Duke University Library, Durham, N. C.; Robert Goodloe Harper to William Sullivan, 2 Nov. 1814, in Harper-Pennington Papers, Maryland Historical Society, Baltimore, Md.; John Jay to Timothy Pickering, 1 Nov. 1814, in Henry P. Johnston, ed., *The Correspondence and Public Papers of John Jay*, 4 vols. (New York: G. P. Putnam's Sons, 1890–93), 4, 378–79; William Polk to Gov. William Hawkins, 17 Oct. 1814, in Raleigh *Minerva*, 21 Oct. 1814; Resolutions of N. Y. Legislature, cited in Georgetown *Federal Republican*, 31 Oct. 1814; New York *Evening Post*, 12 Oct. 1814; Georgetown *Federal Republican*, 11 Oct. 1814; Raleigh *Minerva*, 21 Oct. 1814; Philadelphia *United States Gazette*, 14 Oct. 1814.

[26] Hanson's reaction in particular caused a sensation in New England. See Caleb Strong to Timothy Pickering, 17 Oct. 1814, in Henry Adams, ed., *Documents Relating to New-England Federalism, 1800–1815* (Boston: Little, Brown, 1877), p. 398.

[27] Boston *Gazette*, 7 Nov. 1814.

[28] Otis to Robert Goodloe Harper, 27 Oct. 1814, in Morison, *Otis*, 2, 181. See also Pickering to Strong, 12 Oct. 1814, Strong to Pickering, 17 Oct. 1814, and John Lowell Jr. to Pickering 19 Oct. 1814, in Adams, *New-England Federalism*, pp. 395–400; Pickering to Gouverneur Morris, 21 Oct. 1814, in Lodge, *Cabot*, pp. 536–37; Samuel Taggart to John Taylor, 2 Nov. 1814, in Mary R. Reynolds, ed., "Letters of Samuel Taggart, Representative in Congress, 1803–1814," *Proceedings of the American Antiquarian Society*, 33 (1923), 430–31; Porter, *Jacksons and Lees*, 2, 1122; Boston *New-England Palladium*, 18 and 28 Oct. 1814; Boston *Columbian Centinel*, 19 and 26 Oct. 1814; Keene *Newhampshire Sentinel*, 22 Oct. 1814.

[29] See Taggart to Taylor, 5 June 1812, in Reynolds, "Letters of Taggart," pp. 403–04; Picker-

AM.ST.—3

chusetts Senate in 1814, " has extended its grasp to the ' rightful possessions of the indian tribes,' and a cruel war of extermination, at which humanity revolts, has been prosecuted against them."[30] Sharing Caleb Strong's belief that American Indian policy had been " extremely unjustifiable and inhuman," most New Englanders considered it entirely proper to give the natives a permanent reservation that would not be subject to encroachments from whites.[31] Such a barrier, the Boston *Centinel* said, would benefit the white man as well as the Indian because it would prevent future wars and " check the immeasurable extension of territory, which has always proved the ruin of empires and states."[32]

New England Federalists considered the other terms reasonable too. They regarded the demilitarization of the lakes as sensible, but thought it should be mutual. Nor did they see any cause for alarm over the territorial demands in the wilderness regions of northern Maine and Minnesota. Samuel Taggart called northern Maine (which was then part of Massachusetts) " a cold barren inhospitable region probably not worth one cent per 100 acres." Since it was Republican territory anyway, few Federalists in southern New England would grieve over its loss. They only hoped that it could be exchanged for a renewal of fishing privileges in British waters. If this could be managed, said Taggart, " it would be a good bargain for Massachusetts."[33]

IV

With the publication of the peace terms, then, the division in the party seemed complete: while Federalists from the middle and southern States lined up on the side of the war, their colleagues in New England remained in opposition. But appearances proved deceptive, for no sooner had they

ing to Rufus King, 4 Mar. 1804, Pickering to Strong, 12 Oct. 1814, Strong to Pickering, 17 Oct. 1814, in Adams *New-England Federalism*, pp. 352, 394–96, 399; Proclamation of Gov. Caleb Strong, 26 June 1812, and Address of Mass. Senate, 8 June 1814, in *Niles' Register*, 1 Aug. 1812, p. 355, and 25 June 1814, p. 274; Hartford *Connecticut Courant*, 15 June 1813 and 21 June 1814; Boston *Daily Advertiser*, reprinted in Philadelphia *United States Gazette*, 29 Oct. 1814. New England Federalists who had moved to the West held similar views. See Rufus Putnam to Pickering, 16 June 1813, in Pickering Papers (microfilm), Massachusetts Historical Society, Boston, Mass., reel 30; Manasseh Cutler to Ephraim Cutler, 23 Mar. 1813, in William and Julia Cutler, *Life, Journals, and Correspondence of Rev. Manasseh Cutler*, 2 vols. (Cincinnati: R. Clarke, 1888), 2, 318.
[30] Address of Mass. Senate, 8 June 1814, in *Niles' Register*, 25 June 1814, p. 274.
[31] Strong to Pickering, 17 Oct. 1814, in Adams, *New-England Federalism*, p. 399.
[32] Boston *Columbian Centinel*, 19 Oct. 1814.
[33] Taggart to Taylor, 2 Nov. 1814, in Reynolds, " Letters of Taggart," p. 431. In February of 1815, shortly before peace was restored, Massachusetts officials considered adopting a legislative resolution indicating the state's willingness to give up part of Maine. See Christopher Gore to Rufus King, 11 Apr. 1815, in King, *King*, 5, 476–77.

committed themselves than some papers to the south and west began to echo New England's cry that the terms were not so bad after all.[34] This marked the beginning of a larger shift in these states, one that carried most Federalists back into the anti-war camp. In part, this was due to New England's influence, which, as always, was a potent force in shaping Federalist opinion. But other factors also played a role: the administration's war strategy and politics, and the arrival of favorable diplomatic news from Europe.

The administration's strategic planning bothered Federalists because it continued to focus on Canada. Even though America was on the defensive, Secretary of War James Monroe still talked of taking the war to the enemy.[35] Federalists were no more willing to support a Canadian venture in 1814 than earlier in the war, and Monroe's plans made them wonder if the character of the contest had really changed.[36] They were also angered by the Secretary's scheme for raising a new army by conscripting militia and enlisting minors without the consent of their elders. They regarded the conscription plan as "a palpable and flagrant violation of the Constitution" – a French innovation calculated to destroy the militia and undermine state authority.[37] The minor enlistment proposal was considered no less repugnant as a threat to filial ties and a nullification of state law and contract law. This proposal, according to Thomas P. Grosvenor of New York, would gain no more than a thousand recruits and yet would result in "jeopardizing the good order of the community, violating contracts, disturbing the sacred rights of natural affection, and all the felicities of domestic life." [38]

[34] See New York *Evening Post*, 13 Oct. 1814; Philadelphia *United States Gazette*, 27–28 Oct. 1814, and articles reprinted from Boston *Daily Advertiser* in *Gazette*, 25–31 Oct. 1814; Georgetown *Federal Republican*, reprinted in Charleston *Courier*, 1 Nov. 1814.

[35] See Monroe to William Branch Giles, 17 Oct. 1814, in *American State Papers: Military Affairs*, 1, 515.

[36] See speeches in *Annals of Congress*, 13 Cong., 3 Sess., pp. 76 (David Daggett), 90–91 (Jeremiah Mason), 151 (Christopher Gore), 442 (Cyrus King), 687–88, 791 (Morris Miller), 739, 742 (T. P. Grosvenor), 821 (Z. R. Shipherd), 907–08 (Artemas Ward), 940–44 (Lyman Law), 964–69 (Elijah Brigham). Also New York *Evening Post*, 4–5 Nov. 1814; Alexandria *Gazette*, 17 Dec. 1814; Baltimore *Federal Gazette*, reprinted in Pittsburgh *Gazette*, 21 Jan. 1815.

[37] Quoted words from speech of Robert Goldsborough, in *Annals of Congress*, 13 Cong., 3 Sess., p. 104. See also speeches, ibid., pp. 70–77 (David Daggett), 77–91 (Jeremiah Mason), 95–102 (Christopher Gore), 775–99 (Morris Miller), 819–30 (Z. R. Shipherd), 830–33 (Jonathan O. Moseley), 834–50 (Richard Stockton), 850–60 (Daniel Sheffey), 904–21 (Artemas Ward), 922–28 (William Gaston). Also Federalist press, Oct.–Dec. 1814.

[38] Speech of T. P. Grosvenor, in *Annals of Congress*, 13 Cong., 3 Sess., p. 733. See also speeches, ibid., pp. 720–32 (Cyrus King), 744–49 (Morris Miller). Also Federalist press, Oct.–Dec. 1814.

Disturbed by the administration's military planning, Federalists were also irritated by its political exclusiveness. There was a good deal of talk – even among New Englanders – about the possibility of Federalists joining the cabinet, but nothing came of it.[39] Early in the session a group of Republican Senators had urged the President to take members of the opposition into his cabinet, but Madison had refused.[40] Two months later, when Federalists tried to install Rufus King as president *pro tempore* of the Senate, they were again thwarted. With the President suffering from poor health and the vice-presidency vacant, Republicans were unwilling to put a Federalist next in the line of succession. Annoyed by this rebuff, Federalists murmured that Republicans had no interest in conciliation and could not be trusted.[41]

Exasperated by the administration's war planning and politics, and inspired by New England's example, Federalists in the Middle and Southern States were already deserting the war movement when a new set of British terms was submitted to Congress on 1 December. These showed that Great Britain was willing to restore peace on the basis of *uti possidetus*, meaning that each side would retain whatever territory it held.[42] If the terms were acceded to, title to a few minor forts would change hands and eastern Maine would pass to Britain. This was a settlement that Federalists everywhere could have lived with, and doubtless many Republicans too. Fearing the impact the dispatches might have on the war spirit, Republican Congressmen at first tried to suppress them. And when they were published, the semi-official Washington *National Intelligencer* professed to believe that the prospects for peace were still " very faint." [43] No one was fooled, least of all the Federalists, most of whom thought peace was near.[44] Heartened by the news and anxious for peace, they dis-

---

[39] See speeches in *Annals of Congress*, 13 Cong., 3 Sess., pp. 440 (Thomas Bayly), 472 (Z. R. Shipherd), 948 (Lyman Law). Also Boston *Columbian Centinel*, 31 Aug. 1814; Boston *New-England Palladium*, 2, 6, 9 Sept. 1814; Boston *Gazette*, 5 Sept. 1814; Portsmouth *Oracle*, reprinted in Chillicothe *Supporter*, 19 Nov. 1814; Baltimore *Federal Gazette*, reprinted in Pittsburgh *Gazette*, 21 Jan. 1815; George Hay to James Monroe, 27 Nov. 1814, in Monroe Papers (microfilm), Library of Congress, Washington, D. C., reel 5.

[40] A. C. Hanson to R. G. Harper, 9 Oct. 1814, in Harper-Pennington Papers, Maryland Historical Society, Baltimore, Md.

[41] *Annals of Congress*, 13 Cong., 3 Sess., pp. 110–11; Charles J. Ingersoll, *History of the Second War Between the United States of America and Great Britain*, 2 vols. (Philadelphia: Lippincott, Grambo, 1853), 2, 292–93.

[42] See *American State Papers: Foreign Relations*, 3, 710–26.

[43] Washington *National Intelligencer*, 2 Dec. 1814. The attempt to suppress the documents, unmentioned in the *Annals*, was observed and recorded by a correspondent for the Boston *New-England Palladium*. See issue of 9 Dec. 1814.

[44] See Ebenezer Stott to Duncan Cameron, 12 Dec. 1814, in Cameron Papers, Southern Historical Collection, University of North Carolina Library, Chapel Hill, N. C.; Boston *New-*

continued what little support they were still giving to the war. "The war-pitch," said Republican Congressman Charles J. Ingersoll, "fell as much at Washington as it did in London. The salutary apprehension of October turned to hopeful confidence in December. The nerve of opposition was strung afresh." [45]

Thus by December of 1814, the division that had shown up in the Federalist party two months earlier had largely disappeared. Judging from the party's behavior in Congress, this division apparently did not go very deep anyway, and may have been more a matter of rhetoric than reality. Federalists refused to support the Republicans' troop and trade program in this session and, as the table shows, their cohesion on these measures was over 95 per cent in both houses. [46] The only issue that generated any real difference of opinion was financial policy. Although Federalists voted as a bloc on the various proposals for a national bank (achieving a cohesion of more than 95 per cent), there was an undercurrent of disagreement over the propriety of establishing such an institution when financial conditions were so chaotic. [47] Over tax policy, Federalist opinion varied somewhat more. While a group of Federalists from the Middle States was willing to vote for all the administration's tax bills, a group from New England would support none. Hence in this area of legislation, the party's cohesion fell to 84·1 per cent in the House and 87·3 per cent in the Senate. [48] Even with these differences, however, Federalists maintained their usual high level of agreement for the session as a whole. In the House, their cohesion was 92·7 per cent – down only a few points from the average over earlier sessions; and in the Senate, it was 94·6 per cent, which was actually higher than the average for the previous sessions.

The figures at the bottom of the table show Federalist cohesion levels on all war legislation across the five sessions of Congress. The cohesion achieved on each type of legislation was high, usually over 90 per cent, and more often than not over 95 per cent. On all war measures it was

England Palladium, 9 Dec. 1814; New York *Evening Post*, 5, 7, 8 Dec. 1814; Trenton *Federalist*, 5 Dec. 1814; Philadelphia *United States Gazette*, 13 Dec. 1814, and 6 Jan. 1815; Georgetown *Federal Republican*, 2 Dec. 1814; Alexandria *Gazette*, 3 Dec. 1814; Baltimore *Federal Gazette*, reprinted in Charleston *Courier*, 20 Dec. 1814.

[45] Ingersoll, *History*, 2, 282.

[46] Federalists allowed a state army bill to go through uncontested, but this was consistent with their policy of supporting local defense.

[47] See speeches in *Annals of Congress*, 13 Cong., 3 Sess., pp. 208–14 (Rufus King), 564–65, 568–81, 987–88 (William Gaston), 626–28 (Elijah Brigham), 642–43, 1011–12, 1014–23 (Daniel Webster), 656–65 (A. C. Hanson), 665–85 (T. P. Grosvenor), 686–88 (Morris Miller).

[48] See tables in Hickey, "The Federalists and the War of 1812," pp. 186–87. On all the tax bills combined, New England Federalists voted 24–156, Middle State Federalists 45–51 and Southern Federalists 20–39.

94·4 per cent in the House, and 92·5 per cent in the Senate. This agreement was remarkable, and it both reflected and sustained a larger unity attained by the party during the war. In an analysis of all roll call votes in the House of Representatives during Madison's presidency, Harry Fritz has calculated that Federalists achieved a higher degree of cohesion in the war sessions than in any other between 1809 and 1817.[49] Fritz's study does not extend to the Senate, but it is evident that Federalists in that chamber acted with exceptional harmony during the war too. In both houses of Congress, Federalists probably achieved their highest degree of unity since 1801 — perhaps the highest in the party's history.

V

New England could never claim more than 53 per cent of the party's membership in the House during the war, and never more than 67 per cent in the Senate. Hence the high degree of voting cohesion achieved by Federalists demonstrates her success in forging a united front against the war. Clearly, the traditional picture of the party disintegrating during the war is in error. New England's sectionalism — the threats of nullification and secession, and the Hartford Convention — may have caused anxiety among Federalists elsewhere, but it did not alienate them. New England's national policy, which she consistently pursued throughout the war, was to withhold all support except for defensive measures, and in general other Federalists followed her lead. The Federalist response to the war, in other words, was characterized less by diversity than by uniformity, and this unity was achieved largely under New England's leadership and maintained on New England's terms.

How was New England able to maintain such a firm hold on the party even in time of war? It was as natural for New England to lead the Federalists, as it was natural for Massachusetts to lead New England. The situation was roughly parallel to the relationship between Virginia and the South. And just as Virginia could find sympathetic Republicans in all parts of the Union, Massachusetts could find like-minded Federalists in all sections too. This was chiefly because the policies of the New England Federalists made good sense nationally, as well as regionally, and thus appealed to people in all parts of the country.

[49] Harry Fritz, " The Collapse of Party: President, Congress, and the Decline of Party Action, 1807–1817," Ph.D. dissertation (Washington University, 1971), p. 258. This study is a broadly-based examination of party behavior in the Age of Jefferson. Fritz does not distinguish between war measures and other legislation, and his list of Federalists differs from mine. Even so, his quantitative work is sparkling, and his figures show House Federalists acting with consistently greater cohesion than Republicans throughout the period of his study.

Why did the Federalist party collapse so soon after attaining such a high degree of unity? The party's chief appeal in the Age of Jefferson was that it offered an alternative to Republican foreign policy, an alternative grounded on peace and free trade with Great Britain instead of commercial sanctions and war. When the wars in Europe and America came to an end, the Federalist party lost its main reason for existence. The European situation, so favorable to America during Jefferson's first administration, was again favorable after the Treaty of Ghent, and thus removed the need for an opposition. Moreover, the Federalist party emerged from the war on the wrong side of an American myth. By any reasonable criterion, Republican foreign policy had ended in failure, just as the Federalists had always said it would. The diplomatic goals set in 1806 and renewed in 1812 were uniformly abandoned at Ghent. Yet by the rapid process of mythmaking at which Americans seem to excel, the defeat was converted into a spectacular triumph. In the wake of the belated victory at New Orleans, Federalists were remembered as traitors rather than as prophets. Hence, even though men like John Marshall and Daniel Webster remained active in public life to carry elements of the Federalist tradition into the future, the party itself ceased to function as a national organization and gradually disappeared.

"COOL AND SERIOUS REFLECTION": FEDERALIST ATTITUDES TOWARD WAR IN 1812

Lawrence Delbert Cress

Late in 1811, the United States moved inescapably toward war with Great Britain. Negotiations over American claims to freedom on the high seas had broken down during the previous summer and commercial restrictions once more prohibited the movement of British goods into American markets. With war seemingly just over the horizon, Congress convened faced with the onerous task of improving the nation's defense. For some, however, the next year's prospects were far from gloomy. An anonymous essayist writing in *The Federal Republican* looked forward to war as an agent of national renewal. "[T]he parent of noble feelings and the touchstone, in republics, of real talents and worth," war promised to return the nation to "the scene of American glory in arms," now thirty years past, and to inspire the "heart with hope and confidence." Certainly thoughts of war, even of the glorious Revolutionary War, did evoke the "memory of much evil and suffering," but they also suggested national unity and moral discipline. "A war," wrote the same essayist, "will purify the political atmosphere, and break down the entrenchments by which chicanery fortifies itself in undue prerogatives." It would revive national honor and instill once more the commitment to the common good that had sustained the patriots of the previous generation. In short, "all the public virtues will be refined and hallowed; and we shall again behold at the head of affairs citizens who may rival the immortal men of 1776."[1]

Mr. Cress is a member of the Department of History and Assistant Provost at Texas A&M University. The research for this article was supported by grants from the American Philosophical Society and the College of Liberal Arts at Texas A&M University.

[1] *Niles' Weekly Register*, Dec. 7, 1811, I, 252.

JOURNAL OF THE EARLY REPUBLIC, 7 (Summer 1987). © 1987 Society for Historians of the Early American Republic.

Not everyone, though, greeted the prospect of war or its declaration in June 1812 with such enthusiasm. Historians, of course, have long noted the vocal Federalist opposition to war and the heightened partisanship that it produced. Countless newspaper editorials and pamphlets berated the Madison administration for drawing the United States into a needless war that could only leave American commerce in ruins. For many Federalists, though, Madison's misguided policies threatened consequences more enduring than the disruption of New England's carrying trade. Many feared for the very foundation of American republicanism. Historians of the Federalist party and of the War of 1812 have not ignored the Federalist concern for the safety and well being of the republic. Nevertheless, no attempt has been made to explain in a systematic fashion how war fit into the larger Federalist fear for the republic's future. Neither have historians paid much attention to the prescription for dissent espoused by antiwar clerical and political leaders.[2] This essay seeks to fill these gaps by analyzing the sermons, speeches, and resolutions published for public consumption by the Federalist leadership during the first year of the War of 1812. What did the declaration of war mean to the Federalists? How were vigilant Americans to oppose the misguided policies of the Madison administration? In sum, what was the significance of the war and what political options were possible for men committed to a corporate view of society, suspicious of democratic politics, and certain that anarchy was the surest road to tyranny?

---

[2] General histories of the War of 1812 discuss dissent within the context of state-federal relations, relying primarily on official correspondence. See, for example, Henry Adams, *History of the United States During the Administrations of Thomas Jefferson and James Madison* (9 vols., New York 1921), VI, 398-411; John K. Mahon, *The War of 1812* (Gainesville, Fla. 1972), *passim*; Reginald Horsman, *The War of 1812* (New York 1969), *passim*; and Bradford Perkins, *Prologue to War: England and the United States, 1805-1812* (Berkeley 1961), 418-422. James Banner, *To the Hartford Convention: The Federalists and the Origins of Party Politics in Massachusetts, 1789-1815* (New York 1970), focuses on the ideology of Federalist politics, but he is primarily concerned with how the Federalist party served as a vehicle for the expression of that ideology. Linda K. Kerber, *Federalists in Dissent: Imagery and Ideology in Jeffersonian America* (Ithaca 1970), provides an excellent analysis of Federalist thinking after their fall from power, but she stops short of investigating their attitude toward war and its impact on a republican society. William Gribbin, *The Churches Militant: The War of 1812 and American Religion* (New Haven 1973), discusses the attitude of the clergy toward the War of 1812, but he does not discuss the relationship between antiwar sentiment and fear for the perpetuation of republican values and institutions. For an assessment of the place of republican theory in the Republican party's decision to go to war, see Roger H. Brown, *The Republic in Peril: 1812* (New York 1964), *passim*.

Late in May 1812, Hezekiah Niles, Baltimore's leading Republican editor, predicted that with war the "political atmosphere [will be] purged, a greater degree of *harmony* will exist; and the regenerated spirit of freedom will teach us to love, to cherish and support our unparalleled system of government, as with the mind of one man."[3] Federalists viewed the prospect of war in very different light. Antiwar clergymen were quick to remind parishioners that wars were "ever to be considered as the effects of divine anger, as *whirlwinds* from the Lord." Indeed, they were the greatest expression of God's anger. Famine, pestilence, earthquakes, and fires often reformed and reclaimed the ungodly, but war was the "enemy of every good thing." Morality and religion fled in its path, while "desolation, misery and every evil, follow in its train." War, concluded one Federalist clergyman, made people immoral. The spread of immorality, of course, threatened to do nothing less than to undermine the constitutional balance upon which republican institutions depended.[4]

Republican government depended upon a virtuous citizenry—a citizenry Federalists believed menaced by the social chaos that came with war. "War," proclaimed one opponent of hostilities on the day of national humiliation and prayer called by James Madison on August 20, 1812, "is at once the cause and the effect of great corruption in the principles and manners of the people." The call to arms tore hundreds and thousands of men "from the ordinary occupations of life, from the bosom of virtuous society, [and] from the means of moral and religious instruction." It encouraged them to pursue "every corrupt propensity," exposed them to "every temptation to vice and impiety," and "deluded [them] with an imaginary dispensation from the laws of morality and religion." Army camps—nothing more than

---

[3] *Niles' Weekly Register*, May 30, 1812, II, 210. See also William H. Winder, July 4, 1812, oration, *ibid.*, July 11, 1812, II, 307-308.

[4] Noah Worcester, *The Substance of Two Sermons, occasioned by the late Declaration of War* [delivered at Salisbury, N.H., June 28 and July 5, 1812] (Concord, N.H. 1812), 12; Brown Emerson, *The Equity of God's Dealing with Nations* (Salem, Mass. 1812), 22-23; Benjamin Bell, *A Sermon . . . in Which are Shewn the Evil Effect of War, and When it may be Lawful and Expedient to go to War* [delivered at Steuben, Ohio, Apr. 1813] (Sangerfield, N.Y. 1814), 12. On the civil implications of Christian morality, see Nathan O. Hatch, *The Sacred Cause of Liberty: Republican Thought and the Millennium in Revolutionary New England* (New Haven 1977), *passim*. Hatch argues that during the last half of the eighteenth century New England clergy came to see the primary manifestation of Satan's labors in efforts to undermine political liberty. The millennium depended, then, on the triumph of both American Protestantism and American political liberty.

"schools of depravity"—exposed young men to a world of "no Bible, no prayers, no religious instruction; [and] no Sabbath." Moreover, the profaneness, intemperance, debauchery, idleness, and blasphemy so commonplace among soldiers produced "habits . . . which in great degree disqualify men from being comfortable and useful members of society in time of peace." Life in the ranks transformed benevolent and compassionate men into cruel and savage creatures. Once "honest and useful citizens," residents of the middle Atlantic and New England states were advised, became "legalized robbers" motivated by greed and contemptuous of the public welfare. Referring to the biblical proverb that those who sow the wind must also reap a whirlwind, a New Hampshire clergyman reminded his listeners that "the lusts and passions of individuals" had led many nations down the path to "infamy and ruin." America could not expect to escape history. A disregard for the common good had bred internal disorder in the ancient republics, and, implied the same New Englander, the social disruptions that accompanied military mobilization should give the United States "no reason to expect a long course of tranquility."[5]

The army's pernicious influence was not limited to its own ranks. "The whole mass of the community is infected," declared an anonymous essayist after eighteen months of war. Soldiers home from camp "bring with them loose and vicious habits, by which they contaminate the minds of others." Fighting, stealing, and public profanity, to say nothing of sickness and disease, noted one clergyman, everywhere "mark[ed] the footsteps of an army." On the anniversary of American independence in July 1812, the citizens of Fryeburg, Maine, were reminded that even the Revolutionary War had "poured in upon us, a disregard of the Sabbath and its ordinances; profanity and intemperance [along] with the mighty brook of ills, that follow their train." An ill-advised and unjustifiable war with Great Britain

---

[5] Brown Emerson, *The Causes and Effects of War* [delivered at Salem, Aug. 20, 1812] (Salem, Mass. 1812), 11-12; Samuel Worcester, *Calamity, Danger, and Hope* (Salem, Mass. 1812), 11; Bell, *A Sermon*, 10-11; Noah Worcester, *Abraham and Lot. A Sermon, on the Way of Peace, and the Evils of War* [delivered at Salisbury, N.H., Aug. 20, 1812] (Concord, Mass. 1812), 12; James Sloan, *An address to the Citizens of the United States, But more Particularly those of the Middle and Eastern States* (Philadelphia 1812), 4; Worcester, *Substance of Two Sermons*, 12-13; Philip Van Cortlandt, *Address to the Republican Citizens of the State of New-York* (Albany 1813), 6; William Parkinson, *A Sermon* . . . [delivered in New York, Aug. 20, 1812] (New York 1812), 5-7; Nathan S. S. Beman, *A Sermon* . . . [delivered at Portland, Aug. 20, 1812] (Portland, Maine 1812), 5-7; Arthur J. Stansbury, *God Pleading with America* (Goshen, N.Y. 1813), 20; [Clement Clarke Moore], *A Sketch of Our Political Condition* (New York 1813), 43.

promised even more dire consequences. "The contagion [of war] spread uncontrollably and without bounds," warned a clergyman in Salem, Massachusetts, before the initial campaigns of the war were even underway. He predicted a general decline of morals and manners. Reports from the Ohio Valley during the first year of hostilities indicating that the army's presence had brought vice to villages heretofore unspoiled and blasphemous speech to public inns once safe for the most pious soul confirmed the Federalists' worst fears.[6]

War, of course, had an economic impact. Militia calls and enlistment campaigns disrupted farming and commercial enterprises along the frontier. Plantation masters faced both a personal and an economic risk controlling a slave population, as one Federalist suspected, "restless in their bondage, and . . . easily excited to arms" by British agents. Neither could the capital, industry, and citizens of the eastern states expect to remain unmolested for long. The Atlantic Ocean's undefended 1,500-mile coastline exposed the nation's "most populous and flourishing towns and cities" to the floating batteries of the British navy. The heavy burden of wartime taxation, of course, would rest with equally destructive force on every region of the country. While Federalists meeting in convention in Trenton, New Jersey, in July 1812 asked "every class and description of industrious and GOOD CITIZENS" to consider the economic implications of war, a concerned resident of New Hampshire drew his own conclusion: "Many who are now in affluent circumstances" should, he thought, be prepared to "be reduced to poverty."[7]

An anonymous essayist writing from the perspective of 1814 suggested that the burdens of war would soon strip Americans of their land, opening the way for the creation of "an odious aristocracy" eager "to parcel the lands into lordships; and destroy our republican

---

[6] *A Defence of the Clergy of New-England, Against the Charges of Interfering in our Political Affairs, and Condemning the Policy of the Present War* (Concord, Mass. 1814), 36; Worcester, *Abraham and Lot*, 12-13; Bell, *A Sermon*, 10-11; William Barrows, *An Oration . . .* [delivered at Fryeburg, Maine, July 4, 1812] (Portland, Maine 1812), 15; Worcester, *Calamity, Danger, and Hope*, 11; Beman, *A Sermon*, 7; Parkinson, *A Sermon*, 5-7; [Federalist party], *Proceedings and Address of the Convention of Delegates, to the People of New-Jersey* (Trenton 1812), 9-10.

[7] Emerson, *Causes and Effects of War*, 13-15; *Proceedings and Address to the People of New-Jersey*, 8, 10-14; Worcester, *Abraham and Lot*, 12; Worcester, *Calamity, Danger, and Hope*, 7-8, 10; resolutions of a convention at Albany, New York, Sept. 17-18, 1812, Norfolk *Gazette*, Oct. 2, 1812; resolutions passed by the citizens of Accomack County, Virginia, Aug. 31, 1812, Norfolk *Gazette*, Sept. 7, 1812; Beman, *A Sermon*, 5; Bell, *A Sermon*, 13; James Abercrombie, *Two Sermons* (Philadelphia 1812), 24.

institutions." Nevertheless, it was the threat of anarchy, not aristrocracy, that at the onset of war troubled those most concerned about the adverse impact of war on American freedom. War meant unemployment—"a gloomy pause [in] the activity of the community"—and with it discontent bred of idleness and want. Boston's William Ellery Channing had little faith that "common minds" would withstand the temptation to lash out against all symbols of authority. Unemployed laborers—especially those thrown out of work by the wartime embargo—would come to see "their own government [as] their worst enemy." Civil laws, he contended in July 1812, would soon be treated with contempt and "habits of dissoluteness and intemperance, already too common, will be awfully multiplied."[8]

Reports of smuggling and "other modes of defrauding the government" circulating through New England during the early months of hostilities were solid evidence, Federalists believed, of the moral and political consequences of the economic dislocation that came with war. While Channing predicted the spread of "lawless pleasure or immoral pursuits," others spoke of a general decline of public virtue and a mounting disregard for life, prosperity, and private rights. Federalists found little comfort in claims that those thrown out of work by the curtailment of the carrying trade would find employment under arms. Men called into military service would only return to their communities able "more expeditously, and more certainly, [to] murder their fellow-mortals." Seamen might find berths on the privateers putting out daily to harass British commerce, but that could only serve to replace the respectable merchant marine with a band of lawless and plundering pirates. Neither did the promise of new jobs in the mills expanding to meet the country's wartime demand for manufactured goods ease fears of social discord. The return of cheaper British goods to American markets at war's end would toss the young out of work and the society into further disarray. One troubled opponent of war predicted domestic disruptions of such scale that standing armies would become necessary to maintain public order.[9]

---

[8] *A Defence of the Clergy*, 21-22, 42-44; William Ellery Channing, *A Sermon* [delivered at Boston, July 23, 1812] (Boston 1812), 10-13; Worcester, *Calamity, Danger, and Hope*, 7-8; [John Lowell], *Mr. Madison's War. A Dispassionate Inquiry . . . by a New-Englander Farmer* (Boston 1812), 50; essay from the Boston *Centinel*, in *Niles' Weekly Register*, May 30, 1812, II, 207-208.

[9] Channing, *A Sermon* [1812], 12-13; *Proceedings and Address to the People of New-Jersey*, 10-11; Sloan, *An Address*, 4; [Moore], *Sketch of Our Political Condition*, 41, 43; Worcester, *Abraham and Lot*, 12.

War, then, risked everything dear. Before the first year of hostilities had come to a close, at least one New Yorker was convinced that "habits of despotic authority and abject obedience" acquired through regular association with military institutions had destroyed the republican principles of much of the nation's youth, rendering "them the fit subjects and willing instruments of military despotism." At the very least, war would bring vice and irreligion to the nation, sapping the moral strength of the citizenry. The danger was doubly great for the United States, Federalists agreed, because of its newly established government. American institutions were simply too new, argued a group of dissenting congressmen, too untried, to withstand "situations, calculated to put to trial, the strength of the moral bond, by which they are united . . . . Time is yet important to our country to settle and mature its recent institutions."[10]

In one sense, the declaration of war was only symptomatic of more fundamental problems in American society. Federalist clergy, resurrecting the language of jeremiad commonplace in American pulpits during the wars of the previous half century, called the nation to task for its transgressions against God. Over the past decades the nation had banished religion from its public councils, embracing worldliness and vanity in its place. Believing themselves to be the wisest and most virtuous people on earth, Americans had settled into a false sense of security and confidence. "We have imagined ourselves," warned one clergyman on the occasion of the fast day called by Massachusetts late in July 1812, "secure from the dangers and disasters of other nations; and have refused to take warning from the fallen republics of ancient and modern times." The truth was quite the reverse, argued another cleric on the same day. The flood of licentiousness, which had brought down the judgment of Heaven on the wicked nations of Europe, had spread to the United States: "Impiety and crime of every name and description march forth in defiance of God and man."[11]

---

[10] Van Cortlandt, *Address to the Republican Citizens*, 6; Samuel Whelphley, *The Fall of Wicked Nations . . .* [preached at Newark, Sept. 9, 1813] (New York 1813), 17-23; [George Sullivan *et al.*], *An Address of Members of the House of Representatives . . . to their Constituents, on the Subject of the War with Great Britain* (Alexandria, Va. 1812), 6; [Moore], *Sketch of Our Political Condition*, 43; Bell, *A Sermon*, 12; Sloan, *An Address*, 4, 6; Emerson, *Causes and Effects of War*, 12; Worcester, *Abraham and Lot*, 12; Accomack County resolutions, Aug. 31, 1812, Norfolk *Gazette*, Sept. 7, 1812; *Proceedings and Address to the People of New-Jersey*, 10-13.

[11] Worcester, *Calamity, Danger, and Hope*, 12-14; Emerson, *Equity of God's Dealing with Nations*, 20-22; Stansbury, *God Pleading with America*, 1-20; Worcester, *Substance of Two Sermons*, 10; Freeman Parker, *A Sermon . . .* [delivered at Dresden, July 23,

The nation had sinned. It had turned its back on the God who had made it free and independent. It had allowed individual ambition to replace a commitment to the common good as the driving force in society. For two decades, intoned one New Englander, the lusts and passions of individuals in the pursuit of worldly goods had pushed the nation toward disaster. It had ascribed to men and not to God the prosperity of the post-Revolutionary War years. Worse still, America had been swayed by prejudice and passion to elect the "patrons of evil doers, and persecutors of them who do well," instead of choosing leaders "who fear God and hate covetousness." These men had abused their powers, often "under the guise of friendship, and the insidious delusion of pretended patriotism." Unjust laws, sometimes enforced in a cruel and arbitrary manner, had been passed and the public treasury squandered. Worst of all, a war had been declared that was neither necessary nor in self-defense. "Such Calamitous events are permitted by Providence to occur," reminded James Abercrombie from his pulpit in Philadelphia on the national fast day in 1812, as punishment for a nation's "general defection in religious or moral duties, or [for] an insensible disregard or ungrateful enjoyment of the blessings it may have pleased God to shower down upon them." "God has had very great reason to be offended with us as a people," concluded a New Hampshire clergyman only weeks after war was declared. "He has watched our ungrateful and evil treatment of him; and now we have reason to tremble at his reproof."[12]

Sin had its collective punishments, and war was among them. National salvation, however, depended upon the willingness of individual citizens to turn from their sinful ways and repent. "As the virtue and piety of individuals promote and constitute the security and happiness of the community, so under the infliction of national difficulty or distress, the correction of the errors which induce it, must commence in the reformation of individuals," advised Abercrombie. He pressed his Philadelphia congregation to examine their own lives as the first step toward national repentance. "As a member of a *political and civil association*, have you been obedient to the laws?" he asked. Had they worked to place "men of wisdom, integrity, firmness, magnanimity,

---

1812, and Wiscasset, Aug. 20, 1812] (Portland, Maine 1812), 8-13; Moses Dow, *A Sermon* [delivered Aug. 20, 1812] (Salem, Mass. 1813), 13; Gribbin, *Churches Militant*, 15-39.

12 Emerson, *Equity of God's Dealing with Nations*, 20-22; Abercrombie, *Two Sermons*, 33; Worcester, *Substance of Two Sermons*, 13-15; Stephen N. Rowan, *The Sin and Danger of Insensibility Under the Calls of God to Repentance* (New York 1812), 16-18.

and disinterested attachment" in political office? Had they endeavored likewise to remove men incompetent or unfaithful in their discharge of the public trust? Deference to the corporate character of society was also important. "Have you," he asked his listerners, "acted with kindness and affability towards your equals, with respect and due submission to your superiors, and with mildness and affectionate condescension to your inferiors?" Having failed to do any of these things contributed to the Almighty's displeasure and the consequent "calamaties or evils which have fallen upon your country." All must repent and pray not only for salvation of their souls but also to save "our afflicted country [from] the misery under which she now groans, and the desolation and destruction which threatens so speedily to overwhelm her."[13]

God was a moral governor, Federalists were quick to point out. As a prominent New England clergyman noted late in the war, "a nation has reason for fear, in proportion to its guilt; and a virtuous nation, sensible of its dependence on God, and disposed to respect his laws, is assured of his protection." Therein lies the problem, believed politicians and clergy in 1812. Virtuous nations resorted to war only for self-defense. The United States had gone to war over impressment and the British Orders in Council. News of the latter's repeal had reached the United States only weeks after the declaration of war, while impressment, Federalists agreed, was an issue between Britain and her subjects. In short, the United States was engaged in an unjust and offensive war. Only when the Madison administration had shown that the issues dividing the two countries were great enough to justify war and that force represented a practical means of redressing British wrongs could virtuous citizens rightfully support the war.[14]

The moral consequences of doing otherwise were severe. The culpability of the nation's leadership for engaging in an unjust war was beyond question. Quoting the renowned international jurist, Vattel, one clergyman lumped the Madison administration with the "scourges of the human race, barbarians, enemies to society, and rebels to the law of nation." Moreover, if a free people failed to unseat a leader-

---

[13] Abercrombie, *Two Sermons*, 15-24, 36-41; Emerson, *Equity of God's Dealing with Nations*, 19.

[14] Channing, *A Sermon* (Boston 1814), 7-8; resolution of a convention at Albany, New York, Sept. 17-18, 1812, Norfolk *Gazette*, Oct. 2, 1812; [Massachusetts legislature], Memorial to the honorable the senate and house of representatives of the United States [June 4, 1812], *Niles' Weekly Register*, June 20, 1812, II, 259; Worcester, *Abraham and Lot*, 21-32; Samuel Austin, *The Apology of Patriots, or The Heresy of the Friends of the Washington Peace Policy Defended* (Worcester, Mass. 1812), 18.

ship committed to an unjust war, they were equally guilty as a community and as individuals for the crimes committed in the war: "Each man who volunteers his services in such a cause, or loans his money for its support, or by his conversation, his writings, or any other mode of influence, encourages its prosecution . . . loads his conscience with the blackest crimes, brings the guilt of blood upon his soul, and in the sight of God and his law, is a murderer." Neither the laws of men nor God allowed citizens to hide behind the dictates of their leaders in an unjust war. The common law, John Lowell pointed out, excused not even a slave for committing murder or any other crime at the command of his master.[15]

Individuals had good cause, opponents of the Madison administration agreed, to consider the impact of the declaration of war for another, more secular reason: the nation was entirely unprepared. Connecticut's General Assembly characterized the country as being "without fleets, without armies, with an impoverished treasury, [and] with a frontier by sea and land extending many hundred miles, feebly defended." The administration, a group of dissenting congressmen charged, had rushed "headlong . . . into difficulties, with little calculation about the means and little concern about the consequences" of its actions. With an undistinguished naval force, the United States had declared war on the world's greatest maritime power. Far-flung and prosperous commercial routes were being given up for the precarious profits of privateering. Even more disconcerting, plans were being laid for an invasion of Canada at a time when Great Britain could spread alarm and destruction along the Atlantic seaboard without building a single new ship or hiring an additional soldier. Federalists gathering in New Jersey thought the decision to declare war against one of the most powerful states in Europe exceedingly ill-advised. That the government would assume such risks with little or no chance of success "fills us, and we believe the great body of the people, with grief and amazement."[16]

---

[15] David Osgood, *A Solemn Protest Against the Late Declaration of War* (Cambridge, Mass. 1812), 7-10; [Lowell], *Mr. Madison's War*, 46-48; Emerson, *Equity of God's Dealing with Nations*, 10-13.

[16] Declaration of the [Connecticut] General Assembly, Aug. 25, 1812, *Niles' Weekly Register*, Sept. 12, 1812, III, 24-25; [Sullivan *et al.*], *An Address . . . to their Constituents*, 31; *Proceedings and Address to the People of New-Jersey*, 7-8, 18; Micah Stone, *Danger and Duty Pointed Out* [delivered at Brookfield, Mass., July 23, 1812] (Brookfield 1812), 4; proceedings of a convention at Northampton, July 13, 1812, Norfolk *Gazette*, July 31, 1812; Rhode Island General Assembly, Declaration, May 9, 1812, *Niles' Weekly Register*, May 30, 1812, II, 204; Barrows, *An Oration*, 5-6; Elijah Parish, *A Protest*

Compounding the risks that came with unpreparedness was the political divisiveness that had come with war. Partisanship evoked "all the bad passions of our nature," proclaimed Samuel Worcester at Salem, Massachusetts, in July 1812. The good will, benevolence, and virtue that bound society together were being destroyed by factional infighting. Thus, war threatened to "shake not only the pillars, but the very foundations of the Republick." Predictions of civil war were far from uncommon: that would hardly be an "unprecedented calamity, nor any thing more that we have reason to fear," warned one clergyman. Critics of administration policy noted that even as war was declared idle charges circulated in the Republican press accusing antiwar spokesmen of being opponents of republican government and friends of monarchy. A tract published in Cambridge, Massachusetts, in June 1812 argued that administration efforts to rid itself of legitimate dissent would lead to the violent silencing of the antiwar press and to the end of free speech and hence to civil war. Being men of "Washingtonian principles," unwilling to "stain their hands in the blood of the unjust war," Federalists would be compelled to meet force with force: "thus a civil war becomes as certain as the events which happen according to the known laws and established course of nature."[17] A New Hampshire clergyman warned opponents and proponents of Madison administration policies to "take time for *cool* and *deliberate reflection*. . . . If, in the present state of parties in this nation, the fire of civil war should be kindled, and prevail, it is not probable that it will be extinguished with less sacrifice than the blood of a million of our fellow citizens!"[18]

Political as well as religious leaders opposed to war with Great Britain agreed, moreover, that no political faction could expect to gain from civil war. Governor Caleb Strong cautioned the Massachusetts legislature only a week before the declaration of war that internal division would open the country to foreign conquest. "A state with ten millions of men may be conquered as easily as one with ten thou-

---

Against the War (Newburyport, Mass. 1812), 17-21; Joseph R. Ingersoll, *An Oration* [delivered before the Washington Benevolent Society, July 5, 1813] (Philadelphia 1813), 15-21.

[17] Worcester, *Calamity, Danger, and Hope*, 9; Worcester, *Substance of Two Sermons*, 15, 29-30; Osgood, *Solemn Protest*, 14-15; *Proceedings and Address to the People of New-Jersey*, 17; preamble and resolutions of the Maryland House of Delegates, Dec. 24, 1812, Norfolk *Gazette*, Jan. 1, 1813; Channing, *A Sermon* [1812], 18-19; [Moore], *Sketch of Our Political Condition*, 43; Stansbury, *God Pleading with America*, 16; Abercrombie, *Two Sermons*, 33; Ingersoll, *An Oration*, 21-22; Austin, *The Apology of Patriots*, 11-14.

[18] Worcester, *Substance of Two Sermons*, 15, 29-30.

sand," he warned, "if the people are divided, and one half are willing to assist in subjugating the other." A month later, a Federalist
clergyman predicted that civil war would produce a military despot:
those who survived "the conflagration will be doomed to be his slaves"
and future generations would be left to "groan in bondage, and mourn
for our folly and madness." There was also the fear that civil war
would open the way for the kind of demagoguery that had doomed
the French Revolution to tyranny. Domestic turmoil, Federalists were
convinced, would force the nation to policies from which it might never
recover: "Yea, people may do that in a few moments which they might
have reason to lament to eternity." At the very least, a war among
Americans would leave the land awash "in the blood of its inhabitants."
"Such are gloomy prospects," scolded the same clergyman, "if we
go on to irritate one another, and to abuse the kindness of the Lord."[19]

That God used war to punish wayward Christian nations was a
fundamental tenet of American Protestantism. At the same time,
though, Americans understood that war could be the instrument of
satanic ambition. With the Antichrist identified since the mid-eighteenth
century not with the Pope in Rome but rather, as Nathan Hatch has
pointed out, with "evil and arbitrary civil governments," antiwar
spokesmen moved easily from the sacred implications of war to the
more temporal concern for the foundations of American republicanism.
The declaration of war, argued Elijah Parish, reflected the influence
of France—the primary agent of the Antichrist's ambitions—in the
councils of American government. "If we engage in this war," he
warned, "then . . . we make a common cause with him, and must
share in his approaching destruction." On the domestic front, war
brought with it an expansive and potentially tyrannical civil administration. Swarms of revenue officers, assessors, collectors, customhouse
officers, and their numerous deputies had found their way into every
town and village. Though paid by the people through wartime taxes,
these officials were appointed through "Presidential favor," and it was
with the executive branch that their loyalties lay.[20]

It would have been the rare American who did not recognize the
dangers inherent in government officials beyond the control of the peo-

---

[19] Governor Caleb Strong to the Massachusetts legislature, June 5, 1812, *Niles'
Weekly Register*, June 20, 1812, II, 258; Worcester, *Substance of Two Sermons*, 15, 29-30;
[Moore], *Sketch of Our Political Condition*, 42.

[20] Hatch, *Sacred Cause of Liberty*, 17; Parish, *A Protest Against the War*, 10-17; *A
Defence of the Clergy*, 41-42; Van Cortlandt, *Address to the Republican Citizens*, 6; Bell,
A Sermon, 12-13.

ple. Reviewing the first year of war, Josiah Dunham reminded New Englanders on the anniversary of Washington's birthday in 1814 that independence had come in part as a reaction to the hordes of officials sent by the Crown to the colonies. He claimed that Britain had employed only seven or eight customs officials for the whole of New England, while the Madison administration had appointed untold numbers. In Vermont alone, where the seacoast came no closer than one hundred miles, "a deputy or deputy's deputy" could be found in almost every village. Abuses were certain with "a pimping privileged spy at almost every corner." Reports were commonplace of trunks being ransacked and their contents confiscated on the specious grounds that they contained smuggled goods. Moreover, the proliferation of the customs bureaucracy had opened the way for a more fundamental assault on liberty. The administration's propensity to direct enforcement policy by executive orders—Dunham called them "dictatorical decrees"—challenged the lawmaking powers of elected representatives in Congress. Only "serious and timely attention . . . [to] our constitutional rights" by the state legislatures, argued Federalists, could stop executive branch intrigues from subverting "the first principles of a free government."[21]

Federalists also feared the Republican administration's expanded standing army. The army might well be used to conquer Canada, but afterwards it would be quartered at home. "Every considerable town in New England, that DOUBTS *with regard to the war,*" Dunham warned, will soon know "what is meant, by having 'large bodies of armed troops quartered among them'!" Homes would be converted to barracks, granaries plundered, and pockets rifled "to pay mercenary slaves of that government, which was instituted for your protection." Troops were being used to enforce the law. Worse, soldiers had violated the rights of citizens, imposing nothing less than a "reign of Terror and the Bayonet" in some regions of the country. Such conduct in 1774, Dunham commented sardonically, would have brought the death of every British regular in Boston in less than thirty minutes.[22]

Troubling too was the possibility that the military might overthrow civil authority. Those who doubted that that could happen were simply

---

[21] Josiah Dunham, *An Oration, in Commemoration of the Birth of our Illustrious Washington* (Windsor, Vt. 1814), 17-18, 38; [John Lowell], *Perpetual War, the Policy of Mr. Madison* (Boston 1812), 12-13; preamble and resolutions of the Maryland House of Delegates, Dec. 24, 1812, Norfolk *Gazette*, Jan. 1, 1813.

[22] Dunham, *An Oration*, 18-20, 34-35; John Truair, *The Alarm Trumpet* (Montpelier, Vt. 1813), 25.

wrong, contended a New York essayist. An army of 50,000 had done greater things than conquer a country the size of the United States. A military leader might even be hailed as the savior of the country. The war had already raised fundamental questions about the government's ability to enforce the law and command the allegiance of the people: "Might not the people be induced to believe that he came merely to keep down the turbulent spirits of the country, and to secure tranquility and happiness?" Farther south, "A Loudoun Farmer" reminded Virginians of similar dangers. History abounded with accounts of the collapse of republican institutions under the weight of lesser pressures. "Do we suppose," he asked, that "we possess more virtue, or more devoted patriotism? . . . Look at the list of court retainers and expectants—see the zeal with which they advocate the [illegible] character of their Dragon, and tremble for the existence of institutions, resting upon such fragile props."[23]

The military itself could be destructive, but it was the power that military institutions gave civil authorities that Federalists feared most. As Massachusetts' Governor Strong put it: "A man who has a large army at his control must have the virtue of a Washington, not to make use of it, for his own aggrandizement." Few Federalists thought the Republican leadership capable of such virtue. The county delegates gathering in Northhampton, Massachusetts, in July 1812 thought the army was raised "rather to overawe our peaceful citizens, than to repel foreign aggressions." The military's role in the enforcement of customs regulations was, as the Massachusetts legislature phrased it, "altogether repugnant to the Constitution." A resident of the Ohio frontier feared the rise of a Cromwell, a Caesar, or a Bonaparte, concluding in the spring of 1813 that "we are rapidly verging to despotism." A New Yorker thought the union of civil and military officers under the influence and command of the president contrary to constitutional theory and calculated to destroy civil liberties. Oppressive too were the administration's efforts from the outset of the war to place the state militias under the command of regular army officers. The whole military strength of the country was in the president's hands, concluded one essayist, endangering the soveriegnty of the states themselves.[24]

---

[23] [Moore], *Sketch of Our Political Condition*, 44-45; Alexandria *Gazette*, n.d., reprinted in the Norfolk *Gazette*, Apr. 14, 1813.

[24] Caleb Strong to the Massachusetts Assembly, May 28, 1813, *Niles' Weekly Register*, June 12, 1813, IV, 235; proceedings of the convention at Northampton, July 13, 1812, Norfolk *Gazette*, July 31, 1812; resolutions of the Massachusetts legislature, Dec. 16, 1813, in Dunham, *An Oration*, 40; Bell, *A Sermon*, 13; Van Cortlandt, *Address to the Republican Citizens*, 6; *A Defence of the Clergy*, 42.

While some Federalists thought that the Madison administration would use the army to crush all opposition to the war, others, without doubting that possibility, considered the expanded military establishment to be symptomatic of greater, more long term dangers. A year into the war, when hopes were high in Republican circles for a successful assault on Canada, Caleb Strong raised doubts about the consequences of even a victorious campaign. New territory would bring new power and wealth, and with them would come the pride and arrogance that historically had brought "severe calamities" to republics. With the history of the Roman Empire in mind, Strong argued that foreign conquest inspired "rash counsels and extravagant measures" designed more to indulge the passions and ambitions of leaders than to serve the interests of the citizenry. When republics "acquired the titles of conquerors," the Federalist governor warned, "they have invariably and speedily lost their form of government."[25]

The governor's insights could hardly have surprised New England Federalists. Since the acquisition of Louisiana, they had identified the west with the dilution of eastern political influence and the fracturing of social authority. Indeed, the republic's first wartime celebration of national independence provided an occasion for a searching analysis of the dangers inherent in expanding by military conquest the borders of the republic. William Barrows told his congregation in Fryeburg, Maine, that history spoke like a "voice from the dead" of the "ruinous consequences of waging a war of conquest." Restless ambition "to overleap the bounds of a limited domain" had wrecked popular governments in the ancient republics, robbing them of their vitality and corrupting their institutions. The United States faced a similar fate. The acquisition of new territory would corrupt the simplicity of its republican institutions. The proliferation of territorial officials would dangerously expand presidential patronage. The growth of appointive powers had corrupted England, Barrows reminded his listeners. When the offices of governor general for the Canadas, Nova Scotia, upper and lower Louisiana, and the Floridas fell to the patronage of the president, all power would come to reside with him. If the other branches of government survived at all, they would become only "humble satellites, revolving round this grand luminary of the nation."[26]

---

[25] Caleb Strong to Massachusetts Assembly, May 28, 1813, *Niles' Weekly Register*, June 12, 1813, IV, 235; Dunham, *An Oration*, 31.

[26] Barrows, *An Oration*, 5-14. See also Channing, *A Sermon* [1814], 15. On the longstanding Federalist concern about the acquisition of western territory, see Banner, *To the Hartford Convention*, 27-28, 110-114, and Drew R. McCoy, *The Elusive Republic: Political Economy in Jeffersonian America* (Chapel Hill 1980), 199-200.

But if the acquisition of new territory threatened a dangerous proliferation of executive power, it also portended the dissipation of the
moral and political authority of the national government. "The energy
of government . . . would be lost, in its travel to the frontier of so
mighty an empire," contended Barrows. Allegiances nurtured by
regular and frequent contact would dissolve among a population thinly
scattered over an immense territory. Neither were conquered people
particularly fertile soil for the perpetuation of republicanism. They
knew nothing of the values and virtues necessary to the support of
American institutions. To confer upon them the privileges of citizenship would produce chaos; to do otherwise would necessitate the
maintenance of an expensive military force in the conquered territories.
"On either supposition," argued Barrows, "our Republic must become
such an unwieldy monster, as infallibly to be crushed with its own
weight." The conclusion to be drawn was unavoidable. When the
borders of the United States stretched from Mexico to Hudson's Bay
and from the Atlantic to the Pacific, the social and political fabric
woven under the watchful eye of Washington during the summer of
1787 would be torn asunder—"farewell forever to our Republican
Government; adieu to liberty; farewell to equal rights!"[27]

The times cried out for "cool and serious reflection." Would the
"gratification of some privateersmen compensate the nation for the
sweep of our legitimate commerce" from the sea? Would the conquest of Canada compensate the middle states for the destruction of
New York City? Or would it expiate the loss of New Orleans for the
western states? Many in search of public office and personal gain had
thrown their support behind the administration; "even *many* sincere
friends of their country [had] unthinkingly or rashly" done the same.
But each citizen must decide for himself, advised New Jersey Federalists
gathered in a convention on July 4, 1812. "Let the prudent, the impartial and disinterested—the *Great Body* of FARMERS,
MECHANICS, LABORERS, MERCHANTS"—ask themselves
whether "long and deadly warfare" was more in their interest than
"continued *Peace, Commerce, Agriculture, Security, and Union.*" Prudent
reflection, the Massachusetts legislature believed, would lead citizens
to see war as an inappropriate response to British policies intended
to cripple France and not the United States. National honor was not
at stake. To the contrary, neither national resolve nor individual

---

[27] Barrows, *An Oration*, 10-11; Ingersoll, *An Oration*, 16-17, 21-23; [Moore], *Sketch
of Our Political Condition*, 44-45.

patriotism could be called into question when a country was buffeted
by circumstances beyond its control. No one doubted American courage.
"The world will witness," the New Jersey Federalists argued, "that
it is not *fear*, but *prudence*, and a love of country that restrains them
from *war*." Many nations had lost their liberty in hopeless contests
fought over dubious questions of honor. The American republic's fate
could be otherwise only if the citizenry rejected its leadership's efforts
to engage in a futile struggle over orders in council and impressment.
The blood and treasure of their country, its virtue, religion, and happiness should stand foremost in the American consciousness. "Let it
be our *honor*," the New Jersey convention resolved, "to *prevent* the
introduction of standing armies—and the increase of taxes and public
debt—the distress of private life."[28]

Nevertheless, in the first year of hostilities, Federalists, conscious
of the dangers of anarchy, urged dissent only within carefully defined
limits. "While we remain firm," cautioned one Federalist clergyman,
"we must keep ourselves cool, and take no step but in conformity
to the Constitution and Laws." Random acts motivated by passion
served no one. William Ellery Channing agreed: "Civil commotion
should be viewed as the worst of national evils." Even if the government pursued policies that justified civil disobedience, the citizenry
should consider carefully their duty to submit. "Resistance of established
power is so great an evil,—civil commotion excites such destructive
passions, the result is so tremendously uncertain,—that every milder
method of relief should first be tried, and fairly tried." Indeed, public
spokesmen had an obligation, in times of civil crises, "to avoid all
language and conduct which will produce a spirit of insubordination—a
contempt of laws and just authority." Speaking as "magistrates, soldiers
and citizens," people gathering in Albany, New York, early in the
war announced their determination "to obey with promptness and
alacrity all constitutional requisitions of the proper authorities." New
Jersey Federalists condemned anyone seeking to obstruct the declaration of war "by any irregular opposition—by violence, by menace,
or illegal combinations." They were "too deeply impressed with the
duties of submission to constitutional laws" to do otherwise. Reason
and a commitment to civil liberties, not passionate outbursts, they

---

[28] John H. Church, *Advantages of Moderation* [delivered at Pelham, N.H., Aug.
20, 1812] (Haverhill, Mass. 1812), 9; [Sullivan *et al.*], *An Address . . . to their Constituents*, 3; *Proceedings and Address to the People of New-Jersey*, 13-14; [Massachusetts
legislature], Memorial [June 4, 1812], *Niles' Weekly Register*, June 20, 1812, II, 259.

contended, guided "freemen and good citizens" even when laws "counteract their best and most important interests."[29]

State officials in Connecticut took much the same position. Governor Roger Griswold issued a proclamation on August 6, 1812, decrying opposition to the war, except in a constitutional manner. He called upon the citizens "to discountenance every appearance of menacing the lawful authority of the state and nation, and to promote a spirit of submission to the laws of the land." In Massachusetts, the House of Representatives published a similar call for domestic order within weeks of the declaration of war. Silent submission was impossible. Rights had been neglected, interests ignored, opinions disregarded, and petitions dismissed; nevertheless, tumult and rebellion offered no remedy. The people must "discourage all attempts to obtain redress of grievances by any acts of violence or combinations to oppose the laws. . . . Your habits of obedience to the dictates of duty, your just and temperate views of your social and political obligations, your firm attachment to the Constitution, are pledges," the assembly reminded the citizenry, of "the correctness of your conduct." Later in the summer, Governor Strong issued pleas for a due regard for the laws and Constitution of the republic. Condemning all "violent outrages," he called upon every citizen to "be watchful and determined to prevent tumults and disorders of every kind, by which our internal tranquility would be endangered."[30]

Daniel Webster's address to the Washington Benevolent Society gathered at Portsmouth, New Hampshire, on July 4, 1812, both summarized the early Federalist commitment to peaceful dissent and outlined what was expected of citizens opposed to war with Great Britain. "The disciples of WASHINGTON," he told the assembled gentlemen, "are neither tyrants *in* power, nor rebels *out*." The declara-

[29] Stone, *Danger and Duty*, 6; Channing, *A Sermon* [1812], 17-18; resolutions of a convention at Albany, New York, Sept. 17-18, 1812, Norfolk *Gazette*, Oct. 2, 1812; *Proceedings and Address to the People of New-Jersey*, 6; Austin, *The Apology of Patriots*, 17; [Lowell], *Mr. Madison's War*, 4; Abercrombie, *Two Sermons*, 36-38; Worcester, *Abraham and Lot*, 29; essay in [Baltimore] *Federal Republican*, June 20, 1812, in *Niles' Weekly Register*, Aug. 8, 1812, II, 379.

[30] Proclamation by Governor Roger Griswold, Aug. 6, 1812, *Niles' Weekly Register*, Aug. 15, 1812, II, 389; *Address of the Massachusetts House of Representatives to the People of Massachusetts*, June 25, 1812 (n.p., n.d.), 11-12; Strong to the Massachusetts legislature, Aug. 14, 1812, *Niles' Weekly Register*, Oct. 24, 1812, III, 118; Governor Griswold to the Connecticut legislature, May 1812, *ibid.*, June 6, 1812, II, 226-227; Massachusetts Senate Resolutions, June 26, 1812, *ibid.*, July 11, 1812, II, 309; resolutions of a meeting at Liberty Hall, Boston, July 15, 1812, and at Columbia County, New York, meeting at Hudson, July 8, 1812, in Norfolk *Gazette*, July 24, 27, 1812.

tion of war was part of the law of the land and must be regarded as such. Taxes levied on behalf of the war effort must be paid. Personal service, "to the precise extent of our Constitutional liability," must also be rendered. And, of course, any hostile attack on the United States must be repelled. In sum, all constitutional requisitions by the proper authorities were to be obeyed. "Resistance and Insurrection form no parts of our creed," he declared. Nevertheless, the declaration of war did not require the active support of its opponents. Federalists argued that the Madison administration had no reason to expect more support for the war than it had a right by the Constitution to command. Voluntary enlistment, for example, fell beyond the responsibilities of dissenting citizens as did the purchase of federal loan certificates. "They must," insisted William Ellery Channing, "give no encouragement, no unnecessary voluntary support to the war."[31]

Neither did the declaration of war provide grounds for the government to curtail a citizen's right to free speech or his access to a free press. Federalists dismissed the Republican claim that dissent must cease with the opening of hostilities. Freedom of speech and thought "is an essential principle of Republicanism," advised John Church while celebrating the national fast day in 1812: "Surely we ought not to reproach and abuse persons, for their sober exercise of this freedom." The citizens of Massachusetts, Elijah Mills reminded the Washington Benevolent Society in Hampshire County on July 4, 1813, "have yet to learn the duty of quiet acquiescence, in ruinous measures, or silent submission, to wanton injustice and oppression." Federalists gathered in Albany, New York, resolved "that the doctrine, of late so frequently and *violently* inculcated, that when war is once declared, all enquiry into its [war's] justice and expediency ought to cease, and all opposition to the men in power immediately to be abandoned, is essentially hostile to the vital principles of our republican institutions." Such a doctrine would transform the government into a kind of tyranny, republican in form but despotic and arbitrary in spirit and practice. A declaration of war, reminded Federalists in New Jersey and New York, differed from other laws passed by Congress only in its "dread-

---

[31] Daniel Webster, *An Address delivered before the Washington Benevolent Society* [July 4, 1812] (Portsmouth. N.H. 1812), 21; Channing, *A Sermon* [1812], 17; *Proceedings and Address to the People of New-Jersey*, 14-15; resolutions of a convention at Albany, New York, Sept. 17-18, 1812, Norfolk *Gazette*, Oct. 2, 1812; proceedings of a convention at Northampton, July 13, 1812, Norfolk *Gazette*, July 31, 1812; *Address of the [Massachusetts] House of Representatives*, 13; [Federalist party], *Proceedings of a Convention of Delegates from forty-one Towns in the County of Worcester* (Worcester, Mass. 1812), 18-19.

ful consequences to society.'' It justified neither the violation of constitutional rights nor did it protect ''profligate rulers'' from the indignation and reproach of ''an injured and insulted people.'' Conventions in Worcester and Northhampton, Massachusetts, agreed that in times of public peril the citizenry had a right to assembly and a ''solemn duty boldly to examine the measures of their rulers.'' Otherwise public officials would be shielded from criticism at the very time ''when a rigid scrutiny of their conduct is most necessary for the future safety of the country.'' ''Bad *laws* and misguided councils, measures most fatal to the best interests of society [might] never be changed,'' if the government could use a declaration of war ''to silence complaint.''[32]

But if bad policies were to be changed, they must, argued Federalists, be changed using the institutions guaranteed by republican government. Public meetings were to be called, committees of correspondence and public safety established, and resolutions passed—all for the ultimate purpose of restoring peace ''by the constitutional and speedy effect of your *Elections*.'' While Republicans judged such actions to border on treason, Federalists insisted that the call for the election of antiwar representatives underscored the constitutional character of their dissent. ''Now if rulers do wrong; if they adopt impolitic and ruinous measures; our Republican Constitution of government reserves to us the privilege of electing others to fill their place,'' John Church told the citizens of Pelham, New Hampshire, on the national fast day in August 1812. ''The government and the administration of government are separate and distinct things,'' reminded Federalists meeting in Winchester, Virginia. Indeed, ''an attempt to change the administrators when the public good requires it, is not

---

[32] Church, *Advantages of Moderation*, 10; Elijah H. Mills, *An Oration* [pronounced at Northampton for the Washington Benevolent Society, July 4, 1813] (Northampton, Mass. 1813), 12-13; resolutions of a convention at Albany, New York, Sept. 17-18, 1812, Norfolk *Gazette*, Oct. 2, 1812; *Proceedings of a Convention of Delegates in the County of Worcester*, 9-10; *Proceedings and Address to the People of New-Jersey*, 5-6, 14-15, 17-18; proceedings of a convention at Northampton, July 13, 1812, Norfolk *Gazette*, July 31, 1812; Stone, *Danger and Duty*, 14; Rowan, *Sin and Danger*, 38-39; [Lowell], *Mr. Madison's War*, 48-50, 59-60; Worcester, *Abraham and Lot*, 16; Austin, *The Apology of Patriots*, 15-17; resolutions of a meeting at Liberty Hall, Boston, July 15, 1812, and at Columbia County, New York, meeting at Hudson, July 8, 1812; resolutions of the Maryland House of Delegates, Dec. 24, 1812, *ibid.*, Jan. 1, 1813; resolution of the Pennsylvania House and Senate, Dec. 5, 1812, *Niles' Weekly Register*, Dec. 19, 1812, III, 246; proclamation of Governor Griswold, Aug. 6, 1812, *ibid.*, Aug. 15, 1812, II, 389; Caleb Strong to Massachusetts Assembly, May 28, 1813, *ibid.*, June 12, 1813, IV, 233-236.

to *oppose* the government but is an actual *support* of it," they resolved. The franchise, of course, was not to be misused; motivated by passion, party partisanship, and the hope for the spoils of public office, it easily converted liberty into licentiousness. The rights and liberties of future generations, however, depended upon the enlightened and conscientious discharge of the right to vote. With the election of men moved by a *"love of country, and who will know no guide but the constitution,"* the country could be diverted from the perilous course charted by the Madison administration. Federalists were confident that peace could be restored and by constitutional means. "By the exercise of our Constitutional right of suffrage, by the peaceable remedy of election," Daniel Webster declared, "we shall seek to restore WISDOM to our Councils, and PEACE to our Country."[33]

Of course, the peaceful revolution that leading Federalists espoused during the first year of hostilities never occurred. James Madison was reelected to the presidency late in 1812, and the Republican party held onto its majorities in the House and Senate. Frustrated Federalists—at least those given to more radical solutions to their political dilemma—would in time suggest secession as a reasonable response to the Madison administration's war policies. These better known developments, which culminated in the Hartford Convention, do not, however, accurately reflect attitudes articulated by the Federalist leadership at the outset of hostilities. Early opposition to the country's first formally declared war was tied directly to preserving the political and constitutional order created in 1787.

Federalists began with the assumption, reinforced by the language of the jeremiad, that war placed the foundations of constitutional government in jeopardy. A general disregard for Christian values since the revolution, they argued, had combined with the immorality specifically associated with military mobilization to provoke divine displeasure with the nation and to undermine the virtue essential to a free society.

---

[33] *Proceedings and Address to the People of New-Jersey*, 3-4, 6, 15-17, 24; Church, *Advantages of Moderation*, 8-9; patriotic meeting, Winchester, Va., Aug. 8, 1812, Norfolk *Gazette*, Aug. 28, 1812; proceedings of a convention at Northampton, July 13, 1812, Norfolk *Gazette*, July 31, 1812; Webster, *An Address*, 21; *Proceedings of a Convention in the County of Worcester*, 20-21; Massachusetts Senate Resolutions, June 26, 1812, *Niles' Weekly Register*, July 11, 1812, II, 309; *Address of the [Massachusetts] House of Representative*, 12-14; [Lowell], *Mr. Madison's War*, 48-50, 59-60; resolutions of a meeting at Liberty Hall, Boston, July 15, 1812; Francis Blake, *An Oration* [pronounced at Worcester, July 4, 1812] (Worcester, Mass. 1812), 24-25; Austin, *The Apology of Patriots*, 15-17; resolutions of a convention at Albany, New York, Sept. 17-18, 1812, Norfolk *Gazette*, Oct. 2, 1812.

In short, republicanism was endangered because war assaulted the moral underpinnings of a free society.

War also provided the context for the expansion of potentially tyrannical executive authority, further endangering freedoms gained by the revolution. Charges once leveled at George III were aimed at the Madison administration, providing Federalists with an opportunity to rehash republican theory as old as the English civil war. At the same time, though, grounding dissent in traditional republicanism also served to channel its expression through institutions well founded in the legal and extralegal traditions of American constitutional and political theory. Resolutions passed by state legislatures, proclamations issued from governors' mansions, addresses promulgated by party conventions, and jeremiads delivered from the pulpits of churches often supported by the state provided the principal vehicles for the articulation of antiwar opinion. Mob violence was beyond the pale of legitimate dissent. Classical history provided plenty of evidence of the dangers that popular tumult posed for republican society, as did the recent French Revolution. Even the partisan Washington Benevolent societies around which Federalists gathered—much as the Jeffersonians had rallied around Democratic-Republican clubs two decades before—modeled their conduct after the dignified republicanism of their namesake. Ironically, the Federalist commitment to preserving political stability probably prevented them from mounting a serious effort to derail the Madison presidency during the first year of the war. In the end, the long-term advantages of political stability proved more important to Federalists than the short-term gains available through extra- or unconstitutional measures. Even the most determined opponents of the war proved slow to propose more radical solutions to the crisis faced by Federalists, and then they found most in their party reluctant to follow.

Finally, the hopes for electoral change both suggested the means and defined the limits of acceptable dissent in the Federalist mind. When Daniel Webster spoke of suffrage as the means to restore wisdom to the nation's councils, he was speaking to the broader Federalist insistence that a republican solution was to be found to the political crisis facing America. The ballot was the ultimate remedy for a free society succumbing to misguided leadership and ill-conceived policies. In a basic way, there were few other choices. Believing, as Nathan Hatch has pointed out, that the destiny of America depended on the triumph of both Protestantism and republicanism, Federalists could not separate moral renewal from the preservation of republican values and institutions. Hence, opposition against what Federalists perceived to be an unjust and impolitic war dangerous to the moral foundations of the republic could be founded on nothing less than the Constitution itself. To have opposed the war in any other way risked the further deterioration of public virtue and the certain failure of what one group of New England Federalists called "a form of government, in no small degree experimental."[34]

---

[34] Hatch, *Sacred Cause of Liberty*, *passim*; [Sullivan *et al.*], *An Address . . . to their Constituents*, 6.

American Trade Restrictions during the War of 1812

Donald R. Hickey

For more than six years, from 1806 to 1812, trade restrictions were at the heart of American foreign policy. Although the Jeffersonian Republicans always defended the restrictive system as an alternative to war—as a peaceful means of upholding the nation's rights in the face of European encroachments—they refused to abolish the system even after war had been declared against England in 1812. On the contrary, the record shows that they steadily expanded the system as the nation's military fortunes waned. Indeed, most Republicans regarded trade restrictions not as an alternative to war, but as an indispensable means of prosecuting the war. The restrictive system, in other words, played a central role in Republican strategy for winning the war.

The restrictive system had its origins in the era of the American Revolution. In the 1760s and 1770s, the American colonies had employed nonimportation and nonexportation against the mother country in an effort to force the British to change their tax and trade policies. Although these measures had little impact on British colonial policy, Republican leaders like Thomas Jefferson and James Madison interpreted history otherwise. Convinced that American trade was crucial to British prosperity, they tried to secure congressional approval for economic sanctions in the 1790s. At first their aim was to extract a favorable commercial treaty from Britain, but, after the outbreak of the wars of the French Revolution, they also sought greater respect for American rights. Although Federalists blocked these measures, Republican leaders achieved national power in 1801 and thereafter were in a position to put their views on economic coercion to a full test, not only against England but against France as well.

The restrictive system was launched in Jefferson's second administration in response to Britain's stepped-up war on neutral trade and her impressment of American seamen.[1] The first measure to become law was the partial non-

Donald R. Hickey is assistant professor of history at Wayne State College in Nebraska.

[1] There is no monograph on the restrictive system. For an account that stands above the rest, see Herbert Heaton, "Non-Importation, 1806–1812," *Journal of Economic History*, I (Nov. 1941),

importation act of 1806, which prohibited the importation of selected British manufactured goods. This law was repeatedly suspended and was not implemented until late 1807, when it was joined by a general embargo prohibiting American ships and goods from leaving port. In 1809 these measures were superseded by a nonintercourse law barring trade with Britain and France and their colonies while permitting trade with the rest of the world. When this measure expired in 1810, a period of unrestricted trade followed. This, in turn, came to an end with a presidential proclamation—backed by the nonimportation law of 1811—which prohibited all British imports.[2] The restrictive system passed through several distinct stages—from nonimportation to nonexportation and back again to nonimportation—as Republican leaders searched for the instrument that would have the greatest impact on the European belligerents while doing the least damage to the United States.[3]

The man who was the chief architect of the restrictive system also presided over the War of 1812.[4] Madison, like all good patriots, had supported the interdiction of trade with the mother country in the years before the American Revolution. Like many patriots Madison thought that American economic pressure had been responsible for the repeal of the Stamp Taxes in 1766 and the Townshend Duties in 1770. Thus when the Revolution came to an end in 1783, he favored granting Congress broad powers to restrict commerce in order to win trade concessions from Great Britain. Unable to attain this end, Madison sponsored a navigation act in the Virginia House of Delegates designed to break Great Britain's monopoly of Virginia's trade.[5]

After the national government acquired authority to regulate commerce in the Constitution of 1787, Madison repeatedly sought to use this power against Great Britain. In 1789, in 1791, and again in 1794, he tried unsuccessfully to persuade Congress to enact discriminating duties against England. In 1797,

178-98. Other works that provide considerable insight into the system are Richard Hildreth, *The History of the United States of America* (6 vols., New York, 1854-1855), V-VI; Edward Channing, *A History of the United States* (6 vols., New York, 1905-1925), IV; Henry Adams, *History of the United States* (9 vols., New York, 1889-1891), III-VI; Bradford Perkins, *Prologue to War: England and the United States, 1805-1812* (Berkeley, 1961); Reginald Horsman, *The Causes of the War of 1812* (Philadelphia, 1962); Irving Brant, *James Madison* (6 vols., Indianapolis, 1941-1961), IV-V; Walter W. Jennings, *The American Embargo, 1807-1809* (Iowa City, 1921); Louis Martin Sears, *Jefferson and the Embargo* (Durham, N.C., 1927); Burton Spivak, *Jefferson's English Crisis: Commerce, Embargo, and the Republican Revolution* (Charlottesville, Va., 1979).

[2] This law barred the importation of all British-made goods and of all goods from the British Empire. The act is frequently referred to as a nonintercourse law, but this designation is inaccurate because the law did not prohibit the export of American goods to Britain. For the scope of the law, see Albert Gallatin to Langdon Cheves, June 23, 1812, *The Writings of Albert Gallatin*, ed. Henry Adams (3 vols., Philadelphia, 1879), I, 521-22.

[3] The second nonimportation law belatedly proved its worth by contributing to the British decision to suspend the Orders in Council in June 1812. By then, however, the United States had already declared war.

[4] For a brief discussion of the ideological foundations of James Madison's commercial policy, see Drew R. McCoy, "Republicanism and American Foreign Policy: James Madison and the Political Economy of Commercial Discrimination, 1789-1794," *William and Mary Quarterly*, XXXI (Oct. 1974), 633-46. For an extended treatment of Republican political economy, see Drew R. McCoy, *The Elusive Republic: Political Economy in Jeffersonian America* (Chapel Hill, 1980).

[5] Brant, *James Madison*, I, 91, 141, 148-50, II, 315, 317, 378. See also Drew R. McCoy, "The Virginia Port Bill of 1784," *Virginia Magazine of History and Biography*, 83 (July 1975), 288-303.

when a worldwide food shortage threatened, he enthusiastically recommended an embargo. "In this attitude of things," he exclaimed, "what a noble stroke would be an embargo! It would probably do as much good as harm at home, and would force peace on the rest of the world, and perhaps liberty along with it."[6]

After the Republicans attained power and relations with Britain deteriorated, Madison renewed his plea for trade restrictions. In late 1805 he called for an embargo, convinced that it would "force all the nations having colonies in this quarter of the globe to respect our rights."[7] At the same time he published a two-part article in the semiofficial National Intelligencer recommending a broad range of restrictions against Britain. Madison also helped draft the partial nonimportation law of 1806; he wrote Jefferson's embargo message in 1807; and he published a defense of that measure in the National Intelligencer the day after it became law. When public support for the embargo collapsed in 1809, he proposed the substitution of nonintercourse. Madison was also responsible for reimposing nonimportation against Great Britain in 1811 when France promised to rescind her commercial decrees.[8] In short, the Virginian played an important role in the adoption of all the prewar trade restrictions. By 1812, even though he was prepared to lead the nation into war, Madison had lost none of his enthusiasm for economic coercion.[9] Hence, as the nation's military position deteriorated, he showed a growing interest in bringing the British to terms by expanding the restrictive system.

To enforce the wartime restrictive system, Madison relied on a customs department supervised by a succession of men who served as secretaries of the treasury. Swiss-born Albert Gallatin held this post from 1801 to 1813 and thus was in charge of enforcing the restrictive system from its very inception. Although a loyal and able administrator, Gallatin was a lukewarm restrictionist. When Jefferson had the embargo under consideration in 1807, Gallatin warned him of the dangers. "Governmental prohibitions," he said, "do always more mischief than had been calculated; and it is not without much hesitation that a statesman should hazard to regulate the concerns of individuals as if he could do it better than themselves."[10] To Gallatin, the hope that the embargo would win concessions from Britain was "entirely groundless," and he later told the president that the measure could be enforced only if government officials were given "arbitrary," "dangerous," and "odious" powers.[11] Since Jefferson was determined to give the measure a fair test, Gallatin drafted increasingly draconian legislation, culminating in the enforcement act of 1809, which gave customs officials broad authority to search and to seize property and per-

[6] Brant, James Madison, III, 251–53, 389–93, 434, IV, 397.
[7] Adams, History of the United States, III, 75.
[8] Brant, James Madison, IV, 312, 395, 398–403, 378–79, 481, V, 200. See also Richard Mannix, "Gallatin, Jefferson, and the Embargo of 1808," Diplomatic History, III (Spring 1979), 153–54.
[9] J. C. A. Stagg argues that Madison supported the conquest of Canada as a means of increasing the economic pressure on Britain and her West Indian colonies. The evidence for this claim is slender. See J. C. A. Stagg, "James Madison and the Coercion of Great Britain: Canada, the West Indies, and the War of 1812," William and Mary Quarterly, XXXVIII (Jan. 1981), 3–34.
[10] Gallatin to Thomas Jefferson, Dec. 18, 1807, Writings of Albert Gallatin, ed. Adams, I, 368.
[11] Ibid.; Gallatin to Jefferson, July 29, 1808, ibid., 398.

mitted the routine use of the army, navy, and militia.[12] When the war came, the secretary of the treasury was saddled with the twin burdens of raising money and enforcing the growing number of trade restrictions. Anxious to shed these burdens, Gallatin secured appointment to the peace commission that was sent abroad in 1813.[13]

When Gallatin departed for Europe, his duties were assumed by William Jones, the secretary of the navy, who served as acting secretary of the treasury from May 1813 to February 1814. A Philadelphia shipowner, Jones was not without talent, but he was a poor administrator. Naval and financial problems consumed so much of his time that he could give little attention to the restrictive system.[14] Jones's successor, Scottish-born George W. Campbell of Tennessee, also devoted little attention to the restrictive system. Campbell served as secretary of the treasury for eight months from February to October in 1814. Overwhelmed by the growing financial problems the nation faced, he finally resigned, admitting that he could do little to improve the situation.[15]

Alexander Dallas of Philadelphia assumed the treasury portfolio in October of 1814 and held it for the last four months of the war. A Jamaican-born lawyer educated in Great Britain, Dallas brought great talents and enormous energy to the office. He improved the nation's sagging credit and made a determined bid to stamp out trade with the enemy.[16] He favored prosecuting resident neutrals who were trading with the British, and he was the guiding force behind the strongest trade restriction adopted during the war, the enemy trade act of 1815.[17]

If President Madison relied on the Treasury Department to enforce the wartime restrictive system, he was dependent on Congress to enact the restrictions he favored into law. A majority of Republicans in both houses of the two war Congresses—the Twelfth and the Thirteenth—shared his faith in economic coercion. Some Republicans, especially from Virginia and Pennsylvania, supported the president not only because they believed in the restrictive system but also because they were anxious to follow the administration's lead in the interest of party and national unity. There were some Republicans—like John Clopton of Virginia, Bolling Hall of Georgia, and Elias Earle of South Carolina—who exhibited even greater faith in economic coercion than the president himself. Mainly backbenchers, often southern agrarians who represented districts far from the principal avenues of trade, these archrestrictionists sup-

[12] See *Annals of the Congress of the United States*, 10 Cong., 2 Sess., Jan. 9, 1809, pp. 1798-1804; Leonard W. Levy, *Jefferson and Civil Liberties: The Darker Side* (Cambridge, 1963), 93-141; Mannix, "Gallatin, Jefferson, and the Embargo of 1808," 151-72.

[13] Raymond Walters, Jr., *Albert Gallatin: Jeffersonian Financier and Diplomat* (New York, 1957), 259.

[14] John H. Frederick, "William Jones," *Dictionary of American Biography*, ed. Allen Johnson and Dumas Malone (20 vols., New York, 1928-1936), X, 205.

[15] Philip May Hamer, "George Washington Campbell," *Dictionary of American Biography*, II, 452; Adams, *History of the United States*, VIII, 240-42.

[16] J. Harold Ennis, "Alexander James Dallas," *Dictionary of American Biography*, V, 36-38.

[17] For Alexander Dallas's crackdown on neutral traders, compare George W. Campbell to Hart Massey, Sept. 12, 1814, with Dallas to Perley Keyes, Feb. 8, 1815, General Records of the Department of the Treasury, RG 56 (National Archives).

ported almost every restriction proposed in Congress, whether emanating from the administration or not.

Although Madison could count on a majority of congressional Republicans to support his trade policies, these policies could not always command a majority of votes in Congress. This was in part because of opposition within the Republican party itself. By 1812 there were many Republicans in Congress who no longer shared the president's enthusiasm for commercial restrictions. The most conspicuous opponents were the three young and brilliant South Carolina representatives, John C. Calhoun, William Lowndes, and especially Langdon Cheves. These men agreed with Calhoun that the restrictive system did not suit "the genius of our people, or that of our Government, or the geographical character of our country."[18]

Most Republicans from seaport towns or from river towns close to the sea—especially in the North—also opposed the restrictive system. Men like Samuel Smith of Baltimore, Thomas Robertson of New Orleans, William Rodman of Bristol, Pennsylvania, and Pierre Van Cortlandt, Jr., of Peekskill, New York, had soured on the restrictive system and had concluded that economic coercion was an ineffective weapon that exacted too great a price from their constituents. Also in opposition were the Old Republicans led by the irascible and outspoken John Randolph of Roanoke. This little band of strict constructionists included Edwin Gray of Virginia and Richard Stanford of North Carolina. Although the Old Republicans did not believe the wartime carrying trade was worthy of protection, neither did they think that merchants should be ruined by the laws of their own government. Randolph, who once called the neutral trade a "fungus of war," characterized the restrictive system in late 1811 as "a series of most impolitic and ruinous measures, utterly incomprehensible to every rational, sober-minded man."[19]

The Federalists were in opposition as well. They opposed the restrictive system, as they always had, on the grounds that, by striking at American prosperity and government revenue, it did far more harm to the United States than to either Britain or France.[20] As William Gaston of North Carolina put it, economic coercion was "embarrassing to the finances, oppressive to the community, and inefficient as regards the enemy."[21] Although the Federalists never controlled more than about 35 percent of the seats in either house during the war, by combining with dissident Republicans they could sometimes block restrictive proposals, especially in the Senate.

The first war Congress, which convened in late 1811, at first gave little attention to the restrictive system. Instead, the initial months of the session—

[18] *Annals of the Congress*, 12 Cong., 1 sess., June 24, 1812, p. 1539; *ibid.*, April 9, 1812, p. 1289; *ibid.*, 12 Cong., 2 sess., Dec. 4, 1812, p. 250; *ibid.*, Dec. 7, 1812, p. 298; *ibid.*, Dec. 8, 1812, p. 320.

[19] Hugh A. Garland, *The Life of John Randolph of Roanoke* (2 vols., New York, 1890), I, 233, 291.

[20] The Federalists voted almost unanimously against every commercial restriction enacted between 1806 and 1812. *Annals of the Congress*, 9 Cong., 1 sess., April 15, 1806, p. 240; *ibid.*, March 26, 1806, pp. 877-78; *ibid.*, 10 Cong., 1 sess., April 20, 1808, p. 372; *ibid.*, Jan. 2, 1808, p. 1271; *ibid.*, 10 Cong., 2 sess., Feb. 21, 1809, p. 436; *ibid.*, Feb. 27, 1809, p. 1541; *ibid.*, 11 Cong., 3 sess., March 2, 1811, p. 361; *ibid.*, Feb. 27, 1811, pp. 1094-95.

[21] *Ibid.*, 13 Cong., 2 sess., March 14, 1814, p. 1867.

from November 1811 to April 1812—were devoted to war preparations. By the spring of 1812, with these measures under way, many congressmen were anxious to press ahead with a general embargo as a preliminary to war. On April 1, after repeated urgings from House Speaker Henry Clay, President Madison sent a confidential message to Congress recommending a sixty-day embargo on all American vessels then in port or thereafter arriving.[22] The House Foreign Relations Committee was ready with a bill that Clay insisted was a forerunner of war and not a coercive instrument. It must be viewed, said Clay, "as a direct precursor to war."[23] Although most Republicans shared this view, there were some who supported the bill as a coercive measure.[24] The Senate extended the embargo to ninety days, and the bill, introduced only three days before, was signed into law on April 4.[25] Ten days later, Congress passed a companion measure that prohibited the export of all goods and specie by land or by sea for the duration of the embargo.[26]

The enactment of the ninety-day embargo signaled the likelihood of war, and the Treasury Department was flooded with requests from merchants seeking permission to dispatch ships abroad to bring their property home. Secretary of the Treasury Gallatin asked local customs officials to investigate the legitimacy of these requests, and, if valid, the necessary permits were granted.[27] Because of a specie shortage in England, however, merchants could bring their property home from that country only in the form of British-made goods. It was widely believed that Congress would accommodate the merchants on this issue, and opponents of nonimportation lost little time in seeking changes in the law.[28]

In the spring of 1812, Federalists James A. Bayard of Delaware and James Lloyd of Massachusetts sought to prevail upon the Senate to suspend or repeal the nonimportation law, but without success. A similar proposal offered by Republican Senator John Pope of Kentucky also failed.[29] Opponents of non-

[22] Henry Clay to James Monroe, March 15, 1812, James Monroe Papers (Library of Congress, Washington); Brant, *James Madison*, V, 428; *Annals of the Congress*, 12 Cong., 1 sess., April 1, 1812, pp. 1592-93, 186-87.

[23] *Annals of the Congress*, 12 Cong., 1 sess., April 1, 1812, pp. 1587-88. See also *ibid.*, April 1, 1812, p. 1592; John C. Calhoun to James Macbride, April 18, 1812, *The Papers of John C. Calhoun*, ed. Robert L. Meriwether, Clyde N. Wilson, and W. Edwin Hemphill (13 vols., Columbia, S.C., 1959-1980), I, 100.

[24] James Madison to Jefferson, April 24, 1812, *Writings of James Madison*, ed. Gaillard Hunt (9 vols., New York, 1900-1910), VIII, 188; William Reed to Timothy Pickering, April 25, 1812, Timothy Pickering Papers (Massachusetts Historical Society, Boston).

[25] *Annals of the Congress*, 12 Cong., 1 sess., April 6-9, 1812, pp. 186-92; *ibid.*, April 1, 1812, pp. 1587-98; *ibid.*, April 3, 1812, pp. 1601-14; *ibid.*, April 4, 1812, pp. 2262-64.

[26] *Ibid.*, April 9-14, 1812, pp. 202-04; *ibid.*, April 1-4, 1812, pp. 1617-23; *ibid.*, April 14, 1812, pp. 2269-70. Despite these restrictions, coasting vessels, especially from the southern states, continued to ship flour to Canada. See Joseph Whipple to Gallatin, June 20, 1812, Albert Gallatin Papers (Library of Congress).

[27] See, for example, Gallatin to Thomas Coles, April 28, 1812, General Records of the Department of the Treasury; and Coles to Gallatin, April 29, May 2, and May 6, 1812, *ibid.*

[28] See Dallas to Gallatin, April 5, 1812, Gallatin Papers.

[29] *Annals of the Congress*, 12 Cong., 1 sess., April 2, 1812, pp. 188-89; *ibid.*, April 30, 1812, p. 223; *ibid.*, May 5, 1812, p. 226; *ibid.*, May 6, 1812, pp. 228-35; *ibid.*, May 8, 1812, p. 237; *ibid.*, May 12, 1812, p. 239.

importation fared no better in the House. A bill engineered by Cheves and Lowndes that would suspend the law temporarily was postponed and never taken up again. Later, when the House had the war bill under consideration, Massachusetts Federalist Josiah Quincy moved to make the repeal of nonimportation coincident with the declaration of war, but his amendment was also voted down.[30]

There were some opponents of nonimportation, like John Sevier of Tennessee, who would not vote to suspend the law as long as the nation was at peace. In the hope of picking up these votes, Cheves introduced a bill shortly after the declaration of war that would permit the importation of British-made goods that were considered essential and could not be produced domestically. Cheves defended his bill as a means of securing tax relief, and he produced a letter from Gallatin showing that several classes of proposed war taxes— including the hated internal duties—could be dispensed with if the nonimportation law were modified. The House, however, voted to postpone the bill by a 63 to 58 margin.[31] Postponement carried only with the support of about a third of the Federalists, who would not vote for partial suspension merely to raise revenue to finance a war they opposed. The following day Massachusetts Republican William M. Richardson offered a resolution calling for the unconditional repeal of nonimportation. This time all the Federalists supported the proposal, but it failed when Speaker Clay cast a tie-breaking vote against it.[32]

The defeat of the various proposals to suspend or repeal the nonimportation law showed that the Republican majority in Congress was determined to bring Great Britain to terms not only by employing armed force but by continuing the policy of economic coercion as well. Clay spoke for the majority when he called the restrictive system "a powerful auxiliary of the war." Clay conceded that the nation might be defeated on land and sea. "But if you cling to the restrictive system," he said, "it is incessantly working in your favor," and, if persisted in, it "would break down the present Ministry, and lead to a consequent honorable peace."[33] Calhoun spoke for the other side. He rejected the notion "that if the non-importation act is continued, we shall have a speedy peace." Calling this a "delusive hope," he claimed the restrictive system would "debilitate the springs of war." Calhoun said he was mortified to hear— even from some of those who supported the war—"that it is only by restriction that we can seriously affect our enemies." If this were true, Calhoun asked, then why declare war? "Is it to be an appendage only of the non-importation act. If so, I disclaim it."[34] Although Calhoun and others wanted to jettison the restrictive system, the Republican majority in Congress clearly did not agree.

[30] *Ibid.*, April 10, 1812, pp. 1313–14; *ibid.*, June 4, 1812, pp. 1633–34. Josiah Quincy's proposal was in accord with Federalist expectations that the restrictive system would be repealed once war was declared. See Donald R. Hickey, "The Federalists and the Coming of the War, 1811–1812," *Indiana Magazine of History*, LXXV (March 1979), 74.

[31] *Annals of the Congress*, 12 Cong., 1 sess., June 19, 1812, pp. 1511–12; *ibid.*, June 23, 1812, pp. 1533–34; *ibid.*, June 24, 1812, pp. 1542–44.

[32] *Ibid.*, June 25, 1812, pp. 1544–46.

[33] *Ibid.*, 12 Cong., 2 sess., Dec. 7, 1812, pp. 299–300.

[34] *Ibid.*, 12 Cong., 1 sess., June 24, 1812, p. 1541.

Once it had disposed of proposals to modify the nonimportation law, Congress turned to the subject of enemy trade. This was a complex and murky issue over which opinion varied greatly. There were many Americans, merchants and farmers alike, who opposed any enemy trade act that was likely to limit their wartime economic opportunities. Timothy Pitkin of Connecticut, for example, spoke for Federalist merchants when he tried to convince Congress that no law was necessary because the treason clauses in the Constitution covered the subject. Likewise, Robert Wright of Maryland spoke for Republican export farmers when he insisted that the common law was sufficient to deal with the matter.[35] On several occasions Jefferson, who was in retirement at Monticello, reminded President Madison how important it was to keep these farmers happy. "To keep open sufficient markets," he said, "is the very first object towards maintaining the popularity of the war." Toward this end, Jefferson was willing to sanction a broad range of trade with the enemy under special licenses.[36] Madison was more cautious. He had no objection to American farmers feeding British troops in Europe, but he preferred to rely on neutral bottoms for transportation, believing that the use of licenses was "pregnant with abuses of the worse sort."[37] Madison's solution would please American farmers but was unlikely to satisfy those merchants who were dependent on the export trade.

On June 23, 1812, Calhoun introduced a limited enemy trade bill that merely prohibited the export of military and naval stores and provisions to British North America. In its journey through Congress, however, this bill was amended so much that it was salvaged only by a vote of reconsideration.[38] As finally enacted into law, the bill prohibited not only the export of stores and provisions to Canada but also any seaborne trade with the British Empire. In addition, it established safeguards to prevent British ships under neutral flags from trading in American ports, and it barred Americans from accepting British licenses to trade in British ports. As a concession to American merchants and farmers, the law did not prohibit the use of British licenses to trade in non-British ports.[39]

The nonimportation and enemy trade acts closed most avenues of trade with the British Empire and should have prevented American merchants from

[35] *Ibid.*, June 30, 1812, pp. 1568-69; Bradford Perkins, *Castlereagh and Adams: England and the United States, 1812-1823* (Berkeley, 1964), 9.

[36] Jefferson to Madison, April 17, June 24, and Aug. 5, 1812. *The Writings of Thomas Jefferson*, ed. Andrew A. Lipscomb and Albert E. Bergh (20 vols., Washington, 1903-1905), XIII, 140, 173, 183.

[37] Madison to Jefferson, April 24, 1812, *Writings of James Madison*, ed. Hunt, VIII, 189; *Annals of the Congress*, 12 Cong., 1 sess., Nov. 5, 1811, p. 14. See also Lawrence S. Kaplan, "France and the War of 1812," *Journal of American History*, LVII (June 1970), 38; Brant, *James Madison*, VI, 104.

[38] *Annals of the Congress*, 12 Cong., 1 sess., July 3, 1812, pp. 314-16; *ibid.*, July 5-6, 1812, p. 319; *ibid.*, June 23, 1812, p. 1532; *ibid.*, June 27, 1812, pp. 1560-61; *ibid.*, June 29, 1812, pp. 1563-64; *ibid.*, June 30, 1812, pp. 1568-70; *ibid.*, July 1-2, 1812, pp. 1570-74.

[39] This act is printed in *ibid.*, July 6, 1812, pp. 2354-56. In this version a crucial word—"such" —is omitted from section 7 so that the law appears to prohibit the use of British licenses to trade with *any* port in the world. For a more accurate version, see "An Act to prohibit American vessels from proceeding to or trading with the enemies of the United States, and for other purposes," ch. 129, 1 Stat. 778 (1812).

bringing their property home from Britain and her dependencies. Events in England, however, were to determine otherwise. On June 23, five days after the United State had declared war but a month before news of this development had reached England, the British government suspended the Orders in Council. This apparently paved the way for the restoration of normal trade relations because the American government had earlier said that it would lift nonimportation if the orders were rescinded. American merchants in England, however, were reluctant to ship their property home without official sanction because their goods would be confiscated if for some reason the president chose to continue nonimportation.

Seeking guidance, a group of merchants approached Jonathan Russell, the ranking American diplomat in London. Russell advised them to assume that nonimportation would indeed be lifted. Accordingly, those merchants who already held British-made goods began to ship them to America, while those who held bills of exchange drawn on British firms began to convert their funds into merchandise. When news of the declaration of war reached England at the end of July, the merchants again asked for Russell's advice, and again he advised them to ship their property home.[40]

American merchants in Britain's colonies—particularly in Canada and the Maritime Provinces—responded to the news of war by shipping their property home too. Thus by the end of 1812, merchandise had arrived from various parts of the British Empire whose prime value was about $18 million but whose actual value in the American market was close to $30 million. Since these goods had arrived in violation of the nonimportation law, all were seized by customs officials. The administration sought to keep the shipments under government seal, but federal judges working closely with sympathetic customs officials in Maryland, New York, and New England released the goods under their jurisdiction on bond. Gallatin was dismayed by this development but decided that in fairness to merchants elsewhere the rest of the merchandise should be released as well. As a result, the government was left holding about $18 million in penal bonds and about $5 million in duty bonds.[41]

Normally, the administration might have prosecuted for the full value of the penal bonds, but under the circumstances the merchants seemed entitled to more sympathetic treatment. Most had sent their goods home before learning of the declaration of war, and all their shipments had the stamp of approval of the American charge d'affaires in London. After due consideration, the administration decided to cancel half the value of the bonds and to prosecute for the balance or at least to insist that the merchants loan the government an equivalent sum. The secretary of the treasury had authority to remit fines and

[40] *Annals of the Congress*, 12 Cong., 2 sess., [Nov. 1812], pp. 1267–68.

[41] *Ibid.*, 12 Cong., 2 sess., Nov. 18, 1812, pp. 1253–54; Lemuel Trescott to Gallatin, July 4, 1812, Gallatin Papers; Peter Sailly to Gallatin, July 7, 1812, *ibid.*; Samuel Buell to Gallatin, July 12 and Aug. 8, 1812, *ibid.*; Gallatin to Sailly, Aug. 6, 1812, *ibid.*; and Gallatin to Larkin Smith, Oct. 6, 1812, *ibid.* Although customs officials were generally sympathetic to the importers, some district attorneys—notably Nathan Sanford of New York— tried to put the merchants to as much expense as possible in order to increase their own fees. See letter from "A friend to Jefferson and Madison Administrations" to Madison, Oct. 14, 1812 (with a note by Gallatin appended), James Madison Papers (Library of Congress).

forfeitures, but because of the scope of the problem the administration decided to seek congressional approval first.[42]

While the administration pondered its course of action, merchants were organizing to secure full cancellation of the penal bonds. Merchants from all along the Atlantic seaboard petitioned Congress for relief, and those in the larger cities sent representatives to Washington to defend their interests.[43] The merchants received a sympathetic hearing from many congressmen. The Federalists favored their claims, not only because they traditionally supported the merchants and opposed the restrictive system, but also because they could see no reason for bilking the merchants to pay for an unjust war.[44] Many Republicans supported the merchants as well, believing that they already had suffered enough and ought to be conciliated now that the country was at war.[45] The most outspoken member of this group was Cheves. Convinced that the merchants already had paid more than their fair share of taxes, he said: "I would rather see the seamen of the country impressed on the ocean and our commerce swept from its bosom, than see the long arm of the Treasury indirectly thrust into the pocket of the citizen through the medium of a penal law."[46] A majority of Republicans, however, believed that the merchants ought to be penalized because in violating the law they had aided the enemy and achieved a monopoly of British goods in the American market. Moreover, they regarded this source of revenue as an attractive alternative to internal taxes. As Richard M. Johnson of Kentucky put it: "I am unwilling to fix upon [the American people] internal taxation until it become[s] indispensable, nor to permit [the merchants] to monopolize advantages without an equivalent."[47]

The merchant bond problem was referred to the House Ways and Means Committee, which recommended in November 1812 that the matter be referred back to the secretary of the treasury. This was tantamount to accepting the administration's plan for dealing with the problem.[48] The House spent two weeks wrangling over the matter and, after defeating the committee's resolution and several alternatives, found itself at an impasse. In the meantime, the Senate had passed its own bill directing the Treasury Department to remit all

[42] *Annals of the Congress*, 12 Cong., 2 sess., Nov. 4, 1812, p. 15; *ibid.*, Nov. 18 and Nov. 23, 1812, pp. 1255, 1258; *ibid.*, Dec. 9, 1812, p. 332; *ibid.*, 4 Cong., 2 sess., March 3, 1797, pp. 2953–54; *ibid.*, 6 Cong., 1 sess., Feb. 11, 1800, p. 1437.

[43] *Ibid.*, 12 Cong., 2 sess., [Nov. 1812], pp. 1250–51, 1259–66; *ibid.*, Nov. 10–17, 1812, pp. 1268–76; Nathan Appleton, John Gore, Joseph Sewall, and Giles Lodge to New York merchants, Nov. 2, 1812, Jesse Appleton Papers (Massachusetts Historical Society).

[44] *Annals of the Congress*, 12 Cong., 2 sess., Dec. 14, 1812, pp. 379–93.

[45] *Ibid.*, Dec. 3, 1812, pp. 235–40; *ibid.*, Dec. 7, 1812, pp. 286–98, 305–09; *ibid.*, Dec. 8, 1812, pp. 310–21; *ibid.*, Dec. 9, 1812, pp. 339–49; *ibid.*, Dec. 4, 1812, pp. 241–56; *ibid.*, Dec. 15, 1812, pp. 395–402.

[46] *Ibid.*, Dec. 4, 1812, p. 254; Archie V. Huff, Jr., *Langdon Cheves of South Carolina* (Columbia, S.C., 1977), 70.

[47] *Annals of the Congress*, 12 Cong., 2 sess., Dec. 3, 1812, p. 234; *ibid.*, Dec. 4–5, 1812, pp. 256–63, 267–86; *ibid.*, Dec. 9, 1812, pp. 322–39; *ibid.*, Dec. 10, 1812, pp. 355–61; *ibid.*, Dec. 14, 1812, pp. 365–79.

[48] *Ibid.*, [Nov. 1812], pp. 198–99.

fines and forfeitures incurred in shipments from the British Isles. After insisting on some minor amendments, the House approved this plan by a three-vote margin.[49] Congress then passed two companion bills that provided for remitting fines and forfeitures incurred by merchants who had shipped their property home from other parts of the British Empire.[50]

The rejection of the administration's plan to raise money through the merchant bonds compelled Republican leaders to search for alternative sources of revenue. In order to avoid internal taxes, the House Ways and Means Committee recommended that the nonimportation law be partially suspended, and Cheves again introduced his bill to allow the importation of most British-made goods. To better enforce those restrictions which remained, the bill also contained several administration proposals that would prohibit judges from returning impounded goods on bond and provide for closer inspection of arriving ships.[51] Cheves pleaded with his colleagues to pass the bill, insisting that the disadvantages of nonimportation far outweighed the advantages. "It puts out one eye of your enemy, it is true," he said, "but it puts out both your own. It exhausts the purse, it exhausts the spirit, and paralyzes the sword of the nation."[52] Many Republicans, however, were reluctant to give up this method of coercion. At a town meeting in Baltimore, the Republican majority protested against any changes in the law, arguing that nonimportation was "amongst the most effectual means, which can be used to procure for our Country the blessings of a speedy and honorable peace, and of thus securing its permanent prosperity."[53] Federalists also refused to cooperate with Cheves. According to Thomas P. Grosvenor of New York, they regarded the measure as merely a device "to put further off the dooms-day of direct taxation."[54] Hence they joined with Republican restrictionists to strike out the main clause in the bill. The House passed the remnant, but the Senate showed little interest in the surviving provisions and allowed the measure to die.[55]

Congress next turned its attention to the subject of exports. The enemy trade act should have prevented most exports to the British Empire, but American citizens continued to supply British subjects in Canada and the West Indies, British armies in the Spanish Peninsula, and British fleets in American waters. Most of this trade was conducted under licenses, some 500 of which were issued by British military, naval, and civilian authorities in the first two and a half months of the war.[56] The English government was particularly in-

[49] *Ibid.*, Dec. 14, 1812, p. 33; *ibid.*, Dec. 11, 1812, pp. 364–65; *ibid.*, Dec. 23, 1812, pp. 450–51; *ibid.*, Jan. 2, 1813, p. 1316.

[50] *Ibid.*, Jan. 27, 1813, pp. 1321–22; *ibid.*, Feb. 27, 1813, pp. 1334–35. See also Gallatin to Cheves, Dec. 10, 1812, and James Lloyd to Gallatin, Feb. 19, 1813, Gallatin Papers.

[51] *Annals of the Congress*, 12 Cong., 2 sess., Feb. 15, 1813, pp. 1062–63. The bill is printed in *ibid.*, pp. 1064–65.

[52] *Annals of the Congress*, 12 Cong., 2 sess., Dec. 4, 1812, p. 249.

[53] Memorial of the Citizens of Baltimore, Feb. 18, 1813, Madison Papers.

[54] *Annals of the Congress*, 12 Cong., 2 sess., Feb. 26, 1813, p. 1138; *ibid.*, Feb. 23, 1813, p. 1112; *ibid.*, Feb. 20, 1813, pp. 1091, 1097.

[55] *Ibid.*, Feb. 20, 1813, pp. 1099–1100; *ibid.*, Feb. 23, 1813, pp. 1112–13.

[56] Walter R. Copp, "Nova Scotian Trade during the War of 1812," *Canadian Historical Review*, XVIII (June 1937), 145–46; W. Freeman Galpin, "The American Grain Trade to the Spanish Penin-

terested in facilitating trade to the peninsula because British armies there were dependent upon American provisions. Nor did the American government seek to hamper this trade. The enemy trade act did not prohibit the use of British licenses to trade in non-British ports, and the Treasury Department and Attorney General's office both ruled that the license trade with the peninsula did not violate the law.[57]

President Madison had never been very fond of the license trade, but throughout 1812 he had tolerated it. In early 1813, however, he became incensed when he learned that the British government had issued a circular encouraging officials in the West Indies and South America to favor Federalist New England with the licenses. This policy, Madison told Congress on February 24, 1813, was an "insulting attempt on the virtue, the honor, the patriotism, and the fidelity of our brethren of the Eastern States." In order to spare New England from temptation and to nullify the British policy, Madison asked Congress to outlaw the use of all foreign licenses.[58] The House readily complied with this request, but the bill was killed in the Senate.[59]

In his message to Congress, Madison also asked for a law to bar all exports from the United States in foreign bottoms. Although earlier he had favored the use of neutral vessels, the president was now convinced that most of these ships were "counterfeits" that were "covering and encouraging the navigation of the enemy."[60] The House had already rejected two proposals bearing on the export trade.[61] With Madison's recommendation now before it, however, the House was more amenable to some kind of limitation on exports. To meet the president part way, Calhoun introduced a bill on February 26, 1813, to bar the export of all provisions in foreign bottoms. As a concession to those farmers whose interests would be injured, the measure was to expire on July 1. House Federalists, who disliked the bill, succeeded in making it less palatable—and also more fair—by broadening the prohibition to include all exports. The House passed the bill in this form, but the Senate killed the measure just as it had killed the bill to prohibit the use of foreign licenses.[62]

The proposed ban on exports was the last trade restriction taken up by the Twelfth Congress. Madison's followers may well have breathed a sigh of relief when this Congress adjourned in early 1813, for it had been singularly unwilling to follow the president's lead on trade matters. Although the nonimportation law had been retained and an enemy trade act adopted, the Twelfth Congress had defeated the administration's plan for resolving the merchant bond problem and instead had provided for the full restitution of all mercantile

sula, 1810–1814," *American Historical Review*, XXVIII (Oct. 1922), 29–33; Alfred T. Mahan, *Sea Power in Its Relations to the War of 1812* (2 vols., Boston, 1905), I, 410–11. See also Perkins, *Castlereagh and Adams*, 9n.

[57] Gallatin to Smith, July 24, 1812, Gallatin Papers; Statement of John Purviance and William Pinkney, Oct. 12, 1812, in *Columbian Centinel* (Boston), Oct. 5, 1814.

[58] *Annals of the Congress*, 12 Cong., 2 sess., Feb. 24, 1813, pp. 1116–17.

[59] *Ibid.*, March 3, 1813, p. 121; *ibid.*, March 1, 1813, pp. 1150–51.

[60] *Ibid.*, Feb. 24, 1813, p. 1117.

[61] *Ibid.*, Nov. 6, 1812, pp. 142–44; *ibid.*, Dec. 1–3, 1812, pp. 212–17.

[62] *Ibid.*, March 3, 1813, p. 121; *ibid.*, Feb. 26, 1813, p. 1127; *ibid.*, Feb. 27, 1813, p. 1146; *ibid.*, March 2, 1813, pp. 1163–64.

property. Congress also had rejected administration-backed proposals to bar the return of impounded goods on bond, to provide for closer inspection of arriving ships, to outlaw the use of foreign licenses, and to prohibit exports in foreign bottoms. In each case these measures had gone down to defeat in the Senate.

Although the Twelfth Congress was generally unwilling to strengthen the restrictive system, the federal courts came to the administration's aid, at least on the question of enemy licenses. In May 1813, Joseph Story ruled in the *Julia* case that American vessels using an enemy license were subject to seizure and condemnation. Story's circuit court decision was based on the common law but was upheld by the Supreme Court.[63] Two months later the new Congress, which had more faith in trade restrictions than its predecessor, sustained this decision by passing a bill that outlawed the use of British licenses. Thenceforth, licensed American ships were treated like enemy vessels.[64]

The Thirteenth Congress was more sympathetic to restrictions than the Twelfth had been, but not because it had a larger Republican majority. On the contrary, the Federalists made substantial gains in the congressional elections of 1812, and the proportion of seats held by the Republicans declined from 74 to 64 percent in the House and from 83 to 77 percent in the Senate.[65] However, some Republican opponents of the restrictive system—like Van Cortlandt and Randolph in the House and Philip Reed and Stephen Bradley in the Senate— were not reelected. Others, like Representative Calhoun and Senator Thomas Worthington, were willing to give the restrictive system more support because of the growing evidence of smuggling and the nation's declining military fortunes. The Republican party, in other words, tended to close ranks on this issue. As a result, the new Congress was more receptive to trade restrictions than the old, although it still lagged far behind the president.

In the summer of 1813, President Madison expressed concern over the growing shipments of American provisions to British men-of-war stationed in American waters. Although the court decision and the license law should have curtailed the flow of supplies in American bottoms, many coasters defied the law. In addition, neutral vessels—many of which were actually British— continued to ply this trade as well. Madison was also angered by the British decision to blockade the middle and southern states while leaving New England's ports open. Determined to put an end to the flow of goods to the enemy and to the "insidious discrimination" practiced against the South Atlantic ports, the president sent a confidential message to Congress on July 20, 1813, recommending a ban on all exports from the United States.[66]

[63] William W. Story, ed., *Life and Letters of Joseph Story* (2 vols., Boston, 1851), I, 248; Charles J. Ingersoll, *Historical Sketch of the Second War between the United States of America, and Great Britain* (2 vols., Philadelphia, 1845–1849), II, 40.

[64] *Annals of the Congress*, 13 Cong., 1 sess., July 15, 1813, p. 55; *ibid.*, July 29, 1813, p. 485; *ibid.*, Aug. 2, 1813, pp. 2777–79.

[65] Because of resignations and contested elections, the political composition of Congress was rarely static in any session. The figures presented here are based on the total number of members who sat in Congress long enough to vote on at least one trade restriction. For the tests used to establish party affiliation, see Donald R. Hickey, "The Federalists and the War of 1812" (Ph.D. diss., University of Illinois, 1972), 341–49.

[66] *Annals of the Congress*, 13 Cong., 1 sess., July 20, 1813, p. 500.

The president's proposal was treated roughly in both chambers of Congress. The House referred the message to its Foreign Relations Committee, which recommended against an embargo. The House amended this report to favor the measure and referred the matter to a select committee of five proembargo Republicans. This committee duly reported an embargo bill, which the House passed over Federalist opposition. In the Senate, however, Federalists combined with Republican antirestrictionists to defeat the bill by a two-vote margin.[67] Two days later archrestrictionist Thomas Newton of Virginia suggested that, as an alternative, the House consider banning the export of provisions and naval stores in foreign bottoms. The House, however, refused to act on this proposal.[68] The House also refused to take action on a Senate bill that would have broadened the scope of the enemy trade act.[69]

Blocked in Congress, the administration fell back on its executive authority. On July 29, the day after the embargo was defeated, Secretary of the Navy Jones issued a general order to American naval commanders directing them to seize any vessel, whatever its flag, that was apparently proceeding to enemy ships in American waters or to enemy stations in American territory. A week later, the War Department issued a similar order to the nation's army officers.[70]

Administration officials in 1812–1813 had to contend not only with illegal exports but with illegal imports as well. Smugglers had employed various ruses to circumvent the nonimportation law before the war, and they continued to import British merchandise after hostilities had begun. This illegal traffic was greatest at the nation's peripheries: along the coasts of Massachusetts, Georgia, and Louisiana.

Massashusetts (including Maine) had such an extensive shoreline that it was impossible to keep all British goods out. Small coasters loaded with British merchandise from New Brunswick or Nova Scotia or transshipped from neutral vessels often landed their cargoes under cover of night. British merchants wishing to ship their merchandise directly to the United States could obtain neutral papers from obliging Swedish officials at St. Bart's in the Caribbean.[71] The merchants of Provincetown on the tip of Cape Cod were deeply involved in the illegal import trade. A local revenue official told the Boston collector that "his Inspecters dare not now attempt to search Stores or Houses there, for smuggled Goods, as the mass of the population are interested in their concealment, and so far from giving assistance, threaten such opposition as renders the attempt . . . futile."[72]

Amelia Island, a Spanish possession at the mouth of the St. Mary's River in Florida, was the principal source of British goods for people living in Georgia and other southern states. Shortly before the war, Gallatin received reports

[67] Ibid., 12 Cong., 2 sess., Feb. 23, 1813, pp. 98–101; ibid., Jan. 2, 1813, pp. 500–04.
[68] Ibid., 13 Cong., 1 sess., July 30, 1813, pp. 486–87.
[69] Ibid., June 28–30, 1813, pp. 36–39; ibid., July 1, 1813, p. 382.
[70] Ibid., July 29, 1813, pp. 2544–45; Order of Secretary of War, Aug. 5, 1813, in Niles' Weekly Register, IV (Aug. 14, 1813), 386.
[71] Whipple to Gallatin, June 20, 1812, Gallatin Papers; Henry A. S. Dearborn to Jones, Sept. 21, Oct. 22, and Oct. 30, 1813, General Records of the Department of the Treasury; J. Clason to Madison, Dec. 17, 1813, Madison Papers.
[72] Dearborn to Jones, Dec. 16, 1813, General Records of the Department of the Treasury.

"that British goods to an immense amount have been imported into Amelia Island, with the view of smuggling the same into the United States."[73] Most of this merchandise was no doubt ferried into the country in American or neutral ships.

Lake Barataria, with its ready access to the sea, was the funnel through which British goods flowed into Louisiana. Smugglers and pirates operated openly on this lake, and neither group was above using force against customs officials. The collector at New Orleans repeatedly asked for federal assistance, but Washington officials could do little but recommend that the state supply the muscle to enforce the laws.[74] Because trade was the lifeblood of New Orleans, state officials were not enthusiastic about helping. "I will not dissemble," Acting Secretary of the Treasury Jones told the New Orleans collector in 1813, "that whilst the inhabitants of Louisiana continue to countenance this illegal commerce and the Courts of justice forbear to enforce the laws against the offenders, little or no benefit can be expected to result from the best concerted measures."[75]

When Congress reconvened in late 1813, President Madison again sought to strengthen the restrictive system. The continued evasion of the trade laws and the failure of American arms in Canada had convinced him of the need to broaden the nation's commercial war against the enemy. In a confidential message sent to Congress on December 9, the president said: "To shorten, as much as possible, the duration of the war, it is indispensable that the enemy should feel all the pressure that can be given to it." Toward this end, Madison recommended four new restrictions. To halt the flow of supplies to British armies in Europe and Canada and to British fleets in American waters, he recommended an embargo. To tighten the nonimportation system, he suggested that certain products customarily manufactured in the British Empire— such as rum or woolen and cotton goods—be barred from American ports altogether. Moreover, to prevent the British from fraudulently using neutral flags, he asked Congress to require that the master, supercargo, and at least three-quarters of the crew of foreign vessels trading in American ports be citizens or subjects of the country under whose flag they sailed. Finally, Madison recommended that the ransoming of captured ships and cargoes be outlawed because this practice often served as a cover for trading with the enemy.[76]

The day after Madison's message was read, Felix Grundy of Tennessee introduced a bill from the House Foreign Relations Committee that provided for laying an embargo. Brushing aside Federalist objections, House Republicans

[73] Gallatin to Abraham Bessent, March 17, 1812, ibid.; A. J. Bulloch to Gallatin, Sept. 12, 1811, ibid.

[74] Thomas H. Williams to Gallatin, March 15, 1812, Gallatin Papers; Thomas H. Williams to James Wilkinson, March 14, 1813, Records of the Office of the Secretary of War, RG 107 (National Archives); Jones to P. T. Du Bourg, Aug. 24, 1813, General Records of the Department of the Treasury.

[75] Jones to Du Bourg, Sept. 27, 1813, General Records of the Department of the Treasury.

[76] Annals of the Congress, 13 Cong., 2 sess., Dec. 9, 1813, pp. 2031-32. Ransoming captured vessels was common practice, especially in Long Island Sound. See Coles to Gallatin, July 27 and July 31, 1813, General Records of the Department of the Treasury.

passed the bill by a substantial majority.[77] The Senate, which had killed so many other restrictive proposals—including the previous summer's embargo —was more cooperative this time. This was mainly because three Republicans —William Branch Giles of Virginia, David Stone of North Carolina, and Joseph Anderson of Tennessee—dropped their opposition to the embargo to appease public opinion at home.[78] Once again, Federalist objections were dismissed, and the bill passed essentially unchanged.[79]

This law was far more comprehensive than any previous commercial restriction. All ships were embargoed in port and the export of all goods and produce prohibited. The coasting trade was outlawed except within bays, rivers, sounds, and lakes. Fishing and whaling vessels might go to sea, but only after posting heavy bonds. Government officials were given extensive powers to enforce the law, and the penalties for violation were heavy.[80]

The law was so sweeping that it proved an embarrassment to both the administration and Congress. A week after the measure became law, Treasury Secretary Jones sent a circular to all customs collectors interpreting section ten of the law, which appeared to sanction the seizure of goods on the vaguest of suspicions. Jones told the collectors to impound goods only if circumstances clearly indicated that a violation of the law was intended.[81] Likewise, to relieve some of the unexpected misery caused by the embargo, Congress passed special legislation authorizing Nantucket to trade with the mainland and enabling coasters trapped away from home to return to their native ports.[82]

Even though the administration finally got the embargo it had sought, Congress proved unreceptive to Madison's other restrictive proposals. Most congressmen were unwilling to go as far as the president, especially after the British truce ship *Bramble* arrived in December 1813 with news that Napoleon had been defeated at Leipzig. This shifted the balance of power on the continent to England and her allies, putting an end to Napoleon's Continental System. With most of northern Europe now open to British ships, the restrictive system lost much of its raison d'etre.[83] The news from Europe doomed Madison's hope of shoring up the restrictive system. Although bills were intro-

[77] *Annals of the Congress,* 13 Cong., 2 sess., Dec. 11, 1813, pp. 2033–34, 2048–53.

[78] Jeremiah Mason to Jesse Appleton, Dec. 21, 1813, in George S. Hillard, *Memoir and Correspondence of Jeremiah Mason* (Cambridge, 1873), 70–71.

[79] *Annals of the Congress,* 13 Cong., 2 sess., Dec. 15, 1813, pp. 551–54; ibid., Dec. 16, 1813, p. 561.

[80] *Ibid.,* Dec. 17, 1813, pp. 2781–88. This law was apparently well enforced during the short time it was in operation. The chief violators were American privateers. The officers of these vessels sometimes discharged their crews, sold their provisions abroad, and brought home return cargoes disguised as captured merchandise. See Dearborn to Jones, Jan. 4, 1814, General Records of the Department of the Treasury.

[81] Jones to customs collectors, Dec. 24, 1813, in *Niles' Weekly Register,* V (Jan. 29, 1814), 353–54.

[82] *Annals of the Congress,* 13 Cong., 2 sess., Dec. 29, 1813, p. 564; ibid., Jan. 12–15, 1814, pp. 573–76; ibid., Feb. 21–22, 1814, pp. 636–39; ibid., Jan. 14, 1814, pp. 936–39; ibid., Jan. 18, 1814, pp. 1048–54; ibid., Jan. 23, 1814, pp. 1115–22; ibid., Feb. 3, 1814, p. 1228; ibid., Feb. 5–8, 1814, pp. 1247–55; ibid., Feb. 9, 1814, pp. 1265–69; ibid., Jan. 25, 1814, pp. 2788–89; ibid., March 4, 1814, pp. 2793–95.

[83] John Bach McMaster, *A History of the People of the United States, from the Revolution to the Civil War* (8 vols., New York, 1883–1913), IV, 222–24.

duced to enact his other proposals, in each case they died in one house or the other.[84]

The European news not only killed prospects for additional restrictions, but also added to the growing clamor for the repeal of those measures already on the books, particularly the embargo and nonimportation laws.[85] By the spring of 1814, Madison himself could see the wisdom of repeal. Accordingly, on March 31 he sent a special message to Congress recommending that both laws be rescinded. Goods that were actually owned by the enemy, he said, should continue to be barred from the American market. Moreover, to prevent an unfavorable balance of trade from draining coin from the nation's banks, he asked Congress to prohibit the export of specie.[86]

Madison's message caused an uproar among the most devoted restrictionists in Congress. According to one senator, there was "much pouting and no small degree of execration, I understand, among his zealous supporters, some of whom, I am told, will oppose the Bill with bitterness in the House, as they certainly do out of it."[87] Nevertheless, on April 4, 1814, Calhoun introduced two bills from the House Foreign Relations Committee to repeal the embargo and nonimportation laws while continuing the ban against importing British-owned goods and to prohibit the export of specie. Congress passed the first bill by a substantial majority, although it was opposed by thirty-five die-hard Republican restrictionists in the House and four in the Senate.[88] The bill to bar the export of specie, on the other hand, went down to defeat in both houses.[89]

With the repeal of the embargo and nonimportation laws, Americans gained a significant expansion in their legal right to trade. The restrictions that remained prohibited only trading directly with the enemy, importing enemy-owned goods, or using enemy licenses. Yet just as the United States was lifting its own barriers to foreign commerce, England was moving to seal off this trade. In early 1813 the British had established a blockade of the middle and southern states, a blockade that was subsequently extended to other ports as well. Thus, by the spring of 1814 the entire American coast from Maine to Louisiana was nominally under blockade.[90]

The British blockade did not prevent all American trade, nor was it designed to achieve this end. British officials were willing to permit Americans to supply their subjects in Canada as well as their armies and navies in the New World. Moreover, they were willing to encourage trade that was profitable to British merchants in particular or beneficial to the empire in general. Anglo-

[84] Annals of the Congress, 13 Cong., 2 sess., Dec. 30, 1813, p. 565; ibid., Jan. 31, 1814, p. 613; ibid., March 22, 1814, pp. 678–79; ibid., April 18, 1814, pp. 773–74; ibid., Dec. 30, 1813, pp. 816–17; ibid., Jan. 22, 1814, pp. 1131–32; ibid., Jan. 25–26, 1814, pp. 1134–35, 1144; ibid., Feb. 1, 1814, p. 1199; ibid., Feb. 3, 1814, p. 1229.
[85] Ibid., March 2, 1814, pp. 1771–72; ibid., March 14, 1814, pp. 1866–68.
[86] Ibid., March 31, 1814, p. 694.
[87] Nicholas Gilman to Pierre Van Cortlandt, Jr., April 3, 1814, Correspondence of the Van Cortlandt Family of Cortlandt Manor, 1800–1814, ed. Jacob Judd (Tarrytown, N.Y., 1978), 696.
[88] Annals of the Congress, 13 Cong., 2 sess., April 12, 1814, p. 741; ibid., April 4, 1814, pp. 1946–48; ibid., April 7, 1814, pp. 2001–02.
[89] Ibid., April 16, 1814, p. 773; ibid., April 13, 1814, pp. 2017–18.
[90] Newhampshire Sentinel (Keene), May 14, 1814; Mahan, Sea Power, II, 9–11.

American commerce was particularly brisk along the Florida and Canadian borders. The British government made no effort to interdict this trade, and American officials were unwilling or unable to stop it either.

Amelia Island served as the entrepôt for the export of southern agricultural produce and the import of English manufactured goods. By late 1814 there were close to fifty vessels anchored there taking on American produce. Although these vessels sailed under neutral flags, most were owned by British subjects, and an Englishman residing on the island served as the agent for several companies in Great Britain as well as for American firms based in Richmond, Norfolk, and Charleston.[91]

The northern trade with Canada was of even greater scope. This traffic took two forms: overland from New York, Vermont, and New Hampshire, and by sea from Massachusetts, Maine, and New Hampshire. Overland traders frequently used inland waterways, such as Lake Ontario and the St. Lawrence River, or Lake Champlain and the Richelieu River. Some merchants outfitted privateers on these waters and made dummy captures of goods purchased by their agents in Montreal. Others informed on themselves and by applying to the courts for relief still made a profit. Trade across Lake Champlain was even facilitated by a neutral vessel flying Spanish colors. The seaborne trade, on the other hand, was centered in Halifax until the British captured eastern Maine in 1814, when Castine became the entrepôt. Swedish vessels ran goods from Castine up the Penobscot River to Hampden, and from there the merchandise was distributed to other parts of upper New England. This traffic ran heavily against the United States, draining specie from the nation's banks. Nevertheless, the American government condoned the trade as long as it was conducted in neutral vessels.[92]

The administration took little interest in the Canadian trade early in the war. The War Department even replaced an army officer in Eastport, Maine, who had irritated local inhabitants by enforcing the enemy trade act too zealously.[93] After Napoleon's defeat in 1814, however, British veterans began to pour into Canada, and the trade quickly assumed alarming proportions. Customs officials increased their efforts to halt this trade, but their powers were severely limited. They could not legally search every type of vehicle or

[91] J. V. Mein to John Rutledge, Jr., July 23, 1814, John Rutledge Papers (Southern Historical Collection, University of North Carolina, Chapel Hill); Naval Officer to Department of the Navy, Nov. 11, 1814, in Mahan, Sea Power, II, 185–86; Channing, History of the United States, IV, 540–41.

[92] Chilton Williamson, Vermont in Quandary: 1763–1825 (Montpelier, Vt., 1949), 273; William D. Williamson, The History of the State of Maine (2 vols., Hallowell, Maine, 1832), II, 654; H. N. Muller III, "A 'Traitorous and Diabolical Traffic': The Commerce of the Champlain-Richelieu Corridor during the War of 1812," Vermont History, XLIV (Spring 1976), 78–96; Copp, "Nova Scotian Trade," 141–55; John Chandler to Secretary of War, Nov. 21, 1814, Records of the Office of the Secretary of War; Martin Jennison to Secretary of War, March 23, 1814, ibid.; George Ulmer to William King, Jan. 10, 1813, ibid.; Jacob Ulmer to John Brooks, Sept. 29, 1814, American State Papers: Documents, Legislative and Executive of the Congress of the United States, Class V: Military Affairs (4 vols., Washington, 1832–1860); III, 859; Whipple to Dallas, Dec. 21, 1814, General Records of the Department of the Treasury; J. A. Douglas to Dearborn, Nov. 23, 1814, ibid.

[93] Williamson, History of the State of Maine, II, 639. The officer was George Ulmer.

make preventative seizures, and the enemy trade act did not clearly define those goods that could not be shipped overland to Canada. Revenue officials in Vermont were also hampered by a series of unfavorable judicial decisions. The state courts ruled that inspectors employed by customs collectors had no authority to make seizures and were liable to damages even if merchandise they seized was condemned and forfeited.[94]

Federal attorneys could offer little help to customs collectors because it was difficult to indict and almost impossible to convict smugglers. In some border areas the judges themselves had a stake in the trade.[95] Moreover, the attorney general had ruled that it was not illegal to visit the enemy, and thus the prosecution had to prove that the suspect had passed on "supplies" or "improper information."[96] Canny New England farmers found they could circumvent the law by marching their livestock to the border, where a Canadian cohort would entice the animals across with a basket of corn. And anyone who tried to stop this trade risked a damage suit or worse. In late 1814, for example, two revenue officers were killed and two others wounded in the performance of their duties near Belfast, Maine.[97]

By the time Congress reconvened in September 1814 for its last session during the war, the Canadian trade had become a public scandal. Republican James Fisk of Vermont, whose own state was as guilty as any, lost no time in offering a resolution to strengthen the enemy trade law.[98] Congress, however, devoted the next two months to more pressing matters, waiting for the administration to take the lead on the trade issue. Finally, on November 19, the new secretary of the treasury, Dallas, sent a report to the House Ways and Means Committee outlining the government's enforcement problems and recommending legal remedies.[99]

Armed with Dallas's report, the Ways and Means Committee drew up a new enemy trade bill, which John W. Eppes of Virginia introduced on December 7. This bill passed both houses over Federalist opposition and was signed into law on February 4, 1815.[100] The new law gave government officials more extensive powers than any previous trade restriction, including the enforcement act of 1809 and the embargo of 1813. It authorized customs officials to search without warrant any land or water craft or any person suspected of trading with the enemy and to seize any goods suspected of being illegally imported or of being on their way to the enemy. Upon securing a warrant, customs officials could also search any building suspected of containing goods which were likely to be shipped to the enemy or which might have been imported from enemy

[94] *Annals of the Congress*, 13 Cong., 3 sess., Nov. 19, 1814, pp. 757–61.
[95] Zebulon Pike to Secretary of War, Feb. 15, 1813, Records of the Office of the Secretary of War.
[96] Richard Rush to U.S. Attorney for Massachusetts, July 28, 1814, in *National Intelligencer* (Washington), Oct. 3, 1814.
[97] *Niles' Weekly Register*, VIII (Supplement), 149; H. Storrs to Secretary of War, Oct. 21, 1814, Records of the Office of the Secretary of War; Dearborn to Dallas, Nov. 14, 1814, General Records of the Department of the Treasury.
[98] *Annals of the Congress*, 13 Cong., 3 sess., Sept. 22, 1814, p. 305.
[99] *Ibid.*, Nov. 19, 1814, pp. 757–61.
[100] *Ibid.*, Jan. 25–27, 1815, pp. 181–85; *ibid.*, Jan. 28, 1815, pp. 187–88; *ibid.*, Dec. 7, 1814, p. 757; *ibid.*, Jan. 5, 1815, pp. 1033–38; *ibid.*, Jan. 9, 1815, pp. 1061–62.

territory. Inspectors were classified as customs collectors, and all such officials were empowered to raise posses and rendered virtually immune to damage suits. The penalties set in 1812 for trading with the enemy were increased, and no one was permitted to hover about the border without proper business, or to visit enemy territory, an enemy ship, or an enemy camp in American territory without a presidential or gubernatorial passport.[101]

The enemy trade act of 1815 was the last restrictive measure enacted during the war. It was never fully tested because it expired with the restoration of peace two weeks after it became law.[102] Whether it would have put an end to trade with the British may be doubted. The enforcement machinery of the customs department remained primitive, and people living on the frontiers showed a remarkable determination to keep profitable avenues of trade open. Nevertheless, the law was a suitable capstone to the wartime restrictive system because it showed how far Congress had to go to stamp out illegal trade.

As the passage of this law suggests, the Thirteenth Congress was more willing than the Twelfth to follow the administration's lead on trade matters. Even so, administration officials had been unable to secure approval for a number of trade restrictions they favored. The Thirteenth Congress had refused to enact an embargo in the summer of 1813, although it had adopted this measure later that year. The Thirteenth Congress also had obliged the administration by enacting legislation to ban the use of enemy licenses and to put an end to trade with the enemy. However, the House had killed one administration proposal to outlaw the importation of rum and woolen and cotton goods, and the Senate had blocked two others to prohibit the ransoming of captured vessels and to prevent the return of impounded goods on bond. Moreover, both houses had defeated administration-backed bills to bar the export of specie.

Excluding the two ninety-day preliminaries, the United States employed five trade restrictions during the War of 1812. The nation entered the war with a nonimportation law and adopted a mild enemy trade act in July 1812, a license act in August 1813, and an embargo in December 1813. The nonimportation law and the embargo were repealed in April 1814, but a new and more stringent enemy trade act was adopted in February 1815.

These commercial restrictions were designed to prevent British armies and fleets in the New World from receiving vital supplies and to bring Britain to terms through economic coercion. They failed to achieve either end. The Governor General of Canada, Sir George Prevost, reported in the summer of 1814 that two-thirds of the British army in Canada was eating American beef. According to the customs collector at Portsmouth, New Hampshire, so many cattle were driven into Lower Canada that summer that beef prices in New England rose from four to six dollars a hundredweight.[103]

---

[101] *Ibid.*, Feb. 4, 1815, pp. 1899–1906.

[102] Many provisions of this law were reenacted shortly after the war to prevent smugglers from evading the tariff laws. See *ibid.*, March 3, 1815, pp. 1945–49.

[103] George Prevost to Lord Bathurst, Aug. 27, 1814, in Adams, *History of the United States*, VII, 146; Whipple to Campbell, Aug. 23, 1814, General Records of the Department of the Treasury; Copp, "Nova Scotian Trade," 145. The price of beef also may have risen because of purchases of the American army.

British fleets were equally well supplied. Royal officials sometimes threatened coastal towns with destruction if their needs were not met, and what they could not buy they simply took. But the use of force was rarely necessary. Admiralty procurers paid handsomely in specie for the provisions they needed, and there was no shortage of volunteers to supply their wants. Chesapeake Bay, Long Island Sound, and Vineyard Sound teemed with tiny coasters ferrying supplies to the British fleets stationed there. American merchants reaped direct profits from this trade and could also use the enemy licenses they received to protect their regular coasting trade.[104] Although most of this illegal trade was clandestine, the harbor at Provincetown, Massachusetts, was openly used by British ships seeking provisions or refuge from winter storms. According to one report, small coasters and fishing vessels regularly carried "Fresh Beef, vegitables, and in fact all Kind of supplies" to these ships.[105]

Nor did the trade restrictions win any concessions from the British government. Great Britain refused to surrender to America's demands during the war, and when the British dropped their own territorial aims at the Ghent negotiations in 1814, it was not because of American economic pressure. Rather, it was because of the lack of military progress in America, unfavorable diplomatic developments in Europe, and domestic discontent over taxes.[106]

Given their faith in trade restrictions, it is hardly surprising that the Republicans sought to coerce Great Britain economically during the war and to prevent her from receiving vital supplies from the United States. Nor is it surprising that so many Americans in this freewheeling commercial age were willing to defy their own government in the pursuit of profits. Yet, in the contest between the government and the merchants, the advantage almost always lay with the latter. With extensive land frontiers in the north and south, and an accessible maritime frontier on the east, the administration had neither the manpower nor the legal machinery to stamp out this trade. Revenue officials were not only outmanned and outmaneuvered but had to contend with damage suits and hostile courts as well.[107]

[104] Caesar Rodney to Gallatin (with enclosure), March 20, 1813, Gallatin Papers; Cushing Eells to Madison, May 17, 1813, Madison Papers; William Hawkins to James Iredell, Oct. 8, 1813, James Iredell Papers (Perkins Library, Duke University, Durham, N.C.); Coles to Jones, Jan. 27, 1814, and Dearborn to Campbell, April 2, 1814, General Records of the Department of the Treasury; Dallas to John Hawes, Dec. 3, 1814, ibid.; Independent Chronicle (Boston), July 5, 1813; Copp, "Nova Scotian Trade," 145; Channing, History of the United States, IV, 532, 535.

[105] Dearborn to Jones, Dec. 16, 1813, General Records of the Department of the Treasury.

[106] Perkins, Castlereagh and Adams, 96–100, 110–11, 132; A. L. Burt, The United States, Great Britain, and British North America from the Revolution to the Establishment of Peace after the War of 1812 (New Haven, 1940), 362–63; Fred L. Engelman, The Peace of Christmas Eve (New York, 1962), 283.

[107] No doubt the vast majority of illegal traders escaped detection, but if fines and forfeitures are any indication of the level of activity, there was far more smuggling during the War of 1812 than during the long embargo. In 1808 and 1809 the government collected $38,000 and $74,000 in fines and forfeitures. The corresponding figures for 1813, 1814, and 1815 were $175,000, $264,000, and $190,000. See Adam Seybert, Statistical Annals Embracing Views of the Population, Commerce, Navigation, Fisheries, Public Lands, Post-Office Establishment, Revenues, Mint, Military and Naval Establishments, Public Debt and Sinking Fund of the United States of America (Philadelphia, 1818), 395.

In the end, the various trade restrictions had little effect on Britain's war effort and did little to improve America's bargaining position. Instead, they recoiled upon the United States, reducing American trade and depriving the federal government of much-needed customs revenue. Thus, just as the barrenness of the Treaty of Ghent revealed the failure of the war, so too did it reveal the failure of the restrictive system.

Monetary Aspects of the Treasury Notes of the War of 1812

Donald H. Kagin

Between 1812 and 1815, the United States authorized five Treasury note issues. In total, over $36 million in denominations of $3 to $1000 were emitted. The last issue included small circulating notes in denominations of less than $100. Because of the shortage of adequate circulating medium and revenue to conduct the War of 1812, these notes proved to be extremely useful as they were transferable by delivery and receivable for duties, taxes, and public use at par plus accrued interest. They also served as interest-bearing reserves for banks since they were convertible into any kind of money and bore interest simultaneously. The success of the Treasury notes was demonstrated by the fact that they were fully subscribed and accepted by the banks and merchants. In addition, the small Treasury note issues of 1815 indirectly served to increase the circulating medium of the country. They were used to buy goods and services by individuals, pay custom duties by merchants, and acted as cash reserves for banks, preventing bank notes from being discounted. They thus became the first circulating paper currency issued by the United States after ratification of the Constitution.

IT may come as a surprise to some that the first paper money circulated in the United States after the Constitution was issued in 1815—preceding by 46 years the Demand Notes of 1861. Occasioned by the War of 1812 and the expiration of the charter of the First Bank of the United States, a total of five Treasury note issues were authorized, the last including small circulating notes of less than $100 denominations. Perhaps because of their relative numismatic scarcity and the paucity of information concerning them, there has been little discussion of these precedent-setting remnants of the United States's fiscal past. The circumstances surrounding these first Treasury note issues are discussed here; appendix tables provide systematic quantitative detail.

PRE–1812 FINANCE

From the adoption of the Constitution until the War of 1812, the U.S. Government had financed its deficits by borrowing. Until 1792 major loans were procured primarily from Holland or in funding operations, while temporary or small "bridge" loans were obtained from consor-

Journal of Economic History, Vol. XLIV, No. 1 (Mar. 84). © The Economic History Association. All rights reserved. ISSN 0022-0507.

The author is president of Kagin's Numismatic Investment Corporation, 4 Embarcadero, San Francisco, California 94111.

tiums of prominent capitalists or from the four existing private banks, such as the Bank of North America or the Bank of New York.[1] Once the Bank of the United States was established in 1791, that institution superseded the others in becoming the primary lender of short-term funds to the government (although a few small loans at high rates were sold directly to the public during this period).

Almost all revenues, for whatever purpose, came largely from customs. Between 1801 and 1806 this income amounted from $11 to $13 million annually, with a small supplemental income from the sale of lands, an exiguous revenue with which to fight a world power like Britain.[2]

Until the financial emergencies occasioned by the War of 1812, the U.S. government was firmly committed to a hard money policy. Article 1, sec. 8, paragraph 5 of the Constitution gave Congress the power "to coin money, regulate the value thereof and of foreign coin and fix the standard of weights and measures."[3] While the question of paper money was vigorously debated by members of the Constitutional Convention, both a proposal for the inclusion of a provision authorizing its issue by the national government, and one prohibiting issue were defeated. The political thinking of the time, succinctly expressed by James Madison, was that authorizing the use of paper money might lead to mass abuse and proliferation, reminiscent of the vastly depreciated Continental Currency. Outright prohibition of paper currency, however, would tie the government's hands in case of a temporary emergency. The Constitution, therefore, resolved the dilemma by specifying nothing. It did proscribe, however, the issue of "bills of credit" by the states and, by implication, the same issue by the federal government.

GALLATIN'S RESTRICTIVE POLICY

During the Republican administrations of Jefferson and Madison, the architect of the government's fiscal system was Treasury Secretary Albert Gallatin. Gallatin's major objective was the reduction of the national debt to the exclusion of all other considerations. Up to 1808, Gallatin declined to augment treasury receipts except by temporary loans even though a year later he belatedly conceded the possible need

[1] *Laws of the United States Concerning Money, Banking, Loans, 1778–1909*, National Monetary Commission, compiled by Andrew T. Huntington and Robert J. Mawhinney, Doc. No. 480, Senate 61st Congress, 2nd Session (Washington, D.C., 1910), pp. 29–43.

[2] Albert Gallatin, "Report of the Finances 1807," *Reports of the Secretary of the Treasury of the United States*, Vol. 1 (Washington, D.C., 1837), p. 359, and A. J. Dallas, "Report of the Finances 1815," *Reports*, 2:45.

[3] Foreign coins officially circulated from 1793 until 1797, when a new law declared that only "Spanish milled dollars and parts thereof" were legal tender. This statute remained in effect until 1857.

for internal taxes.[4] It was not until early 1812 that Gallatin's optimism waned, and he intimated that the extraordinary impending expenses of the military and naval services would require funds considerably in excess of current revenue.[5]

With duty revenue down from $13.3 million in 1811 to $9 million in 1812 (mainly a result of the Embargo of 1807–1809) and with a corresponding increase to $22 million in expenditures, Gallatin suggested a 100 percent increase in the tariff. In his report, the Treasury Secretary justified this proposal on the ground that "this mode (increased duties) appears preferable . . . to any internal tax."[6] The result of this policy was the absence of any system by which internal revenues could be collected, an error in policy which Gallatin conceded in 1831 when he admitted that he should have recommended such taxes in 1812.[7]

CONGRESSIONAL WAR LOAN POLICY

Acting upon the Treasury Secretary's recommendation, Congress soon doubled the tariff duties. In February 1812 (four months before war was declared), the House Ways and Means Committee, realizing that merely doubling the tariff would not yield enough revenue, proposed a loan of $11 million which was enacted by a large majority of both houses of Congress on March 14, 1812.[8]

There is some disagreement as to the success of this loan. While only $0.6 million was subscribed to by the public in the first two months, by the end of the year, $8.1 million had been purchased mainly by the larger banks. The lack of enthusiasm for funded loans arose from New England's manifest lack of sympathy for the war coupled with Congress's failure to provide adequate means to pay interest. Thus, Gallatin was soon practically forced to issue Treasury notes.[9]

---

[4] Alexander Balinky, *Albert Gallatin, Fiscal Theories and Policies* (New Brunswick, 1958), pp. 180–88 and Albert Gallatin, "Report of the Finances 1809," *Reports*, p. 401. Also see "Report of the Finances 1811," *Reports*, p. 449.

[5] *Idem.*, "Report of the Secretary of the Treasury, 1811," *Reports*, p. 449. Also in the *Niles Weekly Register*, November 22, 1811 (Washington, D.C.), 2:232. In a letter to the Chairman of the House Ways and Means Committee, Ezekiel Bacon, Gallatin blames the poor state of the finance on the failure of Congress to recharter the Bank of the United States, upon which he had relied heavily for the U.S. government to obtain loans, and also for the Legislature's refusal to double the tariff. Albert Gallatin, "Letter to Ezekiel Bacon, January 10, 1812," *The Writings of Albert Gallatin*, ed. Henry Adams, Vol. I (New York, 1960), pp. 338–40.

[6] Ibid., p. 448.

[7] Albert Gallatin, *The Writings of Albert Gallatin*, ed. Henry Adams, 4 Vols. (Philadelphia, 1879), Vol. III, p. 5.

[8] Ezekiel Bacon, "Ways and Means Report of House, February 17, 1812," *American State Papers, Finance*, U.S. Congress, ed. Walter Lowrie, Vol. II (Washington, D.C., 1832), p. 539.

[9] Rafael A. Bayley, *National Loans of the United States from July 14, 1776 to June 30, 1880* (Washington, D.C., 1882), p. 48, and Henry Carter Adams, *Public Debts: An Essay in the Science of Finance* (New York; Privately printed, 1887), pp. 117–18.

FIRST TREASURY NOTES

Unable to sell long-term debt advantageously and lacking the First Bank of the United States to provide bridge financing, Gallatin recommended the use of Treasury notes. This was not altogether a new suggestion since Gallatin had mentioned that particular mode of public financing as early as February of 1810. Then, in response to an inquiry from the Ways and Means Committee ("Can any other resources, besides taxes and loans, be relied on for immediate revenue?"), Gallatin answered:

Treasury notes bearing interest, and payable to order one year after day, may be annually issued, to a moderate amount, and be put in circulation, both through the medium of banks and in payment of supplies.[10]

The Secretary of the Treasury further cautioned against possible abuses, but maintained that if kept within strict bounds, the notes would facilitate both the collection of the revenue and the loans themselves.

In a letter to Representative Ezekiel Bacon in January 1812, Gallatin repeated his willingness to rely on some use of Treasury notes:

Treasury notes, bearing interest, might to a certain extent be issued, and to that extent diminish the amount to be directly borrowed. The advantage they would have would result from their becoming a part of the circulating medium, and taking, to a certain degree, the place of bank-notes.[11]

This was the first statement by a U.S. Secretary of the Treasury in favor of a federal currency (that is, circulating Treasury notes).

Within six months Gallatin realized that the Treasury was in deep trouble and urged the House Ways and Means Committee to authorize $5 million, in $5\frac{2}{5}$ percent Treasury notes payable one year after date of issue. To enhance their acceptability, he proposed that the notes be receivable by the Treasury for all duties, taxes, or debts due the government.[12] He further recommended in a later message that the notes be fundable into bonds of the loan for which they were intended to be a partial substitute. This would have the double advantage of helping to sell bonds while keeping the issue of the notes within bounds.

DEBATE IN CONGRESS

A bill embodying these ideas was duly reported out of the Ways and Means Committee on June 12; a heated debate ensued. *Niles Weekly*

[10] Albert Gallatin, "Letter to John W. Eppes, February 25, 1810," *Writings*, II: 467–468.

[11] *Idem.*, "Letter to Ezekiel Bacon, January 10, 1812," *Writing*, II: 501. Also in *Letter from the Chairman of the Committee of Ways and Means to the Secretary of the Treasury with the Answer of the Secretary of the Treasury* (Alexandria, 1812), p. 14. Rare Book Room, National Archives, Washington, D.C.

[12] "Letter to Langdon Cheves, May 14, 1812," cited by John J. Knox, *United States Notes* (New York, 1848), p. 22.

Register reported that the controversy over the Treasury notes was the highlight of the legislative session.[13]

Every possible argument ever made against the use of paper money was voiced by the opponents of the bill: They claimed that the notes were not equal in value to gold or silver and would therefore not be taken by banks or people prejudiced against the government paper; that if received, they would circulate at a discount and would further subvert public and private credit; that to allow banks to deposit the notes with the Treasury in exchange for bank paper merely emphasized the description of the government paper; that as with the Continental Currency, these notes would greatly depreciate; that the very need to use them was a confession of impending bankruptcy, and finally; that if they had to be issued, there would have to be a direct tax in order to redeem them.[14]

Proponents of the bill, however, proved more pragmatic. To begin with, they argued, there was a shortage of an adequate circulating medium. Silver already was in short supply because shiny new coins were in demand in Latin America and abroad for the China trade, while gold was undervalued at the mint and hoarded, leaving little to be delivered for coinage. The alleged poor and depreciated quality of many bank notes (especially since the retirement of the Bank of the United States circulating notes), ensured that a soundly managed Treasury note currency would be a welcome addition to the U.S. economic system. Depreciation would be checked by their receivability for taxes and public use while their value would be sustained by the fact that the banks would hoard them as interest-bearing reserves.

The banks will be glad to receive these notes in exchange for their own; . . . the Treasury notes bear a *daily* interest and their own bear none at all. They are *immediately* convertible into any kind of money desired; for the banks always have customers who will use them in payment of bonds due the United States for duties, etc. They are thus better as deposits than specie—gold and silver; for gold and silver lie dormant in the vault—whereas the Treasury notes will be *active* capital, every hour becoming more and more valuable, and as fully competent to all the purposes of the banks as specie, because they will produce it.

From these brief remarks it will appear evident that Treasury notes, the moment they are issued, will be hoarded up by the banks, if they can get them. . . .[15]

The positive arguments, aided by the inability of the opposition to fill the Treasury by any other means, prevailed and the bill authorizing $5 million in Treasury notes passed the House on June 17 by a vote of 85 to 41.[16]

[13] *The Niles Weekly Register*, June 15, 1812, 2:279.
[14] *Annals of the Congress of the United States 12th Congress*, 1st Session, Vol. I (Washington, D.C., 1853) p. 1495–1510.
[15] Ibid. Also *The Niles Weekly Register*, June 13, 1812, 3:300.
[16] Ibid., pp. 1509–10.

Final enactment of the bill came on June 30, 1812, twelve days after war was declared.

TERMS AND SUCCESS

The law, which conformed with Gallatin's proposals, authorized the President to issue up to $5 million in denominations of $100 or more (although only $100 and $1,000 notes were actually issued). They were redeemable one year after issue at 5.4 percent, or 1½ cents a day per $100. All the notes were payable to order, transferable by delivery and assignment on endorsement, and more important, were receivable for duties, taxes, and payments for public lands at par plus accrued interest.[17]

The first issue of Treasury notes was quite successful. By the end of 1812, $3.5 million had been sold to or were contracted for by the banks, the majority of which were located in the Middle Atlantic states.[18] The rest of the bills were disposed of by December 1 of the following year, with New England absorbing a considerable portion of them. All notes, except for a few $100s, were redeemed by the end of 1814 and withdrawn from circulation.[19] Although the initial shock of the war had temporarily depressed the prices of public bonds during late 1812, the new loans and Treasury notes sold at par.[20] An editorial in *Niles Weekly Register* touted the new notes by stating, "This plan appears the most eligible that could possibly have been adopted, as it will mutually accommodate the Government and the people, and be advantageous to both."[21]

There is some question, however, whether these first notes actually circulated. Treasury Secretary Dallas in a letter to William Lowndes, Chairman of the House Select Committee investigating the chartering of the Second Bank of the United States, reported that the Treasury notes had met with opposition and had been willingly accepted only by

---

[17] Bayley, *National Loans*, pp. 48–49. Other major elements provided that 1) the notes were signed by persons designated by the President who were paid $1.25 for every note signed, 2) they were countersigned by the Comptroller of Loans for the state for which the notes were made payable, 3) the Secretary of the Treasury was authorized to borrow upon the security of the notes and pay them to the banks which would receive them at par, 4) interest ceased on the day of payment, and 5) strict penalties were imposed for counterfeiting.

[18] *Niles Weekly Register*, 3:350. Also see *Richmond Inquirer*, February 16, 1814, 2:2. The Treasury Reports, however, state that only $2.8 million were subscribed to by 1813. Davis R. Dewey, *Financial History of the United States* (New York, 1968), p. 137.

[19] "Register of Treasury Notes," Vol. 189, *Record Group 53*, National Archives (Washington, D.C.). Breen erroneously claims March 1813 as the final date of redemption.

[20] Albert Gallatin, "State of Finance, December 1812," *Finance*, II:580.

[21] *Niles Weekly Register* (July 4, 1812), 3:300. It should be noted that, as Walter Breen pointed out, the *Register* had a bias toward Wall Street. Walter Breen, "Promises, Promises," *Numismatic News Weekly*, January 1, 1974.

"necessitous creditors, or contractors in distress, or commissaries, quartermasters, and navy agents acting officially."[22] He went on to point out that even when received they were instantly used to make tax payments to the government, "thus disappointing and defeating the only remaining expectation of productive revenue."[23]

Niles Weekly Register, on the other hand, claimed that the banks were hoarding these notes.[24] No doubt these banks were using the new interest-bearing Treasury notes as reserves, thereby creating a corresponding increase in the money supply.[25] In either case, they were not freely circulating as hand-to-hand currency, which was scarcely surprising in view of the high denominations involved, the transfer-by-endorsement-only rule, and their utility as bank reserves.

NEW WAR LOANS

By the beginning of 1813 it became apparent that the war-loan policy heretofore pursued was hopelessly inadequate. With expenditures running $28.5 million more than receipts, new revenues were an urgent necessity.[26] Yet it was not until the middle of the year that Congress took any new steps to meet the Treasury's expenditures. Even President Madison refused to recognize the facts of life and in an incredibly myopic statement proclaimed that the Treasury receipts up to September of 1812 were "sufficient to defray all the demands of the Treasury . . . (and will) enable us to defray all the expenses of this year."[27]

As a result, instead of immediately implementing new tax programs, Congress, following Secretary Gallatin's monetary suggestions, authorized a new loan of $16 million on February 8. Realizing at the very least that there would be difficulties in selling these bonds, Congress left the rate of interest and sales price to the Secretary's discretion.

The resistance to this new loan was all but total. Even in Congress it was energetically attacked on the ground that no special fund had been set apart for its repayment, and that the war, for which great expenses were to be incurred, should never have been declared in the first

---

[22] A. J. Dallas, "Letter to William Lowndes, November 27, 1814," *Reports*, 1:244.

[23] Ibid.

[24] *Niles Weekly Register* (July 4, 1812), 3:300.

[25] Richard H. Timberlake, *Origins of Central Banking in the United States* (Cambridge, Massachusetts, 1978). Drawing upon statistical information compiled from J. Van Fenstermaker, *A Statistical Summary of the Commercial Banks Incorporated in the United States Prior to 1819* (Kent, Ohio, 1965), Timberlake concluded that "as banks increased their holdings of treasury notes, their own note issues could increase by multiples of the treasury notes obtained. Bank notes were thus used as hand-to-hand currency, and the treasury notes were used mainly as bank reserves in lieu of specie."

[26] "Receipts and Expenditures, from March 4, 1789 to December 15, 1815," *Finance*, 11:920.

[27] James Madison, "Fourth Annual Message, November 4, 1812," *Compilation of Messages and Papers of the President's 1789–1897*, Vol. I.

place.[28] Subscribers were not only quick to realize that there was no redemption fund, but that the war was going badly and would be worse yet if the British could finish off Napoleon and direct their undivided efforts at America. Moreover, Gallatin, frustrated with Congressional reluctance to follow his recommendations, disgusted with the open antagonism displayed by members of his own party, and sensing that it was too late to make the necessary fiscal amends, took a diplomatic leave of absence, thereby abandoning a Treasury mixed in total confusion.[29]

When the new loan was offered on March 12, and again on March 25, only $500,000 was subscribed to on the same terms—6 percent—as the previous loans.[30] The Government was accordingly compelled to sell the rest of the loan stock at a 12 percent discount. Even more embarrassing, the Treasury was forced to make the same concession of a 12 percent discount to those who had earlier purchased loans at par, such as Stephen Girard, David Parish, and John Jacob Astor. The revelation of this did nothing to improve the Treasury's prestige or credit.[31]

SECOND ISSUE OF TREASURY NOTES

The difficulties of floating the $16 million loan along with the necessity of having to borrow $19 million more forced another issue of Treasury notes. As suggested by Gallatin in December, Congress authorized the issue of $5 million in new Treasury notes to replace those of June 1812.[32] The Congressional debate was as arid as before with the bill passing the House 79 to 41.[33] The terms of issue were identical with the preceding notes, with the exception that these were to be redeemed by March 31, 1815, although in the actual event the last payment was not made until the fourth quarter of 1820.[34] Thus by the summer of 1813 the pattern of financing the war had been set; Congress would raise as much as it could in long-term loans and make up the difference by issuing Treasury notes. At the same time, nothing had been done to support this mass of floating currency which now approached $10 million, a sum equal to one year's peacetime revenue.

[28] Bayley, *National Loans*, p. 50.
[29] Gallatin, *Writings*, p. 196.
[30] William Jones, "State of Finance, June 1813," *Finances*, II: 1622–23.
[31] Bayley, *National Loans*, p. 50.
[32] Albert Gallatin, "Report of the Secretary of the Treasury December 1812," *Reports*, p. 469.
[33] Bayley, *National Loans*, p. 50.
[34] W. F. DeKnight, *History of the Currency of the Country and the Loans of the United States* (Washington, D.C., 1897), p. 47.

INTERNAL TAXES

It was at this time that Congress was compelled to consider internal taxes. On May 24, 1813, a full year after the outbreak of war, President Madison called a recalcitrant Congress into special session and told it that the time was long past due for producing a "well-digested system of internal revenue."[35] Spurred by the President's remonstrances and reluctantly recognizing the impossibility of raising all needed funds by borrowing, Congress halfheartedly passed a few direct levies.

There were, however, serious problems associated with collecting this revenue. As Gallatin had dismantled all the internal revenue machinery in 1801–1806, it took a year to collect even the small, inadequate amount legislated. Nor could the Treasury get any bridge financing in the interval. Anti-war proponents, especially in New England, balked at every effort to get them to help. Indeed, the Federalist New England press declared that no true friend of the country would be found among the subscribers to such loans. Opposition was so great that advertisements for war bonds in Boston papers had to promise anonymity to would-be subscribers.[36]

Government finances by the end of 1813 were in poor shape. Anti-war sentiments chilled bond sales as did the Congressional reluctance to provide revenue as backing. Moreover, the banks were either unable or unwilling to lend. Thus the Treasury was compelled to issue even more Treasury notes.

By 1814 the situation was critical. Not only had expenditures risen considerably, but revenue from import duties had drastically declined.[37] Once again Congress resorted to borrowing for its revenue. This time $25 million was authorized—the largest that had ever been attempted and this only after much spirited debate on the entire question of the war.[38] Three subscriptions were offered, each one failing worse than the one before. Discounts up to 20 percent including provisions for accepting subscriptions in Treasury and state bank notes, had to be provided. An additional provision required that if more favorable terms were granted, the same terms had be provided for any previous loans.[39]

[35] *Messages and Papers of the Presidents*, pp. 528–30. The direct tax amounted to $3 million and was assessed in 1814. For a useful table on these taxes, see Dewey, *Financial History*, p. 140.

[36] Gallatin, *Writings*, p. 201.

[37] Estimated expenditures at $43,350,000 and revenue at $16,000,000. Willliam Jones, "State of Finance", *Finance*, 2:651.

[38] Bayley, *National Loans*, p. 52.

[39] *The Richmond Inquirer* (May 7, 1814), 3:2, reported that by May 7, $10 million at 88 percent had been subscribed. In his report on Finances in December 1814, Dallas mentioned that proposals were invited on August 22, 1814 for $6 million at 6 percent; of this only $2,823,300 was subscribed; $100,000 at less than 80 percent; $2,213,000 at 80 percent; $510,300 at 80–88 percent. All but the $100,000 were accepted because there was no prospect of better terms and the money was indispensable. $410,000 of these contracts were reneged on by the banks. Special contracts for loans with the banks were unsuccessful. "Report on Finances December 1814," *Reports*, p. 528.

During the summer and fall of 1814 this latter provision led to considerable speculation and embarrassment, of which further depreciated the value of government stock and marked the lowest point in the government's effort to finance the war.

THIRD ISSUE OF TREASURY NOTES

The same March 14, 1814 Act authorizing a $25 million loan also provided for $10 million of Treasury notes, half of which were considered to be part of the $25 million loan. In his report of December 1813, acting Treasury Secretary Jones urged the further use of Treasury Notes:

> The certainty of their (Treasury notes) reimbursement at the end of the one year, and the facilities they afford for remittances and other commerical operations have obtained for them a currency which leaves little reason to doubt that they may be extended considerably beyond the sum of five millions of dollars, hitherto authorized to be annually issued.[40]

By that time it would appear from the Congressional debates and statements by the Secretary of the Treasury that public policy called for the issue of no more Treasury notes than could be supported by fiscal revenues. Should more be issued, they would be in lieu of or as an adjunct to stock loans.

Although there was an attempt to amend the bill, which would have prohibited the issuance of notes in denominations of more than $100 or less than $5, only three denominations—$1,000, $100, and $20—were issued.[41] The use of a $20 note, even though interest bearing, was a significant departure from previous practices, for they were clearly intended to serve as a *de facto* hand-to-hand currency. Proof of their intended circulation can be found in Tennessee Governor William Blout's October 12, 1814 letter to Treasury Secretary Dallas in which the former stated that he had endorsed $100,000 in Treasury notes, "so that they may go into circulation." Blout subsequently delivered the notes to Postmaster General W. B. Lewis to distribute.[42]

The third issue did not satisfy public demand for a circulating currency, and the general suspension of specie payments outside New England forced a review of Treasury policy. In October, John Eppes, Chairman of the House Ways and Means Committee, solicited from the new Treasury Secretary, Alexander J. Dallas, suggestions on how to

---

[40] William Jones, "Report of Finance, December, 1813." *Reports*, p. 502. There is no corroborating evidence that an annual issuance of $5,000,000 was ever authorized.

[41] Bayley, *National Loans*, p. 52.

[42] "Estimates and Statements by the Registrar of the Treasury," Vol. 145. General Records from the Central Treasury Records, Records of the Bureau of the Public Debt, *Record Group 53*, p. 24.

324

revive and maintain the public credit.[43] Dallas's perspicacious if lengthy reply mentioned the prevailing apprehension over the government's credit and characterized circulating currency as a "copious source of mischief and embarrassment." Exportation and hoarding by individuals of specie, he explained, had considerably diminished the fund of gold and silver coin. Even worse, the suspension of specie payments had "suddenly broken the chain of accommodation that previously extended the credit and circulation of the notes which were emitted in one State into every State of the Union. . . ." "There exists at this time," he continued, "no adequate circulating medium common to the citizens of the United States."[44]

As a remedy he suggested that "under favorable circumstances and to a limited extent an emission of Treasury notes would probably afford relief."[45] He did point out, however, that the notes were "an expensive and precarious substitute for coins and bank notes." The Secretary concluded that the notes might be issued under the auspices of a national bank. "But whether the issues of a paper currency proceed from the national Treasury or from a national bank, the acceptance of the paper . . . must be forever optional with the citizens."[46] In other words, under no circumstances did the Secretary of the Treasury want the notes to be legal tender, although they should be receivable for all public dues and taxes—that is, they were partial legal tender.

In an attempt to establish a uniform national currency, the president called Congress into special session on September 19, 1814. Congress ducked the question, however, when it authorized a $3 million loan subscribable in Treasury notes. No stock was issued under this act, but $1.45 million was borrowed from the banks under special contracts.[47]

FOURTH TREASURY NOTE ISSUE

It was not long after the enactment of this measure that Congress decided to issue more Treasury notes in preference to another issue of stock. With little or no debate, both Houses authorized another issue of $7.5 million. These notes were to be in lieu of Treasury notes authorized by previous loan acts. This December 26, 1814 Act also authorized an additional $3 million of notes to defray the war expenses for 1814. Most of the bill's provisions were identical to the Act of March 4, 1814 and resulted in the issue of a total of $8,318,400.[48] Historian John J. Knox

[43] John W. Eppes, "Letter to Secretary of the Treasury Dallas, October 14, 1814," *Reports*, p. 234.

[44] A. J. Dallas, "Letter to John Eppes, October 17, 1814," *Reports*, pp. 234–36.

[45] Ibid., p. 236 and p. 266; also in *Niles Weekly Register* (Dec. 24, 1814).

[46] *Niles Weekly Register* (Dec. 24, 1814).

[47] *Idem.*, "Report of the Secretary of the Treasury, November, 1815," *Reports*, II:13.

[48] Bayley, *National Loans*, p. 56.

reported that $20, $50, and $100 notes were issued (although there are no records of $50 bills having ever been printed).

It was the unenviable duty of the Secretary of the Treasury to report early in 1815 that the Treasury was virtually empty and without credit. Some $98 million had been borrowed during the war, leaving a funded debt of $68 million, while a deficit of $40 million was estimated for 1815.[49] New loans had been solicited abroad but none was available, fiscal revenues were far from adequate, and a uniform circulating medium still had not been achieved. A new monetary expedient was necessary.[50]

SMALL TREASURY NOTES

In the report of the House Ways and Means Committee (October 10, 1814), Chairman Eppes argued that in order to secure the circulation of Treasury notes, small denominations should be issued. They should be payable to bearer, transferable by delivery, and receivable in all payments for public lands and taxes. Internal revenues should be pledged for payment of the interest, and the notes should be fundable into 8 percent stock or redeemable in specie after six month's notice by the government.[51] This was a radical departure for Dallas, who had never before suggested non-interest-bearing notes as a national circulating medium. These views were repeated at the end of November, when Eppes wrote to Dallas about the proposed National Bank. In his December 1, 1814 reply, Dallas stated that with specie payments suspended a National Bank would be difficult to establish and that the "introduction of a national circulating medium . . ." was necessary.[52] Later that month Dallas reported that "Notes of a smaller denomination than heretofore issued have been prepared. . . ."[53] This is revealing because no Congressional resolution for small Treasury notes was forthcoming until the next month.

On December 11, 1814, Representative Hall of Georgia introduced a resolution that directed the Committee on Ways and Means to inquire into the expediency of authorizing the Secretary of the Treasury to issue notes convenient for circulation. In one of his five resolutions, Hall proposed that these bills "shall be a legal tender in all debts."[54] The House agreed to consider Mr. Hall's resolutions with the exception of the legal tender clause. By a vote of 42 to 95, the first attempt to discuss

[49] Ibid., p. 57.

[50] Albert Gallatin, "Letter to Monroe, October 26, 1814," *Writings*, 1:642.

[51] "Report by John W. Eppes, October 10, 1814," in John Jay Knox, *United States Notes* (New York, 1884), p. 32.

[52] *Niles Weekly Register* (Dec. 2, 1814), 8:266.

[53] A. J. Dallas, "Report on the Finances, December, 1814," *Reports*, p. 529.

[54] *Annals*, 13:3 (Nov. 12, 1814), p. 557.

a legal tender currency was defeated. The entire small Treasury note issue was briefly commented upon and soon laid on the table by a large majority.[55]

A subsequent resolution of January 7, 1815, was introduced by Representative Law of Connecticut. He proposed to make Treasury notes receivable in payment for fines, forfeitures, penalties, and taxes owed to the United States. It seems that, contrary to the reports of the Treasury Secretary, many of the tax collectors were refusing Treasury notes. In spite of this request, the resolution was laid on the table by a vote of 61 to 56.[56] Another motion of Silas Wright of New York that the Ways and Means Committee "look into the expediency of issuing Treasury notes of small denominations" was also laid on the table.[57]

Five weeks later, Secretary Dallas in his annual report, made a proposal similar to Eppes's and Hall's resolutions. Treasury notes amounting to $15 million, he suggested, should be issued in denominations of $100 and upwards bearing interest of 5.4 percent, and those of less than $100 but not less than $20 would either be payable to order and bear interest, or be payable to bearer and not bear interest. Notes under $20 would all be payable to bearer and circulate without interest.[58]

A bill incorporating Dallas's recommendations was introduced in the House on January 30th and referred to the Ways and Means Committee. The bill passed the House on February 11, the Senate on February 21, and became law on February 24, 1815.[59]

As originally proposed, there would have been an issue of $15 million redeemable in five annual installments of $3 million each, for which land tax was pledged. Connected with this scheme was a proposed interest-bearing loan of $25 million. During debate, the bill was amended to reverse the amounts of bonds and Treasury notes, so that there were now to be $25 million of the latter.

While the bill was being considered, Eppes wrote Dallas requesting additional information. Once again Dallas urged the use of small Treasury notes in preference to state bank notes as the national medium of exchange. He warned Eppes, however, that, "considering the outstanding amount of Treasury notes, any new issue should be made to rest upon a basis that will enable the government to employ it both as a circulating medium and as the means of raising money in aid of the revenue."[60]

The treaty of peace with England was received a few days before the

[55] Ibid., p. 559.
[56] *Annals*, 13:3 (Jan. 7, 1815), p. 1045. Also in the *Richmond Inquirer* (Jan. 11, 1815), 2:3.
[57] *Annals*, 13:3 (Dec. 13, 1814), p. 884.
[58] A. J. Dallas, Official Letter, Appendices to Report on Finances October, 1814, *Reports*, pp. 268–69.
[59] *Annals*, 13:3 pp. 1111, 1124, 1133, 1146, 1148, 1177, 258.
[60] A. J. Dallas, "Letter to John Eppes, February 20, 1815," *Reports*, pp. 273–75.

bill passed (rendering it no longer necessary as a war measure), but it was enacted as a means of paying off the arrearages of the war. It was also intended to give a circulating medium to the country superior to state bank notes. Notes issued under this act were denominated "small" if under $100, and "large" if $100 or over. Unlike the first three acts of the series, these notes were not chargeable upon the sinking fund, nor were they payable out of any money in the Treasury not otherwise appropriated as in the previous Act of December 26, 1814. Instead, they rested entirely upon the provision making them fundable into stock. The small notes were fundable in 7 percent stock, the large ones in 6 percent certificates.

Of the $25 million authorized, only $4,979,400 in $100 notes and $3,392,994 in small notes consisting of $3, $5, $10, $20, and $50 notes were actually emitted.[61] The small Treasury notes, however, were re-issued, so that a gross total of $9,070,386 was disbursed.[62]

SUCCESS OF THE TREASURY NOTES

Just how successful were the Treasury notes as a circulating currency? Secretary Dallas in his December 1815 report stated that the notes issued prior to February 24, 1815 were of denominations too high to serve as current medium of exchange. Although the Treasury Secretary was correct in this assumption, the large Treasury notes ($100 and over) indirectly served to increase the circulating money stock. Their utility as short-term (one year) interest earning assets with virtual legal tender status made them extremely desirable as bank reserves. With bank notes no longer refundable in gold (except in New England), and specie no longer available, as economic historian Richard H. Timberlake has pointed out, "what could be more attractive to a bank than reserve assets that are legal tender and yet returned interest income as part of the bank's investment portfolio?"[63]

There were, of course, the usual skeptics. The small Treasury notes, fundable at an interest of 7 percent (though of a convenient denomination for common use, Secretary Dallas asserted), "would be converted into stock almost as soon as they were issued."[64] Even President Madison in his veto message on the Bank of the United States stated on January 30, 1815 that no "adequate advantage arises to the public credit from the subscription of Treasury notes."[65] A more thorough analysis,

[61] William H. Crawford, "Report of the Treasurer," *Reports*, p. 125. The first known transaction in small Treasury notes was $150,000 ordered by Johanthan Smith, Cashier of the Bank of Pennsylvania on June 28, 1815. "Domestic Letters 1814–1816," Vol. 1, *Record Group 53*, Archives (Washington, D.C.), p. 108.

[62] Knox, *United States Notes*, p. 37.

[63] A. J. Dallas, "Report on the Finances, December, 1815," *Reports*, pp. 24–25.

[64] James Madison, "Veto Message, January 30, 1815," *Compilation*, Vol. 1, p. 556.

[65] Richmond *Examiner* (Dec. 31, 1814), 3:2 & 3.

however, reveals not only that the Treasury notes were successful in helping the public credit and as bank reserves, but also that the small Treasury notes did indeed circulate.

An editorial in the *Richmond Examiner* of December 31, 1814 urged more people to accept Treasury notes. They were superior, the writer claimed, to the Exchequer bills of England, and already many people were accepting the notes.[66] The same paper reported on January 10 that the Treasury notes "are rising fast in our market. They were sold yesterday, not merely at their nominal value, but with the interest added."[67]

Both John Jay Knox, writing in 1884, and numismatic scholar Walter Breen assert that the $100 Treasury notes depreciated some 8 to 10 percent. This may have been true in New England against their specie-controlled notes, but published accounts in various papers do not generally bear this out. Indeed, the May 20, 1815 issue of the *Baltimore Sun* stated, "Treasury notes are now in demand and will soon, everywhere, bear a premium nearly equal to the amount of interest they may have accrued on them, on account of the uncommon sums speedily to be paid for duties at our custom-houses."[68] That same day, *Niles Register* quoted a report in the *Boston Patriot* that, "Treasury notes pass at par in Canada. A Canadian will give his hundred silver dollars for a Treasury note of that sum."[69] This is a powerful testimonial when it is remembered that it emanated from the most intensely anti-war city in the nation.

Another editorial in the *Niles Register* surmised that the Boston brokers were angry with the Secretary of the Treasury for not letting them fund Treasury notes on their terms. The editor concluded that this was the reason the Boston brokers had tried to discredit the notes by claiming they had depreciated as a result of the war. This assertion by the Boston merchants, the editor continued, was not a credible one since the duties and taxes for which the Treasury notes were payable (and therefore useful) could retire double the amount of notes in the people's hands.[70] Since the demand for these notes was twice the supply, there was certainly no reason for them to depreciate, but instead they should have and did command a premium.

Two of the best pieces of evidence to support the success of the Treasury notes can be found in two advertisements. In the *Richmond Examiner* of June 7, 1815, a certain Hugh Chambers offered: "Par will be given for One Hundred Thousand Dollars worth of Treasury

[66] Report in the *Niles Weekly Register*, 7:3361.
[67] Breen, in *Numismatic News Weekly*, January 15, 1974, p. 34; and Knox, *United States Notes*, p. 38. Knox makes the additional statement that "after deducting discounts and depreciation," the notes were rapidly funded after December 1814.
[68] Report in the *Niles Weekly Register* (May 20, 1815), 8:203.
[69] Ibid., p. 214.
[70] Ibid., p. 215.

Notes."[71] The other advertiser—this time in the *Washington National Intelligencer* of August 15—offered to pay a premium for Treasury notes.[72] If merchants, albeit speculators, could pay a premium for Treasury notes, it can hardly be asserted that the bills were severely depreciated. Indeed, the only notices in the media that suggested a depreciation in the Treasury notes were found in Boston where a certain banker stated that the 7 percent Treasury notes (and probably all non-New England paper) go at an 8½ to 9 percent discount.[73] This was logical because New England never suspended specie payments. Since specie was the conventional medium, and only New England bank notes were specie-convertible, all other non-convertible money would naturally be discounted. It was also true that premiums were paid for U.S. notes in terms of depreciated bank notes, while the Treasury notes were at a discount for specie.

There is also substantial evidence that the small Treasury notes circulated as currency. The *Niles Register* of June 24, 1815 reported:

Treasury Notes. This species of money, so convenient as a general circulating medium, is above par at Philadelphia and in all parts of the southward and westward—nearly at par in New York, and rapidly rising in Boston. . . .
It is probable that Treasury Notes will immediately become the circulating medium of all the Union; and, perhaps, sound policy may dictate the issue of a large number of small amounts, like bank notes, without interest, as well as to supply the general demand. . . .[74]

In a directive on August 15, 1815, the Treasury Secretary mentions that the circulating medium for local use at that time was cents, Treasury notes and local bank notes.[75] A Boston paper reported a notice by Dallas on December 23, 1815 that because of the suspension of specie payments there was no hard money in the Boston Loan Office to pay off its debts; there were only Treasury notes, which were the "major circulating medium now and the way people pay taxes and duties."[76] In his own December 1815 report, Dallas submitted a table showing $1,365,000 in small treasury notes being sold at a premium of from 2½ percent to 4 percent—a high premium to pay for non-interest-bearing notes convertible into 7 percent stock when other certificates, such as treasury loan certificates, were available at an effective rate of 27 percent.[77] A logical explanation is that these small Treasury notes were valuable as a circulating medium throughout the country, that faith was rising in government bonds, and that funds were needed for customs.

[71] Richmond *Examiner* (June 7, 1815), 3:4.
[72] Washington *National Intelligencer* (August 15, 1815), 1:3.
[73] *Niles Weekly Register* (Dec. 4, 1815), 3:2.
[74] Ibid.
[75] Ibid. (Aug. 26, 1815), p. 439.
[76] Report in the *National Intelligencer* (Jan. 5, 1815), 3:2.
[77] A. J. Dallas, "Report on the Finances, December, 1815," *Reports*, p. 26.

Walter Breen has asserted that $3,218,950 worth were exchanged for stock by October 1, 1815, representing 95 percent of those notes issued.[78] He concludes from these figures that the notes did not circulate, but were immediately funded. But Breen's figures are incorrect. By October 1, 1815 a total of $2,282,850 of notes were issued and only $1,860,000 were paid in for duties and taxes or used in funding. From these figures we realize not only that 81 percent of the small Treasury notes were used for paying taxes or used in funding, but that the notes served a currency purpose by being tax receivable. Furthermore, of the original $2,282,850 in Treasury notes, over $1.3 million went to pay for war supplies and another $645,000 were turned over to pay the dividends on the public debt. The remaining $335,000 was actually sold at premiums of 1¼ to 4 percent (presumably vis-à-vis depreciated bank notes). It is certainly more plausible that most of these notes either circulated, were used as back reserves, or were turned in for taxes, rather than funded at 7 percent as Breen believes.

It is doubtful that the non-interest-bearing small Treasury notes saw much use as bank reserves either. Individuals would deposit the notes or merchants would use them to pay customs duties. The banks would sometimes use the Treasury notes as cash reserves to prevent their own notes from being discounted. Thus the small Treasury notes would again be recycled into the community, acting just as planned—a circulating substitute to specie.

Despite the usefulness of the Treasury notes, Secretary Dallas still viewed them as an embarrassment to the fiscal operations of the government, made necessary by the extraordinary expenses of war. In his December 1816 report, the Secretary recommeded that since temporary loans could be obtained from the newly chartered Second Bank of the United States, "the re-issue of Treasury Notes, of all description, should be discontinued." He therefore suggested that "an appropriation be made during the present session of Congress for the reimbursement of the whole of the Treasury notes issued under the act of the 24th of February, 1815. The Treasury notes issued under the preceding laws have either been reimbursed, or provisions made for that object, during the last quarter of the year."[79]

Again, following the Secretary's recommendations, Congress passed an act on March 3, 1817, repealing all previous Treasury note acts and prohibiting further issue of notes. This law remained in effect for almost 20 years, during which time the legal circulating medium consisted of Spanish and Mexican dollars, occasionally other foreign silver, and notes of the Second Bank of the United States.[80]

Thus ended the first experiment with circulating Treasury notes, one

[78] Ibid., p. 52.
[79] Ibid, p. 75.
[80] Breen, in *Numismatic News Weekly* (January 15, 1974), p. 34.

necessitated (like most currency issues throughout history) by a curren-
cy-hungry war. The introduction of these first Treasury notes caused an
expansion of the money supply and a corresponding rise in prices by
acting as bank reserves. Their utility as legal tender issues, however,
prevented their massive depreciation as was the case for some of the
earlier Colonial issues, the Continental notes of the American Revolution, and later Union and Confederate Civil War notes.

APPENDIX TABLE 1
WAR OF 1812 LOANS
(Amounts in millions of dollars)

Issue Date	Authorized Amount	Amount Sold	Authorized Rate	Rate Sold	Retroactive Discount Clause
March 14, 1812	11.0	11.0	6%	Par	No
February 8, 1813	16.0	16.0	6%	88 1/3%	No
August 2, 1813	7.5	7.5	6%	88 1/4%	No
March 24, 1814	25.0	16.0	6%	85%	Yes
November 15, 1814	3.0	1.5	No Limit	Special Contract	Yes
December 26, 1814	10.0				Yes
February 24, 1815	15.0		7%	95%	Yes
March 3, 1815	18.46				Yes

Source: Rafael A. Bayley, *National Loans of the United States from July 14, 1776 to June 30, 1880*
(Washington, D.C., 1882).

APPENDIX TABLE 2
AMOUNT OF TREASURY NOTES ISSUED
(in dollars)

Issue Date	Amount Issued
June 30, 1812	5,000,000
February 25, 1813	5,000,000
March 4, 1814	10,000,000
December 26, 1814	8,318,400
February 24, 1815	4,969,400 Large Notes
	3,392,994 Small Notes
TOTAL	$36,680,794

Source: "Domestic Letters, 1814–1816," Vol. 1, *Record Group 53*, National Archives (Washington, D.C.).

APPENDIX TABLE 3
AMOUNT OF TREASURY NOTES OUTSTANDING AS OF JANUARY FIRST
(in dollars)

Year	Amount Outstanding
1813	2,835,500
1814	4,907,300
1815	10,646,480
1816	17,619,625
1817	3,450,000

Source: "Domestic Letters, 1814–1816," Vol. 1, *Record Group 53*, National Archives (Washington, D.C.).

APPENDIX TABLE 4
TREASURY NOTE BILL PROVISIONS

Issue Date	Authorized Emission	Amount Sold	Where Issued
June 30, 1812	$5,000,000	$ 5,000,000	Boston, New York, Baltimore, Philadelphia, Washington
February 25, 1813	5,000,000	5,000,000	
March 4, 1814	5,000,000 & 5,000,000 as part of any loan act of that session	10, 000,000	Boston, New York, Philadelphia, Washington, Richmond, Charleston, Savannah
December 26, 1814	7,500,000 as part of loans of 3/24 & 11/15/14 & 3,000,000	8,318,400	
February 24, 1815	25,000,000 Large	4,969,400	
	Small	3,392,994	
	+ reissue	9,070,386	

Note: The large Treasury notes were 7 3/8 by 3 7/8 inches. They were printed on silk-fibered, watermarked paper by MURRAY, DRAPER and FAIRMAN.
Source: "Domestic Letters, 1814–1816," Vol. 1., *Record Group 53*, National Archives (Washington, D.C.).

APPENDIX TABLE 5
AMOUNT OF TREASURY NOTES SOLD AND REDEEMED BY YEAR

Year	Amount Issued	Amount Redeemed
1812	$2,835,500	
1813	6,094,500	
1814	8,297,280	$5,800,000
1815	12,200,000	2,700,000
1816	4,300,000	9,700,000

Source: Alexander J. Dallas, "Report of the Secretary of Treasury, 1815," *Reports of the Secretary of the Treasury of the United States* (Washington, D.C., 1837), Vol. 1, p. 15.

APPENDIX TABLE 6
LIST OF SMALL TREASURY NOTES SOLD

Percent Premium	Amount	Amount of Premium
4	$300,000	$12,000.00
3¼	19,600	637.00
3	89,400	2,682.00
2¾	55,000	1,512.50
2½	281,000	7,025.00
2¼	5,000	112.50
2	340,000	6,800.00
1¾	10,000	175.00
1½	91,000	1,365.00
1¼	74,000	925.00
1¼ with one months' interest deducted	100,000	659.37
	$1,365,000	$33,893.37
Deduct sundry charges incurred:		1,785.73
Net amount of premium received by the United States:		$32,107.64

Source: "Domestic Letters, 1814–1816," Vol. I., *Record Group 53*, National Archives (Washington, D.C.).

Notes and Documents

Enlisted Men in the
United States Army, 1812-1815:
A Preliminary Survey

J.C.A. Stagg

IN recent years historians have shown a renewed interest in the subject of war in early America. Their studies, generally, have pursued two types of inquiry. One, focusing on the Revolutionary period and the formation of the United States, has dealt with how Americans perceived and provided for the common defense within the framework of a republican political culture.[1] The second, ranging more broadly across the eighteenth century, has examined the contexts of military service, particularly the social composition of forces engaged in warfare.[2] Collectively, these studies help explain why Americans, after adopting the Federal

Mr. Stagg is an associate professor of history at the University of Auckland, New Zealand. Acknowledgments: The preparation of this article was assisted by grants from the Penrose Fund of the American Philosophical Society and the Research Committee of the University of Auckland. For drawing the sample on which the article is based, I am deeply indebted to Murray A. McLauchlin. For comments and assistance in various ways thanks are due to Fred Anderson, James M. Banner, Jr., Kenneth A. Lockridge, Michael S. Mayer, and Holly Cowan Shulman.

[1] See E. Wayne Carp, *To Starve the Army at Pleasure: Continental Army Administration and American Political Culture, 1775-1783* (Chapel Hill, N.C., 1984); Lawrence Delbert Cress, *Citizens in Arms: The Army and the Militia in American Society to the War of 1812* (Chapel Hill, N.C., 1982); and Charles Royster, *A Revolutionary People at War: The Continental Army and American Character, 1775-1783* (Chapel Hill, N.C., 1979).

[2] Fred Anderson, *A People's Army: Massachusetts Soldiers and Society in the Seven Years' War* (Chapel Hill, N.C., 1984); Richard Buel, Jr., *Dear Liberty: Connecticut's Mobilization for the Revolutionary War* (Middletown, Conn., 1980); John C. Dann, ed., *The Revolution Remembered: Eyewitness Accounts of the War for Independence* (Chicago, 1980); John E. Ferling, *A Wilderness of Miseries: War and Warriors in Early America* (Westport, Conn., 1980); Mark Edward Lender, "The Social Structure of the New Jersey Brigade: The Continental Line as an American Standing Army," in Peter Karsten, ed., *The Military in America: From the Colonial Era to the Present* (New York, 1980), 27-44; Charles H. Lesser, ed., *The Sinews of*

Constitution of 1787, accepted a professional, regular army for national defense, while at the same time retaining strong suspicions about both the institution and the men whom they feared were most likely to serve in its ranks. A large standing army, composed of propertyless or impoverished men and possibly under the control of politically ambitious officers, could be, it was believed, a threat to the integrity of the republic.[3]

This recent literature has reinforced a much older theme in American military historiography—best exemplified by the writings of Emory Upton—that widely held prejudices against professional, regular soldiers have inhibited the ability of the United States to mobilize and wage war. In no instance has this seemed more true than during the War of 1812.[4] Few historians have ever doubted that the ineffectiveness of the war effort against Great Britain between 1812 and 1815 could be attributed, in part at least, to problems of recruiting and managing an undermanned regular army in a society that was either too heedless of or too hostile to its military needs to provide enough manpower for waging war.[5] Yet studies of the War of 1812 have rarely devoted attention to problems of mobilization, and historians have neglected to examine whether Ameri-

---

Independence: Monthly Strength Reports of the Continental Army (Chicago, 1976); Robert Middlekauff, "Why Men Fought in the American Revolution," *Huntington Library Quarterly*, XLIII (1980), 135-148; Edward C. Papenfuse and Gregory A. Stiverson, "General Smallwood's Recruits: The Peacetime Career of the Revolutionary War Private," *William and Mary Quarterly*, 3d Ser., XXX (1973), 117-132; Howard H. Peckham, ed., *The Toll of Independence: Engagements and Battle Casualties of the American Revolution* (Chicago, 1974); William Pencak, *War, Politics, and Revolution in Provincial Massachusetts* (Boston, 1981); John R. Sellers, "The Common Soldier in the American Revolution," in Stanley J. Underdal, ed., *Military History of the Revolution: Proceedings of the Sixth Military History Symposium, USAF Academy* (Washington, D.C., 1976), 151-161; John Shy, *A People Numerous and Armed: Reflections on the Military Struggle for American Independence* (New York, 1976), esp. 163-254.

[3] For the history of the Continental army and the early U.S. Army see Richard H. Kohn, *Eagle and Sword: The Federalists and the Creation of the Military Establishment in America, 1783-1802* (New York, 1975), and James Kirby Martin and Mark Edward Lender, *A Respectable Army: The Military Origins of the Republic, 1763-1789* (Arlington Heights, Ill., 1982). For a discussion of anti-army prejudice in the early republic see Cress, *Citizens in Arms*, esp. 137-143.

[4] Emory Upton, *The Military Policy of the United States* (Washington, D.C., 1904), esp. 96-142. For a discussion of Upton's influence see Russell F. Weigley, *Towards an American Army: Military Thought from Washington to Marshall* (New York, 1962), 137-161.

[5] Henry Adams, *History of the United States of America* (New York, 1889-1891), VI, 289, 294-295, 337, 389, 390, VII, 380-381, VIII, 17, 216-217, 265, 279, 281; Harry L. Coles, *The War of 1812* (Chicago, 1965), 266; Warren W. Hassler, Jr., *With Shield and Sword: American Military Affairs, Colonial Times to the Present* (Ames, Iowa, 1982), 72-73, 79, 91, 103; J. Mackay Hitsman, *The Incredible War of 1812: A Military History* (Toronto, 1965), 41, 183, 191-192; Reginald Horsman, *The War of 1812* (New York, 1969), 30, 168; Allan R. Millett and Peter

cans' first serious attempt to raise a regular army conformed to their republican preconceptions about the nature of armies generally.[6] As a result, historians today, to measure the success of regular recruiting between 1812 and 1815, continue to rely on nineteenth-century estimates that are probably inaccurate, while of the men who enlisted for service in these years they know nothing. The history of the United States Army in its first full-scale war can thus be identified as an important area for research in the study of the early republic.

The purpose of this article is to initiate discussion on this topic by subjecting to systematic quantitative analysis an old, but almost wholly neglected, source on the army: the twenty-six manuscript volumes entitled "Records of Men Enlisted in the U.S. Army prior to the Peace Establishment, May 17, 1815," held as part of the contents of the Adjutant General's Office (Record Group 94) in the National Archives in Washington, D.C.[7] The article will estimate how many men entered the army during the War of 1812, describe their social origins, and discuss what might be inferred from this material about some of the factors that could have motivated them to enlist. The answers, though in some cases partial and tentative, are significant. They suggest that the army between 1812 and 1815 contained a good many more men than had previously been believed and that the backgrounds of these men reflected a considerable diversity of circumstances. These conclusions, in turn, point to themes in the economy and society of early nineteenth-century America that may have been important in leading so many men to serve in war.

The provenance of the "Records of Men Enlisted in the U.S. Army" is uncertain. Very probably, the registers were compiled from a variety of older military documents sometime between 1879 and 1881; their organization—an alphabetized roll of army enlistments between 1798 and 1815—suggests that they were created to facilitate the handling of pension claims established for veterans of the War of 1812 and for their widows under legislation passed by Congress in 1871 and 1878.[8] These

---

Maslowski, *For the Common Defense: A Military History of the United States of America* (New York, 1984), 102; Russell F. Weigley, *History of the United States Army* (New York, 1967), 118, 120, 121, and *The American Way of War: A History of United States Military Strategy and Policy* (New York, 1973), 47.

[6] A partial exception is J.C.A. Stagg, *Mr. Madison's War: Politics, Diplomacy, and Warfare in the Early American Republic, 1783-1830* (Princeton, N.J., 1983), esp. 144-176. Most discussions of mobilization for the War of 1812 are limited to summaries of the relevant legislation. See, for example, Marvin A. Kreidberg and Merton G. Henry, *History of Military Mobilization in the United States Army, 1775-1945* (Washington, D.C., 1955), 43-60.

[7] The volumes are reproduced on 13 reels of microfilm as part of the Registers of Enlistments in the United States Army, 1789-1914 (M-233).

[8] The volumes are undated, but the inside cover of the first volume contains two scraps of paper bearing the dates "2.11.79" and "Oct 6/81." One of these papers describes the organization of the registers thus: "The arrangement of this Book is

records may contain as many as 90,000 to 100,000 names, but the majority of enlistments fall in the period of the War of 1812. They contain, in varying degrees, the following information about men who served in the army: name, rank, regiment, company commander, height, eye color, hair color, complexion, age, occupation, place of birth, date of enlistment, place of enlistment, recruiting officer, term of enlistment, and a brief service record in the form of "additional remarks."

Exploiting these records is not without its difficulties. Their organization is confusing. The main alphabetical sections containing the names of the enlisted men also include the names of commissioned officers and are interspersed throughout with miscellaneous lists of waiters, washerwomen, civilians, and militiamen. The data they contain are by no means complete for every recruit, particularly for men who enlisted for short terms of service of twelve or eighteen months in 1812 and 1813, though the information is fortunately fairly full for men who served for five years or for the duration of the war.[9] There are inconsistencies in the ways in which data were recorded, especially for reenlistments. The names of some are recorded each time they enlisted for a term, while others appear only once but with a note in the "additional remarks" that they also reenlisted. Since some names were far more widely used than others—there are, for example, fifty-one enlistments under the name of John Campbell between 1812 and 1815—it can be difficult to tell whether such common names belong to different individuals or whether smaller numbers of men were enlisting more than once.

Such problems, though, need not be insuperable. All names other than those of regular recruits can be discarded, while careful scrutiny and systematic comparisons of all the data available for men with common names can usually permit a reasonable guess as to whether such enlist-

---

as follows—All men are arranged under their initials and vowelized. All those who appear under the initials A.A. in the Regular Army are followed by A.A. Miscellaneous (consisting of citizens, wash women, British Vols, Militia etc.), B.A. in the same order and so on to Z.A." For the pension laws of 1871 and 1878 see William H. Glasson, *Federal Military Pensions in the United States*, ed. David Kinley (New York, 1918), 109-113.

[9] In the data sample of 6,370 cases the degree of completeness is as follows: Regiment (6,348), 99.6%; Rank (5,916), 92.8%; Term (5,912), 92.8%; Height (4,672), 73.3%; Age (4,653), 73.0%; Birthplace (4,557), 71.5%; Occupation (4,065), 63.8%; Complexion (4,063), 63.7%; Eye Color (4,062), 63.7%; Hair Color (4,057), 63.6%; Place Enlisted (3,663), 57.5%. When data on one variable are missing, they are often missing on many others, particularly on the eight relating to the recruit's personal description and background. In 1,615 cases (25.3%), data on these eight variables are missing altogether. These cases include 70.3% of the twelve-month men and 55.9% of the eighteen-month men, but only 15.1% of the men who enlisted for five years or for the duration of the war. All quantitative statements in this article are based on a computer-assisted analysis of the registers, using Norman H. Nie *et al., SPSS: Statistical Package for the Social Sciences*, 2d ed. (New York, 1975).

ments were duplications. A much more serious difficulty is simply the overwhelming mass of data about thousands and thousands of men, making the task of drawing a random sample too cumbersome to be considered. Consequently, a systematic sample—starting with a randomly chosen number between one and ten—was taken of every tenth regular recruit who enlisted during the period from January 1812 to February 1815.[10] Since alphabetical listing usually avoids problems of periodicity as a source of bias and is also largely irrelevant to the distribution of most of the variables recorded throughout the population of soldiers, this systematic sample can be fairly considered as equivalent to random sample.[11] The procedure, moreover, produced a very large number of cases—6,370 in all, including 5,350 privates, 450 noncommissioned officers, and 116 musicians.[12] This number, after allowance is made for gaps, inconsistencies, and duplications, is certainly adequate to provide the basis for a statistical and social portrait of regular soldiers in the War of 1812.

The first important question the sample can address is the total number of men who joined the army after January 1812, and that number, furthermore, can be constructed in ways that depict the ebb and flow of enlistments throughout the whole thirty-eight-month period. These were matters about which the War Department was singularly confused between 1812 and 1815, and subsequent investigations made by Congress and the Adjutant General's Office did not greatly clarify them. During the war itself, the staff of that office repeatedly confessed its inability to furnish an accurate return of the army, either for want of reliable, up-to-date recruiting reports, or, more often, for the want of any reports at all.[13] When asked by Congress in November 1814 for a full return of the army,

[10] Jan. 1812 may be fairly considered as the time when recruiting for war started. Congress passed laws on Dec. 24, 1811, for "completing the existing Military Establishment," and on Jan. 11, 1812, "to raise an additional Military Force" ([*Annals of Congress*], *Debates and Proceedings, in the Congress of the United States, 1789-1824* [Washington, D.C., 1834-1856], 12th Cong., 1st Sess., 2227-2228, 2230-2234). The end of the war was officially proclaimed in the United States on Feb. 17, 1815.

[11] For a discussion of systematic samples as equivalents for random samples, see Hubert M. Blalock, *Social Statistics*, 2d ed. (New York, 1972), 514-516, and R. S. Schofield, "Sampling in Historical Research," in E. A. Wrigley, ed., *Nineteenth-Century Society: Essays in the Use of Quantitative Methods for the Study of Social Data* (Cambridge, 1972), 147-154.

[12] Rank was not recorded in 360 cases in the sample while 94 men were described as artificers, seamen, gunners, or laborers.

[13] See, for example, Eustis to Joseph Anderson, June 6, 8, 1812, Letters Received by the Secretary of War, Unregistered Series (M-222), Records of the Office of the Secretary of War (Record Group 107), Nat. Arch., and letters from the Adjutant General to Eustis, Nov. 6, 1812, and to Charles K. Gardner, July 11, 1813, July 25, 1814, in Letters Sent by the Office of the Adjutant General (M-565), Records of the Office of the Adjutant General (Record Group 94), Nat. Arch.

Inspector General Maj. John Bell could respond with certainty only that
13,898 men had been enlisted between February and September 1814.
Admitting that this figure was implausibly low, Bell then declared that
26,017 men "at least" must have been raised since January 1814, to which
he added another estimate, made at the end of 1813, of 8,012 men as the
then "effective strength" of the army. On that basis, he supposed that the
army contained 34,029 men in September 1814.[14]

Even after 1815, when information was more complete than it had been
during the war and could be studied at greater leisure, basic questions
about the size of the wartime army remained unresolved. In response to a
congressional request on the matter in 1858, the Adjutant General
maintained that "the whole number of officers and men in the regular
service during the war [could] not be given"; the "nearest approximation"
he could provide for enlisted men was the following series of figures:
6,385 in July 1812; 17,560 in February 1813; 35,791 in September 1814;
and 31,028 in February 1815.[15] Since 1858, these figures—or very similar
ones—have generally been cited as reflecting the army's annual strength
between 1812 and 1815.[16] At the same time, however, the Treasury
Department provided an estimate of 53,750 as the total number of
noncommissioned officers and enlisted men in service between 1812 and
1815, though the Treasury auditor obtained this figure by making some
allowance for an unspecified number of men who had enlisted for five
years after 1807 and who necessarily served some of their time during the
war.[17] Of course, these two sets of estimates made in 1858 are not strictly
comparable since they addressed different aspects of the problem of army
size, but in varying ways they probably underestimated both the number
of men who enlisted during the war and the number in the ranks at any
given time between 1812 and 1815.

That the number enlisting between January 1812 and February 1815
was greater than has been recognized—and may have exceeded 62,000—
is supported by Table I, a series of monthly enlistment estimates obtained
from the sample of 6,370 and multiplied by ten to provide an estimate of
total enlistments. Men who left the army during the war or who reenlisted
were removed at the appropriate time in order not to inflate either the
monthly estimates or the estimate of the cumulative total of enlistments.
The figures should not be taken as strictly accurate, but there seems no
reason to doubt them as an acceptable approximation or to question the
relative orders of magnitude they suggest.

[14] John R. Bell to Monroe, Nov. 2, 1814, and to George Troup, Nov. 2, 1814,
in Letters Sent by the Adjutant General (M-565).
[15] "Number of Troops In the Last War With Great Britain," 35th Congress, 1st
session, *House of Representatives, Executive Document*, No. 72, 1-2.
[16] See, for example, the almost identical set of figures in United States Bureau of
the Census, *Historical Statistics, Colonial Times to 1970* (Washington, D.C., 1975),
II, 1142. See also Upton, *Military Policy of the United States*, 120, 133.
[17] "Number of Troops," 35th Cong., 1st sess., *House Executive Doc.*, No. 72, 3-4.

TABLE I
ENLISTMENTS, 1812-1815

Month	N	Cumulative Totals
1812		
January-April	2,060	2,060[a]
May-August	8,410	10,470
September-December	3,300	13,770
Total 1812	13,770	
1813		
January-April	8,770	22,540
May-August	8,400	30,840
September-December	4,900	34,640
Total 1813	22,160	
1814		
January-April	10,090	41,160
May-August	8,640	43,210
September-December	6,120	47,740
Total 1814	24,850	
1815		
January-February	1,650	48,920
Total Enlisting		62,430[b]

[a] These figures are multiples of 10 of the sample number of monthly enlistments, from which was subtracted the number of men who left the army after their term expired. The estimated totals do *not* allow for desertions, deaths, sickness, or other reasons for absence, such as furloughs, missing in action, or taken prisoner. Nor do the estimates allow for men serving during the war who enlisted before January 1812.

[b] The total number enlisting is less than the total number in the sample because there are a few cases — 127; 2% of the sample — where either the rank or the month of enlistment is not recorded. These cases therefore do not appear in the monthly totals.

After a slow start in the first four months of 1812, enlistments rose over the summer before falling off to prewar levels by November. Beginning in December 1812, enlistments climbed again and continued upward through May 1813, after which they declined slightly, though not to the lowest levels reached during the previous year. Then, in February 1814, enlistments rose sharply and remained at a high level through September. Nearly 25,000 men enlisted in 1814, constituting almost 40 percent of all enlistments recorded after January 1812. At the end of the war in February 1815, before demobilization began, the number of troops stood at about 48,920.[18]

[18] It makes little sense to assume, on the basis of the figures provided by the Adjutant General in 1858, that the army actually declined in strength between

The growth of the army was by no means steady. Nearly four-fifths of the 4,753 men (79.4 percent) whose term of service is known and who enlisted after January 1812 joined up either for five years or for the duration of the war; the remainder (1,231, 20.6 percent) enlisted for the terms of twelve and eighteen months that were available, as previously noted, in 1812 and 1813. By the end of 1813, when the short terms began to expire, the twelve- and eighteen-month men constituted 35.5 percent of all the enlistments made since January 1812, and the army faced a serious crisis if these soldiers sought discharge instead of reenlisting.[19] Generally, the twelve- and eighteen-month men chose not to reenlist; only 14.0 percent of these men in the sample (172) reenlisted in 1814, while only 4.1 percent (109) of those who enlisted after January 1814 (2,650) can be proved to have enlisted before that date.[20] Consequently, although enlistments rose in the early months of 1814, so too did the number of men leaving the service. By April 1814, the army was losing nearly as many men as it gained, and by June it had actually fallen slightly to 40,890 men. The situation did not stabilize until August 1814, after which the numbers began to increase more steadily, though the rate of monthly enlistments also declined for the remainder of the year. (See Table I.) But most of the men enlisting in 1814 were raw recruits, and the army clearly lacked a core of seasoned soldiers who could play an important role in training new recruits.[21]

The fluctuation of enlistments throughout the war suggests that one of the most important factors governing the army's growth rate was the timing of the implementation of the military laws passed by Congress. The

---

Sept. 1814 and Feb. 1815. Upton attributes the decline to desertion (*Military Policy of the United States*, 123), but it is not clear that the 1858 estimate made any allowance for desertion. Very probably, it did not, since the estimate was supposed to give "the whole number of officers and men in the regular service" ("Number of Troops," 35th Cong., 1st sess., *House Executive Doc.*, No. 72, 1-2). Admittedly, desertion was high in 1814, but so too were enlistments. On the other hand, the 1858 estimate of army strength in Feb. 1815 *may* have made some allowance for the discharge of men enlisted for the duration of the war only.

[19] Secretary of War John Armstrong, while on the northern frontier in the fall of 1813, ordered army officers to reenlist all men whose terms were expiring. See Armstrong to James Wilkinson, Nov. 26, 1813, Orderly Books of the Adjutant General, Aug. 1813-June 1815, Vol. 445, Records of United States Army Commands, 1784-1821 (Record Group 98), Nat. Arch.

[20] These figures do not allow for the men who enlisted for five years in the Additional Military Force of 1808 during the embargo crisis and whose terms were also expiring after the end of 1813. In the sample of 2,485 men who enlisted in 1814, only 15 can be proved to have been previously enlisted in 1808 and 1809. This number is probably too small, but there seems no reason to doubt the more general point that the rate of reenlistment was very low.

[21] For complaints on this score see George Izard's letters to John Armstrong of May 7, June 10, 25, 1814, in his *Official Correspondence with the Department of War, Relative to the Military Operations of the American Army . . . on the Northern Frontier of the United States in the Years 1814 and 1815* (Philadelphia, 1816), 2, 26-30, 36-39.

change of seasons and the rhythm of the agricultural year had far less influence on the temporal pattern of enlistments. This was partly because, as will be seen, men from farming backgrounds did not constitute a majority of recruits, and partly because large numbers were enlisted in urban areas where the change of seasons had less impact on labor markets and the size of the potential pool of recruits than it did in rural areas.[22] Recruiting was slow in the early months of 1812, owing mainly to difficulties inherent in mobilization itself, including the reluctance of the War Department to implement the 25,000-man army bill passed in January 1812. Administration dissatisfaction with this bill then led, in April 1812, to legislation authorizing up to 15,000 enlistments for terms of eighteen months. But enlistments declined after September 1812, mainly due to problems experienced by officers in trying to continue the recruiting service while also preparing forces for the invasion of Canada. Thereafter, the upsurge in recruiting in April 1813 followed the passage of legislation to raise twenty regiments for twelve months, while the high rate of enlistments throughout 1814 seems to have reflected the very strong appeal of the greatly increased money bounty offered by Congress in January of that year. The increased bounty, ironically, was considered necessary to persuade the twelve- and eighteen-month men to reenlist when their terms expired.[23]

Estimates of total size and of monthly enlistments throughout the war do not, of course, reflect the army's "effective strength." This could be eroded by such factors as sickness, desertion, men on leave, men killed or wounded, men dying from other causes—usually camp sickness—and men taken prisoner of war. At times, the incidence of these factors, combined with men being discharged for incapacity or ineligibility, could be sufficiently serious to lead the War Department to discount enlistment totals substantially.[24] A reliable estimate of effective strength, however, cannot be calculated easily, if at all, from the registers, largely because of

[22] For a discussion of the importance of the cycle of the agricultural year see Clarence H. Danhof, *Change in Agriculture: The Northern United States, 1820-1870* (Cambridge, Mass., 1969), 73-74, and James A. Henretta, *The Evolution of American Society, 1700-1815: An Interdisciplinary Analysis* (Lexington, Mass., 1973), 31-39. Only 42.6% of all the recruits enlisted in the months from Oct. to Mar.—when demand for agricultural labor would have been at its lowest—during the period from Jan. 1812 to Feb. 1815. For those who gave their occupation as farmer, the figure is 48.3%.

[23] For the background to this legislation see Stagg, *Mr. Madison's War*, 85-89, 101, 155-176, 279-281, 366-368, 374-375.

[24] See "A Report of the Army—its Strength and Distribution [1814]," where the Inspector General discounted the aggregate strength of the force by 15%, largely because of the "wretched condition" of the right wing of the army under Gen. Izard. James Madison Papers, Library of Congress. See also Bell to Abiel Y. Nicoll, Dec. 14, 1813, Letters Received by the Office of the Adjutant General (M-566), Records of the Office of the Adjutant General, and Armstrong to Troup, Dec. 29, 1813, Daniel Parker Papers, Historical Society of Pennsylvania, Philadelphia.

the nature of the information contributing to any such estimate in the "additional remarks" on the troops. While some sorts of information, such as that on deaths, desertions, and prisoners of war, are recorded in sufficient detail to permit an estimate of their incidence, other relevant data, especially relating to the duration of illnesses, are not precise enough to make accurate estimates of the fluctuations in effective strength. Nonetheless, information from the additional remarks permits absolute calculations of the factors contributing to the effective strength of the army and gives some indication of their relative importance.

Not surprisingly, since the war saw few large-scale battles, the army's losses in men killed and wounded were not great: they amounted to only 3.2 percent (201) of the troops in the sample. A further 2.6 percent (164) of these men were lost to the service while being held prisoner, and 3.4 percent (215) were discharged, usually because too old or incapable of performing military service. Sickness, desertion, and deaths from causes not related to battle, though, were much more important factors constantly undermining effective strength. From the few surviving medical records, it is evident that the army was burdened with large numbers of men afflicted by fevers, agues, hernias, dropsy, diarrhea, dysentery, and venereal disease. The registers reveal that 12.7 percent (807) of the men in the sample were "sick" at least once during their service, and that is probably a conservative estimate of the impact of illness.[25] Moreover, sickness and occasional accidents led to the death in service of 8.2 percent (524) of the sample recruits, while desertion affected the army to the same extent as sickness, 12.7 percent (808) of the sample being recorded as deserters. Since barely one-fifth (161) of these men were ever returned to the ranks, the army, in effect, lost 10.1 percent (647) of its recruits through desertion. Men were also increasingly likely to desert as the war progressed. Only one-fifth (20.2 percent, 163) of the deserters had enlisted in 1812, while one-quarter (26.5 percent, 214) joined the ranks in 1813. But after December 1813, the numbers of deserters rose steeply, a trend that persisted throughout 1814. Nearly half (49.5 percent, 400) of all wartime desertions were recorded for men enlisting in that year.

Why did desertion increase in the last year of the war? It is unlikely that the rise in desertion reflected any tendency on the part of men on short enlistments to quit the ranks before receiving their discharge. In fact, men serving for shorter terms deserted far less frequently than men enlisted for

[25] See, for example, "Register of Patients in the Hospital at Williamsville, 1814-1815," and "Register of the Patients in the Hospital, 9th Military District, 1814-1815," Vols. 552, 680, 683, in Records of United States Army Commands, Nat. Arch.; and more generally see James Mann, *Medical Sketches of the Campaigns of 1812, 13, 14* . . . (Dedham, Mass., 1816). The description of "sick" depended on whether a man ever appeared on a medical report or was admitted to a hospital. Given the fragmentary nature of medical records, company books, and other reports surviving from the early 19th century, this definition produces a conservative estimate of the impact of illness on the army.

longer terms.[26] A more probable explanation is the temptation presented by the changes in the money bounties offered to recruits in 1814. Not only were bounties greatly increased—from $16 to $124—but most of the money was paid to the recruit in advance of his service. Previously, recruits received $16 at the start of their term and three months' pay ($24) at the end, but in 1814 they received $50 on enlistment, $50 on being mustered into a unit, and the remainder at the end of service.[27] Earlier in the war, Secretary of War John Armstrong warned Congress against such bounty legislation, observing that "bounties given at the close of service have many advantages over those given before service begins. The former tie men down to their duty; the latter furnish if not the motive, at least the means, of debauch and desertion."[28] The desertion levels of 1814 seem to have borne out Armstrong's fears.

Clearly, then, the effective strength of the army between 1812 and 1815 was always much less than the number of men who actually entered the ranks, and even at its greatest size, in February 1815, the military establishment was still below the 59,179 enlisted men authorized by Congress. Nevertheless, the army did recruit, and probably retained, a greater number of men during the War of 1812 than the War Department knew at the time or historians have realized. The full significance of that fact must await further discussion, but it surely suggests that many of the difficulties experienced in prosecuting the war reflected inefficiencies in army organization and training rather than any very serious obstacles encountered in recruitment.[29] And the fact that reasonably large numbers of men enlisted as regular soldiers therefore raises the questions of what sort of men they were and why so many decided to join the ranks.

At first sight, early nineteenth-century America might seem an unpromising place to recruit a substantial regular army. After all, what sort of men would volunteer for the risks and hardships of a soldier's life in a prosperous society where nearly three-quarters of the gainfully employed population were engaged in agricultural pursuits, where little more than 7 percent of the total population resided in urban areas, and where

[26] Of deserters whose term of enlistment is known (772), only 8.8% (68) had enlisted for either 12 or 18 months, while the remaining 91.2% (704) had enlisted for five years or for the duration of the war.

[27] Compare the bounty provisions of the military laws of Jan. 11, 1812, and Jan. 27, 28, 1814.

[28] Armstrong to David R. Williams, Feb. 10, 1813, Reports to Congress from the Secretary of War, 1803-1870 (M-220), Records of the Office of the Secretary of War.

[29] The perception of contemporaries, admittedly, was rather different. Both John Armstrong and James Monroe, while administering the War Department, concluded that voluntary enlistments were too unreliable a source of recruits, and both came to advocate some form of conscription of the state militias. See Stagg, *Mr. Madison's War*, 366-367, 456-459.

republican values conferred scant prestige on the profession of arms?[30] One might assume that recruits must have been largely marginal farmers or destitute unskilled laborers, including sizable numbers of such disadvantaged groups as immigrants and blacks—but, as will be seen, a description of the army between 1812 and 1815 resists such easy suppositions. The soldiers were, in fact, not drawn predominantly from any particular region or social groups, and the diversity of their origins makes it difficult to deduce their motives for enlisting. Nonetheless, the behavior of large numbers of men is likely to fall into observable patterns, and these patterns can at least illuminate, if not in individual cases fully explain, some of the social forces operating on men as they made the decision to serve in war.

The great majority of recruits—86.8 percent of those whose birthplace is known—were native-born Americans. A comparison of the distribution of their birthplaces with the distribution in 1810 of the white male population aged sixteen to forty-five—the group most likely to perform military service—can provide a rough idea whether these native-born men originated disproportionately in any particular area of the country. As Table II shows, the New England states, which furnished one-third (33.1 percent) of the native-born recruits, were most overrepresented in the army, since less than one-quarter (24.5 percent) of the nation's white population of military age resided in New England in 1810. The South Atlantic states (below the Mason-Dixon line) were also generally overrepresented—with 32.9 percent of the troops and 27.1 percent of the white population of military age—while the Middle Atlantic region, with slightly less than one-third (31.3 percent) of the troops, was represented in near proportion to its share (33.2 percent) of the white male population of military age. The newer western states and territories were greatly underrepresented.

Foreign-born enlistees composed 13.1 percent of the total for whom birthplaces are known. The percentage of immigrants in the army—after making some allowance for the absence of accurate controlling data—was probably only slightly higher than the best estimates available of the percentage of immigrants (11.1) in the total population in 1810.[31] Over half of the foreign-born recruits (52.7 percent) were born in Ireland, with most of the others coming either from elsewhere in the British Isles, from Canada, or from Europe, mainly France and Germany. (See Table III.)

[30] See Henretta, *Evolution of American Society*, 193, and Curtis P. Nettels, *The Emergence of a National Economy, 1775-1815* (New York, 1962), 387.

[31] A more precise statement is impossible since there are no reliable estimates of the number of immigrants in the population between the Revolution and 1820. For a discussion and the estimate of 11.1% for 1810 see J. Potter, "The Growth of Population in America, 1700-1860," in D. V. Glass and D.E.C. Eversley, eds., *Population in History: Essays in Historical Demography* (London, 1965), 666-667, 672. Richard H. Kohn has pointed out that immigrants in the ranks, when compared with the number of immigrants of the same age in the population, may not have been as overrepresented in the army as is sometimes assumed ("The Social History of the American Soldier: A Review and Prospectus for Research," *American Historical Review*, LXXXVI [1981], 557).

TABLE II
BIRTHPLACES OF NATIVE-BORN RECRUITS

Place of Birth	N	%	% of Adult White Males, 16-45 Years, 1810[a]
Maine	194	4.9	3.8
Massachusetts (except Maine)	425	10.7	8.1
New Hampshire	209	5.3	3.5
Vermont	123	3.1	3.6
Connecticut	292	7.4	4.2
Rhode Island	68	1.7	1.3
Totals	1,311	33.1	24.5
New York	565	14.3	16.1
New Jersey	232	5.9	3.8
Pennsylvania	442	11.1	13.3
Totals	1,239	31.3	33.2
Delaware	57	1.4	1.0
Maryland	236	6.0	4.3
Virginia	459	11.6	9.3
North Carolina	319	8.1	6.2
South Carolina	183	4.6	3.7
Georgia	49	1.2	2.6
Totals	1,303	32.9	27.1
Ohio	12	0.3	3.8
Kentucky	33	0.8	5.3
Tennessee	39	1.0	3.5
Louisiana	8	0.2	—
D.C. and Territories	14	0.4	2.6
Totals	106	2.7	15.2
Grand Totals	3,959	100.0	100.0

[a] Source: 1810 Census

Before 1812, recruiting regulations stipulated that soldiers should be adult male citizens, but thereafter such provisos were not enforced against immigrants—many of whom may not have been naturalized—and, as the war progressed, they were also applied less severely to blacks.[32] How

[32] Legislation governing the Peace Establishment of 1802 and the Additional Military Force of 1808, which were not at full strength in Jan. 1812, required the enlistment of "citizens," but legislation after Jan. 1812 called only for the enlistment of "effective, able-bodied" men. For the army's willingness to enlist immigrants see Thomas Cushing to Messrs. Whiting and Ames, June 24, 1812, Letters Sent by the Adjutant General (M-565). The enlistment of blacks was more problematical. In response to requests on the matter in the early months of the war, the War Department was cautious, believing that blacks might be enlisted but

TABLE III
BIRTHPLACES OF FOREIGN-BORN RECRUITS

Place of Birth	N	%
England	68	11.4
Wales	6	1.0
Scotland	21	3.5
Ireland	315	52.7
Great Britain	3	0.5
France	41	6.9
Holland	13	2.2
Switzerland	6	1.0
Germany	55	9.2
Poland	2	0.3
Russia	1	0.2
Sweden	4	0.6
Denmark	3	0.5
Spain	11	1.8
Portugal	5	0.8
Italy	3	0.5
Canada	28	4.7
Others (Latin America, Asia)	13	2.2
Totals	598	100.0

many black men there were in the army is difficult to ascertain since the registrars probably did not record racial background as opposed to national origin with any consistency, but the number of recruits (27) who were described as having "black" complexions amounted to 0.6 percent of those (4,063) whose skin color was noted. Not even all of these men were necessarily black: two were born in Ireland and were not described as being "colored men," while at least half a dozen others with "yellow" or "brown" complexions were identified as "colored men." All the recruits described as "colored men" enlisted in the last six months of 1814 and in early 1815, on which basis it is possible to suggest that at least 280 to 370 blacks may have been in the ranks by the end of the war.[33]

---

preferably only as musicians. See "Confidential Report of Alexander Smyth, Acting Inspector General," June 23, 1812, in Confidential Inspection Reports, 1812-1820, Records of the Office of the Adjutant General. Not until 1814 did the War Department unequivocally endorse the enlistment of blacks. See Armstrong to James Mease, Aug. 6, 1814, Letters Sent Relating to Military Affairs (M-6), Records of the Office of the Secretary of War.

[33] The only blacks in the sample whose racial origin was consistently recorded are a group of 22 men, mostly laborers and seamen, recruited into the 26th Infantry in Pennsylvania by Lt. Philip Bezeau in the last six months of the war. A few others, very probably blacks but not recorded as much, were recruited in New England.

Men, of course, did not necessarily enlist in the states where they were born, and the distribution of enlistments throughout the Union will provide insights into the movements of the men after their birth and some indications as to where the army concentrated its recruiting efforts. As Table IV shows, New York produced by far the largest number of enlistments, reflecting both the large size of that state's population of military age and, more important, the fact that it was also the main theater of war between 1812 and 1815.[34] A more sensitive indicator of the success of recruiting throughout the Union is the ratio of enlistments to the white male population aged sixteen to forty-five. As already noted, men of this age group, numbering 1,119,844 in the 1810 census, were the most likely to perform military service, and they responded most strongly to recruiting officers in New York and the frontier regions of New England, especially Vermont and the District of Maine. (See Table IV.) Considering the strategic importance of New York and Vermont for the war against Canada, it is hardly surprising that the army recruited intensively in those states, but it may be worth pointing out as well that upstate New York, Vermont, and Maine were also areas where Republican party policies, for a variety of local reasons, traditionally enjoyed stronger support than they did in other parts of New England and New York. For all these reasons, therefore, these areas provided significantly more recruits from their populations of military age than did other parts of the country.[35]

Comparison of places of birth and enlistment also reveals that many recruits had moved about considerably before entering the ranks. Excluding the foreign-born, the sample contains both the birth and enlistment places for 3,088 native-born enlistees, of whom only 1,576 (51.0 percent) were recruited in the state of their birth. The persistence rates of the recruits in the states of their birth were, therefore, with some exceptions, quite low. (See Table V.) In most respects, the geographical mobility of the recruits conformed to population shifts occurring throughout the nation, and the movements of the men broadly reflected the population losses of coastal regions to rapidly expanding frontiers. (Cf. Tables II and

[34] The Ninth Military District, comprising most of upstate New York, was by far the largest military organization in the country. By 1813, its staff numbered 35% of the entire army staff. The district, which included both the main army camp at Greenbush and the naval base at Sacketts Harbor, commanded the routes that led to the Niagara frontier and the Champlain Valley. See Walter Lowrie and Matthew St. Clair Clarke, eds., *American State Papers. Documents . . . of the Congress of the United States . . .*, Class V: *Military Affairs*, I (Washington, D.C., 1832), 385-388.

[35] For the tendency of frontier regions in New England and New York to support the Republican party see Ronald F. Banks, *Maine Becomes a State: The Movement to Separate Maine from Massachusetts, 1785-1820* (Middletown, Conn., 1970), 10, 47-50; Dixon Ryan Fox, *The Decline of Aristocracy in the Politics of New York* (New York, 1919), 48-51; and William A. Robinson, *Jeffersonian Democracy in New England* (New Haven, Conn., 1916), 37-49, 160-170.

TABLE IV
ENLISTMENTS BY PLACE OF RECRUITMENT

State	N	%	White Male Population 16-45 Years[a]	Recruits/10,000 White Males, 16-45 Years
New York	772	21.1	180,661	427
Pennsylvania	499	13.6	148,396	336
Maine	180	4.9	42,482	424
Massachusetts (except Maine)	262	7.2	90,872	288
Virginia	296	8.1	104,040	285
Vermont	180	4.9	40,469	445
Maryland	176	4.8	47,943	367
North Carolina	167	4.6	69,086	237
Connecticut	165	4.5	47,579	347
South Carolina	154	4.2	41,421	372
Tennessee	135	3.7	39,443	342
New Hampshire	104	2.8	39,396	204
Georgia	100	2.7	28,547	351
Kentucky	97	2.6	59,325	163
Ohio	89	2.4	42,950	207
New Jersey	88	2.4	42,625	206
Louisiana	58	1.6	—	—
Rhode Island	28	0.8	14,015	200
Delaware	14	0.4	11,016	127
D.C. and Territories	99	2.7	29,578	—
Totals	3,663	100.0	1,119,844	

[a] Source: 1810 Census

IV.) Of the men born in Old Massachusetts (that is, exclusive of Maine) who left the state, for example, nearly three-fifths (57.8 percent) moved to other parts of New England, principally to Maine and Vermont, while the remainder (42.2 percent) left the region altogether, mostly for New York or Pennsylvania.[36] These last two states, furthermore, became the home of more than three-quarters (76.5 percent) of all the recruits who were born in and left New Jersey. In areas south of New York, a general drift of the population to the south and the west can be detected. Among the Virginia-born men who left their native state, over half (52.1 percent) moved to North Carolina, Kentucky, and Tennessee, while a small number (9.4 percent) migrated to the Old Northwest, mainly into Ohio.[37]

[36] For a similar pattern in out-migration from New England see Lois Kimball Mathews, *The Expansion of New England: The Spread of New England Settlement and Institutions to the Mississippi River, 1620-1865* (Boston, 1909), 139-170.

[37] For southern migration patterns see William O. Lynch, "The Westward Flow of Southern Colonists before 1861," *Journal of Southern History*, IX (1943), esp. 306-309, and John D. Barnhart, "Sources of Southern Migration into the Old Northwest," *Mississippi Valley Historical Review*, XXII (1935), 58-59.

TABLE V
PERSISTENCE OF RECRUITS IN STATE OF BIRTH

State	N Born	N Recruited	% Persisting
Maine	155	121	78.1
Massachusetts (except Maine)	342	152	44.4
New Hampshire	164	66	40.2
Vermont	100	53	43.0
Connecticut	211	90	42.7
Rhode Island	52	14	26.9
New York	439	319	72.7
New Jersey	196	51	26.0
Pennsylvania	345	208	60.3
Delaware	43	6	14.0
Maryland	178	77	43.3
Virginia	344	158	45.9
North Carolina	253	107	42.3
South Carolina	152	82	53.9
Georgia	38	30	78.9
Kentucky	25	9	36.0
Tennessee	25	18	72.0
Louisiana	5	4	80.0
Ohio	9	4	44.6
D.C. and Territories	12	7	58.3
Totals	3,088	1,576	51.0

Many recruits, however, had moved from their place of birth to a town or city rather than to a distant frontier. At least 1,408 (38.4 percent) of the sample troops for whom place of enlistment is recorded (3,663) were recruited in urban locales of 2,500 people or more. In fact, in six states—Old Massachusetts, Connecticut, Rhode Island, Pennsylvania, Maryland, and Louisiana—over half the recruits were enlisted in urban areas, and the towns and cities of these states contributed a significantly larger percentage of recruits than the urban percentage of the population. (See Table VI.) It should be pointed out, however, that the recruiting methods of army officers probably contributed considerably to this result. Many officers clearly disliked recruiting in the countryside; finding the business there often difficult, unrewarding, and uncongenial, they preferred to concentrate on towns and cities.[38] One unhappy officer reported, after

[38] The impression that army officers preferred to recruit in urban areas can be easily gained by surveying their correspondence with the Adjutant General and is powerfully reinforced by scores of letters from officers complaining bitterly of the practical difficulties of recruiting in the more isolated, rural parts of the country. For the case of Pennsylvania as an example see the letters to the Adjutant General of the Fourth Military District, William Duane, from the following: John Arrison, Aug. 4, 10, 1813; George Brent, Sept. 4, 1813; Dominick Cornyn, who wrote 27 letters on the subject between June and Aug. 1813; Samuel Dewey, July 4, 1813;

TABLE VI
RECRUITING IN URBAN AREAS

State	% of Population in Urban Areas 2,500 or More[a]	% of Recruits Enlisted in Urban Areas
Maine	3.1	15.0
Massachusetts (except Maine)	21.3	58.8
New Hampshire	3.2	22.1
Connecticut	6.1	58.8
Rhode Island	23.4	92.9
New York	12.7	44.8
New Jersey	2.4	18.2
Pennsylvania	12.8	58.3
Maryland	12.2	60.2
Virginia	3.2	41.9
South Carolina	5.9	8.4
Georgia	2.1	11.0
Kentucky	1.1	5.1
Ohio	1.1	14.6
Louisiana	22.5	62.1

[a] Calculated from tables in George Rogers Taylor, "American Urban Growth Preceding the Railway Age," *Journal of Economic History*, XXVII (1967), 311-315. Taylor does not list towns of over 2,500 in Vermont, Delaware, North Carolina, and Tennessee in 1810.

being ordered to show the flag in the "respectable" village of Haverstraw, New York, that he could enlist only one "poor drunken devil," and he further complained that there were "no mails here and no printer and I have had to send my printing to Newburgh. Nor can I get music." Concluding that his prospects were dim, he implored his commanding officer, successfully, to send him to Troy, Utica, or Kingston.[39]

Significant questions arise from the occupational structure of the recruits and concern the behavioral patterns and characteristics that might be associated with men pursuing certain occupations. Specifically, was the army between 1812 and 1815 recruited largely from unskilled and marginal men who turned to military service as the only employment readily available to them? The answer, at first sight, is probably negative,

William Downey, Sept. 3, 1813; Frederick Evans, June 28, 1813; Patrick Forde, July 13, 1813; and Robert Hall, June 9, 1813—all in Letters Received by the Adjutant General (M-566). It is also possible that extensive urban recruiting contributed to the slowing urban growth rate between 1810 and 1820. Between 1812 and 1815 the army removed thousands of men from towns and cities but did not necessarily discharge them there. See David T. Gilchrist, ed., *The Growth of the Seaport Cities, 1790-1825* (Charlottesville, Va., 1967), 25-53.

[39] James McLean to Jonas Simonds, Apr. 19, 1812, "Letters Sent and Received, 6th Infantry, 1811-1813," Records of United States Army Commands.

TABLE VII
OCCUPATION OF RECRUITS

	All Recruits		Native-Born		Foreign-Born	
Occupation	N	%	N	%	N	%
Farmer	1578	39.0	1463	42.6	67	13.3
Laborer	578	14.2	421	12.2	134	26.6
Artisan	1508	37.0	1271	37.0	198	39.2
Seamen	211	5.1	154	4.4	51	10.1
Miscellaneous	190	4.7	130	3.8	54	10.8
Totals	4065	100.0	3439	100.0	504	100.0

though the situation is complex and differed markedly for native-born and foreign-born recruits. The two largest groups among the recruits whose occupations were recorded were those described in the registers as "farmers" and artisans of various kinds, with 39 and 37 percent of the enlistments respectively.[40] Laborers, who might be expected to have been more numerous, by contrast made up only 14.2 percent. Seamen and men in other miscellaneous occupations such as clerks, cartmen, boatmen, barbers, tobacconists, and schoolteachers—with 5.1 and 4.6 percent each—composed the remainder. Immigrants, however, were more than twice as likely as native-born Americans to have been recruited from the laboring, seafaring, and miscellaneous occupations. The great majority of native-born men (79.6 percent), on the other hand, were either farmers or artisans. (See Table VII.)

It is often argued that the soldiers of America's colonial and early national wars were drawn largely from among the population of younger adult males, at least in comparison with soldiers who served in the armies of Great Britain and France at the end of the eighteenth century.[41] The mean and median ages of the 1812-1815 recruits—26.8 years and 24.7 years—might seem to confirm this generalization, but the impression may be misleading, especially when one takes into consideration both the age structure of the occupational groups in the U.S. Army and the fact that regulars in European armies generally served far longer than their American counterparts. Table VIII shows that by far the youngest men to serve in the War of 1812 were farmers, with a median age of 22.8 years. Their mean age, however, was 25.1, which suggests that they included a

[40] For convenience, the category of artisan was created by grouping 107 occupations listed in the registers.

[41] See, for example, Anderson, People's Army, 53-58, 238; Lender, "The Social Structure of the New Jersey Brigade," 29; Martin and Lender, Respectable Army, 90-91; Papenfuse and Stiverson, "General Smallwood's Recruits," WMQ, 3d Ser., XXX (1973), 120-121; and Sellers, "Common Soldier in the American Revolution," in Underdal, ed., Military History of the Revolution, 154-155.

TABLE VIII
AGE OF RECRUITS

	N	Mean Age	Median Age
All Recruits	4,653	26.8	24.7
Farmers	1,561	25.1	22.8
Laborers	574	26.6	24.6
Artisans	1,498	27.9	26.2
Seamen	209	27.6	26.3
Misc. Occupations	185	28.8	28.2
Foreign-Born	588	30.5	29.5

substantial minority of older men.[42] Other occupational groups in the army were rather older than the farmers, with artisans being older than laborers, while seamen and men from miscellaneous occupations were older still, the latter group having mean and median ages of 28.8 and 28.1. And the oldest group of all was the foreign-born, with a mean age of 30.5 and a median age of 29.5. By comparison, evidence for the British army during the American Revolution describes the typical soldier as "a mature man of about thirty years of age," but he had also averaged nearly ten years' service, having enlisted at around age twenty.[43] The fact that about one-half of the American recruits of 1812-1815 entered the army after the age of twenty-five, at a time in their lives when many men would have preferred to be settling into their vocation, suggests that they were by no means largely drawn from among the youngest men who might have served.

Regarding motives for enlisting, examination of the characteristics and behavior of these groups suggests the influence of different sets of circumstances, all of them of considerable complexity. Farmers, for example, were predominant among men enlisting in some parts of New England, especially the frontier regions of Maine and Vermont, and also among men from South Carolina, Georgia, and Tennessee. (See Table IX.) Just over half (53.9 percent) of the native-born farmers whose place of enlistment is known (1,139) were recruited in the state of their birth,

[42] More than one-third (35.2%) of farmers were older than the mean age of farmers.

[43] Sylvia R. Frey, *The British Soldier in America: A Social History of Military Life in the Revolutionary Period* (Austin, Tex., 1981), 23-26. Men in the French army also seem to have enlisted, on average, at about twenty years of age. See André Corvisier, *L'Armée Française de la Fin du XVIIᵉ Siècle au Ministère de Choiseul: Le Soldat* (Paris, 1964), II, 616-626; John A. Lynn, *The Bayonets of the Republic: Motivation and Tactics in the Army of Revolutionary France, 1791-94* (Urbana, Ill., 1984), 44-55; and Samuel F. Scott, *The Response of the Royal Army to the French Revolution: The Role and Development of the Line Army, 1787-93* (Oxford, 1978), 7-9.

TABLE IX

DISTRIBUTION OF RECRUITS' OCCUPATIONS BY STATE OF RECRUITMENT

Place of Enlistment	N	Farmers		Laborers		Artisans		Seamen		Miscellaneous	
		N	%	N	%	N	%	N	%	N	%
Maine	165	96	58.2	32	19.4	26	15.8	9	5.4	2	1.2
Massachusetts (except Maine)	235	81	34.5	27	11.5	83	35.3	34	14.5	10	4.3
New Hampshire	98	59	60.2	3	3.1	29	29.6	5	5.1	2	2.0
Vermont	160	112	70.0	6	3.8	35	21.9	4	2.5	3	1.9
Connecticut	150	74	49.3	1	0.7	61	40.7	12	8.0	2	1.3
Rhode Island	15	7	46.7	2	13.3	3	20.0	2	13.3	1	6.7
New York	661	192	29.0	111	16.8	269	40.7	33	5.0	56	8.5
Pennsylvania	445	58	13.0	103	23.1	242	54.4	21	4.7	21	4.7
New Jersey	72	15	20.8	11	15.3	41	56.9	3	4.2	2	2.8
Maryland	137	22	16.1	23	16.8	70	51.1	16	1.7	6	4.4
Delaware	12	2	16.7	7	58.3	1	8.3	2	16.7	–	–
Virginia	266	99	37.2	29	10.9	99	37.2	21	7.9	18	6.8
North Carolina	147	66	44.9	24	16.3	47	32.0	8	5.4	2	1.4
South Carolina	145	92	63.4	12	8.3	35	24.1	–	–	6	4.1
Georgia	94	74	78.7	4	4.3	14	14.9	1	1.1	1	1.1
Ohio	74	29	39.2	23	31.1	21	28.4	–	–	1	1.4
Kentucky	74	35	47.3	16	21.6	21	28.4	–	–	2	2.7
Tennessee	82	54	65.9	13	15.9	14	17.1	1	1.2	–	–
Louisiana	46	19	41.3	7	15.2	11	23.9	2	4.3	7	15.2
D.C. and Territories	89	22	24.7	23	26.1	36	40.9	2	2.2	6	6.8
Totals	3,167	1,208		477		1,158		176		148	

while the remainder had all experienced some degree of geographical mobility. This was particularly true for farmers born in the long-settled coastal states such as Massachusetts, New Hampshire, Connecticut, Rhode Island, New Jersey, Maryland, and North Carolina. (See Table X.) Yet even for farmers recruited in the states where they were born, it is also possible that some may have already left home and moved, probably to a nearby town or city. Nearly one-quarter (23.0 percent) of all farmers were recruited in towns and cities, and their concentration in such places was especially high among recruits in Rhode Island, Old Massachusetts, Connecticut, Pennsylvania, and Louisiana, where 85.7, 44.4, 63.5, 65.1, and 57.9 percent, respectively, of the farmer recruits were enlisted in urban areas. (See Table XI.)

The fact that so many men from farming backgrounds were young, mobile, and recruited in urban areas suggests that to describe them simply as farmers may be misleading. More than likely, this "farmer" group comprised men in a variety of situations. Younger men in the northern states, particularly if they were younger sons from large families with fathers who could not provide them with an adequate inheritance, may have seen in the army a chance to escape from their limited circumstances while also improving their long-term prospects. Slightly older men, who, it is worth noting, seem to have been close to the mean age for marriage— at least in New England—could have already been confronting the problems of establishing themselves and might have similarly turned to the army in response.[44] Furthermore, marginal farmers in the northern states often supplemented their incomes with part-time trades, of which shoemaking was the most important.[45] Since they made frequent trips to town to sell their wares, some of these men undoubtedly joined the army

[44] For discussion of the problems of inheritance, marriage, the viability of farm units, and migration in the northern regions in the late eighteenth and early nineteenth centuries see Philip J. Greven, Jr., *Four Generations: Population, Land, and Family in Colonial Andover, Massachusetts* (Ithaca, N.Y., 1970), esp. 241-258; Douglas Lamar Jones, *Village and Seaport: Migration and Society in Eighteenth-Century Massachusetts* (Hanover, N.H., 1981), 17-21, 41-51, 63-69, 97-102, 104-121; Joseph F. Kett, *Rites of Passage: Adolescence in America, 1790 to the Present* (New York, 1977), 29-31; and John J. Waters, "Family, Inheritance, and Migration in Colonial New England: The Evidence from Guilford, Connecticut," *WMQ*, 3d Ser., XXXIX (1982), esp. 77-86. For data on the average age at first marriage for males at about 25-26 years see Daniel Scott Smith, "The Demographic History of Colonial New England," *Journal of Economic History*, XXXII (1972), 177, and Maris A. Vinovskis, *Fertility in Massachusetts from the Revolution to the Civil War* (New York, 1981), 42-49.

[45] Paul G. Faler, *Mechanics and Manufacturers in the Early Industrial Revolution: Lynn, Massachusetts, 1780-1860* (Albany, N.Y., 1981), 9, 10, 81, 82; Paul E. Johnson, "The Modernization of Mayo Greenleaf Patch: Land, Family, and Marginality in New England, 1766-1818," *New England Quarterly*, LV (1982), 488-516; Jonathan Prude, *The Coming of Industrial Order: Town and Factory Life in Rural Massachusetts, 1810-1860* (New York, 1983), 7-8.

Table X
Persistence Rates of Native-Born by Occupational Groups

State	Farmers			Artisans			Laborers		
	N Born	Recruited N	%	N Born	N	%	N Born	N	%
Maine	81	69	85.1	20	13	65.0	30	25	83.0
Massachusetts (except Maine)	119	52	43.6	126	57	45.2	20	12	60.0
New Hampshire	96	43	44.7	41	15	36.5	5	1	20.0
Vermont	63	35	55.5	15	6	40.0	11	2	18.1
Connecticut	82	38	46.3	75	34	45.3	13	1	7.7
Rhode Island	16	5	31.2	13	1	7.6	5	1	20.0
New York	143	99	68.2	133	99	74.4	59	51	86.4
New Jersey	36	8	22.2	103	29	28.1	22	8	36.3
Pennsylvania	46	23	50.0	174	114	65.5	63	45	71.4
Maryland	32	14	43.7	88	35	39.7	15	6	40.0
Delaware	6	1	16.7	19	1	5.2	7	3	42.9
Virginia	146	74	50.6	92	48	52.1	33	12	36.3
North Carolina	124	54	43.5	48	27	56.2	31	14	45.1
South Carolina	97	58	59.7	23	15	65.2	14	5	37.5
Georgia	26	26	100.0	6	3	50.0	2	0	0.0
Ohio	3	2	66.6	2	1	50.0	4	3	75.0
Kentucky	10	4	40.0	5	3	60.0	6	0	0.0
Tennessee	10	9	90.0	2	0	0.0	4	3	75.0
Louisiana	1	1	100.0	—	—	—	1	0	0.0
Totals	1,139	615	53.9	985	501	50.8	295	192	65.0

357

TABLE XI
PERCENTAGE OF FARMERS FROM EACH STATE RECRUITED IN URBAN AREAS

Place	Percentage
Maine	13.5
Massachusetts (except Maine)	44.4
New Hampshire	16.9
Connecticut	63.5
Rhode Island	85.7
New York	28.1
Pennsylvania	65.1
New Jersey	6.6
Maryland	22.7
Virginia	38.4
North Carolina	16.7
South Carolina	2.2
Georgia	6.8
Ohio	10.3
Kentucky	11.4
Louisiana	57.9

on such occasions, though whether they were recorded as farmers or artisans by recruiting officers is uncertain.

In the South, farmers who signed on would have been drawn from across the spectrum of agricultural occupations held by the "plain folk" of that region. In the Atlantic coastal states, their numbers probably included a mixture of tenants and laborers, some of whom were already migrating in search of fresh opportunities in response to the difficulties of making a living from low-priced crops on lands of declining fertility.[46] In the backcountry and frontier regions, many farmers were engaged in both growing crops and grazing herds of cattle and hogs in the forests. They, too, were men frequently on the move, especially if they drove their livestock long distances to urban markets.[47] For all these men, north and south, it was often difficult to make farming yield more than a subsistence,

[46] For discussion of conditions for small farmers, tenants, and laborers in the South see Richard R. Beeman, *The Evolution of the Southern Backcountry: A Case Study of Lunenburg County, Virginia, 1746-1832* (Philadelphia, 1984), 170-172; Willard F. Bliss, "The Rise of Tenancy in Virginia," *Virginia Magazine of History and Biography*, LVIII (1950), 427-441; Avery Odelle Craven, *Soil Exhaustion as a Factor in the Agricultural History of Virginia and Maryland, 1606-1860* (Urbana, Ill., 1926), 118-120; Jackson Turner Main, "The Distribution of Property in Post-Revolutionary Virginia," *MVHR*, XLI (1954), 241-258; Robert P. Sutton, "Sectionalism and Social Structure: A Case Study of Jeffersonian Democracy," *VMHB*, LXXX (1972), 75-77; and Hugh Hill Wooten, "Westward Migration from Iredell County, 1800-1850," *North Carolina Historical Review*, XXX (1953), 62-69.

[47] The growing literature on the farmers and livestock herders of the southern frontier is conveniently discussed in John Solomon Otto, "The Migration of the Southern Plain Folk: An Interdisciplinary Synthesis," *Jour. So. Hist.*, LI (1985), 183-200. See also Otis K. Rice, *The Allegheny Frontier: West Virginia Beginnings, 1730-1830* (Lexington, Ky., 1970), esp. 158-169.

and land was by no means easy to acquire, least of all in long-settled or densely populated areas where pressure of population on agricultural resources had been restricting opportunity since at least the middle of the eighteenth century. As a consequence, men in their twenties customarily had to consider a number of ways, including laboring and migration, to get a start in life, and in this context military service offered some advantages.[48] The pay of a soldier was not always competitive with rural wage labor rates, but at least it promised to be steady rather than seasonal, and the large land and money bounties offered for service by 1814 would have attracted young farmers seeking to improve their holdings or acquire fresh land.[49]

Accordingly, many of the farmers in the army might have been better described, without injustice, as agricultural laborers at that point in their lives, and they often traveled considerable distances as they moved from place to place, seeking opportunities to augment their rather meager means.[50] As their movements took them to towns, it is hardly surprising that many of them were enlisted there. Some may even have gone to town for that very purpose, while others perhaps impulsively enlisted in town on a visit or a "frolic," possibly a drunken one. One of the more common grounds for requesting discharge from the army was the claim, made either by the recruit or more often by his wife or parents, that enlistment had occurred away from home and under the influence of drink.[51] For all these farmers, therefore, enlistment might be seen as another aspect of their geographical mobility, which had become so prominent a feature of rural life in early nineteenth-century America.

Compared with the "farmers" in the army, artisan recruits were drawn largely from the Middle Atlantic states. (See Table IX.) Not surprisingly perhaps, they tended to be rather more geographically mobile than farmers—barely half (50.8 percent) of the native-born artisans had

[48] See Percy W. Bidwell, "The Agricultural Revolution in New England," *AHR*, XXVI (1921), 698-700; Robert A. Gross, "Culture and Cultivation: Agriculture and Society in Thoreau's Concord," *Journal of American History*, LXIX (1982), 51; James A. Henretta, "Families and Farms: *Mentalité* in Pre-Industrial America," *WMQ*, 3d Ser., XXXV (1978), 26-32; and Darrett B. Rutman, "People in Process: The New Hampshire Towns of the Eighteenth Century," in Tamara K. Hareven, ed., *Family and Kin in Urban Communities, 1700-1930* (New York, 1977), 16-33.

[49] For military service as a means of advancement see Anderson, *People's Army*, 38-39; for data on wage rates during the War of 1812 see Stagg, *Mr. Madison's War*, 170, 173, 276, 325, 337, 456.

[50] For other discussions of rising rates of geographical mobility in the late 18th and early 19th centuries see Robert Doherty, *Society and Power: Five New England Towns, 1800-1860* (Amherst, Mass., 1977), 33-43; James T. Lemon, *The Best Poor Man's Country: A Geographical Study of Early Southeastern Pennsylvania* (Baltimore, 1972), 72-85; and Stephanie Grauman Wolf, *Urban Village: Population, Community, and Family Structure in Germantown, Pennsylvania, 1683-1800* (Princeton, N.J., 1976), 329-332.

[51] See, for example, Thomas Tinsbloom to Eustis, June 14, 1812, and P. Adams to Eustis, June 17, 1812, in Letters Received by the Adjutant General (M-566).

remained in the state of their birth—and 47.0 percent of all artisans were recruited in urban locales. (See Table X.) While artisans as a group might seem to be greatly overrepresented in the army, they were probably not so if allowance is made for the importance of towns as recruiting areas.[52] But, apart from the propensity of officers to seek recruits in towns and cities, what accounts for the readiness of so many men from urban and artisan backgrounds to join the ranks? Almost all artisans, it should be noted, were likely to have suffered some degree of hardship from the economic instability in America's coastal cities that was provoked by administration policies of commercial restriction and war between 1807 and 1815, while in the same period real wages declined and economic inequality increased.[53] Furthermore, artisan recruits were drawn overwhelmingly from the building and clothing trades (60.5 percent), and by far the largest single artisan group to enlist was shoemakers (19.2 percent). Other trades providing substantial numbers of recruits were those of carpenters (15.2 percent), blacksmiths (11.8 percent), tailors (5.6 percent), hatters (4.1 percent), and weavers (3.3 percent). (See Table XII.) There must thus have been particular reasons that led these skilled men to enlist.

By the first decade of the nineteenth century, workers in some building and clothing trades were being adversely affected by economic change, particularly by new ways of organizing production and by the development of larger markets. To reduce costs and to supply these expanding markets, both export and domestic, successful masters in the clothing and

[52] Estimating the percentage of artisans in the work force in cities is a difficult matter. Allan Kulikoff and Sean Wilentz believe that in Boston and New York in the 1790s 49.1% and 52.6%, respectively, of the work force were artisans. Kulikoff, "The Progress of Inequality in Revolutionary Boston," *WMQ*, 3d Ser., XXVIII (1971), 377; Wilentz, *Chants Democratic: New York City and the Rise of the American Working Class, 1788-1850* (New York, 1984), 27. By comparison, the percentage of artisans, where occupation is known, among the men enlisted in Boston, Baltimore, New York, and Philadelphia was 36.0, 47.1, 44.1, and 43.7, respectively.

[53] Howard B. Rock, *Artisans of the New Republic: The Tradesmen of New York City in the Age of Jefferson* (New York, 1979), 77-100. For a discussion of declining real wages see Donald R. Adams, Jr., "Wage Rates in the Early National Period: Philadelphia, 1785-1830," *Jour. Econ. Hist.*, XXVIII (1968), esp., 415-425. The literature on increasing poverty in urban areas after the Revolution is a substantial one; see especially John K. Alexander, "Poverty, Fear, and Continuity: An Analysis of the Poor in Late Eighteenth-Century Philadelphia," in Allen F. Davis and Mark H. Haller, eds., *The Peoples of Philadelphia: A History of Ethnic Groups and Lower-Class Life, 1790-1840* (Philadelphia, 1973), 13-36; Alexander, *Render Them Submissive; Responses to Poverty in Philadelphia, 1760-1800* (Amherst, Mass., 1980), esp. 11-25; Kulikoff, "Progress of Inequality in Revolutionary Boston," *WMQ*, 3d Ser., XXVIII (1971), 375-412; Raymond A. Mohl, *Poverty in New York, 1783-1825* (New York, 1971), 14-34; and Billy G. Smith, "The Material Lives of Laboring Philadelphians, 1750 to 1800," *WMQ*, 3d Ser., XXXVIII (1981), 163-202. The situation in Baltimore seems to have been more stable; see Charles G. Steffen, *The Mechanics of Baltimore: Workers and Politics in the Age of Revolution, 1763-1812* (Urbana, Ill., 1984), 3-26.

TABLE XII
ARTISAN GROUPS IN THE ARMY[a]

	N	%
Building Trades	380	25.2
Clothing Trades	532	35.3
Food Trades	83	5.5
Marine Crafts	53	3.5
Metal Crafts	229	15.2
Woodworkers	112	7.4
Other Crafts	119	7.9
Totals	1,508	100.0

[a] The classification of trades comes from Allan Kulikoff, "The Progress of Inequality in Revolutionary Boston," *William and Mary Quarterly*, 3d Ser., XXVIII (1971), 411-412.

shoe trades, sometimes with access to merchant capital, were resorting to cheaper labor. Usually, they employed apprentices, but the use of women and sometimes slaves was not unknown. The development of this "market trade" or "slop trade"—largely for the southern states—undermined conditions for journeymen, who in many cases were reduced to mere wage laborers with little hope of rising to master status. Carpenters, especially those engaged in shipbuilding, similarly found themselves working as wage laborers for large masters.[54] These changes led to increasing inequality of wealth within artisan groups, while journeymen, to preserve their handicraft traditions and their conditions of work, began to organize craft unions.[55] Craft action could sometimes succeed, but its instigators, especially shoemakers, lost a number of "conspiracy" trials after 1800 that weakened their organizations.[56] Increasingly hard-pressed,

[54] The "classic" analysis of the problems of declining artisan groups was first put forward by John R. Commons. See his introductory essay to Commons *et al.*, *A Documentary History of American Industrial Society*. Vol. III: *Labor Conspiracy Cases, 1806-1842* (New York, 1910), 19-58. More recent studies usually build on, or modify, this analysis. See Faler, *Mechanics and Manufacturers*, 8-27, 77-86; Ian M. G. Quimby, "The Cordwainers Protest: A Crisis in Labor Relations," *Winterthur Portfolio*, III (1967), 83-101; Rock, *Artisans of the New Republic*, 239-257; Sharon V. Salinger, "Artisans, Journeymen, and the Transformation of Labor in Late Eighteenth-Century Philadelphia," *WMQ*, 3d Ser., XL (1983), 62-84; Steffen, *Mechanics of Baltimore*, 27-50, and "Changes in the Organization of Artisan Production in Baltimore, 1790 to 1820," *WMQ*, 3d Ser., XXXVI (1979), 101-117; and Wilentz, *Chants Democratic*, 30-60, 97-103.

[55] Increasing inequality within artisan groups is noted by Kulikoff, "Progress of Inequality in Revolutionary Boston," *WMQ*, 3d Ser., XXVIII (1971), 387; Steffen, "Changes in the Organization of Artisan Production," *ibid.*, XXXVI (1979), 104-105; and Rock, *Artisans of the New Republic*, 254.

[56] See Rock, *Artisans of the New Republic*, 273-288. Strike action, particularly by shoemakers in Philadelphia in 1806 and in Baltimore and New York in 1809, is discussed in the literature cited in notes 53 and 54. See also Morton J. Horwitz, *The Transformation of American Law, 1780-1860* (Cambridge, Mass., 1977), 3, 22.

many artisans, most of them, judging by their ages, very probably thwarted journeymen, entered the army after 1812, where some of them, by promotion to noncommissioned officer's rank, achieved a degree of success.[57]

Laborers joined the army in all parts of the Union. Their places of recruitment show no very marked geographical concentrations, with the possible exception of Pennsylvania where 23.1 percent of recruits were from this unskilled background.[58] (See Table IX.) As a group, depending on the demand for their services, laborers could be geographically mobile or immobile, and drawn from both rural and urban areas. In states where significant numbers of laborers were recruited—such as Massachusetts, New York, and Pennsylvania—they seem to have been much less geographically mobile than other occupational groups; 65 percent of all native-born laborers enlisted in the state of their birth. (See Table X.) Laborers, like farmers, tended to be among the younger recruits, but a number of circumstances also differentiated some of them from farmers. Many more laborers (36.9 percent) were recruited in urban areas than were farmers, and a significant number of laborers (24.1 percent) were also foreign-born, far more so than was the case with farmers (4.3 percent). It would seem, then, that the laborer recruits were of two sorts: a larger number of marginal men from rural backgrounds who had not moved far, if at all, from their place of birth in search of opportunity, and a smaller group of unskilled urban workers, including some of the less successful immigrants in the coastal cities.[59]

Seamen and men in miscellaneous occupations were drawn from a small pool spread over the coastal states. (See Table IX.) Enlistees with these backgrounds had experienced a greater degree of geographical mobility than did those in other occupational groups, included a greater number of foreign-born men, and were recruited to a far greater extent in urban

[57] For a discussion of the argument that in artisan groups journeymen might be distinguished from masters on the basis of age, with the former likely to be under 30 years of age and the latter over, see Thomas Smith, "Reconstructing Occupational Structures: The Case of the Ambiguous Artisans," *Historical Methods Newsletter*, VIII (1975), 135. Artisans were more likely to become noncommissioned officers than any other occupational group. Of 275 noncommissioned officers in the sample whose occupations are known, 129 (46.9%) were artisans; 89 (32.4%) farmers; 21 (7.6%) laborers; 7 (2.5%) seamen; and 29 (10.5%) from miscellaneous occupations.

[58] For evidence of laborers concentrating in Philadelphia see Priscilla Ferguson Clement, "The Transformation of the Wandering Poor in Nineteenth-Century Philadelphia," in Eric H. Monkkonen, ed., *Walking to Work: Tramps in America, 1790-1935* (Lincoln, Neb., 1984), 59-64.

[59] For a similar argument on the degree of geographical immobility for laborers relative to other occupational groups see Georgia C. Villaflor and Kenneth L. Sokoloff, "Migration in Colonial America: Evidence from the Militia Muster Rolls," *Social Science History*, VI (1982), 554-555.

TABLE XIII
OCCUPATIONAL PERCENTAGES BY ENLISTMENT TERM

	Farmers	Laborers	Artisans	Seamen	Miscellaneous
12 months	3.6	2.1	3.0	12.0	4.8
18 months	4.5	3.3	4.1	3.3	2.1
5 years	45.3	57.3	51.5	31.3	45.8
War	46.6	37.3	41.4	53.4	47.3
	100.0	100.0	100.0	100.0	100.0

areas.[60] While it is almost impossible to generalize from the data about why men in the miscellaneous occupations joined the army, seamen may have had more easily identifiable motives. Between 1807 and 1815, commercial restriction and the war itself badly disrupted the work patterns of large numbers of seamen, while other forms of employment, such as naval service and privateering, do not seem to have absorbed the surplus in the nation's ports.[61] Clearly, many seamen decided on a period of military service as a temporary alternative to their normal vocation, an impression that is strengthened by the fact that seamen recruits showed a far stronger preference for the short terms of service than did men from other occupations. (See Table XIII). Moreover, given the frequency, particularly in New England, with which men from farming backgrounds went to sea to earn money before returning to the land, it is quite possible that seamen may have regarded military service as a way of advancing this goal as well.[62]

Finally, it might be noted that the recruits' dissatisfaction with army life—as measured by the incidence of desertion—was shared fairly equally among all occupational groups. The occupational profile of deserters conforms closely to the distribution of occupations among the recruits as a whole. (Cf. Tables VII and XIV.) Men who did desert, though, were of

[60] In cases where place of birth is known for occupational groups, 24.8% of the seamen and 29.3% of the men in miscellaneous occupations were foreign-born, and 63.4% and 62.0% of these groups respectively were recruited in urban areas. For the native-born seamen and men in miscellaneous occupations, the persistence rates in the states of their birth were 47.2% and 41.1% respectively.

[61] The U.S. Navy did not expand during the war to the same extent as the army, while seamen from the port cities do not seem to have transferred in any number to the service on the Great Lakes. See William Jones to Madison, Oct. 15, 26, 1814, Madison Papers, Lib. Cong. Alternatively, privateers by no means relied exclusively on seamen for crews, while the demand for such crews also fluctuated greatly. Moreover, privateering, like naval service, could be extremely dangerous, and privateer crews usually received no pay unless they took prizes. See Jerome R. Garitee, The Republic's Private Navy: The American Privateering Business as Practiced by Baltimore during the War of 1812 (Middletown, Conn., 1977), 127-142.

[62] See Samuel Eliot Morison, The Maritime History of Massachusetts, 1783-1860 (Boston, 1921), 105-111.

TABLE XIV
OCCUPATIONAL PROFILE OF DESERTERS

Occupation	N	%
Farmer	207	37.1
Laborer	83	14.9
Artisan	219	39.2
Seamen	28	5.0
Miscellaneous	21	3.8
Totals	558	100.0

two sorts. The first was a larger group of younger, native-born men, drawn more from the Middle and South Atlantic states than from elsewhere in the Union; 60.1 percent of the deserters whose age is known (626) were under twenty-six years of age, suggesting that older recruits may have felt greater reason to remain in service to collect their bounties, and over two-thirds of them (67.7 percent) had been born in the coastal states south of New England. The second group comprised a smaller number of foreign-born men, among whom those born in England, Scotland, France, and Spain made up a larger percentage of the deserters than they did among the foreign-born recruits as a whole.[63] Desertions were probably more likely to occur among troops based in the northern states than elsewhere in the Union, particularly among troops enlisted in Pennsylvania, 20.8 percent of whom abandoned the ranks. Many of these desertions almost certainly occurred in Philadelphia, where the army concentrated large numbers of recruits on military posts with lax security, from which men could escape all too easily and disappear into the city.[64]

In conclusion, this examination of the social composition of the United States Army between 1812 and 1815 reveals that reasonably large numbers of men were willing to enlist, induced to do so, in part, by a variety of social and economic factors. And it seems clear that these recruits, with the exception of the handful who were discharged for being too old or otherwise incapable of performing military service, were not drawn from the poorest, the most unfortunate, and the least productive

[63] In cases where the birthplace of deserters is known (646), 84.6% (547) were native born and 15.3% (99) were foreign-born. Among the foreign-born deserters, Irishmen made up only 45.4% as compared with their 52.6% of the foreign-born in the army as a whole. All other foreign-born groups were overrepresented among the foreign-born deserters.

[64] In his half-yearly report on posts in Philadelphia, Assistant Inspector General Robert Sterry emphasized that their use merely as recruiting depots was bad for discipline, and he pointed to the lack of facilities to confine offenders, including the absence of fences and picket guards, especially in the Province Island Barracks. Sterry to Armstrong, July 10, 1814, Letters Received by the Adjutant General (M-566).

men in American society. Furthermore, the number of men in service from such groups as blacks, seamen, and unskilled laborers was also too small to support the contention that the army was recruited from among those who might be described as belonging to an underclass of the permanently disadvantaged. In short, the United States could not have raised an army of any significant size at all after 1812 had it been necessary to rely on the availability of large numbers of permanently impoverished or indigent men. A broader range of men from more ordinary backgrounds had to be attracted in order to swell the ranks to the levels that were attained. At the same time, the men who did enlist were not exactly a cross section of the male population of the Union. Such groups as farmers, blacks, and westerners—not to mention men of high social status—were underrepresented in varying degrees, while artisans, urban dwellers, and New Englanders were unusually conspicuous.

But if it is inaccurate to describe the soldiers of 1812-1815 merely as poor or destitute, it can be suggested that they were men of largely respectable social status who were, nonetheless, in varying ways, close to the margins of that respectability. One factor that may have united many recruits in their decision to enlist, especially the farmers, artisans, and seamen, was that they were all men, probably more so than others in their occupations, who had felt the impact of either short-term disruption of their livelihoods, as in the case of the seamen, or, as in the case of the farmers and the artisans, of longer-term changes that were reshaping the economy and society of the early republic. The effects of economic instability provoked by national commercial and foreign policies after 1807, the pressures of population growth and related problems of maintaining viable agricultural units, the restructuring of traditional crafts and manufactures, and the experience of geographical mobility in response to these changes can all be surmised in the backgrounds of large numbers of the men who entered military service after 1812.[65] To men affected by such changes, enlistment may have appealed as one way of coping with, or escaping from, the circumstances they were facing, though this is not to say that they therefore chose a soldier's life *as a profession*. Conditions of army service were hard and hazardous, a reality clearly reflected in the rates of sickness, death, and desertion. Of those recruits who had an opportunity to reenlist during the war, very few took it, and for the vast majority one term of service was probably all they wanted. If then, as is often maintained, the War of 1812 marked a transitional phase from America's colonial premodern past toward its national, modernizing future, the soldiers who chose to fight it may have done so, in part, because they had already felt directly many of the forces producing that transformation.

[65] See Rowland Berthoff, *An Unsettled People: Social Order and Disorder in American History* (New York, 1971), 127-173; Richard D. Brown, *Modernization: The Transformation of American Life, 1600-1865* (New York, 1976), 106-127; and Henretta, *Evolution of American Society*, 192-200, 213-214.

THE PETERSBURG VOLUNTEERS, 1812-1813

by Lee A. Wallace, Jr.[*]

War against Great Britain was declared on June 18, 1812, with a determination to conquer Canada. The first offensive was Brigadier General William Hull's advance into Canada from Detroit on July 12 with an army composed largely of militia. The outposts of Fort Malden at Amherstburg, where most of the enemy was concentrated, were contacted, but Hull, overestimating their strength by tenfold, hesitated to attack. Further unnerved by the British capture of Fort Michilimackinac, which guarded the entrance to Lake Michigan, he withdrew on August 8 to Detroit. On August 16 Hull, after offering less than token resistance, was bluffed into surrendering Detroit with the entire garrison. This humiliating capitulation left the British in control of Lake Erie and the Michigan Territory. Indignation over the surrender swept the country, and there was a general outcry against Hull.[1]

On September 1 a requisition was made on Virginia for 1,500 armed militia infantrymen to march as soon as possible to the Northwestern Army in Ohio. The next day Governor James Barbour called for the quota to be drawn from the militia regiments in the counties of Brooke, Cabell, Greenbrier, Hampshire, Hardy, Harrison, Kanawha, Lewis, Mason, Monongalia, Ohio, Preston, Randolph, Tyler, and Wood.[2] Point Pleasant, on the Ohio River in Mason County, was designated as the rendezvous where the militiamen would be organized into regiments and battalions under the command of Brigadier General Joel Leftwich of Bedford County.[3] By October 12 there were 1,311 men encamped at Point Pleasant with marching orders to join the Pennsylvania militiamen at Wooster, in Wayne County, Ohio.[4]

[*] Mr. Wallace, of Falls Church, is an historian with the National Park Service.

[1] A court martial found Hull guilty of cowardice and neglect of duty, and sentenced him to be shot. President James Madison, because of Hull's services in the American Revolution, spared his life. Hull was dropped from the army and spent his remaining years writing in defense of his campaign.

[2] William Eustis, secretary of war, to Governor James Barbour, September 1, 1812, Executive Papers (September 1812), Virginia State Library, Richmond, Virginia; *The Enquirer*, Richmond, Virginia, September 8, 1812. All of the named counties are now in West Virginia.

[3] *Virginia Argus*, Richmond, Virginia, September 3, 1812. Leftwich was elected by the General Assembly, January 19, 1809, as brigadier general of the 12th Brigade, Virginia Militia (*Calendar of Virginia State Papers and Other Manuscripts*, edited by William P. Palmer *et al.* [Richmond, 1875-1893], X, 43), which was composed of regiments in the counties of Bedford, Campbell, Franklin, Henry, and Patrick.

[4] Brigadier General Joel Leftwich to Governor Barbour, October 12, 1812, Executive Papers (October 1812).

In Petersburg, the organization of a company of volunteers was already underway. A public meeting was held in the town courthouse on September 8 with Nathaniel Friend presiding, which adopted a resolution providing for the appointment of a committee of twelve to raise funds for the benefit of the company by public subscription. Another resolution expressed the sentiments of the gathering: "That the town of Petersburg will ever hold in high rememberance, those Noble & Patriotic young men, who, unmindful of every other consideration, save love of country, have volunteered their services to retrieve the reputation of the republic, so shamefully, ignominously and disgracefully sullied by the imbecile [if not treacherous] conduct of General Hull." [5]

Raised as a volunteer infantry company to be mustered into federal service for a period of one year, the Petersburg company was not a part of the quota requested of Virginia on September 1, 1812. The company was reported as having 75 enrolled on September 10, and that as soon as their uniforms were completed, they would march to Washington and tender their services to the president. It was expected that the strength would reach at least 100 before their departure.[6] The company met on September 12 and elected its officers, Captain Richard McRae, First Lieutenant William Tisdale, Second Lieutenant Henry Gary, and Ensign Shirley Tisdale.[7]

The original plan for the entire company to march to Washington was abandoned, and about September 16 Captain McRae and Lieutenant Tisdale left Petersburg for the capital. In Richmond they visited Governor Barbour, carrying with them a letter of introduction from an M. Barbour of Petersburg, urging His Excellency "to pay them all due respect and giving them every facility in your power to accomplish their object in Washington." [8] News of President Madison's acceptance of the company's services reached Petersburg before the return of the two officers on September 25.[9] The company was under orders to march for Ohio as soon as practicable, and it was thought that they would leave about October 10.[10]

---

[5] *Virginia Argus,* September 17, 1812. Nathaniel Friend was mayor of Petersburg, 1812-1813, and Edward Pescud, secretary of the meeting, served as mayor, 1818-1819.

[6] *Virginia Argus,* September 10, 1812.

[7] *Ibid.,* September 14, 1812.

[8] M. Barbour to Governor Barbour, September 15, 1812, Executive Papers (September 1812).

[9] Petersburg *Republican* quoted in *The Enquirer,* September 29, 1812; *Virginia Argus,* October 1, 1812. Captain McRae returned with the commissions of the company's four officers. The commissions were made out about September 21, but the compiled service records in National Archives Record Group No. 94 indicate that the appointments for these officers were back-dated to September 12, 1812, the day on which they were elected.

[10] *Virginia Argus,* October 1, 1812.

Eulogistic press accounts left little doubt that the Petersburg Volunteers were the finest body of young patriots ever to be raised for the service of the country. They were credited with having the firmness of character, "which will ever command respect—that glow of patriotism, which is the presage of their future glory and renown in the annals of their country—and that nobleness of soul which disdains fear, and is a stranger to dishonor." They would, predicted the writer, become "as celebrated in the war of their country as the immortal band who defended the pass of Thermopylae." [11] One Petersburg correspondent, in a letter to the Richmond *Enquirer*, declared: "This company is composed not of the dregs of society, culled from the by-lanes & alleys of the town; but of the flower of our youth and the best blood of our country. . . . They have left the caresses of friends, and the soft repose of their private life, to tread the snows of Canada and the inhospitable wilds of the Savage." [12] Another letter, in the *Virginia Argus*, revealed that the men would march supplied with every comfort imaginable, and that the ladies of Petersburg had prepared the company's flag and were busily employed in completing the uniforms and knapsacks. [13]

Twelve of the fourteen men from Amelia County who had joined the Volunteers met on October 14 at the courthouse on their way to Petersburg. Among the crowd gathered to see them off were a number of Revolutionary War veterans, and it was said to have been "a proud scene, indeed, to see the soldier of '76 clasp the hand of the young soldiers of 1812, one by one, bestowing on them their thanks, their praises; the old soldiers then formed themselves in a line, and as the young patriots marched off, gave them 3 cheers." [14]

On October 16 the company of Petersburg Volunteers was enrolled in the service of the United States for a term of twelve months. Besides the officers previously elected, the company was comprised of the following: Sergeants—Robert B. Cook, John Henderson, James Stevens, Samuel Stevens; Corporals—George T. Clough, Joseph C. Noble, John Perry, Joseph Scott, Thomas G. Scott, Norborne B. Spotswood; Musicians—Daniel Eshon, James Jackson; Privates—Richard Adams, Andrew Andrews, John W. Bentley, Joseph R. Bentley, Thomas B. Bigger, John Bignall, Robert Blick, Daniel Booker, George Booker, Richard Booker, Edward Branch, Richard H. Branch, Edmund Brown, George Burge, William Burton, James Cabiness, James G. Chalmers, Edward

---

[11] *Virginia Argus*, September 14, 1812.
[12] Reprinted in the *Virginia Argus*, October 12, 1812.
[13] *Ibid.*, October 12, 1812.
[14] *The Enquirer*, October 23, 1812.

Cheniworth, William R. Chives, Thomas Clarke, Moses Clements, Reuben Clements, Edward H. Cogbill, Samuel Cooper, George Craddock, James Cureton, William B. Degraffenreidt, George P. Digges, Grieve Drummond, Laven Dunton, Alfred O. Eggleston, James Farrar, John Frank, Frederick Gary, James Gary, Edmund S. Gee, Edmund M. Giles, Leroy Graves, George Grundy, George W. Grymes, Nathaniel Harrison, William Harrison, John C. Hill, Jacob Humbert, James Jeffers, William Lacy, William Lanier, William R. Leigh, Herbert C. Lofton, Alfred Lorrain, Roger Mallory, David Mann, Joseph Mason, Nicholas Massenburg, Benjamin Middleton, Samuel Miles, Anthony Mullen, Edward Mumford, James Pace, Benjamin Pegram, Thomas W. Perry, James Peterson, Richard Pool, John Potter, Evans Rawlings, John Rawlings, William P. Rawlings, George P. Raybourne, George Richards, John H. Saunders, Thomas Scott, Richard Sharp, John Shelton, John Shore, John H. Smith, John Spratt, Robert Stevens, Ezra Stith, John F. Wiley, David Williams, James Williams, Samuel Williams, Nathaniel H. Wills, Daniel Worsham, Thomas Worsham, and Charles Wynne.[15]

The long-awaited day for the departure finally arrived October 21, 1812. At an early hour the company and citizens began to assemble on Centre Hill, and by ten o'clock the spacious ground was filled. An hour later a hollow square was formed for the flag presentation ceremony. The flag, made by the "fair hands" of Petersburg, was presented on their behalf to the Volunteers by Benjamin Watkins Leigh, an illustrious son of Chesterfield County, Petersburg lawyer, and civic leader, who was to become one of Virginia's most distinguished statesmen.[16] In a "concise but eloquent and impressive harangue," Leigh told the Volunteers "to bear in sacred rememberance the

[15] Compiled service records, Captain Richard McRae's Co., filed under "Major Alexander's Independent Battalion Virginia Volunteers (War of 1812)," National Archives, Record Group No. 94. The file heading is curious in that Alexander's battalion consisted of only one Virginia company, McRae's, and two from Pennsylvania. A roster of the company may be found in the *Petersburg Intelligencer*, October 23, 1812. A broadside in commemoration of the Petersburg Volunteers, 8″ x 11½″, of an undetermined date prior to 1845, in the Centre Hill Mansion Museum in Petersburg, features a roster of the company, with the omission, however, of Private John McClellan, who was enlisted between May 31 and October 16, 1813. The roster on the broadside was reproduced in Henry Howe, *Historical Collections of Virginia* (Charleston, S. C., 1845 [reprinted, 1969]), pp. 245-246. Another broadside, 13½″ x 18½″, in commemoration of McRae's company, printed by James Monroe Hamilton Brunet of Petersburg in 1849 is displayed at Centre Hill. It is similar, including the same roster, but more elaborate than the older one, and is printed on silk.

[16] Benjamin Watkins Leigh (1781-1849) attended the College of William and Mary and in 1802 began law practice in Petersburg. He was first lieutenant of the Petersburg Republican Light Infantry from 1805 until 1807, when he was elected captain. Leigh had resigned by October 1812 (*The American Constellation*, Petersburg, Virginia, October 7, 1834). After serving in the House of Delegates, 1811-1813, he removed to Richmond.

fair donors and to preserve from hostile hands, this proud evidence of their regard for the honor and happiness of the company." Captain McRae, accepting the flag on behalf of Ensign Tisdale, who was absent, acknowledged the obligation the company was under to defend the flag at every hazard.[17]

Following the ceremony, the company formed in ranks and took up the line of march for their departure. Preceded by the militia cavalry, the officers of the 39th Regiment of militia, the Senior Volunteers, and the Petersburg Republican Light Infantry, the Volunteers, accompanied by carriages filled with ladies and followed by a large crowd of citizens, marched down Sycamore Street into Bollingbrook Street and across Pocahontas Bridge.[18] As they passed over the bridge, a small cannon on the armed schooner *Washington* from New York acknowledged the Volunteers with a salute. When they reached Haxall's lane, leading to Violet Bank, the Senior Volunteers and some of the citizens turned back. The procession continued to Swift Creek, where there was a brief halt for refreshments provided by John Edwards and William Rowlett. Here the Republican Light Infantry and many of the citizens dropped out. The Volunteers, followed by the cavalry, militia officers, and people who had joined in from the countryside, continued the march to Ware Bottom Church, where they made camp for the night, probably in a grove of trees near the spring, which was a short distance from the church.[19] A "plentiful dinner, and other refreshments," provided by citizens of Chesterfield County, was partaken, after which the cavalry and militia officers and others left the Volunteers for their first encampment.[20]

The next day, as the company neared Richmond, they were met by the cavalry and other militia companies of the city, with several bands, and escorted to Capitol Square, where they were welcomed by Governor Barbour amid the cheering of an immense crowd. On Saturday, October 24, a public dinner, arranged by the officers of the 19th Regiment (City of Richmond) of militia, was given for the Volunteers at Buchanan's Spring.

[17] *The Enquirer*, October 27, 1812. An ensign, the lowest commissioned rank in the infantry, was charged with carrying the unit's colors.

[18] The Senior Volunteers, apparently composed of citizens over military age, was organized at the outbreak of the war as a home guard company and still existed in 1814. The Petersburg Republican Light Infantry, a volunteer militia company attached to the 39th Regiment (Petersburg), had been organized in 1805.

[19] Ware Bottom Church was built in 1723 and has long since disappeared. A rough boulder marks the approximate site, south of the present road (Route 10) to Hopewell, about 300 yards east of the railroad overpass.

[20] *Petersburg Intelligencer*, October 23, 1812; *The Enquirer*, October 27, 1812.

Over 600 attended, with the governor presiding. As it was also muster day for the 19th Regiment, the uniformed companies were present in full dress and armed. At the center and the largest of the five tables were officers of the Revolutionary War, the governor, and the Petersburg Volunteers. Seated at the next two tables were the Richmond companies, and the remaining two tables were occupied by citizens who had subscribed for the dinner. The *Enquirer* described it as "the most sumptuous and animated feast which we have ever seen." [21]

Soon after the Volunteers arrived in Richmond they were visited by the celebrated Methodist missionary and church historian, the Reverend Jesse Lee, a native of Prince George County, and a veteran of the American Revolution, who was eminent in the early growth of Methodism in Virginia.[22] A member of the company, Alfred M. Lorrain, later to become a Methodist of considerable fame, recalled years later that Lee "recognized almost each soldier as the son of some highly esteemed friend." [23] The Volunteers solicited a sermon from Lee, and on the appointed day, the company marched to his church, which was soon packed with citizens and soldiers. The text of the sermon, directed at the youth of Richmond, was "Shall your brethren go to war, and ye sit here?" [24]

There was considerable agitation in the Richmond newspapers for the organization of a volunteer company in the city. After praising Petersburg for its company, the *Virginia Argus* on October 12 asked: "Why does not

---

[21] *The Enquirer*, October 27, 1812. Buchanan's Spring was west of the city, just north of Broad Street near Harrison Street.

[22] Jesse Lee (1758-1816) was a Methodist zealot before he was drafted into the army in 1780. Refusing to bear arms throughout his three months of service, Lee served as a wagon driver, sergeant of pioneers, and acted as an unofficial chaplain. He labored for Methodism for the remainder of his life and has been ranked near Bishop Francis Asbury. Relations between the two were intimate, but they did not always agree. Lee was the author of *A Short History of Methodists in the United States*, published in 1810.

[23] Alfred M. Lorrain (1791-1863) was born in Chester Town, Kent County, Maryland, but while an infant, his family moved to Petersburg, Virginia. In 1804 he went to sea as a cabin boy and was a sailor for seven years, ending his nautical career as a second mate. After his service with the Petersburg Volunteers during the War of 1812, Lorrain was converted to Methodism and in New Orleans in 1822, he was licensed to preach. He moved to Xenia, Ohio, the same year and from 1824 to 1861 traveled on almost all of the Ohio circuits. He was a frequent contributor to the *Ladies Repository* and from 1854 to 1855 edited the *Western Seamans' Pilot*. At the request of the conference held in Springfield, Ohio, in 1861, he wrote his autobiography, *The Helm, the Sword, and the Cross: A Life Narrative*, published in 1862. He was also the author of two volumes of "sea sermons" (*Minutes of the Annual Conferences, M. E. Church, Cincinnati Conference, 1863*; William Coyle, editor, *Ohio's Authors and Their Books* [Cleveland, 1962], p. 395).

[24] Alfred M. Lorrain, *The Helm, the Sword, and the Cross: A Life Narrative* (Cincinnati, 1862), pp. 100-102. The text is from Numbers 32:6.

Richmond follow her example? We can only sigh over the apathy which hangs over the metropolis." In complimenting the appearance of Captain McRae's company, the *Enquirer* on October 23 stated: "Richmond ought to have sent forth a compatriot band to have fought by your side; but *she* sleepeth in inglorious repose. Shame, shame, on the Metropolis of Virginia." The *Argus* of October 26 proclaimed its confidence in the raising of a Richmond company, and pointed out that "nothing is now wanting but the appearance of three or four distinguished young republicans, whom we could readily name, to raise the standard of their country—and hundreds of the flower of our youth would in one week join them and rally around it. Let but the experiment be made we can almost vouch for its success." The cries of the press were not in vain for in November the Richmond Washington Volunteers was organized.[25] The Reverend Mr. Lee's sermon reverberated in the announcement which appeared in the *Argus* on November 5: "A roll is opened in this City for a company of Volunteers. 50 enterprising spirits have already put down their names—Will you join them? Will you follow the glorious steps of Petersburg? Or 'while they go to the battle, will you sit here' in inglorious ease?"

Ordinarily the War Department furnished arms for volunteer organizations raised for federal service, but the expansion of the army had seriously depleted the government's stock. Aware of this, Captain McRae applied to the state for arms and cartridge boxes, which would be, in effect, issued on a loan basis to the federal government. The governor and Council agreed to grant McRae's request, but before arms could be carried from the state, there had to be assurances from federal authorities that the Commonwealth would be remunerated for any arms lost.[26] McRae sent two requests for these assurances to Washington, but there were no acknowledgements. Finally, on October 27, McRae, writing from Petersburg, where he-had returned be-

---

[25] The Richmond Washington Volunteers under Captain Richard Booker (1790-1853) left Richmond in July 1813 and was subsequently attached to the 20th Regiment of U. S. Infantry, which participated in the St. Lawrence Campaign. On December 29, 1813, Major General James Wilkinson, commanding the Northern Army, with headquarters at Malone, New York, published orders expressing appreciation for the services of the Volunteers, and ordered them to march for Richmond to be discharged from service (*Virginia Argus*, November 19, 1812, July 15, 1813; *Niles' Weekly Register*, IV, 5-6; "Thanks in General Orders to the Richmond Volunteers, War of 1812," *Virginia Magazine of History and Biography*, II [1894], 94-95; Certificate No. 11066WC, Mrs. Selna Booker, Pension Files, National Archives, Record Group No. 15). See also "War's Wild Alarm," *VMHB*, XLIX (1941), 217-233.

[26] Captain Richard McRae to Governor Barbour, October 11, 1812; Governor Barbour to Captain McRae, October 12, 1812; filed in the compiled service record of Captain Richard McRae, Alexander's Independent Battalion Virginia Volunteers (War of 1812), National Archives, Record Group No. 94.

cause of illness, sent another letter, stating that he had been waiting for an answer " 'till patience ceased to be a virtue," and that the company, detained in Richmond since October 21 for want of arms, was "impatient to be on the march." A postscript noted that he had been advised that the Council of State would deliver the arms to the Petersburg Volunteers, "relying on receiving the sanction & assurance of the General Government." [27] About October 29 the Volunteers received an issue of arms from the state, and on October 31 the adjutant general in Washington notified McRae that the arms furnished to his company by the executive of Virginia would be returned by the federal government when called for. [28]

On November 2 the Petersburg Volunteers marched from Richmond, escorted from the city by the volunteer companies of the 19th Regiment, the governor and other officials, and hundreds of citizens. "These men," commented the *Enquirer*, "have exhibited among us, an example of decorum and good conduct, which confers the highest credit upon them. . . . Blessings go with them! And may victory perch upon their banners." The company, it was reported, intended to camp for the night at a Mr. Williamson's eight miles from the city. [29]

Throughout their journey westward, the company was graciously received and plied with an abundance of food and drink, to the extent that they passed almost through the state without having to purchase provisions. [30] Upon their arrival at Louisa Court House, they were treated to "a fine soldier's dinner," consisting of "a Good Beef, Mutton, Shoat and Bacon, together with whiskey and Country brandy." While encamped at Major Branham's place in Louisa County, one of the Volunteers wrote on November 8 of their reception there: "We met with the same marks of respect. Capt. Wm. Wash. of this county, sent a fine stalled Beef, Major C. Quarles a plenty of good Cyder, Major Branham and others Vegetables, Straw & Our company are in good health and high spirits." [31]

The Volunteers stopped at Monticello on November 9 for a visit with the sixty-nine-year-old former president, and as Lorrain remembered it:

---

[27] McRae to Thomas H. Cushing, Adjutant General of the United States, October 27, 1812; filed in the compiled service record of Captain McRae, National Archives, Record Group No. 94.

[28] *The Enquirer*, October 30, 1812; Cushing to McRae, October 31, 1812, filed in compiled service record of Captain McRae, National Archives, Record Group No. 94.

[29] *The Enquirer*, November 3, 1812.

[30] McRae to James Madison, July 5, 1814, Madison Papers, Manuscripts Division, Library of Congress.

[31] *The Enquirer*, November 17, 1812.

We drew up, in military array, at the base of the hill on which the great house was erected. About half way down the hill stood a very homely old man, dressed in plain Virginia cloth, his head uncovered, and his venerable locks flowing in the wind. Some of our quizzical clique at once marked him as a fit subject of fun. "I wonder," said one, "what old codger that is, with his hair blowing nine ways for Easter Monday." "Why, of course," said another, "it is the overseer, and he seems to be scared out of a year's growth. I suspect he never saw gentlemen volunteers before." But how were we astonished when he advanced to our officers and introduced himself as THOMAS JEFFERSON! The officers were invited in to a collation, while we were marched off to the town, where more abundant provision had been made.[32]

From Charlottesville the company pushed across the Blue Ridge, passed through White Sulphur Springs, and, by way of the Great Kanawha River, reached Point Pleasant on the Ohio River. Unable to cross the river because of the ice, the company went into camp near the village for about two weeks. Here Captain McRae, who had been absent because of illness since late in October, rejoined his company. One member wrote that the captain "was received with every testimony of joy, almost bordering on phrenzy," and that "the inhabitants thought we were taking leave of our senses."[33]

As soon as conditions permitted the Volunteers struck tents and began the move across the river. About six of the company, impatient to reach the other side, commandeered a skiff belonging to a young inhabitant, who vigorously protested with a determination not to let the volunteers use his boat. A number of the villagers and about half the company collected at the scene, but the apparent beginnings of a brawl developed into a mutual admiration for the parties. The owner of the skiff long remembered his experience with the Petersburg Volunteers as a lesson in life, to the extent that he wrote of it in an article which appeared thirty-one years after the incident.[34]

After a fatiguing march of about sixty miles from Point Pleasant, the Volunteers on December 22 reached Chillicothe, then the capital of Ohio. It was reported that "a finer company . . . or more elegantly uniform, has

---

[32] Lorrain, *The Helm, the Sword, and the Cross*, p. 103. Two contemporary accounts, however, state that the entire company, and not just the officers, were entertained by Jefferson (*The Enquirer*, November 20, 1812; *Niles' Weekly Register*, III, 202).

[33] *Petersburg Intelligencer*, quoted in *The Enquirer*, January 7, 1813.

[34] "Scene at Point Pleasant," *American Pioneer*, II (April 1843), 174-175. The article was published pseudonymously under "Clio," with an editor's note that "The gentleman who communicated the above, could not be induced to have his proper name inserted. He is a respectable citizen of Cincinnati at this time" (*ibid.*, p. 175). The Point Pleasant story also appears in Henry Howe, *Historical Collections of Virginia*, pp. 246-247.

probably never passed through this place. They certainly do much honor to the state from which they came." The Volunteers were provided quarters in the statehouse, and on December 24 the Ohio legislature sponsored a Christmas Eve dinner for them at Buchanan's hotel. On the following day they were given another dinner, by the citizens of the town.[35]

Appointed to the command of the Northwestern Army on September 12, 1812, Major General William Henry Harrison, with headquarters at Franklinton within the present site of Columbus, undertook laborious preparations for a campaign to regain Detroit and advance into Canada. The public clamoured for a winter campaign without delay, and Harrison optimistically began preparations for it, although much more time was needed to train undisciplined troops and collect supplies. His plan was to move the army in three "wings," and have them converge at the Rapids of the Maumee River, held by the British since the loss of Detroit. Typhus fever and a shortage of clothing and provisions forced the left wing, made up of General James Winchester's Kentuckians, to halt at the beginning of December and go into winter quarters. The center wing reached the Maumee, but failing to secure a lodgement, fell back to Fort M'Arthur, forty miles from the river. The right wing occupied Lower Sandusky (later Fremont), but could move no further. In short, by the time the Petersburg Volunteers reached Chillicothe, Harrison's campaign had pretty well bogged down because of the inability to transport badly needed supplies over the muddy and mostly impassable roads.[36]

Ensign Tisdale, who had been sent ahead to contact General Harrison, rejoined the company at Chillicothe on December 23 with orders that they were to march for Upper Sandusky as soon as possible. The general, Tisdale reported, had known nothing of the company's coming, otherwise he would have sent pack horses to expedite the march.[37] As the Volunteers left Chillicothe on or about December 26, a northwester brought rain and then snow, which covered the countryside. Forcing their way through mud, ice, and snow, and across swollen streams, they reached Franklinton.[38] From there the march was continued over almost impassable roads, and on January 6, 1813, the company reached Worthington, where they were put up in the

[35] *The Supporter*, Chillicothe, Ohio, December 26, 1812; *Niles' Weekly Register*, III, 282; *The Enquirer*, January 5, 1813.

[36] Robert B. McAfee, *History of the Late War in the Western Country* (1816), (Bowling Green, Ohio, 1919), pp. 159, 182-191, 209-213.

[37] *The Enquirer*, January 7, 1813.

[38] Lorrain, *The Helm, the Sword, and the Cross*, p. 107.

local taverns.[39] Here they found Captain Daniel L. Cushing's company of the 2nd Regiment of U. S. Artillery, also en route to Upper Sandusky, and experiencing great difficulty in making their way with two wagons heavily laden with ammunition and baggage. On January 8 the march was resumed by way of Delaware, which Lorrain described as being "a handsome village—the *ultima Thule* of American civilization, as far as our route was concerned." [40] Only one cabin was passed as the company marched forty miles through the cold, desolate, snow-covered country to Upper Sandusky, which was reached about January 10, after a march of 110 miles from Chillicothe.

Meanwhile, Winchester's command had broken camp and on January 10 was encamped at the Rapids of the Maumee, awaiting Harrison, who was expected on January 20. From the Rapids they would march against Malden. Soon after reaching the Rapids, Winchester received a request for help at Frenchtown (later Monroe) on the River Raisin in Michigan, thirty-five miles north of the Rapids and eighteen miles from Malden. On January 17 most of his forces left the Rapids and, after a sharp action the next day, captured Frenchtown. Winchester with the remainder of his army, excepting about 300, left the Rapids on January 19 and arrived at Frenchtown the next day. Although a victory had been gained, Winchester was now dangerously situated within enemy-held territory, far in advance of support by Harrison.

News of Winchester's move to the Rapids reached Harrison at Upper Sandusky on the night of January 16, and the next day he started for the Rapids by way of Lower Sandusky to order up the troops stationed there. Orders were given directing the Petersburg Volunteers and other units at Upper Sandusky to proceed to the Rapids using the new road by way of the Portage River, a distance of sixty miles.[41] All were expected to depart on January 18, but as a lieutenant of Cushing's artillery wrote a few days later: "From one dam'd thing & another, being out of order & wanting repairs, we have not got started as yet." [42] On the morning of January 21 the march began, with Major Robert Orr of the Pennsylvania line in command. There

---

[39] Harlow Lindley, editor, *Captain Cushing in the War of 1812* (Columbus, 1944), p. 76. This publication includes Cushing's Orderly Book, several letters, and a roster of his company; cited hereinafter as Lindley, *Cushing*.

[40] Lorrain, *The Helm, the Sword, and the Cross*, p. 107.

[41] Alexander A. Meek to General John S. Gano, January 18, 1813, in "Selections from the Gano Papers, III," *Quarterly Publication of the Historical and Philosophical Society of Ohio*, XVI (1920), 28.

[42] Meek to Gano, January 25, 1813, "Selections from the Gano Papers, III," *Quarterly Publication of the Historical and Philosophical Society of Ohio*, XVI (1920), 33.

were, besides the Petersburg Volunteers, Captain Cushing's artillery and six companies of militia. With them were twenty pieces of artillery and a large quantity of military stores and baggage transported on wagons and sleds. After marching for nine miles, they went into camp for the night by a "little stream of very good water." [43]

On the morning of January 23 news was received of Winchester's capture of Frenchtown, but later in the day a courier arrived with the sad tidings that the British and Indians had recaptured Frenchtown, that most of Winchester's men had been killed or captured, and that Harrison expected an attack on his position at the Rapids. Major Orr was ordered to leave one company as guards for the artillery and baggage, which had to be left behind, and march at once to the Rapids with the remainder of his men. Camp was made early in the evening, and a heavy rain was falling at dark as Major Orr held council with his officers to make preparations for the next day's forced march to join Harrison. [44]

Before daylight on January 24, Orr's troops were on the road. In the lead was a train of 450 pack horses laden with salt and flour. A continual rain softened the snow into mud, which the animals churned into what Cushing described as a "bed of mortar about a foot deep." [45] His artillery, save one 6-pounder, had been left behind, and those of his company who were not struggling with it through the mire marched through the swamp beside the road. One of the Petersburg company, writing of the grueling experience, declared:

That day I regretted being a soldier. On that day we marched thirty miles, under an incessant rain; and I am afraid you will doubt my veracity when I tell you, that in 8 miles of the best road, it took us over the knees and often to the middle. The Black Swamp (4 miles from the Portage river, and 4 miles in extent) would have been considered impassable by all but men determined to surmount every difficulty to accomplish the object of their march. In this swamp you lose sight of *terra firma* altogether—the water was about 6 inches deep on the ice, which was very rotten, often breaking through to the depth of four or five feet. [46]

Moving along the same road General Hull had used the summer before, they reached the Portage River. There they learned that Harrison had left the

---

[43] Lindley, *Cushing*, pp. 77-78.
[44] *Ibid.*, pp. 78-79.
[45] *Ibid.*, p. 79.
[46] Letter from a private in McRae's company to a friend in Petersburg, March 28, 1813, published under "Picture of a Soldier's Life," in *Niles' Weekly Register*, IV, 166-168.

Rapids and had fallen back seventeen miles to the Portage. It was still raining when they camped for the night, their clothing was drenched, and the tents had been left behind. Fires were built with considerable difficulty, and although they had no cooking utensils and but few provisions, the Petersburg Volunteers managed a fairly decent supper. Flour was procured from the nearby packhorses and baked into bread in ashes. A hog was killed, butchered, and the pork broiled on the coals—"a sweeter meal I never partook of," was the opinion of at least one volunteer.[47]

When reinforcements could be collected, Harrison proposed a return to the Rapids. Meanwhile, an attack on the position at the Portage was not held improbable, and for several nights, wrote one of the Petersburg Volunteers, "we went to sleep with our muskets in our arms, and all our accoutrements fixed for action." [48] Delayed on his march from Lower Sandusky by heavy rains which began on January 24, General Leftwich with his Virginia brigade, a regiment of Pennsylvanians, and a considerable amount of artillery, reached the Portage on January 30.[49] With his forces now at about 1,700, Harrison moved up to the east side of the Maumee River, and on February 2 established camp at the foot of the Rapids. The arrival of more Pennsylvania troops nine days later raised Harrison's strength to slightly over 2,000.

Work soon began on the construction of a strongly fortified position with eight blockhouses, elevated battery emplacements, powder magazines, and a palisade 2,500 yards in circumference. Five 18-pounders, six 12-pounders, six 6-pounders, and three howitzers were placed in position as the fort's construction progressed.[50] Daily the men were set to work cutting trees, splitting logs, digging, and in other endless tasks necessary for the completion of the fort, which was named for Ohio's governor, Return Jonathan Meigs.[51] It was an unusually severe winter, and the frozen ground required the most strenuous use of the spade and wielding of the mattox and pickax. Alfred Lorrain recalled that: "This season of fatigue was replete with hardships, as it was in the depths of winter, and we suffered from many priva-

---

[47] "Picture of a Soldier's Life," *Niles Weekly Register*, IV, 167.

[48] *Ibid.*

[49] McAfee, *History of the Late War in the Western Country*, pp. 259-260.

[50] "Journal of the Northwestern Campaign of 1812-13, . . . Bvt. Lieut.-Colonel Eleazer D. Wood, Capt. Corps of Engineers, U. S. Army," in George W. Cullum, *Campaigns of the War of 1812-5, against Great Britain, Sketched and Criticised; with Brief Biographies of the American Engineers,* (New York, 1879), pp. 370-373; cited hereinafter as Wood's "Journal."

[51] The origin of Governor Meigs's singular name is discussed in Benson J. Lossing, *The Pictorial Field-Book of the War of 1812* (New York, 1868), p. 255n.

tions. However our bodies and minds were actively employed which rendered our condition far preferable to what followed." [52]

The Petersburg company was sent out with a detachment of about 600 on the evening of February 9 to attack an estimated 200 Indians reported to be some fifteen miles down the Maumee. Marching on ice for most of the way, they reached the area in which the Indians were supposed to be about 4 o'clock in the morning, and in battle order they quietly advanced. "I could hear the men cocking their pieces," wrote one of the Volunteers, "our company to a man, were even at that moment cheerful and gay! fear was far distant from our ranks." Much to their disappointment, the Indians had left, and after a pursuit of about eight miles, the detachment gave up and returned to Fort Meigs.[53] Again, on March 4, Captain McRae's company was sent out, this time with a party which was to cover the retreat of an unsuccessful expedition fitted out from the fort on February 26 to burn the British brig *Queen Charlotte* at Malden. They met the expedition at the mouth of Lake Erie, and returned with them to the fort on the following day.[54]

In late January the Petersburg Volunteers and two companies of twelve-month volunteers from Pennsylvania were organized into a battalion under Major John B. Alexander, who was promoted from captain of the Greensburgh Riflemen, a small company of about twenty-three.[55] The other company was Captain James R. Butler's Pittsburgh Blues, which had a total strength of about thirty-nine.[56] The two Pennsylvania companies, both of which had seen action at the battle of Missineway, November 18, 1812, did not reach Fort Meigs until March 18.[57] Major Alexander, wrote one of McRae's company, "is as fine a fellow as I ever knew—The most perfect

[52] Lorrain, *The Helm, the Sword, and the Cross*, p. 124.

[53] Lindley, *Cushing*, p. 87; "Picture of a Soldier's Life," *Niles' Weekly Register*, IV, 167.

[54] Lindley, *Cushing*, pp. 89-90; "Picture of a Soldier's Life," *Niles' Weekly Register*, IV, 167.

[55] Greensburgh (Pennsylvania) *Gazette*, quoted in *The Enquirer*, February 9, 1813; Pittsburgh *Gazette*, January 29, 1813; compiled service record of Captain John B. Alexander, Alexander's Independent Battalion Volunteers (War of 1812), National Archives, Record Group No. 94; Muster Roll, Captain John B. Alexander's Company, Volunteer Riflemen (Pennsylvania), December 31, 1812, National Archives, Record Group No. 94 (Entry 55, Muster Rolls of Volunteer Organizations: War of 1812).

[56] Muster Roll, Captain James R. Butler's Company Light Infantry (Pennsylvania), January 18, 1813, Alexander's Independent Battalion Volunteers (War of 1812), National Archives, Record Group No. 94 (Entry 55). For a history of the Pittsburgh Blues, see John H. Niebaum, "The Pittsburgh Blues," *Western Pennsylvania Historical Magazine*, IV (1921), 110-122, 175-185, 259-270; V (1922), 244-250.

[57] Lindley, *Cushing*, p. 88; Niebaum, "The Pittsburgh Blues," *Western Pennsylvania Historical Magazine*, IV (1921), 261.

harmony exists between the Pittsburg company and ours . . . a generous emulation exists among them, . . . officers and men mingle together; we visit each others tents of an evening, sing, tell stories, play music, and drink grog, when we can get it; which by-the-bye, is not often the case, suttlers not being permitted to sell spirits in the camp." [58]

Soon after their arrival at the Rapids the Volunteers suffered their first loss, Private Andrew Andrews, who died from "diseases of a severe climate." [59] Conditions within the camp were far from healthful, with mud and water covering the ground, even within the tents. Worse still was the lack of wood for fires. As the timber had been cut for a long distance around the fort, wood had to be collected and hauled in by teams, for which there was "not a bushel of forage." On March 8 Private Edmund S. Gee died, and a companion who was present wrote: "I saw him breathe his last—we consigned him to his mother earth with all the decency our circumstances would permit. . . . All the battalion attended the funeral—likewise general Leftwich, who requested the chaplain to perform a funeral service, a thing not done on any similar occasion." [60] Corporal James Stevens died on March 17, and two days later Captain Cushing noted in his journal: "Our men are very sickly; no wonder lying in mud and water and without fire; not less than two or three men died every day, and I expect the deaths to increase unless the weather changes very soon." [61]

The advance to Malden set for early February was abandoned, and with the departure of the Kentucky and Ohio militia, whose terms of service had expired, there was no hope for a campaign until spring. Harrison left on March 5 to make arrangements for more troops, and, on the same day, his engineer officer, Captain Eleazer D. Wood, went to superintend the building of fortifications at Lower Sandusky. General Leftwich, now in command, was charged with completing Fort Meigs, but Wood, who returned on March 18, found that "this phlegmatic, stupid old granny, so soon as General Harrison left camp, stopped the progress of the work entirely, assigning as a reason that he couldn't make the militia do anything," and that Leftwich had even permitted the timber brought in for building blockhouses to be used as fuel. [62]

[58] "Picture of a Soldier's Life," *Niles' Weekly Register*, IV, 167.

[59] Letter by Richard McRae, April 20, 1854, filed with the compiled service record of Private Andrews, Captain McRae's Company, Alexander's Independent Battalion Virginia Volunteers (War of 1812), National Archives, Record Group No. 94.

[60] "Picture of a Soldier's Life," *Niles' Weekly Register*, IV, 167.

[61] Lindley, *Cushing*, pp. 91-92.

[62] Wood's "Journal," pp. 378-397.

The strength of the garrison was seriously depleted on April 2, when Leftwich and his brigade, with most of the Pennsylvania militia, left for their homes, their terms of service having ended. Wood wrote, "And away went every Virginian belonging to the drafted militia, without the least concern as to what became of those they left behind, or caring whether the enemy or ourselves were in possession of the camp, so long as they could escape from the defense of it." [63] With Leftwich's departure, the command of Fort Meigs devolved upon Major Amos Stoddard, 2nd Regiment of Artillery, veteran of the American Revolution, lawyer, and former acting governor of Louisiana.[64]

A fifteen-gun salute on April 12 welcomed the return of Harrison with 200 regulars and militia. More arrived later, and by April 23 the garrison had an effective strength of about 1,600.[65] Work continued feverishly on completing the fort and readying it for the siege, which was now more than a possibility. It had been known for several weeks that Colonel Henry Proctor was collecting his forces at Malden and Detroit, and on April 18 word came that the attack would be in about twelve days.[66] The forces which embarked at Malden on April 24 numbered slightly over 2,000, including 413 of the British 41st Regiment of Foot, 468 Canadian militiamen, and about 1,200 Indians.[67] Landing at the mouth of the Maumee, they moved up the north bank of the river, and established their main camp about two miles below Fort Meigs. While battery positions were being prepared nearly opposite Fort Meigs, the Indians crossed the river and surrounded the fort in the rear and on the flanks.

Inside the fort Harrison put his men to work throwing up the "grand traverse," which could be erected only after determining the location of the enemy batteries. It was an earthen embankment twelve feet high and extended through the middle of the fort, where the tents of the garrison were pitched, and parallel with the batteries across the river. The tents which had been left to conceal the construction of the traverse were removed,

---

[63] *Ibid.* Letters were received from Harrison on March 29 urging the Virginia and Pennsylvania brigades to stay a few days longer, and Cushing, who does not appear to have shared Wood's harsh opinion of the Virginians, wrote: "These calls and invitations will not do; the government has not been punctual enough in paying their troops for them to stay longer" (Lindley, *Cushing*, p. 94). In February 1822 Leftwich was appointed major general, 1st Division, Virginia Militia (*Calendar of Virginia State Papers*, X, 502). He died on April 20, 1846.

[64] Stoddard was wounded during the siege, and died on May 11 of tetanus.

[65] Lindley, *Cushing*, p. 125.

[66] *Ibid.*, pp. 96, 100.

[67] Alexander C. Casselman, editor, *Richardson's War of 1812* (Toronto, 1902), pp. 165-166.

and bombproofs were dug in its base on the sheltered side. As the men were completing the traverse and removing the tents, the batteries played on the surrounding Indians with grape and canister and bombarded the British at work on their emplacements across the river.[68]

The British on the night of April 30 towed a gunboat up the river to a position near the fort, and after firing thirty rounds, which were ineffective, withdrew before daylight. Late on the morning of May 1 the batteries on the opposite shore opened and during the day expended about 250 rounds, but without much injury to the fort. Not more than two were killed and four wounded. During the night the firing was just enough to keep the garrison from rest. A heavy fire from all four of the enemy's batteries began on the morning of May 2, and, with the Indians firing from the treetops nearest the fort, continued all day. Harrison's losses were four killed and seven wounded.[69]

Working largely at night, the British established a battery consisting of a light gun and a mortar on Harrison's side of the river in a broad ravine about 300 yards on the right of the fort. With these pieces and the batteries across the river, Fort Meigs was subjected to a galling cross fire. Some 516 rounds were discharged at the fort on May 3, but the garrison suffered few losses. On May 4 Harrison refused Proctor's demand for a surrender, and late that night he received the good news that General Green Clay's Kentucky brigade of 1,200 would soon arrive.[70] With the day there came a loss to the Petersburg Volunteers, Second Lieutenant Gary, who died after a long illness.[71]

May 5 was the momentous day of the siege and is the date upon which the fame of the Petersburg Volunteers largely rests. On Clay's arrival 846 of his brigade, under Colonel William Dudley, landed on the north side of the river and captured the enemy's batteries, which were without the support of infantry. Instead of returning to the fort after spiking the guns as ordered, the Kentuckians lingered about, some going in pursuit of the fleeing Indians. Three companies of the 41st Regiment, some Canadian militia, with Tecumseh and his Indians, rallied and drove in between Dudley's men and the

---

[68] Wood's "Journal," pp. 389-390; Lindley, *Cushing*, p. 102.

[69] *Ibid.*, pp. 102-103.

[70] Green Clay (1757-1826), a native of Powhatan County, Virginia, migrated to Kentucky about 1777. He had little schooling, but with a knowledge of surveying, and by acquiring land, accumulated a fortune. He served in both houses of the legislature and became a major general in the Kentucky militia at the outbreak of war in 1812.

[71] *The Enquirer*, June 4, 1813.

river, killing and capturing the entire force save about 170 who managed to escape to Fort Meigs.[72]

While the British batteries were being spiked, the remainder of Clay's brigade on the south bank of the river fought their way to Fort Meigs, arriving in time for three companies of the Kentuckians to join a sortie on its way out to engage the Indians on the left flank of the fort. A detachment from Alexander's battalion, comprised of McRae's company and the Pittsburgh Blues, was included in the sallying party. The Indians were driven back into the woods a half a mile or so, but the pursuing troops, becoming reckless and overconfident, very nearly experienced a disaster like that suffered by Dudley's men on the north bank.[73]

Harrison ordered a sortie against the battery in the ravine on the right of the fort. In support of the battery Proctor had the grenadier and light infantry companies of the 41st Regiment, two companies of Canadian militia, and Tecumseh with some 500 Indians; in all, about 850.[74] Under the command of Colonel John Miller, 19th U. S. Infantry, the sortie consisted of detachments from seven companies of the 19th and 17th U. S. Infantry regiments, Captain Uriel Sebree's company of Kentucky militia, and Major Alexander's battalion of volunteers. The Petersburg Volunteers was the largest of the battalion's companies, with 64 men under First Lieutenant Tisdale, who commanded in the absence of Captain McRae, who was ill as were many others in the company.[75] The Pittsburgh Blues, led by First Lieutenant Matthew Magee in place of Captain Butler, who was indisposed, numbered about 25.[76] No more than a dozen or so of the Greensburgh Riflemen, under Lieutenant Peter Drum, participated.[77] In all, Miller had about 350 men.

The troops were assembled in a small ravine just beyond the southeast wall of the fort, out of the enemy's sight. Lieutenant Tisdale, nicknamed

---

[72] McAfee, *History of the Late War in the Western Country*, pp. 291-295.

[73] *Ibid.*, pp. 288-289; *Niles' Weekly Register*, IV, 210; Niebaum, "The Pittsburgh Blues, Part III," *Western Pennsylvania Historical Magazine*, IV (1921), 261; Lorrain, *The Helm, the Sword, and the Cross*, p. 133.

[74] McAfee, *History of the Late War in the Western Country*, p. 290.

[75] *The Enquirer*, June 4, 8, 1813; see also Muster Roll, Captain McRae's Co., May 31, 1813, Alexander's Independent Battalion Volunteers (War of 1812), National Archives, Record Group No. 94 (Entry 55).

[76] Niebaum, "The Pittsburgh Blues," *Western Pennsylvania Historical Magazine*, IV (1921), 181-182; Muster Roll, Captain James R. Butler's Co., February 28, 1813-May 31, 1813, Alexander's Independent Volunteer Battalion (War of 1812), National Archives, Record Group No. 94 (Entry 55).

[77] Muster Roll, detachment of Volunteer Riflemen under command of Lieutenant Peter Drum, May 31, 1813, Alexander's Independent Volunteer Battalion (War of 1812), National Archives, Record Group No. 94 (Entry 55).

"Old Sluefoot" by the men, paced back and forth in front of the company, urging them to rush forward with a tremendous shout. Harrison, after passing through the ranks offering encouragement, took a post at a nearby battery to observe the attack. The word was given, and moving out of the ravine at trail arms, they advanced up a hill in full view of the enemy. As they reached the top, the companies of the 41st Regiment opened fire but inflicted few casualties. Miller's lines moved out on a plain some 200 yards in width, and after advancing about 50 yards, halted, closed ranks, and, with the Petersburg company on the right flank, charged, firing as they went. The Indians, firing from the woods with considerable effect, came very near turning the right of Miller's line and getting into the rear, which could have been disastrous. As they were driving the enemy back in confusion and spiking the gun and mortar in the battery, Sebree's company, outflanked by the enemy, became locked in a hand-to-hand struggle, which ended when Harrison sent in a company of regulars. About noon the fighting ceased, and Miller, his objective accomplished, returned to the fort with 42 prisoners.[78]

The casualties of the sortie were reported as 30 killed and about 90 wounded, of whom Alexander's battalion had two killed, both members of the Pittsburgh Blues, and 29 wounded.[79] Seventeen of the Petersburg Volunteers were wounded, most of the wounds were slight, but three proved fatal. On May 10 Nicholas Massenburg died, George Booker died on May 12, and George Clough on May 18.[80] The company's number of casualties was largely attributed to its exposed position on the right flank during the assault.[81]

Harrison wrote of the "intrepidity" of the Petersburg Volunteers in his report of May 9, and Captain Wood noted in his journal: "The company of volunteers from Petersburg (Virginia) particularly distinguished them-

---

[78] Wood's "Journal," pp. 399-400; Lorrain, *The Helm, the Sword, and the Cross*, pp. 133-136.

[79] *Niles' Weekly Register*, IV, 192; Wood's "Journal," p. 400.

[80] Muster Roll, Captain McRae's Co., Alexander's Independent Battalion Virginia Volunteers (War of 1812), February 8-May 31, 1813, National Archives, Record Group No. 94 (Entry 55). Two others wounded in the sortie were Sergeant Herbert C. Lofton (promoted March 17, 1813); Corporals Joseph Scott, Thomas G. Scott; Musician Jackson; and Privates Blick, Cooper, Chives, Drummond, Leigh, Thomas Perry, Stith, Thomas Scott, Samuel Williams, and John F. Wiley. The muster roll does not substantiate the wounding of the following as indicated on the broadsides in the Centre Hill Mansion Museum: Musician Eshon, and Privates Edmund Brown, Joseph Mason, and Samuel Stephens. An ode to the memory of George Booker by "J. T. W." of Amelia County, June 30, 1813, appeared in the *Virginia Argus*, July 8, 1813.

[81] *The Enquirer*, June 3, 4, 8, 1813.

selves by their intrepid and cool conduct, while approaching the batteries under a heavy fire of musketry." [82] No lesser tribute, however, was paid the Volunteers by an unknown post rider, who declared that they "fought like devils." [83]

Sergeant John Henderson of the Petersburg Volunteers had charge of a battery served by others of his company. One of them, John Shore, who was said to have been largely responsible for the organization of the company, was wounded by a splinter and died of lockjaw on May 8. A letter to his brother in Petersburg disclosed that the battery was "manned by the Petersburg Volunteers—a Battery, my dear sir, that did more execution among the enemy than any other at Fort Meigs." [84] Harrison in his report on May 9 wrote that "The battery managed by Sergt. Henderson was as the enemy confessed—managed with peculiar efficacy & effect with respect to the sorties which were made on the 5th inst." Henderson, recommended for promotion by Harrison, was commissioned a lieutenant in the 2nd Regiment of Artillery. In July one of the fort's batteries was named in his honor.[85]

The end of the siege on May 9 left Fort Meigs with 81 killed and 189 wounded. Along with the many who were too sick for active duty, the wounded suffered much from the extreme wet and cold. Many of them lay on rails to keep above water until they could be placed in the blockhouses converted into temporary hospitals.[86] Dysentery prevailed in the fort, and on May 20 it was said that not more than twenty of the Petersburg Volun-

---

[82] *Niles' Weekly Register*, IV, 211; Wood's "Journal," p. 400.

[83] *The Enquirer*, June 4, 1813.

[84] *The Enquirer*, May 29, 1813. "Captain Jack Shore," wrote Lorrain, was "the darling of our crew," and as a kinsman of General Harrison, "had more than once taken tea with his distinguished cousin, 'sub rosa,' in the grand marquee" (*The Helm, the Sword, and the Cross*, pp. 138-139).

[85] *The Enquirer*, June 8, 1813; Lindley, *Cushing*, p. 47; compiled service record of John Henderson, Captain McRae's Co., Alexander's Independent Battalion Volunteers (War of 1812), National Archives, Record Group No. 94. Henderson was described by the *Petersburg Intelligencer* as a "true honest son of Hibernia," who had "served for many years in the floating dungeons of Britain," and had "migrated to this land of liberty, in search of those blessings and privileges denied of him in the country of his nativity. He entered the ranks here with all that zeal and devotion so characteristic of the Irish" (*Virginia Argus*, May 31, 1813). He was commissioned on June 20, 1813, but his career in the regular service was not especially commendable. At Fort Meigs, July 21, 1813, he was tried, but acquitted on six charges which involved "Unexemplary & disorderly conduct, . . . being in a evident state of inebriety" (Lindley, *Cushing*, pp. 52-53). Henderson was dismissed from the service on April 2, 1818 (Charles K. Gardner, *A Dictionary of the Army of the United States*, 2nd edition [New York, 1860], p. 224), and is believed to have been the John F. Henderson who died in New Orleans, Louisiana, in 1858 (Petersburg, Virginia, *Daily Express*, June 5, 1858).

[86] Wood's "Journal," pp. 401-402.

teers were fit for duty.[87] Cushing wrote on May 22 that several of the sick had died, and "not more than could be expected, considering the fatigue and the badness of the weather they have experienced for the last thirty days."[88] At the end of the month the rolls of the Petersburg company noted 41 men as sick. John Cureton died on June 13, Corporal John Perry on the 14th, and three days later, William Lacy and George P. Raybourne died. On June 16 Captain McRae, who seems to have been sick for much of his time in service, with several of his company, Lieutenant Magee of the Pittsburgh Blues, and some from Cushing's artillery company left for Cleveland where it was hoped they would regain their health.[89]

On July 21, Proctor, now a major general, returned for another try at Fort Meigs, then under the command of General Clay, and found the fort stronger than before. A ruse to draw the garrison from the fort into the open to be ambushed failed, and on July 28, the "second siege" was lifted. Proctor then moved down the Maumee, along Lake Erie, and up the Sandusky River, to attack Fort Stephenson at Lower Sandusky, ten miles from Harrison's main supply depot at Seneca Town. Harrison moved his forces closer to the depot, leaving in command of Fort Stephenson twenty-one-year-old Major George Croghan, 17th U. S. Infantry, who had distinguished himself in Miller's sortie at Fort Meigs.[90] Croghan had only 160 men and one iron 6-pounder to defend the fort, which was attacked on the first of August.

A severe cannonade by the British on the first day had little effect. The 6-pounder occasionally replied, and was shifted about to give the impression of more artillery. Late on August 2 the 41st Regiment advanced 400 strong, with an assault column coming within 50 yards before it was discovered. Musketry sent their lines into confusion, but they rallied and swarmed into the ditch just outside the palisade. A masked port was opened, and the 6-pounder sent forth a deadly fire of grape and slugs into the ranks of the redcoats. Another assault was attempted and again with the same result. Proctor gave up and left that night for Malden with almost 100 casualties. In the fort there had been one killed and seven slightly wounded. Petersburg's link with the determined defense of the fort and the 6-pounder, later dubbed

---

[87] *Virginia Argus*, June 3, 1813.

[88] Lindley, *Cushing*, p. 108.

[89] *Ibid.*, p. 112. The Richmond, Virginia, *Daily Compiler*, June 29, 1813, reprinted a notice from the Petersburg *Republican*, which stated that John Perry had died on June 10.

[90] George Croghan (1791-1849), a Kentuckian, attended the College of William and Mary, 1809-1810. At the battle of Tippecanoe he served as a volunteer aide-de-camp to Harrison, who recommended his appointment as captain in the regular army.

"Good Bess," is found in Harrison's report of the action, which in part read: "A young gentleman private in the Petersburg Volunteers, of the name of [Edmund] Brown, assisted by five or six of that company and of the Pittsburgh Blues, who were accidently in the fort, managed the six pounder which produced such destruction in the ranks of the enemy." [91] Another of the Petersburg company with the 6-pounder was Edward Mumford. [92]

After Fort Stephenson, Harrison began organizing his forces for an offensive against Malden by water, the success of which depended upon the control of Lake Erie. The garrison of Fort Meigs was reduced in size, and leaving 300 men there, including about twenty of the Petersburg Volunteers under Lieutenant Tisdale, General Clay on August 18 marched with the balance to Harrison's headquarters at Lower Seneca Town. [93] There, on August 28, Alexander's battalion was broken up when the Pittsburgh Blues and the Greensburgh Riflemen were discharged, their terms of enlistment having expired. Within a period of three weeks, when the Petersburg Volunteers were at Fort Meigs and Camp Seneca, the ranks of the company were reduced by the deaths of Samuel Miles, William Lanier, William P. Rawlings, and Samuel Williams, who had been among the wounded on May 5.

The Petersburg company was now attached to Lieutenant Colonel James V. Ball's squadron of about 400 "chosen men," selected to be the first to land on the Canadian shore. In a letter from Camp Seneca on September 10 one of the Volunteers said: "I now write you for the last time (in all probability) from this place, as we shall move from this post in four or five days for Malden. . . . Our troops, throughout the whole camp, are in high spirits, and pant for the moment when they shall encounter the enemy." Another of the company wrote: "I merely wish to inform you, the time has at last arrived, when we have to march for Canada . . . should I come off even as well as at Fort Meigs, I would be contented." [94]

Tisdale's detachment left Fort Meigs on September 7 and on the 11th rejoined the company at Lower Sandusky. En route, on Lake Erie, they had

---

[91] *Niles' Weekly Register*, IV, 389.

[92] General Orders, Headquarters, Seneca Town, August 8, 1813, in Lindley, *Cushing*, p. 55. Since 1850 "Good Bess" has occupied a position on the site of Fort Stephenson in the heart of Fremont, Ohio; see Julia M. Haynes, "Fremont in History," *Ohio Archaeological and Historical Publications*, X (1901-1902), 49-66, and Lossing, *The Pictorial Field-Book of the War of 1812*, p. 507n.

[93] *Virginia Argus*, September 8, 1813.

[94] *Ibid.*, September 27, 1813.

been within a short distance of the two fleets during the famous battle of September 10, in which Commodore Oliver Hazard Perry defeated the British and opened the way for Harrison's invasion of Canada. At least three of the Petersburg company had answered to the call for volunteers to serve with the fleet. Private John H. Smith was one. Another was one of the two Harrisons, but which of them, William or Nathaniel, is undetermined. Former Sergeant John Henderson, then a second lieutenant in the 2nd Artillery, also volunteered and was posted in the tops with a musket. All three escaped injury.[95]

The army embarked on September 20 for the rendezvous points at Put-in-Bay Island, Bass Island, and Middle Sister Island, about twelve miles off the Canadian shore. On board Perry's ship, the schooner *Ariel*, late in the evening the officers, having dined, were on deck enjoying the cool breeze. Major John Chambers, volunteer aide to General Harrison, and future governor of the Iowa Territory, was approached by one of the Petersburg Volunteers, who asked if it would be possible to obtain a cup of coffee, saying that he was still weak from malaria and had been unable to eat the cold and coarse rations issued to the company. Chambers felt powerless to grant the request, but within a half an hour, and to his gratification, the entire company was relishing an excellent hot supper, thanks to Commodore Perry who, after overhearing the conversation, had ordered its preparation.[96]

Late in the afternoon of September 27 Harrison's army landed about three miles below Malden, which was occupied the same day. Sandwich and Detroit, just across the river, were entered on September 29. With his forces increased by the arrival of Colonel Richard Johnson's Mounted Regiment of 1,000 Kentuckians, Harrison went in pursuit of the enemy. The victory at the Battle of the Thames, 56 miles east of Detroit on October 5, ended in the disgrace of Proctor and the death of Tecumseh, but, more important, it brought to an end the fighting in the Northwest. The Petersburg Volunteers, in the rear guard, did not arrive in time to share in the fighting. "I for one was right glad of it," Lorrain recalled, "for our time of service was now expired, and the word[s] 'home, sweet home,' seemed to gather additional charms every day."[97] The release of the volunteer troops in the

[95] John Cook Wyllie, editor, "'Observations Made During a Short Residence in Virginia,' In a Letter from Thomas H. Palmer, May 30, 1814," *Virginia Magazine of History and Biography*, LXXVI (1968), 409; *Virginia Argus*, September 30, 1813.

[96] James Cooke Mills, *Oliver Hazard Perry and the Battle of Lake Erie* (Detroit, 1913), p. 174.

[97] Lorrain, *The Helm, the Sword, and the Cross*, p. 153.

army began soon after their return to Detroit. There on the public parade ground the Petersburg company was discharged by the following order:

General Orders   Head-Quarters Detroit—17th October, 1813

The term of Service for which the Petersburg Volunteers were engaged, having expired, they are permitted to commence their march to Virginia, as soon as they can be transported to the South side of the Lake.

In granting a discharge to this Patriotic and Gallant Corps, the General feels at a loss for words adequate to convey his sense of their exalted merits. Almost exclusively composed of individuals who had been nursed in the lap of ease, they have, for twelve months, borne the hardships, and privations of Military life in the midst of an inhospitable wilderness, with a cheerfulness and alacrity which has never been surpassed. Their conduct in the Field has been excelled by no other Corps; and whilst in Camp, they have set an example of Subordination and Respect for Military Authority to the whole Army. The General requests Captain M'Rae, his Subalterns, Non-Commissioned Officers and Privates, to accept his warmest thanks—and bids them an Affectionate Farewell.

By Command,

ROBERT BUTLER,
Acting Assistant Adjutant General[98]

Muskets were turned in and the company began its long journey homeward. They waited for about a week in Cleveland, expecting to receive their final pay, but when the paymaster, James G. Chalmers, a member of the company, failed to appear, the Volunteers broke up into "little social bands, in different routes," Lorrain recalled, for Petersburg.[99] A number went to Pittsburgh, still hoping to meet Chalmers, but after about ten days they started for home. Lorrain and three of his intimate friends, who do not appear to have been with the group at Pittsburgh, traveled to Petersburg by way of Winchester and Fredericksburg. From Petersburg on November 12 it was announced that three of the company had arrived on the 9th and "nearly all the rest, we understand, are on the way, by different routes, and may be shortly expected to arrive. With the exception of Captain McRae, the Members of the Company generally . . . enjoy good health."[100]

---

[98] *The Enquirer*, November 16, 1813.

[99] Lorrain, *The Helm, the Sword, and the Cross*, p. 154. Chalmers was alleged to have lost the money gambling. Finally, forty years after the Petersburg Volunteers had been discharged, Congress, on March 3, 1853, appropriated $10,334.31, to be paid to the survivors, or their heirs. The provision was included in the act making an appropriation for the support of the army for the year ending June 30, 1854; see George Minot, editor, *The Statutes at Large and Treaties of the United States of America. From December 1, 1851, to March 3, 1855*, X (Boston, 1855), 217.

[100] *Virginia Argus*, November 14, 1813.

The firing of cannon at dawn and sunrise on January 8, 1814, opened the festivities honoring the returned Volunteers. Three guns fired at noon brought the militia companies, the Volunteers, and many citizens to Centre Hill, where after salutes were rendered to the company, the procession left for Poplar Spring, within the grounds which later became known as Poplar Lawn. There Postmaster Thomas Shore, brother of the lamented John Shore, who died at Fort Meigs, delivered the oration, in which he declared: "The pride of Sparta were the heroes of Thermopylae, the pride of Virginia the heroes of Fort Meigs." Appropriate selections were rendered by the band, and all joined in the singing of patriotic airs. The hall in which the dinner was held that afternoon was bedecked with a variety of flags, "among which waved conspicuously the war worn banner of the heroes of Fort Meigs." [101] This was not the only observance that year in connection with the Petersburg Volunteers. A number of the veterans who had removed to Richmond borrowed two field pieces from the state, and on May 7, the *Enquirer* reported: "We understand that the National Salute fired in this city on Thursday [May 5] was to commemorate the Anniversary of the Sortie from Fort Meigs." [102]

Traditionally, President Madison reviewed the company on its way home in 1813, and at the time conferred upon Petersburg a sobriquet, "The Cockade City of the Union," which is usually shortened to "The Cockade City." Madison, searching for something complimentary to say, possibly thought of the leather cockade ornamenting the soldiers' hats. Thus, Petersburg in furnishing the volunteer company which had served so well at Fort Meigs, was the ornament, or cockade, of the Union. There seems to be some historical basis for this cherished legend, but contemporary evidence as to exactly *when* the incident occurred is lacking. As the Volunteers traveled homeward in separate groups Madison could not have reviewed the company in its entirety, but it may have been that some of the returning soldiers stopped to see him in Washington. Another possibility is that the sobriquet was conferred at the time McRae was in Washington during July 1814 settling accounts with the War Department.[103]

---

[101] *Virginia Argus,* January 17, 1814; *The Enquirer,* January 11, 1814.

[102] Executive Papers (May 1814), Virginia State Library.

[103] The Madison Papers (Library of Congress) include two letters written by McRae while in Washington in 1814, but there is no evidence that he met the president. It is plausible that the sobriquet was conferred *before* the company left for the war, when McRae and Tisdale visited Washington in September 1812, at which time they did see Madison. Had the company been reviewed at any time by Madison, it is unlikely that Alfred Lorrain would have failed to record the event in *The Helm, the Sword, and the Cross: A Life Narrative.*

Whatever may have been the circumstances of its origin, the sobriquet does not seem to have come into general usage until several decades after the war. On March 14, 1817, General Harrison, upon special invitation by the citizens of Petersburg and the veterans of the Volunteers, was honored with a public dinner at Poplar Spring. Many toasts were given, but nowhere in them, or in the lengthy press accounts of the occasion, do we find mention of "The Cockade City of the Union." [104] Lafayette visited Petersburg on October 29-30, 1824, and at the ball following the banquet given in his honor on the first night "A crowd of the Canada volunteers from Petersburg, were by name introduced to him. He received them with a soldier's hand, and looked upon them with a soldier's eye." Another dinner was given him at Niblo's Tavern on the second night, and immediately after a toast was drunk in his honor, the 67-year-old general rose, and gave the following: "The Petersburg Volunteers and the Petersburg Canada Company in the late war." [105] Again, in the newspaper accounts of these events covering two days, we find no mention of the "Cockade City." There were other occasions where, seemingly, Petersburg's appellation would have been mentioned. Finally, on July 4, 1838, a toast was drunk to the town of Petersburg: "The Cockade of the Union, a proud cognomen won by her gallantry in the late war; may she maintain it to the last moment of her existence." [106] The sobriquet, "The Cockade of the Union," was phrased the same in 1843, 1846, and in 1848, and throughout this period there were references to the "Cockade Town" in the press.[107] "City" first appeared in the sobriquet after 1850 when Petersburg became a city, and to this day it has continued as "The Cockade City of the Union."

Interestingly, it is "The Cockade City of the Union" on the monument to McRae and the Petersburg Volunteers erected in Blandford Cemetery in 1857. Apparently, no one questioned the inscription.[108] The story of this imposing monument begins with the tragic death of McRae, who had left Petersburg for Washington on May 29, 1854. On June 1, after a squall, his

---

[104] *The Enquirer*, March 25, 1817.

[105] *Ibid.*, November 5, 1824.

[106] *The American Constellation*, July 6, 1838.

[107] *The Republican*, June 26, 1843, December 4, 1846, August 9, 1848. *The Little Cockade*, a newspaper edited by Supple and Ellyson, appeared in January 1841, but was short-lived. A copy dated January 26, 1841 (Vol. I, No. 3) is in the collections of the Petersburg Public Library.

[108] The inscriptions on the monument, now weather-worn and barely legible in places, are fortunately recorded in M. Clifford Harrison, *Home to the Cockade City* (Richmond, 1942), pp. 32-34.

body was found floating in the Potomac at the mouth of Aquia Creek. There were wounds about the head and foul play was generally suspected, but the mystery has never been resolved. He was interred in Blandford Cemetery with military honors on June 4. Funds for a monument were raised by popular subscription in 1856, and on January 12, 1857, the marble shaft was erected, not only to honor McRae but as a memorial to his company. The gilded eagle with spread wings on top of the shaft and the iron fence ornamented with military trophies were added a little later.[109]

Superlatives for the Petersburg Volunteers would have to include John F. Wiley, Thomas Bell Bigger, and Reuben Clements. Wiley, who had been among the wounded at Fort Meigs, represented Amelia County in the House of Delegates, 1835-1837, 1840-1841, and in 1843 was elected councillor of state. He was re-elected in 1846, and as senior councillor in 1848, Wiley was lieutenant governor. In 1849 he was elected again, and served until the expiration of his term in 1852.[110]

Thomas Bigger removed to Richmond after his return from the war. In 1844 he was appointed postmaster and served until his resignation in 1862. He joined the Richmond Light Infantry Blues in 1820 and was captain of the company from 1832 until 1839, when he was commissioned as lieutenant colonel of the 19th Regiment, Virginia Militia. He was later made colonel of the regiment and in 1845 resigned his commission. Bigger was among those who accompanied the remains of Captain McRae from Richmond to Petersburg in 1854. When he died at the age of 86 on May 5, 1880, the 67th anniversary of the sortie at Fort Meigs, the *Daily Dispatch* declared him as the last survivor of the Petersburg Volunteers.[111] This was erroneous for in Petersburg a former corporal of the company, Reuben Clements, was still very much alive and quite active.[112]

On August 5, 1848, Clements and Captain McRae, the only survivors of the company then left in town, had been guests of honor at the dinner given for Petersburg's two companies just returned from Mexico, and among the many toasts was one to them as "The representatives of another age, and

[109] *Daily South-Side Democrat*, Petersburg, Virginia, June 2, 1854; *Daily Richmond Enquirer*, June 5, 6, 7, 1854; *Daily Express*, Petersburg, Virginia, May 19, June 17, 1856, January 13, 1857, March 3, 5, 1857; James G. Scott and Edward A. Wyatt, IV, *Petersburg's Story: A History* (Petersburg, 1960), p. 128.

[110] Earl G. Swem and John W. Williams, *A Register of the General Assembly of Virginia 1776-1918* (Richmond, 1918), pp. 139, 141, 149; *The Republican*, August 9, 1848.

[111] Richmond *Daily Dispatch*, May 6, 1880.

[112] Clements was promoted to corporal sometime between May 31 and October 16, 1813 (Compiled service record, Reuben Clements, Alexander's Independent Battalion Virginia Volunteers [War of 1812], National Archives, Record Group No. 94).

other scenes—an age and scenes that won glory to our country. . . ." [113] Clements was custodian of the flag carried by the Volunteers, and in 1854 he loaned it to Captain Joseph V. Scott of the Petersburg Grays to be carried in a parade. It was a tragedy, to say the least, when the flag was destroyed in a fire which swept through Scott's room on Bollingbrook Street.[114] In 1861 Clements saw companies of Petersburg youth march away for the second war since his own, 49 years before. Not long after the death of Bigger in Richmond, the old veteran had a fall and suffered complications which eventually led to his demise on October 7, 1881, at the age of 91 years. On Sunday, October 9, the Petersburg Grays, Petersburg Artillery, Old Grays Association, and the Association of Mexican War Veterans turned out to bury in Blandford Cemetery with military honors the remains of the last known survivor of the Petersburg Volunteers.[115]

[113] *The Republican*, August 9, 1848. The Brunet broadside lists twelve survivors of the Petersburg Volunteers, July 4, 1849: Richard McRae, Reuben. Clements, Petersburg; Thomas B. Bigger, John Bignall, Richmond; John Wiley, Amelia County; Edward H. Cogbill, Chesterfield County; John H. Saunders, Powhatan County; Alfred O. Eggleston, Cincinnati, Ohio; Shirley Tisdale, Thomas Clarke, Alabama; Nathaniel H. Wills, Tennessee; and Anthony Mullen, whose residence was unknown. Alfred Lorrain, however, was still living in Ohio, and John Henderson is believed to have been still alive. Pension files in the National Archives (Record Group No. 15) show that Saunders left Powhatan County in 1852 for Richmond, where he died on April 23, 1861; Thomas Clarke died in Marengo County, Alabama, on February 3, 1851; and Nathaniel H. Wills died on December 6, 1857, at Jonesboro, Tennessee.

[114] *Index-Appeal*, Petersburg, Virginia, October 8, 1881. Joseph V. Scott, son of Joseph Scott, who was wounded at Fort Meigs, and died at the age of 60 on March 16, 1846, served as captain of the Petersburg Grays, 1847-1860. In April 1861 he was elected captain of the Cockade Rifles, which became Co. E, 3rd Regiment of Virginia Volunteers (1861-1865). He was promoted to major on November 6, 1861, to lieutenant colonel on April 27, 1862, and was mortally wounded on June 30, 1862.

[115] *Index-Appeal*, October 11, 1881.

THE FOG AND FRICTION OF FRONTIER WAR:
THE ROLE OF LOGISTICS IN
AMERICAN OFFENSIVE FAILURE
DURING THE WAR OF 1812

JEFFREY KIMBALL
Miami University

T HE theme of American offensive defeat has been a pervasive and enduring one in military historiography of the War of 1812, for American armed forces failed to accomplish their overriding strategic mission of conquering British North America.[1] To some extent another theme has counterbalanced it: American pride and honor were snatched from the jaws of defeat through the limited successes of William Henry Harrison and Oliver Hazard Perry in the Old Northwest, Andrew Jackson's defeat of the Indians in the Old Southwest, a few dramatic tactical victories on land and the high seas, and the defensive victories that came at the end of the war at Baltimore, Plattsburg, and New Orleans. Nevertheless, Americans did fail to conquer Canada; and in the attempt to explain it military historians have suggested at least five major military causes of offensive defeat. First, Americans were so strategically ignorant they did not clearly recognize those geographical points in Canada which would have been most strategically efficacious; consequently, they attacked the wrong places. Second, American wartime leadership was incompetent, especially in the theater of war and on the field of battle. Third, Americans put excessive reliance on citizen militia and volunteers, as opposed to well-trained regulars. Fourth, Americans lacked adquate logistical capability. Fifth, the British and Canadians made a small but effective defensive effort.[2]

The charge that Americans were strategically ignorant rests on the assertion that they did not appreciate the relatively greater strategic and logistic importance of Northeastern, as compared with Northwestern, targets of invasion. As J. F. C. Fuller put it, Americans "had overlooked the fact that the his-

323

toric front door to Canada was to be found on Lake Champlain
and not at Detroit or Niagara." From this point of view the
problem of conquering Canada was metaphorically similar to
the hewing of a tree whose trunk was the St. Lawrence River,
for Upper and Lower Canada depended for their defense on the
flow of men and supplies that came upriver from Montreal and
Quebec. "The best strategy," according to Harry L. Coles,
"would have been to concentrate on severing the trunk as near
the roots as possible.... The taking of Montreal... would have
assured the fall of all that lay above."[3]

There is abundant evidence, however, that Americans were
very much aware of the relative importance and promise of
Northeastern Canadian objectives. The plan of invasion for
the year 1812, for instance, which many historians have taken
as a prime example of the allegedly unfortunate American
propensity to squander resources and energy in the
Northwest, did in fact look to the capture of Montreal and
ultimately Quebec. On paper at least it was a unified plan with
interrelated parts, calling for four simultaneous offensives.
Major attacks were to be aimed at Montreal in the East and
Fort Malden in the West; in the center, minor, diversionary,
holding attacks were to be directed against Kingston and the
Niagara peninsula on either end of Lake Ontario. The plan
failed; but as President James Madison reminded Major
General Henry Dearborn, these "simultaneous invasions of
Canada at several points, particularly in relation to Malden
and Montreal, might have secured the object of bringing all
Upper Canada and the channels communicating with the
Indians under our command, with ulterior prospects towards
Quebec." Explaining the plan to Thomas Jefferson, he wrote:
"It would probably have been best, if it had been practicable in
time, to have concentrated a force which could have seized on
Montreal & thus at one stroke have secured the upper Province
and cut off the sap that nourished Indian hostilities. But this
could not be attempted without sacrificing the Western & N.W.
Frontier." Thus, the purpose of Brigadier General William
Hull's offensive was primarily to defend the Northwest
against the "inundation of savages under the influence of the
British establishment near Detroit. Another reason . . . was
that the unanimity and ardor of Kentucky & Ohio [militia]
promised the requisite force at once for that service, whilst it

was too distant from the other points to be assailed."[4] In 1812 and in subsequent years Americans were not oblivious to the strategic advantage of concentrating their effort against Montreal. But in the circumstances of the time they felt they had to take other strategic, political, logistical, and manpower considerations into account while choosing their targets and implementing their plans.

If in fact it can be said that Americans attacked the wrong places, it was not because they lacked the ability to identify military objectives.[5] Rather, it was because they lacked either the ability to attack them, or, if attacking, the ability to capture, hold, and exploit them. In what did this inability consist? Unfortunately, the best answer that can be gleaned from the history books is what is left when the above first cause is removed: offensive failure was due to some combination of all the other causes—incompetent leadership, unreliable militia, poor logistic capability, and British/Canadian resistance. In their predominantly narrative accounts, historians have rarely attempted to explain in any systematic, analytic way the nature of the relationships between and the impact of these contributory causes of offensive defeat.[6] Logistics, of all the causes, has probably received the least scrutiny, for historical narratives usually focus on leadership, tactics, and strategy. Those historians who have paid it some attention have tended to view its delimiting impact on strategy narrowly, as simply a matter of excessive supply costs in the face of chronic specie scarcity, or as a question of naval superiority on the Great Lakes, etc. But if understood as the administrative and transportation means by which the armed forces were supplied with subsistence and materiel in order to accomplish their strategic and tactical aims, logistics played a more complex and significant role in American offensive defeat.[7] Americans were attempting to wage an offensive war on a thousand mile frontier, directing and supplying it from coastal towns several hundred miles away during the pre-industrial, pre-railroad, pre-telegraph era. Their administrative and transportation systems, operating across long distances over poor roads through wilderness areas, severely limited their ability to support armies on the northern frontier that were large and powerful enough to overcome the inherent advantages of defensive warfare. This logistic delimitation was probably the most important—though not the only—contributory cause of American offensive failure.

As Leonard D. White noted in his monumental study of Jeffersonian administration: "Given the state of the means of communication from 1800 to 1830, it may be doubted whether it would have been physically possible to mount an effective campaign on any substantial scale. Even where integrity, good will, and harmony of purpose prevailed, nature, not yet subdued by man, interposed stupendous obstacles." But this was only a tangential remark, one which White did not analyze. Even though he recognized that overland communication was a "fundamental handicap" to effective management of offensive war, he failed to explore its functional interrelationships with command and administration. Instead, he focused his attention on the incapacity of leaders, the weakness of administrative doctrine, and the structural anomalies of the administrative system. "Apart from the incapacity of men," he argued, "it was the lack of system and comprehension of the function of top executives and commanding officers in a military situation that is impressed upon the mind." Not one of the top leaders, including the President, the Secretary of State, the Secretary of War, and the generals, "performed correctly the function which his office imposed upon him. No one had . . . a reasoned conception of function and duty that would have provided an intelligent means of coping with the emergency."[8]

White also pointed an accusing finger at the organizational deficiencies of the administrative system itself, especially as they related to supply. The key element in the system was the Secretary of War, for the person holding the office was both the army's chief supply officer and its chief strategist. He was both by default, there being no military chief of the administrative, or "housekeeping," staff and no general-in-chief as there had been during the Revolution. The dual nature of the office held out the possibility of successfully coordinating strategy and logistics, but unfortunately for the Americans there were certain statutory and structural weaknesses in the command and administrative system which hampered the secretary in performing his dual role. As White pointed out, he was overburdened with routine administrative duties while lacking sufficient administrative and clerical assistance to free him for more important duties. In addition, he had to cope with such functional incongruities as the overlapping of Quartermaster General and Commissary General responsibilities, which in effect meant that he, the Secretary of War, had the onerous and fallible task of specifying the kinds of supplies purchased by each department in the varying circumstances at the frontier areas. When Congress enacted a new law creating an administrative general staff of the army in March 1813, the act also eliminated the confusing language which had led to the duplication of quartermaster and commissary functions. However, the overall logistical impact of the reform was negligible, because the disunified, decentralized general staff did not serve to coordinate the activities of the many subordinate staff officers throughout the country, most notably those of the assistant quartermasters and commissaries. By default that task also remained the direct responsibility of the Secretary of War.[9]

Without doubt these onerous, routine administrative duties adversely affected the performance of the secretary as chief supply officer and chief strategist. They were probably not as important, however, as those problems which White did not examine, those which resulted from the simple fact that the secretary resided in Washington, D. C.; and the campaigns were fought hundreds of miles away. One of the most serious difficulties sheer distance presented was the inevitable lag in communications between the secretary in Washington and his generals in the field, for even under the best of circumstances it could take a letter between one and two weeks to cross the distance between the capital and the frontier. On 18 June 1812 Secretary of War William Eustis compounded the problem when he sent notification of the declaration of war to General Hull through the regular mail service. Hull's army was then plodding through the northern Ohio wilderness toward Detroit. The letter finally arrived at Hull's camp on the Maumee River on 2 July, one day too late to prevent disaster. On 1 July Hull had sent his heavy baggage, medical supplies, and official papers to Detroit on the unarmed schooner *Cuyahoga*. The British, having learned of the declaration of war earlier, snapped up the *Cuyahoga* as it sailed past Fort Malden. It was the first in a series of blows that, several weeks later, would persuade Hull to surrender; but it was not an unusual occurrence in this frontier war.[10]

The delays incurred in communicating orders, intelligence, and supply requests across long distances was a circumstance that enveloped Americans in what Karl von Clausewitz called the "fog of war"—that twilight of uncertainty and ignorance about the data of war which "gives to things exaggerated dimension and unnatural appearance."[11] Usually applied to uncertainty about enemy strength and intentions in operational situations, the "fog of war" concept is also useful for interpreting the uncertainty and ignorance of Americans toward their own activities in command and administrative situations. The Secretary of War was often in the dark about the movements and intentions of his own commanders as well as those of the British. On the other hand, commanders who required the cooperation of the secretary and of other frontier commanders, or who needed the swift clarification of orders, were often in a fog about what assistance they could expect and about what to do in a particular situation. One of the most ludicrous examples of this form of the fog of war occurred in February and March of 1814 on the New York frontier. Major-General Jacob Brown, misinterpreting Secretary of War John Armstrong's confusingly written orders—which in turn had been based on faulty information—marched his Left Division 250 miles from Sackets Harbor to Buffalo. It was definitely not what Armstrong had wanted him to do. Ultimately, though, Brown's mistaken but irrevocable march resulted in a Cabinet decision to direct the major American offensive for that year toward the Niagara peninsula.[12]

The military district system of command—a system in which major generals responsible only to the Secretary of War commanded the nine military districts of the country—further complicated the problem of the fog of war.[13] Offensives on the northern frontier usually required the cooperation of commanders in District No. 8 (Kentucky, Ohio, Indiana, Michigan, Illinois, and Missouri) and District No. 9 (northern New York and Vermont). But cooperation depended on the ability of the secretary to coordinate their efforts—to see to the timely launching of attacks or the shifting of troops, supplies, and means of transportation from one district to another. Given the state of communications, it was a system that frequently broke down. It discouraged field commanders, retarded expeditious action, prevented appropriate responses to the ebb and flow of events, and precluded cooperation between districts. In 1812, British Major General Isaac Brock found the task of defeating Hull's offensive eased when Americans were unable to coordinate their attack in the Northwest with their attacks in New York. James Wilkinson and Wade Hampton's abortive combined offensive from northern New York against Montreal in 1813 was a notorious case of command confusion, lack of cooperation between commanders and the secretary, and resulting logistical breakdown.[14] Problems could orginate at the district commander's end of the chain of command, too, because he might feel that circumstances warranted a change in plans, a privilege he could claim on the basis of immediate knowledge of the situation. However necessary or significant a change was, the decision, because of communications lag, was irreversible and could result in altering previously determined strategy. One of the more momentous of such changes in strategy was Dearborn's decision in April 1813 to attack York, a secondary objective, instead of Kingston, a primary objective. But in this case all was not lost, because the Americans succeeded in destroying the ammunition, guns, and naval stores destined for Robert H. Barclay's British fleet on Lake Erie. The British shortage of heavy guns in the battle of Lake Erie later in the year was one of the major causes of Barclay's defeat, finally making possible the American reconquest of Detroit and capture of Fort Malden.[15]

The absence of army-navy unity of command also contributed to the fog of war. Cooperation between military and naval commanders on the northern frontier and Great Lakes depended upon a complicated four-way correspondence between themselves and the Secretaries of War and Navy.[16] While it was often cordial, it also proved unsatisfactory and sometimes disastrous. General Brown, who planned to invade the Niagara peninsula in 1814 and link up with forces stationed in Detroit, required the logistical assistance of the Lake Erie fleet. But to his dismay he learned at the last moment that the navy had decided to withdraw from the operation in order to attack a small British naval post in Lake Huron, whose size and importance had been exaggerated by espionage reports. For Brown it was the first of a series of naval disappointments.[17]

The fog of war was only one of the afflictions of the command and administrative system. Another was the "friction of war." "All appears so simple . . . in War," Clausewitz explained, "but the simplest thing is difficult. These difficulties accumulate and produce a friction. . . . Through the influence of an infinity of petty circumstances, which cannot properly be described on paper, things disappoint us, and we fall short of the mark."[18] The friction of war made its effect felt most keenly in the area of supply. In theory, once the government decided upon a particular plan of campaign, the Secretary of War could issue orders to the Commissary General in Philadelphia to prepare sufficient amounts of clothing, hospital stores, camp equipage, guns, powder, and ammunition. He could instruct the contractor to make deposits of food at convenient depots in the district. Orders could be sent to the assistant quartermasters to transport the materiel to the appropriate points on the frontier, to construct barracks for the troops, and to prepare means of transportation for the offensive. But the system never worked in reality as it was supposed to in theory. Clothing might not be ready on schedule; supplies could be lost along the way through theft, damage, or careless bookkeeping; wagons could break down without the necessary tools on hand to repair them; materials for constructing barracks might not be immediately available. The contractor or an assistant quartermaster might require additional funds, because the cost of supplies and food had been underestimated or prices had risen. Moreover, they might require scarce specie because some banks would not accept Treasury notes or drafts on the Secretary of War. Until the funds were provided, delay in supplying the army could force a change in plans, and a change in plans could cause further delay. Only the general could know how many wagons or boats would be required for the campaign, but they might not be obtainable because the secretary had not authorized their purchase. On the other hand the general might not know how many wagons or boats were required because he did not know how many troops he would receive.

Friction—or things going wrong—occurs in all wars. For the Americans in the War of 1812, however, administrative malfunctioning, complicated by the fog of war, made it all the more difficult to cope with. One of the results was supply shortage. Only a modicum of supplies and shelter may have been necessary to initiate preparations for a campaign; but serious shortages retarded recruiting, delayed mobilization, adversely affected the health and morale of troops, and ruined offensives.[19] During the winter of 1812-1813, four hundred men died of pneumonia at Greenbush, New York, because of inadequate shelter, fuel, clothing, and medical care. In November 1814 General Brown complained that "five men have perished by disease to one who has fallen by the sword," mainly because of the "infamous" quality of clothing and shoes and because winter clothing always arrived on the frontier in the dead of winter rather than in the fall. In northwestern Ohio in November 1812 General William Henry Harrison postponed his anticipated advance upon Detroit until he could accumulate more rations and supplies. But during the ensuing winter his troops continued to be ill-housed, poorly clothed, inadequately fed, and generally short of all supplies—despite vast expenditures of money and laborious effort. Under the circumstances Secretary of War Amstrong had little choice in the spring but to order Harrison to halt his attempts to retake Detroit by land and to wait for Commander Oliver Perry to gain control of Lake Erie.[20]

Human error, incompetence, administrative dysfunction, the lag in communications, the fog of war—all these things helped create logistical friction. But probably the most important cause, as Erna Risch insists, was simply the supreme difficulty of transporting supplies. "The great defect," lamented General Harrison, "is in the means of transportation." Most manufactured military goods had to be procured from the older cities and towns near the Atlantic coast. When practicable, these were transported by river; but most of the materiel was carried overland from the littoral to and through the trans-Appalachian frontier on roads and traces that left much to be desired, those nearest the frontier being the worst of all.[21] Traveling long distances, supply trains encountered the inevitable friction of war; and progress by heavily loaded wagons and packhorses was extremely slow.[22] Among the transportation sources of friction were terrible road conditions, bad weather, accidents and injuries, shortages of medical supplies and repair parts, and scarcity of local sources of food and forage.

The experience of Assistant Quartermaster Captain Joseph Wheaton illustrated the problems encountered by other quartermasters. Wheaton's supply train of 37 wagons, 8 gun carriages, 2 "travelling Forges," and 304 horses left Pittsburgh on 22 November 1812, bound for Harrison's headquarters and forward supply base at Upper Sandusky, Ohio, over 250 miles away. Rain, hail, snow, "extreme deep roads, bad bridges, and worse crossings, with the addition of frozen ground" slowed his pace to six miles per day and forced the caravan to stop frequently for reshoeing of horses and repairing of wheels, axles, and axletrees. On 8 December Wheaton halted the march at Canton, Ohio; for the train had used up its supply of food, forage, horseshoes, nails, axles, axletrees, and chains. Bureaucratic red tape and stock shortages at Pittsburgh had prevented Wheaton from taking all of the repair parts he needed. Eight blacksmiths and four wagonmasters worked around the clock to make the necessary parts and repairs, but some of the parts and all of the food and forage had to be purchased in the neighborhood. "With the road swept of provisions of every kind by those who have gone before me and by some whose wanton conduct has set an example," he wrote the Secretary of War, the price of every item had risen enormously.

One week later the train finally left Canton. Fourteen miles down the road one of the teamsters caught his leg between a wagon wheel and a tree, stripping skin and flesh from his thigh. Leaving the train, Wheaton brought the injured man back to Canton for treatment; and he and a physician worked through the night to mend the wound as best they could. In the meantime, "pioneers" from the Pennsylvania militia detachment accompanying the train had to cut a new road for twelve miles, part of the state road having been found impassable. On 19 December, thirty miles through "mud and mire" from Canton, Wheaton's train stopped for a full day at Wooster to make the usual repairs.

On 27 December Wheaton reached Mansfield, fifty miles from his ultimate destination. He spent three days making more repairs and procuring corn from the Mohican River settlement, eighteen miles off the main road. En route from Canton, Wheaton had bought and hired additional teams of horses and oxen in order to collect the public stores that the

Quartermaster's Department had previously deposited in depots scattered along the route. The animals, who now numbered 690 horses and 15 oxen, were consuming huge amounts of hay and corn; and nearly one-third of the horses were needed to carry forage alone. Wheaton expected to arrive at Upper Sandusky in another week or less, and despite tribulations and delays—or perhaps because of them—he was pleased with his progress. He had made the journey from Pittsburgh to Mansfield in only thirty-six days, while other quartermasters had averaged sixty-two.[23]

Transportation problems not only restricted the speed and volume of supply but raised the cost of supply to enormous sums. According to one oft-quoted source, Balthasar H. Meyer, the government paid from $1,100 to $1,600 to transport each cannon sent from the Atlantic coast to Lake Erie in 1813. The $400 cost of transporting one cannon to the Niagara front in 1814 was less, but it nevertheless matched the original cost of the piece and was a sum greater than the cost of transporting one cannon across the Atlantic from Liverpool, England. Transportation expenses also helped raise the price of food and forage. On the Detroit frontier in 1813, pork was $127 per barrel, flour was $100 per barrel, and oats were $60 per bushel.[24] The specie shortage caused a costly form of inflation as some merchants accepted Treasury notes, drafts on the Secretary of War, and bank notes only at discount. However, had more specie been available to the government and its agents, the cost of supply would still have been great, because of the cost of feeding transport animals, the increased demand for scarce frontier agricultural products, the loss of supplies and animals en route to their destination, the practice of hiring civilian teamsters, wagons, horses, and oxen, and the one-way traffic exchange.[26] Given inherently great transportation costs, the tenuous financial condition of the government simply caused additional costs and delays in delivering supplies.

It was, nevertheless, still possible to transport supplies over the long land routes from the littoral to the frontier, as from Philadelphia via Pittsburgh to Upper Sandusky, because supply trains could resort to local, albeit scarce, sources of forage until they reached the forward supply bases near the northern frontier.[27] But the resort to reliable, adequate local sources of forage was not possible on the frontier itself. Literally the advanced region of settlement and civilization facing a hostile power, the "northern frontier" was an apt contemporary title for the theater of operations. With only six persons on the average per square mile in a fifty to one-hundred mile band of territory along the border, it was impossible for an army to live off the countryside in the Napoleonic manner.[28] Armies deployed on the Canadian border had to be supplied from the forward bases, which were at least fifty to one-hundred miles away in southern Ohio, western Pennsylvania, central New York, and Vermont. Much of this region itself contained only two to six persons per square mile, but there were several sections with as many as eighteen and more: northern Vermont and the Connecticut River valley; wedges of settlement from Albany to the Genesee country in western New York and north along Lake Champlain; southwestern Pennsylvania at the Forks of the Ohio; and a wide strip of territory in southern Ohio along the Ohio River. Although these were still pioneer areas, much of the army's food could be procured from them.[29]

On the frontier, however, the inherent disadvantages of a subsistence system of supply trains and depots employing animal drawn vehicles were magnified. Transportation costs were greater, even over short distances; and they rose geometrically as the distance from the base increased, since each vehicle had to return to base after delivering a cargo of supplies, and extra food and forage had to be carried for the logistics personnel and animals. Horses fed only on grain and hay; and even though oxen could forage in fields and woods, they could not rely on a wild food supply. Ox-drivers, moreover, were scarce and expensive. From its base of supply, an army could be effectively provisioned at a maximum distance of about ninety miles, or six to seven days by wagon at an optimistically average pace of fifteen miles per day. If packhorses had to be resorted to because of poor road conditions or a shortage of wagons and teamsters, then the effective operational distance might be reduced by as much as two-thirds, to thirty miles. If the army advanced and the distance and the time required to supply it increased, then so did the need for more wagons, horses, and teamsters. Eventually, however, the wagons or the packhorses would have to carry more forage for the teams than flour and other supplies for the troops. This point would be reached at a distance of about 135 miles from base using wagons and 45 miles using packhorses, whereupon the possibility of supplying the army would be practically eliminated. Even at shorter distances, the hundreds of wagons, horses, and oxen required to maintain an army for any length of time were often unobtainable on the frontier, either because of unavailability or excessive cost.[30] The establishment of food storage depots along the supply route in advance of forward bases was an expensive, difficult, and only partially effective expedient. In northern Ohio by as early as the end of 1812, for example, grain was so scarce that quartermasters had to make purchases south of Chillicothe in order to place deposits 120 miles away at the forward base of Upper Sandusky, which was another 120 miles or so from Detroit. On the northern New York front the northernmost depot was Plattsburgh, about twenty miles south of the Canadian border and almost eighty miles north of the forward supply base of Whitehall. As General Hampton discovered in November 1813, forage was non-existent between Plattsburgh and the border, and roads could not support wheeled traffic during wet seasons. Supplies could only be moved on soldiers' backs.[31] Despite forage scarcity on the Niagara front, relatively better road conditions and relatively high agricultural productivity in central and western New York in 1814 made it possible to store food and forage in depots between the Genesee River forward bases and the Niagara River frontier and, therefore, to support the army at Buffalo. But forage scarcity and other overland transportation difficulties delayed or prevented the transport of clothing and cannon from eastern New York.[32]

All of this meant that the limit of advance for an American army relying on overland supply was roughly the Canadian border or a short distance beyond it. Even had more specie and more recruits been available, overland transportation alone would have caused serious problems and certainly limited the size of armies and their mobility on the frontier.

To attempt to conduct an offensive under these conditions, moreover, created tremendous planning problems. As one contractor explained to Secretary of War Armstrong, depots or magazines had to be established and stocked well in advance along the route of march "in places best calculated for the accumulation of the surrounding country, whilst at the same time they should possess the advantages of water communication to such points as the army may concentrate" from time to time. Planners had to take into consideration the contemplated size of the army, the duration of the campaign, the amount of local food supplies that might be available in friendly or enemy territory, and the time of the year when roads would be impassable and water routes blocked by ice. With this information the general and the contractor could decide where to purchase flour and meat and where to establish depots, and determine whether it would be possible to supply the army. Too often, however, such careful planning was not done. In fact, the government usually decided upon plans of campaign so late in the year that contractors had to buy victuals when they were in great demand and prices had already risen.[33] And besides subsistence the army had to transport its ordnance, ammunition, medicine, extra muskets, and the rest of the impedimenta.

The army's inability to forage on the march and its dependence on supply from bases and depots in the rear limited its size, reduced its speed and mobility, confined it to specific and vulnerable lines of operation, forced it to advance on a narrow front, and eliminated the possibility of substantial penetration. This was why Henri Jomini pointed out that "from a military point of view the offensive has its . . . bad sides."[34] Unless the invader could reduce his supply train by using water transportation, invasion might be out of the question, or if attempted, doomed to failure. Only naval superiority on the Great Lakes held out the chance of turning the tables. With it one could concentrate troops and supplies faster at critical points in all seasons except midwinter, communicate with distant posts more speedily, threaten the enemy's land line of communications and supply depots near the shore, and, perhaps more important, force the enemy to move by land. Without naval superiority on the lakes, the Duke of Wellington observed, "it is impossible . . . to maintain an army in such a situation as to keep the enemy out of the whole frontier, much less to make conquest."[35] In 1812 the Americans' lack of foresight gave the British temporary and tenuous superiority on the lakes, which Brock used to great advantage in defeating the Americans at Detroit and Niagara. The Americans finally gained control of Lake Erie in late 1813, making possible Harrison's reconquest of Detroit; but on the other lakes the balance of power alternated indecisively.

Both belligerents in the struggle learned, however, that the supplies required for naval construction created their own logistic problems, which might detract from the army's effort.[36] In addition, naval superiority was not in itself a complete solution to the problem of supplying an offensive against a determined defender. The navy must not only maintain supremacy on its particular lake, but also supply the army. The army would still depend on overland supply from the hinterland to the port of embarkation and from the port of disembarkation into enemy territory. Continued American control of Lake Erie after Harrison's victory on the Thames River did not in itself permit them to extend their conquests through the Upper Canadian peninsula. By the spring of 1814 the Americans could only manage to support about 1,600 men at and around Detroit. Because of sickness, the effective force was about 800; and because of provisions shortages, Lieutenant Colonel Anthony Butler occasionally had to send foraging expeditions deep into Upper Canada to supplement the ration.[37]

It is from the perspective of logistical fog and friction that American leadership and troop performance must be judged. "In all military operations, we must, as you know," Secretary Armstrong wrote, "begin with the belly."[38] Granted, there were defeats attributable mainly to the mistakes or incompetence of leaders, or to ill-trained, unwilling militia, volunteers, and even regulars. When it came to offensive warfare at least, no one, from the President to the common soldier, seemed to possess a sufficient quantity of that quality White described as "a reasoned conception of function and duty" and Clausewitz called "character"—the mental strength, moral power, and force of will needed at decisive moments to dominate intelligently whatever event or crisis emerged.[39] But perhaps there are times when the obstacles people encounter cannot be overcome by any amount of character, especially in the face of determined enemy resistance. It is worth noting that the British, who are generally credited with having better leaders and troops, also failed to achieve offensive victory when, having accumulated numerical and qualitative troop preponderance in some areas, they moved to the attack in

1814. Each campaign must be analyzed on its own specific merits. But in the view of the war as a whole perhaps the best overall explanation for American offensive defeat is that they had, from the start, ambitiously reached for all of Canada without the wherewithal to take and permanently hold any part of it.[40] Fighting a war that had resulted from the complex conflicts of the Age of Democratic Revolution, they nevertheless lacked the revolutionary striking and staying power of mass armies and steam propulsion. All they—or the British— could do was manage to fight an ineffectual border, frontier war with a few thousand milita and regular soldiers and sailors supplied by beasts of burden. "Nature, not yet subdued by man, interposed stupendous obstacles."[41]

NOTES

[1]Despite historiographic disagreement about whether the conquest of Canada was a cause or a political goal of the war, there is virtual unanimous agreement that conquest of Canada was the main strategic objective. Americans used the word "Canada" to refer at different times to Upper and Lower Canada as well as to all of British North America. Although the words "strategy" and "logistics" were not part of the era's vocabulary, military leaders of necessity observed the concepts.

[2]This list, which for practical purposes includes only the direct military related causes, not the "underlying" social, economic, political, or ideological causes, is based on a reading of many or most of the major and minor histories of the War of 1812. For good published bibliographies, see: Harry L. Coles, *The War of 1812* (Chicago: University of Chicago Press, 1965); John K. Mahon, *The War of 1812* (Gainesville: University of Florida Press, 1972); and Morris Zaslow, ed., *The Defended Border: Upper Canada and the War of 1812* (Toronto: Macmillan Co. of Canada, 1964).

[3]J. F. C. Fuller, *The Decisive Battles of the United States* (London: Hutchinson & Co., 1942), p. 81; Coles, *War of 1812*, p. 43, and see pp. 107, 111, 136, 143-144, 163, 241, 258-262. Similar criticism of American strategy may be found in these representative works: Henry Adams, *History of the United States during the Administrations of James Madison* (1889-91; rpt. Bks. V-IX in 2 vols. New York: Albert & Charles Boni, 1930), Bk. VI, pp. 317, 338, Bk. VII, pp. 144-147, Bk. VIII, pp. 91, 93, 99-102; Irving Brant, *James Madison: Commander in Chief*, VI (New York: Bobbs-Merrill Co., 1961), 46; J. Mackay Hitsman, *The Incredible War of 1812: A Military History* (Toronto: Univ. of Toronto Press, 1965), pp. 240-241; Alfred Thayer Mahan, *Sea Power in Its Relations to the War of 1812* (1905; rpt. Boston: Little, Brown & Co., 1919), I, 304-313, II, 29; C. P. Stacey, "An American Plan for a Canadian Campaign," *American Historical Review*, 46 (1941), 348-358.

[4]Madison to Jefferson, 17 August 1812, Madison to Dearborn, 9 August 1812, *The Writings of James Madison*, ed. Gaillard Hunt (New York: G. P. Putnam's Sons, 1908), VIII, 211, 206. Other contributors to the plan were Albert Gallatin, John Armstrong, William Hull, Henry Dearborn, and William Eustis.

Henry Adams, ed., *The Writings of Albert Gallatin* (Philadelphia: J. B. Lippincott, 1879), I, 340-353; John Armstrong, *Notices of the War of 1812* (New York: Wiley & Putnam, 1840), I, 236-237; *Report of the Trial of Brig. General William Hull, taken by Lt. Col. Forbes* (New York: Eastburn, Kirk, 1814), pp. 27-36; H. A. S. Dearborn, *Defence of Gen. Henry Dearborn* (Boston: E. W. Davies, 1824), p. 3; Eustis to Hull, 24 June 1812, Eustis to Dearborn, 9 April, 26 June 1812, Records of the Office of the Secretary of War, Letters Sent (Military Books), Record Group 107, National Archives.

[5]It is highly speculative whether Montreal was indeed the best target. To seize it Americans would have needed to: (1) control Lake Champlain and the St. Lawrence River; (2) overcome many natural and military obstacles south of Montreal in a wilderness area; (3) beseige Montreal; (4) out-concentrate the British at the very heart of their defensive system; (5) defend Montreal against counterattack. New England's lukewarm support for the war only added to these inherent difficulties. For a British view, see Frederick De Gaugreben, "Memoir on the Places Which Ought to be Fortified for the Defence of Lower Canada, June 1, 1815," (F) Military and Naval Figures, Nineteenth Century Pre-Confederation Papers, MS. Group 24, Public Archives of Canada. For a description of British strategy, which stressed the defense of Montreal at the expense of everything else to the west, see: A. M. J. Hyatt, "The Defence of Upper Canada in 1812," Thesis Queen's University 1961, pp. 24-29; Hitsman, *Incredible War of 1812*, pp. 243-249; Hitsman, "Sir George Prevost's Conduct of the Canadian War of 1812," *Canadian Historical Association Report* (1962), pp. 34-43; John K. Mahon, "British Command Decisions in the Northern Campaigns of the War of 1812," *Canadian Historical Review*, 56 (1965), 219-237. Perhaps it would have been best for the Americans to have concentrated on taking Kingston and territory to the west, for they could transport men and supplies easier to the west. Much depends on whether it was American policy to take all or part of British North America. When Gallatin suggested a limited western offensive in 1812, the idea was rejected. Gallatin, "Agenda," n.d. [ca. 12 July 1812], Madison Papers, Ser. 2.

[6]The narrative tradition continues in recent works. See, e.g., Reginald Horsman, *The War of 1812* (New York: Alfred Knopf, 1969) and Mahon, *War of 1812*, especially p. vii. For a critique of the narrative tradition in military history, see John Keegan, *The Face of Battle* (New York: Viking Press, 1976).

[7]Brereton Greenhous, "A Note on Western Logistics in the War of 1812," *Military Affairs*, 34 (1970), 41-44; Mahan, *Sea Power*, passim; for a good discussion of the meaning of logistics, see Richard M. Leighton and Robert W. Coakley, *Global Logistics and Strategy, 1940-1943*, Ser. 1, Vol. IV of *The United States Army in World War II*, ed. Kent Roberts Greenfield (Washington: Office of the Chief of Military History, 1955), 3-17.

[8]Leonard D. White, *The Jeffersonians: A Study in Administrative History, 1801-1829* (New York: Macmillan Co., 1951), pp. 215, 216, 222-223.

[9]White, *The Jeffersonians*, Chs. xv, xvi, xvii. See also Erna Risch, *Quartermaster Support of the Army: A History of the Corps, 1775-1939* (Washington: Office of the Chief of Military History, 1962), pp. 141-142.

[10]Alec R. Gilpin, *The War of 1812 in the Old Northwest* (East Lansing: Michigan State Univ. Press, 1958), pp. 52-54; Milo Quaife, "General Hull and His Critics," *Ohio State Archeological and Historical Quarterly*, 47 (1938), 168-182; Mahon, *War of 1812*, p. 44.

[11]Karl von Clausewitz, *On War*, trans. J.J. Graham (1873; rpt. London: Lowe & Brydone, 1966), I, 106, 48-49, 75-76. Michael Howard and Peter Paret translated this passage somewhat differently. *On War*, ed. and trans. Howard and Paret (Princeton: Princeton Univ. Pres, 1976), p. 140.

[12]Jeffrey P. Kimball, "The Battle of Chippawa: Infantry Tactics in the War of 1812," *Military Affairs*, 31 (1967-68), 169-186.

[13]Some contemporaries and some historians suggested that the problems resulting from geographical distribution of command might have been alleviated through the creation of the post of general-in-chief. But anti-military suspicions and personal rivalry between Armstrong and James Monroe prevented the creation of such a post. Brant, *Madison*, VI, 166, 226; Harry Ammon, *James Monroe: The Quest for National Identity* (New York: McGraw-Hill, 1971), pp. 313-327. Even with this office, the problems of communicating between district commanders and the general-in-chief, on the one hand, and between the general-in-chief and Washington and other coastal cities, on the other, would have been as great as the problems of the existing system.

[14]Madison to Armstrong, 3 August 1814, Letters and Other Writings of James Madison (New York: R. Worthington, 1884), III, 417-419; Mahon, *War of 1812*, pp. 202-215.

[15]C. P. Stacey, "Another Look at the Battle of Lake Erie," *Canadian Historical Review*, 39 (1958), 41-51.

[16]See White, *The Jeffersonians*, Chap. xix, for naval administration.

[17]John Sinclair to William Jones, 19, 27 May 1814, Letters Received by the Secretary of the Navy (Captains' Letters), RG 45, National Archives; Armstrong to Brown, 10 June 1814, Military Books, RG 107.

[18]Clausewitz, *On War*, trans. Graham I, 77-78. Cf. *On War*, trans. Howard and Paret, p. 119.

[19]Marguerite M. McKee concluded that there was never a time when the defeat or failure of a campaign could be entirely blamed on supply shortages. Following the lead of Emory Upton, she blamed failure on incompetent generalship and overreliance on militia. But this was an unwarranted conclusion and reflected an overly narrow conception of logistics. "Service of Supply in the War of 1812" (4th Paper), *Quartermaster Review*, 7 (1927), 32.

[20]Dearborn to Morgan Lewis, December [?] 1812 (ltr. 180), Dearborn to Lewis, 3 September 1812 (ltr. 65), Dearborn to Eustis, 24 November 1812 (ltr. 107), Letters and Orders of General Dearborn, Letterbook No. 2, New York Historical Society. See also, James Mann, *Medical Sketches of the Campaigns of 1812, 13, 14* (Dedham, Massachusetts: H. Mann & Co., 1816); Brown to Secretary of War (SW), 29 November 1814, Registered Letters Received, RG 107, National Archives; Harrison to SW, 15 November 1812, in *Governors Messages and Letters: Messages and Letters of William Henry Harrison*, ed. Logan Esarey, II (Indianapolis: Indiana Historical Commission, 1922), 213; Risch, *Quartermaster Support*, pp. 171-172. Cf. Mahon, *War of 1812*, p. 132.

[21]Risch, *Quartermaster Support*, p. 162; Harrison to SW, 15 November 1812, *Messages and Letters of Harrison*, ed. Esarey, II, 212; Curtis P. Nettels, *The Emergence of a National Economy, 1775-1815* (New York: Holt, Rinehart & Winston, 1962), pp. 270-283; Tench Coxe, "Digest of Manufactures," *American State Papers: Finance* (Washington: Gales & Seaton, 1832), II, 666-812. In a very few of these cases transportation was by steamboat.

[22]For overland transportation, the following published sources were especially useful: *American State Papers: Military Affairs*, I; *American State Papers: Miscellaneous*, I; G. P. T. Glazebrook, *A History of Transportation in Canada* (Toronto: Ryerson Press, 1938); Oliver W. Holmes, *Conquering the Wilderness*, Vol. V of *History of the State of New York*, ed. Alexander C. Flick (New York: Columbia Univ. Press, 1934); John Melish, *Military and Topographical Atlas of the United States* (Philadelphia: J. Melish, 1815); Balthasar

H. Meyer, Caroline E. MacGill, et al., *History of Transportation in the United States before 1860* (Washington: Carnegie Institution, 1917); Nettels, *National Economy;* Charles O. Paullin ed., *Atlas of the Historical Geography of the United States* (Washington and New York: Carnegie Institution and American Geographical Society, 1932).

[23]Wheaton to SW, 14, 22, 31 December 1812, Registered Letters Received, RG 107; Wheaton to SW, 1, 8 December 1812, *Letters to the Secretary of War, 1812, Relating to the War of 1812 in the Northwest,* Vol. VI of *Document Transcriptions of the War of 1812 in the Northwest,* ed. Richard C. Knopf (Columbus: Ohio Historical Society, 1959), 575, 580; William Piatt to Wheaton, 27, 28 November 1812, *Letters to the Secretary of War,* pp. 570, 571. Wheaton apparently paid as much as $0.625 a bushel for corn, $2.50 for oats, and $20.00 a ton for hay. In 1818 the price of these items at Zanesville was $0.335 to $0.50 a bushel for corn, $0.25 to $0.335 for oats, and $9.00 to $10.00 for hay delivered. Percy W. Bidwell and John I. Falconer, *History of Agriculture in the Northern United States, 1620-1860* (Washington: Carnegie Institution, 1925), p. 176.

[24]*Transportation in the U.S.,* pp. 91-92; McKee, "Service of Supply" (4th Paper), p. 31; Meyer, *Transportation in the U.S.,* pp. 91-92. In 1818 pork sold at Zanesville for $4.50 to $5.00 cwt. and flour, $5.00 to $5.75 a barrel (196 lbs). Bidwell and Falconer, *History of Agriculture in the Northern U.S.,* p. 176. At Cincinnati and Pittsburgh, flour sold at $6.50 a barrel in 1815. Thomas S. Berry, *Western Prices Before 1861* (Cambridge: Harvard Univ. Press, 1943), p. 160.

[25]Greenhous, "A Note on Western Logistics," pp. 41-44, argued that Meyer's figures were exaggerated and exceptional and that the real logistical problem was not poor transportation but scarcity of specie. He gave the figure of $15.00 per barrel for the price of flour at Fort Meigs. But this lonely outpost was over 60 miles south of Detroit through the terrible "black swamp." According to McKee, "Service of Supply" (3rd Paper), n. 130, p. 38, flour at Fort Meigs in January 1814 was $19.61 per 96-lb. barrel. At Cincinnati and Pittsburgh, flour sold at $9.00 a barrel in late 1814, when prices peaked. Prices at Detroit would have been considerably higher because of added transportation costs. Moreover, while the government was short of specie, specie itself was not scarce on the frontier. Berry, *Western Prices,* pp. 159-160, 366-367. Nevertheless, agricultural prices were still high during the war. See Risch, *Quartermaster Support,* pp. 135-180, for some of the interrelated causes of high prices, including transportation as the most important. Transportation, moreover, did more than raise the costs of supply; it caused frictions and weakened offensives.

[26]Many wagons returned to the east empty. Berry, *Western Prices,* p. 74.

[27]By forward bases I mean those bases which were on the northern and western limits of local sources of forage (though forage was sometimes scarce south and east of forward bases). The major forward bases of subsistence were: Piqua, Sandusky, and Upper Sandusky on the northwest frontier; the Genesee River on the Niagara frontier; Oswego on the eastern Lake Ontario frontier; and Whitehall on the Lake Champlain frontier. Such places farther north and west as Fort Defiance, Fort Meigs, Buffalo, Sackets Harbor, and Plattsburgh were depots and bases of operations.

[28]Assuming that for a brief period of time a given region could support one soldier for each inhabitant, then the foraging area required to feed an army near the border would be roughly 40 times larger than in France, whose population density was 250 per square mile. A force as small as 5,000 men would have the impossible task of foraging in an area of over 850 square miles, which

in any case could support them only briefly. This analysis is in part based on certain mathematical calculations in John G. Moore, "Mobility and Strategy in the Civil War," *Military Affairs*, 24 (1960), 68-77. Wheat and corn yields per acre in 1812 were comparable with those in 1860. *Historical Statistics of the United States* (Washington: Government Printing Office, 1961), Ser. K 83-97.

[29]Paullin, *Atlas of Historical Geography*, Plate 76D; for sources of wheat, cattle, hogs, horses, salt, rum, and whiskey, see: Nettels, National Economy, pp. 283-305; Bidwell and Falconer, *Agriculture in the Northern U.S.*, pp. 169-177; Ralph H. Brown, *Historical Geography of the United States* (New York: Harcourt, Brace and Co., 1948), pp. 181, 199-200; Paul W. Gates, *The Farmer's Age, 1815-1860* (New York: Holt, Rinehart & Winston, 1960), pp. 23-50. The center of the wheat belt, southeastern Pennsylvania, sometimes supplied northern armies with flour and whiskey when crops failed or when prices were too high near the frontier. Salt pork and packed beef could be procured from as far away as New York City and New Jersey if water routes could be used. Elbert Anderson to SW, 2 January 1813, Registered Letters Received, RG 107. Garrison troops supplemented their diet by fishing and growing vegetables. *Fort Meigs and the War of 1812: Orderly Book of Cushing's Company and Personal Diary of Captain Daniel Cushing*, ed. Harlow Lindley (Columbus: Ohio Historical Society, 1975), pp. 32, 121; David A. Simmons, "The Military and Adminsitrative Abilities of James Wilkinson in the Old Northwest, 1792-1793," *The Old Northwest*, 3 (1977), 244.

[30]James Winchester to John Piatt, 17 November 1812, Piatt Letterbook, MS. Div., Library of Congress; Armstrong to Brown, 10 June 1814, Military Books, RG 107; Harrison to SW, 13, 22 October 1812, and Piatt to Harrison, 17 October 1812, *Messages and Letters of Harrison*, ed. Esarey, II, 177, 181, 183-184. Two-horse wagons, which might carry loads of up to 1,500 lbs., were more often used on the frontier than four- to six-horse wagons. Packhorses might carry 150-250 lbs. Cf. McKee, "Service of Supply" (3rd Paper), n. 130, p. 38. If each horse consumed 25 lbs. of grain per day on the trip going and returning, then at 90 miles wagons would be one-third laden with forage; at 30 miles packhorses would be one-third laden with forage. Return trips took approximately one-third less time, but horses would then have to be rested. These calculations depend on many variables. See also Moore, "Mobility and Strategy," pp. 68-77. Beeves and hogs could generally be delivered on the hoof. *Fort Meigs and the War of 1812*, p. 94. For the army ration, see Risch, *Quartermaster Support*, p. 118.

[31]Risch, *Quartermaster Support*, p. 163; Mahon, *War of 1812*, p. 213.

[32]Brown to SW, 22 June 1814, William Cheever to SW, 23, 24 May, 6, July, 17 August 1814, and Winfield Scott to SW, 17 May 1814, Registered Letters Received, RG 107; Armstrong to Callender Irvine, 18 January 1814, Military Book, RG 107; McKee, "Service of Supply" (4th Paper), pp. 25, 30, 31; Charles W. Elliott, *Winfield Scott: The Soldier and the Man* (New York: Macmillan Co., 1937), p. 162.

[33]Elbert Anderson to SW, 2 January 1813, Registered Letters Received, RG 107. See also Meyer, *Transportation in the U.S.*, p. 62.

[34]*Jomini and His Art of War*, ed., J.D. Hittle (Harrisburg: Stackpole Co., 1947), p. 68.

[35]To the Earl of Liverpool, 9 November 1814, *Supplementary Despatches, Correspondence, and Memoranda of Field Marshal Arthur Duke of Wellington*, ed. [His Son] (London: John Murray, 1862), IX, 425.

[36]In 1814, e.g., Lieutenant General Sir George Prevost, Governor-in-Chief of the Canadas and Commander-in-Chief of British forces, could not send army

reinforcements westward to Kingston because of the heavy logistical demands placed on men, supplies, and transportation by the massive amount of naval construction then taking place at Kingston. Hitsman, *Incredible War of 1812*, pp. 215-219.

[37]Gilpin, *War of 1812 in the Old Northwest*, pp. 237-239. The see-saw naval struggle on Lake Ontario well illustrated the dilemmas of the navies' dual role. See, e.g., C.P. Stacey, "Naval Power on the Lakes, 1812-1814," in *After Tippecanoe: Some Aspects of the War of 1812*, ed. Philip P. Mason (East Lansing: Michigan State University Press, 1963), pp. 49-59.

[38]Armstrong to Brown, 10 June 1814, Military Book, RG 107.

[39]*On War*, trans. Graham, Chapter iii.

[40]Does this mean, as the disciples of Emory Upton and Alfred Thayer Mahan have suggested, that the Americans should have been better prepared, especially by establishing naval control of the lakes and a regular force on the frontier before declaring war? Yes, of course. But how historical and realistic is this criticism? Would the country have supported such expenses and such a course of action during peacetime? That is what Madison meant when he said that it would have been best at the outset to have gained control of the lakes and to have seized Montreal "if it had been practicable in time." Perhaps the Americans should not have declared war or tried to conquer Canada.

[41]White, *The Jeffersonians*, p. 216.

THE SOUTHERN INDIANS IN THE WAR OF 1812: THE CLOSING PHASE

by JOHN SUGDEN

IT has been conventional to equate the conflict between the southern Indians and the United States during the War of 1812 with the Creek war of 1813-1814. More correctly, however, there were three stages of the fighting, each emanating from standing grievances against the Americans nursed by Creek and Seminole bands, but receiving their initial impetus from separate sources. In 1812 and 1813, the Seminoles and their Negro allies, rallied by the Spanish who were concerned to protect their possessions in the south from American filibusters, participated in a number of skirmishes. A second phase of Indian hostility to the Americans, and that most widely known, was ignited primarily by the admonitions of Tecumseh and his followers from 1811 to 1814. The fighting of the so-called Creek War commenced with an engagement at Burnt Corn in the summer of 1813, and lasted until the American victory at Horseshoe Bend in March 1814. Within a few months of their defeat, however, the Indians were reinvigorated by the arrival of British forces in Florida, and the cooperation of the dissident natives with the British forms the closing stage of the conflict. To the collapse of this relationship, consummated by a British failure to uphold those clauses in the Treaty of Ghent which protected the Indians, a subsequent exchange between Indians and Americans, the Seminole war of 1818 acted as a finale, but this last lies outside the scope of the present article.

A clarification of the Indian resistance to the United States in the south during the closing phase of the conflict is here intended. Several previous examinations of this area have been published, but the emphasis of this study, as far as possible, has been upon the Indian viewpoint. However, since the natives left no written records, it necessarily is inferred from the re-

John Sugden is lecturer and research officer at Hereward College, Coventry, and is completing his doctorate at the University of Sheffield, England.

[273]

ports of their British allies.[1] The episode is best interpreted as part of the last, and the largest, of several desperate attempts made by the Indians of the eastern woodlands to arrest the social disintegration, cultural decay, depopulation, and loss of land occasioned by their protracted contact with the white frontier. A militant pan-Indian nativist movement, led by Tecumseh and Tenskwatawa, two Shawnees, developed in the northwest in the years preceding the War of 1812. Assisted by the outbreak of fighting between England and the United States, it eventually swept in some of the southern Indians, those who rose against the Americans in the Creek war. This movement was defeated in the north at Moraviantown in 1813, and in the south at Horseshoe Bend in 1814, but in neither theatre was it completely crushed.

In the summer of 1814 British forces arrived in the south to fortify the remaining Indian dissidents and to supply them with arms and provisions. The Indians welcomed the British as stronger and more steadfast allies than were the Spaniards, their immediate wants were relieved, and there were prospects of driving back the enemy and regaining their lands. Moreover, while many tribesmen in the south refused to commit themselves to war against the United States so long as the Americans retained the military ascendancy, the harsh policies of Andrew Jackson strengthened the hostile nativist faction. Nevertheless, the British invasion failed, and Indian hopes rested upon the Treaty of Ghent of 1814 which invalidated the dispossession of the Creeks by the Treaty of Fort Jackson signed earlier that year. But the Americans continued to uphold the Fort Jackson agreement, and the Indians were unable to persuade the British

---

1.   Mark F. Boyd, "Events at Prospect Bluff on the Apalachicola River, 1808-1818," *Florida Historical Quarterly*, XVI (October 1937), 55-96; John K. Mahon, "British Strategy and the Southern Indians: War of 1812," *Florida Historical Quarterly*, XLIV (April 1966), 285-302; John K. Mahon, *The War of 1812* (Gainesville, 1972); Frank L. Owsley, Jr., "British and Indian Activities in Spanish West Florida During the War of 1812," *Florida Historical Quarterly*, XLVI (October 1967), 111-23. A sound appreciation of the Indian position is evidenced by J. Leitch Wright, Jr., "A Note on The First Seminole War as Seen by the Indians, Negroes and their British Advisors," *Journal of Southern History*, XXXIV (November 1968), 565-75, and in his books, *Anglo-Spanish Rivalry in North America* (Athens, 1971), *Britain and the American Frontier, 1783-1815* (Athens, 1975), and *The Only Land They Knew, The Tragic Story of the American Indians in the Old South* (New York, 1981).

to take up their cause as an infringement of an international treaty. Without that support the nativist movement in the south was powerless to contest further American aggression and the stage was prepared for the Indian removals of the ensuing decades.

Both of the principal Indian groups actively in opposition to the Americans at the time of the British invasion of the south in 1814 had been involved in the earlier conflict with the United States. One, the Seminole, had probably heard of Tecumseh's inflammatory talk to the Creeks in 1811, and according to tribal tradition two of the influential Seminole chiefs, Ben Berryman and Cappachamico, had been among those who heard the Shawnee at Tuckabatchee.[2] But whatever support Tecumseh might have reaped for his inter-tribal confederacy among the Seminoles and their Negro allies, a more potent influence was that of the Spanish. Spain, at this time, controlled the Florida peninsula and a strip of land south of the thirty-first parallel running westwards along the Gulf to the Mississippi. Between 1810 and 1813, however, Georgians and Tennesseans, supported cautiously by the American government and aware of internal unrest among the Spaniards, managed to wrest Baton Rouge, the area west of the Perdido, Mobile, and Amelia Island from Spain. To secure his country's possessions from further aggression the Spanish governor, Sebastián Kindelan, incited the Seminoles and Negroes against the American interlopers in 1812. Many of the Negroes were refugees from American plantations who had found considerable freedom and status among the Seminoles; they particularly feared the increase of American interference in Florida. Furthermore, the destruction of some Indian towns by American forces in 1813 gave additional cause for Seminole hostility towards the United States.[3]

The other major Indian opponents of the Americans were the "Red Stick" Creeks of Alabama. Their resentment had been long brewing. Creek society had been fraught with excessive

---

2. A. W. Crain to Lyman C. Draper, January 11, 1882, Draper Collection Wisconsin Historical Society, Madison, Wisconsin, Vol. 4, YY, 16.
3. The best studies of this conflict are Rembert W. Patrick, *Florida Fiasco: Rampant Rebels on the Georgia-Florida Border, 1810-1815* (Athens, 1954); Edwin C. McReynolds, *The Seminoles* (Norman, Oklahoma, 1957). See also Julius W. Pratt, *Expansionists of 1812* (New York, 1949), 60-125, 189-237.

interference from the United States since the Treaty of Coleraine in 1796. Benjamin Hawkins, the American agent, tried to dominate the Creek National Council, to which delegates from all the Creek towns were invited. He also wanted to centralize Indian society by issuing certificates to Creeks intending to hunt or trade, testifying to their reliability. By the administration of public order rather than the allowance of its management to the clan, town, or individual, Hawkins also contributed towards this trend. Further, he encouraged agricultural development and production for the market. His efforts tended to promote the settlement of the Indians outside of the villages, away from the communal influences, and the development of ownership of private property and individualism. Many of the traditional Creek villages went into decline, some of the land was exhausted, and the sense of communal responsibility among the Indians was eroded.[4]

A schism rapidly appeared in Creek society. The so-called "progressive" faction, strong among the Lower Creeks of the Chattahoochee, Flint, and Ocmulgee rivers, adhered more strongly to the American program; the nativist or Red Stick Creeks, prevalent among the more remote Upper Creeks of central Alabama, espoused tribal independence and a separate cultural identity. The anger of the Red Stick Creeks against the Americans was enhanced by incursions onto Indian lands. Not only were the Spaniards being pressed in the south by the United States, but the newly organized Louisiana Territory, the growth of American settlements along the Cumberland River, and the perennial expansion attempts by Georgians, created among the Indians the feeling that they were being encircled by the United States and that such activity would lead to

---

4. For the Creek war, see R. S. Cotterill, *The Southern Indians: The Story of the Civilized Tribes Before Removal* (Norman, 1954), 146-93; McReynolds, *Seminoles*, 52-62; Angie Debo, *The Road to Disappearance* (Norman, 1941), 66-83; Merritt Bloodworth Pound, *Benjamin Hawkins, Indian Agent* (Athens, 1951); Frank L. Owsley, "Benjamin Hawkins, the First Modern Indian Agent," *Alabama Historical Quarterly*, XXX (Summer 1968), 7-13; H. S. Halbert and T. H. Ball, *The Creek War of 1813 and 1814* (University, Alabama, 1969); Frank Herman Akers, *The Unexpected Challenge: The Creek War of 1813-14* (Ph.D. dissertation, Duke University, 1975); John Spencer Bassett, ed., *Correspondence of Andrew Jackson*, 6 vols. (Washington, D. C., 1926-35), I, II; Theron A. Nunez, "Creek Nativism and the Creek War of 1813-14," *Ethnohistory*, V (Winter, Spring, Summer 1958), 1-47, 131-75, 292-301.

exorbitant demands for Indian land. Tracts on the Georgia frontier, along the Ocmulgee and the Oconee, were ceded to the United States by the Creeks in 1802 and 1805, and a horse path was blazed across Indian territory between the Ocmulgee River and Mobile. In 1811, the Americans peremptorily demanded that the Creeks allow a north-south road to pass through their lands to connect white settlements on the Tennessee River with Fort Stoddert near Mobile.

This was the situation into which Tecumseh, in 1811, introduced his call for the tribes to unite, to reassert traditional Indian values and culture, and to resist further territorial encroachment by the Americans. Before the close of 1812, the Red Sticks had developed a militant, anti-American nucleus of warriors who looked to Tecumseh for leadership and who were able to increase their influence among the Creeks. In 1813 a civil war between the Red Stick and Americanized Creeks broke out, which in the summer escalated into a confrontation between the nativists and the Americans. The fighting ended with Jackson's victory over the Red Sticks at Horseshoe Bend and the cession of some 23,000,000 acres of Creek land to the United States at the Treaty of Fort Jackson on August 9, 1814.

The defeated Red Sticks made their way into Pensacola where the Spanish afforded them a refuge. There they heard of the Fort Jackson treaty and their anger increased. The terms were imposed upon Red Sticks and friendly Creeks alike, and without the representation of the former, whose presence, no doubt, was considered unnecessary. About half of the Creek territory was ceded in reparation to the United States and no payment was to be made for it. Later, in 1817 and 1853, $195,417.90 was given to the friendly Creeks as compensation for the damage done them by the Red Sticks but during the forty years following the annexation, the United States Treasury realized over $11,250,000 from the land.[5] Naturally, the Red Sticks repudiated the cession immediately and it served to alienate some Creeks, such as the Big Warrior, who had been friendly to the United States.

It is difficult to estimate how many Red Sticks survived the war of 1813-1814. Various assessments of the size of the Creek nation, and the census of 1832, when the population may have

5. Debo, *Road to Disappearance*, 83.

recovered, would indicate that the tribe consisted of some 25,000 people. At the most there were about 5,000 warriors.[6] More than half, perhaps sixty per cent of these, went over to the Red Sticks during the conflict.[7] Many, undoubtedly, were lost in the fighting although the casualties ascribed to the hostiles by American commanders during the campaigns were grossly inflated.[8] Hundreds of them managed to escape to the south, reportedly those from eight towns. In June 1814 some 200 warriors were believed to be at Pensacola and about 1,500 more were reportedly on the Escambia River.[9] British reports indicated that about 800 warriors eventually gathered about Pensacola and that 1,300 others remained on the Alabama as "prisoners of war," although this last figure is likely not very accurate.[10] It seems, however, that in the late summer of 1814 perhaps as many as 1,000 warriors who had resisted the American forces remained at large as potential enemies of the United States. Among those at liberty were some of the most implacable of the Red Stick leaders. A number of the principal hostile chiefs, such as High Head Jim, had been killed, and others, among them Menawa and Paddy Walsh, were in hiding. Some, such as William Weatherford, whom British reports suggest later fought for the Americans against his former colleagues at Pensacola, had surrendered.[11] But two of the most influential Red Sticks remained prepared to resume the conflict, Peter McQueen and Josiah Francis (Hillis Hadjo), both of whom had been fomentors of the rebellion.

Both men had a history of antagonism to the United States. Francis, the son of an Englishman and a Creek, was a leader of the Tuskegee Creeks and had risen to prominence as a prophet ministering the revitalization cult introduced by Tecumseh. Early in 1813, he had been in contact with the Spanish, and

6. Ibid., 103; Mary Jane McDaniel, *Relations Between the Creek Indians, Georgia and the United States* (Ph.D. dissertation, University of Mississippi, 1971), 2-3.
7. Akers, *Unexpected Challenge*, 137.
8. The British estimate of 1,800 warriors killed was also too high. "Return of the Muscogee or Creek Indians," War Office, Public Records Office, London (hereinafter cited as WO), class 1/folio 143/pp. 174-75.
9. Cotterill, *Southern Indians*, 190; Harry Toulmin to Andrew Jackson, June 22, 1814, Bassett, *Correspondence of Jackson*, II, 9-11.
10. "Return of the Muscogee or Creek Indians," WO/1/143/174-75.
11. Unsigned letter from Pensacola, July 19, 1814, Cochrane Papers, National Library of Scotland, Edinburgh (hereinafter cited as CP), 2328, 32.

in the summer he may have accompanied the expedition to
Pensacola which led to the first skirmish of the Creek war at
Burnt Corn.[12] His movements, thereafter, are obscure and
controversial. It has been asserted that at the time of the attack
on Fort Mims in August 1813, he led a party against Fort Sinque-
field, or that he was busy establishing his Indian town known as
the "Holy Ground."[13] However, according to Edward Nicolls, a
British agent who knew the chief well, "Frances told me that
while he was attacking Fort Mims the blacks were the first in,
and I have one man who killed seven Americans in that affair."[14]

McQueen, probably the son of James McQueen, a Scots
frontiersman, was a leader of the Tallahassee Upper Creek band
and had been present at the Creek victories at Burnt Corn and
Fort Mims. According to Nicolls, he and Francis led the Creeks,
who, in a three-day battle on January 24-26, 1814, turned
Jackson's army back to Fort Strother, and who, with eighty
warriors, defeated General John Floyd's superior force at Calabee
Creek on January 27, 1814. Both chiefs fled to Pensacola after
the defeat at Horseshoe Bend; McQueen escaped after he was
captured on the Tallapoosa in April.[15]

At Pensacola the Indians depended upon help from the
Spanish. By the middle of 1813 there were only about 500
Spanish troops in West Florida, and Spain, locked in combat
with the French in Europe, was unable to send them any substantial reinforcement. Confronted with the obvious American
threat, Juan Ruiz Apodaca, captain general of Cuba, and Mateo
González Manrique, the governor of Pensacola, were ready to
arm the Indians and provision them in case they would be needed
to bolster the weak Spanish defenses.

Another possible source of support for the Red Sticks was
the British. As early as the previous September and November,
the Indians had appealed through Governor Charles Cameron,
at New Providence in the Bahamas, for assistance, suggesting
that contact might be made through the Apalachicola River. Not

---

12. Halbert and Ball, *Creek War of 1813 and 1814*, 125.
13. Ibid., 184; Nunez, "Creek Nativism," 168.
14. Edward Nicolls to Alexander Cochrane, August 12, 1814, CP, 2328, 59-
62; see also Nicolls to John Philip Morier, September 25, 1815, WO/1/
143/137-39.
15. George Stiggins, a Creek half breed, is in error in suggesting that
Francis fled to Pensacola after the destruction of his town in December 1813. Nunez, "Creek Nativism," 172-73.

until early in 1814, however, did Earl Bathurst, secretary of state
for war in London, give instructions to the British navy to
support the Creeks.[16] The delay caused the Indians to despair,
but their defeat in March, the loss of their fields and homes, and
the appalling material conditions in which they were compelled
to cluster about Pensacola merely accentuated their need for
the British. Red Stick resentment of the United States was also
growing. "Our Case is really miserable and lamentable," they
told the British who eventually arrived at Apalachicola, "driven
from House and Home without Food and Clothes to cover our
Bodies by disasters and an Enemy, who has sworn our ruin, and
hovering about Pensacola and its Vicinity, where We can get
now [sic] Assistance, as the Spanish Government tells Us that
it is scarsely [sic] able to support its Own Troops." Nevertheless,
they "have Determined to make no Peace with the United States
of America without the British Government's Consent."[17] The
same truculent attitude was forcibly put to Benjamin Hawkins,
the American Indian agent: "We have lost our country and re-
treated to the sea side, where we will fight till we are all destroyed."[18]

Both the Seminoles and the Red Stick Creeks, despite their
defeat in an unequal contest with the United States, were spoil-
ing to renew the fighting, and the British were willing to oblige
them. In Europe the war with France was drawing to a triumphant close, and an able admiral, Alexander Cochrane, had
been appointed commander in chief of the American station to
coordinate a campaign against the United States seaboard.
Cochrane, as well as his predecessor, Admiral John Borlase
Warren, had been aware of the possibilities of using southern
Negroes and Indians in the subjugation of the American south,
and he now moved quickly to respond to Bathurst's instructions.[19] A British expeditionary force was sent to assist the
Indians.

Captain Hugh Pigot, of the frigate *Orpheus*, was employed
to make the first contact. He was given a message from Cochrane

16. Mahon, *War of 1812*, 341; Owsley, "British and Indian Activities,"
   111-15; Earl Bathurst to Charles Cameron, March 30, 1814, CP, 2338, 34.
17. Joshua Francis, Yahollasaptko, Hopoyhisihlyholla to British Commander at St. George's Island, June 9, 1814, CP, 2328, 28-29.
18. Debo, *Road to Disappearance*, 82.
19. Wright, *Britain and the American Frontier*, 162-65; Cochrane to George,
   Earl Spencer, March 13, 1797, CP, 2568, 49-50.

to the Indian chiefs and carried blankets and other presents, supplied by Governor Cameron, together with 2,000 muskets and ammunition. Accompanied by Lieutenant David Hope of the *Shelbourne,* Pigot sailed for Apalachicola Bay, and anchored there on May 11, 1814. He landed his acting lieutenant of Royal Marines, George Woodbine, who had been given the shore rank of brevet captain of marines and a provisional appointment as British agent to the southern Indians. Woodbine quickly induced some Indians aboard the British vessels on May 20. The following day Corporal James Denny and Sergeant Samuel Smith of the marines were set ashore to instruct the warriors in the use of small arms. A loghouse was erected upon Vincent Island, stores were landed, and ammunition distributed.[20]

The base was then extended up the Apalachicola River. On May 25, Woodbine reached Prospect Bluff, where he accepted from the local Indians power to direct operations. He urged them to spare the lives of any American prisoners in the forthcoming campaigns. A start was made upon erecting a fort with a powder magazine. Since provisions for the Indians, including flour and red paint, were inadequate, an important feature of the bluff was the existence there of the trading store belonging to John Forbes and Company of Pensacola. It was eventually seized, and its caretakers, Edmund Doyle and William Hambly, entered Woodbine's service as interpreters. Nevertheless, there were neither field pieces nor the supplies necessary to begin an offensive against Fort Mitchell, eighty miles upriver, and the Indian parties had to be content for some time with their capture of one Wilson, an American "spy."[21]

Predictably, the advent of the British was welcomed, particularly by three groups, the Seminoles, the Red Stick Creeks, and many of the Negroes. The Indians and Negroes who first rallied around Woodbine were mainly Seminoles, under the old chief Thomas Perryman, and Cappachamico, head of the Mikasuki Seminole band. The chiefs were pleased to support the

---

20. Hugh Pigot, April 13, 1814, CP, 2328, 1-2; Pigot to George Woodbine, May 10, 1814, ibid., 3-6; Pigot to James Denny and Samuel Smith, May 21, 1814, ibid., 9; Pigot to Cochrane, June 8, 1814, Admiralty Papers, Public Record Office, London (hereinafter cited as ADM), class 1/folio 506/pp. 394-99.
21. Woodbine to Pigot, May 25, 1814, CP, 2328, 14-15; Boyd, "Events at Prospect Bluff," 74-75; Woodbine to David Hope, May 31, 1814, CP, 2328, 13.

campaign against the Americans. The hostility of the Seminoles
to the United States, as well as the attraction of British presents,
arms, and provisions, guaranteed immediate support for
Woodbine. The agent was also aware of the recalcitrant Red
Sticks, who, destitute and unarmed, sheltered about Pensacola.
They were unable apparently to obtain supplies from either
the Spaniards or John Forbes and Company, the Indian traders.
Consequently, a young warrior called Yellow Hair was dispatched
by Woodbine to Pensacola to carry the news of the British
landing to the followers of Francis and McQueen. There was an
immediate response. McQueen, with twenty-five men, left for
Apalachicola by boat. Durgan with a party of twenty, and other
groups, followed shortly afterwards. Francis found passage to
Apalachicola on a British schooner, and as word spread, numbers
of Negroes fled from American plantations to join the British
standard.[22]

An estimate of the Indian forces in alliance with the British
at this time reveals the continued hostility of the Seminole and
Red Stick bands to the United States. Woodbine assessed his
support from villages along the upper Apalachicola River as:
Yawolla, ten warriors; Tamathea or Tamathla and Ochesee, 150;
Tochtohuli, 100; Oaketee Ockanee, 250; Saockulo, fifty; Fowl-
town, 300; Euchee, twenty; Tallasee, thirty; Canholva, fifteen;
and Emasee, fifty, for a total of 975 warriors. To these were added
the men of other Seminole and Creek villages: the Chihaw Lower
Creeks on the upper Flint River, 400; the Indians at Red
Ground, twenty; Cheskee Tallosa, sixty; Kivah Rawon and
Cedar Creeks, 100; Mikasuki Seminole, 700; the Tallasees, 200;
and the Pensacola Red Sticks, 800. In all there were 3,255 men,
of whom 2,800 were immediately ready to take up arms. While
these estimates included some boys between the ages of ten and
fourteen, they were not disconcerting to the British, who believed that only some 1,200 Creek warriors remained faithful to
the Americans.[23]

The forces enumerated by Woodbine represented the
survivors of the Indian bands who had already tried their

---

22. Woodbine to Pigot, May 25, 1814, ibid., 12-13; Woodbine to Hope, May
   31, 1814, ibid., 13; Toulmin to Jackson, June 22, 1814, Bassett, *Correspondence to Jackson*, II, 9-11; letter from Pensacola, June 8, 1814,
   ibid., 7; John Gordon to Jackson, July 20, 1814, ibid., 17-18.
23. Woodbine-Pigot information, CP, 2326, 151-59.

strength against the Americans, and it was possible that others might later join them. An attempt was made to sow disaffection among the Creeks who, under Big Warrior, had remained friendly to the United States and whose strength the British estimated to be some 1,200 men. These Indians, however, had not yet been alienated from the Americans by the Fort Jackson treaty, which lay in the future, and the bitterness which they felt to the Red Sticks as a result of the Creek civil war had not been forgotten. More important, they had witnessed the futility of nativist resistance to the United States and were shrewd enough to realize the danger of committing themselves to the British while the Americans remained in control of the south.

At the same time, even the "progressive" Creeks were disturbed by the repeated encroachment upon Indian land, and they were willing to court the British. Woodbine dispatched emissaries to the main Lower Creek towns of Coweta and Cussita, conveying the message of pan-Indianism that had once belonged to Tecumseh. The Creeks, he said, should unite with the Chickasaws, Choctaws, and Cherokees against the Americans. Meetings were held in the Creek country, and thanks were returned to the British for the presents that had been received. It was acknowledged that the unification of the tribes had long been the cherished desire of the Creeks and that they had never ceased their fidelity to the British crown and their claims upon British protection. But for the time being, that was as far as they were willing to go.[24]

The Indians assembling at Apalachicola, in the meantime, were amenable to British suggestions. On May 28 Woodbine harangued the local Seminoles, emphasizing the strength of the British king and his determination to help the Indians. "He wants to protect all Indians," the warriors were told, "and to make them into one family that they may unite and drive the children of the bad spirit out of their lands and hunting grounds." But the war must be fought according to the standards of British humanity, and rewards were offered for prisoners delivered to the soldiers.[25] The chiefs signed a bizarre document

24. Creek Nation to Cochrane, CP, 2328, 18-19; Benjamin Hawkins to John Armstrong, July 13, 1814, *American State Papers*, 38 vols. (Washington, D.C. 1832-61), *Indian Affairs*, Class II, 2 vols., I, 860.
25. Woodbine to the Indians, May 28, 1814, CP, 2328, 15.

pledging themselves to preserve the lives of captives: "In the name of all the chiefs of the Creek Nations now assembled in arms against the Americans we promise to spare the lives of all the prisoners taken, whether man, woman or child, and to give them up to Captain Woodbine of the Royal Marines who has informed us that they would be a gratefull [sic] present to our Father King George."[26]

The Indian response to Woodbine convinced Pigot that if sufficient stores could be arranged the tribesmen could become an important military force. Forty pistols, powder and ball, eleven barrels of cornpowder, drums, a launch and equipment, 100 pounds of tobacco, seventy-five blankets, sixty gallons of wine, a coat, and an epaulet were unloaded, and Pigot left Apalachicola carrying Seminole addresses to Cochrane. He left Woodbine, Denny, and Smith behind to work with the Indians. He ordered Captain Nicholas Lockyer of the sloop *Sophie* to take under his command the *Childers* and *Shelburne*, make contact with the Pensacola Red Sticks, and maintain a supply from New Providence to Apalachicola.[27]

Cochrane was no less enthusiastic than Pigot, whose report he forwarded to the Admiralty together with his own observation that if 3,000 British troops were landed at Mobile, and were joined by the Indians, Jean Lafitte's Baratarian privateers, and the Spanish, they "would drive the Americans entirely out of Louisiana and the Floridas."[28] To follow up Pigot's mission, the admiral organized an expeditionary force of 114 men, two howitzers, and a field piece to convey to Apalachicola 300 suits of clothing, 1,000 stand of arms, and other provisions for the Indians.[29] In an exhortation to the chiefs, Cochrane explained that "your Father King George will not suffer his Indian Children to be made Slaves of by his rebellious Subjects" and that the men and arms had been sent to support them. He contended that the United States would leave the Indians "not one foot

---

26. Thomas Perryman and Cappachamico, pledge, May 28, 1814, ibid. These chiefs were Seminoles, but at this time the Seminole bands regarded themselves as part of the Creek Nation.
27. CP, 2326, 160; Pigot to Nicholas Lockyer, June 11, 1814, CP, 2328, 24-25; Thomas and William Perryman, Cappachamico and other chiefs to Cochrane, 1814, ADM/1/506/402-03; Pigot to Cochrane, June 8, 1814, ibid., 394-99.
28. Cochrane to Admiralty, June 20, 1814, ADM/1/506/390-93.
29. Ibid., July 23, 1814, ADM/1/506/478-79.

of land . . . to the Eastward of the Mississippi" and that the message must be circulated to the Negroes of Georgia and the Carolinas and to any Indians friendly to the Americans. Significantly, Cochrane referred to the large British forces being prepared for the attacks on the American seaboard and added that, in the event of a peace, "your rights will not be forgotten." These promises were to be important to the Indians, who would, in time, expect the British to fulfill them.[30]

On June 30 Woodbine was appointed auxiliary captain of the Corps of Colonial Marines, of which the expeditionary force to be embarked was the basis; the balance would be recruited from loyalists and Negroes. To command the expedition, Cochrane selected from his flagship, *Tonnant*, Major Edward Nicolls of the Royal Marines, a man of attested gallantry, known as "Fighting Nicolls." He has been described by one historian of the marines as "possibly the most distinguished officer the corps ever had."[31] In July 1814 Nicolls was ordered to place himself at the head of the irregular operations in the American South and was empowered to raise 500 men as a colonial regiment in support of the Indians. During the next four years, Nicolls developed a close relationship with the Indians, and he became their most consistently outspoken white champion.

His instructions enjoined him both to raise and command a colonial regiment and to instruct, assist, and direct the Indians in military matters. He bore with him a copy of Pigot's report and of Cochrane's proclamation to the natives which would serve as letters of introduction. Cochrane permitted Nicolls considerable freedom of action, providing he refrained from acts of hostility to the United States within Spanish territory, except in self defense. The troops and stores were embarked at New Providence aboard the *Hermes* (Captain William Henry Percy), and the *Carron* (Captain Robert Cavendish Spencer), largely upon the orders of Governor Cameron. Cochrane had Cameron

---

30. Cochrane to Indian chiefs, June 29, 1814, ADM/1/505/163-64.
31. P. C. Smith, *Per Mare Per Terram: A History of the Royal Marines* (St. Ives, Huntingdon, 1974), 45. A sketch of Nicolls is contained in ibid., 45-47. See also William James, *Naval History of Great Britain*, 6 vols. (London, 1878), III, 197-99, 291-96, IV, 221, 347, 431; Admiralty *Navy Lists* (London, issues between 1814 and 1864); Cochrane to Woodbine, June 30, 1814, CP, 2326, 190-91; Nicolls, Memorial, 1817, WO/1/144/419-22; Nicolls, Commission, July 4, 1814, CP, 2326, 192-93.

informed that Britain's only intention was to "preserve the Indians from being destroyed by the United States." The admiral, in his proclamation, had promised the Indians two field pieces, 2,000 stand of guns, and 1,000 swords, and Nicolls drew upon Cameron for two long twenty-four pounders, launches and flatboats, belts, fowling pieces, powder flasks, flints, sabres, buttons, jackets, epaulets, vermillion, and $100 worth of presents.[32]

Before Nicolls reached Apalachicola Bay in August 1814, a new development had increased the prospects of the Indians' engaging the American forces, and they were, themselves, the cause of the changing circumstances. Andrew Jackson, district commander of the American troops, had viewed with alarm the resurgence of the Indian cause. He complained to Governor Mateo González Manrique of Pensacola that the British had been allowed to mobilize upon Spanish soil against the United States, and that the Spaniards themselves were harboring refugee Red Sticks. McQueen and Francis, Jackson maintained, should be surrendered to the Americans. In view of the aggressive attitude of Jackson and the Americans to both the Creeks and the Spaniards in recent years, these aggrieved protestations failed to impress Manrique.[33] Nevertheless, the governor was alarmed. The solution to the problem was not easy to find. While the Spanish were too weak to successfully contest the United States, they feared that an attempt to improve their position might cost them any remaining American goodwill. Confronted by the threat from Jackson, but unwilling to act in any way that might antagonize the Americans, they vacillated. Governor Manrique refused to sever connections with his Creek allies and sent appeals for help to his superior, Apodaca, at Havana, but he shrank from too vigorous a defense of Pensacola. Apodaca, on his part, was willing to allow Nicolls's Indians and British to operate as they desired, provided that they recognized Spanish control of St. Marks, St. Augustine, and Pensacola, but he refused to give direct aid.[34]

32. Cochrane to Nicolls, July 4, 1814, ADM/1/506/480-85; Cochrane to Admiralty, July 23, 1814, ibid., 478-79; Cochrane to Cameron, July 4, 1814, CP, 2328, 30; Nicolls to Cochrane, July 27, 1814, ibid., 54-55; Cochrane to William Henry Percy, July 5, 1814, ADM/1/506/486-87.

33. Jackson to Mateo González Manrique, July 12, 1814, Bassett, *Correspondence of Jackson*, II, 15-16; Gordon to Jackson, July 20, 1814, ibid., 17-18; Manrique to Jackson, July 26, 1814, ibid., 20-21.

34. Cameron to Ruis de Apodaca, July 29, 1814, CP, 2328, 40; Percy to

Unaware of the frustrations to be imposed upon them in their dealings with the Spaniards, the British were determined to employ their Indian allies, if necessary, in a resolute defense of Pensacola. Learning of the apprehensions of the Spanish governor there, Woodbine, at Apalachicola, abandoned his plans to attack an American post, Fort Hawkins, and set his forces in motion towards the Spanish town. Sergeant Smith, who had been given the local rank of lieutenant, and the Seminole leaders, Thomas and Benjamin Perryman, were instructed to march from Apalachicola to Pensacola with 300 men, while Woodbine embarked with the stores on the *Sophie* and the *Cockchafer* to arrive at his destination on July 28.[35]

When Nicolls arrived at Prospect Bluff in August, therefore, Woodbine was absent, although Smith and Denny were drilling Indians in the adjacent countryside and other natives were daily arriving to receive provisions and arms. For the first time Nicolls was awakened to the animosity many of the destitute Indians bore the United States. Commenting upon one group of eighty who arrived at the Bluff, he wrote, "such objects I never saw the like of, absolute skin and bone, but cheerfull [sic] and resolved to do their utmost against the common enemy. An old man told me, when I asked him how far it was to where the enemy were, and if he new [sic] the way to lead me to them, he said it was seven days journey to them [about 300 miles] that he could not miss the way for it was marked by the graves of his five children." However, attention was now pivoted upon Pensacola, and Nicolls did not remain at Prospect Bluff. Leaving some arms there, he sailed for the Spanish town, arriving there on August 24 and manning one of the forts.[36]

The arrival of Nicolls at Apalachicola had marked a further advance in the fortunes of the Indians hostile to the United

---

Cochrane, August 4, 1814, ibid., 43; Nicolls, August 4, 1814, ibid., 52-53; David Hope to Cameron, July 29, 1814, CP, 2338, 47; letter from Havana, August 8, 1814, Arsène Lacarrière Latour, *Historical Memoir of the War in West Florida and Louisiana in 1814-15* (Philadelphia, 1816), Appendix 2, v-vii.

35. Woodbine to Lockyer, July 30, 1814, CP, 2328, 39; Woodbine to Samuel Smith, July 21, 22, 1814, ibid., 33-34; Woodbine to Cochrane, July 25, 1814, ibid., 35-36; Woodbine to Cameron, July 26, 1814, ibid., 37; Woodbine to Cochrane, August 9, 1814, ibid., 56-57.

36. Nicolls to Cochrane, August 12, 1814, ibid., 59-61; Percy, September 9, 1814, ibid., 74-80.

States. Their requests had been partly responsible for bringing the British to Apalachicola, and the advent of Woodbine and Nicolls helped them satisfy their immediate needs of food, clothing, and arms. There were also prospects of reversing the military position in the south. Excited by the thought of major British conquests and the promise of being included in any peace settlement, the Indians saw a possible opportunity to regain their lost territories and to expel the rapacious American invaders. Nor was their confidence in the British entirely misplaced. Cochrane had remonstrated with his government on behalf of the Indians in June 1814, and on December 7, 1814, reiterated his concern: "The imbecility of the Spanish Government in West Florida and their natural jealousy leave the Americans every opportunity of encroaching upon the Indians, and as it appears to be the object of the American Government, to cut off all communications between the Indians and Great Britain, by driving the Creeks out of their country and possessing both sides of the Apalachicola, I trust that in any future negotiations of a pacific nature, stipulations will be made for repossessing the Indians of the Territory they have been deprived of."[37]

Not the least important consequence of the British intervention, therefore, was the renewed hope and the fillip it gave to the nativist morale. Cochrane received a proclamation from Nicolls, McQueen, Francis, Cappachamico, and Hopoy Mico which voiced their intention to "live or die free of which we have given hard proof by choosing to abandon our Country rather than live in it as slaves." They described the Spanish as "weak, frail friends," but the Indians had been impressed with British verve: "since your sons came here . . . we walk like men in their streets."[38]

If the arrival of the British had stiffened the resolve of the Indians, it was not, by itself, sufficient to win over to the nativists those tribesmen who had been willing to accept American domination. The battle lines remained largely as before, the difference being simply that the belligerent Seminoles and surviving Red Sticks could now call upon the British,

37. Cochrane to Admiralty, December 7, 1814, ADM/1/505/150-51; Cochrane to Admiralty, June 22, 1814, ADM/1/506/343.
38. Peter McQueen, Francis, Cappachamico, and Hopoy Mico to Cochrane, September 1, 1814, ADM/1/505/165-66.

as well as the Spanish, for support. Their morale and prospects had improved, but military superiority in the south still remained firmly with the United States. That being so, the Creeks under the Big Warrior, the Choctaws, the Chickasaws, and the Cherokees continued overtly to remain friendly to the Americans. If they were to align with the nativists, a major military breakthrough by the British would be necessary. There are reasons to believe that had the British achieved such a success most of the southern Indians, despite the machinations of American agents, would have joined their Seminole and Red Stick brethren. Much restrained discontent existed among the tribesmen, and it was enhanced in the summer of 1814 by the harshness of Jackson's Indian policy.

To some extent the extremity of Jackson's dealings with the Indians reflected his concern at the implications of the British arrival at Apalachicola. As early as July, after receiving definite news of the landing, Jackson induced the United States to reappraise its plans to disband the militia. He argued that Pensacola should be occupied since it provided a haven from which hostile Indians might raid American settlements.[39] Jackson issued an ultimatum to the remaining recalcitrant Creeks, demanding that they surrender by August 1.[40] At Fort Jackson on August 9 he imposed upon the tribe his treaty, seizing about half of their land in order to separate the Indians from their potential allies, the Spaniards. The belief that the treaty of Fort Jackson would cement the Indians in friendship to the United States was, perhaps, a cynical one. On August 10 Jackson recommended that food and clothing be distributed to the neutral Creeks, "or necessity will compel them to embrace the proffered friendship of the British. . . . To clothe the whole number will cost a considerable sum; but this sum would be very inferior to the Value of the territory ceded to the United States; in addition to which I may observe, that the cession has made them our friends, and will in future effectually prevent their becoming our enemies."[41]

Unable, however, to understand the form of friendship that deprived them so unjustly of about half of their land, even the

---

39. Jackson to Armstrong, July 24, 1814, Bassett, *Correspondence of Jackson,* II, 19-20; Jackson to David Holmes, ibid., 18-19; Jackson to Armstrong, July 30, 1814, ibid., 22-23.
40. Jackson to John Coffee, July 17, 1814, ibid., 16-17.
41. Jackson to Armstrong, August 10, 1814, ibid., 24-26.

pacific Creeks grew restless. The Big Warrior, who had held fast to the Americans throughout the Creek war, was regarded with suspicion by Jackson's colleagues. The general even demanded a liberal policy to be pursued with the Choctaws, hitherto considered as a neutral or friendly tribe, to check the growth of dissension.[42] While Jackson alternated a cool hand of charity with an iron fist, Indians were reported to be "pouring" into the British camps for arms. The Big Warrior established amicable relations with the Seminoles and was alleged to have "cut" with the Americans; plans were afoot to reconcile him with the Red Sticks. Cherokee, Choctaw, and Chickasaw delegates contacted Nicolls, and some Shawnees from the north relayed the news that "they are coming to join us right through the enemy's country. The chiefs all believe it but it appears very improbable to me. . . . When I asked one of their messengers what they did for provisions he replied most seriously that in their first attack they destroyed 500 of the Americans and barbacued [sic] the fattest of them and since that they never were in want."[43] There were, therefore, constant demands upon the British for supplies. At Apalachicola British vessels unloaded provisions and arms for transportation in shallow boats up the river to Prospect Bluff where Lieutenants Mitchell and Sergeant were strengthening the fort there. Ships also visited Pensacola. Yet at both places it was necessary to send out parties of Indians to forage, and on September 4 one group attacked a house near Mobile, killing or capturing a white man and three Negroes. The incident prompted Jackson to demand the seizure of Pensacola and the construction of an American fort upon the Apalachicola.[44]

The Treaty of Fort Jackson probably pushed many wavering Indians towards the nativists and the British, and it multiplied the resentment of others. Cochrane and Nicolls appeared to be the only immediate means whereby lost lands might be regained, but, notwithstanding this, if an intertribal alliance was to be

---

42. Ibid., August 5, 1814, ibid., 30-31; Jackson to Rachel Jackson, August 28, 1814, ibid., 35; W. C. C. Claiborne to Jackson, August 29, 1814, ibid., 35-36; Big Warrior to Hawkins, August 25, 1814, ibid., 36; James Monroe to Jackson, September 5, 1814, ibid., 43; Jackson to Monroe, October 14, 1814, ibid., 72-74.
43. Nicolls to Cochrane, August 12, 1814, CP, 2328, 59-61. The reference is presumably to the battle of Frenchtown, January 22, 1813.
44. Jackson to Monroe, September 5, 1814, Bassett, Correspondence of Jackson, II, 42; Jackson to Manrique, September 9, 1814, ibid., 44-56.

consummated, the necessity for British victories in the field was paramount. Unfortunately, their first attempt to both display their own martial prowess and to employ their existing Indian allies degenerated into a humiliating fiasco. To strengthen his hold upon the Gulf coast, Nicolls attempted to capture Mobile, a garrison with only some 158 fit men at the time of his attack.[45] At Pensacola Nicolls had at his disposal a number of men from his colonial marines, a few British vessels, and the Indians. The latter were daily increasing. They arrived as destitute refugees, many in so poor a condition that they were not immediately serviceable as a military force. It was estimated in August by Captain Lockyer that 1,000 Indians were at Pensacola, of whom 700 were warriors. Woodbine placed their strength even higher at 2,000, of whom 800 were fighting men. Some of these Indian forces had come from Apalachicola. Their chiefs were McQueen, Francis, John of the Attassees, Old Factor of the Euchees, Hopoeth Mico of the Four Nations, and Colonel Perryman of the Seminoles. It is probable that they were respectably armed. Lockyer distributed six cases of arms and eight kegs of powder to the Pensacola Red Sticks, and munitions had also been ferried from Apalachicola.[46] A setback, however, to Nicoll's attempts to recruit men for an assault upon Mobile occurred at the beginning of September when Lockyer failed to win the allegiance of the Baratarian pirates under the command of the Lafitte brothers.[47]

About 190 Indians participated in the attack upon Mobile on September 12-15, 1814; 130 warriors were on board the four British ships and sixty were ashore with Lieutenant Castle. During an engagement between the vessels and the batteries of Fort Bowyer both Percy and Nicolls, aboard the *Hermes*, were wounded. Nicolls lost the sight of his right eye. Nor more successful were Captain Robert Harvey and a shore party, who advanced on September 14 with a howitzer to within 800 yards of the fort but who were compelled to retreat before heavy American fire. The following day the vessels stood in while

45. Jackson to Monroe, September 17, 1814, ibid., 50-51.
46. Lockyer to Cochrane, August 12, 1814, CP, 2328, 67-68; Woodbine to Cochrane, August 9, 1814, ibid., 56-57; Nicolls, expenses, enclosed in Nicolls to John Barrow, August 21, 1815, WO/1/143/123-27.
47. John Sugden, "Jean Lafitte and the British Offer of 1814," *Louisiana History*, XX (Spring 1979), 159-67.

the troops approached along the beach to fire upon Fort Bowyer with the howitzer. The latter expended all its available shells and case shot without success, and an attempt was made to storm the American positions by landing parties from the boats supported by Indians on the shore. When these efforts also proved futile, the whole British and Indian force fell back to Pensacola. Their performance had been a lamentable one; they had lost the *Hermes*, which ran ashore, and thirty-two men killed and thirty-seven wounded aboard the ships. Scant casualties—four killed and five wounded—had been inflicted upon the enemy. Indian participation in the affair seems to have been minimal.[48]

The reverse at Mobile deprived the British of an opportunity to advance their cause among the uncommitted Indian tribes, but it was scarcely significant compared with the importance attached to the defense of Pensacola. This Spanish town had been a traditional prop of Creek independence of the United States since the post-revolutionary time of Alexander McGillivray. It had supplied ammunition and shelter to the Red Sticks in their war of 1813-1814, and its capture could not fail to impress Indians throughout the south. It became increasingly clear that the Americans would make an attempt against Pensacola, and the debacle at Mobile served to increase the necessity for Jackson to do so. Aware of the weakness of the Spaniards, he was prepared to force the issue with Governor Manrique. On August 24 Jackson repeated his allegations that the Spanish were harboring Indians hostile to the United States.[49] Manrique, in reply, recalled recent American aggression against Spain's possessions and declared the Treaty of Fort Jackson to be void, a matter that would be taken up with his home government in Spain.[50] Jackson was unimpressed. He mobilized his militia, which included, significantly, 700 Choctaws, and eventually marched upon the town. An admonition of October 21 from Secretary of State James Monroe ordered the general not to take "measures which

48. Nicolls to Cochrane, August 12, 1814, CP, 2328, 59-61; Percy to Cochrane, September 16, 1814, ibid., 83-87; Robert Harvey to Nicolls, September 20, 1814, ibid., 91; Cochrane to Admiralty, December 7, 1814, ADM/1/505/150-51; list of casualties, ibid., 161-62.
49. Jackson to Manrique, August 24, 1814, Bassett, *Correspondence of Jackson*, II, 28-29.
50. Manrique to Jackson, August 30, 1814, ibid., 37-40.

would involve this Government in a contest with Spain" but arrived too late to interfere with the expedition.[51]

The British and Indian participation in the defense of Pensacola proved to be both ineffective and fraught with difficulties. Provisioning the large numbers of Indians assembling there was perennially embarrassing, for, although some supplies were brought in by sea, most had to be purchased locally and shortages and profiteering drove up prices. Difficulties were constantly encountered in procuring clothing, blankets, needles, vermillion, ammunition, salt, and food. Woodbine lacked sufficient ready cash and found himself dredging his private resources and borrowing to meet the outlay, and, since American supplies were gradually stifled, Nicolls reported the necessity of smuggling flour into Pensacola.[52] British inability to meet all the accounts of the Pensacola merchants immediately did not improve their relationships with the local residents, but a more contentious matter still was Nicolls's recruitment of slaves to the fury of the slaveholders. The blacks had not rallied to the British standard as readily as had the Indians, and only about eighty of them were at this time assembled at Prospect Bluff. Others were with Nicolls at Pensacola, and some of them were claimed as the property of local dignitaries, such as the Indian trader John Forbes. Since the British had announced on August 26 and August 29 that neutral rights would be safeguarded, and Nicolls was present at Pensacola as an ally of the Spaniards, there was logic in the complaints of Forbes and other slaveowners that they had been poorly treated.[53] It is impossible to determine how far the Negroes had been impressed by Nicolls, or whether they were simply enlisting with the British to take advantage of their standing offer of land in the colonies open to slaves volunteering for service. Whatever the truth of the matter, however, it held important implications for Indian resistance in the south, because during the ensuing decades the communities of largely

51. Monroe to Jackson, October 21, 1814, ibid., 79-80; Jackson to Monroe, October 26, 1814, ibid., 82-83.
52. Woodbine to Nicolls, October 3, 1814, CP, 2328, 95; Woodbine to Nicolls, September 27, 1814, ibid., 93; Woodbine accounts, ibid., 100, 107; Nicolls to naval commissioners, October 1814, ibid., 102.
53. John Forbes and thirty-three Spanish inhabitants to Manrique, March 1815, ibid., 148-51.

free Negroes located in the Seminole country were to be principal forces in the fight against tribal removal.[54]

The Negro issue at Pensacola intensified difficulties which had already developed among the Indians, the British, and John Forbes. The Red Sticks charged that Forbes had so stifled supplies of ammunition to Indians during the Creek war that they had been compelled to retreat to Pensacola. This was all the more irritating, since lands on the Apalachicola River had been ceded to Forbes's company by Seminoles and Creeks in 1804 and 1811 conditional upon Forbes's operating an Indian trade with regulated prices. Under this front, the warriors alleged, Forbes had attempted to settle Indian land. In addition to the native grievances, the British had evidence that Forbes was now committed to a south dominated by American rather than British, or even Spanish, suzerainty, although his company continued to operate out of Pensacola. One partner, James Innerarity, was, in 1816, major of the American town of Mobile and colonel of the Mobile militia, and he was in regular contact with his brother, John Innerarity at Pensacola. In an intercepted letter of 1814 to Doyle and Hambly at Apalachicola, it was revealed that Forbes himself, in St. Augustine, had urged his employees to dissuade the Indians from joining the British. It was comparatively easy, therefore, for the Indians and the British to regard the Forbes company as a source of espionage and as an obstruction to their efforts.[55]

The problems with Forbes and other Pensacola residents did not end when the British eventually departed. At that time Nicolls made efforts to settle debts with the local merchants, and in February 1815 Cochrane appointed a committee to investigate and liquidate claims upon the British. However, the admiral declared that he had no power over any Negroes except those actually taken by the British Marines; he assumed no responsibility for those still with the Indians. This did not appease all slaveowners, and Forbes and Company continued to agitate

54. Kenneth Wiggins Porter, "Negroes and the Seminole War, 1817-1818," *Journal of Negro History*, XXXVI (July 1951), 249-80; Porter, "Negroes and the Seminole War, 1835-1842," *Journal of Southern History*, XXX (November 1964), 427-50.
55. Owsley, "British and Indian Activities," 118-19; Boyd, "Events at Prospect Bluff," 61-65; Indian chiefs to British government, March 10, 1815, WO/1/143/147-50; Nicolls to Cochrane, March 1816, WO/1/144/151-53.

upon this account and was able to obtain the arrest and imprisonment of Woodbine at New Providence in October 1815
on charges of appropriating slaves. As late as 1854, John
Innerarity was claiming indemnification for forty-five slaves from
the British. Such discontent was probably due in part to the
attempt of the British after the war to fulfill their obligations
to the enlisted Negroes. Although an effort was made to persuade the latter to return to their former masters, they were
offered the choice of enlisting in the West Indian Regiments or
of taking small pieces of land in the West Indies as free settlers.
Alternatively, they might remain at the fort at Prospect Bluff,
or on the Suwannee River, or live with the Indians. To the
chagrin of Innerarity and his colleagues, many of the Negroes
preferred these courses to returning to their masters.[56]

More important than these disputes, however, in the defense
of Pensacola, was the friction between Nicolls and Governor
Manrique. Strained relations between the two made any concerted effort impossible. Manrique was unwilling to antagonize
Jackson unnecessarily realizing his weak position in the event
of an American attack. He sought to retain control of the defense of Pensacola; whereas Nicolls and Captain James Alexander
Gordon of the *Seahorse*, who arrived with the *Mars* and the
Shelburne, demanded a more aggressive approach to the
problem. The Spanish, Nicolls reported, were "slumbering
amidst the threatened storm," but, apart from launching weak
Indian sorties against American forces which flitted about the
area, there was little he could do without more cooperation.[57]
In an attempt to reverse the lethargy in the defense, the British,
somewhat arbitrarily, interfered with Manrique's supervision
of the preparations to resist Jackson's army. On November 2,
they threatened to evacuate their forces unless Fort Barrancas

56. Nicolls to Gordon, November 7, 1814, CP, 2328, 114; British public
    notice, March 9, 1815, ibid., 165; claims of Forbes and others for
    Negroes, ibid., 172-79; Cochrane to John Wilson Croker, February 25,
    1815, ADM/1/508/570-71; Cochrane to Robert Cavendish Spencer, George
    Taylor, and Robert Gamble, February 17, 1815, ibid., 572-74; Cochrane
    to Pulteney Malcolm, February 17, 1815, ibid., 562-63; Nicolls to
    Hawkins, April 28, 1815, WO/1/143/161-62; WO/1/144/155-70; "Docu-
    ments Relating to Colonel Edward Nicholls and Captain George
    Woodbine in Pensacola, 1814," *Florida Historical Quarterly*, X (July
    1931), 51-54; Wright, "Note on First Seminole War," 569; Boyd, "Events
    at Prospect Bluff," 72, 74.
57. Gordon to Cochrane, November 18, 1814, CP, 2328, 109-11; Nicolls to
    Apodaca, November 9, 1814, ibid., 103-04.

and the harbor entrance were placed under the joint control of Manrique and Nicolls.[58] In reply the governor explained that "it was not in the power of the Governor to declare war."[59]

On November 3-5, the Indians and their families were moved across Pensacola Bay to a place of greater safety, and the next day the Americans opened fire upon Fort St. Miguel, near the town, partly manned by the British. Jackson called upon the Spaniards to surrender and while Manrique replied that he would repel any attack upon the town, his hand was weakened by the attitudes of his British allies, who believed that a successful defense was no longer possible. Gordon brusquely informed the governor that 600 Indian warriors had been sent to Apalachicola, and that "the enemy had already got possession of a post that he [Manrique] should have defended, that from his conduct, I was certain he had betrayed his trust, and as it was my duty to provide for the safety of the troops and the ships under my orders, I should destroy the Barrancas and the Fort on Santa Rosa, embarking the Spanish troops who choose to come off whenever I saw the enemy in possession of the town. By my direction the fort on Santa Rosa was destroyed that evening."[60]

Pensacola was stormed by Jackson's force on November 7; little resistance was offered. The following day Nicolls sent away the Indian rear guard, 200 Spanish soldiers were embarked from Barrancas, the guns were spiked, surplus arms and stores destroyed, and the fortifications blown up. The squadron remained in the harbor only long enough to cover the retreat of the Indians. Then it left with all but one of the ships sailing for Apalachicola with the British and Spanish forces. Because the British vessels were busy elsewhere, Manrique's soldiers did not leave Apalachicola and return to Pensacola until the summer of 1815.[61]

---

58. Nicolls and Gordon to Manrique, November 2, 1814, ADM/1/505/71; Nicolls and Gordon to Manrique, October 11, 1814, CP, 2328, 96; Nicolls to Apodaca, November 9, 1814, ibid., 103-04.
59. Gordon to Cochrane, November 18, 1814, ibid., 109-11.
60. Ibid.; Manrique to Jackson, November 6, 1814, Bassett, *Correspondence of Jackson*, II, 93.
61. Gordon to Apodaca, November 9, 1814, ADM/1/505/169-70; Gordon to Cochrane, November 18, 1814, CP, 2328, 109-11; Jackson to Monroe, November 14, 1814, Bassett, *Correspondence of Jackson*, II, 96-99; Cochrane, February 17, 1815, ADM/1/508/556-61.

Jackson's occupation of Pensacola represented the second defeat for the infant British-Indian alliance, and a more serious one than Mobile. It strongly indicated the military preeminence of the United States, and must have counteracted the headway which the British and their Indian allies had made among the neutral tribes. Seven months earlier, the fall of Pensacola would have been disastrous for the nativists, since it had been the major source of succour for Francis and McQueen's Red Sticks. In November, however, Apalachicola offered an alternative, especially as the position was being gradually strengthened. The British, supervised by Lieutenant Christie of the Royal Artillery, completed their fort at Prospect Bluff on the east bank of the river, and another fort was built at the forks of the Apalachicola. The immediate consequence of the fall of Pensacola, therefore, was a transfer of the Indian strength to Apalachicola, where they continued to assemble and arm. Jackson was disturbed by the concentration, but an American expedition against the Indians under Major Uriah Blue was not successful.[62]

In November Nicolls's principal objective was to maintain a force which could collaborate with Cochrane's invasion fleet, then assembling in the West Indies. At Apalachicola three companies of Negro Colonial Marines had been formed, and a fourth was in the process of organization. There was still hope of harnessing the neutral Creeks, for whom £500 worth of presents were being prepared, and the Cherokees, who received British arms. It is not inconceivable that the arrival in the Gulf of Mexico of Cochrane's forces at the end of the month encouraged more Indians to join the British. On December 22, 1814, for example, the 1,100 warriors, 450 women, and 755 children at Apalachicola were joined by 500 newcomers, "several wavering towns" having "lately joined us from the American Lines," and early in January "two different Indian tribes from the neighbourhood of the American lines," some 1,100 men, arrived.[63] Probably there were over 2,000 Indian fighting men gathered at the Bluff at the time, although British

---

62. Nicolls to Cochrane, August 12, 1814, CP, 2328, 59-61; Boyd, "Events at Prospect Bluff," 71-73; Jackson to James Winchester, November 22, 1814, Bassett, *Correspondence of Jackson*, II, 104-07.

63. Robert Henry to Cochrane, December 22, 1814, CP, 2328, 126; William Rawlins to Cochrane, January 16, 1815, ibid., 136-37; Nicolls to Cochrane, December 3, 1814, ibid., 117-18.

estimates held that 3,551 warriors were available for service. Of these 1,421 resided on or near the Apalachicola River, 800 were Red Sticks, 400 were Chihaw Lower Creeks, 760 were Seminoles or Mikasuki, and 170 were Negroes from the area eastwards of the Flint and the Apalachicola rivers. None of the neutral tribes had come over to the British, although it is possible to argue that the Choctaw were substantially with the Americans. The most promising recruits were still the Big Warrior Creeks, who were believed to have 2,540 warriors, of whom some 1,300 had been with the Red Sticks during the Creek war.[64]

During this period the relationship between the nativists and Nicolls and Woodbine matured into one of mutual affection. Working daily with the Indians, the two British officers developed a respect for their allies which stands in stark contrast to the bigoted arrogance with which they were regarded by many British leaders.[65] Among the chiefs at Apalachicola who were frequently in British company were McQueen, Francis, John, Old Factor, Hopoeth Mico, Perryman, Cappachamico, and Hopoy Mico; the latter two, both Seminoles, had remained at Prospect Bluff during the operations at Pensacola. Cappachamico and Perryman were reported much annoyed with John Forbes, and with other Indians, confiscated the company's property at the Bluff and rescinded the land grants made earlier to the traders. In particular, the "brave and faithful old Chief" Cappachamico, as Nicolls called him, bore such a grievance against Forbes that he vowed his death. It was this warrior, who, with Perryman, Francis, and others, visited Cochrane's flagship, the *Tonnant*, when it arrived in Apalachicola Bay late in 1814, and who, in company with Hopoy Mico, Francis, and some colleagues, was entertained aboard the *Erebus* when it arrived in the bay in January 1815.[66]

For all their understanding, however, Nicolls and Woodbine, like most white men who met Indians, did not doubt that aboriginal society was inferior to that of their own. A philanthropic sentiment was present. Woodbine, for instance, proudly

64. "Return of Muscogee or Creek Indians," WO/1/143/174-75.
65. For example, compare Mahon, *War of 1812*, 352, with Jane Lucas de Grummond, *The Baratarians and the Battle of New Orleans* (Baton Rouge, 1961), 68-69.
66. Nicolls to Cochrane, December 3, 1814, CP, 2328, 117-18; David Ewen Bartholomew to Cochrane, February 6, 1815, ibid., 145; Nicolls, expenses, enclosed in Nicolls to John Barrow, August 21, 1815, WO/1/143/123-27.

declared that "the lessons of humanity, inculcated in the minds
of our aggrieved red brethren have not been thrown away." As
he confided to Nicolls, "Their having given up unhurt to
yourself all the prisoners captured by them since your arrival,
makes me feel not a little proud in having been the first instrument of inducing them to lay aside the tomahawk and the scalping knife." The warriors were even willing to "liberate their
slaves, tho' they were to lose what they cost them." "The Indian
character," he believed, "has been much mistaken and has been
most unjustly stigmatized as bloody and ferocious. You have
been long enough among them to observe many most amiable
traits in them, which only want the fostering hand of instruction
and the light of christianity to mature. You often said that
with a little trouble and expense these our loyal brethren might
be civilized. Be assured, Sir, it is the truth and a very few
thousands expended on that laudable object would insure to
Great Britain thousands of most faithful and obedient subjects
whose loyalty has stood unshaken to our Sovereign [in] spite of
all the allurements held out to them by the Americans."[67]
Patronizing as many of these remarks may have been, they
reflect a recognition by both Nicolls and Woodbine of qualities
in the Indians missed by many contemporaries.

Inevitably, the concentration of men at the Bluff posed the
usual problem of supplies. Considerable quantities of provisions
and munitions were required. The *Alceste,* for example, landed
thirty-seven cases of arms and casks of flints, five bales, nine
cases, four casks, eighteen bundles, ten cradles, and four bags
of "sundry stores," 200 barrels of ball cartridges, 1,600 sand
bags, three cases of tools, seventy-five shovels, and other imple-
ments.[68] In November the *Seahorse* and the *Childers* deposited
stores, three six-pounder pieces, and $4,000; $3,000 was for the
use of Woodbine and the balance for Nicolls.[69] The attrition was
particularly severe upon food supplies. In December twelve
barrels of flour were consumed each day, and in times of acute
stress Nicolls was compelled to send the warriors into the woods
to hunt.[70] Even the river exacerbated the difficulties, for the

67. Woodbine to Nicolls, October 27, 1814, CP, 2328, 145.
68. List of goods aboard the *Alceste,* ibid., 108.
69. Gordon to Cochrane, November 19, 1814, ibid., 111-12.
70. Nicolls to Cochrane, December 3, 1814, ibid., 117-18; Rawlins to Senior
    Officer, Pensacola, January 16, 1815, ibid., 138.

ebbs in the Apalachicola obstructed the shallow-draught vessels which conveyed provisions to Prospect Bluff, and the bar in the bay sometimes necessitated the lightening of the victualling ships before they could pass towards the river mouth. Thus, the *Erebus*, which arrived off St. George's Island on January 22, 1815, was not able to shift supplies up the Apalachicola until the twenty-eighth.[71]

Nevertheless, a formidable force of men was assembled and maintained at Prospect Bluff, and their use was planned as part of the British invasion of the south. On December 5, 1841, Cochrane and Major General John Keane issued a proclamation to the Indians asserting that the war aims of the British included "the restoration of those lands of which the People of Bad Spirit have basely robbed them [the Indians]" which was to act as a clarion call for battle.[72] The Indians were to harrass the Georgian frontier and to link up with Admiral George Cockburn, who was operating upon the Atlantic seaboard against Florida and Georgia, while Cochrane himself struck at New Orleans. Later, in February, it was envisaged that they might act in a diversionary role by attacking Fort Stoddert on the Tombigbee River and threatening Mobile. Unfortunately, although, as late as January 1815, Prospect Bluff was strengthened by the addition of two long sixes and a company of the West India Regiment, the forces there were used in a fragmentary and ineffective manner. During the period November to February, fifty Mikasukis moved south to attack the frontier, Woodbine tried to make contact to the northeast with Cockburn, Nicolls took fewer than 100 Seminole, Creek, and Choctaw warriors to participate in the abortive British attack upon New Orleans, and some men were sent towards Mobile to cooperate with General John Lambert's troops there. Nothing of importance was achieved by any of these parties.[73] Worse still, the major British invasion of the south misfired. In December and January General Edward Pakenham's army was disastrously defeated at New Orleans, and

---

71. Bartholomew to Cochrane, January 31, 1815, ibid., 142; Rawlins to Cochrane, December 21, 1814, ibid., 122.
72. Cochrane and John Keane, proclamation to the Indians, December 5, 1814, WO/1/143/159.
73. Cochrane to John Lambert, February 3, 1815, ADM/1/508/566-69; Cochrane, February 14, 1815, ibid., 535-38; Nicolls to Cochrane, December 3, 1814, CP, 2328, 117-18; Bartholomew to Cochrane, January 31, 1815, ibid., 143.

while Cockburn raided the coasts in January, and Lambert's force captured Fort Bowyer the following month, no major progress had been made before hostilities between Britain and the United States finally came to an end.

At the close of the War of 1812, therefore, the Indian service with the British had been singularly unsuccessful. Large numbers of Seminoles and Red Sticks had assembled to fight their American foes, and although they had loyally accepted British direction, they were witness to a series of reverses: the repulse at Mobile, the loss of Pensacola, and the rout at New Orleans. The warriors themselves had hardly been in battle, and their losses were trivial. "I have had 4, 8, and 13 of them killed in different affairs," wrote Nicolls more than a year later.[74] In February 1815, the Americans may have appeared far from secure, but they had preserved their control of the south, and in such circumstances the Seminoles and the Red Sticks could expect little support from the other Indians who were more amenable to the United States.

At best, the nativists could claim to have been rescued from distress and to have received food and arms. But their lands were still in the hands of their enemies, and their ability to maintain their independence was almost as precarious as it had been before the British arrived. Nevertheless, there were still those promises made by Cochrane that the Creeks would not be forgotten in the event of peace. If the British had failed the Indians militarily, it remained to be seen if, by diplomacy, their pledges could be fulfilled.

When Admiral Cochrane had first written in June 1814 to Whitehall, arguing that the Indians should be included in a peace, he was preaching to the converted. As early as August 29, 1812, General Isaac Brock, who owed so much to Tecumseh and his followers in the campaign which saved Canada from invasion that year, had urged the British government to protect his Indian allies in peace negotiations, and by the end of 1812 he had obtained from Earl Bathurst, colonial secretary, a promise to that effect. The lesson was reinforced by the Canadian fur trade interest. It agitated for the preservation of Indian hegemony over the lands of the lakes and the northwest which would afford the traders access to that prime hunting area. In 1814, when the war in Europe ended, such ideas seemed feasible;

---

74. Nicolls to Cochrane, March 1, 1816, WO/1/144/139-42.

Britain would be free to concentrate its resources towards a military victory sufficient to warrant the imposition upon the United States of a settlement that would protect the Indian lands. Catching this mood, in May and June interested parties clamoured in the British press for the creation of an Indian buffer state in the northwest.[75]

However, Viscount Castlereagh, the British foreign secretary, was in no position to ask prolonged military operations of a war- and tax-weary Britain. While he hoped that the 1814 campaigns would weaken the hand of the United States, he feared that an extensive war would raise opposition to his government at home. Moreover, he had, of course, little if any commitment to the Indian cause. Nevertheless, he instructed his three commissioners negotiating with the American diplomats at Ghent to insist "as a *sine qua non* of peace" upon "an adequate arrangement" of Indian interests. This, he suggested, might be obtained by both Britain and the United States guaranteeing "the Indian possessions as they shall be established upon the peace, against encroachment on the part of either state," thus creating between Canada and the United States a buffer which would reduce, he believed, tension between the two countries.[76]

The Americans were, naturally, astonished by such suggestions when the peace negotiations opened in Ghent in August 1814, and the British commissioner, Henry Goulburn, coupled the idea of the barrier state with the *sine qua non*. Indeed, as late as January 1814, James Monroe had been proposing his own solution to British and American friction over the Indians by means of a British cession of Canada.[77] By August, the Americans

---

75. Isaac Brock to Liverpool, August 29, 1812, William Wood, ed., *Select British Documents of the Canadian War of 1812*, 4 vols. (Toronto, 1920-28), I, 506-09; Brock to George Prevost, September 18, 1812, ibid., 592-94; George Clifford Chalou, "The Red Pawns Go to War: British-American-Indian Relations, 1810-1815" (Ph.D. dissertation, Indiana University, 1971), 139, 188-89; Bradford Perkins, *Castlereagh and Adams: England and the United States, 1812-1823* (Berkeley, 1964), 64, 82-84; Charles M. Gates, "The West in American Diplomacy, 1812-1815," *Mississippi Valley Historical Review*, XXVI (March 1940), 502; Fred L. Engelman, *The Peace of Christmas Eve* (London, 1962).
76. Castlereagh to William Adams, Lord James Gambier, and Henry Goulburn, July 28, 1814, Charles W. Vane, ed., *Correspondence, Despatches and Other Papers of Viscount Castlereagh, Second Marquess of Londonderry*, 12 vols. (London, 1848-54), X, 67-72.
77. Monroe to the American commissioners, January 28, 1814, James F. Hopkins and Mary W. M. Hargreaves, eds., *The Papers of Henry Clay*, 5 vols. (Lexington, 1959-63), I, 857-62.

were on the defensive, but their commissioners undoubtedly considered the idea of an Indian barrier state, which would pose a threat to the expansion of the United States, as preposterous. It would restore to the Indians a recognition of their sovereignty over the lands they occupied, and it would impeach American jurisdiction over the northwestern territory, concepts satisfactorily conceded to the advantage of the United States by the British in 1783. Moreover, since the Americans were determined to settle the northwest, the creation of the barrier state would amount to a virtual cession of territory by the United States. As described by Goulburn on August 9, the Indian land would not be alienable either to Britain or the United States, and Castlereagh was persuaded to consider the Greenville treaty line of 1795 as a basis for discussion of boundaries. Although the American diplomats lacked instructions which would enable them to deal with the matter, they expressed contempt for the British proposals. Henry Clay, one of the American commissioners, referred to "the absurdity, to say the least of it, of Great Britain attempting, without powers, to treat for savage tribes, scattered over our acknowledged territory, the very names of which she probably does not know."[78]

On August 25 the American commissioners rejected the conditions of the Indian buffer state and British control of the lakes, leaving Britain with the alternatives of climbing down over the Indian issues or of risking what Castlereagh termed an "imprudent" military campaign.[79] Lord Liverpool, the British prime minister, doubted that his government could guarantee inalienable Indian lands, since the tribes themselves might wish to sell territory to the United States. Concerned that the peace negotiations would be ruptured, he suggested a modification to the *sine qua non* which established it in its final form.[80] It would certainly have been difficult to justify to the British public the maintenance of the war on a question so remote to them as the fate of the American Indian. Sir James Mackintosh, for one, expressed agreement with the Americans, and stated in the

---

78. Henry Clay to Monroe, August 18, 1814, ibid., 962-68; Castlereagh to the British commissioners, August 14, 1814, Vane, *Papers of Castlereagh*, X, 86-91.
79. Castlereagh to Lord Liverpool, August 28, 1814, ibid., 100-02.
80. Liverpool to Henry Bathurst, September 14, 15, 30, 1814, Francis Bickley, ed., *Report on the Manuscripts of Earl Bathurst* (London, 1923), 286-89, 294-95.

House of Commons that it was impossible to contemplate prohibiting land sales "from the savages." It would, he suggested,
"arrest the progress of mankind" and "condemn one of the most
favoured tracts of the earth to perpetual sterility." His views
were similar to those of one of the American commissioners,
John Quincy Adams.[81]

Article 9 of the final treaty was the crucial item. "The United
States of America," it read, "engage to put an end, immediately
after the ratification of the present treaty, to hostilities with all
the tribes or nations of Indians with whom they may be at war
at the time of such ratification, and, forthwith, to restore to such
tribes or nations respectively, all the possessions, rights and
privileges which they may have enjoyed or been entitled to in
1811, previous to such hostilities. Provided always that such tribes
or nations shall agree to desist from all hostilities against the
United States of America, their citizens and subjects, upon
the ratification of the present Treaty being notified to such tribes
or nations, and shall so desist accordingly."[82] Its implications for
the southern Indians were evident, even though the British
diplomats envisaged that they were working on the behalf of
the northern tribes alone. The Treaty of Fort Jackson of August
9, 1814, had already been declared by the nativists and the
Spaniards to be null. Now, by international treaty, the United
States also invalidated Jackson's dispossession of the Creeks,
since, by Article 9 of the Treaty of Ghent, the Indians were to
be restored "all the possessions, rights and privileges which they
may have enjoyed or been entitled to in 1811."

Cochrane received news of the peace in February 1815, but
he remained ready to resume operations if the treaty was not
ratified. On February 14 he wrote Nicolls, requesting him to
advise the Indians to cease hostilities and await the consumma-
tion of the treaty and the consequent restoration of their lands.
Various precautions were, in the meantime, to be taken to ensure
the safety of the Indians at Apalachicola. The munitions,
presents, and stores were to be turned over to them, and the
warriors might be permitted to retain the field guns if they
considered them necessary for their defense. Nicolls's marines,

81. *Parliamentary Debates* (London, 1815), XXX, 529-30; Allan Nevins, ed.,
    The Diary of John Quincy Adams, 1794-1845 (New York, 1951), 131, 133.
82. *Parliamentary Debates*, XXX, 216-17.

the coloured colonial marines, and the company of the 5th West India Regiment at the Bluff were not to be withdrawn until the peace was finally concluded. In addition, General Lambert was asked to place a British regiment and two more West India regiments at Apalachicola, and the ships were to remain in support.[83] In March additional supplies of corn were sent to the Indians in the *Norge* and the *Meteor*. That military campaigning was not yet considered inconceivable is indicated by a scale of allowances devised only a little before this time to provide inducements to the Indian chiefs.[84]

The Indians and some of the British seem to have been sufficiently naive to believe that the Americans would restore the lands "ceded" in 1814, but from this delusion they were rapidly awakened. On April 28, 1815, Nicolls, who had remained at Apalachicola after the troops were withdrawn, felt obliged to protest to the American agent, Benjamin Hawkins. He enclosed a copy of Article 9 and complained that a few days previously a number of Americans had attacked a Seminole town of Chief Bowlegs, killing a man and wounding another, and stealing cattle. The Indians, however, had refrained from any acts hostile to the United States, and, indeed, had resolved to communicate with the Americans as little as possible. Consequently, Nicolls warned the latter not to encroach upon Indian territory or to communicate directly with the natives, and to evacuate the lands Jackson had sequestered as guaranteed by Article 9. To emphasize the point, Nicolls enclosed an Indian pledge, signed by Hopoeth Mico, Cappachamico, and Hopoy Mico, in which the Indians, declaring themselves "a free and independent people," gave their promise to abide by the treaty.[85]

Unfortunately, Nicolls's tone was likely to aggravate rather than to placate the American temper, and his letter was treated

---

83. Cochrane to Nicolls, February 14, 1815, ADM/1/508/531-32; Cochrane, February 17, 1815, ibid., 556-61; Cochrane to Pulteney Malcolm, February 17, 1815, ibid., 562-63; Cochrane to John Lambert, February 17, 1815, ibid., 564-66.
84. Malcolm to Nicolls, March 5, 1815, Foreign Office Papers, Public Record Office, Kew, England (hereinafter cited as FO), class 5/folio 139/p. 181; Cochrane, instructions to Nicolls, March 9, 1815, ibid., 185; Scale of Allowances Proposed to be Given to the Indians when Assembled to Aid in Operations against the United States, 1815, CP, 2330, 171a.
85. Nicolls to Hawkins, April 28, 1815, WO/1/143/161-62; pledge of Hopoeth Mico, Cappachamico, and Hopoy Mico, April 2, 1815, FO/5/139/187.

with derision. Hawkins commented that the Indian signers were Seminoles, not Creeks, rather speciously, since the former tribe had lost lands on the lower Chattahoochee and the Flint as a result of the Fort Jackson treaty, and Jackson himself resented the continued interference of the British agents and the "bare faced effrontery" of the letter. As a result, Nicolls again wrote Hawkins on May 12, complaining that while one of the Indians had executed a tribesman for stealing cattle belonging to the United States, Chief Bowlegs's village had once more been attacked by American filibusters, and two people had been murdered. Notwithstanding, he continued, he had the previous day arranged for four chiefs in different parts of the Indian country to be designated upholders of the law and to accept responsibility for its maintenance. In view of this, the Americans should evacuate the lands of the Indians according to the Ghent treaty. More antagonistic was the tactless announcement by Nicolls that he had furnished the Indians with arms and ammunition for their defense and had prepared an offensive and defensive treaty between Britain and the chiefs which was to be taken to London for ratification.[86]

The new "treaty" was an attempt to provide for the needs of both Nicolls and the Indians, and it proclaimed also its value to British interest generally. With the war over, Nicolls faced the prospect of unemployment with half pay, and he had neither received his salary for the last year nor a confirmation of the pay and allowances offered him by Cochrane when he was appointed to the provincial rank of colonel of the colonial regiment. Furthermore, service with the Indians had enjoined severe expenses which had eroded Nicolls's personal resources. The cost of his entertainment of leading chiefs alone, up to December 7, 1814, had amounted to $1,952, of which Cochrane had repaid $500 in February 1815. As late as August of that year, however, Nicolls was in debt to the extent of £442. To banish these embarrassments, he hoped to remain in the south as an Indian superintendent, representing British interests, and, from the confiscated land formerly occupied by Forbes and Company, to administer a profitable Indian trade.[87]

86. Jackson to Hawkins, August 14, 1815, Bassett, *Correspondence of Jackson*, II, 214-15; Nicolls to Hawkins, May 12, 1815, WO/1/143/165-66.
87. Nicolls to Bathurst, May 5, 1817, WO/1/144/417-18; Nicolls, Memorial, ibid., 419-22; expenses enclosed in Nicolls to John Barrow, August 21,

The treaty was drafted at the British fort on the junction of the Chattahooche and Flint rivers on March 10, 1815, and signed by thirty chiefs, including Hopoeth Mico, Hopoy Mico, Cappachamico, and Francis. The Forbes grants were declared invalid, and the British were asked to provide trade through the Alabama, Apalachicola, and St. Marys rivers. The Indians swore obedience to the British, and denounced sales of native land without British consent. They offered to grant territory to any subjects of Britain sent to stay with them. The chiefs promised to "do our best to protect and defend them in their lands and property."[88]

There can be no doubt that the chiefs feared the loss of British support, especially as famine, accentuated by the large numbers of Red Stick refugees in Seminole country, was still present. The document also drew attention to some of their earlier grievances predating the Creek war of 1813, such as the wagon road blazed through the Indian land from Hartford, Georgia, to Mobile, and the activities of Creek Chief William McIntosh. The latter, the Indians stated, had been sent by the Creeks to remonstrate with the Americans over the road and the encroachments upon the Tombigbee, Coosa, and Alabama rivers, but he had been bribed and had sold a large tract about the Oconee and the Ocmulgee rivers to the United States.[89] Nicolls had shown little discretion in detailing the trade agreement to Hawkins, because the Treaty of Fort Jackson, which the Indians considered anulled, had itself been concocted as a device to separate the Creeks, by a land cession, from interference by the Spaniards. To demand the restoration of those territories and in the same breath to provide further evidence for the necessity of the cession was the ultimate folly. Couched in such a truculent manner, and furnishing further grounds for suspicion of the Indians, Nicolls's communications only served to reinforce the political expediency of the Treaty of Fort Jackson, and the Americans found it convenient to ignore Article 9.

After one more attempt to protest at the running of the Fort Jackson line, Nicolls, accompanied by Francis, his son, his in-

---

1815, WO/1/143/123-27; Nicolls to Barrow, August 24, 1815, ibid., 131-33; Wright, "Note on First Seminole War," 570-71.

88. Indian agreement, March 10, 1815, WO/1/143/147-50.
89. Ibid., William McIntosh was concerned in a land cession to the United States in 1805.

terpreter, and his servant, who had been deputized by the Indians to place their complaints before the British government and to give a calumet of peace to the prince regent, left for England. Early in August Nicolls installed the Indians at his home, Durham Lodge, near Eltham, Kent, and then hurried to London, where he arrived on the evening of August 14. He solicited an interview with Bathurst, but there was little response apart from an order from the earl that some pistols be presented to Chief Francis for his trouble. In a detailed letter, Nicolls explained that the chief had been delegated to present a communication to the British government on behalf of the southern Indians. Various needs of the natives were articulated, including winter clothing for the visitors, the desire for an Indian trade and a communication line with the British in the West Indies through Apalachicola, and the wish of Francis that his son remain in England to receive an education. Probably hoping to invoke ministerial responsibility, it was stated that before the Creek war the Red Sticks had obtained from the governor of Canada a letter urging them to commence the war but that none could read it.[90]

It appears that Nicolls was also canvassing for monetary rewards, according to a memorial to Bathurst, in which he itemized the remuneration which the leading chiefs and agents should receive. Hopoeth Mico, "the young king of the Four Nations," he hoped, would be awarded £300 and the half pay of a major, £146 per annum. This last perquisite should also be bestowed upon Cappachamico and the Mikasuki, Hopoy Mico. Francis and Talmuchees Hadjo (presumably McQueen) were each worth £300 and the half pay of a captain, £95.16.3 per annum. Pensions of £63.17.6 per annum, the half pay of a lieutenant, it was suggested, should be assigned to each of six other chiefs, and to First Lieutenant William Hambly of the Colonial Battalion of Black Marines, head interpreter, and to Lieutenant Castle. Nine other interpreters should each receive £40 and Woodbine, £95.16.3 a year. Finally, rewards of 5,831 each of hoes, axes, and

---

90. Nicolls to Hawkins, June 12, 1815, WO/1/143/151; Nicolls to John Philip Morier, September 25, 1815, ibid., 137-39; expenses of Nicolls, ibid., 141; Nicolls to John Wilson Croker, August 15, 1815, ibid., 103; Nicolls to Bathurst, August 1815, ibid., 107-08.

knives were requested for the Indians and the issuance of a license for regular trade.[91]

To these appeals the government turned a deaf ear, although on March 12, 1816, Cochrane himself wrote in support of the Creeks, highlighting the disparity between the Fort Jackson and Ghent treaties, and explaining that he had not known of the former agreement when Captain Robert Cavendish Spencer had finally withdrawn the troops. The Red Sticks, he stated, could not be bound by a treaty they had not signed. Eventually, in the early summer of 1816, Francis did obtain an interview with Bathurst. He was accompanied by one Faden as interpreter, since Nicolls was ill, but received little more than sympathy. Although the chief received handsome presents during his visit, the central aims of his mission had been frustrated.[92] Fired as he was by an almost fanatical hatred of Americans, he could not induce the British government to enforce the stipulations made on behalf of the Indians in the Treaty of Ghent, nor bring them to underwrite the establishment of a permanent British trade with the southern Indians which would have enabled them to remain independent of the United States. The shallow altruism which had characterized the cabinet's Indian policy was at last exposed, and further attempts by Francis to obtain a hearing do not appear to have been successful. Nicolls fared the worse for the visit, for he entertained the Indians at his house during the whole period of their stay in England at great personal expense, and he was compelled eventually to memorialize the treasury for relief from a debt of £378.2.6 in 1817.[93]

Francis did not, however, sail for the West Indies until De-

---

91. Nicolls, Memorial to Bathurst, 1815, CP, 2575, 120-21.
92. Cochrane to Bathurst, March 12, 1816, ibid., 140-41; Nicolls to Cochrane, July 26, 1816, ibid., 157; letter to Henry Goulburn, May 13, 1816, WO/1/144/263. A list of presents considered suitable for the Indians (ibid., 21-28) refers to two ploughs and two harrows in addition to numerous agricultural and domestic utensils, blankets, and cotton. Some of these items, axes, spades, shovels, scythes, hammers, grindstones, rakes, hoes, and nails, were shipped out for Francis, according to J. Barker to George Harrison, January 2, 1817, ibid., 409. In addition the three Indian delegates received suits, sabres, dirks, rifles, and a few agricultural and household instruments while they were in London (Nicolls, expenses, WO/1/143/141).
93. William Pole to Bathurst, August 16, 1816, WO/1/144/309-10; Nicolls to Bathurst, enclosing memorial, May 5, 1817, ibid., 417-22. Francis's attitude is revealed in Nicolls, December 19, 1815, CP, 2328, 182, which states: "He (Francis) sweares he will kill every American in the province as soon as he returns."

cember 30, 1816. In September of that year, when he was preparing to leave, Nicolls attempted to retrieve more from the visit by requesting Bathurst to supply funds for the education of the chief's son in England, and eventually he managed to procure a sum of £100 which was to be given to Francis by Governor Cameron at New Providence.[94] The Creek's ensuing departure marked a further retreat of the British on the matter of the Indian allies, and the point was underlined by the cabinet responses to protests lodged by Indians at Apalachicola even before Francis had left London. Early in 1816 a memorial, allegedly from some of the head chiefs of the Choctaw, Creek, and Cherokee, was sent to Cameron pleading for British interference in the question of their rights as guaranteed by the peace. Significantly, the three signers included, at last, the leaders of the hitherto pro-American Creek faction, including Big Warrior (Tustennuggee Thlucko) and Little Prince. Bathurst seemed disposed to act upon the complaint. He forwarded it to the foreign office, observing that the Indians possessed a claim to British intervention, and he instructed Governor Cameron to inform the Indians that the British minister in Washington would raise the matter with the United States.[95]

Nothing, apparently, was done, however, and the inactivity brought two Indian deputies to the Bahamas in January 1817, reporting that the Americans had destroyed the fort at Prospect Bluff and were building posts upon Indian land, while the warriors lacked muskets, ammunition, and British help. Although their message was passed through the usual channels to the foreign office, neither it nor further representations of the Indians for a trade with the West Indies or even the removal of the Creeks to another British colony appear to have accomplished anything.[96] With the refusal of the British to uphold the provisions made for the Indians in the Treaty of

---

94. Nicolls to Goulburn, December 21, 1816, WO/1/144/399-400; Nicolls to Goulburn, January 7, 1817, ibid., 403-04; Nicolls, September 24, 1816, ibid., 347-48; Bathurst to Cameron, January 11, 1817, FO/5/127/151.
95. Cameron to Bathurst, March 23, 1816, ibid., 142-44; Goulburn to William Hamilton, May 17, 1816., ibid., 145; Bathurst to Cameron, June 8, 1816, ibid., 147.
96. Indian chiefs, December 19, 1816, ibid., 157-58; Cameron to Bathurst, January 10, 1817, ibid., 153; Goulburn to Hamilton, June 26, 1817, ibid., 155.

Ghent, the War of 1812 among the southern Indians may be said to have come to an end.

British promises to the Indians that their rights would not be ignored in the event of a peace had come to nothing. At the time of the so-called first Seminole war of 1818 a final appeal was made to the British through Alexander Arbuthnot, a trader from Nassau, New Providence, then residing with the southern Indians. According to the wishes of the chiefs, especially "King Hatchy," but presumably also Francis, who "has been called by his people to put himself at their head" and was camped "at Spanish Bluff" with 1,000 to 1,200 men, mainly Red Sticks, word was sent to Cameron, Charles Bagot, and Nicolls that the Indians were in desperate need of assistance.[97] Nicolls, in particular, was stung by the American execution shortly afterwards of his "noble" friend Francis, and he tried hard to persuade his government to intercede on behalf of the natives but without success.[98] For the cabinet the affair became nothing more than another passing incident.

In resigning their interest in the Indian problem, the British signalled the passing of aboriginal America east of the Mississippi. The expansion of the United States could have been arrested only by a bulwark of overwhelming power, one which, conceivably, only the British, with the aid of large numbers of Indians, would have been capable of establishing. Without Britain's aid, Indian confederacies could not hold the west; their efforts to do so were gallant, but futile. Within a few decades, in both the north and the south, the remnants of the once-proud tribes were dispossessed and removed to areas west of the Mississippi.

It is possible that the dispossession of these Indians might have been deferred had Britain and her native allies enjoyed greater military fortune in the War of 1812. In the northwest, Tecumseh and his warriors had helped contain the American offensive for over a year with few British troops to support them, while in the south the Creeks had employed thousands of American soldiers before their defeat at Horseshoe Bend in March 1814. In both theatres, the principal nativist strength had been broken before the arrival of the major British forces in 1814. Had the

---

97. Alexander Arbuthnot to Nicolls, January 30, 1818, FO/5/139/203-04.
98. Nicolls, June 27, 1818, ibid., 173.

maximum Indian and British power in the north and the south coincided, and greater success attended some of their efforts, it is possible that a defeat of sufficient magnitude might have been inflicted upon the Americans to have at least delayed the dispossession of the Indians.

The result, in the final reckoning, would have been the same. It is true that many of the British officers had learned to like and sympathize with the Indians, men such as General Isaac Brock, the Indian agent Matthew Elliot, Cochrane, Nicolls, and Woodbine, the men who knew them best. But no nation would, of course, have been prepared to commit the resources that would have been necessary to preserve the Indian homelands, not even Britain, which owed so much to the natives for the defense of Canada. The British, no less than the Americans, adhered to the principles of economic and population growth and territorial expansion which had no place for aboriginal America. Given the proximity of the aggressive nations of America and Europe, bent upon fulfilling "manifest destiny," the Indian might, briefly, be able to capitalize upon international rivalries to his advantage, but the ultimate preservation of his homeland was not possible.